SYSTEMS
ANALYSIS and DESIGN

Second Edition

SYSTEMS
ANALYSIS and DESIGN
Second Edition

Gary B. Shelly

Thomas J. Cashman

Judy Adamski

Joseph J. Adamski

boyd & fraser publishing company

An International Thomson Publishing Company

Danvers • Albany • Bonn • Boston • Cincinnati • Detroit • London • Madrid • Melbourne
Mexico City • New York • Paris • San Francisco • Singapore • Tokyo • Toronto • Washington

SHELLY
CASHMAN
SERIES

Executive Editor: Jim Quasney
Series Coordinator: Tracy Murphy
Project Manager: Ginny Harvey
Director of Production: Becky Herrington
Production Manager: Peter Schiller
Composition: Mike Bodnar, Betty Hopkins
Interior Design: Betty Hopkins & Associates
Cover Design: Ken Russo

 © 1995 boyd & fraser publishing company
One Corporate Place • Ferncroft Village
Danvers, Massachusetts 01923

 International Thomson Publishing
boyd & fraser publishing company is an ITP company.
The ITP trademark is used under license.

Printed in the United States of America

For more information, contact boyd & fraser publishing company:

boyd & fraser publishing company
One Corporate Place • Ferncroft Village
Danvers, Massachusetts 01923, USA

International Thomson Publishing Europe
Berkshire House 168-173
High Holborn
London, WC1V 7AA, England

Thomas Nelson Australia
102 Dodds Street
South Melbourne 3205
Victoria, Australia

Nelson Canada
1120 Birchmont Road
Scarborough, Ontario
Canada M1K 5G4

International Thomson Editores
Campose Eliseos 385, Piso 7
Col. Polanco
11560 Mexico D.F. Mexico

International Thomson Publishing GmbH
Konigswinterer Strasse 418
53227 Bonn, Germany

International Thomson Publishing Asia
221 Henderson Road
#05-10 Henderson Building
Singapore 0315

International Thomson Publishing Japan
Hirakawacho Kyowa Building, 3F
2-2-1 Hirakawacho
Chiyoda-ku, Tokyo 102, Japan

ISBN 0-87709-631-7

1 2 3 4 5 6 7 8 9 10   BC   9 8 7 6 5

This book was designed using Windows 3.11, QuarkXpress 3.31 for Windows, and CorelDraw 3.0 & 5.0 for Windows.

CONTENTS

SYSTEMS ANALYSIS

CHAPTER *3*

Determining Requirements

P
H
A
S
E

2

TRADE
O F F

CHAPTER 10

Software Design and Completing the Systems Design Phase

Chapter Case Study 10

Minicase Studies 10

Student Case Study 10

TRADE OFF

Tradeoff in this Chapter:
Designing Single-User versus Multiuser Processing Modes........10.15

PHASE 4

SYSTEMS DEVELOPMENT

CHAPTER 11

Project Management and Costs

TRADE OFF

CHAPTER 12

Programming, Testing, and Documentation

TRADE OFF

PHASE 5

SYSTEMS IMPLEMENTATION AND EVALUATION

CHAPTER 13

Systems Implementation and Evaluation

TRADE OFF

CHAPTER 14

Systems Operation

Chapter Case Study 14

Minicase Studies 14

Student Case Study 14

TRADE OFF

Index

PREFACE

This textbook emphasizes a practical approach to learning systems analysis and design. It incorporates salient material from, and is based on the methodology and pedagogy of, earlier works by Gary B. Shelly and Thomas J. Cashman.

Numerous realistic examples support all definitions, concepts, and techniques. The examples and cases are drawn from actual systems projects. This enables students to learn in the context of solving realistic problems, much like the ones they will encounter in industry. In this textbook, students learn what works and what they need to know on the job. The many figures throughout the book clarify the narrative and reinforce important points. In addition, numerous tips are provided for many topics. For example, the coverage of screen design includes tips and guidelines for effective design results.

This textbook allows students to *do* systems analysis and design right from the start. They can begin their project work in Chapter 2.

Content

Chapter 1 presents the basis for this book — a five-phase systems development life cycle approach to conducting a systems project. Coverage of electronic data interchange (EDI) is also included.

Chapter 2 covers the initiation of systems projects, feasibility, and other project start-up activities.

Chapter 3 focuses on requirements determination and consolidates presentation of all fact-finding techniques and communication skills.

Chapter 4 features structured analysis — specifically data flow diagrams, data dictionaries, structured English, decision tables, and decision trees.

Chapter 5 concentrates on alternative techniques such as prototyping and computer-aided software engineering (CASE) tools. The chapter also includes coverage of outsourcing and software package evaluation and selection. Coverage of state-transition diagrams in this chapter can be skipped without loss of continuity.

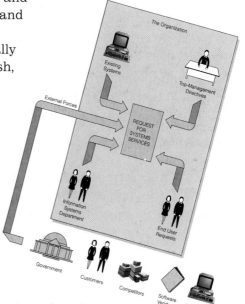

Chapters 5 and 11 include discussions of software change control. The requirements of an information system frequently change during systems development; these chapters stress the importance of instituting and following a means for controlling these changes.

Chapters 5, 9, and 10 include discussions of object-oriented analysis, design, and databases.

Chapters 6 and 7 provide a practical, balanced treatment of output and input design. Text-based and graphical user interfaces are equally covered.

Chapter 8 and Chapter 9 are dedicated to file design and database, including normalization, and entity-relationship diagrams. Chapter 8 covers general file concepts; this chapter can be skipped or assigned as review if students have learned about file

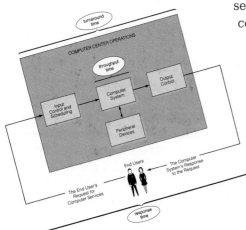

organization in another course. Also, the file organization sections can be skipped without loss of continuity. Chapter 9 covers databases and file/database design.

Chapter 11 on project management and costs can be assigned any time after Chapter 1.

Chapter 14, a unique chapter on operations, includes coverage of such topics as system performance, system maintenance, and system obsolescence.

Finally, coverage of various topics throughout the book are integrated. For example:

- Prototyping and CASE tools are integrated.
- Volume calculations and sizing factors appear whenever appropriate so students recognize the need to determine them throughout the systems development life cycle.
- Emphasis is placed on the end products of each systems development life cycle phase. This helps students realize how important the intermediate end products are to the success of the final system.

Tradeoffs

Integrated discussions of some of the tradeoffs that systems analysts must make in carrying out their responsibilities are found throughout the textbook. Tradeoffs are designated by the tradeoff logo shown on the left.

Each tradeoff presents an issue or problem with alternative solutions and the advantages and disadvantages of each solution. Students need to know that various alternatives are available at each step of systems development and that more than one correct solution to a question or problem may be possible. The topics covered in these tradeoff discussions are listed in the Contents.

Cases

his textbook includes three types of cases: Chapter Case Study, Minicase Studies, and Student Case Study.

■ Chapter Case Study — James Tool Company

This is a practical, solved, on-going case study presented at the end of each chapter. It reinforces chapter material with realistic situations and solutions.

■ Minicase Studies

Each chapter has at least two minicase studies; each contains questions for the student. The minicases contain enough information for the student to solve a problem limited to a topic or topics covered in the chapter.

Student Case Study — Western Dental Clinic

This is a practical, on-going case study that reinforces chapter material by requesting students to provide the solutions. Instructors can select one or more of the Student Assignments for each installment of the case.

Chapter pedagogy

Each chapter begins with Objectives and an Introduction that give students an overview of what they will learn in the chapter. Besides the cases, each chapter also concludes with a Summary, which recaps the key concepts of the chapter. This is followed by Review Questions, which are simple tests of recall, and Discussion Questions, which can be used in class or as written assignments for more thoughtful consideration and debate of chapter material.

Supplements

Instructor's Materials

This supplement, written by the authors, provides Lesson Plans with teaching tips. It also includes a Test Bank with answer key, and answers and solutions to all Review Questions, Discussion Questions, Minicases, and Student Case Studies.

Transparency Masters

Also available are Transparency Masters, one for each illustration in the book. Suggestions for when to use these visual aids are keyed into the Lesson Plans in the Instructor's Materials.

MicroExam IV

MicroExam IV, a computerized test-generating system, is available free to adopters of this textbook. It includes all of the questions from the Text Bank included in the Instructor's Materials for this book. MicroExam IV is an easy-to-use, menu-driven package that provides instructors testing flexibility and allows customizing of testing documents. For example, a user of MicroExam IV can enter his or her own questions and can generate review sheets and answers keys. MicroExam IV will run on any IBM compatible system with two diskette drives or a hard disk.

NetTest IV

NetTest IV allows instructors to take a MicroExam IV file made up of True/False or Multiple Choice questions and proctor a paperless examination in a network environment. The same questions display in a different order on each PC. Students have the option of instantaneous feedback. Tests are electronically graded, and an item analysis is produced.

Visible Analyst Workbench

A CASE workbench package, *Visible Analyst Workbench (VAW) — Student Edition*, can be bundled with this textbook so each student has a personal copy. The package includes a tutorial manual and software to provide students with powerful CASE tools using typical college or university resources. Both DOS and Windows versions are available.

VAW— Student Edition supports the Planning, Analysis, and Design phases of the SDLC and has a fully functional and accessible Repository with extensive reporting capabilities. It includes various cross model analysis, reports, and matrices. Diagram types supported include functional decomposition diagrams, data flow diagrams, entity relationship diagrams, and structure charts. Model techniques include: Yourdon, DeMarco, Constantine, Page-Jones, Gane & Sarsen, Chen, Martin, and Bachman. It also allows multiple models to be used for different phases of the SDLC, and system outputs can be easily included in a word processing or desktop publishing package. Because the VAW — Student Edition is also one of the easiest tools on the market to use, it is perfect for an introductory systems analysis and design course.

VAW — Student Edition includes all the operational and functional capabilities of the professional versions, with the following constraints:

- One Project (running on the single-user system at a time)
- Project is limited to 10 diagrams per type supported
- No Custom Symbol Generator (for flowcharting, etc.)
- No import capabilities

Adopting schools that bundle VAW — Student Edition with this *Systems Analysis and Design Second Edition* can receive up to two free copies from Visible Systems Corporation (617-890-2273), one for each 25 copies sold to the bookstore. Schools can also purchase additional copies (single-user or multiuser configurations) for their laboratory facilities at a minimal price from Visible Systems Corporation whether or not they bundle VAW — Student Edition with this textbook. For more information about bundling this CASE package with *Systems Analysis and Design Second Edition*, contact your ITP representative or call 800-423-0563.

Acknowledgments

Systems Analysis and Design Second Edition would not be the quality textbook it is without the contributions of many people. We want to express our appreciation to the following individuals who worked diligently to assure an excellent publication: Becky Herrington, director of production and art coordinator; Peter Schiller, production manager; Ken Russo, senior illustrator and cover design; Mike Bodnar, Greg Herrington, Dave Bonnewitz, and John Craig, illustrators; Betty Hopkins, typographer; Melissa Dowling LaRoe, copy editor; Nancy Lamm and Marilyn Martin, proofreaders; Ginny Harvey, editorial assistant; Tracy Murphy, series coordinator, and Jim Quasney, series editor.

Special thanks go to the following reviewers of *Systems Analysis and Design Second Edition:* Deborah Fansler, Purdue University Calumet; Donald Gottwald, Walsh College; Priscilla Grocer, Bristol Community College; Mary Kuehn, Oakton Community College; Karen Nantz, Eastern Illinois University; Ludwig Slusky, California State University Los Angeles; and James Woolever, Cerritos College.

CHAPTER 1

Introduction to Systems Development

Objectives

You will have mastered the material in this chapter when you can:

- Define information system and explain its components and characteristics
- Describe the common business information systems and their primary features
- Discuss the six different types of information systems
- Explain the informational needs and responsibilities of the different levels within a business organization
- Describe the phases and objectives of the systems development life cycle
- Explain the use of software tools in the development of information systems
- Discuss the functions performed by the information systems department
- Discuss the responsibilities, required skills, and opportunities for the systems analyst position

Introduction

ave you ever seen newspaper headlines similar to the following?

IRS Computers Audit Record Number of Tax Returns
Bank Teller Charged in $8 Million Computer Fraud
Computer Skills Needed for Today's Jobs
Computer Failure Halts Shuttle Launch
Wall Street Computers Handle Growing Stock Trading Volume
Retail Stores Support New Computerized Checkless Debit Card

Newspaper headlines are not our only view of today's widespread use of computers. The use of computers in today's world is commonplace. We take computers for granted and expect them to work perfectly; that is, to be reliable, fast, accurate, and easy to use. We become impatient and upset when computers are less than perfect. Usually it's only when there is a malfunction that we notice the impact of computers on our lives. The fact that it is news when a computer malfunctions is one indication that computers work consistently well. The computer's usefulness, however, does not happen by magic. It takes talented people working together to unleash the computer's power. This chapter serves to introduce you to the concepts, processes, and methods through which people develop practical and reliable computer-based applications.

Systems and procedures

As it conducts its business, a company performs many functions in a specified manner. As examples, a company writes payroll checks for its employees and fills orders for customers who buy its products. The manner in which these functions are performed depends upon the needs of the business and the requirements that must be satisfied for each function. A **procedure** is defined as the series of steps followed in a regular, specified order to accomplish one end result. One procedure for a company is the writing of employee payroll checks, and a second procedure is the filling of customer orders.

A **system** is defined as a set of procedures used to accomplish specific results. A company's payroll system, for example, determines the accurate pay for each employee as a specific result. To achieve this result, the payroll system consists of many procedures. Among these procedures are the addition of employees to the company's records, the calculation of taxes, and the writing of employee paychecks.

Procedure 1: Employee fills out deduction form for credit union dues.

Procedure 2: Employee submits completed form to credit union for approval and processing.

Procedure 3: Credit union representative gives approved form to Payroll Department clerk for processing.

Procedure 4: Payroll and union deduction are computer processed.

Procedure 5: Employee recieves paycheck with union dues deducted.

Figure 1-1   *Example of a system to deduct credit union dues.*

Systems take many forms, and the procedures that are incorporated into a given system are very diverse. For example, consider a system to build a complex rocket engine and a system to allow employees to deduct money from their paychecks for the credit union. These systems are quite different from one another, yet both are governed by a set of procedures that either the individuals in the manufacturing plant must follow to build the engine or the employees must follow to deduct money for the credit union (Figure 1-1).

At the simplest level every system follows the model shown in Figure 1-2. Inputs are processed to produce meaningful outputs. Using Figure 1-1 as an example, the employee supplies the input, consisting of the facts entered on the credit union deduction form. The processing is done by the credit union, the payroll department, and the computer program. The credit union approves the deduction, the payroll department establishes the employee's deduction for each pay period, and the computer program actually deducts the proper amount each payroll. The check stub reporting the deduction to the employee and the crediting of the deduction to the employee's credit union account represent the outputs.

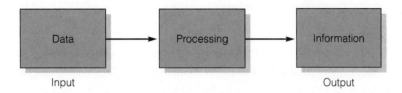

Figure 1-2   *Simple system model.*

System inputs are called data, and system outputs are called information. **Data**, defined as raw facts and figures, are the raw materials of the system. **Information**, defined as data processed for someone's use, represents the finished goods of the system. The objective of processing is to ensure the validity of the incoming data and to convert valid data into timely and accurate information. For the credit union system, the employee deduction form contains data such as Social Security number, employee name, and deduction amount. These data items are processed and retained within the system to be used each pay cycle. The system supplies information to the employee and to the credit union: the deduction amount on the employee's check stub and the transfer of money, respectively. Even in this simple credit union system, multiple data items and multiple outputs are associated with the system. For larger systems there are hundreds or thousands of input data items and information outputs.

A system may be called an **information system**, an **application**, or an **application system**. These terms are used interchangeably in the computer profession; in this book, however, we will primarily use information system.

Information system components

igure 1-3 on the next page expands upon the simple system model of Figure 1-2 to present the complete components of an information system. Notice that we still have data input and information output. The processing portion has been expanded to include five components: people, procedures, hardware, software, and files.

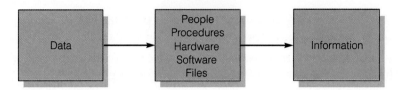

Figure 1-3 *Information system components.*

■ People

The primary reason for the existence of an information system is to provide information to the people in the company. People include both management and end users. **End users** are those people who directly interact with the information system. End users supply data to the information system and receive information from the information system. It is critical that you develop information systems that fulfill the needs of both management and the end users. The success or failure of an information system depends almost entirely on how satisfied the end users and management are with their interaction with the information system. The people component also includes those who work in the information systems department, which is discussed later in this chapter.

■ Procedures

We have already discussed **procedures**, the second processing component. Procedures are typically in written form and also include manuals and other documentation describing the tasks performed by all the people, both the end users and information systems department personnel, involved with the system.

■ Hardware

The **hardware** component consists of all the physical equipment used within the information system. This equipment includes computer hardware, such as computers, scanners, and printers, and noncomputer equipment, such as typewriters and check signature machines. Supplies needed for the hardware's operation, such as ribbons, toner, and paper, and supplies, such as special data collection forms, are also included in this component. Computers are not a required hardware component for every information system. The majority of companies do, however, use computers with their primary information systems.

■ Software

The **software** component consists of both systems software and application software. **Systems software** includes the programs that control the hardware and software environment. These programs consist of the operating system, communications software, and utility programs, which handle common functions such as sorting and copying. Either the hardware manufacturer supplies the systems software, or a company purchases the systems software from a software vendor. Prominent examples of systems software include DOS, Windows, and UNIX.

    Application software consists of the programs that directly support the information system in processing the data to produce the required information. Examples of application software include spreadsheets, word processors, database management systems, payroll, customer order entry, and billing. In some companies the information systems department staff develop all the needed application software. Such software is called a **legacy system**, or **in-house developed software**. Other companies purchase already developed information systems, called **software packages** or **off-the-shelf packages**, from vendors who supply the same software to many other companies. Most frequently, companies use a combination of legacy systems and software packages.

■ Files

Most data processed within an information system must be retained for legal reasons or for future processing needs. This retained data is stored in files and databases on computer secondary storage or in paper and other forms in various office files. These files are a critical information system component because all information either is produced *directly* from data stored in files or is *derived* from data stored in files. Figure 1-4 illustrates these two methods of generating information. The employee's gross pay is derived from a calculation based on the hours worked and rate of pay, both of which are obtained from files. The employee's credit union deduction comes directly from a file. Subtracting the credit union deduction from the gross pay yields the employee's net pay, a second example of derived information.

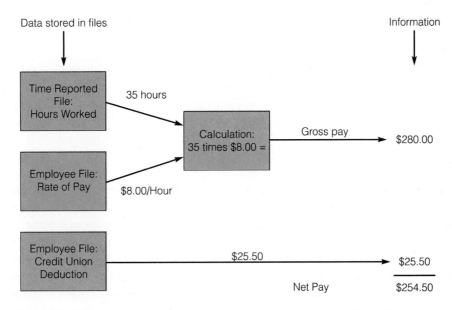

Figure 1-4   *Information can be obtained directly from data stored in a file or derived from data stored in one or more files.*

■ Information system

Now that you are familiar with the components, we can present an improved definition for *information system*. An **information system** is the collection of data, people, procedures, hardware, software, files, and information required to accomplish an organized set of functions. This definition requires that you focus on the information system's components, as shown in Figure 1-3. This focus is important because you cannot develop a successful information system unless you consider all its components and connect them properly.

Business information systems

Each business organization sells specific products or services and has specific goals, methods, and information systems requirements that are set in the organization's underlying corporate culture. A company's **corporate culture** is the set of beliefs, rules, traditions, values, and attitudes that give a company its atmosphere or personality and govern its way of doing business. In order to create an effective information system for a company, you must understand the information system's requirements and the company's goals, methods, and corporate culture.

Although there are a variety of types of business organizations in operation in the world today, companies are generally classified into two basic types:

- Industrial, or production-oriented companies, which produce, sell, and distribute goods
- Service companies, which sell and distribute goods, services, or information

The distinctive characteristic of industrial companies is the *production* of goods, whereas the activities of service companies center on the *selling and distributing* of goods, services, or information. The industrial company usually has a much more complex organizational structure than the service company and has more information systems that are more complex in nature.

Another type of organization is government, which includes city, county, state, and federal governments. Governmental organizations are much like service companies because governments usually provide some type of service or information.

The total business information system of a company normally consists of a series of **subsystems**, many of which are common to all business organizations. In small companies these subsystems might be handled by a single individual. In large companies management personnel, along with related staff, are assigned responsibility for a given subsystem. Figure 1-5 shows the common business subsystems for an industrial organization.

It is customary to consider each of the subsystems shown in Figure 1-5 as a separate information system. Each information system manipulates data to produce information. The purchasing systems manage purchases of goods and services and control payment for these purchases. The production systems manage the manufacturing of products for production-oriented organizations. The finance systems manage the company's financial records. The human resource systems maintain records on employees' employment. The receivables systems manage customer billing and payments. The marketing systems sell the company's products and services.

A breakdown in any one of these information systems can drastically affect a company's success. It is a tribute to modern business management that large organizations, some of which have over a half million employees, can effectively integrate this complex set of systems to produce a successful, profitable business organization.

Four characteristics of business information systems help to define their complexity.

1. Information systems are related to other information systems. For example, some information output from the purchasing systems becomes data input to the production systems and to the finance systems; the arrows in Figure 1-5 illustrate the flow of data between information systems. Thus, what is output information to people responsible for the purchasing systems is input data to those in charge of the other two groups of systems. The finance systems are central to a company's information processing because all other systems feed monetary data to them.

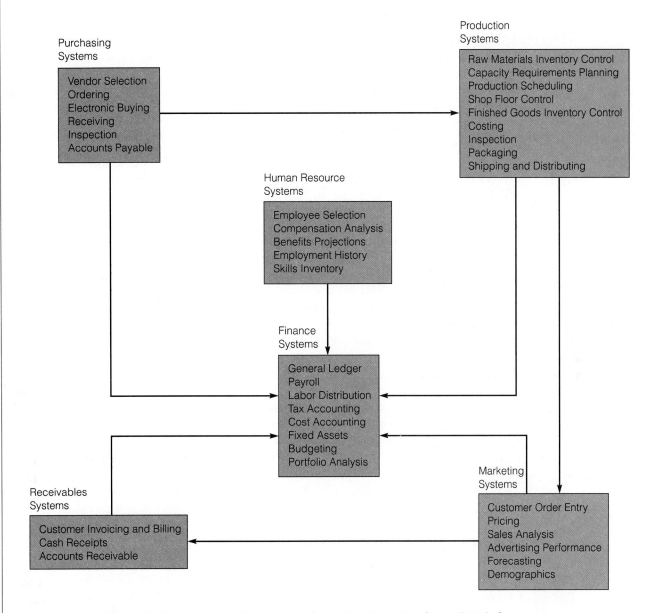

Figure 1-5   *Common business information systems for an industrial organization. Arrows indicate the flow of data from one group of information systems to another group.*

A company's information systems are also related to other companies' information systems. Two examples are the input of a payment from a customer's accounts payable system to a company's cash receipts system and the input of an order from a customer's ordering system to a company's customer order entry system. Many companies use computers to handle this transfer of data with other companies in a process called electronic data interchange. **Electronic data interchange (EDI)** is the computer-to-computer transfer of data between companies. The most popular current uses of EDI are in the areas of purchasing and payment processing. The use of EDI is growing and expanding — the Internal Revenue Service even permits the use of EDI for the filing of individual federal income tax returns.

2. A **boundary** between two systems is where one system ends and the other system begins. The boundary between two systems is not always clear-cut. For example, when are payments received from customers

part of the accounts receivable system, and when are they included in the finance system? If payments received from customers need to be adjusted, must these adjustments take place in both systems? Who makes the adjustments? What procedures and files are involved? If changes occur to the way adjustments are handled, what hardware and software and other information system components are affected? Clearly, it takes coordination and proper system definition to make these boundary judgments.

3. In addition to the common business information systems, there are many specialized information systems. At a school, specialized information systems handle class registration, classroom scheduling, student grading, student loans, and transcript processing. At a hospital facility, specialized information systems manage patient admissions, room and patient scheduling, and insurance billing. Banks, insurance companies, airlines, and every other industry have their own group of specialized information systems that are needed to effectively run their businesses.

4. Large and small companies in the same industry have significant differences in their information system requirements. For example, banks can range in size from a bank with a main office and no branches to a multinational bank with branches in many states and many countries. Both banks have similar fundamental requirements for processing loans, savings, checking, and funds management. The large bank, however, has a much higher volume of customers, transactions, and accounts. The large bank's processing is much more complicated because it needs to be able to pay employees worldwide, and it needs to be able to consolidate information from its branch operations. Finally, the large bank has greater specialization in order to deal with foreign currencies and, most likely, to offer a wider variety of consumer and commercial accounts.

Types of information systems

he types of information systems that use a computer fall into six broad categories: operational systems, management information systems, decision support systems, executive information systems, expert systems, and office automation systems.

■ Operational systems

An **operational system** is designed to process data generated by the day-to-day business transactions of a company. Examples of operational systems are accounting, billing, inventory control, order entry, and the other systems shown in Figure 1-5 on the previous page. Operational systems are also called **transaction processing systems**.

■ Management information systems

When computers were first used for processing business applications, the information systems developed were primarily operational systems. Usually, the purpose was to *computerize* an existing manual system. This approach often resulted in faster processing, reduced clerical costs, and improved customer service. Managers soon realized, however, that computer processing could be used for more than just day-to-day transaction processing. The computer's capability to perform rapid calculations and compare data could be used to produce meaningful information for management. This led to the concept of management information systems.

Although the term management information system has been defined in a number of ways, today a **management information system (MIS)** refers to a computer-based system that generates timely and accurate information for the top, middle, and lower levels of management. For example, to process a sales order, the operational system would record the sale, update the customer's accounts receivable balance, and make a deduction from the inventory. In the related management information system, reports would be produced that show slow- or fast-moving items, customers with past due accounts receivable balances, and inventory items that need reordering. In the management information system, the focus is on the information that management needs to do its job.

■ Decision support systems

Frequently, management needs information that is not routinely provided by operational and management information systems. For example, a vice president of finance might want to know the effect on company profits if sales increase by 10% and costs increase by 5%. This type of information is not usually provided by operational or management information systems. To provide this information, decision support systems have been developed.

A **decision support system (DSS)** is a system designed to help someone reach a decision by summarizing or comparing data from either or both internal and external sources. Internal sources include data from an organization's files, such as sales, manufacturing, or financial data. Data from external sources could include information on interest rates, population trends, or new housing construction. Decision support systems often include query languages, statistical analysis capabilities, spreadsheets, and graphics to help the end user evaluate the decision data. More advanced decision support systems also include capabilities that allow end users to create a model of the factors affecting a decision. A simple model for determining the product price would include factors for the expected sales volume at each price level. With a model, end users can ask *what-if* questions by changing one or more of the factors and seeing what the projected results would be. Many people use electronic spreadsheets for simple modeling tasks.

■ Executive information systems

Many decisions that must be made by management are periodic and predictable. For example, the need for decisions regarding raw material in low supply or a customer with a past due account occur regularly; the types of information required for making these decisions can be predefined; and the appropriate alternative actions can be prespecified. Such decisions, whose needs are periodic, whose information requirements can be predefined, and whose alternatives can be prespecified, are termed **structured decisions**. Semistructured decisions are somewhat predictable and definable, although less so than structured decisions. As an example of a semistructured decision, consider that costs generally rise as a result of inflation; it is likely, therefore, that management will someday need to make a decision about how much, if any, to increase prices in response to rising costs. At the other extreme from structured decisions are **unstructured decisions**, those decisions that cannot be predicted and whose information needs cannot be predefined. Unstructured decision making is most typical of top-level management.

Operational systems and management information systems support structured decision making. Operational systems, management information systems, and decision support systems together support semistructured decision making. However, none of these three types of information systems, used alone or integrated, adequately supports unstructured decision making. A fourth type of information system, the executive information system, has evolved to support the unstructured decision making required of top-level management. An **executive information system (EIS)** combines all the features and capabilities of both management information systems and decision support systems, but in an even more comprehensive, sophisticated, high-level, and flexible way, in order to support the unstructured decision-making needs of top management. Executive information systems are also called **executive support systems (ESS)**.

■ Expert systems

Expert systems combine the knowledge on a given subject of one or more human experts into a computerized system that simulates the human experts' reasoning and decision-making processes. Thus, the computer might also be considered to possess expert knowledge on the subject. Expert systems are made up of the combined subject knowledge of the human experts, called the **knowledge base**, and the **inference rules** that determine how the knowledge is used to reach decisions. Although they may appear to think, the current expert systems actually operate within narrow preprogrammed limits and cannot make decisions based on common sense or on information outside their knowledge base. Expert systems have been successfully applied to problems as diverse as diagnosing illnesses, searching for oil, and making soup. These systems are part of a branch of computer science called **artificial intelligence (AI)**, the application of human intelligence to computer systems.

■ Office automation systems

An organization can operate most effectively if it has efficient communication among all its members. **Office automation systems (OAS)** meet the need for integrated, efficient information exchanges among all the employees in an organization. An office automation system might include some or all of these functions: electronic mail; voice mail; fax; audio/video conferencing; word processing with spell checking, grammar checking, and thesaurus features; an automated calendar; electronic filing; a database management system; a spreadsheet; and a graphics package.

■ The integration of information systems

With today's sophisticated software, you might find it difficult to classify a system as belonging uniquely to one of the six types of information systems. For example, much of today's application software provides both operational and management information system information, and some of the more advanced software even includes some decision support capabilities. Although expert systems still operate primarily as separate systems, one trend is clear: to integrate operational, MIS, DSS, EIS, OAS, and expert system features into each information system.

Organizational levels

I nformation is a company asset, as are employees, equipment and buildings, materials, and money. Information systems exist to provide this information asset to people in the organization. Information requirements vary widely, depending on the person's responsibilities and position within the company. All companies organize in the way shown in Figure 1-6; operational personnel report to lower management, who report to middle management, who report to top management.

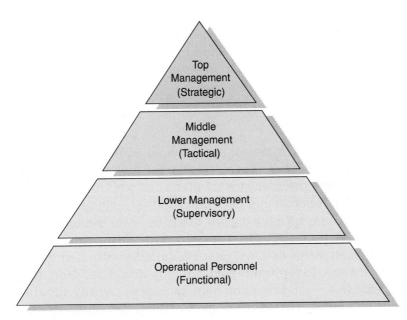

Figure 1-6 *The four levels of an organization and their information systems requirements.*

Taken in turn, we next describe the responsibilities, decision-making styles, and information systems requirements of each of these organizational levels (Figure 1-7).

Organizational Level	Responsibility	Decision Making	Information Systems Requirements
Top Management	Develop long-range goals, plans and strategies	Unstructured	Executive information systems MIS summaries Decision support systems Office automation systems
Middle Management	Develop short-range goals, plans, and tactics	Semistructured	MIS summaries and exceptions Decision support systems Office automation systems
Lower Management	Develop day-to-day plans and supervise operational personnel	Structured	Operational systems details Some MIS summaries and exceptions Office automation systems
Operational Personnel	Perform routine functions	Structured	Operational systems details Expert systems Office automation systems

Figure 1-7 *The four organizational levels and their responsibilities, decision-making styles, and information systems requirements.*

■ Operational personnel

Operational personnel perform a company's repetitive, day-to-day functions following well-defined procedures. Production-line workers, clerks, sales representatives, and auditors are examples of operational personnel.

The interaction of operational personnel with information systems is at the most detailed level; they deal primarily with office automation systems and operational systems, although there is growing use of expert systems by operational personnel. Operational personnel enter company data and receive information that helps them carry out their jobs; as examples, customer orders tell the warehouse clerks which products need to be selected, a sales report tells the sales representatives which customers need to be contacted, and a bank statement tells the accountants which checks have cleared the bank and which are still outstanding. The data items entered by operational personnel form the basis for the information generated for all higher levels of the organization.

■ Lower management

Lower management supervises operational personnel and establishes the day-to-day plans, based on direction and longer-range plans from higher levels of management. Lower management ensures these day-to-day plans and workloads are properly executed by monitoring the work of operational personnel and by making decisions and taking corrective action as necessary. The decisions made by lower management are highly structured: specific events cause specific actions.

Lower management needs detailed operational information and some exception and summary information. **Exception reports** identify deviations from what is defined to be the normal or successful condition and help managers identify situations that require action. Two examples of exception information are a list of customers who are late in making payments and a list of raw materials that must be reordered. Lower management's information needs also are narrow in scope, because lower management requires information only about its specific areas of responsibility. Lower management primarily uses office automation systems, operational systems, and management information systems.

■ Middle management

Middle management focuses on the short-range, tactical time frame, usually in the range of one month to one year. For this time frame, middle management establishes plans and allocates company resources to best meet organizational objectives. Middle management delegates authority to lower management to handle day-to-day business and follows up by directing lower management's activities and monitoring its performance. The decisions made by middle management are semistructured: routine events cause routine actions, but other events require insightful and original actions.

Middle management needs less detailed information and more exception and summary information than does lower management. Two examples of summaries for middle management are salaries by department and sales by geographic region. Middle management's information needs are also broader, because each middle manager is responsible for the operation of several departments. Middle management receives output from management information systems and uses decision support systems and office automation systems.

■ Top management

Top management is responsible for the long-range, strategic time frame measured in one or more years. Top management establishes overall company policies and goals, determines when organizational restructuring must occur, and sets new directions for the company in terms of products, services, and acquisitions.

Because top management is concerned with the entire company, it needs summary-level information, such as total company salaries and sales. Management information systems supply this summary information to top management. Also, top management's decisions center around problems and situations that are unstructured, nonrepetitive, and filled with uncertainty. Thus top management often needs one-time, *what-if* information provided by decision support systems, as well as the more flexible and sophisticated capabilities provided by executive information systems. Top management, similar to the other organizational levels, also uses office automation systems. Finally, top management needs information from outside the company to support its interaction with competitors, governmental agencies, shareholders, and so on.

Systems development life cycle

The information requirements of a company constantly change as the company grows, matures, and reacts to internal and external forces. Consequently, to satisfy a company's information needs, its information systems must constantly change. First, however, the information systems must be constructed, or developed.

The **systems development life cycle (SDLC)** is an organized approach used in companies to develop an information system. The systems development life cycle consists of the following five phases:

1. Preliminary investigation
2. Systems analysis
3. Systems design
4. Systems development
5. Systems implementation and evaluation

In Figure 1-8 on the next page, each phase appears in a box, and arrows connect the inputs and outputs for each phase. We devote the remainder of this book to discussing each systems development life cycle phase in detail, providing first an overview of the phase, and then following with a discussion of specific considerations for the phase. The systems development life cycle is sometimes called the **waterfall model** because the results of each phase flow into the next phase, similar to a series of waterfalls.

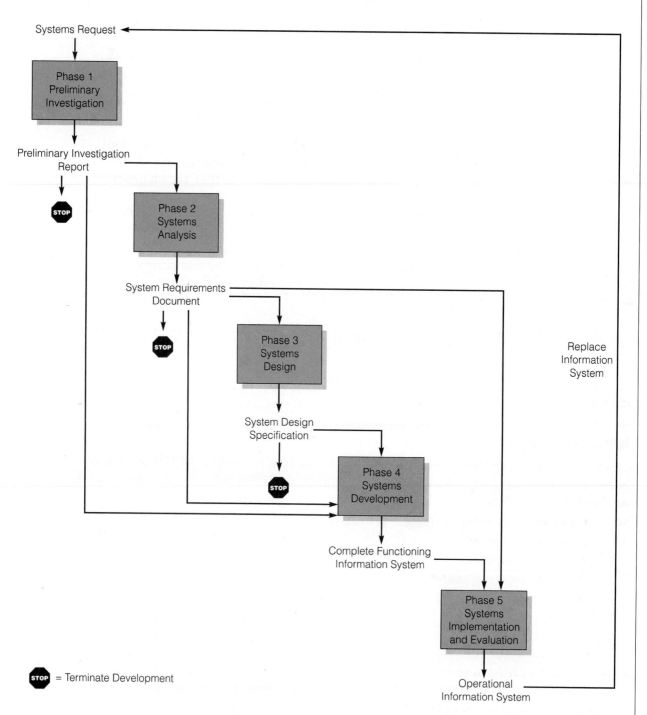

Figure 1-8 *The five phases of the systems development life cycle and their respective outputs.*

■ Preliminary investigation

A written request from management or an end user triggers the start of the systems development life cycle. This written request is called a **systems request**. On the systems request, the end user or manager identifies the information system and the nature of the work that must be done for the information system. The work to be done usually is expressed as a problem statement that is a definition of the deficiencies in the information system or of the improvements desired. The work requested can be substantial; for example, the request could be for the creation of an information system to meet a newly identified business requirement, or it could be for the replacement of an existing information system that can no longer handle changing business requirements. In contrast, the work requested can be minor; the addition of a new report or changes to existing calculations are examples of minor systems requests. Substantial systems requests require many months or years of effort, while some minor systems requests require as little as a few hours of effort.

The purpose of the **preliminary investigation** phase is to identify clearly the nature and scope of the problems mentioned in the systems request. Because identifying the problem is the focus of the preliminary investigation, this phase is sometimes called the *problem definition* phase.

Suppose you were developing an information system. During the preliminary investigation phase you would not conduct a complete examination of the information system and its problems. Instead, your objective would be to spend a limited amount of time to produce the **preliminary investigation report**. This document is a report to management specifying the identified problems within the system and what further action you recommend. As shown in Figure 1-8, you would recommend one of three actions. If no problem exists and no further action is needed, then you will not conduct phases two through five of the systems development life cycle. If the problem and its solution are minor, then your recommended action would be to proceed directly to phase four, systems development. The majority of systems requests, however, require further detailed investigation. In these cases, your recommended action would be to begin the next phase, systems analysis.

■ Systems analysis

The purpose of the **systems analysis** phase is to learn exactly what takes place in the current system, to determine and fully document in detail what should take place, and to make recommendations to management on the alternative solutions and their costs. Through the process of **fact-finding** or **requirements determination**, you first define all the functions performed by the current information system. At the same time, you determine what modifications are needed by the organization in the improved version of the information system.

After you have obtained the facts, you then analyze and evaluate them in a systematic fashion in order to develop alternative plans to solve the problems found in the current information system. This process is called **requirements analysis** (other names sometimes used for this process are *systems definition* and *general design*).

The end product you create for this life cycle phase is the **system requirements document**, which documents all end user and management requirements, all alternative plans and their costs, and your recommendations to management. After you present your results from this phase to management, management decides on the best alternative. Figure 1-8 shows the four possible alternatives. If the selected choice involves the use of a software package, then your company must purchase the package, and you would continue to either phase four, systems development (if package modifications are needed), or phase five, systems implementation and evaluation (if the package can be used as is). If management's choice of alternatives is for a legacy system, then you enter the third phase, systems design. Finally, management might decide to terminate development. Management might choose to terminate development at any point of the SDLC due to high costs, changing priorities, or failure to meet objectives.

■ Systems design

The purpose of the **systems design** phase is to determine *how* to construct the information system to best satisfy the documented requirements. You must design all required information system outputs, files, inputs, application software programs, and manual procedures. Also, you must design the internal and external **controls**, which are computer-based and manual steps that guarantee the information system will be reliable, accurate, and secure.

The design is documented in the **system design specification** (Figure 1-8 on page 1.14) and is presented to management and the end users for their review and approval. Management and end user involvement is critical so there is no misunderstanding about what the information system is to do, how it will do it, and what it will cost. After all systems design steps have been completed and if the development is not terminated, you then enter the next phase, systems development.

■ Systems development

Systems development is the phase during which the information system is actually constructed: application programs are written, tested, and documented; operational documentation and procedures are completed; and end user and management review and approval is obtained. The end product of this phase is a completely functioning and documented information system (Figure 1-8 on page 1.14). As is true with all other phases, the systems development phase ends after management has reviewed and approved all results of the phase.

■ Systems implementation and evaluation

After the systems development phase is completed, you then proceed to **systems implementation** (Figure 1-8 on page 1.14). Activities for this phase include conversion of data to the new system's files, final training of the end users, and the transition from the old system to the new system. It is at this point that the end users and management actually begin to use the constructed information system.

As part of a complete systems development life cycle, provision is made to allow for post-implementation **systems evaluation** at regular intervals. The purpose of these evaluations is to determine if the information system operates as proposed, and if the costs and benefits are as anticipated.

■ After the SDLC: systems operation

A company uses the developed information system to support its business during the **systems operation** phase. During the systems operation phase, changes will need to be made to the information system. These changes are classified as either maintenance or enhancements. **Maintenance** changes are made to correct errors or to conform with government requirements. **Enhancements** are modifications that add or change capability within the system. Adding new information to an existing printed report and the addition of a new report are examples of enhancements.

There are some information systems that have been used for over twenty-five years. Most businesses, however, undergo vast changes and find that their information systems need to be replaced after several years of operation. The replacement of the information system constitutes the end of its **systems life cycle**, which is defined as the systems development life cycle together with the systems operation phase.

■ General considerations

We now can highlight several characteristics of the systems development life cycle that you should keep in mind as you build an information system.

Complete phases in sequence   The successful development of an information system requires that you follow the SDLC phases in order; that is, you must complete one phase before you start on the next phase. When phases are bypassed or are hurried, you can expect problems with the developed information system.

It is our human nature to think ahead to what must be done next, so nothing is wrong with considering the impact on later phases of the decisions you are making in an earlier phase. If you do have an early choice of going in one of two equivalent directions, you would want to recommend the one that would result in a cleaner, more usable system. You can see that completing the phases in sequence does not mean that you must restrict all your thoughts to just the current phase activities.

You can also overlap work you are doing in one phase with the work for the next phase. This is especially important when you work on an information system that must be developed in a faster than desirable time frame.

When you complete a phase, you are not necessarily done with that phase. For example, you might be in phase four, systems development, when new hardware and software become available that causes you to reconsider your systems design and return to phase three. Or, changes to the company's requirements could force you back to the systems analysis phase.

Even though exceptions occur, you will be wise to follow the SDLC phases in order. You will design a better system if you first know all the requirements, and you will develop a better system if you know its design. Furthermore, it is more cost effective to complete one phase before moving on to the next phase. Suppose you complete the systems design phase, but you then discover you have overlooked a number of system requirements. You now have to rework both the system requirements document and the system design specification. This rework results in higher costs than if the requirements were considered originally during the SDLC's second phase. End users and management might also lose faith in your ability and the quality of the developing information system.

Focus on end products   Figure 1-8 on page 1.14 showed the end products for each phase of the systems development life cycle. Each end product represents a milestone or checkpoint in the information system's development and signals the completion of a specific phase.

Management uses each checkpoint to assess where the development stands and where it should go next. Management's choices at each checkpoint are to proceed to a subsequent phase, to redo portions of the work just completed, to return to an earlier phase, or to terminate the development entirely. One major factor in management's decision is the quality of the end product. Because the end products from the SDLC phases are highly visible measures of your progress, be sure you focus on the content and quality of these end products.

Estimate required resources   Cost-effective information systems are important to the success of every organization. Management is keenly interested in your estimates of what it will cost to develop and operate the information system. At the start of each phase, you must provide *accurate* cost estimates for that phase and *projected* cost estimates for all succeeding phases and for the operation of the information system.

During early phases, the projected costs are usually given as a range. For example, at the start of the systems analysis phase, you might estimate it will cost $11,000 for this phase and forecast the costs for all subsequent phases to be in the $30,000 to $50,000 range. When you have a better understanding of the information system at the end of this phase, your projected costs can be refined, say in the $40,000 to $45,000 range.

Management must have a reasonable idea of total costs so it is able to make sound business decisions based on the economics of the development effort. Thus, you must be skilled at estimating costs.

■ Automated tools for systems development

Developing an information system is a complex undertaking, and the systems development life cycle helps you to control this complexity. You use the SDLC as a guideline for what you should do and when you should do it. You also use software packages, called **software tools**, in performing many of the required developmental activities. These software tools make you more productive and help to ensure better quality products.

The software tools include general-purpose products, such as word processors for preparing memos and documents and graphics packages for drawing company organization charts and preparing charts and graphs. You also use specialized software tools that aid you in performing specific developmental activities. These specialized software tools include data dictionaries, report writers, screen generators, program generators, fourth-generation languages, and graphical tools that you use to create organization charts, data flow diagrams, systems flowcharts, and state-transition diagrams. We will present the details of these software tools in later chapters.

When you define an information system's requirements during systems analysis, you could use several of these software tools to develop a prototype of the information system. The **prototype** is an early and rapidly constructed, working version of the information system. The prototype could serve either as the definition of the end users' requirements or as the initial version of an information system. In the latter case, the prototype serves as an alternative to the SDLC approach to systems development. The process of developing a prototype is called **prototyping**.

Computer-aided software engineering (CASE) is the computer automation of the process of developing and maintaining information systems. A **CASE tool** is a software product that automates a specific systems life cycle task. Many CASE tools are integrated and automate multiple activities or phases of the systems development life cycle. We will discuss the prototyping process and CASE tools in Chapter 5.

TRADE OFF

The number of phases in the systems development life cycle is not fixed at five. The systems development life cycle for some companies has as few as four phases, while other companies have as many as twenty or more phases. The purpose of any systems development life cycle is to provide an organized framework for constructing an information system. The exact number of phases is not of great importance; what is important is that a company follows a logical set of steps in developing an information system. Every company's SDLC has at least these major phases: define the requirements, design the system, build the system, and install the system. Companies that have more than these four phases merely have subdivided one or more of these four phases into multiple phases.

Is it better to have more or fewer phases? More phases result in more checkpoints, more end products, and thus, more work. This translates into a greater cost and more time needed to develop the information system. More phases, however, also mean that these checkpoints occur more frequently, allowing a greater chance to attain the development goal. With small information systems, the extra phases might be too burdensome. With a larger development effort, however, the extra phases and additional checkpoints can be useful to help ensure it remains on target.

.The key to successfully developing an information system has nothing to do with the number of phases in the SDLC. The SDLC is simply a framework for developing an information system. The key to success lies in the quality and attitudes of the people who participate in the developmental effort. ■

Information systems department

The **information systems department** develops, maintains, and operates a company's information systems. The structure of the information systems department varies among companies, as does its name and its placement within the organization. Figure 1-9 shows a typical organization for this department in a company that uses a combination of microcomputers and centralized, multiuser computers. The four common functional subdivisions of the information systems department are operations, technical support, applications, and the information center.

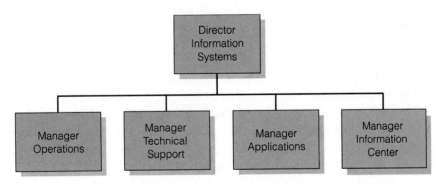

Figure 1-9 *Functional organization of the information systems department.*

The **operations** group is in charge of the centralized computers, the data communications equipment, and centralized peripheral devices, such as printers and optical scanners. This group also schedules the execution of batch jobs, distributes printed output, performs centralized data entry, and serves as the first line of contact when end users have problems with their operational information systems.

The **technical support** group installs and supports systems software, such as the operating system, data communications software, language and editor processors, and centralized database management systems. This group also serves in an advisory and support capacity to the other groups within the information systems department.

The **applications** group analyzes, designs, programs, tests, installs, and maintains the company's centralized information systems. If the company uses software packages, the applications group also installs, upgrades, and maintains these packages. Members of this group are the key liaisons with the end users.

Personnel in the **information center** train and support end users and management in the use of microcomputers within their departments. This support includes training for software packages, such as word processors and spreadsheets, single-user information systems, and networked applications, and extracting and feeding data between the microcomputer and centralized computer environments. The information center supports the end users in their **end user computing**, which is the development of an entire information system, or portions of an information system, by the end users in the organization.

The systems analyst position

Most systems analysts are employed in a company's information systems department. Some companies, however, have certain systems analysts report to the management within a specific end user area; in these cases, the systems analyst becomes an expert on the detailed needs of the department and on how best to blend computer technology with its business processing requirements. Other companies hire **consultants**, people who do not work for the company, to perform systems analyst functions on an as-needed basis.

■ Responsibilities

The **systems analyst** is the person who investigates, analyzes, designs, develops, installs, evaluates, and maintains a company's information systems. On large projects, the systems analyst works as a member of a team from the information systems department, while on smaller efforts, the systems analyst might be the only assigned individual. Whether working as a member of a team or alone, the systems analyst must interact with end users, company management, and others from the information systems department.

The systems analyst is responsible for a large variety of activities, specifically those activities that constitute the systems life cycle. Some of these activities are technical in nature, such as the selection of hardware and software packages, the design of computer files, and the training of end users on the use of computer technology. Other activities relate to the company's business. Recommending improvements to business procedures and designing a new payroll check are just two examples.

The systems analyst must create **project plans**, which are schedules of who is to do what by when, and must estimate costs for the work to be accomplished. Because people must be kept informed of progress and accomplishments, the systems analyst must write memos, reports, and documentation, and must give presentations and lead meetings.

■ Required skills and background

A systems analyst must have strong skills in the application of computer technology to a company's information systems. In addition to the technical skills in computer concepts, tools, and techniques, a systems analyst must possess a knowledge of the company's business, as well as an understanding of business in general.

A systems analyst interacts with people at all levels of the organization from top-level executives to clerks. Frequently, the analyst needs to deal with people from outside the company, including software and hardware vendors, customers of the company, and government officials. Thus, the systems analyst must have strong people skills and must be able to relate to people's needs, gain their confidence, and sell them on his or her recommendations. An ability to communicate is crucial. Communication includes not only oral and written skills, but also the ability to read what others write and to listen to what others say. Often a systems analyst must lead a team to develop an information system. When functioning as a team leader, the systems analyst must have leadership skills in planning, estimating, and controlling the project and in motivating others.

A systems analyst must be comfortable dealing with complex problems and with ambiguity and uncertainty. Creativity and analytical skills are important in coping under these circumstances.

Because business requirements and computer technology change rapidly in today's world, the systems analyst must have a strong desire to learn and to keep current with these rapid changes. Formal training in schools and at seminars and workshops are helpful to the systems analyst, as are memberships in professional associations and the reading of journals, periodicals, and books.

Companies today require their newly hired systems analysts to have at least a two-year degree in computer information systems, computer science, business, or a closely related field. Experience as a programmer is also frequently required. Figure 1-10 shows the suggested qualifications for a systems analyst at a typical company.

Qualifications: Systems Analyst

Formal Education

Two-year degree in computer information systems, computer science, business, or a closely related field.

Skill Prerequisites

Works well with people at all organizational levels.

Communicates effectively orally and in writing.

Understands business information systems and their impact on the organization.

Exercises mature judgment and can make independent decisions.

Understands computer hardware and software technologies and their applications to business information systems.

Functions well in team leadership and project management positions.

Experience

Minimum of three years experience as a programmer.

Figure 1-10   *Suggested qualifications for the systems analyst position at a typical company.*

■ Career opportunities

The demand for systems analysts is projected to remain strong in the United States through the 1990s. Computer technology continues to change at a rapid pace, and companies need people with strong analytical skills and training to help them employ this technology effectively in their organizations. The systems analyst position is very challenging and rewarding, and the salary is respectable. A career as a systems analyst can be very fulfilling.

Because talented systems analysts are knowledgeable in both technical and business areas, opportunities for promotion to supervisory positions are available in the information systems department and in end user departments. For the first time in the late 1980s, companies began naming to president and chief executive positions people who started in information systems departments as systems analysts. If a person has the right background, skills, attitude, and some luck, then prospects as a systems analyst are unlimited.

The responsibilities of a systems analyst employed at a small company are quite different from those at a large company. If you are starting out as a systems analyst, is it better to try for a position at a small or large company?

First of all, do not be misled by job titles. Some positions titled systems analyst require nothing more than programming or computer operations responsibilities. In other cases, systems analyst responsibilities are found under job positions titled computer specialist, programmer/analyst, systems designer, software engineer, programmer, and a number of others. Be sure the responsibilities of the position are clearly stated before you accept the position.

In small companies, a systems analyst usually does a little bit of everything, becoming a generalist in all areas of information systems development, maintenance, and operation. At large companies, a systems analyst focuses on a narrower area of information systems development or maintenance, becoming a specialist in that area. You might consider neither of these extremes to be at all desirable. If so, a medium-sized company might allow a degree of specialization within several areas.

If you prefer variety in what you do each day, then a small- or medium-sized company would suit you best. If you enjoy only a small number of information systems activities, then consider a medium- to large-sized company. Of course, you have more responsibility and control in a smaller company, whereas the promotional opportunities and financial rewards are generally greater in larger companies. ■

CHAPTER CASE STUDY

James Tool Company — Introduction and Background

James Tool Company is a continuing case study that is used throughout this book to illustrate the concepts and techniques of information systems development. The case study reinforces the chapter material and presents information systems development in a practical setting.

James Tool Company was organized in 1967 by Howard James. He believed that he could fill a void in the machine tooling industry by providing tooling and dies to smaller manufacturing plants that could not profitably produce those items themselves.

James Tool Company incorporated within the state of California and started with six employees. Because of clever marketing, competitive pricing, and timely product production, James Tool Company has grown to 456 employees. The employees consist of five officers of the company, office and clerical help, and foremen and workers within the shops that produce the tools.

The organization chart of top-level management is shown in Figure 1-11. The four vice presidents report to the president of the company, Howard James.

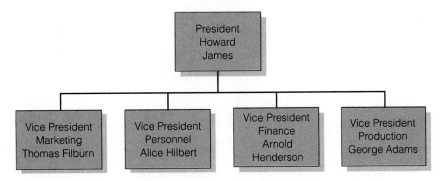

Figure 1-11   *Organization chart of James Tool Company.*

Figure 1-12 on the next page shows a more detailed organization chart of the high-level management positions within James Tool Company. Notice that the director of information systems, David Green, reports to Arnold Henderson, the vice president of finance. The director of the payroll department, Jim McKeen, also reports to Henderson.

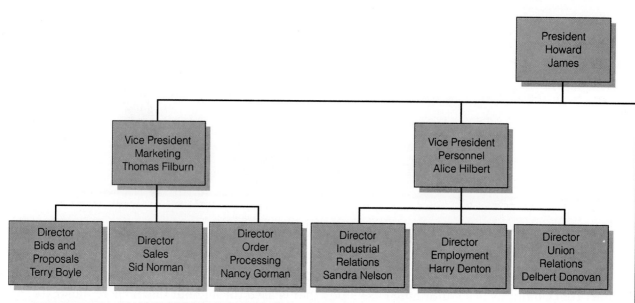

Figure 1-12 *Detailed organization chart of James Tool Company.*

The management structure of the information systems department includes: the director, David Green; an applications manager, Clyde Harland; a technical support manager, Mel Bagai; and an operations manager, Jane Miller. Figure 1-13 illustrates the organizational structure of the information systems department.

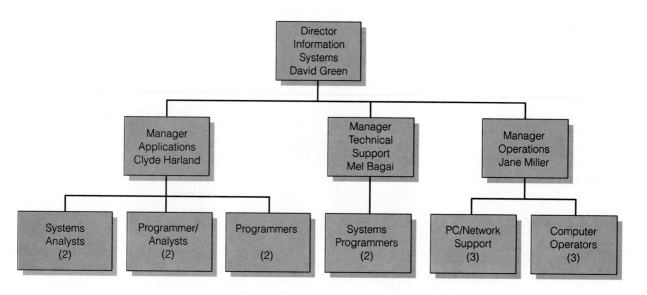

Figure 1-13 *Organization chart of the information systems department of James Tool Company.*

As shown in Figure 1-13, the systems analysts, programmer/analysts, and programmers report to Clyde Harland, the manager of applications. The primary functions of the systems analysts are to analyze and to design information systems, while the programmer/analysts spend their time both analyzing and designing systems and writing application programs. The programmers' primary work is to write programs.

The technical support manager and the systems programmers are responsible for the systems software on all computers used within the company. They also advise and support the other two groups within the information systems department.

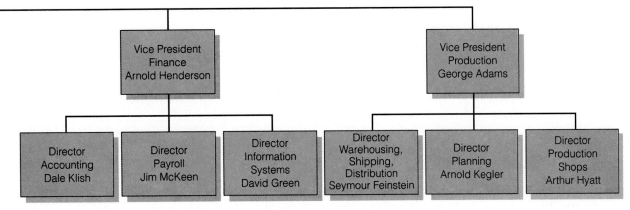

Figure 1-12   (continued)

The operations manager and her people install and support all the diverse computer equipment at James Tool Company. Three people within this group handle PC and network support; three others focus on centralized processing functions.

Summary

In this chapter, we began our study of information systems and their development. The essential components of an information system are people, data, procedures, hardware, software, files, and information. An information system can be created (legacy system) or purchased (software package).

The six categories of common business information systems for an industrial organization are finance, human resources, purchasing, production, marketing, and receivables. Four special characteristics of business information systems that help to define their complexity are: systems are related to one another, system boundaries are difficult to define, companies have many specialized information systems, and large and small companies have different information system requirements.

The six types of information systems are operational systems, management information systems, decision support systems, executive information systems, expert systems, and office automation systems. These types of information systems are used in various degrees by people at different organizational levels in a company; these organizational levels consist of operational personnel, lower management, middle management, and top management. Each organizational level has different responsibilities and different information requirements.

The systems development life cycle (SDLC) is an organized approach used in companies to develop an information system. The SDLC consists of these five phases: preliminary investigation, systems analysis, systems design, systems development, and systems implementation and evaluation. Software tools are used during systems development for productivity, cost, and quality reasons. Many of these software tools support prototyping and computer-aided software engineering. After an information system is developed, a company uses the information system to support its business processing during the systems operation phase of the systems life cycle.

The information systems department develops, maintains, and operates a company's information systems. The systems analyst investigates, analyzes, designs, develops, installs, evaluates, and maintains information systems.

Review Questions

1. What is a procedure? How are procedures related to systems?
2. What are other names used for input and for output as related to an information system?
3. Describe the components of an information system.
4. What is a file? Explain derivable information.
5. Provide a definition for information system and explain its significance.
6. List the six groups of common business systems.
7. Define EDI and give an example of its application.
8. What are the six types of information systems and what are their characteristics?
9. Name the four organizational levels and explain the information requirements for each level.
10. Give a definition for systems development life cycle (SDLC).
11. List and briefly explain the five phases of the systems development life cycle.
12. What is a systems request and what is its importance to the systems development life cycle?
13. What are the two types of changes made to an information system during systems operation?
14. Name the end products created at the end of each phase of the systems development life cycle.
15. Explain the use of a prototype in the systems development life cycle.
16. What is computer-aided software engineering?
17. What are the four common functional subdivisions of the information systems department?
18. What does a systems analyst do? Name six skills that a systems analyst should have to be effective.

Discussion Questions

1. Present an argument for and an argument against the following proposition: The heart of a company is centered around the information systems operation. Because members of information systems management are knowledgeable in all phases of the business, a company should therefore draw exclusively from information systems management to fill vacancies in top-level management, such as presidents and vice presidents.
2. Discuss the advantages and disadvantages of having the information systems director report to the chief financial officer of the company, such as the vice president of finance.
3. Some companies have a high-level information resource management department instead of an information systems department. This department handles traditional information systems functions. In addition, this department is responsible for all company information, such as telephones, fax, photocopy machines, and document management. What are the advantages and disadvantages of this approach?
4. Schedule a visit to the information systems department of your school or a nearby company. Prepare a diagram similar to Figure 1-5 on page 1.7 that shows the information systems your school or the company uses. If possible, classify whether each information system is an operational, MIS, DSS, EIS, expert, or OAS system.
5. Schedule a visit to the information systems department of your school or a nearby company. Does the department use an SDLC to develop its information systems? If it does use an SDLC, how many phases does it have, and how do these phases differ from those presented in this chapter? If it does not use an SDLC, what methodology does it use and why?
6. Schedule a visit to the information systems department of your school or a nearby company. Prepare a complete organization chart of the department and describe the functions carried out by each unit in the department.

MINICASE STUDIES

Green Pastures Limited

Kirby Ellington graduated with a two-year degree in microcomputer programming and worked as a programmer for three years at a large insurance company in Hartford, Connecticut. Kirby was responsible for maintenance programming on the company's credit insurance information system. He was competent in carrying out his duties, but he wanted to advance to a systems analyst position and did not feel this opportunity was forthcoming at the insurance company.

Kirby answered an ad he saw in a computer periodical for a systems analyst position at Green Pastures Limited, located in Plattsburgh, New York. Kirby decided to add to his resume that he had over two years experience as a systems analyst and had been the lead systems analyst for two major projects at the insurance company. When Green Pastures reviewed Kirby's resume, the company was impressed with his systems analyst and leadership experience and flew him in for an interview.

During the interview Kirby communicated well and appeared to be knowledgeable about programming, microcomputer software packages, such as spreadsheets and word processors, and all the latest microcomputers on the market. This fit in well with Green Pastures' needs, because it had only just started using computers in their business six months ago, when three microcomputers were installed in the company's office headquarters. Because Green Pastures had no one with computer experience on staff, it felt a systems analyst would be able to develop the specialized information systems it needed. Green Pastures offered Kirby a job as a systems analyst, and he accepted the offer.

Kirby initially did a great job at Green Pastures. He was able to help everyone with his or her spreadsheet and word processing problems and advised Green Pastures on the purchase of a database management package. Kirby next started to develop a billing information system. He had really enjoyed the C programming language when he was in school and decided to use this language for the billing system.

After four months of work, Kirby finished the billing system. The clerks at Green Pastures began using the system and encountered immediate problems. The clerks had difficulty understanding what they should do and when they should do it. Although there was no documentation or written directions for the system, Kirby was always available to help them out. The clerks spent one week entering data and making corrections to the data until all the input was correctly entered, and the time came to print the billing statements. The printing went well, and the statements were mailed out to customers.

Two days later, Green Pastures began receiving calls from irate customers complaining about the errors in the billing statements they had just received. After a thorough review, they discovered that all the billing statements were wrong and would have to be redone manually.

Question

1. Who is at fault for the problems with the billing system? Why?

Ridgeway Company

Ridgeway Company is an organization whose main business is the purchase and development of recreational land. Sales during the past year have exceeded thirty million dollars.

Senior-level management of Ridgeway Company includes George Ridgeway, president; Helen Hill, senior vice president; and three vice presidents who report directly to Hill: Luis Sanchez, vice president, finance; Trinh Lu, vice president, administration, research and development; and Thomas McGee, vice president, operations. Arnold Logan reports directly to the president in a staff capacity as the company's land development consultant.

Ridgeway Company recently acquired a large recreational complex containing both a tennis club and a golf course. Now named the Ridgeway Country Club, the facilities include twenty lighted tennis courts, an eighteen-hole golf course, a pro shop that sells tennis and golfing supplies and related items, a clubhouse containing a restaurant and bar, and other recreational facilities, including a swimming pool and exercise room. Thomas McGee is the senior management-level person in charge of the Ridgeway Country Club.

Ridgeway Company recently acquired a minicomputer system, including a high-speed printer and high-capacity tape and disk storage devices.

Linda Usher, as director, heads the information systems department and reports directly to the vice president of finance. Reporting directly to Usher are a manager of systems development, a manager of systems management, and a manager of operations.

Questions

1. Prepare an organization chart of the top-level management of Ridgeway Company.

2. Add the organizational structure of the information systems department to the top-level organization chart.

Linda Usher recently met Arnold Logan for lunch. Linda was surprised at the invitation, and Logan's secretary had given her no reason for this informal meeting. After some small talk, Arnold suddenly said, "I need your help, Linda. Several months ago, I bought a microcomputer for my office. Believe me, I wasn't trying to get around your department. It's just that I know you folks are all very busy, and I thought this was something I could do without bothering you."

Noting Linda's encouraging nod, Arnold continued. "All I needed was a program to help me keep track of how many members use each of the Ridgeway Country Club's facilities. I figured it would help me predict future usage, spot trends, and point out potential problems of over-demand for certain facilities. For example, I'm sure we will need to build several additional tennis courts someday soon. I didn't think it would be a big deal to get a computer program to help me figure out how soon we'll need them. The store where I bought the microcomputer recommended a spreadsheet package that has statistical capabilities. They said it was very popular and would do exactly what I wanted. But it isn't working out. I had originally planned to keep track of weekly usage, but now I realize that in some cases I need daily or even hourly figures. But the package can't handle that many different numbers. And I can't get it to do the seasonal analyses I need. So now what should I do?"

By now Linda looked very serious. "Arnold, this is a common story. It happens all the time. People think that if you simply turn on a computer and start up a package, everything is possible. But it doesn't work that way. Computers and packages are just tools. You still have to first figure out exactly what you want to do before you can determine what tools you need to do it."

"I appreciate that now," Arnold said, "but what I want to know is how I can salvage what I've already done. Do you have a few minutes this afternoon to look at what I've got on the microcomputer and tell me how I can make it do what I want?"

"It isn't going to be that easy," Linda quietly responded. "I can't come up with answers that quickly. We need to look carefully at exactly what it is you want to do, what kinds of information you need from the system, and what data you have available. Only then will we be able to determine the kind of computer system you need. Maybe then we'll be able to find a microcomputer package that will do the job. Or maybe we'll determine that a specialized information system must be written for your specific needs. That system might be one that would run on your micro, or maybe it would have to be written for Ridgeway's minicomputer. But frankly, Arnold, this will all take time. There are no magic shortcuts."

Questions

3. What mistakes did Arnold make?
4. Do you think Linda's assessment is correct? Do microcomputer systems need the same kind of systems development life cycle that large mainframe systems do?

STUDENT CASE STUDY

Western Dental Clinic — Introduction and Background

Western Dental Clinic is a continuing case study that is used throughout the book to give you practical experience in the development of an information system. You should complete all case study assignments for a chapter after you have completed your study of that chapter.

Introduction

Early in 1984, Robert O'Donnell, D. D. S., and Sophia Kozlaw, D. D. S., decided to combine their individual dental practices in Sioux Falls, South Dakota, to form the Western Dental Clinic. Carl Rivera, D. D. S., an orthodontist, joined the clinic in late 1984. In 1986, an oral surgeon, Stephen Garvin, D. D. S., and a periodontist, Colette Early, D. D. S., joined the group, and the practice moved to its current location next to a new mall in the fastest-growing section of the city.

At the present time, the staff of Western Dental Clinic includes those five dentists, five dental technicians, four hygienists, and six office staff workers. Western Dental Clinic's motto is *Full Family Service* and the practice has grown considerably since it began in 1984.

Western Dental Clinic currently has a patient base of 5,500 patients from 1,800 different households. Western's patients are employed by 250 different employers, many of which provide dental insurance policies for their employees. Consequently, Western Dental Clinic currently has to deal with thirty-four different insurance companies.

Emily Hendricks, who has been with Western Dental Clinic since its inception, is the office manager. In addition, Hendricks, assisted by Chris Brown, handles office payroll, tax reporting, and profit distribution among the associates. Susan Gifford is responsible for maintenance of all the patient records. Most of the paperwork concerning insurance reporting and accounting is handled by Tom Capaletti. Mary Ann Carruthers has the primary responsibility for the appointment book; her duties include making reminder calls to all patients the day before an appointment and preparing daily appointment lists for all the dentists and hygienists in the clinic. Carla Herrara is primarily concerned with ordering and organizing office and clinic supplies.

Each of the six office workers has one or more primary responsibilities; however, all members of the staff help out whenever necessary with patient records, insurance processing, and appointment processing. In addition to their regular responsibilities, all six office workers are involved in the preparation of patient statements at the end of each month.

Student Assignments

1. Western Dental Clinic is currently not computerized in any way. Do you think the clinic could profitably computerize all or part of their office procedures? If you, a computer professional, could do anything you wanted for Western Dental Clinic, which operations would you computerize? Which would you do first?

2. Prepare an organization chart of the office staff at Western Dental Clinic.

PHASE

1

Preliminary Investigation

CHAPTER 2

Preliminary Investigation

Objectives

You will have mastered the material in this chapter when you can:

- Explain why and how systems projects are initiated
- Explain how systems projects are evaluated
- List the objectives of the preliminary investigation phase
- Describe what activities occur during the preliminary investigation phase
- Describe what takes place at the completion of the preliminary investigation phase

Introduction

In this chapter we examine the first phase of the systems development life cycle: the preliminary investigation. During this phase, the systems analyst determines whether the development of the requested system is justified. First, we look at why and how ideas for systems projects originate. Then, we examine the criteria used to evaluate systems projects. Next, we study the preliminary investigation itself — first by discussing its objectives and then by studying the activities that take place during this investigation. Finally, we look at the activities that complete the preliminary investigation phase.

Origination of systems projects

■ Reasons For Systems Projects

Every business organization is a system that exists to pursue and achieve one or more goals. A **goal** is an end that the organization is striving to attain. Even if the goals have not been explicitly stated by the organization, goals influence and direct all the activities of that organization. Goals are usually stated in very broad terms. For example, a typical business might strive to maximize profits, or to maximize market share, or to maximize return on investment. A company also might have a goal to make a positive contribution to the community in which it operates or a goal to minimize its negative impact on the environment.

An **objective** is a task that will help achieve a goal. For the goal of maximizing profit, for example, there may be several supporting objectives, such as producing a product that is competitive, marketing the product effectively, handling order entry and billing rapidly and accurately, and managing inventory efficiently. Thus, objectives are more concrete, measurable, and specific than goals. An example of a specific objective is to reduce current inventory costs by 10%.

All the assets and resources of a business organization enable the organization to attain its objectives. For example, manufacturing equipment is used to create the product, marketing department employees market the product, shipping department employees package and send the product to customers, and so on. Similarly, computer systems exist to support the organization's objectives. For example, a computerized order entry system provides rapid and accurate processing of customer orders; a computerized inventory system provides the information necessary for assessing, controlling, and reducing inventory costs.

Changes in an organization's objectives or formulation of new objectives can trigger the need for a systems request. A **systems request** is a formal request for the services of the information systems department. The systems request might result in the development of a new computer system or enhancements to an existing computer system. The recognition of problems or errors in a current computer system, which can undermine its ability to support the organization's objectives, might also trigger a systems request.

You might find it useful to classify the reasons for systems requests by the type of improvement required, as shown in Figure 2-1. The five types of desired improvement are service, performance, information, controls, and economy.

Service   Requests are often aimed at improving service to the customers or the end users of the organization. Simplifying the registration process at a college, streamlining the processing of insurance claims at a hospital, providing more up-to-date and useful information on customer statements — all such activities would improve service to customers or end users of the organization. This improved service, in turn, results in an increase in customer and end user satisfaction, which clearly benefits the organization.

Performance   The current system might not perform as well as it must. Reports might take too long to prepare, or **response time**, which is the amount of time between an end user making a request and the computer furnishing a response, might be too long.

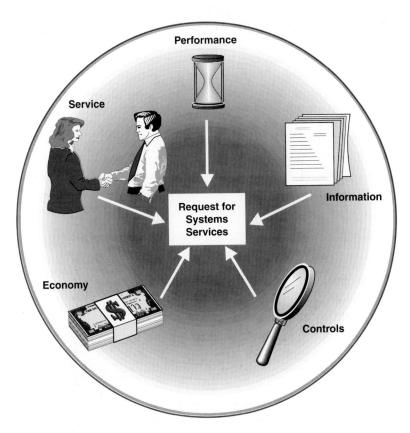

Figure 2-1   *Desired improvements that can trigger systems requests.*

Information   Information produced by the system might be inadequate or incomplete. In other cases, information might be complete, but not produced in a timely manner. In still others, the information might not be available to those who need it.

Controls   The controls in an existing system might be inadequate, allowing erroneous data to enter the system. For example, if an invalid customer number is input to an order entry system, the system should immediately reject that customer number and require that a valid number be input. Otherwise, the error would not be detected until after the order has been filled and a clerk begins to prepare the address label. At that point, the clerk would detect the invalid customer number and would be unable to prepare the address label. Consequently, organizational resources would have to be applied to finding the original order and correcting the erroneous customer number. On the other hand, the controls might be excessive in a system. If a system requires input of redundant data or takes too long verifying every input item, undue burden might be imposed on the end users or even on the customers of the organization.

Economy   Features in the current system might be more costly than they need to be. The system might not use computer resources as efficiently as it could, or possibly does not utilize newly available, more efficient technology. Perhaps entering data is a more cumbersome process than it needs to be, thus wasting the time of data entry personnel and, consequently, wasting money.

■ Sources of systems projects

Who initiates systems projects? We can trace the origination of systems projects to the five sources shown in Figure 2-2.

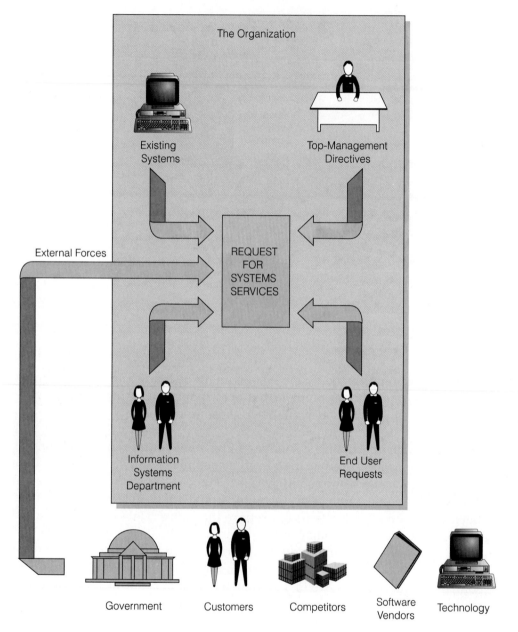

Figure 2-2 *Five common sources of systems project requests.*

End user requests   As end users within various departments in the organization learn the capabilities of computers, they are likely to make numerous requests for computer services. For example, end users might request a new sales analysis report, mailing labels, or an updated inventory report. They might be dissatisfied with the current system and point out inadequacies in it. They might feel that the current system has not kept up with the growth of the organization or with changing requirements. They might become aware of factors that were not known or did not exist when the current system was developed.

Top-management directives   Directives from top management are a second source of systems projects. These directives can result from the need to meet a new organizational objective, the need for additional information for decision making, a new activity being established within the business, new management, or other new requirements.

Existing systems   Errors or inefficiencies within existing systems can trigger requests for systems projects. System errors should certainly be corrected, but the systems personnel in many organizations spend too much time *fire fighting*. When they are fire fighting, systems analysts are reacting to problems as they are detected, immediately making the changes necessary to solve the problem. If fire fighting becomes the basis of all systems activity, the entire business system becomes a patchwork of corrected or improved systems with little consideration to the business organization as an integrated whole.

Information systems department   A fourth source of systems projects is the information systems department's own recommendations for projects. The value of such projects, of course, depends on the department's knowledge of the operations and needs of the organization. Such systems projects can lead to the development of useful and efficient systems. Information systems departments, however, might tend to design large-scale management information systems that are more sophisticated and expensive than needed for the effective operation of the business. Many of these large-scale information systems, after hundreds and even thousands of hours of effort, have never been successfully implemented. Thus, management has become increasingly wary of large projects proposed by information systems departments.

External forces   Agencies outside the organization can dictate changes to existing systems or the creation of new systems. For example, government tax regulations or reporting requirements often change. A software vendor might issue a new release of a computer system package used by the organization. Competitors might offer new computer-supported services that the organization must also consider offering in order to stay competitive. Important customers might impose requirements that have an impact on existing systems. Automobile companies, for example, have the power to force their suppliers to process orders in a certain way. Insurance companies can force hospitals or clinics to submit claims in a specified fashion. Sometimes, advances in technology push development of systems in particular directions. For example, the development of the technology used in the scanners now common in grocery store check-out lanes led to a very different approach to the check-out process. This process, which relies heavily on an underlying computerized system, has greatly changed the job of store clerks and made them much more efficient. Without this breakthrough in technology, the opportunity to develop such a system would not have existed.

■ Request form and procedure

Many organizations use a special form for systems requests; Figure 2-3 on the next page is a sample systems request form. A properly designed form streamlines the process of making a request and also assures that all such requests are made with a uniform format. The form should be as easy to use and as nonintimidating as possible. Clear documentation of how to use the form should appear on the form itself or in a procedures manual that explains how to fill out systems requests. The form should contain enough space for all the required information and should include directions concerning what supporting documents should be attached to the form. Some organizations use e-mail to communicate their systems requests; this allows them to maintain an electronic record of all requests.

REQUEST FOR INFORMATION SYSTEMS SERVICES

DATE: _____

SUBMITTED BY: _____

TITLE: _____

DEPARTMENT: _____

PHONE: _____

Request for:

[ ] MODIFICATION OF EXISTING SYSTEM

[ ] NEW SYSTEM

DESCRIPTION OF REQUESTED SYSTEMS SERVICE:
(attach additional documents as necessary)

(to be completed by the Information Systems Department)

DATE:

ACTION:

Figure 2-3 *Sample systems request form.*

Once a systems request form has been completed and submitted, a systems analyst or information systems manager will examine the request and determine what resources will be required for the preliminary investigation. Then, a designated manager or a committee will decide whether to proceed with a preliminary investigation.

Evaluation of systems requests

■ Systems review committee

Some organizations assign responsibility for evaluating systems requests to one manager. This manager might be the director of information systems or a high-ranking executive in another area of the company. Other organizations use the committee method to evaluate systems requests. This committee is often called the **systems review committee**. It may also be called a **steering committee**, a **management committee**, a **computer policy committee**, or an **advisory committee**. In any case, the function is the same: to evaluate systems projects.

Using a committee to evaluate systems requests, instead of relying on the judgment of a single individual, draws upon the knowledge and skills of a wide range of individuals with specialized talents within the business organization. A typical evaluation committee consists of the information systems director and several upper-level executives of the company. Although the committee approach has the advantage of utilizing the talents and knowledge of several people, the responsibility for successful development of the system rests with the information systems department. Therefore, the information systems director must ensure that all committee members are aware of any difficulties that might be encountered with a new or changed system.

A committee has the added advantage that it is often better able to establish priorities than is a single individual. Further, the approval of projects is far less likely to be affected by the bias of any one person.

On the other hand, approval of requests must wait until the committee meets. This can delay crucial projects. Often, to make sure such projects are not delayed, committee members will communicate through memos and e-mail. Another disadvantage of a committee is that each committee member has individual biases and interests. These biases and interests might lead committee members to favor projects that will improve their own departments or those aligned politically with them over projects that might benefit other departments in the organization. Those committee members, therefore, who are more highly positioned or who are politically stronger might have their projects approved with higher priorities than the projects favored by others on the committee. At the very least, contention among committee members might add time to committee deliberations and delay committee recommendations.

In some companies, a single individual is responsible for evaluating systems requests. An individual is able to respond to systems requests faster than a committee. The individual, however, might be biased toward certain projects and be unduly influenced by particularly powerful individuals in the organization. ■

■ Evaluation of projects

Within most organizations, the demand for systems services exceeds the capacity of the information systems department to carry out the requested activities. Thus, the systems review committee faces the task of evaluating all requests for services, rejecting some, and selecting and establishing priorities for those requests that appear to offer the greatest benefit to the organization.

For instance, the committee might receive a request to investigate errors occurring in payroll, a request to design a new inventory control system, a request for new sales analysis reports, and a request for the computerized billing of customer accounts. With a limited number of systems analysts on staff, which of these projects would be considered for further study? By what criteria does the committee evaluate and decide on the priorities for the many and varied requests that the information systems department is likely to receive? The committee's first step in the evaluation of a systems request is to determine its feasibility.

■ Feasibility

A systems request has **feasibility** if the request can be successfully implemented. When you analyze feasibility, you must consider three separate types: technical, operational, and economic. These three types of feasibility are equally important. As shown in Figure 2-4, a proposed systems request that fails to satisfy any one of the three types of feasibility is said to be *infeasible*, or not feasible.

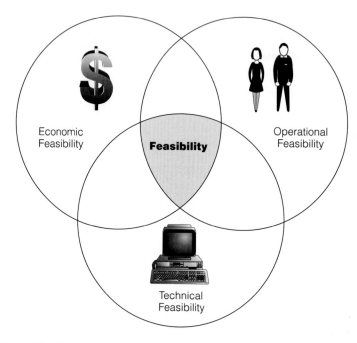

Figure 2-4   *Systems request feasibility requires satisfying three types of feasibility: technical, operational, and economic.*

Technical feasibility   A systems request is technically feasible if the organization has or can obtain the equipment and personnel to develop (or purchase), install, and operate the system. When determining technical feasibility, you need to consider many issues. The following questions illustrate some of the technical feasibility issues that must be resolved.

- Does the organization have the equipment necessary for the system? If not, can it be acquired?
- Does the organization currently have the needed technical expertise? If not, can it be acquired?
- Does the equipment that is proposed for the system have the required capacity? If not, can it be expanded?
- Will the combination of hardware and software be able to supply adequate performance? In answering this, you must consider the impact to the end users already using the hardware, as well as the new end users of the proposed system.
- Will the system be able to handle the projected growth of the organization over the next five years?

Operational feasibility   A systems request is operationally feasible if it is highly likely that the system will be used once it has been developed and implemented. If the end users resist a new system, the system might not be used to its full potential. In that case, the benefits the organization hopes to achieve will not occur. To determine operational feasibility, you need to consider many issues. The following questions illustrate some of the operational feasibility issues that must be resolved.

- Does management support the project? Do the end users support the project? Is the current system well-liked and effectively used? Do the end users see the need for a change?
- How will the end users be involved in planning for the new system? The more involvement they have and the earlier in the project this involvement occurs, the less resistance the end users will have to the new system.
- Will the new system ever produce poorer results than the present system? For example, will any information be less accessible to the end users? Will performance suffer for any new function? If so, is there an overall gain to the organization that outweighs these individual losses?
- Will customers be adversely affected? Might some customers be lost? Will the organization's goodwill with its customers be damaged?
- Is the schedule for development of the system reasonable?

Economic feasibility   A systems request is economically feasible if the projected benefits of the proposed system outweigh the estimated costs involved in developing (or purchasing), installing, and operating it. To determine economic feasibility, you need to ascertain the following:

- The estimated cost of the people needed to develop the system.
- The estimated cost of additional needed equipment.
- The estimated cost of developing or purchasing the necessary software (cost can be a combination of development and purchase costs if the organization purchases a software package and then makes modifications to it).
- The estimated benefits that will result from the proposed system.
- The estimated cost of *not* developing the system.

■ Determining feasibility

The first step in the evaluation of a systems request is an initial determination of feasibility. Those requests that do not meet an initial feasibility test should immediately be rejected, and the systems request form should be returned to the requester with an explanation of the reasons for rejection. For example, a request for the preparation of a report that is needed only once could require extensive input design, preparation, and programming effort. *One-time* reports are often more efficiently prepared using manual methods instead of using a computer. In other cases, end users might be able to use special report writing software tools to produce the reports themselves without assistance from the information systems department. In that case, devoting information systems department resources to the production of the report might not be economically feasible.

Similarly, a systems request that requires the use of hardware that does not exist should be recognized immediately as technically infeasible. This systems request, too, should be rejected.

You should keep in mind that currently infeasible systems requests can become feasible in the future and be resubmitted for evaluation. When the necessary hardware, software, or expertise become available, problems of technical feasibility can be eliminated. Developmental or equipment costs might decrease, or the value of benefits might increase to the point that a particular systems request becomes economically feasible. Also, attitudes within the organization might change to such a degree that a systems request that was initially determined to be operationally infeasible becomes feasible.

Conversely, an initially feasible project can become infeasible. As the project progresses through the systems development life cycle, the conditions that affect feasibility might be altered. Economic conditions might change, or actual or projected costs might be higher than originally anticipated, making the project economically infeasible. Attitudes or politics within the organization toward the project could deteriorate to such a degree that the project becomes operationally infeasible. A previously unknown constraint could render the project technically infeasible. Feasibility analysis is, therefore, an ongoing process that must be performed during *all* phases of the systems development life cycle.

■ Criteria used to evaluate systems requests

After rejecting infeasible systems requests, the committee must then establish priorities for the remaining feasible systems requests. Under normal circumstances, the rule is to favor those projects that provide the greatest benefit to the company at the lowest cost in the shortest period of time. Many factors, however, influence a decision on the selection and scheduling of systems projects. The following questions might be asked during the project evaluation process.

- Will the proposed system or changes in the current system reduce costs? Where? When? How? How much?
- Will the system save money or improve revenue for the company? Where? When? How? How much?
- Will the systems project result in better information or produce better results? How? Are the results measurable?
- Will the customers be better served?
- Will the organization be better served?
- Can the project be implemented in a reasonable time period? Will the results be lasting?
- Are the necessary resources (i.e., money, people, and equipment) available to proceed?
- Is the project absolutely necessary? Projects for which management is given a choice of doing or not doing are often called **discretionary projects**. Projects where no choice exists are **nondiscretionary projects**. Adding a new report for an end user to an existing information system is an example of a discretionary project, while adding a new required federal regulatory report is an example of a nondiscretionary project.

To obtain positive answers to all these questions is unusual. Some proposed systems might not reduce costs but will provide more timely management reports. Other systems might substantially reduce costs but require the purchase or lease of additional hardware. Some systems might be very desirable but require several years of development before the benefits would begin to apply.

For the best possible results, you should evaluate a project based on its tangible factors. A **tangible factor** is a factor that can be assigned an actual or approximate dollar value. A reduction of $8,000 in annual processing costs is an example of a tangible factor.

Often, the project evaluation decision also involves consideration of intangible factors. An **intangible factor** is a factor for which it is difficult to assign a dollar value. Acquiring more accurate information, enhancing the organization's image, and improving customer service are examples of positive intangible factors. In many cases, such intangible factors weigh heavily in the decision for or against a systems project.

If a particular project is nondiscretionary, is it really necessary for the systems review committee to evaluate the project? Because the project *must* be done, the committee must necessarily approve it. Some people argue that it is pointless, therefore, to bother the committee with nondiscretionary systems requests. Besides, waiting for committee approval can unnecessarily delay critical nondiscretionary projects.

Others argue that by submitting *all* systems requests to the systems review committee, the committee is continually aware of all the projects that are occupying the resources of the information systems department. As a result, the committee can better assess the priority of discretionary projects and schedule them more realistically. Additionally, the committee might need to prioritize nondiscretionary projects whenever funds or staff are limited.

Some organizations permanently schedule a portion of the time of one or more systems analysts for nondiscretionary project work. Many nondiscretionary projects are, in fact, quite predictable. Two examples are the annual updates to tax percentages used in a payroll system and the quarterly changes to the legal and regulatory requirements in an insurance processing system. Other nondiscretionary projects are not so predictable, but management can be reasonably certain that such projects will arise. By permanently assigning resources for nondiscretionary projects, these organizations can react immediately to nondiscretionary systems requests and can keep the systems review committee informed of all such projects without first obtaining their full review and approval. ■

Preliminary investigation objects

After an approved systems project has been assigned a priority, the information systems director will direct that a preliminary investigation be undertaken. A **preliminary investigation** involves one or more systems analysts investigating a systems request for the purpose of determining the true nature and scope of the problem and recommending whether a systems analysis of the current system is desirable. Suppose, for example, that a request for systems services concerned complaints that a payroll system was not functioning properly. As a systems analyst, you would perform a preliminary investigation to determine if the complaints were justified. If the results of your preliminary investigation indicated that a problem did exist and could be resolved by a redesign of the current system, you would then submit a report to management recommending a systems analysis of the payroll system.

The purpose of a preliminary investigation is to gather enough information to determine if the information or problems specified in the systems request warrant conducting subsequent phases of the systems development life cycle. The preliminary investigation is *not* a comprehensive data-gathering activity. You are not expected to define *all* the problems in a system, and you should not attempt to propose an absolute solution to the problem stated in the original systems request. Instead, you should meet the five objectives described on the following pages and illustrated in Figure 2-5 on the next page.

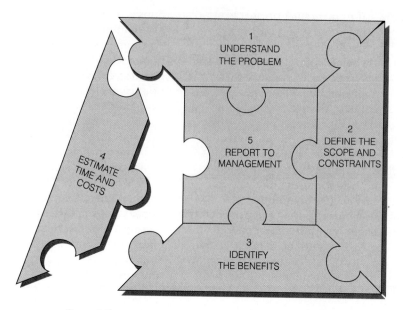

Figure 2-5 *The five objectives of the preliminary investigation phase.*

1. Understand the true nature of the problem.
2. Define the scope and constraints of the proposed systems project.
3. State the benefits that are likely to occur if the proposed systems project is completed.
4. Specify time and money estimates for the next SDLC project phase, systems analysis, and for subsequent developmental phases.
5. Present a report to management describing the problem and detailing recommendations relative to the desirability of conducting a systems analysis of the current system.

■ Understand the problem

One of the key objectives in the preliminary investigation is to gain an understanding of the true nature of the problem and the reason for the systems request. In many cases, the *stated* problem in the systems request is not the *real* problem. The stated problem might be only a symptom of the real problem or might actually be a problem solution; the underlying cause of the problem or the problem itself might not be identified in the systems request. For example, a request for additional hardware (needed because the current computer system is not fast enough) might point to an actual problem of poor systems design, improper scheduling, or even poor operations and programming. Similarly, a systems request for a new report listing customer complaints by product line is actually a statement of a problem solution — the actual problem might be inadequate quality control in the manufacturing plant.

When interacting with end users, you should be careful in your use of the word *problem*, because it generally has a negative connotation. When you ask end users about their problems, some will focus on *only* the obvious faults within the current system; they might not mention desirable features not present in the current system or possible improvements in areas of the system that are currently functioning satisfactorily. You can be more successful in defining the problem if you concentrate your questioning of the end users on specific improvements and on additional capabilities. Using this approach, you determine those opportunities that will improve the end user's job, instead of focusing only on what is wrong today. This is a positive approach that can be more effective in gaining a clear understanding of existing problems.

■ Define the project scope and constraints

Project **scope** is the range, or extent, of the project; scope helps to establish the boundary of the systems request. Defining scope requires precise statements of the problem. For example, the problem statement *payroll is not being produced accurately* can lead to a significantly different project scope than the statement *union dues are not being properly deducted from employees' pay*. Likewise, a statement that the scope of the systems project is to *redesign the accounts receivable system* is significantly different from a statement that the scope is to *correct billing errors*.

Determining who is affected by the problem and who could be affected by the problem's solution is one part of defining scope. To determine the people affected, you must first determine all the business functions involved in the problem. Then, you will be able to identify all the internal organizational units affected by the problem and its potential solutions.

The scope of the project also limits the solutions that you can impose. If you set no limits, you might be tempted to investigate unrelated systems, and a project scheduled for completion in several weeks could take months or even years to complete.

Along with defining the scope of the project, you need to determine the system constraints. A **constraint** is a condition, restriction, or requirement that *must* be met for the system to be viable. A constraint can involve hardware, software, time, policy, law, or cost. System constraints further define or clarify scope. For example, if the system must function on existing equipment, then this is a constraint that must be identified and considered, because it affects potential problem solutions. *The system must interface with the existing accounts payable system, the system must accept input from the fifteen remote sites, the system must produce statistics for the government on hiring practices*, and *the system must be operational by March 1* are all examples of system constraints. Note that constraints are yes or no conditions; a system either meets or does not meet a constraint. When determining and evaluating constraints, keep in mind the following factors:

- Present vs. future. Is the constraint something that must be met as soon as the system is developed or modified? Or is the constraint necessary at some future time?
- Internal vs. external. Is the constraint due to a requirement within the organization, or is it imposed by some external force, such as government?
- Mandatory vs. desirable. Is the constraint mandatory? That is, is it absolutely essential that the constraint be met? Or is it merely desirable? If desirable, how important is the constraint? One common failing is to list all constraints as mandatory. As a result, all possible constraints are built into the system, unnecessarily increasing development time and costs.

Present, external, and mandatory constraints are usually fixed and must be met by the system as it is currently being developed or modified. Constraints determined to be future, internal, and desirable can possibly be postponed to a future follow-up project. Even so, all such constraints should be identified now; a future constraint postponed to a follow-up project, for example, could affect the systems design approach chosen during the current project.

You must clearly and completely define the scope and constraints of the project so there will be no misunderstandings concerning the system under consideration. Always try to avoid a situation where a manager assumes that the system will contain a certain feature and supports the system because of that feature, but later finds that the feature is not included. Providing a clear definition of the scope and constraints helps to avoid such misunderstandings.

The definition of the problem to be solved and the scope and constraints of the systems request are critical to the process of identifying the best solutions to the problem. Some systems analysts have a tendency during the preliminary investigation to recommend a complete study of the entire information system when a less costly approach, in terms of time and effort, could be equally effective in solving the organization's problems.

■ Identify the benefits

The third objective of the preliminary investigation is to identify the tangible and intangible benefits that are expected to result from the systems request. These benefits, along with the estimates of costs that you will provide, will be used by management when it decides whether to pursue the project beyond the preliminary investigation phase.

Tangible benefits are those that can be stated in terms of dollars. Such tangible benefits can result from a decrease in expenses, an increase in revenues, or both. For example, one expected benefit of a proposed system might be to reduce overtime costs or eliminate the need to hire additional staff. The proposed system might improve customer service, thereby measurably increasing sales and decreasing the percentage of merchandise returns. A proposed inventory control system might enable the organization to maintain a smaller inventory, leading to the benefit of lowered inventory storage costs.

Intangible benefits are those that cannot be stated in terms of dollars. Nevertheless, you should also try to identify all relevant intangible benefits. For instance, the proposed system might relieve the tedium of a particular task, thus improving employee morale and job satisfaction and decreasing turnover. More timely information might benefit the organization by improving the decision-making process. A proposed system might enhance the image of the organization. Such intangible benefits, although not quantifiable, might help the organization attain its goals; therefore, they should be identified and documented.

■ Estimate the costs

The fourth objective of the preliminary investigation is to develop specific time and money estimates for the systems analysis phase, the second phase of the systems development life cycle. You should consider the following issues when you make your estimates.

1. What information must you obtain, and what is the volume of information that you must gather and analyze?
2. What sources of information will you use, and what difficulties will you encounter in gathering and analyzing the information?
3. How many people will you interview, and how much time is required to interview the people?
4. How much time and how many people are required to analyze the information gathered and to prepare a report indicating the findings and alternative solutions to the problem?

In addition to accurate estimates for the systems analysis phase, you also should provide ballpark estimates of the money and time requirements for all subsequent project phases. Such estimates are often stated in rather broad ranges, such as $90,000-$120,000, or 8-12 months. Management needs a general idea of the resource requirements for the entire project to be able to weigh the estimated total costs against the estimated total benefits and then to make a decision based on knowledge of the entire project.

■ Report to management

The purpose of the preliminary investigation is to clarify the systems request and the practicality of pursuing solutions by obtaining an overview of the current system and its problems. The preliminary investigation also provides an opportunity to determine more accurately the projected cost of the complete analysis. The preliminary investigation takes a minimal amount of time to get a better handle on the request so impractical projects are terminated with a minimum expenditure of time and money and management can weigh the estimated value of the project against those of other proposed projects in order to establish priorities for the scheduling of projects. To inform management of the results of the preliminary investigation, you present a report to management, who then decides whether the systems analysis phase should take place.

Preliminary investigation activities

o ensure success when conducting a preliminary investigation, you should perform the seven steps described below and illustrated in Figure 2-6 on the next page. These steps apply regardless of the size of the systems project.

1. Obtain an authorization for the preliminary investigation.
2. Identify the information that you need to gather.
3. Obtain organization charts for those departments undergoing study to determine who should be interviewed.
4. Conduct interviews to obtain information.
5. Review current system documentation and observe current operations to obtain information.
6. Analyze the gathered information.
7. Present your results and recommendations to management.

■ Authorization to proceed

A systems project often results in a significant change from the usual mode of operation within a company. As a consequence, you might encounter resistance during your preliminary investigation. This is not the problem it was a few years ago, because end users today are more likely to be aware of the potential benefits to be derived from a new system. It is still an issue to be considered, however. In addition, a preliminary investigation can often require the involvement of personnel who are not the direct end users of the system. These people might not immediately understand the potential organizational benefits of the study, and yet their cooperation is essential to the success of the project.

Before beginning the preliminary investigation, therefore, you should obtain an authorization from management. In prior years, this often took the form of a formal *letter of authority*. Today, however, organizations are more mature, and a variety of methods are used to authorize the preliminary investigation and to communicate your involvement to others in the organization. An approved systems request and written directions from the systems review committee are normally sufficient. In addition, a launch meeting of key managers and information systems personnel often serves the same purpose. Regardless of the manner in which you obtain authorization, the organization's personnel do need to know that you have been authorized to proceed with the systems project.

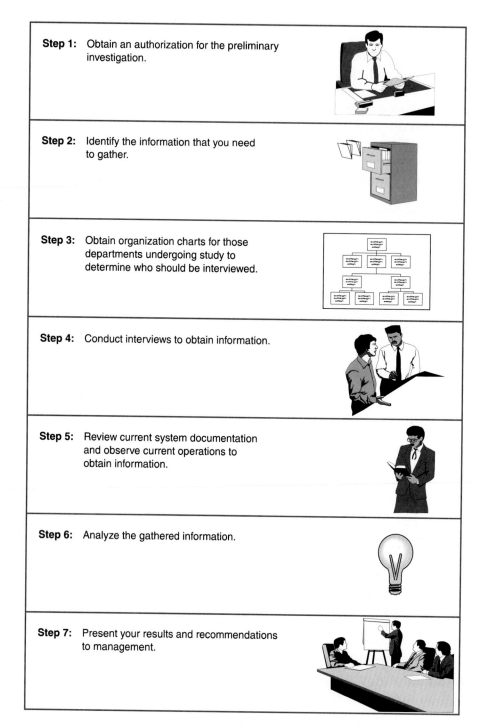

Step 1: Obtain an authorization for the preliminary investigation.

Step 2: Identify the information that you need to gather.

Step 3: Obtain organization charts for those departments undergoing study to determine who should be interviewed.

Step 4: Conduct interviews to obtain information.

Step 5: Review current system documentation and observe current operations to obtain information.

Step 6: Analyze the gathered information.

Step 7: Present your results and recommendations to management.

Figure 2-6 *Preliminary investigation activities.*

■ Identify needed information

You should prepare a list of the information you need to obtain during the preliminary investigation phase. The basis for this information consists of the objectives for this phase that we discussed earlier: understand the problem, define the scope and constraints, identify the benefits, estimate the costs, and report to management. From this list of needed information, you can prepare a schedule of the remaining activities for the preliminary investigation phase.

■ Organization charts

In many instances you will not know the organizational structure of the departments around which the problem centers. You should, therefore, obtain organization charts for these departments to help determine the appropriate individuals to interview during the preliminary investigation. Organization charts often can be obtained from the company's personnel department. If such charts are not available, you should obtain the necessary information from department personnel in order to construct the charts. Even when organization charts are available, you should verify that the charts are updated and accurate. Additionally, organization charts show the formal structure of an organization, not the informal organizational structure. Because it is often through the informal structure that things are accomplished and decisions are made in an organization, you should know and deal diplomatically with both organizational structures.

■ Conduct interviews

The primary method of obtaining information during the preliminary investigation is the interview. You must be sure to interview those individuals who can best assist you to define the problem and to identify potential solutions.

An interview should be approached as logically as computer programming. Remember that the purpose of the interview, and of the preliminary investigation in general, is to uncover facts about the existing system. Its purpose is not to convince others that a new system is needed. Thus, your primary role in an interview is to be a *listener*.

When you conduct interviews during the preliminary investigation, you must be quite selective in who you interview. Because the preliminary investigation is not designed to learn every detail of a given system, you must not spend time interviewing everyone who has anything at all to do with the system. Concentrate instead on those persons who know the most about the system, so you can gain an accurate picture of the current system.

Generally, you will interview people in managerial or supervisory positions during the preliminary investigation. These people should have sufficient knowledge of the system and its problems to give you a good idea of the overall operation and to help you identify the potential benefits of completing the systems request. In rare instances, however, you may have to interview persons at other levels within the company during the preliminary investigation in order to get a sufficiently clear understanding of the system.

■ Review current processing

Although the interview is an extremely important method of obtaining information, you might often find it necessary to further investigate the manner in which the current system works. One other useful fact-finding method is to review the documentation of the current system. Documentation may not be up-to-date, so you should verify this with the end users to ensure you are receiving accurate and complete information. Another fact-finding method is to observe the current system in operation. You might watch workers as they carry out their normal tasks. You might choose to trace or follow the actual paths taken by input source documents or output reports. You should pursue these investigations until you have enough information to be able to determine current problems and potential solutions.

■ Analyze the information

Once you have gathered all the information you identified as necessary in step 2, you are ready to analyze the information, to identify alternatives with their associated costs and benefits, and to determine a recommended course of action. In this preliminary investigation phase, there are generally only three alternatives. If you determine that there is no problem, then no further action is necessary. If the problem and its solution are both minor, you might recommend proceeding directly to the systems development phase. Most often, however, your recommendation will be to undertake systems analysis, the next phase of the SDLC.

Preliminary investigation completion

■ Report

After you conduct a preliminary investigation, you must report your findings either to the systems review committee or to top-level management. The report should include what you found concerning the operation of the system in question, the problems that appear to be present in the system, and your recommendations for future action. This report is presented in written form and is usually prepared using a word processor. You also must make an oral presentation of your preliminary investigation results.

While the format of the preliminary investigation report varies from one organization to another, you often will organize it as shown in Figure 2-7.

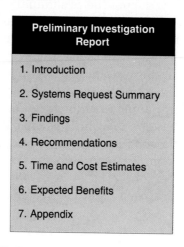

Preliminary Investigation Report

1. Introduction

2. Systems Request Summary

3. Findings

4. Recommendations

5. Time and Cost Estimates

6. Expected Benefits

7. Appendix

Figure 2-7   *The organization of a preliminary investigation report.*

The report typically includes the following seven sections.

1. The first section is simply an introduction to the report. It contains a brief description of the system that was investigated, as well as the name of the person or group who carried out the investigation, and the name of the person or group who initiated the investigation.

2. This section summarizes the original systems request. The summary is necessary so readers of the report will understand why the investigation was initiated.

3. The third section presents the findings of the preliminary investigation, including a description of the true nature and scope of the proposed project and the conclusions you have reached.

4. Next, the report contains the recommendations for further action by the information systems department. Members of management make the final decisions concerning future action, and they do not always follow the recommendations of the information systems department. In most cases, however, those recommendations weigh heavily in management's decision making.

5. One of the factors that will influence management's decision is the cost of the recommendation of the information systems department. Include an estimate of time and cost, therefore, if you recommend further action. You must make management aware of all costs whenever any type of system activity is to take place.

6. The next section contains the anticipated benefits of implementing the recommendations. Whenever asked to spend money and commit other resources, management must be told the results it can expect from the expenditures.

7. Include an appendix if you need to attach supporting information. For example, you might list the interviews you conducted, the documentation you reviewed, and other sources of information you obtained for the preliminary investigation phase. You do not need to attach detailed reports of the interviews you conducted or other lengthy documentation. It is critical, however, that you retain these documents to support your findings and to serve as sources for future reference.

■ Presentation

In the presentation you make at the end of the preliminary investigation, you need to inform the audience of what is currently taking place within the system, direct their attention to the problems that have been occurring within the system and why they have been occurring, and present a recommendation relative to whether a full-scale systems analysis should take place.

In the next chapter, we discuss detailed suggestions for making presentations as we study the presentation at the end of the systems analysis phase.

CHAPTER CASE STUDY

James Tool Company — Preliminary Investigation

■ Background

Shortly after James Tool Company was created in 1967, the management team began to use a service bureau to handle payroll processing and standard accounting systems, such as accounts payable and general ledger. This service bureau, Brafford Services, uses its own mainframe computers to contract with James Tool Company and dozens of other companies to process these companies' common business systems.

James Tool Company rapidly grew in size, and by 1976, management determined that it would be more productive and cost effective to purchase its own mainframe computer for the processing of its manufacturing functions and other specialized systems, such as marketing and labor distribution. At this same time, James Tool Company established an information systems department to develop and maintain the manufacturing and other systems. James Tool Company has been very progressive in its use of computer technology and has continued to upgrade its computer environment and application systems over the years. In addition to a recently upgraded mainframe computer, the company currently has microcomputers installed in most offices and in many shop floor locations. Payroll processing has remained with Brafford Services, however, because it was believed that the payroll function was being correctly and efficiently managed.

During the past several months, however, complaints have come from both employees and the unions that union dues have not been handled properly. They cite an increasing number of instances in which union dues have not been properly deducted from payroll checks and in which the checks paid to the unions were incorrect. In addition, company auditors have filed several complaints that the amounts deducted from payroll checks did not match the amounts paid to the union. Payroll clerks within James Tool have had to work overtime to correct all reported errors and to issue hand-typed checks to employees and the union.

Arnold Henderson, the vice president of finance, has discussed these problems with both Jim McKeen, the director of the payroll department, and Delbert Donovan, the director of union relations. In addition, Henderson has become increasingly concerned with the amount of money being spent for overtime pay in the payroll department. McKeen has indicated that this outlay of overtime money is necessary, because the demands of the payroll operation require more people than are available and his budget will not allow for the hiring of more personnel.

■ The request for information systems services

Arnold Henderson decided to ask the information systems department to investigate the payroll application system. He completed the Request for Information Systems Services, shown in Figure 2-8 and forwarded it to the information systems department for action.

REQUEST FOR INFORMATION SYSTEMS SERVICES

DATE:	September 9, 1996
SUBMITTED BY:	Arnold Henderson
TITLE:	Vice President
DEPARTMENT:	Finance
PHONE:	X138

Request for:
[x] MODIFICATION OF EXISTING SYSTEM
[ ] NEW SYSTEM

DESCRIPTION OF REQUESTED SYSTEMS SERVICES:
(attach additonal documents as necessary)

There have been some problems in our payroll system. In particular, an extraordinary amount of overtime has been paid to payroll department employees. In addition, some problems have been encountered in the deduction of union dues from employees' checks, and the unions have been complaining to me about this problem. I have spoken with Jim McKeen, director of the payroll department, and he says the only problem is lack of personnel - he wants two more people. I think, however, that there may be more to it than that, so I would like you to look into the situation. Please contact me at your earliest convenience.

(to be completed by Information Systems Department)

DATE:

ACTION:

Figure 2-8 Arnold Henderson's request for information systems services.

As you can see in the request, Henderson specified problems with the payroll system and requested assistance. In no way did he identify the causes of the problems nor did he propose a solution. This is a typical example of a systems request that the information systems department receives from employees outside the department who know of a problem but who know neither the cause nor the solution.

When Clyde Harland, the manager of applications, received Henderson's Request for Information Systems Services, he began the process of determining if a preliminary investigation was warranted. Harland first contacted David Green, the director of the information systems department. Together, they decided that the information systems department would likely find problems in the current payroll process, because it had been developed in 1981. Harland assigned systems analyst Don Mard to the task of conducting the preliminary investigation of the payroll system. David Green then advised Henderson that Mard would begin a preliminary investigation of the payroll system the following week.

Henderson then wrote and distributed the memo shown in Figure 2-9. Notice that the memo gives high-level management approval for the preliminary investigation phase. The memo gives few details, but it alerts employees that Don Mard will conduct an authorized investigation and requests their full cooperation.

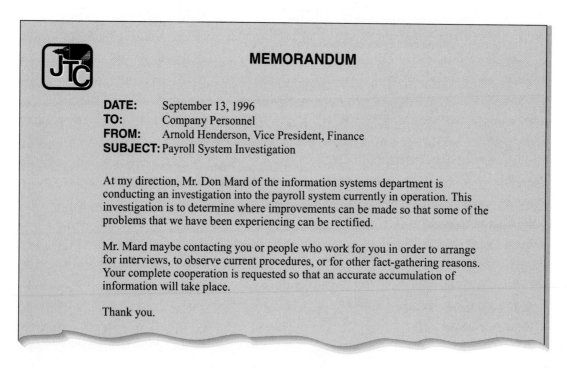

MEMORANDUM

DATE: September 13, 1996
TO: Company Personnel
FROM: Arnold Henderson, Vice President, Finance
SUBJECT: Payroll System Investigation

At my direction, Mr. Don Mard of the information systems department is conducting an investigation into the payroll system currently in operation. This investigation is to determine where improvements can be made so that some of the problems that we have been experiencing can be rectified.

Mr. Mard maybe contacting you or people who work for you in order to arrange for interviews, to observe current procedures, or for other fact-gathering reasons. Your complete cooperation is requested so that an accurate accumulation of information will take place.

Thank you.

Figure 2-9   *Arnold Henderson's memo announcing the start of the payroll system preliminary investigation.*

■ Organization charts

To begin the preliminary investigation, Don Mard requested an organization chart of the payroll department from Arnold Henderson. Henderson suggested that Mard contact Jim McKeen, director of the payroll department.

When Mard called Jim McKeen, McKeen informed him that the personnel department had job descriptions for all payroll department employees and that they also should have formal organization charts of the company. When Mard contacted the personnel department, he was informed that personnel did not have any organization charts, but they did have job descriptions for the employees in the payroll department. The vice president of the personnel department, Alice Hilbert, suggested that Mard contact Henderson; she was sure his office had organization charts for those departments under his control!

From the information received from personnel and from additional contact with Henderson, Don Mard constructed the organization chart shown in Figure 2-10.

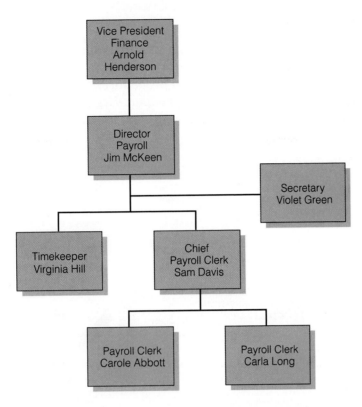

Figure 2-10 *Payroll department organization chart at James Tool Company.*

■ Interviews

Don Mard decided that he should interview Arnold Henderson and Jim McKeen, as well as Delbert Donovan, the director of union relations.

Henderson proved to be a good source of general information concerning problems that have been occurring within the payroll system. Also, Henderson provided Mard with the costs of the current system.

In his meeting with Delbert Donovan, Mard learned more about the reported union deduction errors. He also learned that the company uses no standard form to notify the payroll department when an employee joins a union. Donovan explained that instead of using a form, he immediately sends a memo to Jim McKeen detailing the pertinent facts.

Jim McKeen has the responsibility of managing the payroll department and, therefore, is in daily contact with the problems and procedures in the department. In the interview meeting, McKeen told Mard that the only problems with union deductions occur when formerly nonunion employees first join one of the unions. McKeen admitted that occasionally in such situations the deductions required for union dues do not begin immediately, but he clarified that it was not his payroll clerks who were at fault. He suggested that Mard look elsewhere for the source of the problem. McKeen then explained that it was the responsibility of the director of union relations to notify the payroll department, via e-mail or telephone, whenever an employee joins a union.

McKeen offered his opinion that the payroll process generally worked fine. He stated that if he were allowed to hire two additional payroll clerks, no further problems with the payroll system would occur. After the meeting with McKeen, Mard decided that perhaps McKeen's answers were somewhat prejudiced. McKeen has worked with the existing payroll system for many years. As the current director of the payroll department, McKeen might be unwilling to say that there could be departmental personnel problems that contribute to the payroll problems. And McKeen seemed to feel he already knew the solution to the payroll problem: add to his staff by hiring two more people.

■ Review Current Documentation

After interviewing Henderson, Donovan, and McKeen, Mard wanted to find out more about the actual sequence of operations that takes place within the current system. He consulted the current documentation of the system and found step-by-step procedures for the preparation of the payroll. He reviewed these written procedures with the timekeeper, Virginia Hill, and the chief payroll clerk, Sam Davis, and learned that the procedures were outdated; the actual sequence of events in the payroll process is as illustrated in Figure 2-11.

Step 1: A newly hired employee completes an Employee Master Sheet in the personnel department. A copy of this sheet is sent to the payroll department.

Step 2: From the Employee Master Sheets, time cards are prepared and distributed before the employees arrive at work for the week.

Step 3: Employees check in and out on a time clock Monday through Sunday.

Step 4: The time cards are collected Monday morning and returned to payroll. The timekeeper copies pay rates from the Employee Master Sheets to the time cards, which are then sent to Brafford Services.

Step 5: Brafford Services processes the time cards and prepares the paychecks and payroll register.

Step 6: The time cards, paychecks, and payroll register are received from Brafford Services. The chief payroll clerk creates the union reports.

Figure 2-11   *Sequence of events in the payroll processing at James Tool Company.*

Mard noted that a number of forms (for example, employee master sheets, time cards, payroll registers, and paychecks) are prepared and used in the current payroll system. In this preliminary investigation phase, he is not concerned with the detailed information that appears on each form. He would gather such information only after management has authorized the systems analysis phase.

■ Presentation of findings

After Mard conducted his investigation, he analyzed his findings, prepared the preliminary investigation report, and began to plan his presentation to management. The memo to Arnold Henderson that accompanied the written report and announced the time and location of the presentation is shown in Figure 2-12.

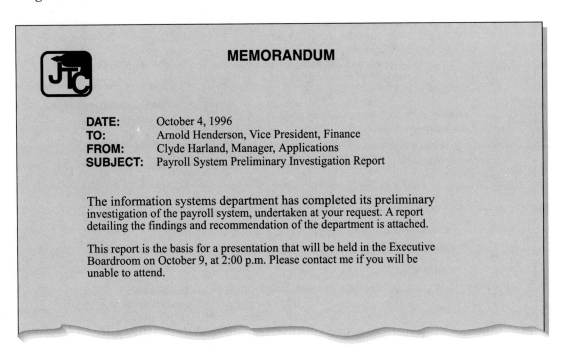

MEMORANDUM

DATE: October 4, 1996
TO: Arnold Henderson, Vice President, Finance
FROM: Clyde Harland, Manager, Applications
SUBJECT: Payroll System Preliminary Investigation Report

The information systems department has completed its preliminary investigation of the payroll system, undertaken at your request. A report detailing the findings and recommendation of the department is attached.

This report is the basis for a presentation that will be held in the Executive Boardroom on October 9, at 2:00 p.m. Please contact me if you will be unable to attend.

Figure 2-12   Cover memo for the James Tool Company preliminary investigation report.

Figure 2-13 on the next two pages shows the preliminary investigation report that Mard prepared for the payroll system. After the report was submitted to Arnold Henderson, he and other upper-level managers of James Tool Company attended the presentation. After a question and answer session, the managers discussed the findings and recommendations and agreed that the payroll system should be fixed. Thus, Arnold Henderson approved the systems analysis phase, the next step in the systems development life cycle.

PRELIMINARY INVESTIGATION REPORT

James Tool Company Payroll System
Prepared: October 4, 1996

INTRODUCTION
The information systems department has completed a preliminary investigation of the payroll system. This investigation was prompted by the September 9, 1996 request from Arnold Henderson, vice president, finance.

SYSTEMS REQUEST SUMMARY
Two problems were cited in the original request for information systems services:
1. Deductions for union dues from employees' checks are not correct, especially for those employees who join the union after employment.
2. Payroll department overtime charges have been excessive.

FINDINGS OF THE PRELIMINARY INVESTIGATION
The following problems were found with union deductions:
1. There is no formalized procedure by which the department of union relations notifies the payroll department of an employee's change of union status.
2. The payroll processing contracted from Brafford Services does not currently include the union reports necessary for verification and reporting of union deduction totals. These reports are manually prepared by the payroll department clerks.

The following factors were found to contribute to the payroll department overtime problem:
1. The current payroll procedures were developed in 1981, when there were 42 employees, and have not been significantly modified since. There are currently more than 450 employees. The payroll department has been incurring overtime charges only recently, suggesting that current procedures have now surpassed the limit on the number of employees that can be handled efficiently.
2. When the payroll department receives notification of an error in deducting union dues, a new paycheck must be prepared, and the payroll register and union reports must be manually corrected.

-1-

Figure 2-13 *Page 1 of the James Tool Company preliminary investigation report.*

RECOMMENDATIONS

The problems identified in the preliminary investigation will not disappear on their own. In fact, further growth of the company will only place additional burdens on existing payroll processing. The information systems department, therefore, recommends a system analysis of the current automated payroll processing at Brafford Services and the manual payroll processing at James Tool Company.

TIME AND COST ESTIMATES

We estimate that two work weeks are required for an analyst to perform the systems analysis recommended above.

We estimate that one work week of time is required from persons outside the information systems department for the purposes of interviewing and supplying information to the investigating analyst.

The following is our estimate of the total costs for performing the systems analysis:

2.0 weeks	—	Systems analyst	@ $750/week	$1,500.00
1.0 week	—	Outside personnel	@ $600/week	600.00
			Total:	$2,100.00

Our ballpark estimate for the total project effort is two to four months elapsed time at a cost of $7,000 to $12,000.

EXPECTED BENEFITS

At the conclusion of the systems analysis phase, the information systems department expects to have defined in detail the problems that exist in the payroll system and will present alternative solutions for these problems. The recommended solutions will eliminate or substantially reduce overtime and eliminate errors in the deduction of union dues. The solutions, therefore, should reduce overall costs, improve employee and union relations, and streamline processing procedures.

Figure 2-13 (continued)   Page 2 of the James Tool Company preliminary investigation report.

Summary

The preliminary investigation is the first phase of the systems development life cycle. Systems projects are initiated to improve performance, information availability, economy, controls, or service so the organization can better meet objectives in support of its goals. End user requests, top-management directives, existing system errors and inefficiencies, the information systems department, and external forces are the sources of systems projects.

The systems analyst should first evaluate the feasibility of the systems request. If the systems analyst immediately determines that the request is not technically, operationally, or economically feasible, the systems request can be rejected with a minimum of cost and effort. Feasible systems requests are evaluated in terms of their expected costs and benefits, both tangible and intangible. Those requests that are approved are then scheduled for a preliminary investigation.

The purpose of the preliminary investigation phase is to gather enough information for management to determine if the next phase, systems analysis, is warranted. The five basic objectives of the preliminary investigation are:

1. Determine and understand the true nature of the problem.
2. Define the scope and constraints of the systems request.
3. Identify the benefits of resolving the problem.
4. Estimate costs for subsequent project development phases.
5. Prepare a report and presentation to management covering the information learned during the preliminary investigation phase, along with a recommendation for further action. If the recommendation is to proceed with the systems analysis phase, the report and presentation includes estimates of time and staffing requirements, costs, benefits, and expected results for that next phase of the systems development life cycle.

Review Questions

1. What is a goal? What is an objective? How are they different? How are they related?
2. What possible types of desired improvement can cause the initiation of a systems request?
3. By what other names might the systems review committee be known?
4. What is the role of the systems review committee?
5. Is systems review always done by a committee of people, or can it be done by a single individual? What are some advantages and disadvantages of a committee approach?
6. What is feasibility? List and briefly discuss the three kinds of feasibility. At what point(s) in the systems development life cycle could a systems request or a proposed solution be determined infeasible?
7. What is a discretionary project? What is a nondiscretionary project?
8. What is scope?
9. What is a constraint? In what three ways are constraints classified?
10. List and briefly describe the seven basic sections of the preliminary investigation report.
11. What is the purpose of the preliminary investigation?
12. How do tangible benefits differ from intangible benefits?

Discussion Questions

1. One source of new systems projects is a top-management directive. You are the director of the information systems department, and you receive a directive from the vice president of marketing to write a program to prepare 200 mailing labels on the computer for a one-time mailing of advertising literature. As systems director, you know that the mailing labels can be prepared more efficiently by merely assigning a clerk to prepare the mailing labels using the mail merge function of the word processor on the marketing department's personal computer. How would you handle this situation?

2. The vice president of accounting says to you, the director of information systems, "this systems development life cycle stuff takes too much time and money." He tells you that his people know what they are doing and that all systems requests coming from his department are necessary and important to the organization. He suggests that the information systems department bypass the initial steps for any accounting department request and immediately get to work at the solution. What would you say to him?

3. What would you do as a systems analyst if a vice president of your company came to you and insisted that a system be computerized, but, at the conclusion of the preliminary investigation phase, you knew that the system could not be cost-justified?

4. Do you think the absence of a systems review committee at James Tool Company has contributed in any way to the difficulties they are now experiencing with the payroll system? Do you think the lack of a systems review committee adversely affects the resolution of problems?

MINICASE STUDIES

Gallagher Imports

Four months ago, Douglas Highstreet was hired away from an advertising agency to become the director of marketing for Gallagher Imports. Highstreet recently submitted a systems request for the redesign of customer statements to the information systems department at Gallagher. Julie Hippen, the systems analyst assigned to do the preliminary investigation, first interviewed Highstreet to determine the reasons for the request. Highstreet explained that the current statements are much too unattractive and dull. "Gallagher Imports needs to update its image," he explained. "We have to convince our customers that Gallagher Imports is current with contemporary ideals and tastes. And the best place to start is with the monthly statements we send them. We need something more eye-catching, more artistic, more modern!"

Julie next interviewed the director of accounting, George Parker, who oversees the accounts receivable (A/R) computer system. The monthly customer statements are output from that A/R system. Parker told Julie that no problems with the A/R system have been reported, and no complaints from the customers about the statements have ever been received. He assured Julie that the current forms were clear and easy to understand.

Confused, Julie decided she should talk with Barbara Hennessey, the manager of customer relations. Hennessey assured Julie that Gallagher Imports was having no problems with its customers. She even showed Julie the latest annual report, which clearly showed that Gallagher Import's annual sales were increasing at a healthy pace.

Questions

1. Do you think this a feasible project? Discuss.
2. What should Julie do next?

Ridgeway Company

At Ridgeway Company, senior vice president Helen Hill, vice president of finance Luis Sanchez, and director of information systems Linda Usher comprise the permanent steering committee that approves and schedules all systems projects.

Thomas McGee, vice president of operations, recently talked to Hill about the committee's work. "It just isn't fair," McGee began, "for the committee to be able to turn down projects that one of my facility managers thinks is worthwhile. After all, Ridgeway runs all the facilities as separate profit centers. The Country Club pro shop, the golf course, the restaurant and bar, and the tennis club all have their own budgets. When the information systems department does a project for one of them, the facility is charged for all development costs. My pro shop manager, Chris Connely, is planning to submit a request for a computerized inventory system for his shop. We have the figures to prove that the system will save the pro shop and the company money in the long run. The pro shop has the funds to pay for the system development, but what's so frustrating is that after all our planning, the committee might say no-go. I can see why the committee has to have the power to set priorities and schedules, but if we are willing to pay for a system, and if we believe the system is worthwhile, why should the committee be able to veto it?"

Questions

1. Is a project that is good for the pro shop necessarily good for the company? For what valid reasons might the steering committee turn down this project request?

2. How should Hill respond to McGee's complaint?

G. H. Ames & Company

Neal Killian, a systems analyst at G. H. Ames & Company, is often assigned responsibility for maintenance changes to the company's sales analysis system. He recently noticed that the frequency of requests for fixes and additions to that system was increasing. Neal mentioned this to his manager, Dana Payne, who asked if the marketing department had registered any specific complaints about the system. When Neal admitted that he was unaware of any such complaints, Dana said, "Then don't worry about it."

Questions

1. Do you agree with Dana Payne's decision? Why or why not?

2. If the frequency of fixes and enhancements on the sales analysis system is increasing, what are some possible causes?

3. How else could Dana Payne have responded to Neal's concerns?

STUDENT CASE STUDY

Western Dental Clinic — Preliminary Investigation

Introduction

Western Dental Clinic's office manager, Emily Hendricks, recently has asked permission to hire an additional office clerk. She feels the current staff can no longer handle the growing workload. The associates discussed Hendricks' request during their meeting. The associates were not surprised that the office staff was beginning to be overwhelmed by the constantly growing workload. Because the clinic was busier and more profitable than ever, they all agreed that Western could certainly afford to hire another office worker. Then, Dr. Early voiced another idea: to investigate the possibility of computerizing the office systems. Early suggested that a computer could keep track of all the patients, appointments, charges, and payments, thus relieving the office staff of much of its overwhelming paperwork. All the associates were enthusiastic about the possibilities and voted to follow up on the suggestion. Early agreed to head up the project.

Because no member of the clinic staff was a computer expert, Early decided to find a computer consultant to study the current office systems and recommend a course of action. Several friends recommended Jim Archer, a local independent computer consultant who was known to be very knowledgeable about computerized business applications.

Student Assignments

1. Assess the initial feasibility of this project.

2. Dr. Early arranges an introductory meeting between the associates of Western Dental Clinic and Jim Archer to determine if there is mutual interest in pursuing the project. What should the associates try to learn about Jim Archer? What should Jim Archer try to learn in this meeting?

3. Western Dental Clinic decided to contract for the services of Jim Archer to perform a preliminary investigation. If you were Jim Archer, what would your plan of action now be? What information is needed? From whom would you obtain it?

PHASE 2 Systems Analysis

CHAPTER 3

Determining Requirements

Introduction

In the preliminary investigation phase, your job is to determine if a problem does in fact exist. In the **systems analysis phase,** your objective is to learn exactly what takes place in the current system, to determine and fully document what should take place, and to develop and make recommendations to management.

We begin this chapter with an overview of the systems analysis phase and then look at the general characteristics of systems analysis. Next, we discuss the requirements determination stage of the systems analysis phase. We begin the discussion of this stage by describing the information you need to collect. Then, we examine techniques for determining system requirements: interviewing, data collection, observation, questionnaires, and research. Then, we look at how you record these system requirements. Next, we provide an overview of requirements analysis, the second stage of the systems analysis phase, which is covered in detail in the next two chapters. Finally, we discuss effective presentation techniques.

Systems analysis overview

During the systems analysis phase, the emphasis of your investigation is on *what* is taking place. You must obtain answers to many questions about the current system. For example, you must determine what procedures and documents are used and what people are involved in each operation. Also, you need to know what transactions are processed and what information is generated and used within the system. At the same time, you must determine what is desired by the end users. You must learn such things as the strengths of the current system, procedures that should be eliminated, and improvements that are needed. Moreover, as you analyze this information, you must answer two additional questions: you must determine *why* system activities are being performed as they are and *where* improvements and changes should be made.

Management uses the following simple three-step approach to decision making that is equally applicable to the task of systems analysis.

1. Get the facts.
2. Analyze the facts.
3. Make a decision.

During systems analysis you *get the facts* by a process called **requirements determination**, also known as **fact-finding**, which is the subject of this chapter. During **requirements analysis**, the subject of the following two chapters, you *analyze the facts* and organize, document, and present the facts to management, who then *makes a decision*. Thus, this simple three-step approach provides a sound framework with which to solve systems problems. Figure 3-1 illustrates the application of these three steps to the systems analysis phase of the systems development life cycle.

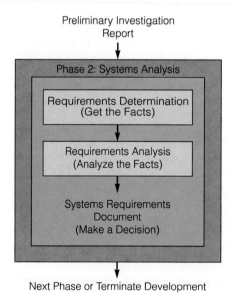

Figure 3-1   *The three steps of decision making and their application to the systems analysis phase of the systems development life cycle.*

During the systems analysis phase, you use the same techniques you used during the preliminary investigation phase. The major difference between the two phases is the depth of the process. During the preliminary investigation, you attempt to get only an overview of the system, whereas during systems analysis, you must investigate the system in depth.

Software tools have been developed to assist you in analyzing the facts that you collect during the systems analysis phase; we will examine these software tools later in the text. Unfortunately, no software tools have been developed for fact-finding. This chapter will present many valuable tips and ideas, but remember that no magic framework guarantees that all the necessary facts have been gathered and understood. Only by being careful and thorough in your fact-finding, while utilizing all your analytical skills, can you help ensure that your investigation will be comprehensive.

Systems analysis characteristics

The systems analysis phase is a complex undertaking because information systems are large, difficult to define, and subject to change. Additionally, a system problem might be ill-defined initially because of uncertainty about its true nature and scope. As the analysis proceeds, the problem can evolve or change. Furthermore, several potential solutions are normally possible, but only one can be chosen. Even when the chosen solution is later being developed, the organization, the participants in the problem, and the environment in which the organization operates, are all continually changing.

During systems analysis, you must interact with end users at various organizational levels. In addition, you must be able to understand and integrate the system needs of all the end users, who can have different, and occasionally conflicting, objectives.

The size of the information system also contributes to the complexity of systems analysis. Some systems are truly enormous, with hundreds or even thousands of procedures, inputs, reports, and other outputs. Usually, a team of systems analysts is assigned to large system projects. Additional effort is required to coordinate the systems analysts and to manage all the details associated with these very large systems.

The systems analysis phase requires you to obtain complete answers to the questions *who*, *what*, *when*, *where*, and *how*. With each of these five questions, you also must ask *why*, as you seek answers for questions, such as:

1. Who? Who performs each of the procedures within the system? Why? Is the correct person performing the activity? Could the job duties be assigned to someone else?

2. What? What is being done? What procedures are being followed? Why? Why is this process necessary? Often, procedures have been followed for many years and no one knows why. You should question why a procedure is being followed at all.

3. Where? Where are operations being performed? Why? Where could they be performed? Could they be performed more efficiently elsewhere?

4. When? When is a procedure performed? Why? Why is it being performed at this time? Is this the best time?

5. How? How is a procedure performed? Why? Why is it performed in that manner? Could it be performed better, more efficiently, or more cost-effectively in some other manner?

Figure 3-2 on the next page summarizes the questions asked during systems analysis and categorizes them by the stage in which they must be answered: during requirements determination or during requirements analysis.

Requirements Determination		Requirements Analysis
What is done?	Why is it done?	What should be done?
Where is it done?	Why is it done there?	Where should it be done?
When is it done?	Why is it done at this time?	When should it be done?
Who does it?	Why does this person do it?	Who should do it?
How is it done?	Why is it done this way?	How should it be done?
Why is it done?	Why should it be (or not be) done?	Should it be changed (or eliminated)

Figure 3-2   *Questions in systems projects classified by the stage of the systems analysis phase in which they must be answered.*

Systems requirements

■ Typical system requirements

A **system requirement** is a feature that must be included in an information system in order for the system to be acceptable to the end users. Determining all the system requirements is essential, because these documented requirements form the basis for further development of the new system. The documented requirements also later serve as a standard against which the finished system is compared to determine its acceptability.

We classify system requirements into five categories: outputs, inputs, processes, timings, and controls. Some examples of typical system requirements within each of these five categories follow.

Outputs

- On a weekly basis, the system must produce a report showing the part number, description, quantity on hand, quantity allocated, quantity available, and unit cost of all parts, sorted by part number.

- On a daily basis, the system must produce an Accounts Receivable Transaction Register, in account-number sequence, showing the account number, charges, payments and credits, old balance, new balance, and amount over credit limit for all accounts with activity that day.

Inputs

- The information on approved Customer Account Applications, including date, account number, name, address, telephone, standard industrial classification code, and credit limit, is used to add a new customer to the system.

- Final grade information is input to the system on machine-scannable forms prepared by the instructor. Each form, which is identified by course code and section code, includes a series of student numbers, student names, and final grades.

Processes

- Student records must be accessible by either the student name or the student number.

■ As the final step in the year-end processing cycle, the system deletes terminated employee records.

Timings

■ Monthly statements are prepared no later than the end of the third business day of each month.
■ Class lists are produced within five hours after the end of final registration.

Controls

■ An employee record may be added, changed, or terminated only by a member of the personnel department.
■ The manager of the sales department must approve orders that will cause customers' balances to exceed their credit limits.

■ Volumes, sizes, and frequencies

As you determine the system requirements, you also must gather quantitative information about both current and future volumes, sizes, and frequencies for all the outputs, inputs, and processes. For example, for an output report such as an Accounts Receivable Transaction Register, you would determine that you need to print the account number, charges, payments and credits, old balance, new balance, and amount over the credit limit for all accounts with activity. You also need to determine quantitative information about the report, such as how often the report is printed and how many report copies are generated.

In order to estimate the size of the report, you need to determine the number of accounts that have activity on a typical day, as well as the highest and lowest number of active accounts expected on any given day. You must also estimate how these numbers are expected to change in one, two, or five years.

Why do you need to ask all these questions about a printed report? One reason is that printing volume affects hardware decisions; high enough volume would require an additional or a faster printer, for example. Another reason is that efficient and realistic scheduling of printing operations and timely delivery of finished reports require accurate estimates of print volume. Additionally, realistic print volume estimates help determine accurate cost estimates for expenses such as paper and storage.

You must ask similar kinds of questions about all other system outputs, such as screen displays and data files, as well as all inputs and all processes. You might determine the frequency of on-line student history queries, the time required to enter a query, and the average response time for each such query, for example. With that information, you then could estimate the amount of time the two terminals in the student records office are tied up with such requests. Or you might learn that a proposed month-end customer information file must, by law, be saved for seven years. If the information is to be saved on tape, and if you calculate that five tape reels are needed for one month's file, then you would determine that the company would have to provide for the purchase and storage of 420 (5 tapes/month x 12 months/year x 7 years) tape reels.

Other critical analytical determinations include the usage, scheduling, and procurement of hardware; the size, type, and activity level of files; response times; processing schedules; and costs. All these determinations depend on accurate quantitative information about volumes, sizes, and frequencies.

■ Codes

Documenting existing codes and identifying potential new codes is a necessary step you must perform in requirements determination, because end users work with codes in every information system. A **code** is a sequence of letters or numbers that represents an item of data that is more lengthy, cumbersome, or ambiguous. You encounter codes constantly in your everyday life. For example, student numbers are codes used to concisely and unambiguously identify students. There might be three Susan K. Arnolds enrolled at your school, but only one of them has student number 268960. Your zip code contains quite a bit of information compressed into five digits. The first digit identifies one of ten geographical areas of the nation. The first three digits together identify a major city or major distribution point. The full five digits identify an individual post office, an area within a city, or a specific delivery unit. For example, consider the zip code 98465. That first digit 9 indicates a West Coast location in Washington, Oregon, or California. The 984 identifies Tacoma, Washington. And finally, the 98465 uniquely (and more concisely) points to Tacoma Community College, Tacoma, Washington. If you use the nine-digit zip code, then the additional four digits pinpoint the mailing location to a specific street mailbox or post office box.

Codes serve several useful purposes. Very often, codes serve as unique identification. Codes are shorter than the data they represent and, therefore, save storage space and costs, reduce transmission time, and decrease data-entry time. Codes such as zip codes are used to efficiently classify and sort data. Codes can also be used to conceal information; the coded wholesale price on a retail price tag, for example, is easily deciphered by the sales people but not by customers. Conversely, codes can be used to reveal information; one example is a seven-digit part number for which the last two digits represent the supplier number. Finally, codes can reduce data input errors when the coded data is easier to remember and enter than the original data; when only a finite number of easily checked codes are allowable; or when something within the code itself can provide immediate verification.

End users must deal with coded data, so the coding schemes used must be acceptable to them. If end users find an existing coding scheme acceptable, then devising a completely new, different coding scheme is probably unnecessary. If you find that a data item is not coded but might be coded advantageously, you must consult the end users about the design and use of a coding scheme and get their approval on its use. They might already have a coding scheme in place for their own internal use, or they might suggest very good reasons for not coding the particular data item.

We will now look at these most commonly used coding schemes: sequence codes, block sequence codes, classification codes, alphabetic codes, mnemonic codes, significant digit codes, derivation codes, cipher codes, action codes, and self-checking codes.

1. **Sequence codes** are numbers or letters assigned in sequence. Such codes contain no additional information other than an indication of order of entry into the system. For example, employee numbers that are issued consecutively serve to uniquely identify particular employees. You also can tell that employee number 584 was hired some time later than employee number 433, but the code furnishes no exact knowledge of the starting date of either person's employment.

2. **Block sequence codes** use blocks of numbers for different classifications. College courses are usually assigned numbers using a block sequence code. 100-level courses, such as Chemistry 110 and Mathematics 125, are freshman-level courses, whereas numbers in the

200s indicate sophomore-level courses. Within a particular block, the sequence of numbers might have some additional meaning, as for example when English 151 is the prerequisite for English 152.

3. **Classification codes** distinguish one group of items from another. For example, a local department store might use a two-character code to identify the department in which a product is sold: WW for women's wear, HW for hardware, and PD for housewares.

4. **Alphabetic codes** are actually just abbreviations. One example is the standard two-character postal codes for state names: NY represents New York, ME represents Maine, and MN represents Minnesota.

5. **Mnemonic codes** use a combination of easily remembered letters and symbols. The three-character airport codes you see on luggage tags are mnemonic codes: LAX represents the Los Angeles airport, ORD is Chicago's O'Hare Airport, and GRR is the Grand Rapids, Michigan airport.

6. **Significant digit codes** distinguish items using a series of subgroupings. For example, an inventory location code could consist of a two-digit warehouse code, followed by a one-digit floor number, a two-digit section code, a one-digit aisle number, and a two-digit bin number. Figure 3-3 illustrates the inventory location code 11205327. What appears to be a large eight-digit number is actually five smaller numbers, each of which has significance.

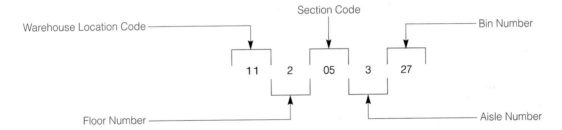

Figure 3-3 *Significant digit code example using an inventory location code.*

7. **Derivation codes** use pieces of different item attributes, or characteristics, to build the code. Most magazine subscription codes are of this type. One popular magazine's subscriber code consists of the five-digit zip code, followed by the first, third, and fourth letters of the last name, the last two digits of the house number, and the first, third, and fourth letters of the street name. This magazine's subscriber code for one particular subscriber is illustrated in Figure 3-4.

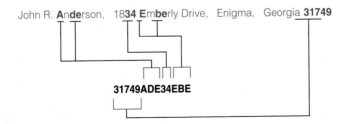

Figure 3-4 *Derivation code example using a magazine subscriber code.*

8. **Cipher codes** use a keyword to encipher (encode) a number. A retail store might use the word CAMPGROUND to code wholesale prices, where the letter C stands for 1, A for 2, and so on. Thus, the code of GRAND indicates that the store paid $562.90 for the item.

9. **Action codes** indicate what action is to be taken with an associated item. For example, you might be required to enter a student number and an action code to a computerized query/update program. The code D indicates that you want to display the student's record, the code A indicates that you want to add a record for the student number, and the code X indicates that you want to exit the program.

10. **Self-checking codes** use a check digit to verify the validity of a numeric code. One scheme for a four-digit self-checking code calculates a check digit by multiplying the first digit by 1, the second digit by 2, and so on. Then, those products are summed. If the sum contains more than one digit, the digits in the sum are added until there is finally a one-digit answer. That final answer is the check digit, which is appended to the numeric code. In this coding scheme, 1302-6 is a valid code because the result of the calculation is 6, which matches the given check digit. This calculation is shown in Figure 3-5. Also illustrated in that figure is the erroneous code 7198-3. At least one of the five digits in this code is wrong because the calculation result is 5, which does not match the given check digit 3.

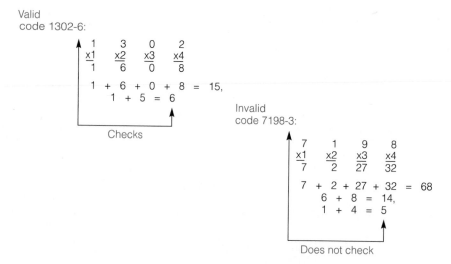

Figure 3-5   *Self-checking code examples.*

It is possible to build a useful code by using a combination of two or more of these coding schemes. But in general, the simpler the coding scheme, the better. A code could be devised that uses so many features of these different coding schemes that the resulting code is too difficult to remember, decipher, or verify. Obviously, coding should not be so complex that the advantages of coding are overpowered by the difficulty of working with the particular coding scheme. Keep in mind the following useful tips when you develop a code.

Keep codes concise.   Don't create codes that are longer than necessary. If you need a code number to identify each of 250 customers, you do not need a four-digit code.

Allow for expansion.   A coding scheme must allow for reasonable growth in the number of assigned codes. If the company currently has eight warehouses, you should not use a one-digit code for the warehouse number. If three more warehouses were added, the code would have to be lengthened to two digits or changed to a character code in order to identify each of the eleven warehouses.

Keep codes stable.   Codes that have to be changed cause problems during the changeover period; changing all the stored occurrences of a particular code, changing all documents containing the old code, and getting all the end users to switch from the old to the new code instantaneously is a troublesome process. Invariably, both the old and new codes are used for some interim period, and special procedures are required to handle that situation.

Make codes unique.   Codes used for identification must be unique to have meaning. If HW can mean either Hardware or Housewares, the code has no utility.

Use sortable codes.   If products with three-digit codes in the 100s or the 300s are of one type, while products with codes in the 200s are of another type, a simple sort will not group all the products of one type together.

Avoid confusing codes.   Do not, for example, code some part numbers with two letters, a hyphen, and one digit, and others with one letter, a hyphen, and two digits. Avoid allowing either a letter or a number to occupy a given position within a code. Imagine the problems with a five-character code 5ZO81 that can easily be misread as 5ZO8I, or 52O81, or even totally incorrectly as S20BI!

Make codes meaningful.   Codes must be easy to remember, useful for the people who must deal with them, convenient to use, and easy to encode and interpret. Using SW as a code for the southwest sales region, for example, has much more meaning than does 14. Also, ENG is obviously more convenient for everyone to deal with than either XQA or 132 as the code for the English department.

Use a code for a single purpose.   Do not use a single code to classify two or more unrelated attributes. For example, a single code that identifies the department in which an employee works, as well as the employee's insurance plan type, is unwieldy. It will surely be difficult to identify all the subscribers of a particular plan, or all the workers in a particular department, or both. A separate code for each separate characteristic makes much more sense.

Keep codes consistent.   If the payroll system is already using two-digit codes for departments, do not create a new, different department coding scheme to be used in the personnel system. If these two systems are already using two different coding schemes, you should try to convince the end users of the two systems to adopt just one, consistent department coding scheme.

Interviews — an important fact-finding technique

By now you realize that systems analysts spend a great deal of time talking with people both inside and outside the information systems department. Much of this time is spent in interviewing people to collect information, so it is critical that you have the skills to properly plan, conduct, and document interviews. An **interview** is a planned meeting during which you obtain information from another person. The process of interviewing consists of these six steps.

1. Determine who to interview.
2. Establish objectives for the interview.
3. Prepare for the interview.
4. Conduct the interview.
5. Document the interview.
6. Evaluate the interview.

■ Determine who to interview

Even if you eventually ask all the right questions, if you do not ask the right questions of the right people, you will never get an accurate picture of the system under study. Also, you want neither to waste your time asking unproductive questions nor to waste the time of the people you interview. Thus, you must first carefully determine who should be interviewed.

During the preliminary investigation, you most likely dealt only with middle- or upper-level management. Also during this first phase, you determined the formal organizational structure of all levels of personnel for all areas associated with the system. During the systems analysis phase, however, you will interview people from all levels of the organization. Also, you now must consider the different, informal structures that might exist within the organization. Such informal structures are usually based on interpersonal relationships but might have developed from previous formal organization structures, physical proximity, time- or labor-saving shortcuts, and so on. In the informal structure, some people have more influence or knowledge than is evident or expected from their position in the formal organization. You should, therefore, be alert to informal organizational structures that might affect the system being investigated. Your knowledge of the formal and informal structure will help you determine who to interview during the systems analysis phase.

■ Establish objectives for the interview

Once you decide who to interview, you must establish objectives for each interview. You must determine the general areas to be discussed and the specific facts you require for each of those general areas. In addition, you must plan to solicit ideas, suggestions, and opinions from those you interview.

The objectives of an interview depend on the role of the person being interviewed. Different information is obtained from a vice president of the company than from a clerk. From upper-level management, you learn about the big picture, the system as a whole. Specific details about processes are best learned from the people who actually perform the processes.

The interview objectives also vary, depending on the stage of the investigation. For example, if the investigation is just beginning and this is your first interview with a particular individual, you will discuss different aspects of the system than if your requirements determination effort is nearly complete. By setting down all the objectives for an interview, you create a framework for the interview. This framework then guides you as you decide on the specific questions you will ask and how you will ask those questions.

■ Prepare for the interview

Once you determine the objectives for an interview, you must prepare for the interview. Careful preparation is essential because the probability of gaining the required information by merely sitting down to chat is quite small.

You should schedule a meeting with the person to be interviewed for a given day at a given time. It is also best to call ahead about an hour before the meeting to be sure that the interviewee will be available. Remember that your interview is an interruption of the interviewee's routine responsibilities. Other business might arise for the interviewee to cause a postponement of the meeting. If this occurs, you should schedule another appointment.

Keep department managers informed of your meetings with their staff members. Sending a memo to each department manager listing your planned appointments is one excellent way to keep them informed. Figure 3-6 on the next page is an example of such a memo.

You should prepare your interview questions ahead of time. If your interview objectives are well defined, you should be able to structure your questions without too much difficulty. Not all questions can be planned in advance; often unexpected subjects will arise that you will also need to pursue. Without a prepared list of questions, however, you might not be able to satisfy the objectives of the interview.

Your objectives also influence the way you ask your questions. Two types of questions are open-ended questions and closed-ended questions. **Open-ended questions** are questions that are designed to permit spontaneous and unguided responses. Open-ended questions are most useful when you are trying to understand a larger process or when you want to draw out the interviewee's opinions, attitudes, or suggestions. *How are the checks reconciled?* and *What added features would you like to have in the new billing system?* are open-ended questions. **Closed-ended questions** are questions that limit or restrict the response. You would use closed-ended questions when you are seeking more specific information or need verification or clarification of facts. Examples of closed-ended questions are *How many microcomputers are there in this department?*, *Are most of your reconciliation problems due to inadequate documentation or to poorly trained clerks?*, and *Would changes in the reconciliation procedure documentation help eliminate reconciliation problems?*

MEMORANDUM

Creative Computer Solutions

DATE: October 1, 1996
TO: Ramon Ruiz, Vice President, Finance
FROM: Betty Searle, Systems Analyst
SUBJECT: Bonus Compensation System Meetings

I have been assigned to the systems analysis phase of the new bonus compensation system. I need to collect all the detailed processing requirements for this system, and I have scheduled a series of meetings with members of your staff. The current schedule of meetings is:

Ernie Kubinski, October 4 at 9:00 a.m.

Rosa Kavanaugh, October 4 at 10:00 a.m.

Dyanne Gendron, October 7 at 1:00 p.m.

I might need to meet with others in your department or schedule follow-up meetings with the above individuals. I will keep you informed of these meetings as I schedule them. I plan to complete the systems analysis phase by the end of October, and I will send you a copy of the system requirements document at that time. If you have any questions or suggestions, please contact me at extension 371.

Figure 3-6   *Sample informational memo sent to the head of a department.*

When you have completed a list of questions and topics you want to discuss, send this list to the interviewee several days before the meeting. This allows time for the interviewee to prepare for the interview. Furthermore, you often can avoid the need for a follow-up interview because the interviewee will be prepared at the first meeting. As illustrated in Figure 3-7, you should also include in this memo a confirmation of the purpose, date, time, and location for the interview.

MEMORANDUM

DATE: October 1, 1996
TO: Rosa Kavanaugh, Compensation Manager
FROM: Betty Searle, Systems Analyst
SUBJECT: Bonus Compensation System Meetings

I would like to confirm our meeting on October 4 at 10:00 a.m. in your office. As part of my information gathering for the new bonus compensation system, I need to know all details about the steps you and your staff perform in processing bonus compensation. I plan to ask the following questions:

1. What portion of bonus compensation processing is handled within your department?

2. What other areas of the company are responsible for different aspects of bonus compensation? How do these other areas interact with your department?

3. What procedures do you handle and what specific steps are involved?

4. What improvements would you like to see in the bonus compensation processing when we implement this system on the computer?

5. Are portions of bonus compensation processing confidential? What special security requirements are needed?

If you have written procedures, standard forms, or special calculations for the bonus compensation system, please have them available for me to review during our meeting. I will need my own copies of some of this material, but we can decide which material should be copied during our meeting.

Please contact me if something comes up and we have to reschedule our meeting.

Figure 3-7   *Sample memo sent to an interviewee to confirm a planned interview.*

If the interviewee uses documents in his or her job and you have questions about these documents, you will want such documents available during the interview. Include a list, therefore, of all the documents you plan to discuss during the interview in the memo you send to the interviewee. If you are unsure that the interviewee uses specific documents, you should make a general request for documents (as in the memo in Figure 3-7).

■ Conduct the interview

After you determine who to interview, establish your objectives, and plan for the interview, you are ready to conduct the interview. The model for a typical interview is to introduce yourself; summarize the project objectives and progress; summarize your interview objectives; ask your questions, generally going from open-ended to closed-ended questions; summarize the main points covered in the interview; specify what is to be done next by you and the interviewee — for example, that you will send a follow-up memo and that the interviewee will prepare a benefits estimate; and thank the interviewee.

Establishing a rapport between you and the interviewee is important, especially in a first interview. If the interviewee feels comfortable and at ease with you, you are more likely to receive more complete and candid answers to your questions.

Your primary responsibility during an interview is to *listen* to the answers. All too often, systems analysts do not listen properly to the answers given and, instead, hear only what they expect to hear. You must carefully and actively listen to the actual words being said and must be aware of the non-verbal communication taking place.

After asking a question, you should allow the person enough time to think about the question and to formulate an answer. Studies have shown that the average maximum pause between one person speaking and another person speaking during a conversation is three to five seconds; after this period of time, one or the other will begin to talk. But when you are conducting an interview, you must allow more than the average maximum time for the interviewee to answer a question. You will find that this kind of patience requires practice in many actual interview situations.

There are two schools of thought about the best location for an interview. Some believe that interviews should take place in the interviewee's office, whereas others argue that a neutral location, such as a conference room, is better.

It is important for the interviewee to feel comfortable during the interview. For this reason, many people believe that the interviewee's own office is the ideal location. A second argument in favor of using the interviewee's own office is because in his or her own office the interviewee has the easiest access to supporting material that might have to be reviewed during the interview. If you have alerted the interviewee in advance with a complete list of the interview topics and required materials, however, the interviewee can bring all the necessary materials to a conference room or other neutral location before the start of the interview.

Supporters of neutral-location interviews emphasize the importance of conducting an interview with a minimum of interruptions. In this way, both the interviewer and the interviewee can concentrate completely on the questions and subject matter. Also, an interruption-free interview means that the interview will take less time, thereby saving valuable time for both participants.

If, however, the meeting does take place in the interviewee's office, you should tactfully suggest that all calls and interruptions be held until the conclusion of the interview. ■

At the conclusion of the interview, you should verbally synthesize and summarize the interview to the interviewee. By reviewing your understanding of the facts stated during the session, the interviewee can immediately correct any misunderstandings you may have formed.

■ Document the interview

After you conduct the interview, you must take definite steps to ensure that you don't forget the information from the interview. One step involves setting aside time immediately after the interview to record what transpired during the meeting.

Although there are pros and cons about taking notes during an interview, the accepted view is that note taking should be kept to a minimum. You should write down a few key items with which to jog your memory, but you should not act as a secretary taking dictation. Too much writing distracts the person being interviewed, and in general, fails to establish the necessary rapport.

Set aside time immediately after the interview to record the facts that were discussed and to evaluate the information that you received. Studies have shown that 50% of a conversation is forgotten within 30 minutes. Therefore, based on the notes you took, you should immediately record the facts from the interview so you will not forget them. You can prepare a narrative describing what took place, you can record the answers you received next to the questions on your prepared question list, or you can draw a diagram with a supporting narrative.

You should send a memo to the interviewee expressing your appreciation for the time he or she spent both in preparation for the interview and during the interview itself. In this memo, you should document the date, time, location, and purpose of the interview; the memo should then report the facts that you discussed so the interviewee has a written copy of the interview results and can correct any misconceptions you have formed.

Tape or video recorders can be effective tools during an interview. Many people, however, feel threatened by the presence of recorders, and you do want the interviewee to be candid and to feel at ease. Even careful use of tape or video recorders might make the interviewee uncomfortable and the interview difficult to complete. You might tend to rely too much on the recorder and forget to listen carefully to the responses to your questions and have to come back another day to ask the follow-up questions you missed the first time. If you are discussing personalities, internal politics, or sensitive information, you should not record the discussion. Finally, each interview is twice the normal length, because you listen to or view the recorded interview after going through the interview itself.

If you find difficulty taking brief notes during an interview and later filling in the details, however, you could tape the interview. You will have a complete record of the interview and can transcribe the interview at a later time.

Because some people dislike recorded sessions, you should take special steps if you want to use a tape or video recorder. Discuss the use of the recorder with the interviewee at the beginning of the interview. Assure the interviewee that you will erase the tape after you transcribe your notes later that same day. Tell the interviewee that you will stop and back up the tape at any time during the interview at his or her request. If you have sensitive questions, or the interviewee wants to answer a question without being recorded, you can turn off the tape for a period of time during the interview. ■

■ Evaluate the interview

In addition to recording the facts obtained in an interview, you should analyze the interview and the person interviewed. Many facts that were stated in the interview might have been biased by one or more circumstances. For example, the interviewee might be attempting to protect an empire and could believe that any knowledge he or she reveals will destroy that empire. Such a person might not actually lie when asked questions, but yet might not give complete answers.

In other circumstances, the interviewee might have very strong opinions about the system under study. Such a person could intentionally or unintentionally so distort the facts that much of the information gained is questionable or even useless. Other interviewees might want to be so helpful that they answer questions when in fact they do not know the answer. In all these cases, you must distill the proper answers from those that might not be correct.

■ Unsuccessful interviews

No matter how well you prepare for interviews, some are not successful. One of the primary reasons might be that you and the interviewee do not get along with each other. This can be caused by several factors. For example, you and the interviewee might simply have a personality conflict, or the interviewee might be anti-computer and afraid that you are there to eliminate his or her job. The interviewee might be involved in an internal political problem that prevents him or her from cooperating.

In other interview situations, the interviewee might give only short or incomplete responses to your open-ended questions; then, you should restrict your questions to closed-ended ones. If asking closed-ended questions still does not help, you must find a way to conclude the meeting with as much tact as possible.

It is obviously a waste of two peoples' time to continue an interview that is not producing results, no matter what the cause. At an appropriate time, you should state that you have all the information you need and terminate a nonproductive interview. It is possible that at a later time the interviewee will be more cooperative. You also might find the information you seek elsewhere. In those cases where the failure to obtain the necessary information in a particular interview jeopardizes the overall success of the project, you must inform your supervisor, who should decide what action should occur. Your supervisor might contact the interviewee's supervisor, ask another systems analyst to interview the person, or take some other form of action to get the needed information.

Other important fact-finding techniques

There are several standard fact-finding techniques. Although interviewing is the most commonly used, the others are also valuable and effective techniques for requirements determination. During a typical project, you can use a variety of these fact-finding techniques, the most used of which are data collection, observation, questionnaires, and research.

■ Data collection

During the requirements determination process, you should review the existing system documentation in order to understand the system's operating procedures and documents. Be aware, however, that sometimes system documentation is not up-to-date. Some documented forms might no longer be used or might have been changed. Some documented procedures might have been modified or eliminated. You should obtain, therefore, copies of the *actual* forms and operating documents that are currently used in the system. You should obtain blank copies of forms, as well as samples of actual completed forms. You can usually obtain document samples for a particular procedure when you interview individuals associated with that procedure. If the current information system is computerized, you might need to review the application programs to obtain some of the required information.

■ Observation

Another fact-finding technique is the observation of current operating procedures. Often, it takes observation of a system in action to fully understand that system's requirements. Seeing the system in action gives you an additional perspective to supplement what you have heard and read. During observation, you might solidify your hazy understanding of the system and its procedures. You might also correct any misconceptions or erroneous impressions you had formed. In addition, by personal observation you can verify statements made in interviews, as well as determine if procedures operate as specified in the system documentation. You might even discover that neither the system documentation nor the statements from those interviewed truly reflect the system in operation.

Personal observation can also provide advantages that will become significant during later phases in the systems development life cycle. For example, recommendations often receive better acceptance when they are based on personal observation of actual operations. Also, personal observation helps you acquire the know-how you will need if you are asked to assist or supervise the testing or installation of the changes that have been recommended. You also become better acquainted with the operating personnel who will be implementing the new or changed system.

Plan your observations in advance by preparing a checklist of the steps that you want to observe and the questions you want to ask. Consider the following issues when you prepare your checklist.

1. Ask sufficient pertinent questions to ensure that you thoroughly understand the present operations of each procedure. This is especially important for identifying the methods used to handle exceptions or problems that are not covered by standard operating procedures. For example, what happens in a payroll system if an employee loses a time card? What is the procedure if an employee checks in five minutes late but works ten minutes overtime? Often, the rules for exceptional cases such as these are not written down or formalized. As a result, you must attempt to document all the exception-handling procedures.

2. Observe all the steps in a processing cycle and note the output from each procedural step.

3. Examine each pertinent form, record, and report. Determine the purpose each item of information serves.

4. Consider the work of each person associated with the system, keeping in mind the following questions: What information is received from other people? What information is generated by this person's work? What tools are used in the procedure? To whom is the information passed? What questions do the workers ask each other? How fast must each step be done? How much concentration does each step require? How often do interruptions occur? How often must a worker take a break from a concentrated activity?

5. Consult those receiving current reports to determine if the reports they receive are complete, timely, accurate, and in the most useful form. Inquire as to what information they receive can be eliminated or improved, and what information they do not presently receive would be helpful.

When you observe individuals performing tasks, you should be aware of a phenomenon called the **Hawthorne Effect**. The name comes from a study performed in the Hawthorne plant of Western Electric Company in the 1920s. The purpose of the study was to determine whether various types of changes in the work environment would improve worker productivity. The surprising result was that worker productivity improved *whether the environmental conditions were made better or worse!* The conclusion drawn was that the workers' productivity improved because they knew they were being observed.

As you observe workers doing their jobs, keep the Hawthorne Effect in mind. Normal operations might not always run as smoothly as your observations indicate. Workers might also be nervous when you observe them. Before you observe them, therefore, you might meet with them and their supervisors to discuss your plans and objectives and to help establish a good working relationship with them.

■ Questionnaires

In large systems projects where it is not possible to interview all individuals associated with the system, the questionnaire can be a valuable tool. A **questionnaire** is a document containing a number of standard questions that you ask of a large number of people. Questionnaires are used to obtain information such as work loads, reports received, volumes of transactions handled, types of job duties, difficulties, and opinions of how the job could be better or more efficiently performed. Figure 3-8 shows a sample questionnaire that illustrates a variety of question and response formats.

Apply the following rules when you design a questionnaire.

- Make the questionnaire as brief and easy to answer as possible.
- Arrange the questions in a logical order.
- Phrase questions to avoid misunderstandings.
- Phrase questions to avoid giving clues to expected answers.
- Avoid questions that require long, narrative answers.
- Avoid questions that appear threatening to a person's job.
- Determine carefully what questions are required to obtain the information you desire.
- Test the questionnaire whenever possible on a small test group of subjects before handing out the questionnaire formally.

PURCHASE REQUISITION QUESTIONNAIRE

Pat Kline, Vice President, Finance, has asked us to investigate the purchase requisition process to see if it can be improved. Your input concerning this requisition process will be very valuable. We would greatly appreciate it if you could complete the following questionnaire and return it by March 8 to Dana Juarez in information systems. If you have any questions, please call Dana at x2561.

_____

1. How many purchase requisitions did you process   _____
   in the past five working days?

2. What percentage of your time is spent processing   [ ] under 20%
   requisitions?   [ ] 21-39%
                                                          [ ] 40-59%
                                                          [ ] 60-79%
                                                          [ ] 80% or more

3. Do you believe there are too many errors   [ ] yes
   on requisitions?   [ ] no

4. Out of every 100 requisitions you process, how   [ ] fewer than 5
   many contain errors?   [ ] 5 to 9
                                                          [ ] 10 to 14
                                                          [ ] 15 to 19
                                                          [ ] 20 to 29
                                                          [ ] 30 to 39
                                                          [ ] 40 to 49
                                                          [ ] 50 or more

5. What errors do you most often   [ ] Incorrect charge number
   see on requisitions? (Place a 1 next [ ] Missing charge information
   to the most common error, place   [ ] Arithmetic errors
   a 2 next to the second most common   [ ] Incorrect discount percent used
                                        [ ] Missing authorization
                                        [ ] Other (please explain)

                                        _____

                                        [ ] Other (please explain)

                                        _____

6. If the currently used purchase requisition form were to be redesigned,
   what changes to the form would you recommend?

_____
_____
_____
_____
_____
_____

(Please attach another sheet if necessary)

Figure 3-8   *Sample questionnaire.*

When you must ask a large number of individuals a series of identical questions, a questionnaire can be advantageous to use. Conversely, if you require information from only a few people, then you would likely choose to interview each person individually. Is it better to interview or use a questionnaire in those situations that don't fall neatly into either extreme? Often, you have a choice of a number of people from whom you could obtain necessary information. Is it better to interview just a few of these people or to send questionnaires to all of them?

The interview is, by its very nature, more intimate and personal. People who would be unwilling to put critical or controversial comments in writing might talk more freely in person. Moreover, during a face-to-face interview, you can immediately react to anything the interviewee says. If surprising or confusing statements are made, you are free to pursue the topic with additional questions. In addition, during a personal interview, you can be alert for clues to help you determine if responses are knowledgeable and unbiased.

An interview is a costly and time-consuming process, however, and it requires the dedicated time of both the interviewer and the interviewee for the duration of the interview. Add to this the interviewee's preparation time, plus all the preparation and follow-up work the interviewer must do. The total cost can be significant. Of all the fact-finding techniques, the personal interview is usually the most expensive.

A questionnaire provides many people with the opportunity to provide input and suggestions. This participation can be a very important human relations factor, because people who have been asked to contribute their knowledge and opinions to a systems project often view that project with greater favor. Also, the recipients can answer questionnaires at their convenience; it isn't necessary to set aside a significant block of time as one must do for an interview. Questionnaires can be answered privately, so the respondents might be more candid than they would be in an interview. The questions in the questionnaire are also presented consistently to all respondents without interviewer bias.

On the other hand, questionnaire preparation is an art. It does take time to prepare an effective questionnaire and to design questions that elicit exactly the desired information. All too often, a question can be misinterpreted, and you cannot clarify the question as you can in an interview. The subsequent interpretation of answers is also subject to inaccuracies. Furthermore, some questionnaire recipients view questionnaires as intrusive, time consuming, impersonal, and tedious.

As you can see, both interviewing and questionnaires have advantages and disadvantages. To select the best fact-finding technique in a particular situation is not always easy. ■

■ Research

Research represents yet another important fact-finding technique. Research can involve reviewing journals, periodicals, and books that contain information relevant to the task at hand. Research can involve attending professional meetings and seminars. Formal and informal discussions with other professionals in related areas also can shed valuable light on the problem. And finally, research can involve site visitations.

A **site visitation** is a visit to another installation to see one of its systems in actual use. For example, if you are doing a systems analysis on your organization's personnel system, you might want to see how another company's personnel system works. Most often, you use a site visitation when you are considering the purchase of an application software package. The package vendor is usually happy to suggest possible sites to visit. A vendor is likely to suggest only satisfied customers, however, so you should be aware that such sites constitute a biased sample. Because a single site visitation seldom gives you a true picture, you should, whenever possible, visit more than one installation. Keep in mind that the Hawthorne Effect, which was discussed in relation to observation, is also relevant to site visitations.

Before the visit, you should prepare as you would for any meeting. Make contact with the appropriate manager and indicate your purposes for the visit. Decide what questions you will ask and what processes you will observe. While you are visiting the site, you will want to determine how well the system works, what problems there are with the system, details about the support provided by the vendor (both type and quality of support), the quality of the documentation of the system, and so on.

Recording the facts

■ The need for recording the facts

We cannot overemphasize the importance of adequate records of interviews, facts, ideas, and observations. You might have difficulty appreciating the significance of particular facts in a sea of facts, and you might easily forget ideas and understandings as you move from procedure to procedure through a system. The basic rule, therefore, is to *write it down*. You should document your investigations according to the following principles.

- Record all information as you obtain the information.
- Use the simplest recording manner possible consistent with completeness.
- Record your findings in such a way that they can be understood by someone who is not a member of the information systems staff.
- Arrange your documentation so related information can be easily brought together and coordinated.

Often, systems analysts use specialized forms for documenting a system, such as special forms for interviews and special forms for summarizing document contents. One type of documentation is a narrative in a list format in which you make simple statements about what is taking place, specify problems that are apparent, and make suggestions for improvement. Other forms of documentation include diagrams, flowcharts, sample forms, and screen dumps.

■ Writing tips

Good writing is important. Other people judge you by your writing. Grammatical mistakes, typographical errors, and spelling mistakes cause readers of your documents to judge you poorly and, consequently, to downgrade or dismiss what you are trying to say. The points you are trying to make will be lost.

If you have not already taken a writing class, and if it is at all possible to fit one into your program, we strongly encourage you to do so. If you have a choice of writing classes, pick one that is oriented toward business writing. Any writing class, however, will be well worth your time. You should find the following general writing tips useful when you are recording the facts.

- Avoid the passive voice.
- Don't make your writing overly complex. Be as concise as possible without losing meaning.
- Make sure that each paragraph conveys a single idea.
- Make sure that subjects and verbs agree in number. Make sure that nouns and pronouns agree.
- Try to get some variety in your sentence structure and length. Don't be stilted.
- Use lists when appropriate. Readers usually find it easier and quicker to gather information from a list than from a narrative.
- Avoid using longer words than necessary. The purpose of the document is not to impress your audience with the size of your vocabulary.

- Avoid repeating the same word too often. Use a thesaurus to help you find synonyms for words you find yourself repeating frequently. If you are using a computerized word processor to prepare your documents, you might be able to access an online thesaurus.
- Check your spelling. Computer word processing systems offer online spelling checkers. Be aware, however, that a spelling checker will flag only those words that do not match any word in its dictionary. Misspelling the word *their* as *there*, for example, will not be caught because *there* is a legitimate word.
- Check your grammar. There are computerized tools to assist in this process also. Again, you should be aware that the tool is just an aid. You should not assume that the computer will find all the problems.

Requirements analysis overview

Requirements analysis is the second major stage of the systems analysis phase. During requirements analysis, you organize the facts you obtained during the requirements determination stage. Your objective is to develop a logical user-oriented design of the information system. The methods and tools you use to accomplish this are covered in the next two chapters.

Two important tasks conclude the systems analysis phase. The first task is the creation of a formal report, the system requirements document, that details everything that you have learned and concluded about the information system. This formal report serves as the starting point for systems design, the next phase in the systems development life cycle.

The final task of the systems analysis phase is the formal presentation of your findings. Even though the audience has already received your formal report, this oral presentation is necessary and very important.

Presentations

You have already seen the need for a presentation at the end of the preliminary investigation phase. Once you have documented the system and developed possible solutions, you must make another presentation, this time at the end of the systems analysis phase. In some organizations you might be required to give more than one presentation at this point, each tailored for a specific audience. A presentation to middle management is always required. In addition, you might have to give a more technical presentation to other members of the information systems staff or a more high-level presentation to top management. In other organizations, only one presentation is given with all interested people in attendance; in this case, you should target the presentation for the decision makers. Based on the information you present, management will decide whether to proceed with the design of a new system. Because presentations can influence whether management accepts your findings, a look at some of the techniques for making effective presentations is worthwhile.

■ Presentation techniques

Your presentation consists of two major stages: preparation for the presentation and the presentation itself. Listed on the next page are the six steps of presentation preparation.

1. Define the audience.
2. Define the objectives.
3. Organize the presentation.
4. Define terms.
5. Prepare presentation aids.
6. Practice.

Define the audience   Before any detailed planning for the presentation takes place, you must define the audience to whom you will make the presentation. In general, you will make the presentation to persons in management positions. These management positions, however, can vary from the manager of a department to the president of the company. The depth of the material you present should be matched to your audience. If the audience includes lower- and middle-level managers, then you should present material in some detail. If only top-level management is in attendance, then an overview presentation is more appropriate.

Define the objectives   The objective of any communication is to produce a mental picture in the mind of the receiver that duplicates the picture in the mind of the sender. Therefore, you must define the picture you want to send to your presentation audience. Make your picture clear, concrete, and measurable, so that you focus your presentation planning on achieving your objectives.

In general, the objectives of a management presentation concerning the systems analysis phase are to:

- Inform management of the status of the current system.
- Describe your findings concerning the current system problems.
- Explain the alternative solutions that you have developed.
- Provide detailed cost and time estimates for the alternative solutions.

These general objectives serve as guidelines for determining and organizing the specific items that you will include in your presentation. Without a definition of objectives, you are not likely to be able to plan a presentation that adequately informs management of the results you have achieved and the decisions that they must make.

Organize the presentation   Next, you must organize the presentation to meet the objectives for the defined audience. The sequence in which you present material is critical. If the material is presented in an illogical and unorganized manner, your audience can become confused and unsure about what you are saying. You then will have wasted all the good work you put into your investigation and analysis of the system.

In addition, you must emphasize the proper topics. In general, you should emphasize the problems encountered, the solutions proposed, and the costs of these solutions. In other words, your listeners will want to hear what is wrong, how it can be fixed, and how much it will cost to fix it. In most cases, the audience is not concerned with the details of the system's operation. Any member of the audience can consult the details in the documentation you have prepared, or you can answer his or her questions about specific details after the meeting.

Define terms   You might find yourself planning to use terminology that will not be familiar to everyone in the audience. You should avoid specialized or technical terminology whenever possible. You also should not assume that the terminology used within the application system under study will be familiar to the entire audience. If you suspect that even one listener might not be familiar with a term you plan to use, either find another way to say what you want to say or else define the term. Your material must be understandable to all the participants.

Prepare presentation aids   Studies show that 75% of everything we learn is learned through seeing. Only 13% is learned through hearing, and the remaining 12% is learned through the other senses. Therefore, you should supplement your presentation with helpful, appropriate visual aids. A visual aid can help to dramatize, reinforce, or demonstrate a point; in some cases, you can even condense a verbal narrative by using a visual aid that more rapidly and succinctly illustrates the information you wish to convey. Visual aids also help the audience to follow the logic of your presentation and help to refocus an audience member's attention on the topic if his or her attention momentarily wanders during the presentation. Visual aids direct some of the audience attention away from you; this can be helpful to you if you are nervous when you give the presentation. Visual aids also provide you with cues to remind you what to say next.

Some suggestions for material that can be illustrated visually include: performance trends, performance comparisons, cost trends, costs versus benefits, document flows, and bottlenecks. If a chart, diagram, graph, or picture is not appropriate, then prepare short lists to highlight the key points of your presentation.

You can use several different types of visual aids. Some of the more useful are chalkboards, flip charts, overhead transparencies, slides, films, and video tapes. These materials, used either separately or together, can greatly add to the effectiveness of a presentation. When you prepare your visual aids, you should make sure that all such material is clear, uncluttered, and to the point. Verify ahead of time that the visual material can be easily viewed from everywhere in the room, even for someone sitting in a far corner. One additional word of warning: because physical and mechanical equipment can fail or may not always be available, you must be prepared to give your presentation without your visual aids.

Computerized presentation/graphics software, if available, should be used for your visual aids. With such a product, you can prepare a complete visual aid program that includes sophisticated sound, color, video, and animation effects. Presentation/graphics packages enable you to create an attractive and effective multimedia presentation quickly and easily. As is true with all tools, however, you must exercise restraint when preparing a visual aid program using a presentation/graphics software package. It can be tempting to use (and overuse) every possible effect. Instead of saving preparation time, you might end up spending even more time adding and fine-tuning features; you might even create a visual program that overwhelms rather than supplements the points you are trying to make with your presentation.

Practice   After all the preparation has been completed, you are nearly ready to make the presentation. One important element is missing, however, and that is *practice*. You should never go into a presentation without first thoroughly reviewing all the material that you will present and previewing the presentation in your mind. In most cases, you will benefit by going through several rehearsals with your visual aids to be sure that all the necessary material is ready and that the timing of the presentation is correct. You must feel confident that you will be able to keep a smooth, enlightened presentation going; rehearsing several times will make you comfortable enough with the material to help build your confidence.

You might be tempted to write out exactly what you plan to say in the presentation and to read through your prepared script when you practice. This is not a good idea.

There are two likely outcomes from reading your presentation, and neither is desirable. First, you might resort to reading from the script during the presentation. As a result, you lose eye contact with your audience and sacrifice the opportunity to watch your audience, gauge their reactions, and adjust to those reactions. Moreover, the audience will know you are reading, and they will either tune you out or wonder why they need you to read the presentation material for them when they could just as easily read the material themselves. Second, you might be tempted to memorize your presentation when you have a prepared script. The presentation ends up sounding memorized and stilted. You will also find it difficult to change or adjust the presentation in response to audience reactions when you recite from memory. If you have memorized your presentation and suddenly go blank, what do you do? Even if you have your memorized script available to use, you have already lost your audience's attention and their confidence in you.

It is much better to prepare an outline of your presentation and to practice from the outline. Then, when you make the actual presentation, your notes can consist of that same outline. You won't be tempted to read your notes, you won't have to struggle to remember the exact words you planned to say, and you will be able to establish a rapport with your audience.

Because management often has important business occur unexpectedly, the length of time scheduled for your presentation might be reduced shortly before or during your presentation. You should always have prepared, therefore, an abbreviated version of your presentation to give when the length of your presentation must be abruptly shortened.

■ The presentation

When you give the actual presentation, keep the following points in mind to maximize your chances for success.

- Sell yourself and your credibility.
- Control the presentation.
- Answer questions appropriately.
- Use good speaking techniques.

Sell yourself and your credibility   In order to be successful in a presentation, you must sell yourself and your credibility. A brilliant presentation will not convince management that the system should be designed and implemented if management is not sold on the individual who gave the presentation. On the other hand, many systems that are not truly deserving have been implemented because the systems analyst did an excellent sales job in a presentation to management.

You must give a presentation that shows confidence about the subject and your recommendations. You should avoid any conflicts with the people attending the presentation. If anyone directs critical remarks to you, face the criticisms honestly and directly.

You will have a successful presentation only if you thoroughly know the material you are presenting. When you know the material and have properly prepared for the presentation, you will have the best chance to sell yourself and your credibility.

Control the presentation   Because you give the presentation and preside over the discussions, you must control the presentation. You must direct the audience's attention to those things that are important.

Even though you might be more familiar with the subject material than many or all of your listeners, you must not appear to be taking a superior attitude toward the audience. The audience rapport that you desire can be achieved through adequate preparation so that the material you present is appropriate for your audience. You should also maintain eye contact with the audience so people feel you are talking directly to them. Humor, when appropriate, can have a very good effect on an audience. But don't insert irrelevant jokes in your presentation just because you think it should include a little humor.

Answer questions appropriately   Inevitably, the audience will have questions during or following a presentation. Sometimes the questions can be quite difficult. You must listen very carefully to a question being asked and then give a straightforward response that answers the question.

Too often, systems analysts respond with an answer that either does not directly address the question or that, although technically correct, is not in terms that can be understood by the person asking the question. Inappropriately answered questions cause the audience to feel that you are not relating to them and is a sure means of quickly losing control of the presentation.

Use good speaking techniques   You should keep several effective speaking techniques in mind while making your presentation. Most accomplished speakers concentrate on using good voice and accent, making no distracting movements, and having a relaxed approach. Another important element of effective speaking is the pace at which you deliver the presentation. If the pace is too fast for the audience, they will be lost and will lose interest. On the other hand, if the pace is too slow, the audience will lose their concentration and the presentation will not be effective. We must again emphasize that you should not read your speech.

Most of us are nervous when we face an audience. The following suggestions might help you to control your nervousness.

1. Control your environment. If your hands are shaking, don't hold notes. If your knees are knocking, stand behind something. If you are most nervous when the audience is looking right at you, use visual aids to direct their attention away from you. Concentrate on using a strong, clear voice.

2. Turn your nervousness to your advantage. Most people do their best work when they are under a little pressure or tension. View your nervousness as a stimulus.

3. Avoid meaningless filler words and phrases, such as okay, alright, you know, like, um, and ah.

4. Practice!

Some people are naturally gifted speakers. Many are not. Fortunately, giving a presentation is an area where proper preparation and practice can often overcome most shortcomings. Thus, you should spend a great deal of time in preparation and practice, especially if you are at all uncomfortable with your speaking ability. If you have not already taken a speech course, we strongly encourage you to do so. Most schools offer a speech or public speaking course, and many businesses and organizations offer similar classes.

Systems analysis phase skills

Many systems analysts find interviewing, performing the other fact-finding techniques, documenting, and making presentations to be the most difficult parts of their jobs. The skills necessary to be competent at these activities are nontechnical skills; these skills are far removed from computer technology and from a scientific basis compared to systems design activities, programming, testing, and other activities that occur during later phases of the systems development life cycle. In the next two chapters, we examine the more technically oriented activities of the systems analysis phase — the activities that take place during the requirements analysis stage of systems analysis.

CHAPTER CASE STUDY 3

James Tool Company — Determining Requirements

James Tool Company's vice president of finance, Arnold Henderson, had submitted a request for information systems services to investigate problems with the company's payroll system. Clyde Harland, the manager of applications, assigned systems analyst Don Mard to conduct a preliminary investigation to study the payroll system's problems.

Mard's investigation revealed that the payroll problems are primarily caused by the lack of a formal notification procedure for union status changes and by the payroll department's need to manually prepare required union reports. Consequently, the payroll clerks work excessive overtime hours to overcome these problems.

The information systems department has recommended that a detailed study be conducted for these problem areas in the payroll system. Arnold Henderson has given his approval for such a study. Thus, the second phase of the systems project, the systems analysis phase, has now begun.

■ Interview — personnel department

Based on job descriptions supplied by the personnel department and a list of the payroll department employees, Mard constructed a payroll organization chart during the preliminary investigation phase. As the first step in the detailed investigation, Mard also prepared an organization chart for the personnel department. These two charts are illustrated in Figures 3-9 and 3-10.

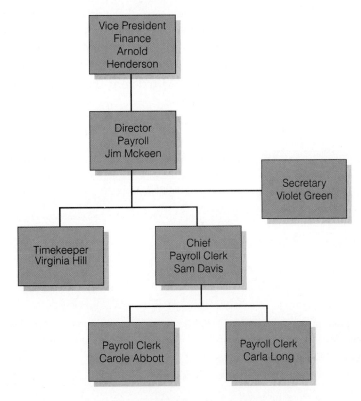

Figure 3-9   *Payroll department organization chart at James Tool Company.*

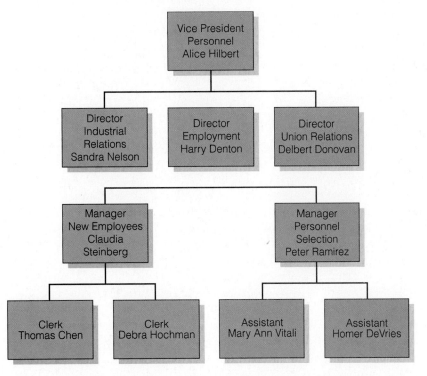

Figure 3-10   *Personnel department organization chart at James Tool Company.*

Mard decided that he should track the information flow pertaining to an employee's union status. The original recording of union status would take place when the employee is first hired, Mard believed, and so after reviewing the personnel department organization chart, he decided to interview Claudia Steinberg, who has the primary responsibility for completing the personnel records of newly hired employees and forwarding those records to the payroll department.

After making an appointment with Steinberg, Mard sent the memo shown in Figure 3-11 to her director to inform him of that meeting.

MEMORANDUM

DATE: October 14, 1996
TO: Harry Denton, Director of Employment
FROM: Don Mard
SUBJECT: Payroll System Investigation

The information systems department is investigating detailed improvements to the payroll system. We are particularly interested in tracking procedures concerning an employee's union status.

I plan to meet with Claudia Steinberg of your department on October 18, at 10:00 am., to discuss this topic.

I might need to meet with other staff in your department and will keep you informed of these meetings as they occur. We will also advise you of our findings as we progress through this project phase.

Figure 3-11   Memo to Harry Denton.

Mard also sent a memo to Steinberg listing the planned interview questions and requesting copies of relevant forms. That memo is shown in Figure 3-12.

MEMORANDUM

DATE: October 14, 1996
TO: Claudia Steinberg
FROM: Don Mard
SUBJECT: Payroll System Investigation

As per our telephone conversation, I will meet with you on October 18 at 10:00 a.m. in your office. If this will not be convenient for you, please let me know.

I would like to discuss all the procedures you follow for initially recording employee information relevant to the payroll preparation. I plan to ask the following questions:

1. Is there a standard form on which the initial employee information is recorded?

2. If so, does that form include an indication of union membership?

3. How is the payroll department notified about a new employee and informed of pay rate, union status, and so forth?

4. How are changes recorded to the initial information about an employee recorded? Is a standard form used for this purpose?

If there are any standard forms used as I've described, it would be very helpful for me to have copies of them. Would you be willing to provide blank copies of any such forms and also copies of such forms completed with actual employee information?

I look forward to meeting with you.

Figure 3-12 Preinterview memo to Claudia Steinberg.

In the interview, Steinberg explained that when an employee is hired, the personnel department completes an Employee Master Record. Steinberg gave Mard a blank copy of that form, as well as a sample of a completed form. She explained that because payroll and personnel information is confidential, the sample she prepared for Mard was for a fictitious employee but was otherwise realistic in all respects. The sample Employee Master Record prepared by Claudia Steinberg is shown in Figure 3-13 on the next page. Completed Employee Master Record forms are immediately sent to the payroll department, where they are filed in alphabetical order by name, Steinberg explained.

EMPLOYEE MASTER RECORD

SOCIAL SECURITY NUMBER _____261-24-9021_____

NAME _____Avcollie_____ _____David_____ _____Lee_____
          last   first   middle

ADDRESS _____7148 Grove Road_____ _____Manchester_____ _____CA_____ _____92101_____
              street address   city   state   zip code

JOB CLASSIFICATION _3C_ STARTING DATE _3/10/97_ DEPT. _04_

PAY RATE _$8.80/Hour_ UNION AFFILIATION _Machinists_

DEDUCTIONS: Federal Income Tax Exemptions _3_____

              Credit Union Deduction _____

Figure 3-13 Sample Employee Master Record.

When questioned about the procedures that are followed when an employee's status changes, Steinberg explained that the Deduction and Pay Rate Change Form shown in Figure 3-14 is used for this purpose. Whenever the personnel department is notified of a change for an employee, a change form is completed and sent to the payroll department, where it is filed behind that employee's original Employee Master Record.

DEDUCTION AND PAY RATE CHANGE FORM

SOCIAL SECURITY NUMBER _____

NAME _____
         last   first   middle

DEDUCTION CHANGE [ ] Income Tax Exemptions Old _____ New _____
                       Credit Union Deduction Old$ _____ New$ _____

PAY RATE CHANGE [ ] Old$_____ New$_____

EFFECTIVE DATE _____/_____/_____

Figure 3-14 Deduction and Pay Rate Change Form.

Mard noted that there was no place on the Deduction and Pay Rate Change Form for indicating union membership changes. Steinberg explained that the union is supposed to notify the personnel department, specifically the director of union relations, Delbert Donovan, about any such union change. Donovan then informs the payroll department, where, Steinberg believed, the change is noted on the original Employee Master Record.

After concluding the interview with Claudia Steinberg, Don Mard prepared the interview documentation shown in Figure 3-15. He also sent to Steinberg the follow-up memo shown in Figure 3-16 on the next page, to which he attached a copy of the interview documentation.

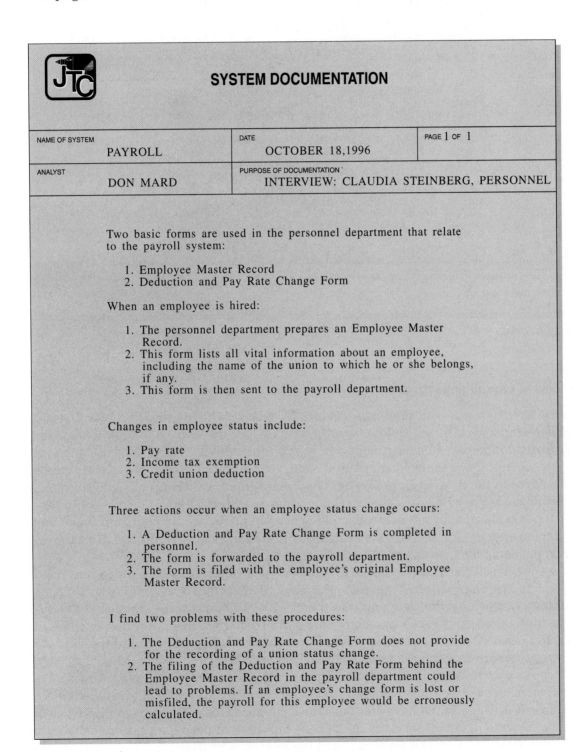

SYSTEM DOCUMENTATION

NAME OF SYSTEM	DATE	PAGE 1 OF 1
PAYROLL	OCTOBER 18,1996	

ANALYST	PURPOSE OF DOCUMENTATION
DON MARD	INTERVIEW: CLAUDIA STEINBERG, PERSONNEL

Two basic forms are used in the personnel department that relate to the payroll system:

1. Employee Master Record
2. Deduction and Pay Rate Change Form

When an employee is hired:

1. The personnel department prepares an Employee Master Record.
2. This form lists all vital information about an employee, including the name of the union to which he or she belongs, if any.
3. This form is then sent to the payroll department.

Changes in employee status include:

1. Pay rate
2. Income tax exemption
3. Credit union deduction

Three actions occur when an employee status change occurs:

1. A Deduction and Pay Rate Change Form is completed in personnel.
2. The form is forwarded to the payroll department.
3. The form is filed with the employee's original Employee Master Record.

I find two problems with these procedures:

1. The Deduction and Pay Rate Change Form does not provide for the recording of a union status change.
2. The filing of the Deduction and Pay Rate Form behind the Employee Master Record in the payroll department could lead to problems. If an employee's change form is lost or misfiled, the payroll for this employee would be erroneously calculated.

Figure 3-15 *Documentation of the interview with Claudia Steinberg.*

MEMORANDUM

DATE: October 18, 1996
TO: Claudia Steinberg
FROM: Don Mard
SUBJECT: Payroll System Investigation Meeting Results

Thank you for meeting with me on October 18 and explaining the information flow associated with an employee's union status. I have attached my documentation of the interview; the documentation represents my understanding of the information flow and points out two problems I believe exist with the current procedures.

Please review the attached documentation. If you have any corrections or additions to the documentation, please call me at extension 2046 before October 25. I will advise you of our final recommendations from the payroll system investigation before the end of the month.

I appreciate the time that you spent with me and that you spent preparing the sample forms.

Figure 3-16 Postinterview memo to Claudia Steinberg.

Interview — payroll department

Mard's next interview was with chief payroll clerk Sam Davis. During the interview, Davis stated that when an employee is hired, an Employee Master Record is completed in personnel. This form is then forwarded to the payroll department, where one of the payroll clerks files the form with the other master forms. Davis then explained that each week a payroll clerk types a time card for every hourly employee in the firm. In Figure 3-17, you will see a time card that Davis prepared for Mard's sample Employee Master Record. Davis explained that in addition to the period ending date, a payroll clerk types in the employee's name, Social Security number, department, and union number, if any. The timekeeper enters the pay rate, which is confidential, on the time card after the end of the week when the completed cards are collected.

After the payroll clerk has prepared all the new time cards, Davis explained that the time cards are sorted by name within department number. Then, prior to the employees arriving for work on Monday morning, the clerks pick up the prior week's time cards and distribute the new time cards in the time clock racks located in each of the departments. Every day, each employee checks in and out on the time clock that automatically records on the time card the time the employee reports for work and the time the employee leaves work.

The clerks deliver the prior week's time cards to the timekeeper, who rearranges all the cards into alphabetical sequence. The timekeeper then matches the time cards against the Employee Master Records and copies the pay rates onto the corresponding time cards. A payroll clerk delivers the time cards to Brafford Services, the service bureau that prepares the James Tool Company payroll. When Brafford Services has completed the payroll, a Brafford employee returns the time cards, along with the completed paychecks, payroll register, and other reports to Davis.

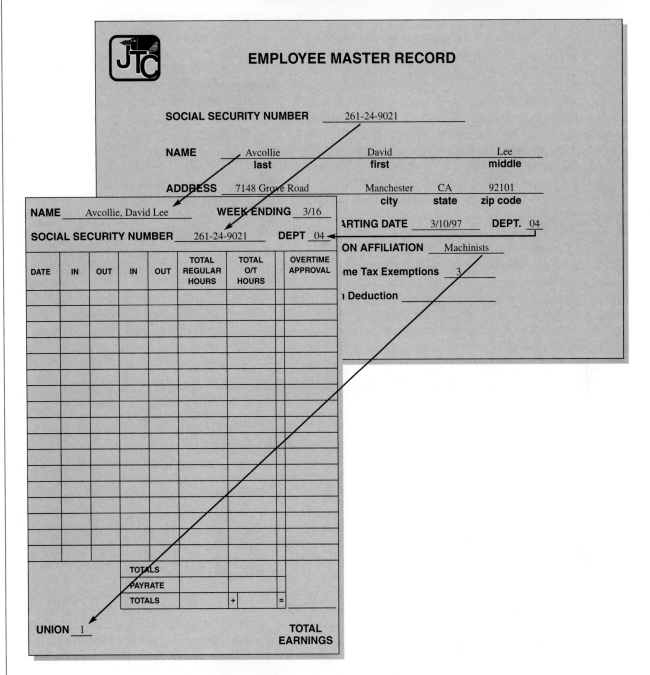

Figure 3-17 *Example of time card preparation at James Tool Company.*

Once each month, Davis uses the payroll registers and the Employee Master Records to manually prepare reports of dues collected, one report for each of the four unions represented within James Tool Company. When the reports are finished, the payroll director, Jim McKeen, writes a check to each of the unions for the total amount of dues deducted for that month for that union. This entire process, as described by Davis, matched in all important aspects Mard's understanding of the process after his interview with McKeen during the preliminary investigation. This process is illustrated in Figure 3-18 on the next page.

Step 1: A newly hired employee completes an Employee Master Sheet in the personnel department. A copy of this sheet is sent to the payroll department.

Step 2: From the Employee Master Sheets, time cards are prepared and distributed before the employees arrive at work for the week.

Step 3: Employees check in and out on a time clock Monday through Sunday.

Step 4: The time cards are collected Monday morning and returned to payroll. The timekeeper copies pay rates from the Employee Master Sheets to the time cards, which are then sent to Brafford Services.

Step 5: Brafford Services processes the time cards and prepares the paychecks and payroll register.

Step 6: The time cards, paychecks, and payroll register are received from Brafford Services. The chief payroll clerk creates the union reports.

Figure 3-18 *Sequence of events in the payroll processing at James Tool Company*

Mard noted that the Employee Master Record (Figure 3-13 on page 3.34) includes the name of the union to which an employee belongs, whereas the time card shows a number in the union field (Figure 3-17 on the previous page). Davis explained that the clerks can type a single number faster than they can type the union name. The relationships between union name and union number and the weekly dues for each of the unions are specified in the payroll procedures manual. Davis provided Mard with a copy of the relevant page of that manual, as shown in Figure 3-19.

**JAMES TOOL COMPANY
SYSTEMS AND PROCEDURES**

PAYROLL
page 18

VII. UNION DEDUCTIONS

Deductions for union membership are taken from the pay of those employees who are members of a union. The union dues are deducted every pay period, and the amount deducted is placed in an account. On the 15th of each month, the total applicable amount deducted from paychecks since the 15th of the prior month is paid to the unions. The following procedure should be used to calculate and record the deductions made for each union employee.

A. UNIONS AND RATES

The following unions have employees in James Tool Company. Their corresponding weekly dues are given.

1. Machinists Union $1.50/week
2. Electricians Union $2.00/week
3. Plumbers Union $2.25/week
4. Teamsters Union $3.00/week

B. DEDUCTION PROCEDURE

1. From the Employee Master Records, determine the union affiliation, if any, for each employee (see Exhibit 1).

2. From the weekly dues in (A) above, determine the amount to be deducted from the paycheck.

Figure 3-19 A page from the James Tool Company's Payroll Procedures Manual.

Mard then asked if Davis knew why Brafford Services could not produce the necessary union reports. Davis stated that even though the payroll is run weekly, the collected union dues are reported and paid to the unions once a month. Because the two cycles do not match, Brafford Services cannot calculate and prepare the union reports and checks, he explained. Mard then asked why the unions were paid monthly instead of, say, every four weeks. Davis said he thought there was some reason why it had to be done monthly, but he admitted that he did not know the reason.

Davis then showed Mard the sample Union Deduction Register shown in Figure 3-20. Davis had prepared this sample for the first complete union reporting period that the fictitious employee would have worked. For each union, this report lists that union's member employees, their earnings and applicable union deductions for each week in the reporting period, and their total union deductions for that period. Two copies of this report are prepared each month, one of which is distributed to the unions.

JAMES TOOL COMPANY
UNION DEDUCTION REGISTER

UNION Machinists   PAGE 1

LOCAL NUMBER 328   PERIOD 03/16/97 - 04/15/97

EMPLOYEE NAME	SOCIAL SECURITY NUMBER	WEEK ENDING DATE	WEEKLY EARNINGS	UNION DUES	TOTAL UNION DUES THIS PERIOD
Avcollie, David Lee	261-24-9021	3/23	361.90	1.50	
		3/30	352.00	1.50	
		4/06	352.00	1.50	
		4/13	352.00	1.50	
		4/20	352.00	.60	6.60
Bombeck, Estelle Louise	. . . . .	3/23	. . . .	1.50	
	. . . . . .	. . . . . .	. . . . .	. . . .	

Figure 3-20   Sample Union Deduction Register.

At first, Mard was confused by the figures shown in the report. He asked why the union dues were not $1.50 for every week. Davis explained that $1.50 would indeed have been deducted from this employee's paycheck every week. But for the week ending 4/20 (which is a Sunday), the first two of the five workdays of the week are the 14th and 15th. Those two days fall into the given union reporting period, Davis explained, and so two-fifths of that $1.50, or $.60, would be applied to the sample month. The remaining three-fifths, or $.90, would apply to the following month. Most months, Davis added, dues from both the first and last weeks of the reporting period have to be allocated to the appropriate period. But in the sample month, the Saturday of the prior week happened to be the 15th, so no allocation was necessary. Mard began to understand why the union reports were being prepared manually.

■ Interview — Brafford Services

Don Mard decided that he should next talk with someone at Brafford Services. He learned from Jim McKeen that Linda DeMarco serves as Brafford's customer representative, so Mard scheduled an appointment with DeMarco.

When Mard arrived at Brafford, DeMarco greeted him warmly. She explained that she had planned to schedule a meeting with members of James Tool Company's payroll department within the next month or two to discuss developments at Brafford Services. However, because Mard was now working with the payroll system, this meeting would save DeMarco a trip to James Tool Company. Even though she was not yet prepared with all the details, the two of them could talk about those developments that day. Abandoning his interview plan for the moment, Mard asked to what developments she was referring.

"The payroll system that you people are using, which we call GAPP, for Generalized Automated Payroll Program, was originally developed here at Brafford in 1967," DeMarco began. "In fact, James Tool Company was one of our very first customers. And so, of course, we feel great loyalty and affection for your firm. Anyway, GAPP has obviously been modified and updated since 1967 to take advantage of advancing technology. But let's face it, notwithstanding the patches, GAPP is an antique! But I have exciting news. A few months ago, Brafford management finally gave the go-ahead to develop a new, state-of-the-art payroll system. We are going to call it CHIPS, for Comprehensive High-powered Interactive Payroll System. I am really looking forward to working with your company when you switch over to CHIPS," DeMarco said.

Mard took a few moments to consider this surprising development. He then asked what would happen with GAPP. DeMarco stated that GAPP would be available to customers for another year or two, but that Brafford Services would make no further changes or enhancements to that system. Wasting Brafford's resources on an obsolete system would not make sense, DeMarco explained.

Mard had been hoping that some of James Tool's payroll problems could be solved with a few changes to the Brafford payroll system that James Tool used. That, he now realized, was impossible, and so he decided to learn more about CHIPS.

Mard described the union situation at James Tool Company, the reporting requirements, and the problem with the mismatched cycles, and asked if CHIPS would handle that. DeMarco commented that because Mard had briefly described that same situation when they had set up this meeting, she had checked into it. She pointed out that James Tool was their only customer with more than one union. Consequently, Brafford Services had concluded that programming CHIPS to handle multiple unions did not make economic sense. DeMarco suggested that perhaps a special add-on module could be written, once CHIPS was up and running. Brafford could do that kind of job on a contract basis, DeMarco added.

Mard then asked when the new system would be available, and what the weekly charges for the system would be. DeMarco stated that current plans were to begin offering CHIPS in the last half of the next year. She explained that because the system was still in development, she couldn't be more specific about timetables and costs. She was sure, however, that the monthly fee for CHIPS would not be more than 30% higher than the current GAPP charges. She then gave Mard a preliminary copy of the CHIPS documentation that the Brafford Services development programmer had prepared.

As Mard was preparing to leave, DeMarco urged him to keep in touch. In the next few months, she explained, plans for CHIPS would become more firm, and she would then be able to answer all his questions.

■ New plans

When Mard returned from his meeting with DeMarco, he immediately went to his manager, Clyde Harland. After Mard had recounted his visit at Brafford Services, Harland phoned David Green, the director of information systems. Within the hour, Harland and Mard were meeting with Green in his office, where Mard again recounted the details of the Brafford visit. Green asked for Mard's opinion of how this new development affected the current systems analysis phase. Mard explained that one of the identified problems, the lack of formal procedures for reporting union status changes, still appeared to be easily solvable by instituting a new form or changing an existing one. But Mard admitted that he saw no obvious solutions for the union dues reporting problems except to change the scope of the project immediately.

Green, Harland, and Mard then analyzed the situation. All agreed that because of the upcoming changes with the Brafford Services arrangement, the current payroll system project would have to be changed, canceled, or postponed. As input for that management decision, they totaled the costs of the project to that point and prepared estimates for a detailed investigation of the entire payroll system.

Later that week, Green met with Arnold Henderson, vice president of finance, to discuss the new developments and options. After meeting with his payroll director and consulting with other James Tool Company vice presidents, Henderson approved the systems analysis plan that Green had proposed. James Tool Company would obviously have to have a new payroll system, one way or another.

■ Payroll reports

Don Mard, a systems analyst, and Howard Coswell, a programmer/analyst, were assigned to the revised system project. Because they now had to determine the requirements for the complete payroll system, Mard and Coswell conducted follow-up interviews with Jim McKeen and Sam Davis, as well as the timekeeper and both payroll clerks. During these payroll department interviews, the payroll staff prepared samples of all the existing payroll reports.

The first report is the Payroll Register, a sample of which is shown in Figure 3-21. On this report, all employees are listed, one employee per line, along with their earnings, deductions, and net pay. This register is used by James Tool Company as a record of payments to employees. Brafford creates three copies of this report each week. One copy is sent to Arnold Henderson, one copy goes to Jim McKeen, and the third copy is used within the payroll department for determining how much money James Tool owes to the federal government, the state government, and the unions for the deductions that have been made for taxes, Social Security, and union dues.

JAMES TOOL COMPANY
PAYROLL REGISTER

WEEK ENDING 03/23/97   PAGE 1

EMPLOYEE DATA		EARNINGS			DEDUCTIONS					NET PAY	
EMPLOYEE NAME	SOCIAL SECURITY NUMBER	REGULAR EARNINGS	OVERTIME EARNINGS	TOTAL EARNINGS	FEDERAL TAX	FICA	STATE TAX	CREDIT UNION	UNION DUES	NET AMOUNT	CHECK NUMBER
Avcollie, David Lee	261-24-9021	352.00	9.90	361.90	46.40	23.04	7.60		1.50	283.36	02232
Bard, William Avon	· · · ·	· · · ·	· · ·	· · · ·	· · · ·	· · ·	· ·	· ·	· ·	· · ·	00233
Bombeck, Estelle L.	· · · ·	· · · ·	· · ·	· · · ·	· · · ·	· · ·	· ·	· ·	· ·	· · ·	00234

Figure 3-21   Sample Payroll Register.

A second payroll report is the Employee Compensation Record (Figure 3-22). This report shows year-to-date payroll information for each employee. As was true with the Payroll Register, Brafford prints three copies of this report. One copy is sent to Henderson, one to McKeen, and the third is filed in the payroll department.

JAMES TOOL COMPANY
EMPLOYEE COMPENSATION RECORD

EMPLOYEE NAME _____ Avcollie, David Lee _____   **MARITAL STATUS** _____ Married _____

EMPLOYEE ADDRESS __ 7148 Grove Road, Manchester, CA 92101 ____   **NUMBER OF EXEMPTIONS** _____ 3 _____

SOCIAL SECURITY NUMBER ____ 261-24-9021 _____   **DATE EMPLOYED** _____ 03/10/97 _____

UNION AFFILIATION _____ Machinists _____   **DATE TERMINATED** _____

WEEKLY PAYROLL										YEAR TO DATE								
EARNINGS				DEDUCTIONS					NET PAY		EARNINGS			DEDUCTIONS					NET PAY
WEEK ENDING	REGULAR EARNINGS	OVERTIME EARNINGS	TOTAL EARNINGS	FEDERAL TAX	FICA	STATE TAX	CREDIT UNION	UNION DUES	NET AMOUNT	CHECK NUMBER	REGULAR EARNINGS	OVERTIME EARNINGS	TOTAL EARNINGS	FEDERAL TAX	FICA	STATE TAX	CREDIT UNION	UNION DUES	NET AMOUNT
3/16	352.00		352.00	45.00	22.40	7.40		1.50	275.70	01845	352.00		352.00	45.00	22.40	7.40		1.50	275.00
3/23	352.00	9.90	361.90	46.40	23.04	7.60		1.50	283.36	02232	704.00	9.90	713.90	91.40	45.44	15.00		3.00	559.06

Figure 3-22   Sample Employee Compensation Report.

The weekly Overtime Report, which lists every employee who worked overtime that week, is sent to Arnold Henderson. A sample of that report is shown in Figure 3-23. When Coswell interviewed Henderson about this report, Henderson stated that he consulted it occasionally but admitted that he did not need the report every week.

JAMES TOOL COMPANY
OVERTIME REPORT

WEEK ENDING ____ 03/23/97 _____   **PAGE** ___ 1 ___

EMPLOYEE NAME	DEPARTMENT	HOURS OF OVERTIME	OVERTIME COMPENSATION
Avcollie, David Lee	04	0.75	9.90
Dubichek, Alexander	02	2.50	24.75

Figure 3-23   Sample Overtime Report.

The most important output from the payroll system is the payroll check, a sample of which is shown in Figure 3-24. From the sample you can see that the payroll check output consists of the payroll check itself as well as a stub that lists the hours worked, the amount of gross pay, all the deductions from the gross pay, and the net pay (which corresponds to the amount that is written on the check). The pay stub also shows year-to-date totals. The payroll checks, with the stubs attached, are distributed weekly to the employees.

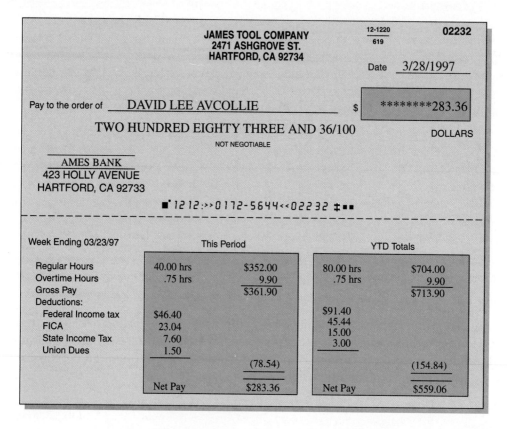

Figure 3-24 *Sample paycheck (with attached stub).*

Coswell and Mard determined that weekly production of all but one of these output reports was deemed necessary. The Overtime Report, however, could be eliminated from the weekly processing schedule and could instead be prepared on a demand or as-needed basis.

Summary

The systems analysis phase consists of obtaining answers to the questions who, what, where, when, how, and why. The systems analysis phase is the second phase of the systems development life cycle and consists of two stages: requirements determination and requirements analysis. During requirements determination, you collect the requirements for the new information system, concentrating on requirements for the outputs, inputs, processes, timings, and controls. You also collect quantitative information concerning volumes, sizes, and frequencies for all outputs, inputs, and processes.

We considered the reasons for coding of data and examined several commonly used coding schemes. We also presented several useful tips for data coding.

We then began our examination of specific techniques used in the requirements determination effort, which is the first part of the systems analysis phase, and during all other phases of the systems development life cycle. We discussed interviewing in detail, including how to determine who to interview, how to set interview objectives, and how to prepare for, conduct, and analyze interviews. Then, we examined the other fact-finding techniques of data collection, observation, questionnaires, and research.

Our next discussion focused on the need to record the information you collect and considered aspects of good writing. Then, we concluded the chapter by studying presentations. Before you give a presentation, you should first define the audience, set your presentation objectives, organize your material, define all technical terms, prepare supplementary presentation aids, and then practice. Finally, we discussed what you should do during a presentation to help ensure its success, including techniques for selling yourself, controlling the presentation, answering questions, using good speaking techniques, and controlling your nervousness.

Review Questions

1. The systems analysis phase is divided into what two stages?
2. What is an informal organizational structure? Why is it important?
3. Systems analysis consists of obtaining answers to what five questions? What additional question is asked in the process of answering each of those five questions?
4. What is a system requirement? Into what categories can system requirements be classified?
5. What is a code? What purpose might a code serve?
6. What are the most commonly used coding schemes? Briefly describe each.
7. What are the two different types of questions? How do these different question forms affect the answers given?
8. Why might an interview be unsuccessful? If an interviewee is not answering your questions satisfactorily, what should you do?
9. Should you take notes during an interview? Should you use a tape or video recorder?
10. What is the Hawthorne Effect? Why is it significant?
11. To what three different audiences might you have to give a presentation? How would the presentation differ for each? If only one presentation is given with all interested parties in attendance, to whom should the presentation be primarily addressed?
12. What should you do or not do if your hands shake while you give a presentation? If your knees knock? If you are nervous when people are looking at you?

Discussion Questions

1. A group meeting is sometimes suggested as a useful compromise between interviews and questionnaires. In such a group meeting, one systems analyst meets with and asks questions of a number of end users at one time. Discuss the possible advantages and disadvantages of such a group meeting. (*Hint:* Consider the advantages and disadvantages of interviews and questionnaires and consider which of those advantages might be compromised and which of the disadvantages might be alleviated. Also, consider additional factors introduced by the very nature of a group meeting.)

2. Some authorities feel that during the presentation, the job of the systems analyst is to sell to management the one solution that the information systems department believes will offer the greatest benefit to the company. Other authorities argue that the job of the systems analyst is to present objectively all alternative solutions and to have management assume all responsibility for deciding on the solution to be taken. Which position do you support and why?

3. In the James Tool Company case in this chapter, the systems analyst investigating the payroll system asked for copies of *actual* reports and completed forms. Instead, he was given *simulated* copies prepared with fictitious data. Do you feel that simulated copies were appropriate in this case? What if the investigation instead had involved a customer billing system for a manufacturing firm such as James Tool Company? What about a customer billing service for a health clinic? Do you think that allowing a systems analyst to see only simulated documents is a good idea in general? At some point in the development of a new system, might it not be necessary to trust a systems analyst with confidential information?

4. In the James Tool Company case in this chapter, Don Mard met with Linda DeMarco of Brafford Services. Mard abandoned his planned set of questions when DeMarco began to explain the new payroll system developments at Brafford. What questions would you have originally planned to ask DeMarco if you, instead of Mard, had been assigned to the project?

5. Assume that you, not Don Mard, had met with Linda DeMarco of Brafford Services during the James Tool Company case. Write a follow-up letter to DeMarco that describes the information collected from her during the interview.

6. Look through magazines or textbooks to find examples of each of the following types of visual aids: bar chart, pie chart, graph, table, diagram, and a list of key points. How clear, meaningful, and effective do you think each is? Find at least one visual aid example that you feel could be improved; describe its shortcomings and prepare an improved version of it.

7. Attend a speech or presentation and analyze its effectiveness. Consider the speaker's delivery and how he or she organized the material, used visual aids, and handled audience questions. Describe specifically how the speech or presentation was most effective, as well as how it could have been improved.

8. Attend a speech or presentation, and then prepare an outline of the material presented. Was the material logically organized? If not, prepare a more logical outline for that same material. Did the speaker use visual aids? Prepare a visual aid you believe the speaker could or should have used.

9. Prepare and practice telling a humorous anecdote, and then tell it to the class. Have your audience comment on your performance and offer suggestions for improvement.

Baxter Community College

Baxter Community College is a two-year school in New Hampshire. The records office at Baxter currently manually maintains the alumni records. Twice a year, Baxter mails requests for donations to the alumni. For each such mailing, the envelopes are hand-addressed or typed. The college has recently decided to produce an alumni newsletter, for which six issues a year are planned. The registrar had been wanting a computerized alumni system for some time. Because mailing labels will be needed at least eight times a year, he is convinced that the system is necessary and justifiable and, therefore, has asked the college's computing services department to develop such a system.

Todd Wagner is the systems analyst assigned to the alumni system project. He conducted the preliminary investigation and prepared a report at the end of that investigation. After reading the report, the registrar immediately gave the go-ahead for the systems analysis phase, saying that a presentation of the findings was unnecessary. Wagner then conducted the systems analysis phase and prepared a recommendation for a new alumni system with online update and query features. He discussed his ideas with his boss and several co-workers, and all felt that Wagner's ideas were excellent. Wagner then prepared and sent to the registrar the final report for the systems analysis phase.

This time, the registrar did not waive the presentation. Instead, he requested that the college president, the provost, and all the administrative vice presidents be invited to attend. The registrar wanted to be sure that he would have administrative support and funding for the new alumni system. All the records office clerks were also invited to attend the presentation.

Unfortunately, Wagner's car wouldn't start the morning of the presentation. As a result, he arrived twelve minutes late for the presentation, out of breath and disheveled. He immediately apologized and began to set out his notes. He then noticed that there was no easel in the room to hold his flip charts. Consequently, he moved a table closer to the front wall, placed the flip chart on the table and propped it against the wall, and began his presentation.

The flip chart wasn't very steady in that position, however, so Wagner had to constantly stand next to it to hold on to it. In order to flip to the next chart, Wagner had to juggle the entire flip chart. He was so busy with the charts that he didn't notice that people in the back of the room were straining to see the charts. The registrar finally interrupted to point out that the charts couldn't be seen by everyone. Wagner rushed out of the room to find an easel. When he finally returned with an easel, he found that several of the attendees had left. He did finish the presentation but with little of his original enthusiasm.

Questions

1. List every mistake that Wagner made, and for each, describe what he should have done instead.
2. What do you think Wagner should do now to try to salvage the alumni project?

Hoober Industries

Michelle Quinn was recently hired as an information systems analyst at Hoober Industries. This new job represented a promotion for her, because she had been a programmer at her previous job. Quinn's first assignment at Hoober Industries was a preliminary investigation concerning a request for enhancements to an existing computer system. Quinn's boss had been very pleased with her work on that phase, and so Quinn subsequently was assigned to do the systems analysis phase on the system.

During the preliminary investigation, Quinn had had a brief interview with Raymond Morgan, the one person at Hoober Industries most knowledgeable about the existing system procedures. A more detailed, comprehensive interview with Morgan was now appropriate. Morgan would be describing many critical details about the system operations in this interview, and Quinn was nervous about comprehending and remembering all the discussed material. So she hid a small tape recorder in her purse and switched it on just before the interview. That night at home, Quinn replayed the tape many times, transcribing all that Morgan had said. The next day at work she wrote up the interview documentation on the basis of those transcribed interview notes.

Questions

1. What do you think of Quinn's actions?
2. What else might Quinn have done to ensure that she understood and retained the information revealed during the interview?

Campus Life Today Magazine

Tanna Carpenter, who recently graduated with a two-year degree in journalism and another in computer science, has just been hired by *Campus Life Today*. That magazine, which has current and future post-secondary students as its target audience, is planning an upcoming article about computer science students at schools exactly like yours. Tanna's first assignment is to interview current computer science students from several schools for that article.

Questions

1. Make a list of the kinds of topics you, as a student, would be interested in reading about in such an article.
2. Make a list of questions that you might ask a computer science student if you were Tanna. Include both open-ended and close-ended questions.
3. Conduct interviews in class, with half the students assuming Tanna's role and the other half playing the interviewee.
4. Document the information covered in one or more of the interviews.

STUDENT CASE STUDY

Western Dental Clinic — Determining Requirements

Introduction

Western Dental Clinic is considering computerizing one or more of its office systems. The associates at Western hired Jim Archer, a local computer consultant, to perform a preliminary investigation. Archer had several meetings with Dr. Colette Early, one of Western's associates, to discuss the office record and accounting systems. Emily Hendricks, the office manager at Western Dental Clinic, participated in one of those meetings.

In a report submitted to the associates at the end of his investigation, Archer recommended a detailed analysis of the patient record system, the patient and insurance billing systems, and the patient scheduling system. Archer believed that Western would most benefit from automating these three systems. Although any one system could be automated independently of the others, Archer recommended analyzing all three systems simultaneously. There would be, Archer stated, significant interactions among these three systems. The best systems design would result if the three systems were automated concurrently, Archer concluded.

Archer presented his findings and recommendations at a meeting of the associates. After answering several questions, Archer left the meeting so the associates could privately discuss the matter. Dr. Early began the discussion by stating that she had been favorably impressed with Archer's knowledge and professionalism in the meetings she had with him, as well as from his report and presentation.

She recommended accepting his proposal and hiring him immediately to conduct the systems analysis phase. Dr. Kozlaw, however, was not as enthusiastic as Dr. Early. Dr. Kozlaw pointed out that such a study would certainly disrupt office procedures. The staff already had more work than they could handle, Kozlaw argued, and having Archer around taking up their time with his questions would only make the situation worse. Dr. O'Donnell countered that the office work load was going to increase in any event, and that it was critically important to find a long-term solution to the problem. After some additional discussion, Dr. Kozlaw agreed with Dr. O'Donnell's assessment. The associates then voted to hire Jim Archer to perform the systems analysis phase he had recommended.

Student Assignments

1. Review the office organization chart you previously prepared for Western Dental Clinic. List the individuals you would interview during the systems analysis phase.

2. Prepare a list of objectives for each of the interviews you would conduct.

3. Prepare a list of specific questions to be asked of each of the individuals you will interview.

4. Conduct the interviews (contact your instructor).

5. Prepare a written report of the information gained from each of the interviews.

CHAPTER 4

Analyzing Requirements

Objectives

You will have mastered the material in this chapter when you can:

- Explain the importance of structured analysis and name its components
- Discuss the purpose of data flow diagrams, and draw and describe the symbols used in constructing them
- Define the different types of data flow diagrams and their purposes
- Explain how to level and balance data flow diagrams
- Draw a complete set of data flow diagrams for an information system
- Describe how a data dictionary is used and what it contains
- Compare and contrast the use of structured English, decision tables, and decision trees to specify an information system's process descriptions
- Explain the relationships among the data flow diagrams, data dictionary, and process descriptions within an information system

Introduction

Systems analysis is a two-stage process. During the first stage, requirements determination, you use appropriate fact-finding techniques to determine the detailed requirements of the proposed information system. This first stage was the subject of Chapter 3. In this chapter and in Chapter 5, we will discuss the second stage of systems analysis: requirements analysis. During requirements analysis you analyze the information system's requirements and then organize, document, and present the requirements to management.

In this chapter, you will learn about structured analysis, which is the most popular technique used for requirements analysis. Specifically, you will learn about the components of structured analysis: data flow diagrams, the data dictionary, and process descriptions.

Structured analysis

The primary objective of the systems analysis phase is to document *all* the end user requirements for the proposed information system and present these requirements in the system requirements document.

You can use a large variety of methods to document the end user requirements. Most of these documentation methods have been used at various times during the past forty years. Since the late 1970s, however, **structured analysis** has become the dominant technique for documenting end user requirements. You can use structured analysis without using a computer as an aid. Of greater interest and importance, structured analysis is a central component of many computer-aided software engineering (CASE) software products. We will discuss CASE in Chapter 5.

Most information systems are of substantial size and complexity; thus, methods for analyzing and controlling this size and complexity make invaluable tools for the systems analyst. Structured analysis provides methods to the systems analyst for analyzing, organizing, controlling, and documenting large, complex information systems. This is the major reason for the popularity and usefulness of structured analysis during requirements analysis. Of course, structured analysis is also applicable for use with smaller information systems.

Structured analysis is most appropriate for use with business information systems because these systems are predominantly data-driven systems. That is, the input of data initiates procedures that transform data from one form into another form or into information. To document an information system's data and the data's transformations, structured analysis uses three components: data flow diagrams, a data dictionary, and process descriptions. Each of these components is discussed in detail in the remainder of this chapter.

Data flow diagrams

 data flow diagram shows how data moves and changes through an information system in a graphical, top-down fashion. Systems analysts use data flow diagrams, often referred to as **DFDs**, to produce a logical model, or **essential model**, of an information system in a simple, direct way. Data flow diagrams are *not* used to show the logic of a program or any detailed processing logic.

■ Data flow diagram symbols

Data flow diagrams are drawn using the four symbols shown in Figure 4-1. These four symbols are the most commonly used for DFDs and are referred to as **Yourdon DFD symbols**; however, there are alternative symbols used for DFDs that serve similar purposes. Our standard practice is to use capital letters for the names used with each symbol in our DFDs when we refer to the names in the textbook.

| Symbols | Symbol Names | Examples |

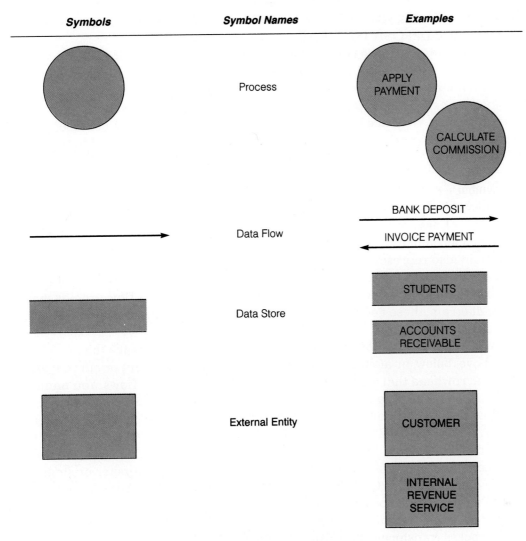

Figure 4-1 Data flow diagram symbols, symbol names, and examples.

Process symbol   A **process** modifies, or changes, data from one form to another form; that is, data is input to a process, and the process transforms this data to produce output data of a different content or form. The process for calculating gross pay, for example, uses pay rate and hours worked data to produce the employee's gross pay. Examples of processes include preparing vendor checks, posting customer payments, calculating taxes, determining past overdue accounts, adding new credit card members, searching for dean's list students, and categorizing patients based on their medical diagnoses.

The symbol for a process is a circle, or bubble. You place the name of the process inside the circle. You name the process to identify the function it accomplishes. A process name consists of a strong, active verb, followed by a descriptive, singular noun; there might be an intervening adjective to clarify the process name. Examples of process names are APPLY PAYMENT, CALCULATE COMMISSION, ASSIGN FINAL GRADE, VERIFY ORDER, and FILL ORDER.

The details of a process are not shown in the data flow diagram; these details are documented in the process descriptions, which we discuss later in this chapter. For example, you might have a process symbol named DEPOSIT PAYMENT on your data flow diagram. The actual detailed data used, the detailed information created, and the detailed steps taken in DEPOSIT PAYMENT would not be shown in the data flow diagram. To understand these details, you would need to look at the supporting process description that would be titled DEPOSIT PAYMENT.

In data flow diagrams we consider a process to be a *black box* for which we know the general inputs, outputs, and function, but not the underlying details. Using a black box approach allows us to represent the processing flow of an information system in a series of increasingly detailed pictures without cluttering the more general pictures with unnecessary details. We place the details where they will not obstruct, confuse, or clutter our overall top-down view of the system — as separate descriptions linked to the associated DFD process symbol by the process name.

Data flow symbol   A **data flow** is a pathway by which data moves from one part of the information system to another part. A given data flow in a data flow diagram represents a specific piece of data or set of data. For example, a data flow could represent a single data item, such as employee name, student number, total sales amount, or letter grade. A data flow could also represent a set of data, such as a class roster that consists of all student numbers and names for a specific class, or a bank deposit that consists of a filled-in deposit slip with its related checks. The detailed contents of a data flow are not shown in a data flow diagram; these details are defined in the data dictionary, which we describe later in this chapter.

The symbol for a data flow is a line with an arrowhead. You place the name of the data flow above, below, or alongside the line. The line can be straight or curved, and it has a single arrowhead that shows the direction in which the data flows. You name the data flow to identify the data it represents. A data flow name consists of adjectives (if necessary) and a singular noun. Examples of data flow names are BANK DEPOSIT, INVOICE PAYMENT, STUDENT GRADE, ORDER, and COMMISSION. Exceptions to the singular-name rule are data flow names, such as GRADING PARAMETERS, where the use of the singular could mislead you to think there is a single parameter or single item of data. Use a name such as CLASS DETAIL instead of CLASS DETAILS, however, because the former name does not lead to a similar misinterpretation.

Figure 4-2 shows typical examples of data flow and process symbol connections. Because a process transforms data from one form to another form, at least one data flow must enter each process symbol, and at least one data flow must leave each process symbol, as they do in the CREATE INVOICE process. A process symbol often has more than one outgoing data flow, such as in the GRADE STUDENT WORK process, or more than one incoming data flow, such as in the CALCULATE GROSS PAY process. Finally, each data flow is connected to at least one process symbol; some data flows, such as ACCEPTED ORDER, connect to two processes. In a completed DFD, each end of a data flow line must be connected to another symbol, but the end opposite a process symbol connection can be connected either to a process symbol or to one of the other two DFD symbols.

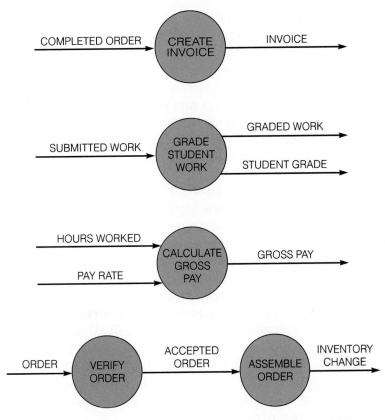

Figure 4-2 *Examples of correct combinations of data flow and process symbols.*

Figure 4-3 shows two data flow and process connections you must avoid. APPLY INSURANCE PREMIUM is a **spontaneous generation** process, which is a process that has no input. CALCULATE GROSS PAY is a **black hole** process, which is a process that has no output. Neither a spontaneous generation process nor a black hole process is possible. A process acts on data, which must be represented by an incoming data flow, to produce modified data, which must be represented by an outgoing data flow. You have to guard against these incorrect connections when doing DFDs by hand; CASE tools, however, alert you to these situations automatically.

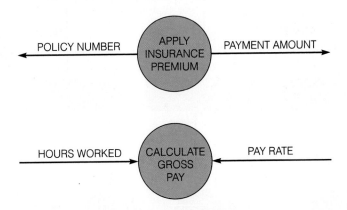

Figure 4-3 *Examples of **incorrect combinations** of data flow and process symbols. APPLY INSURANCE PREMIUM has no inputs and is called a spontaneous generation process. CALCULATE GROSS PAY has no outputs and is called a black hole process.*

Data store symbol   A **data store** is a data repository. You use a data store in a data flow diagram when the system must store data because one or more processes need to use the stored data at a later time. For example, you need to store student scores on tests and assignments during the semester so you can assign final grades at the end of the semester. As another example, you need to store employee salary and deduction data during the year so you can report earnings and withholdings to the government and the employee at the end of the year. The detailed contents of a data store are not shown in a data flow diagram; these contents are defined in the data dictionary.

The length of time that the data is stored is unimportant — it can be seconds or years. What is important is that a process needs access to the data at some later time. The specific medium (disk or file folder, for example) used for the data store is also unimportant because we are concerned with the logical, not the physical, requirements of the information system. **Logical requirements** are the information system's requirements and the relationships among these requirements, independent of how they will be physically accomplished. **Physical requirements** combine the logical requirements and their implementation with specific physical devices, systems software, and so on.

The symbol for a data store is two parallel lines. You place the name of the data store between the lines. You name the data store to identify the category of data it contains. A data store name is a plural name consisting of adjectives (if necessary) and a noun. Examples of data store names are STUDENTS, ACCOUNTS RECEIVABLE, PRODUCTS, DAILY PAYMENTS, PURCHASE ORDERS, OUTSTANDING CHECKS, CREDIT INSURANCE POLICIES, and EMPLOYEES. Exceptions to the plural-name rule are collective nouns that represent multiple occurrences of objects. For example, GRADEBOOK represents students and their scores.

A data store must be connected to a data flow with a process at the other end of the data flow. Figure 4-4 illustrates typical examples of data stores in a data flow diagram. In each case, the data store has at least one incoming and one outgoing data flow, and a process symbol appears on the other end of the data flow.

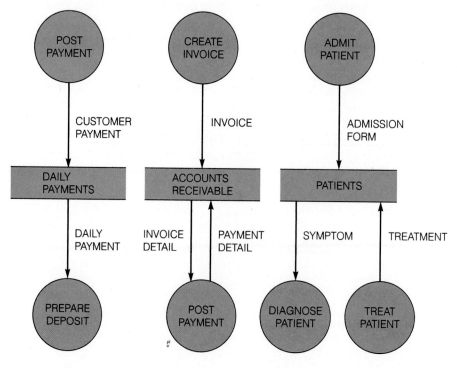

Figure 4-4 *Examples of correct uses of data store symbols in a data flow diagram.*

Violations of the rule that a data store must have at least one incoming and one outgoing data flow are shown in Figure 4-5. In the first example, two data stores are incorrectly connected, and in the second two examples, a data store lacks either an outgoing or incoming data flow.

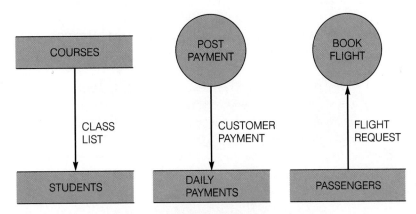

Figure 4-5 Examples of **incorrect uses** of data store symbols: two data stores cannot be connected by a data flow without an intervening process, and each data store should have an outgoing and incoming data flow.

External entity symbol   An **external entity** is a person, department, outside organization, or other information system that provides data to the system or receives data or information from the system. External entities show the boundaries of the information system or the information system's interactions with the outside world. For example, a customer submitting an order is an external entity because the customer supplies data to the order system. Other examples of external entities include a patient supplying medical data, a home owner receiving a property tax bill, a warehouse receiving product shipping information, a credit agency sending a company the credit ratings of its customers, and an accounts payable system receiving data about a company's purchases.

External entities are also called **terminators**. An external entity that supplies data is called a **source**, or **origin**. An external entity that receives data is called a **destination**, or **sink**.

The symbol for an external entity is a rectangle. You place the name of the external entity inside the rectangle. An external entity name is the singular form of the name of the department, outside organization, other information system, or person (by category or position, but not by the individual's name). Examples of external entity names are CUSTOMER, STUDENT, EMPLOYEE, MEMBER, SALES REP, WAREHOUSE, ACCOUNTING, BANK, INTERNAL REVENUE SERVICE, CREDIT UNION, PAYROLL SYSTEM, GENERAL LEDGER SYSTEM, and PRODUCTION MANAGEMENT.

An external entity might be a source, a destination, or both, as shown in Figure 4-6 on the next page. An external entity is always connected by a data flow to a process.

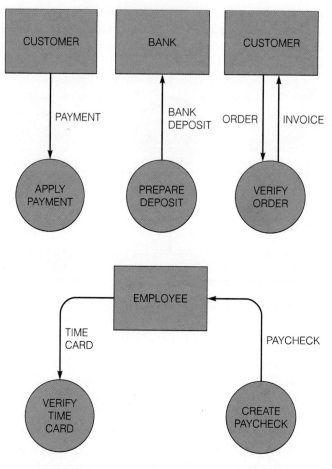

Figure 4-6   *Examples of correct uses of external entities in a data flow diagram.*

Figure 4-7 shows violations of the rule that an external entity must be connected by a data flow to a process.

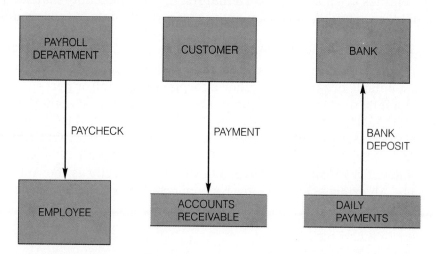

Figure 4-7   *Examples of **incorrect uses** of external entity symbols. An external entity must be connected by a data flow to a process, not directly to a data store or to another external entity.*

■ Context diagrams

To demonstrate how to construct data flow diagrams, we will use as examples three information systems of differing complexities. The simplest example is a grading system teachers use to assign final grades to students, based on the scores the students receive for the work they complete. The second, more complex example is an order system that a company uses to fill customer orders and to account for payments against the orders. The most complex example we will show is a manufacturing system used to manage and control the production and sale of a company's products.

The first step in constructing a set of data flow diagrams for an information system is to draw a DFD called the context diagram. A **context diagram** is a data flow diagram that shows the boundaries of the information system. The context diagram is a top-level view of the information system. To draw a context diagram, you place one process symbol representing the entire information system in the center of the page. You then draw all the external entities around the perimeter of the page and use data flows to properly connect these external entities to the central process. You do not show any data stores in a context diagram because data stores are internal to the system.

How do you know what external entities and data flows must be placed in the context diagram? You review the information system's requirements in detail to extract all external data sources and destinations. During this review and analysis be sure to record the name of the external entities, the name and content of the data flows, and the direction of the data flows. If you do this carefully, you should have no difficulty drawing the context diagram. Your task of review and analysis is made easier if you clearly defined the boundaries and scope of the information system when you undertook requirements determination in the systems analysis phase.

Figure 4-8 is the context diagram for our grading system example. The GRADING SYSTEM process is at the center of the diagram. The three external entities of STUDENT RECORDS SYSTEM, STUDENT, and TEACHER are placed around this central process. The data interactions between the information system and the external entities occur through six different data flows. The STUDENT RECORDS SYSTEM external entity supplies data through the CLASS ROSTER data flow and receives data through the FINAL GRADE data flow. The STUDENT external entity supplies data through the SUBMITTED WORK data flow and receives data through the GRADED WORK data flow. Finally, the TEACHER external entity supplies data through the GRADING PARAME-TERS data flow and receives data through the GRADE REPORT data flow.

The context diagram for a more complex example, an order system, is shown in Figure 4-9 on the next page. Notice that the ORDER SYSTEM process is at the center of the diagram, and the five external entities of CUSTOMER, WAREHOUSE, SALES REP,

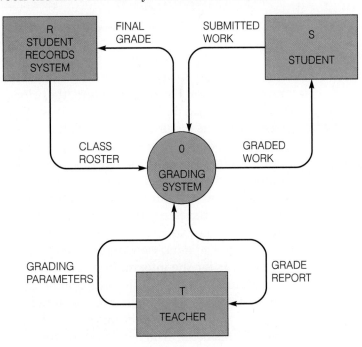

Figure 4-8　Context diagram DFD for the grading system.

BANK, and ACCOUNTING surround the process. Three of the external entities, SALES REP, BANK, and ACCOUNTING, have single, incoming data flows: COMMISSION, BANK DEPOSIT, and CASH RECEIPTS ENTRY, respectively. The WAREHOUSE external entity has one incoming data flow, PICKING LIST (which is a report that shows the items ordered and their quantity, location, and sequence to pick from the warehouse), and one outgoing data flow, COMPLETED ORDER. Finally, the CUSTOMER external entity has two outgoing data flows, ORDER and PAYMENT, and two incoming data flows, ORDER REJECT NOTICE and INVOICE.

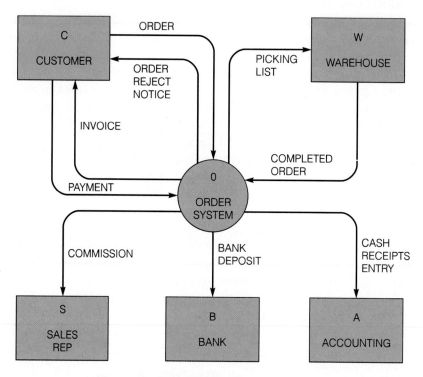

Figure 4-9 *Context diagram DFD for the order system.*

The context diagram for the order system is more complex than the context diagram for the grading system because it has two more external entities and three more data flows. The order system, therefore, has a greater level of interaction with data sources and destinations outside the information system; but we cannot say that the order system is more complex than the grading system just by comparing their context diagrams. Generally, you would consider one information system to be more complex than another if its external entities, data stores, data flows, and processes are greater in number and of a more intricate nature. The context diagram tells you only the number of entities that are external to a particular information system. An information system's complexity is based on its total complexity, not just on the number of its external interfaces. Thus, you cannot use a context diagram alone to determine a system's complexity. You must view the rest of the DFDs and other structured analysis components for the information system in order to determine the system's complexity.

Figure 4-10 shows the context diagram for our third example, the manufacturing system. Because this information system supports the entire production flow of a company, you would expect this system to be very complex. The context diagram seems to verify this belief. The context diagram has thirteen external entities and eighteen data flows!

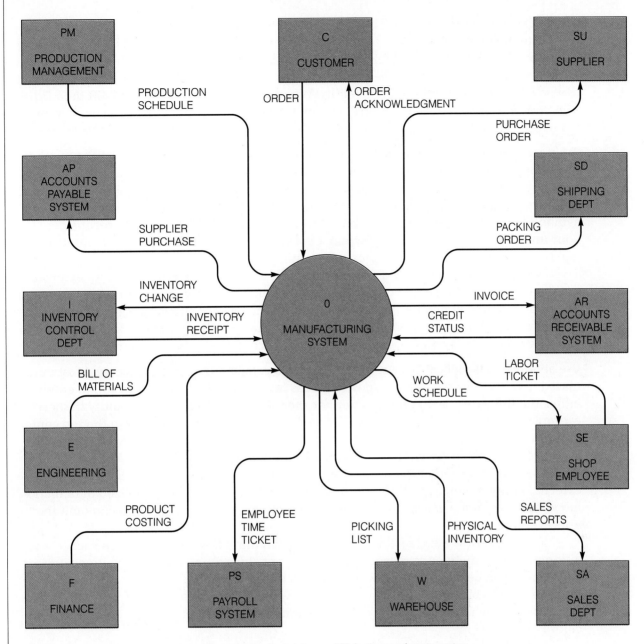

Figure 4-10 *Context diagram DFD for the manufacturing system.*

■ Conventions for data flow diagrams

Figures 4-8 through 4-10 depict conventions you should use in your data flow diagrams. Be guided by the following rules for these conventions when constructing your diagrams.

Each context diagram must fit on one page This one-page rule applies to every data flow diagram you construct.

The process name in each context diagram should be the name of the information system Examples in Figures 4-8 through 4-10 are GRADING SYSTEM, ORDER SYSTEM, and MANUFACTURING SYSTEM. You use the system name as the process name because the context diagram shows the information system and its boundaries. On lower level DFDs, you would conform to the naming convention for a process of a verb followed by a descriptive noun.

Use unique names within each set of symbols Referring to Figure 4-10 on the previous page as an example, you must have only one external entity named CUSTOMER and only one data flow named PURCHASE ORDER in this diagram. Whenever you see the external entity CUSTOMER on one of the other manufacturing system's DFDs, you know that you are dealing with the same external entity. Whenever the PURCHASE ORDER data flow appears, you also know that you are dealing with the same data flow. This convention also applies to data stores.

Avoid crossing lines, if at all possible One way to achieve this goal is to restrict the number of symbols in any data flow diagram. On lower-level diagrams where multiple processes are shown, you should limit yourself to no more than nine process symbols on any one diagram. An additional and more important reason for this limit is that more than nine symbols is a signal that your diagram is too complex and that you should reconsider your analysis of the information system. On rare occasions, this nine-symbol limit rule can be relaxed for the most complex information systems.

Another way to help avoid crossing lines on a diagram is to duplicate an external entity or data store. If you do duplicate a symbol on a diagram, make sure you document this duplication to eliminate the possibility of confusion. You should place a special notation inside the duplicated symbols to signify that they are duplicated on the diagram. An asterisk next to the symbol name, for example, might be used for this purpose.

Use abbreviated identifications when you are using a computerized data dictionary Most automated data dictionaries, which we will discuss later in this chapter, allow you to enter either the full name or an abbreviation for the full name. Each external entity in these examples has a unique one- or two-character abbreviation that appears in the top center of the rectangle. For the manufacturing system in Figure 4-10 on the previous page, we have used a C to represent CUSTOMER, an AP for the ACCOUNTS PAYABLE SYSTEM, an I for the INVENTORY CONTROL DEPT, and so forth. You can use either the full external entity name or the abbreviation to gain access to the computerized data dictionary. If you are not using an automated data dictionary system, then you can omit the abbreviation.

Each data flow also has an abbreviated form that allows you to access your automated data dictionary more easily. You do not show data flow abbreviations in your DFDs, however, because data flow names tend to be long names that are difficult to place in a readable manner along the data flow lines. The additional placement of the data flow abbreviation would make this placement task even more difficult and would clutter the diagram.

Each data store also has a short two- or three-character abbreviated name placed inside the data store symbol along with the full data store name. This serves a purpose similar to that of the abbreviation for an external entity and the abbreviation for a data flow.

Use a unique reference number for each process symbol instead of an abbreviation as is done with the other DFD symbols. You use the process reference number to point to the DFD that contains the next level of detail for that process. For example, on the highest level DFD, the context diagram, always place a reference number of 0 (zero) inside the process symbol that represents the entire system. To find the detail for process 0, you find the DFD that is identified as diagram 0.

■ Diagram 0

A context diagram provides a general view of an information system, because the entire information system is represented by a single process symbol. Other data flow diagrams show more details of the information system. The first of these more detailed diagrams is diagram 0. **Diagram 0** is a data flow diagram that gives a more detailed view of an information system than does the context diagram. On diagram 0 (the digit zero, not the letter O) you show the major processes, data flows, and data stores for the information system. In addition, you repeat the external entities and data flows that appear in the context diagram.

Let's look at the grading system's context diagram and diagram 0 together, as shown in Figure 4-11 on the next page, to help demonstrate the relationship between them. Notice that the three external entities (STUDENT RECORDS SYSTEM, STUDENT, and TEACHER) and the six data flows (FINAL GRADE, CLASS ROSTER, SUBMITTED WORK, GRADED WORK, GRADING PARAMETERS, and GRADE REPORT) appear in both diagrams. In addition, process 0 (GRADING SYSTEM) in the context diagram has been expanded in diagram 0 by showing it in greater detail. Specifically, this one process has been replaced by four processes, one data store, and five new data flows. We have given the data store GRADEBOOK an abbreviation of D1.

Notice that each process in diagram 0 has a reference number: ESTABLISH GRADEBOOK is 1, ASSIGN FINAL GRADE is 2, GRADE STUDENT WORK is 3, and PRO-DUCE GRADE REPORT is 4. These reference numbers are significant only in that they represent the diagram numbers for more detailed data flow diagrams, if these diagrams are necessary. If more detail is needed for ESTABLISH GRADEBOOK, for example, you would draw a diagram 1, because 1 is the reference number for this process.

The process reference numbers do not imply that the processes are accomplished in a sequential order. Most information systems do not have a series of sequential processing steps. Each process is considered always to be available and active, awaiting data to be processed. If there is a true, established sequence in which the processes must be completed, you must document the sequence elsewhere, because data flow diagrams do not convey this information.

The FINAL GRADE data flow output from the ASSIGN FINAL GRADE process is a diverging data flow that becomes an input to the STUDENT RECORDS SYSTEM external entity and to the GRADEBOOK data store. A **diverging data flow** is a data flow in which the same data travels to two or more different locations. Diverging data flows occur infrequently and typically represent multiple-part forms that are sent to two or more recipients. More frequently, different processes, external entities, and data stores require different data flows, and you use separate lines to indicate the separate data flows. As an example from Figure 4-11 on the next page, notice the separate data flows (STUDENT GRADE and GRADED WORK) output by the GRADE STUDENT WORK process. If the logical requirements demand that the same output data flow be used in two or more locations, however, then a diverging data flow is the best way to show this flow, because showing two identical data flows as separate data flow lines would be misleading.

Because diagram 0 is a more detailed or expanded version of process 0, diagram 0 is called an **exploded** version of process 0. Other names for exploded are **partitioned** and **decomposed**. Sometimes process 0 is said to be the **parent** of diagram 0, and diagram 0 is the **child** of process 0. Alternative names for diagram 0 are the **overview diagram** and the **level-0 diagram**.

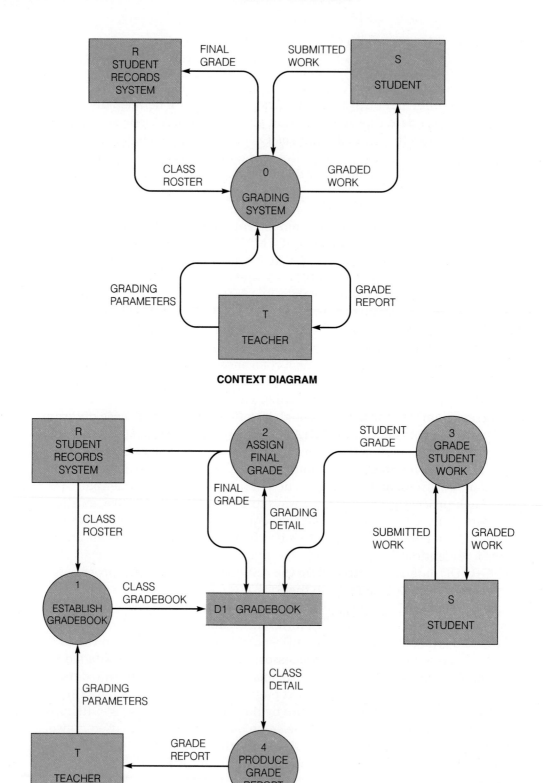

CONTEXT DIAGRAM

DIAGRAM 0

Figure 4-11 *Context diagram and diagram 0 DFDs for the grading system.*

The grading system is simple enough that you do not need any additional data flow diagrams to provide a visual model of this information system. The details of the one data store and the ten data flows are placed in the data dictionary, and the details of the four processes are defined through the process descriptions and are also placed in the data dictionary. Each of the four processes in Figure 4-11 is called a functional primitive. A **functional primitive** is a process that consists of a single function and is not exploded further. You would give the detailed specifications of a functional primitive in one of your process descriptions in the data dictionary.

The order system's diagram 0 is shown in Figure 4-12. Process 0 on the order system's context diagram has been exploded to three processes (FILL ORDER, CREATE INVOICE, and APPLY PAYMENT), one data store (ACCOUNTS RECEIVABLE), two new data flows (INVOICE DETAIL and PAYMENT DETAIL) and one diverging data flow (INVOICE). Let's walk through the Figure 4-12 data flow diagram to be sure we can follow what is being modeled.

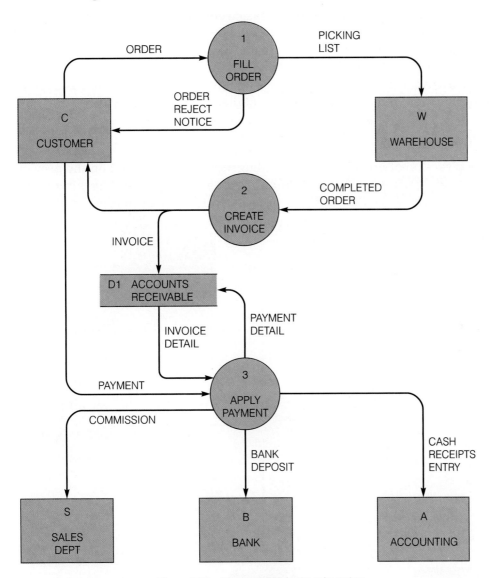

Figure 4-12 *Diagram 0 DFD for the order system.*

- A CUSTOMER submits an ORDER. The FILL ORDER process acts on the order, either sending an ORDER REJECT NOTICE back to the customer or sending a PICKING LIST to the WAREHOUSE. Notice that we do not show either conditional or repetitive steps in data flow diagrams. Either a functional primitive for FILL ORDER or the process description for FILL ORDER will clarify any conditional or repetitive detail.

- A COMPLETED ORDER from the WAREHOUSE is input to the CREATE INVOICE process, which outputs an INVOICE to both the CUSTOMER and to the ACCOUNTS RECEIVABLE data store.

- A CUSTOMER makes a PAYMENT which is processed by APPLY PAYMENT. APPLY PAYMENT requires INVOICE DETAIL input from the ACCOUNTS RECEIVABLE data store along with the PAYMENT. APPLY PAYMENT also outputs PAYMENT DETAIL back to the ACCOUNTS RECEIVABLE data store and outputs COMMISSION to the SALES REP, BANK DEPOSIT to the BANK, and CASH RECEIPTS ENTRY to ACCOUNTING.

This walk-through has illustrated the basic requirements of the order system. You might have questions about some aspects of the system, but these questions would be answered by looking at more detailed diagrams. Two more order system data flow diagrams provide these further details. Although the CREATE INVOICE process is a functional primitive, the other two processes in Figure 4-12 on the previous page are not functional primitives, and each has a more detailed data flow diagram.

■ Lower level diagrams

The exploded version of FILL ORDER from diagram 0 in Figure 4-12 on the previous page is shown in Figure 4-13. This new data flow diagram is called diagram 1 because it is the decomposition of the FILL ORDER process, which has a reference number of 1.

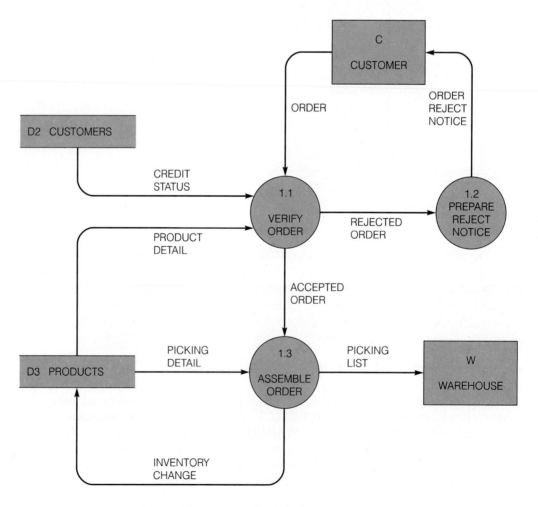

Figure 4-13 Diagram 1 DFD, detail of FILL ORDER, for the order system.

Leveling FILL ORDER consists of three detailed processes: VERIFY ORDER, PREPARE REJECT NOTICE, and ASSEMBLE ORDER. All processes on more detailed data flow diagrams are numbered using a decimal notation consisting of the parent's reference number, a decimal point, and a sequence number within the new diagram. The parent process of diagram 1 is process 1, so the processes in Figure 4-13 have reference numbers of 1.1, 1.2, and 1.3. If process 1.3, ASSEMBLE ORDER, were to be decomposed further, then we would do so in a diagram 1.3, and the processes in diagram 1.3 would be numbered 1.3.1, 1.3.2, 1.3.3, and so on. This reference numbering technique allows us to link all data flow diagrams in an orderly fashion.

This reference numbering technique is part of the leveling of data flow diagrams. **Leveling** is the DFD technique of representing the graphical model of an information system first as a single process, and then in greater and greater detail, until the only processes are functional primitives. Leveling is simply the more common term for exploding, partitioning, or decomposing the processes in the data flow diagrams. Leveling is an appropriate term to describe this technique because data flow diagrams are a top-down, or general-to-detail, picture of an information system. Each *level* from the top to the bottom shows increasing details about the information system.

Diagram 0 represents the highest level view of the information system when you consider the leveling concept. Because we fully represent the grading system by a context diagram and a diagram 0, the grading system has just one DFD level. The order system needs two DFD levels. Both these systems are simple ones, needing few DFD levels. Very large information systems, such as the manufacturing system, however, could require as many as six or more DFD levels.

Not all processes must be exploded the same number of levels. The order system's diagram 0 shown in Figure 4-12 on page 4.15 has one functional primitive process, CREATE INVOICE, but the other two processes are exploded one additional level. Although it is not necessary to explode all processes down to equivalent levels, try to avoid leveling that is too uneven because uneven leveling is often a symptom of the improper analysis of an information system. If you develop a set of data flow diagrams that has one process exploded two levels while another process is exploded six levels, for example, then you should consider redrawing your DFD logical model of the information system. Making several sketches is a common occurrence. Most systems analysts find that partitioning an information system into an acceptable model is an iterative process.

Figure 4-14 on the next page is equivalent to Figure 4-13 and is the more common way of showing data flow diagrams below the context diagram level. The difference between these two diagrams is that the CUSTOMER and WAREHOUSE external entities have not been drawn in Figure 4-14. As a result, the ORDER, ORDER REJECT NOTICE, and PICKING LIST data flows are missing a DFD symbol at one end. Most people draw DFDs in this manner because they do not feel that the missing symbols are required to understand the diagram, and they believe that including the symbols clutters the diagram unnecessarily. Because the missing symbols appear on the parent diagram, you could refer to that diagram if you need to know the source or destination of the data flows. We do not conform to this approach because we prefer to minimize the need to refer back and forth between diagrams. Either approach is acceptable, as long as you are consistent. You should follow whichever approach your instructor directs you to follow or whichever your company adopts as a standard.

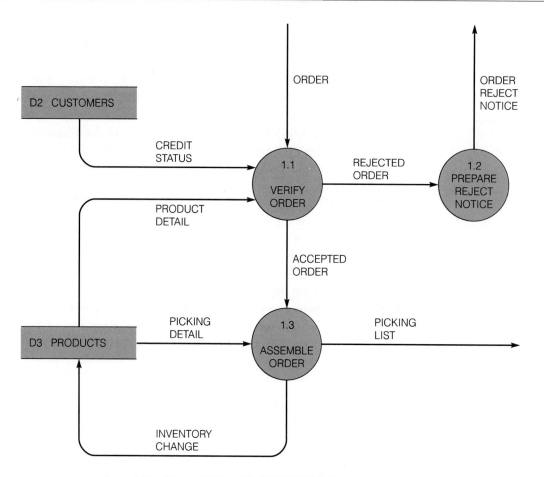

Figure 4-14 *Diagram 1 DFD, detail of FILL ORDER, for the order system. This diagram does not show the symbols that connect to data flows entering or leaving FILL ORDER on diagram 0 (compare to Figure 4-13 on page 4.16).*

Suppose you were omitting connecting symbols, as is done in Figure 4-14, and you exploded the VERIFY ORDER process of Figures 4-13 and 4-14. Which symbols would not appear on diagram 1.1, and which data flows would be unconnected on one end? The symbols that would not appear are the CUSTOMER external entity, the CUSTOMERS and PRODUCTS data stores, and the PREPARE REJECT NOTICE and ASSEMBLE ORDER processes. The data flows that would be unconnected at one end are ORDER, CREDIT STATUS, PRODUCT DETAIL, REJECTED ORDER, and ACCEPTED ORDER. The WAREHOUSE external entity and the PICKING LIST, PICKING DETAIL, and INVENTORY CHANGE data flows also would not appear, but data flows and symbols not connected to the exploded process never appear in the lower-level DFD, regardless of the method of diagramming you choose.

You will occasionally encounter one special situation concerning data stores. Sometimes an information system has a data store with output data flows only, which indicates that the information system accesses or retrieves data from the data store but does not change the data in the data store in any way. In this case, the data in that data store must be created and changed by some other information system. The CUSTOMERS data store in Figure 4-13 on page 4.16 and Figure 4-14 illustrates this special situation.

Balancing   Your data flow diagrams must be accurate and consistent because DFDs must represent the system's requirements without introducing ambiguities and errors. One way you gain consistency is by ensuring that each functional primitive is defined by a process description and that each data store, data flow, and process is defined in the data dictionary. Ensuring that your data flow diagrams are balanced is another measure of consistency. A **balanced** data flow diagram is one that has the parent process's input and output data flows preserved on the child data flow diagram.

Figure 4-14 is a balanced data flow diagram because it is balanced with its parent process FILL ORDER shown in Figure 4-12 on page 4.15. The ORDER data flow is input to both FILL ORDER and diagram 1, and the PICKING LIST and ORDER REJECT NOTICE data flows are output from both FILL ORDER and diagram 1. Because the data flow diagrams do not show the data dictionary entries, you would need to verify that all Figure 4-14 processes, data flows, and data stores are defined in the data dictionary to ensure that this data flow diagram is completely consistent.

Data stores Figure 4-15 shows the order system's diagram 3, the detail of APPLY PAYMENT. The data store DAILY PAYMENTS appears on this diagram, but it did not appear on diagram 0 nor on diagram 1. Why? The reason is that when you draw data flow diagrams, you place a data store on the highest level data flow diagram that has two or more processes using that data store. Neither diagram 0 nor diagram 1 requires the use of the DAILY PAYMENTS data store. Only when you reach diagram 3 do you have a need for DAILY PAYMENTS. The POST PAYMENT process in diagram 3 must store CUSTOMER PAYMENT data because both the DEPOSIT PAYMENT and PREPARE ACCOUNTING ENTRY processes require the use of this data at a later time.

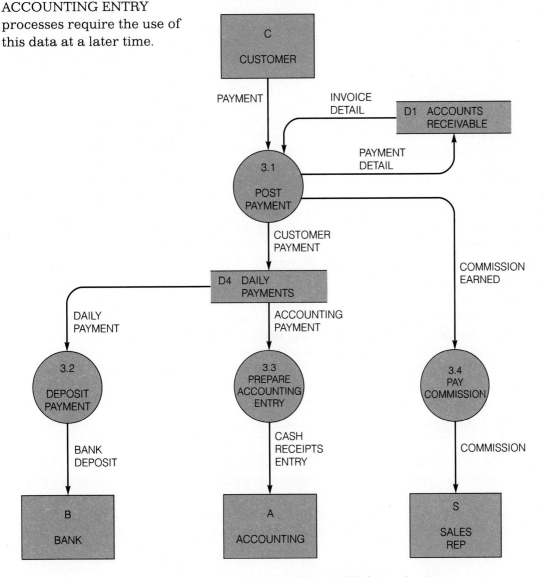

Figure 4-15 *Diagram 3 DFD, detail of APPLY PAYMENT, for the order system.*

Similarly, the CUSTOMERS and PRODUCTS data stores in Figure 4-13 on page 4.16 and Figure 4-14 on page 4.18 appear for the first time on a lower level diagram and are internal only to the FILL ORDER process. This is another example of how you can control the amount of detail in your data flow diagrams. You defer details as long as possible; that is, you defer details to the lowest possible DFD level.

How do you learn to develop a set of data flow diagrams for an information system? You must follow a number of tips and guidelines, many of which we have discussed in this chapter. As with many other aspects of information system development, however, you will become proficient only through practice and experience. You must consider many tradeoffs as you develop a logical model of an information system. Each system's requirements provide a unique set of circumstances. No textbook can anticipate what every possible circumstance might be. Experience in constructing data flow diagrams provides you with knowledge about different situations and tradeoffs and how best to resolve them.

A set of data flow diagrams is a graphical, top-down model of an information system. Because you must verify the validity of your DFD model, you must review the set of diagrams with the end users and obtain their approval of the model. Typically, you conduct the end user review of the diagrams in a top-down fashion.

What about an overall strategy for developing a set of data flow diagrams? From the definition and use of data flow diagrams and from our treatment of them in this chapter, you might infer that you also must develop them in a top-down fashion. If so, you would start by creating the context diagram, followed by diagram 0, then all the child diagrams for diagram 0, and so on. Some systems analysts are successful with this top-down strategy.

Other systems analysts follow a bottom-up strategy. Following a bottom-up strategy, you first identify all functional primitives, data stores, external entities, and data flows. Then, you group closely related processes with appropriate other symbols to develop the bottommost diagrams. Next, you group these diagrams in a logical way to form the next higher level. You continue to work your way in this fashion to diagram 0.

Now take a moment to review Figure 4-16 that shows diagram 0 for the manufacturing system, whose context diagram appeared in Figure 4-10 on page 4-11. This information system is large enough that each process in diagram 0 actually represents an entire system. Diagram 0 is just one of dozens of acceptable ways you can partition a manufacturing system into its component systems. Recall that we recommend that you have no more than nine process symbols in a diagram. Figure 4-16 has only four process symbols — imagine how much more complicated and confusing the figure would be with nine or more process symbols.

In fact, there are so many detailed processes, data stores, and data flows in this manufacturing system and in similarly complex information systems, that neither a pure top-down nor a pure bottom-up strategy might be successful. In complex cases, you might use a combination of the top-down and the bottom-up strategies. You could start with a bottom-up approach, then find problems and have to work your way back down before continuing back up again. Or you could start at the top, working your way down and then back up repeatedly. In either case, you would find the diagramming process to be an iterative process.

If people who review your data flow diagrams find them correct and simple to follow, then you know you have chosen the proper strategy. Most likely, your particular strategy will depend on your personal preferences and the circumstances of the information system you are modeling. ■

Data dictionary

 e use data flow diagrams to present a graphic, top-down logical model of an information system. This logical model is an organized, structured view of the information system's data and the data's transformations without the clutter of details. We place the detailed data definitions and processing rules in a data dictionary, which is the second component of structured analysis.

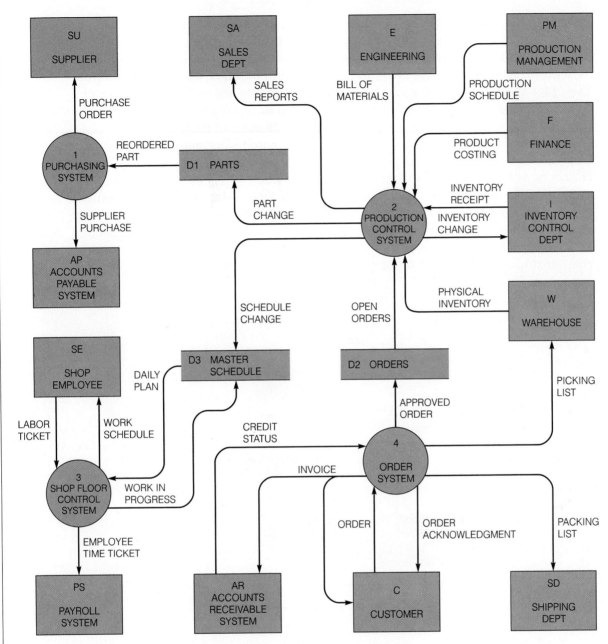

Figure 4-16 *Diagram 0 DFD for the manufacturing system.*

A **data dictionary** is a central storehouse of data about an information system's data and the data's transformations. You use the data dictionary throughout the systems development life cycle and during systems operation to document the detailed facts about an information system. The data dictionary is such a vital tool that you would want to use a data dictionary even if you are not using the structured analysis approach.

Few companies today do not use a data dictionary software package. These software packages range from stand-alone data dictionaries to those data dictionaries that are integrated into sophisticated CASE products. Most database management systems use a data dictionary; if you have used a database, you have probably used its data dictionary.

You can store a wide variety of facts about an information system in a data dictionary. During structured analysis, you document in the data dictionary the contents of the data flows, data stores, external entities, and processes that appear in the information system's data flow diagrams. You also define and describe all data elements and meaningful combinations of data elements. A **data element** is the smallest piece of data that has meaning within an information system. Examples of data elements are student grade, salary, Social Security number, account balance, and company name. Examples of meaningful combinations of data elements are student name, which consists of first, middle, and last names; and birth date, which consists of birth month, day, and year. Data elements are also called **data items** and **fields**.

Figure 4-17 shows the data dictionary and the items defined in it during structured analysis. Two significant relationships among these items exist, as shown by the direct connections between items in Figure 4-17. One relationship is based on data elements, and the other relationship is based on data flows. First, related and meaningful combinations of data elements compose the data flows and data stores in our data flow diagrams; these combinations of data elements are usually called records. Second, data flows are connected to data stores, external entities, and processes. Documenting these relationships in our data dictionary is important, so that the data dictionary is consistent with the data flow diagrams.

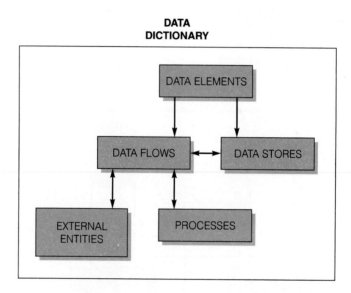

Figure 4-17 *The data dictionary, the items defined in the data dictionary, and the relationships among these items.*

■ Documenting data elements

In the data dictionary, you must document every data element in the information system. You define the following characteristics of each data element, as shown in the two examples in Figure 4-18.

**DATA ELEMENT
DATA DICTIONARY FORM**

DATA ELEMENT NAME:
ALTERNATE NAMES:

TYPE AND LENGTH:
OUTPUT FORMAT:
DEFAULT VALUE:
PROMPT / COLUMN HEADER:
SOURCE:
SECURITY:

RESPONSIBLE END USER:

ACCEPTABLE VALUES:
OTHER VALIDATION:

DERIVATION FORMULA:

DESCRIPTION AND COMMENTS:

**DATA ELEMENT
DATA DICTIONARY FORM**

DATA ELEMENT NAME:
ALTERNATE NAMES:

TYPE AND LENGTH:
OUTPUT FORMAT:
DEFAULT VALUE:
PROMPT / COLUMN HEADER:
SOURCE:
SECURITY:

RESPONSIBLE END USER:

ACCEPTABLE VALUES:
OTHER VALIDATION:

DERIVATION FORMULA:

DESCRIPTION AND COMMENTS:

Figure 4-18   *Two different data elements documented on a typical form used to record facts for the data dictionary.*

1. *Data element name.* This is the standard name for the data element. This name should be the one that is most meaningful to the majority of the end users.

2. *Alternate names.* Alternate names are any other names for the standard data element name. These other names are called **synonyms**, or **aliases**. For example, you might have a data element named CURRENT BALANCE. Various end users might refer to this data element by alternate names, such as OUTSTANDING BALANCE, CUSTOMER BALANCE, RECEIVABLE BALANCE, or AMOUNT OWED.

3. *Type and length.* Type refers to whether the data element contains numeric, alphabetic, or character values. Length is the maximum number of characters for an alphabetic or character data element, or the maximum number of digits and number of decimal positions for a numeric data element.

4. *Output format.* This is the arrangement of the data element when end users see it printed on reports or displayed on screens. The output format is also called the data element's **edit mask**.

5. *Default value.* This is the value for the data element if a value is not otherwise entered for it.

6. *Prompt/column header.* This is the default display screen prompt or report column heading when the information system outputs the data element. The prompt or column header is also called the data element's **field caption**.

7. *Source.* The source specifies the origination point for the data element's values. The source could be a specific form, a department or outside organization, another information system, or the result of a calculation.

8. *Security.* Security tells you who has access or update privileges for this data element.

9. *Responsible end user.* You identify the end user(s) responsible for entering and changing values for the data element.

10. *Acceptable values* and *Other validation.* You must specify the data element's **domain**, which is the set of values permitted for the data element. These values can be discrete and either specifically listed or referenced through a table of values, or the values can be continuous over a listed range of values. You would also specify if a value for the data element is optional. Some data elements have additional validity rules; for example, an employee's salary must be within the range defined for the employee's job classification.

11. *Derivation formula.* If the data element's value is the result of a calculation, then you show the formula for the data element.

12. *Description and comments.* This part of the data element's documentation allows you to provide additional definition, description, or commentary.

■ Documenting data flows

You must document every DFD data flow in the data dictionary. You define the following characteristics of each data flow, as shown in Figure 4-19.

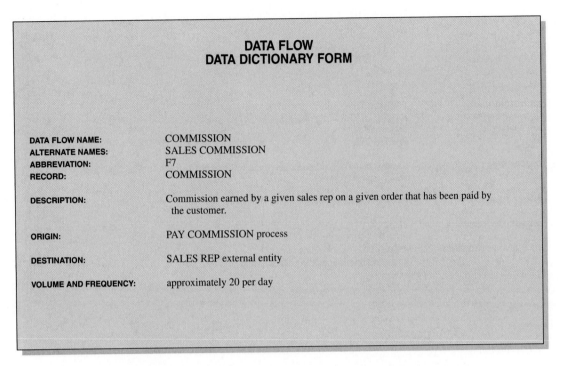

DATA FLOW
DATA DICTIONARY FORM

DATA FLOW NAME:	COMMISSION
ALTERNATE NAMES:	SALES COMMISSION
ABBREVIATION:	F7
RECORD:	COMMISSION
DESCRIPTION:	Commission earned by a given sales rep on a given order that has been paid by the customer.
ORIGIN:	PAY COMMISSION process
DESTINATION:	SALES REP external entity
VOLUME AND FREQUENCY:	approximately 20 per day

Figure 4-19 *Sample data dictionary form used to record facts about data flows.*

1. *Data flow name.* This is the data flow name as it appears on the DFDs.

2. *Alternate names.* These alternate names are the aliases for the DFD data flow name.

3. *Abbreviation.* This abbreviation is a very short name synonymous with the data flow name. The abbreviation provides a quicker way of accessing an automated data dictionary for a given data flow.

4. *Record.* Each data flow represents a group of closely related data elements; that is, a record. In most data dictionary systems, records are defined separately from the data flows and data stores. It is good documentation practice to define records separately, so more than one data flow or data store can use the same record, if necessary.

5. *Description.* This characteristic describes the data flow and its purpose.

6. *Origin.* The origin is the DFD beginning, or source, for the data flow. The origin can be a process, a data store, or an external entity.

7. *Destination.* The destination is the DFD ending point(s) for the data flow. The destination can be a process, a data store, or an external entity.

8. *Volume and frequency.* The volume and frequency describes the expected number of occurrences for the data flow per unit of time.

■ Documenting data stores

You must document every DFD data store in the data dictionary. You define the following characteristics of each data store, as shown in Figure 4-20.

DATA STORE
DATA DICTIONARY FORM

DATA STORE NAME:	PRODUCTS
ALTERNATE NAMES:	PARTS, INVENTORY ITEMS
ABBREVIATION:	D3
RECORD:	PRODUCTS
DESCRIPTION:	The raw materials, subassemblies, and finished goods for the products manufactured.
INPUT DATA FLOWS:	INVENTORY CHANGE
OUTPUT DATA FLOWS:	PRODUCT DETAIL PICKING DETAIL
VOLUME AND FREQUENCY:	4500 to 5000 total product records 2 to 20 additions and changes per month

Figure 4-20   Sample data dictionary form used to record facts about data stores.

1. *Data store name*. This is the data store name as it appears on the DFDs.

2. *Alternate names*. These alternate names are the aliases for the DFD data store name.

3. *Abbreviation*. This abbreviation is a very short name synonymous with the data store name. The abbreviation is shown on all data flow diagrams and provides a quicker way of accessing an automated data dictionary for a given data store.

4. *Record*. This entry gives the record name in the data dictionary for the data store.

5. *Description*. This characteristic describes the data store and its purpose.

6. *Input data flows*. These are the standard DFD names for the data flows entering the data store.

7. *Output data flows*. These are the standard DFD names for the data flows leaving the data store.

8. *Volume and frequency*. The volume and frequency describes the estimated number of records stored in the data store. You should also specify any growth and change statistics for the data store.

■ Documenting processes

You must document every DFD process that is a functional primitive in the data dictionary. You define the following characteristics of each process, as shown in Figure 4-21.

**PROCESS
DATA DICTIONARY FORM**

PROCESS NAME: VERIFY ORDER

PURPOSE: Determines if an incoming customer order should be accepted based on the customer's credit standing and each product's availability.

INPUT DATA FLOWS: ORDER, CREDIT STATUS, PRODUCT DETAIL

OUTPUT DATA FLOWS: REJECTED ORDER, ACCEPTED ORDER

Figure 4-21 *Sample data dictionary form used to record facts about processes.*

1. *Process name.* This is the process name as it appears on the DFDs.

2. *Purpose.* This is a very brief statement of the process's general purpose. You document the detailed steps that comprise the process in the process description.

3. *Input data flows.* These are the standard DFD names for the data flows entering the process.

4. *Output data flows.* These are the standard DFD names for the data flows leaving the process.

5. *Process description.* You document the detailed steps for the process. We have not included this entry in Figure 4-21, because we will discuss process descriptions in the next section.

■ Documenting external entities

You will find that not every systems analyst documents external entities in the data dictionary, but we recommend you do, so that the data dictionary can serve as a complete documentation package. If you do document external entities, then you define the following characteristics for them, as shown in Figure 4-22.

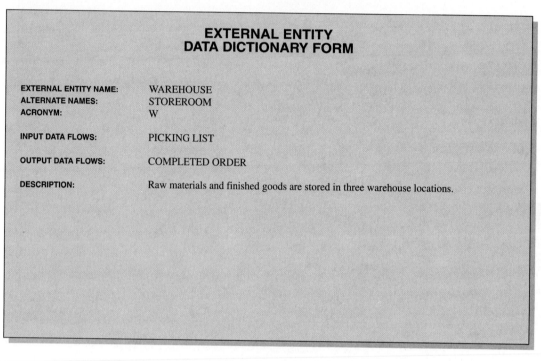

**EXTERNAL ENTITY
DATA DICTIONARY FORM**

EXTERNAL ENTITY NAME:	WAREHOUSE
ALTERNATE NAMES:	STOREROOM
ACRONYM:	W
INPUT DATA FLOWS:	PICKING LIST
OUTPUT DATA FLOWS:	COMPLETED ORDER
DESCRIPTION:	Raw materials and finished goods are stored in three warehouse locations.

Figure 4-22   Sample data dictionary form used to record facts about external entities.

1. *External entity name.* This is the external entity name as it appears on the DFDs.

2. *Alternate names.* These alternate names are the aliases for the DFD external entity name.

3. *Acronym.* This acronym is a very short name synonymous with the external entity name. The acronym should appear on all data flow diagrams to provide you with a quicker way of accessing an automated data dictionary for a given external entity.

4. *Input data flows.* These are the standard DFD names for the data flows input to the external entity.

5. *Output data flows.* These are the standard DFD names for the data flows leaving the external entity.

6. *Description.* You describe the external entity and its purpose.

■ Documenting records

Data elements are logically combined to form records. These records are the unit components of data flows and data stores. You must document all records in the data dictionary. You define the following characteristics of each record, as shown in Figure 4-23.

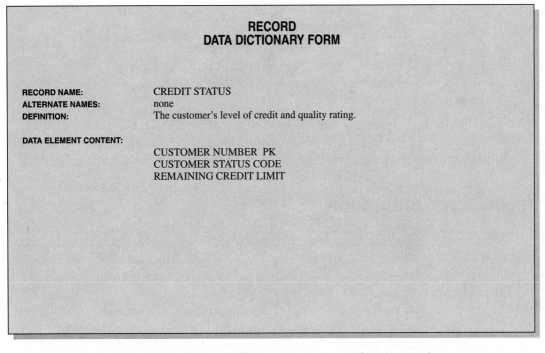

RECORD
DATA DICTIONARY FORM

RECORD NAME: CREDIT STATUS
ALTERNATE NAMES: none
DEFINITION: The customer's level of credit and quality rating.

DATA ELEMENT CONTENT:

CUSTOMER NUMBER PK
CUSTOMER STATUS CODE
REMAINING CREDIT LIMIT

Figure 4-23 *Sample data dictionary form used to record facts about records.*

1. *Record name.* This is the record name as it appears in the related data flow and data store data dictionary entries.

2. *Alternate names.* These alternate names are the aliases for the record name.

3. *Definition.* This is a brief definition for the record.

4. *Data element content.* You list all the data elements that are included in the record. The data element names must match exactly with those you entered in the data dictionary. Identify any data element that will serve as a primary key. A **primary key** is a data element that uniquely identifies a given instance of a record from all other instances of the record. The CREDIT STATUS record in Figure 4-23, for example, has a primary key of CUSTOMER NUMBER (we have used PK to identify the primary key), which serves as our way to distinguish one customer from all other customers.

■ Data dictionary reports

The data dictionary serves as the central repository of documentation for an information system. Many computerized data dictionaries that are components of CASE software products provide additional benefits, such as verifying that your data flow diagrams are balanced. Some packages perform the balancing task automatically, whereas other packages produce various balancing reports that you can review for completeness and consistency.

The data dictionary contains facts about the information system's DFD components, records, and data elements, and the relationships among these items. Consequently, you can obtain a wide variety of reports from an automated data dictionary system. The following are a few example reports that most data dictionary systems produce.

- An alphabetized list by name of all data elements
- A report by end user department of data elements that must be updated by that department
- A report of all data flows and data stores that use a particular data element
- Detailed reports showing all characteristics of data elements, records, data flows, processes or any other selected item stored in the data dictionary

An automated data dictionary can generate these as printed reports or output them to display screens. We will describe more features of data dictionaries when we discuss prototyping software tools and CASE software products in the next chapter.

Process description tools

Each data flow diagram functional primitive represents a specific, detailed procedure or policy. You must document each functional primitive if you want to have a complete logical model of the information system. In documenting the functional primitives, be accurate, complete, and concise. You could use standard English narratives to document each functional primitive, but standard English tends to be wordy and ambiguous, and so it is not really appropriate for structured analysis. Instead, you should use structured analysis's third component: the process description.

A **process description** documents the details of a functional primitive in a precise and concise way. You must have one process description for each functional primitive. Structured analysis's process description language is based on the fundamental principle of structured design and programming — that all problem solutions can be expressed by appropriate combinations of three logical building blocks, or structures:

1. **Sequence** — the completion of one process step in sequence after another process step.
2. **Selection** — the completion of one of two process steps based on the results of a test or condition.
3. **Iteration** — the completion of a process step repeated until the results of a condition terminates this repetition. Iteration is also called **repetition** and **looping**.

All process description tools for structured analysis are based on these three logical building blocks. The process description tools most often used are structured English, decision tables, and decision trees. You can use one or any combination of these tools for a given information system; you must decide which is the best tool to use.

■ Structured English

Structured English is a subset of standard English that is used to describe logical processes precisely and concisely. When you use structured English, you must conform to the following rules:

1. Use only the three building blocks of sequence, selection, and iteration.
2. Use indentation for readability.
3. Use a limited vocabulary of terms defined in the data dictionary and certain reserved words to describe the processing rules and building blocks.

Figure 4-24 shows a sample process description using structured English. We have numbered the lines for our discussion here (this is not done with typical structured English). Structured English might look familiar to you because it is similar to *pseudocode*, which is used for program design. The difference between structured English and pseudocode is that structured English must be readable to the end users and is used to represent logical processes. Thus, structured English does not have technically-oriented and implementation-oriented details as does pseudocode.

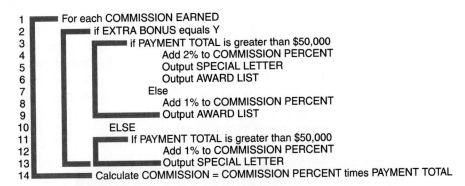

```
1    For each COMMISSION EARNED
2        if EXTRA BONUS equals Y
3            if PAYMENT TOTAL is greater than $50,000
4                Add 2% to COMMISSION PERCENT
5                Output SPECIAL LETTER
6                Output AWARD LIST
7            Else
8                Add 1% to COMMISSION PERCENT
9                Output AWARD LIST
10       ELSE
11           If PAYMENT TOTAL is greater than $50,000
12               Add 1% to COMMISSION PERCENT
13               Output SPECIAL LETTER
14   Calculate COMMISSION = COMMISSION PERCENT times PAYMENT TOTAL
```

Figure 4-24   *Sample structured English process description. Structured English is an organized way of describing what actions are taken on data. This structured English example describes a commission calculation policy.*

Notice that the capitalized words in Figure 4-24 are all terms from our data dictionary; you should similarly use data dictionary terms to ensure consistency between the process descriptions and the data dictionary. The other words are words that we reserve to describe the building blocks and the process steps in the functional primitive. Examples of these reserved words are *For each*, *If*, and *Output*.

Indenting the lines improves the readability of the structured English by showing how the various lines relate to each other. Lines 2 through 14 are indented under the iteration control statement on line 1. Likewise, lines 3 through 13, 4 through 9, and 12 and 13 are indented under their respective selection control statements on lines 2, 3, and 11. Examples of sequences of statements are lines 4 through 6, 8 through 9, and 12 and 13.

If you follow these structured English rules, your process descriptions should be understandable to the end users, who must confirm that the process is correct, as well as to the system designers, who must design the information system from these same descriptions.

■ Decision tables

A **decision table** is a tabular description of a selection structure. A decision table often is a better tool than structured English for describing a selection process with many complex conditions because you can easily spot inconsistencies. Figure 4-25 shows the general format of a decision table.

Condition Heading	Decision Rule Numbers
Condition Statements	Condition Entries
Action Statements	Action Entries

Figure 4-25   *General format for a decision table.*

A specific example of a decision table, the PAY COMMISSION selection from Figure 4-24 on the previous page, is shown in Figure 4-26. At the top left you place a heading that names the decision table. Under the heading you enter the conditions, one condition per line. For PAY COMMISSION, you have two conditions under the heading of PAY COMMISSION: EXTRA BONUS and PAYMENT TOTAL > $50,000. Then, under the conditions, you enter the actions that can occur based on the results of the conditions. We have entered the four actions shown in Figure 4-26.

Pay Commission	1	2	3	4
EXTRA BONUS	Y	Y	N	N
PAYMENT TOTAL > $50,000	Y	N	Y	N
Add 2% to COMMISSION PERCENT	X			
Add 1% to COMMISSION PERCENT		X	X	
Output SPECIAL LETTER	X		X	
Output AWARD LIST	X	X		

Figure 4-26   *Sample decision table process description. Decision tables help you quickly determine the course of action based on two or more conditions. This decision table is based on the commission calculation policy described in Figure 4-24 on the previous page. For example, if the payment total is over $50,000 but no extra bonus is to be paid, the policy is to add 1% to the commission percent and to output a special letter to the sales representative.*

Because each condition is either true or false (yes or no), the number of rules doubles each time you add a condition. For example, with one condition there are two rules, with two conditions there are four rules, with three conditions there are eight rules, and so on. Number the rules at the top right in sequence, starting at 1. Because our example has two conditions, we have entered decision rule numbers 1 through 4.

Under the decision rule numbers in the condition entries area, enter all possible combinations of Y/N (for yes and no) to account for all possible combinations of the conditions. Finally, place an X in the action entries area for a column to indicate which action statements are completed based on the status of the conditions for that column. For example, we add 1% to COMMISSION PERCENT and output a SPECIAL LETTER when there is no EXTRA BONUS, but the PAYMENT TOTAL > $50,000.

Decision tables are easy to construct and verify. Because you do not use extraneous words with a decision table, you will often find decision tables easier to account for all situations for the given conditions than is the case with other ways of documenting a process.

■ Decision trees

A **decision tree** is a graphic representation of a selection structure. The graphic representation is in the form of a tree with the roots at the left and the branches to the right. A decision tree is useful in the same situations as is a decision table. In fact, you can consider a decision tree and a decision table to be equivalent, but in different forms — a graph versus a table.

We have taken the same PAY COMMISSION conditions and actions and shown them in Figure 4-27 as a decision tree. A decision tree is read from left to right. You place the actions at the far right and the conditions along the various branches. Because our example has two conditions with four resulting sets of actions, our example has four terminating branches along the right side of the tree.

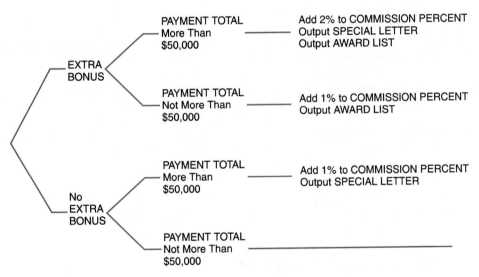

Figure 4-27 *Sample decision tree process description. Similar to a decision table, a decision tree illustrates the action to be taken, based on the given conditions, but presents it graphically. This decision tree is based on the commission calculation policy described in Figure 4-24 on page 4.31. For example, if the payment total is over $50,000 but no extra bonus is to be paid, the policy is to add 1% to the commission percent and to output a special letter to the sales representative.*

In actual practice, most systems analysts use structured English and decision tables instead of decision trees due to personal preference rather than any inherent, major disadvantage of decision trees. Because you can represent all three building blocks using structured English, most systems analysts predominately use structured English and reserve decision tables for complex selection situations.

We have used the tools of structured analysis in this chapter to discuss the development of a logical model for the new information system. The structured analysis tools also can be used to develop physical models of information systems. A **physical model** shows *what* the system's requirements are and *how* they are implemented. During the systems design phase, you will create a physical model of the new information system. This physical model follows from the logical model and the specific way you will implement the requirements.

Many systems analysts do not develop the logical model of the proposed information system as their first model during systems analysis. Recall that as you progress through analysis you study the existing information system to understand how the existing requirements are carried out. You also establish what modifications to the existing requirements are needed in the new system. Many systems analysts create a physical model of the current system and then a logical model of the current system before tackling a logical model of the new system. By doing this, they can assure themselves and others that they completely and accurately understand the what and how of the current system.

If you follow this sequence when you develop an information system, you develop a total of four models: the physical model of the current system, the logical model of the current system, the logical model of the new system, and the physical model of the new system. The major benefit to this approach is that you obtain an understanding and verification of the current system's functions before addressing modifications and improvements. This benefit is important because mistakes made early during systems development, either oversights or misunderstandings, will be carried out through the rest of the life cycle. Such mistakes lead to a poorer quality system and unhappy end users, and incur additional costs to correct. Another advantage of the four-model approach is that the requirements of a new information system are usually similar to those of the current information system. This is true especially in those cases where the development is based more on new computer technology than on a large number of new requirements. Modifying the current system logical model to the new system logical model in these cases is fairly trivial.

The major disadvantage to the four-model approach is the added time and cost required to develop the two models for the current system. Time is a critical factor; most developmental efforts have extremely tight schedules, often not allowing the time to create the current system models. Additionally, the end users and your bosses want to see you making progress on the new system. To them, spending too much time on the current system seems to be counterproductive to the objective. Finally, if you truly know the new system's requirements, then spending time documenting a system that is being replaced doesn't seem reasonable. ■

Automated structured analysis

Structured analysis, as well as all other requirements analysis techniques, requires considerable clerical work to organize and document the new information system. When you do this manually, requirements analysis techniques are tedious and error prone. Fortunately, many excellent CASE software products support the structured analysis technique. These automated CASE tools reduce the amount of clerical work required to organize and document an information system and minimize the chance for error. We will discuss these CASE tools in the next chapter.

CHAPTER CASE STUDY 4

James Tool Company — Analyzing Requirements

Don Mard, a systems analyst, and Howard Coswell, a programmer/analyst, continued their progress on the payroll system project for James Tool Company. Mard and Coswell had completed their detailed interviews and other fact-finding activities and felt they understood how the current system operated and what new requirements were desired by the end users. It was now time for them to organize, analyze, and document the payroll system by preparing a logical model.

■ Data flow diagrams

Together, Mard and Coswell reviewed the collected set of requirements and decided that their first step would be to prepare a context diagram DFD. Mard was most familiar with the overall scope of the payroll system, so he sketched out the context diagram shown in Figure 4-28. On a Friday afternoon, Mard walked Coswell through the diagram and asked for criticisms on the top-level payroll system flow.

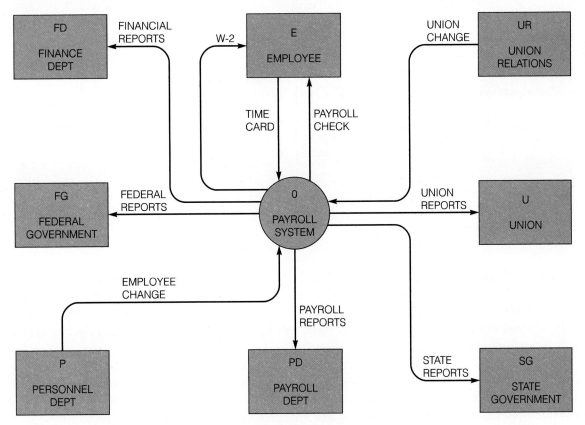

Figure 4-28 *Initial context diagram DFD for James Tool Company's payroll system.*

Mard and Coswell agreed that an employee submits a time card and receives a payroll check every week. At the end of the year, the payroll system produces a W-2 form for each employee. The personnel department submits employee changes, and the payroll system outputs state and federal governmental reports and reports to the finance and payroll departments. The union and the union relations department connections also appeared to be accurate.

Coswell, however, was bothered that so many outputs were based on relatively few inputs. Although Mard reminded Coswell that this was not an unusual situation, Mard suggested they independently review payroll system requirements over the weekend and discuss the diagram again on Monday.

The weekend review turned out to be a wise strategy. Coswell was pleased he had discovered from his interview documentation that the payroll department enters payroll changes, so they adjusted the context diagram accordingly. Mard also had detected an error: the payroll system sends accounting entries to the accounting department. Based on these changes, Mard redrew the context diagram, as shown in Figure 4-29.

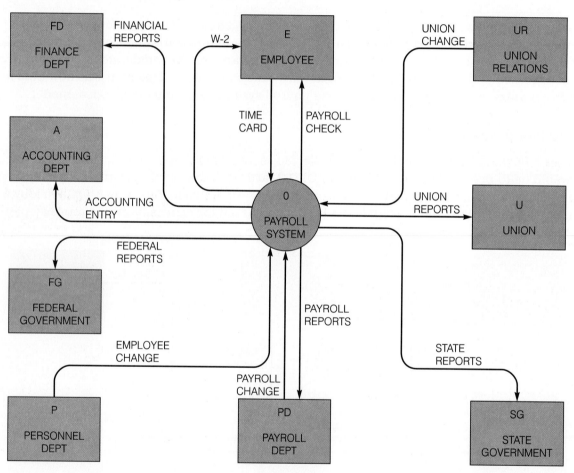

Figure 4-29 *Second context diagram DFD for James Tool Company's payroll system.*

Mard and Coswell now felt comfortable with the context diagram and scheduled a meeting for the next day with Jim McKeen, the director of the payroll department, to review their context diagram with him. In preparation for the meeting, Mard and Coswell brainstormed their ideas about the payroll system's major processes, data stores, and data flows, and then reviewed the system's requirements the rest of the day.

The next day, Mard and Coswell discussed the context diagram with McKeen, who had several significant suggestions. McKeen first noted that the personnel department never directly enters data into the payroll system. All employee changes are forwarded by the personnel department to the payroll department, where the changes are entered. McKeen had these other comments.

- The state and federal governments send tax changes periodically. These changes are inputs to the payroll system.
- All the financial reports, except for the Employee Overtime Report, should be distributed instead to the accounting department. Mard and Coswell admitted they had overlooked this change to the current processing — now that it was mentioned, they both clearly recall Henderson wanting this change.
- Once a month, the bank submits all cleared payroll checks to the payroll department. McKeen reminded the analysts that the payroll system takes care of its own reconciliation of checks.

Following the meeting, Mard and Coswell prepared the final payroll system context diagram, as shown in Figure 4-30. This data flow diagram reflects all the oversights they had found and all the changes McKeen suggested.

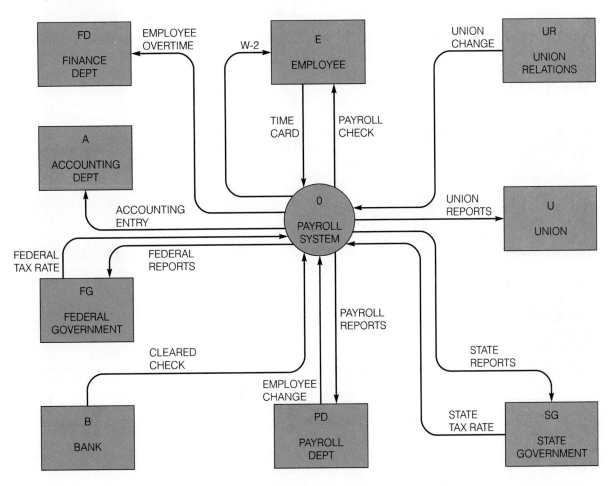

Figure 4-30   *Final context diagram DFD for James Tool Company's payroll system.*

While their conversation with McKeen was still fresh in their minds, Coswell proposed they construct the diagram 0 DFD. After several false starts and several versions, they were able to complete the diagram 0 presented in Figure 4-31 on the next page. They decided the major processes were the check reconciliation subsystem, the union subsystem, the payroll employee subsystem, and the payroll accounting subsystem.

Over the next few days, Mard concentrated on partitioning the payroll employee subsystem and the union subsystem, while Coswell developed the lower-level diagrams for the other two subsystems. The union subsystem was straightforward; diagram 4, shown in Figure 4-32 on page 4.39, was the only further level required.

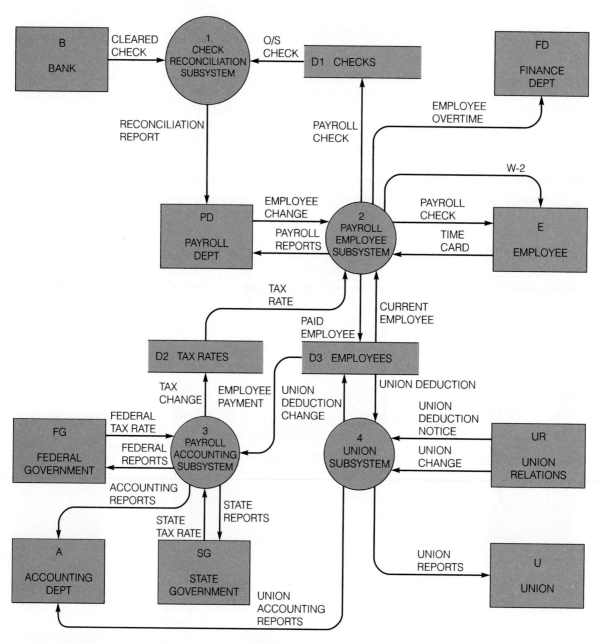

Figure 4-31 Diagram 0 DFD for James Tool Company's payroll system.

The logical model for the union subsystem would fix all existing problems with the processing of union dues. First, the union relations department would use a new form to initiate changes to an employee's union deduction. The payroll department would use this form as the official notification to change the union dues deduction for that employee. The union relations department would use a second new form to notify the payroll department of all changes to union dues amounts, union numbers, and union names. In addition to changes to employees' deductions and to the unions themselves, the planned new forms would also handle additions and deletions. Mard anticipated that the new forms would eliminate the problems with improper union dues deductions.

Figure 4-32 also demonstrates how Mard expected to correct the other problems connected with union dues. Immediately after the weekly running of each payroll, all employee union dues deductions would be extracted and retained until it was time to pay the unions.

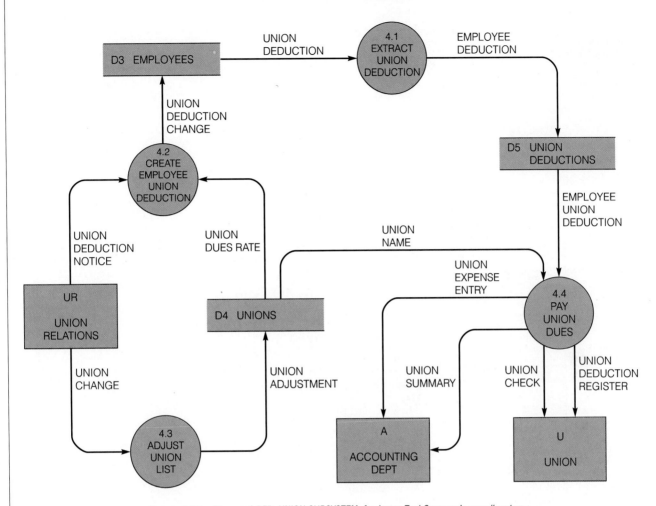

Figure 4-32 Diagram 4 DFD, UNION SUBSYSTEM, for James Tool Company's payroll system.

Delbert Donovan, director of union relations, had recently written Mard a memo, informing him that he had received agreement from the unions to change the union payment frequency from once a month to once every four weeks. This payment cycle would better coincide with the company's payroll cycle and eliminate the complications of splitting dues deductions across two different union payment periods. As a result, Mard planned to pay the unions and report to the unions and to the accounting department once every four weeks. In this way, he believed, the union dues would be paid accurately to the unions, the amounts deducted from the payroll checks would match the amounts paid to the unions, and the excessive amount of payroll staff overtime would be reduced, if not eliminated.

■ Data dictionary and process descriptions

As they constructed the data flow diagrams for the payroll system, Mard and Coswell also developed the data dictionary entries with supporting process descriptions. The union subsystem in Figure 4-32, for example, has two local data stores: UNIONS and UNION DEDUCTIONS. Mard prepared the data dictionary entries shown in Figure 4-33 on the next page for these two data stores. He then prepared the data element entries for both data stores; the three data dictionary entries for the data elements in the UNIONS data store are shown in Figure 4-34 on pages 4.41 and 4.42.

**RECORD
DATA DICTIONARY FORM**

RECORD NAME: UNIONS
ALTERNATE NAMES: none
DEFINITION: A union's code, name and weekly dues.

DATA ELEMENT CONTENT: UNION NUMBER PK
UNION NAME
UNION WEEKLY DUES

**RECORD
DATA DICTIONARY FORM**

RECORD NAME: UNION DEDUCTIONS
ALTERNATE NAMES: UNION DUES DEDUCTIONS
DEFINITION: A detailed recording of an employee's union dues deductions.

DATA ELEMENT CONTENT: SSN
EMPLOYEE NAME
UNION NUMBER
WEEK ENDING DATE
WEEKLY EARNINGS
UNION DUES

Figure 4-33 *Data dictionary definitions for the two records local to the UNION SUBSYSTEM: UNIONS and UNION DEDUCTIONS.*

DATA ELEMENT
DATA DICTIONARY FORM

DATA ELEMENT NAME:	UNION NUMBER
ALTERNATE NAMES:	none
TYPE AND LENGTH:	A 1
OUTPUT FORMAT:	X
DEFAULT VALUE:	none
PROMPT / COLUMN HEADER:	UNION NUMBER
SOURCE:	Union Relations Department
SECURITY:	Union Relations Department (update)
RESPONSIBLE END USER:	Union Relations Department
ACCEPTABLE VALUES:	any one-character unique value
OTHER VALIDATION:	none
DERIVATION FORMULA:	none
DESCRIPTION AND COMMENTS:	A one-character code that identifies each union. Must be a unique value.

DATA ELEMENT
DATA DICTIONARY FORM

DATA ELEMENT NAME:	UNION WEEKLY DUES
ALTERNATE NAMES:	UNION DUES, EMPLOYEE UNION DUES
TYPE AND LENGTH:	4 N, 2 decimal
OUTPUT FORMAT:	Z9.99
DEFAULT VALUE:	none
PROMPT / COLUMN HEADER:	UNION DUES
SOURCE:	Union Relations Department
SECURITY:	Union Relations Department (update)
RESPONSIBLE END USER:	Union Relations Department
ACCEPTABLE VALUES:	any number
OTHER VALIDATION:	none
DERIVATION FORMULA:	none
DESCRIPTION AND COMMENTS:	The weekly dues for an employee who belongs to a particular union.

Figure 4-34 *Data dictionary definitions for the three data elements in the UNIONS record.*

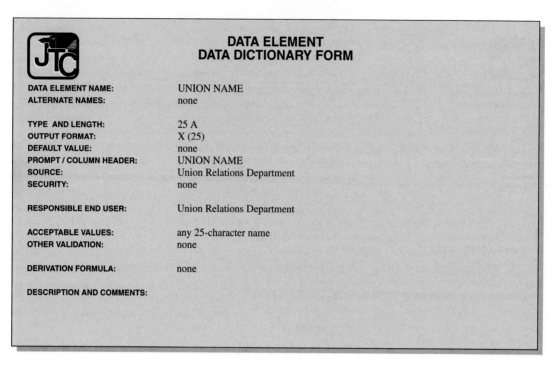

Figure 4-34 (continued)

Mard spent the next two days documenting the data flows and external entities for the union subsystem, along with all applicable data elements. He then carefully documented the four union subsystem processes, as shown in Figure 4-35.

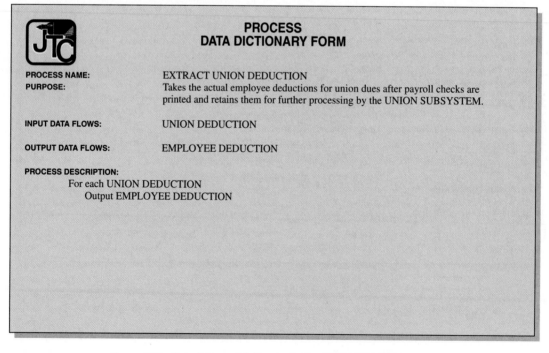

**PROCESS
DATA DICTIONARY FORM**

PROCESS NAME: EXTRACT UNION DEDUCTION
PURPOSE: Takes the actual employee deductions for union dues after payroll checks are
                          printed and retains them for further processing by the UNION SUBSYSTEM.

INPUT DATA FLOWS: UNION DEDUCTION

OUTPUT DATA FLOWS: EMPLOYEE DEDUCTION

PROCESS DESCRIPTION:
          For each UNION DEDUCTION
              Output EMPLOYEE DEDUCTION

Figure 4-35   Data dictionary definitions for the four UNION SUBSYSTEM processes.

PROCESS
DATA DICTIONARY FORM

PROCESS NAME: ADJUST UNION LIST

PURPOSE: Verifies each union change (add, delete, or change) and updates the list of unions and their weekly deduction rates.

INPUT DATA FLOWS: UNION CHANGE

OUTPUT DATA FLOWS: UNION ADJUSTMENT

PROCESS DESCRIPTION:
    For each UNION CHANGE
        If UNION CHANGE data elements valid
            Output UNION ADJUSTMENT

PROCESS
DATA DICTIONARY FORM

PROCESS NAME: CREATE EMPLOYEE UNION DEDUCTION

PURPOSE: Verifies each employee's union deduction change (add, change, delete), verifies the weekly dues rate, and modifies the employee's payroll union deduction.

INPUT DATA FLOWS: UNION DEDUCTION NOTICE, UNION DUES RATE

OUTPUT DATA FLOWS: UNION DEDUCTION CHANGE

PROCESS DESCRIPTION:
    For each UNION DEDUCTION NOTICE
        If UNION DEDUCTION NOTICE data elements valid
            Verify UNION DUES RATE
            Output UNION DEDUCTION CHANGE

Figure 4-35   *(continued)*

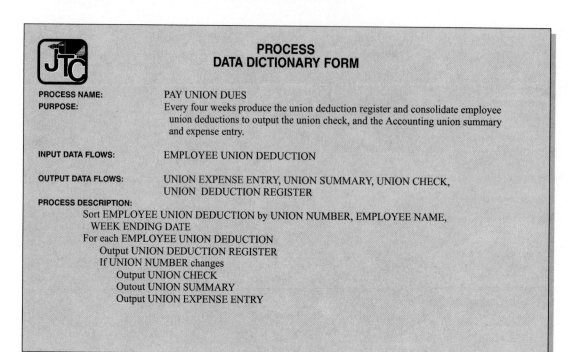

Figure 4-35 *(continued)*

Having completed his documentation of the union subsystem, Mard met with McKeen and Donovan to review the proposed model for this subsystem. After a thorough discussion of all proposed changes and processing, McKeen and Donovan approved the model.

Mard and Coswell continued their analysis and documentation of the payroll system for the next several days. As they completed a model of a portion of the information system, they would meet with the appropriate end users at James Tool Company to review the model, make adjustments to the model, and obtain the end users' approval. After Mard and Coswell had finished the complete payroll information system logical model, they turned their attention to completing the rest of the system requirements document.

Summary

In this chapter, we examined structured analysis, the most widely used requirements analysis methodology. You can use structured analysis to analyze and document the logical model for business information systems of all sizes and levels of complexity. Structured analysis has three components: data flow diagrams, the data dictionary, and process descriptions.

Data flow diagrams graphically depict the data's movement and transformations through an information system. Data flow diagrams use four symbols: the process transforms data, the data flow shows data movement, the data store shows data at rest, and the external entity represents an agent connected to the information system but outside the system's control. You use various naming, numbering, and annotating conventions to link the set of data flow diagrams and to make them readable.

Data flow diagrams are hierarchical with the context diagram at the topmost level. The context diagram represents the information system's scope, in that it establishes its external connections, not its internal workings. Diagram 0 displays the information system's major processes, data stores, and data flows and is the exploded version of the context diagram's process symbol, which represents the entire information system. Lower-level data flow diagrams reveal more and more detail of the information system in an organized manner through the leveling technique of numbering and partitioning. Leveling continues until you reach the functional primitive processes, which are not decomposed further and are documented through process descriptions. All diagrams must be balanced, which is a measure of their consistency and accuracy.

We next examined the data dictionary, which is the central documentation tool for structured analysis. In the data dictionary, you document all data elements, data flows, data stores, processes, external entities, and records. By consolidating your documentation in one location, you can more easily verify your information system's accuracy and consistency and can generate a variety of useful reports.

You document each functional primitive process using the process description tools of structured English, decision tables, and decision trees. Structured English uses a structured subset of natural English that allows you to define each process with combinations of the fundamental building blocks of sequence, selection, and iteration. For documenting selection situations, you can use a tabular style with decision tables or a graphical style with decision trees.

Review Questions

1. What are the advantages of using structured analysis? Why is structured analysis most appropriate for use with business information systems?
2. Define data flow diagram and name and draw its four symbols.
3. Define process and draw the symbol used for a process in a data flow diagram. Give four examples of good process names.
4. Define data flow and draw the symbol used for a data flow in a data flow diagram. Give four examples of good data flow names.
5. Define data store and draw the symbol used for a data store in a data flow diagram. Give four examples of good data store names.
6. Define external entity and draw the symbol used for an external entity in a data flow diagram. Give four examples of good external entity names.
7. What is a context diagram, and what symbol is not used in this diagram?
8. Explain how you would measure an information system's complexity.
9. Describe two ways to avoid crossing lines on a data flow diagram.
10. What is the relationship between a context diagram and diagram 0?
11. What is meant by an exploded data flow diagram?
12. Where are the details of data flows, data stores, and processes documented?
13. Explain the data flow diagram leveling technique.
14. What is a balanced data flow diagram?
15. What do you document in a data dictionary when you use structured analysis?
16. List and describe six characteristics you would define in a data dictionary for a data element.
17. List four characteristics you would define in a data dictionary for the following:
    a. a data flow
    b. data store
    c. process
    d. external entity
    e. record
18. Name and describe the three building blocks of problem solving.
19. What is structured English?
20. What is the difference between a decision table and a decision tree, and when would you use each of these tools?

Discussion Questions

1. We defined a balanced data flow diagram as one that has the parent process's input and output data flows preserved on the child data flow diagram. In other words, balance is a downward attribute in that all data flows must be preserved as you level the data flow diagrams downward. What about the reverse? Must balance occur as you proceed upward in your leveling? Defend your position with examples and reasons.

2. None of the data flow diagrams in this chapter has two-headed data flows — that is, data flows with arrowheads on both ends. Is it appropriate to use two-headed data flows? If so, under what conditions and why? If not, give your reasons.

3. A systems analyst attended a week-long workshop on structured analysis. When she returned to her job, she told her boss that structured analysis was not worth the time to learn and use on the job. Her view was that it was too academic and had too much new terminology to be useful in a practical setting. Do you agree or disagree? Defend your position.

4. The structured English shown below represents a company's order processing policy.
   a. Create a decision table to represent this policy.
   b. Draw a decision tree to represent this policy.

```
If ORDER AMOUNT exceeds $1,000
    If CUSTOMER has any unpaid INVOICE over 90 days old
        Do not issue ORDER CONFIRMATION
        Write message on ORDER REJECT REPORT
    Otherwise (account is in good standing)
        Issue ORDER CONFIRMATION
Otherwise (ORDER AMOUNT is $1,000 or less)
    If CUSTOMER has any unpaid INVOICE over 90 days old
        Issue ORDER CONFIRMATION
        Write message on CREDIT FOLLOW-UP REPORT
    Otherwise (account is in good standing)
        Issue ORDER CONFIRMATION.
```

MINICASE STUDIES 4

Ridgeway Company

Ridgeway Company, whose main business is the purchase and development of recreational land, has successfully managed the Ridgeway Country Club for the past three years. When they originally acquired the club, it had twenty lighted tennis courts, an eighteen-hole golf course, a swimming pool, a pro shop selling tennis and golfing supplies and related items, and a clubhouse containing a restaurant, bar, and exercise room.

Over the past two years, Ridgeway Company has expanded the facility by adding a second eighteen-hole golf course, a second swimming pool, and twenty more lighted tennis courts. Ridgeway Company has completed the construction of the first ten condominiums as part of a ten-year plan to build a total of sixty on club property. Because the facility sits on the shores of a lake, Ridgeway recently changed the name of the club to the Blue Waters Country Club.

Memberships at the facility are limited to 2,000 full members with unlimited privileges and 1,000 social members who are permitted use of the clubhouse and swimming pools only. There is a waiting list for both types of memberships. A full member buys a share in the club. Each member pays monthly dues: $150 for a full member, and $50 for a social member. Thomas McGee, vice president of operations, manages the club's operations.

Ridgeway management has funded a project to develop a new membership billing system for the Blue Waters Country Club. The requirements for this system are detailed as follows.

Two types of sales forms are used. One sales form is used for recording tennis and golf lessons, purchases in the pro shop, and recording the rounds of golf played by a member and his or her guests. This first sales form is a pressure-sensitive form that has two parts: the member is given the top copy, and the second copy is forwarded to the corporate accounting department. The second sales form is used for purchases made in the restaurant and bar. The tear-off receipt at the bottom is given to the member, and the rest of the form is sent to the corporate accounting department.

Members must sign both types of sales forms and place their member numbers on the form. The accounting department receives the sales slips and posts them to an account ledger for each member of the club. Posted on each account line is the date of the charge, a description of the charge including where the charge occurred, the amount of the charge, and the running balance.

The data on the member's account ledger is the same data that appears on the invoice, which is a monthly statement, that is sent to each member at the end of each month. Also included on the statement is the member's monthly dues. Each member is required to make a minimum amount of purchases each month: $100 for a full member, and $35 for a social member. If a member's purchases for the month exceeds the minimum, the member pays the amount of the purchases. Otherwise, the member pays the minimum amount. A member makes an average of fifteen charges in a month. Only the statement is mailed to the member. Corporate accounting retains their copies of the charge slips for a period of one year in case a member disputes a charge.

A name and address file of all members is kept on 3-by-5-inch index cards in the corporate accounting department.

A monthly summary sales report is sent to the president, George Ridgeway. This report shows total sales by club area (pro shop, restaurant, tennis lessons) and an overall total.

Thomas McGee receives three reports once a month. The daily sales report gives total sales in the restaurant, in the bar, and in the pro shop by day, plus total sales by day. Overall totals for the month for the three areas and a grand total also appear on the daily sales report. The monthly member sales report lists all members alphabetically and their total purchases for the month. The final report is an exception report, listing alphabetically all members who made no purchases during the month.

Questions

1. Prepare the context diagram for the billing system.
2. Prepare the diagram 0 data flow diagram for the billing system.
3. If any processes on diagram 0 need to be partitioned, prepare the second-level diagrams for these processes.
4. For each data store, list the data elements that would be found in that data store.

Genealogy System

Peggy and Steven Corbett have been tracing their family history for the past year and are beginning to become overwhelmed by all the data they have gathered. Their daughter, Cathy, recently completed a course in systems analysis and design, and they have asked her to create a genealogy system for them to use on their home personal computer.

The Corbetts want to enter data about their ancestors. This data is to include name, gender, and place and date of birth. If applicable, they also want to enter the place and date of the death and the burial of the individual. The Corbetts have narratives they would like to enter in a free-form manner. They want to keep track of marriage data, which includes the place and date of the marriage. Also they need to enter marriage relationships: husband and wife, and children.

Because they are likely to make mistakes, they want to be able to change or delete any data they enter. They also would like to view on the display screen any data they have entered.

Cathy determines that three reports are needed. These reports will be used for reference by the Corbetts and also might be sent to relatives to keep them up-to-date on the family history project and to solicit further information from them.

The individual report lists alphabetically each family member and his or her birth place and date. The family report lists all marriages alphabetically in sequence by husband name and includes the names and places and dates of birth of the husband, wife, and children, as well as the date and place of the marriage.

Finally, the descendents report lists an individual and all the marriages and descendents of that individual (and each descendent's marriages), one person per line. Each line would show the ancestor's name, date of birth, and date of death, if applicable. Each marriage line would show the spouse name and date of the marriage. The children of an individual would be printed indented three positions from the parent, their children would be indented three positions from them, and so on.

Questions

1. Prepare a complete set of data flow diagrams for this genealogy system.
2. For each data store, list the data elements that would be found in that data store.

Western Dental Clinic — Analyzing Requirements

Introduction

Jim Archer completed his detailed interviews at Western Dental Clinic. He then reviewed all current reports and observed one morning's operations at the facility. Archer learned that five reports were needed at Western Dental Clinic.

A daily appointment list is created for each provider. This list shows all scheduled appointment times and patient names, along with the services to be performed on each patient. The services are identified by both the service code and an abbreviated service description. Also needed on a daily basis is a call list, which shows the patients who are to be called to be reminded of their next day's appointments. Shown on the call list are the patient name, telephone number, appointment time, and provider.

The provider report is needed on a weekly basis. This report lists each of the nine providers and each provider's charges generated both on a month-to-date (MTD) and on a year-to-date (YTD) basis.

The fourth report is the statement, a preprinted form usable in a windowed envelope. The statement is produced monthly for selected patients. Statement header information includes the statement date, household head name and address, the previous month's balance, the total household charges MTD, the total payments MTD, and the current balance. The bottom section of the statement lists every activity for the month in date order. For every service performed, there is a line showing the patient's name, the service date, the service description, and the service fee. For every adjustment and payment received, there is a line showing the date and amount. If the payment was received from an insurance company, then that source is noted on the line. A running balance appears at the far right of each activity line.

Western Dental Clinic employees would find mailing labels helpful so that they can automate the mailing of reminder postcards. These postcards are sent to patients when it is time to schedule their next appointment. The postcards are currently mailed out twice each month.

Archer began to organize the facts he had gathered on the Western Dental Clinic operation in order to prepare the system requirements document. The tools he used were data flow diagrams, a data dictionary, and process descriptions.

Student Assignments

1. Prepare the context diagram and diagram 0 for the Western Dental Clinic system.

2. Prepare the lower-level data flow diagrams for the Western Dental Clinic system.

3. Prepare a list of all the data stores and data flows needed for the system; under each data store, list the data elements that each requires.

4. Prepare the data dictionary entries for three of the system's functional primitives.

5. Insurance processing must be included in the Western Dental Clinic system. Prepare the context diagram and diagram 0 for the version of the information system that includes both the base requirements and the insurance requirements. What additional data elements are required when you include the insurance processing?

CHAPTER 5

Completing the Systems Analysis Phase and Considering Alternative Tools

Objectives

You will have mastered the material in this chapter when you can:

- Evaluate alternative information system solutions and select the viable alternatives
- Explain the advantages and disadvantages of constructing your own information system versus purchasing an application software package
- List the steps in purchasing a software package
- Define outsourcing and end user computing, and give the reasons for their growing importance
- Explain the differences between a request for proposal and a request for quotation
- Describe the contents of the system requirements document and explain its purpose
- Discuss the reasons why requirements change over time, and explain why change control is needed
- Describe the prototyping process, its components, and its advantages and disadvantages
- Describe the different types of computer-aided software engineering (CASE) tools, and explain how CASE fits into the systems development life cycle
- Discuss the object-oriented approach to systems analysis
- Explain the purposes of systems flowcharts and state-transition diagrams

Introduction

The objectives of the systems analysis phase are to determine, to analyze, to organize, and to document the detailed requirements of a new information system. In Chapters 3 and 4, we discussed techniques and tools for determining and analyzing requirements. In this chapter, we examine the remaining steps of the systems analysis phase: the evaluation of alternative solutions, the preparation of the system requirements document, and the presentation that concludes this phase.

This chapter also describes alternative tools and approaches you can use to complement or replace the ones we have covered in Chapters 3 and 4. First, we present prototyping and its role in the systems development life cycle. Next, we examine computer-aided software engineering (CASE) and its growing importance to information systems development. Finally, we describe two alternative graphical tools: systems flowcharts and state-transition diagrams.

Evaluating alternatives

After constructing the logical model of the proposed information system, you are ready to consider solutions that might satisfy the information system's requirements. The two primary solutions you consider are the development of in-house software and the purchase of a software package. You should also consider other potential solutions, such as contracting with another company to develop the system and letting the end users develop their own system. Frequently, you must also make choices among hardware alternatives. We will first consider the software alternatives.

■ Software alternatives

When evaluating software alternatives, you most often choose between in-house developed software and software packages. **In-house developed software** is software developed by the technical staff in a company's information systems department. A **software package** is an information system written by another company and available for purchase. A software package is also called **commercial application software**. Software companies that specialize in developing software for sale are called **software publishers** or **software vendors**.

Software packages are available to handle almost all types of industrial, service, and governmental activity. **Horizontal application software** is a software package that can be used by many different types of organizations. Accounting packages are a good example of horizontal applications because they apply to most organizations. In contrast, a software package developed to handle the requirements of an information system for a specific type of organization is called **vertical application software**. Examples of industrial and service organizations that have special information system requirements include colleges, banks, hospitals, insurance companies, construction companies, real estate firms, and airlines. A typical company might use vertical application software for industry-specific systems and horizontal application software for some of its common business systems.

Developing Your Own Software Because software packages are available to handle most horizontal and vertical needs, why would you choose to develop your own information system? The reasons why you might choose to develop your own software are to satisfy unique requirements, to minimize change to business procedures and policies, to meet the constraints of existing systems, to meet the constraints of existing technology, and to utilize new technology.

Satisfy unique requirements. The most common reason for developing your own software is that your company has unique requirements that no software package can satisfy. An example would be a company's system to keep track of data for the semiannual incentive program of its sales representatives. Another situation that creates unique requirements occurs when a company develops innovative products or services to gain an edge over its competitors; for example, a Wall Street firm might need computer support for a newly developed type of investment that has just received regulatory approval. If software packages do not exist, or if they do not handle significant portions of the requirements, then in-house developed software might be the only choice.

Minimize change to business procedures and policies. A company might also choose to develop instead of buy software when existing software packages would handle its processing requirements far too differently than the company would find acceptable. Most software packages necessitate some degree of change to a company's way of doing business. If the degree of change is too severe, however, a company might elect to develop its own information system.

Meet the constraints of existing systems. A third reason to develop instead of buy software is that the new software must work with a company's existing information systems. You might be developing a new company budgeting system, for example, that must be integrated with existing accounting systems; that is, the new system must update data stored in existing accounting files and display data elements from the new budgeting system on current reports and terminal screens. Finding a software package that works correctly with the existing accounting system is unlikely. If you did want to utilize a software package to handle your budgeting requirements, you would probably have to replace the accounting system with a software package that integrates accounting and budgeting.

Meet the constraints of existing technology. Another reason to develop instead of buy software is that the new software must work with existing hardware and its systems software. If your company has an IBM mainframe or compatible computer, for example, you will be able to choose from a large number of software packages. Because IBM dominates the mainframe market, software package vendors prefer to concentrate on the IBM market where they have their greatest potential for sales. On the other hand, if you have another mainframe manufacturer's computer, your choice of software packages will be much more limited. If none are available or acceptable, then you must develop your own information system or switch to hardware that offers what you need.

Utilize new technology. A final reason to develop instead of buy software is that you want the software to work with newly developed hardware or systems software that you have just acquired. Available software packages might not work with the new technology, at least for some period of time while the software vendors enhance their packages. When scanners were first introduced, for example, each retail store chain had to develop its own information systems to interact with them. As a second example, when OS/2 first became available, several months elapsed before the first vendors were ready to market their PC software packages to run under OS/2.

Figure 5-1 on the next page summarizes the reasons why companies develop their own information systems and why companies purchase software packages.

Reasons for In-house Developed Software	Reasons for Purchasing a Software Package
Satisfy unique requirements	Less expensive
Minimize change to business procedures and policies	Less time to implement
Meet constraints of existing systems	Fewer errors
Meet constraints of existing technology	Already in use in many companies
Utilize new technology	Fewer technical staff required for development
	Upgrade versions from vendor

Figure 5-1 *The decision to make or buy an information system involves balancing the reasons for developing an information system against the reasons for purchasing a software package.*

Buying a Software Package Whenever available software packages might satisfy the requirements of an information system under development, you should investigate these packages as possible solutions. The reasons you might consider the purchase of a software package over in-house developed software are: a package is less expensive, it requires less time to implement, it has fewer errors, it is already in use in many companies, it requires fewer technical staff for development, and it is upgraded by vendors.

Package is less expensive. Software vendors spread the cost of their package development over many companies. Compared to an in-house developed system, therefore, a software package is less expensive.

Package requires less time to implement. Because the package has already been designed, programmed, tested, and documented, the time normally spent completing these steps is eliminated. However, when you purchase a package, you must still install it and integrate it into your company's processing environment; these steps might require weeks or months to complete.

Package has fewer errors. Other companies have been using the package, and critical errors should already have been detected and corrected by the software vendor.

Package is already in use in many companies. This means you can contact the end users in these companies to get their impressions and recommendations about the software package. You can also observe the package in operation and, in some cases, experiment with the package before making a purchase decision.

Package requires fewer technical staff for development. Some companies that often use software packages further reduce expenses by reducing the number of programmers and systems analysts they employ. Other companies still retain high levels of technical staff; their programmers and systems analysts develop greater numbers of information systems whose requirements cannot be satisfied by software packages.

Package is upgraded by vendors. A software vendor upgrades a package by adding improvements and enhancements to create a new version, or **release**. A new version typically interacts with new equipment and operating environments and complies with new laws and regulatory requirements. A new release of a software package, for example, might support a popular laser printer that has recently come to market. As another example, a software vendor will update its payroll package to conform to recently enacted federal and state tax changes. In all cases, the vendor does the work and your company benefits from its work.

Installing a new release must be planned and coordinated, however, just as any other information system change, and you must pay for the new release. Also, if you have modified the standard package in any way, you must reapply the modifications to new releases, because a software vendor will not support its package if you have modified it. Finally, a new release might have unknown errors; waiting a few months for other companies to find these errors and for the software vendor to install corrections for them is usually a sound plan.

Customizing Software Packages You might not be able to find a software package that satisfies the precise requirements of the new information system. If this is the case, the primary options are either to build your own information system or to purchase a package and change your way of doing business in order to match the package's processing scheme. A third option, however, is to purchase a customized software package. A **customized software package** is a software package you or the vendor specially modify or a vendor develops at your request to meet your specifications.

A package is customized in one of three ways. The first way to customize happens when the vendor's standard package, called an **off-the-shelf package**, falls short of meeting a company's requirements in just a few critical areas. If, in all other areas, the package is suitable and attractive to the company, then you can negotiate with the vendor for package enhancements to meet these requirements; the software vendor, however, will charge an extra fee for the package enhancements. The vendor might agree to the package enhancements because it plans to permanently include these modifications in future versions of its package. Or, the vendor might create this customized version of its package for your sole use in order to make a sale and gain you as a potential customer for its other software packages.

The second way to customize a package is for a company to purchase the package and make its own modifications. This option might be a possibility when the package comes close to satisfying the requirements and the vendor will not make your requested changes. The systems analysts and programmers who make the modifications will be unfamiliar with the package, however, and will, therefore, need time to learn the package and make the modifications correctly.

The third way to customize occurs when a vendor's basic package has a standard central processing core with supplemental components that are customized on an individual basis. A vendor takes this approach when the specific application system cannot easily be standardized to satisfy all customers. A human resource system is often offered in this way, because each company handles its employee benefits, compensation analysis, and other personnel-related processing in unique ways.

Some of the advantages of a software package might be lost or lessened when a package is customized. If the vendor does the customization, it will charge more and need more time to deliver the modified package. Errors might be introduced during customization. Finally, though vendors upgrade their standard software packages, they might not upgrade customized versions. If you want to use a new release of the package and you have a customized version, you will probably have to apply the custom modifications to the package's latest release.

■ Selecting software packages

The selection of a software package involves five steps: evaluate the information system requirements, identify potential software vendors, evaluate software package alternatives, make the purchase, and install the software package.

Evaluate the Information System Requirements Based on your analysis of the information system's requirements, you are responsible for identifying the system's key features, summarizing its volume and growth figures, and specifying its external constraints. Some examples follow that can help you in this process.

Identify the key features of the information system. If a company has employees nationwide, for example, then its payroll system must be able to deduct income and unemployment taxes for each state. Therefore, automatic deduction of employee and company payroll taxes in all states should be listed as a key feature.

Summarize the information system's current volume and future growth over the next three to five years. Figure 5-2 shows a volume summary for a company's order entry system. Volume figures provide important constraints for both the software package and the hardware that the package will use. You want to ensure that the package and the hardware will be able to handle present and future transaction volumes and file storage requirements.

ORDER ENTRY SYSTEM VOLUME SUMMARY		
FILE SIZES: **NUMBER OF**	**CURRENT**	**IN 3-5 YEARS**
Products	2,240	3,200
Warehouses	2	5
Customers	11,750	24,500
Sales Reps	40	70
TRANSACTIONS: **NUMBER DAILY**		
Orders	155	400
Order Lines	545	1,500
Invoices	210	550
Payments	175	550

Figure 5-2 *A volume summary showing current and future growth for an order entry system.*

Specify the information system's external constraints by identifying the hardware and software with which the system must work. If the new system must transfer data to or receive data from an existing system, for example, then you must identify this constraint. An example would be a payroll package that feeds data to the general ledger, where all accounting transactions are summarized, and to the check reconciliation system, where outstanding and cleared checks are processed. In addition, if you already have a particular type of computer, you will probably want to find software for that computer. On the other hand, if you do not have any equipment, make the decision about the software *first* — the software is the most important element in any system.

The typical way that you represent the information system's requirements when you consider software packages is in a request for proposal. A **request for proposal (RFP)** is a written list of the information system requirements that is given to prospective software vendors. RFPs help the vendors determine if they have a product that is a possible software solution. Just as the size and complexity of information systems varies, so too do RFPs. RFPs for simple information systems might be only a single page consisting of the key features and a volume summary. RFPs for large information systems might consist of dozens of pages that identify both key and optional features. An example of a page from an RFP, with sample vendor comments included, is shown in Figure 5-3.

**REQUEST FOR PROPOSAL
ACCOUNTS PAYABLE**

Features	Standard Feature	_Comments_
1. Interface to general ledger	✓	
2. Matching to receiving documents	✓	
3. Matching to purchasing documents	✓	
4. Automatic check printing	✓	
5. Recurring payments		_Planned For Next Release_
6. Flexible payment selection	✓	
7. Checking statement reconciliation		_Will Do On Custom Basis_
8. Consolidated check preparation	✓	
9. Duplicate invoice check		_No Plans For This Feature_
10. Manual check processing	✓	

Reports		
1. Vendor listing	✓	_By Vendor Name_
2. Invoice register	✓	
3. Check register	✓	
4. Cash requirements	✓	_Weekly & Monthly_
5. Detail aging	✓	_30, 60, 90, 120 + Days_
6. Form 1099 reports		_Planned For Next Release_
7. Account distribution	✓	
8. Bank statement reconciliation		_Will Do On Custom Basis_

Figure 5-3 _A request for proposal (RFP) documents the key features that are needed in a software package. This sample RFP has sample vendor comments included._

Identify Potential Software Vendors After you know the software features you need, your next step is to locate vendors selling packages that might satisfy these needs. If the software will be implemented on a personal computer, one place to look is a local computer store. Most computer stores have a wide selection of application software packages and can suggest several alternatives to consider. If you have prepared an RFP, even a simple one, the RFP will help the store representative to narrow the choices.

If software is required for a minicomputer or a mainframe, however, you won't find it at the local computer store. For this type of software, which can cost tens to hundreds of thousands of dollars, the best place to start is with the computer manufacturer. In addition to providing software themselves, most manufacturers have lists of software companies that they work with — companies that specialize in developing software for the manufacturer's equipment.

Another place to find software suppliers, especially for vertical applications, is to look in industry trade publications, which are magazines written for specific businesses or industries. Companies and individuals who have written software for these industries often advertise in the industry trade publications. An auto parts store that is looking for an inventory management system, for example, might find several packages advertised in automobile industry publications. Some industry trade groups also maintain lists of companies that provide specific software solutions.

For horizontal applications, most computer magazines publish regular reviews of individual packages and often have annual reviews of several packages of the same type. Independent market research and analysis companies, such as DataPro and Auerbach, also sell comparative analyses of software packages.

Another way to identify software suppliers is to hire a knowledgeable consultant or to contract with an information systems consulting company. Although the fees paid to consultants increase the overall software investment, the added cost is usually worthwhile, considering the real cost of making a bad decision. Many consultants specialize in assisting companies of specific sizes in specific vertical markets to identify and implement software packages. You could start looking for a consultant by contacting professional organizations in your industry.

A final place to investigate package possibilities is to contact your competitors. As a professional courtesy, your competitors will often tell you which packages they use and their level of satisfaction with the packages.

Evaluate Software Package Alternatives   After you have identified possible software package solutions, you must compare them and select the best choice(s). You should obtain information about the packages from a variety of sources. These sources include vendor presentations, literature, and documentation; evaluations in trade publications and from market research companies; and answers to the questions you ask of the software vendors. Then, you objectively match each package against the RFP features and give each package a rating. If some key features are more important than others, then give those key features a higher weight than the less important features.

The next step is to talk to existing users of the software package. For minicomputer and mainframe software packages, software vendors routinely provide user references. For personal computer packages, if the computer store cannot provide references, call the software vendor directly. User references are important because if a software package works for companies like yours, it probably will work for you. Vendors and computer stores, however, try to screen dissatisfied clients from their reference lists, so you should not be surprised if you receive only positive feedback.

Finally, have the end users try the software package. For a small information system, using a demonstration copy of the package at the computer store to enter a few sample transactions might represent an acceptable test of the package. For large information systems, you and the end users might require one or more days of testing either at the vendor's office or at your own facility to be sure that the package meets your needs.

If you are concerned about the capability of the package to handle a certain transaction volume efficiently, you should perform a benchmark test. A **benchmark test** involves measuring the time a package takes to process a set number of transactions. For example, a benchmark might consist of measuring the time a particular package takes to produce a sales summary report using 1,000 sales transactions. Comparing the time they require to perform the same task using the same data and the same equipment is one way of measuring the various packages' relative performance. For horizontal applications, many computer magazines publish regular product comparisons of several packages of the same type with benchmarks included. Figure 5-4 shows a benchmark comparison of six low-end desktop publishing software packages.

Source: *InfoWorld* June 18, 1990

BENCHMARKS

INFO WORLD

Low-End Desktop Publishing Software*

	Avagio Version 1.1	Express Publisher Version 1.1	Finesse Version 3.1	GEM Desktop Publisher Version 2.01	PFS:First Publisher Version 3.0	Publish It Version 1.12
Flyer document (two-page file)						
Open document	0:11	0:05	0:06	0:10	0:04	0:06
Jump to last page	0:03	0:02	0:01	0:01	0:03	0:02
Change view	0:07	0:01	0:01	0:01	0:01	0:02
Save and continue	0:05	0:03	0:01	0:12	0:06	0:04
Print	4:50	2:04	5:50	3:51	0:14	5:01
Newsletter document						
(four-page file)						
Open document	0:15	0:09	0:10	0:19	0:06	0:20
Jump to last page	0:03	0:03	0:01	0:02	0:03	0:02
Change view	0:12	0:01	0:02	0:06	0:01	0:04
Save & continue	0:05	0:05	0:02	0:23	0:15	0:12
Print	9:59	5:16	10:44	7:36	37:43	10:30
Prnbench ASCII						
Flow text	0:13	0:54	0:45	0:05	0:07	0:31

*Times in minutes:seconds.

Figure 5-4 *Many computer publications regularly evaluate and compare application software packages. This product comparison shows benchmarks for six low-end desktop publishing software packages.*

Make the Purchase   When you purchase software you usually do not own it. What you are actually purchasing is a **software license**, which gives you the right to use the software under certain terms and conditions. One of the typical terms and conditions allows you to use the software on a single computer only, or on two or more computers — but not at the same time. Other license restrictions include prohibitions against making the software available to others and making modifications to the software. For personal computer users, software license terms and conditions usually cannot be modified. For minicomputer and mainframe users, however, terms of the license agreements can be negotiated and, therefore, should be carefully reviewed by management and the legal department.

Although most software packages are purchased products, some packages, especially mainframe systems software such as database management systems, are not purchased outright. These packages must be leased for a period of time and paid for on a monthly basis as stipulated in the lease agreement. You can also pay a monthly or annual fee for a maintenance agreement with the vendor. **Maintenance agreements** give you the right to contact the vendor for assistance when you have problems or questions with the package. For most minicomputer and mainframe packages, a maintenance agreement gives you the right to obtain new releases of the package at no charge or at a reduced rate. For personal computer packages, you must mail in a registration card; the vendor then contacts all registered owners whenever a new release is available and offers the new release for purchase at a reduced price.

Install the Software Package After you have acquired the software package, the final step is to install the package. For small information systems, installation could be a one-day task. For large information systems, installation of a complete software package might be scheduled over a period of a year or more. If the software package is customized, then even more work must be coordinated and a correspondingly longer period of time required. To install the software package, you must complete typical implementation activities. Examples of implementation activities are loading the software on your computer system, testing the software, training the end users, and converting data to the system's files.

■ Outsourcing

So far we have discussed these three primary software alternatives: developing your own software, buying an off-the-shelf software package, and buying a customized software package. Two additional alternatives companies have been considering and selecting more frequently over the past few years are outsourcing and end user computing.

Outsourcing is the use of outside companies to handle a portion of a company's work load. Outsourcing is a general term applied to all aspects of a company's business — from the purchase of parts that a company formerly manufactured to the shifting of information systems' work from employees to outside contractors. Companies are turning to outsourcing as a means of controlling the growing costs of its information systems department while at the same time dealing with rapid technological change and the resulting obsolescence of computer equipment.

Companies have been outsourcing more and more of their internal information systems workload. More companies are turning to the oldest form of outsourcing, **systems management**, or **facilities management**, in which a company contracts with an outside firm to run its computer operations. Outsourcing is experiencing high growth rates in several other diverse areas. Examples of outsourcing include educational and training services, the management of a company's personal computers and their standard software packages, the installation and maintenance of a company's networks, and full responsibility for the development and maintenance of all information systems. The major information systems consulting firms and hardware manufacturers have special divisions established to deal with various outsourcing alternatives.

Another example of outsourcing is the joint development of customized vertical application software packages between a company in a specific industry with an outside software vendor. Each party supplies specific expertise: the company knows the application, and the vendor knows how to construct and market information systems. The vendor develops the package to meet the exact requirements of the company. Because the package is tailored to the company's requirements and to its operating environment, the package is more efficient and less costly to operate than a standard software package. The vendor sells the package to other companies involved in that specific vertical market. The joint-developing company recovers some of its development investment by saving money on future maintenance from the vendor and by making money from royalties on package sales.

Some companies require additional programmers, systems analysts, and other technical personnel for a few months to a year or two to handle peak work loads. Rather than hire these people and then have to let them go, companies will often deal with a contract personnel firm. A **contract personnel firm** supplies needed technical personnel for contracted periods of time at a set per-hour rate. A company might also turn to a contract personnel firm when it needs someone with specialized skills or knowledge for short periods of time.

■ End user computing

End user computing is the last software alternative we will discuss. **End user computing** is the development of an entire information system, or portions of an information system, by the end users in a company. Companies usually restrict end user computing to microcomputer-based applications that are limited to the end user's department and that are not integral to the company's essential information processing. To develop their own systems, end users typically use spreadsheets, database management systems, and other microcomputer packages. Fourth-generation tools and single-user application packages might also be used. The information center unit within the information systems department is responsible for supporting end user computing. This department determines which support products to use, where they will be purchased, and how they will be maintained and upgraded.

Most companies have a large backlog of development and maintenance work scheduled to be done by the information systems department. Consequently, small information systems that benefit individual end users or that are less visible or of lower priority are not developed unless the end users develop them. End users also can develop one-time only printed reports and screen inquiries and do what-if analyses against information systems installed on the company's minicomputers and mainframes.

If you are assigned to analyze the alternative solutions for an information system, you should not let end users develop any portion of the system that will affect other parts of the information system or other end users in the organization. If an end user needs to perform analysis or processing that does not affect other end users or critical information systems in any way, then you certainly should consider end user computing as an alternative.

■ Systems analyst involvement with the various software alternatives

The software alternatives differ in the amount of systems analyst involvement required for the remaining phases of the systems development life cycle. The in-house developed software alternative, for example, requires a much higher level of systems analyst involvement than does the end user computing alternative. Figure 5-5 illustrates the degree of systems analyst involvement for each software alternative in a continuum from high to low involvement.

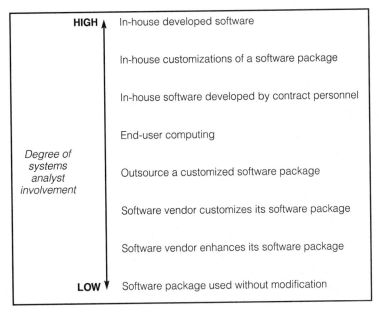

Figure 5-5   *The degree of systems analyst involvement in the remaining phases of the systems development life cycle for the various software alternatives.*

■ Hardware alternatives

The requirements of a new information system might necessitate the acquisition of additional hardware. If so, then you should select hardware similar to the way in which you select software packages; that is, the selection of hardware involves five steps: evaluate the information system requirements, identify potential hardware vendors, evaluate hardware alternatives, make the purchase, and install the hardware.

When you select hardware, you frequently know the specific products you need. If you do, then instead of a request for proposal, you prepare a request for quotation or a request for bid. A **request for quotation (RFQ)**, or **request for bid (RFB)**, solicits price and related information from vendors for the specific hardware products and/or software you need and specify in your proposal.

Special situations might require that you select a combination of hardware and software from vendors as a total solution for a specific information system. If this occurs, then you would prepare a proposal for a turnkey system. A **turnkey system** is a complete information system that includes all hardware, systems and application software, documentation, training, installation, and support from an outside vendor. You usually encounter the need for turnkey systems in smaller companies that lack the technical staff to develop and support their own computer information systems. The advantage of selecting a turnkey system is that a company has to deal with only a single vendor for the entire system. You will often find minicomputers and personal computers used with turnkey systems.

If you are purchasing hardware, such as printers, computers, and workstations, then you need to plan and complete the necessary site preparation activities. Site preparation can range from clearing a space on an office desk for a new workstation to the installation of special raised floors, water pipes, electrical lines, and backup storage batteries for a large mainframe computer.

Most companies use in-house developed software and a mixture of software packages, outsourcing, and end user computing. Even a single information system might use a combination of software alternatives. A company might purchase a standard software package to handle its payroll processing, for example, then develop its own software to handle specialized interfaces between payroll and its other information systems, and have end users prepare several reports and queries needed for internal departmental use.

The evaluation and selection of alternatives is not a simple process. Your objective is to obtain the best product at the best price, but what the true cost and actual product quality will be for any of the alternatives is often difficult to predict. With such a large number of possible alternatives, how do you select the one best alternative? Several factors help ease your burden and provide some degree of sanity to the selection process.

First, in most cases, you will be a member of an evaluation and selection team. The collective viewpoints of the team members help to ensure that critical factors are not overlooked and that a workable alternative is selected.

Key end users should be members of the selection team, because the end users best know their needs and must be sure they can live with the chosen alternative. The information system is theirs, not yours, and the end users should feel a sense of ownership for the information system. The information system benefits the end users, so they should be the driving force behind the alternative selection process. Your role is to advise and to deal with technical considerations and to help guide the selection process.

You must also be aware that neither the systems analyst nor the selection team is responsible for selecting the one best alternative. The final alternative selection is management's decision. The selection team's task is to eliminate the alternatives that will not work and to rank those alternatives that will work. The alternatives that appear to be possible solutions are called **viable alternatives**, which simply means they are the workable, or feasible, alternatives. The team then recommends one viable alternative with its rationale to management, although in some cases, more than one alternative might be recommended with the tradeoffs among the alternatives given to management. Management then selects the alternative it believes to be the best. In some cases, management's choice might not be one of the alternatives you recommended, because management has a different perspective than that of the team and considers different factors. If you conduct the evaluation correctly, you ultimately supply management with the facts it needs to make its selection decision. ■

Completion of systems analysis

reparing and distributing the system requirements document, preparing and making presentations of your analysis, and establishing procedures for controlling future changes to the system requirements are the activities that complete the systems analysis phase.

■ System requirements document

The **system requirements document** presents the detailed requirements for the new information system, describes the alternatives considered, and specifies your recommended course of action. The system requirements document serves as the baseline from which systems design will begin and against which the operational system will be measured in terms of its performance, accuracy, and completeness. You can consider the system requirements document to be a contract that details what must be delivered by the system developers to the end users. Therefore, the document should be written in the end users' language so they can understand it, suggest improvements to it, and approve its final version. The system requirements document is also called the **software requirements specification**.

Because the system requirements document will be dozens or even hundreds of pages in length, you must format and organize it so it is easy to read and reference — you should have a cover page, a detailed table of contents, an index, a glossary of terms, and all pages numbered in sequence.

The contents of the system requirements document varies, depending on the company and the complexity of the information system. Most system requirements documents have a structure similar to that shown in Figure 5-6.

SYSTEM REQUIREMENTS DOCUMENT

Table of Contents

1. Management Summary

2. Information System Background

3. Functional Requirements

4. Environmental Requirements

5. Alternatives

6. Recommended Alternative

7. Time and Cost Estimates

8. Appendices (as needed)

Figure 5-6 *The organization of a typical System Requirements Document.*

1. The *Management Summary* is a concise summary of the critical points contained in the rest of the document. Company executives expect to find in the Management Summary all the facts they need to know in order to make a decision; supporting details for these facts are found elsewhere in the document, so they can read the details if necessary. The summary sketches the objectives of the system, outlines the developmental efforts to date, summarizes the costs and benefits of the most viable alternatives, and recommends the best alternative solution. The Management Summary is normally two to three pages in length and is usually the last section of the document that you write. The Management Summary is also called an **executive summary**, or **management overview**.

2. In the *Information System Background* section, you give details about the background of the information system and a recap of the developmental effort to date. The Information System Background describes the problems with the current system, details the benefits and objectives of developing the new system, identifies the information system project's scope, summarizes the results of the preliminary investigation phase, and describes the major steps and accomplishments of the systems analysis phase.

3. The *Functional Requirements* section contains the logical design of the new information system. You put the information system's data flow diagrams, data dictionary entries, and process descriptions in this section. For very large information systems, some systems analysts include in this section only the top-level DFDs and the data dictionary entries and process descriptions directly related to them. In this case, the systems analyst places the lower-level logical design in a separate appendix. The functional requirements are also sometimes called **functional specifications**, or **software specifications**.

4. The *Environmental Requirements* provide the constraints under which the information system must operate. In this section, you document the operating constraints, external constraints, hardware and systems software constraints, control requirements, and security requirements. Operating constraints include volumes, sizes, frequencies, and timing considerations, such as reporting deadlines, online response times, and processing schedules. External constraints include any statutory restrictions and requirements by regulatory and governmental agencies; examples are data retention requirements and privacy considerations. Your system might also have other types of external constraints to define, such as EDI or credit bureau interface requirements.

5. In the *Alternatives* section you document all the alternatives that you considered during the systems analysis phase. For the infeasible alternatives, you state what the alternative is and why it is not feasible. For the feasible alternatives you describe the alternative and give its advantages and disadvantages and summary costs and plans.

6. In the *Recommended Alternative* section you give the rationale to support your choice of the one best alternative. If you cannot narrow down your choice to one alternative, then you must discuss in detail each of the alternatives you favor; you need to include in this discussion the tradeoffs among the alternatives so management can make an informed decision.

7. In the *Time and Cost Estimates* section, you provide estimates for each viable alternative. These estimates consist of detailed estimates for the next phase of systems design and revised projections for the remainder of the systems development life cycle. You need to estimate costs, schedules, and staffing requirements for each feasible alternative.

8. You should include several *Appendices* if they are needed. If the material you need to include is important enough, you should consider adding another separate section to the document instead of using an appendix. Frequently, the system requirements document has a separate appendix with copies of important documents from the first two phases; for example, you could include the systems request and the preliminary investigation report in such an appendix. You might want to have another appendix that contains your information sources and references; it is here you would include sample questionnaires, sample forms, lists of interviews with end users and software package vendors. Other examples of information you could include in separate sections or in appendices are testing criteria, conversion requirements, and any expected changes to the information system, if you are developing the information system in a series of releases.

■ Presentations

The presentation given to company management at the end of the systems analysis phase is one of the most critical milestones in the entire systems development life cycle. At the presentation, or as a result of what occurs at the presentation, management makes major decisions and commitments for the ultimate disposition of the information system.

Prior to the presentation you give to company management, you usually give two other presentations. You give one presentation to key individuals in the information systems department to inform them of your progress and recommendations and to be sure that you have their support. You give a second presentation to the end users to solicit their approval of the system requirements document.

The system requirements document is the basis for all three presentations, and it should be distributed to key end users, key information systems personnel, and management a week or two before the presentations to give these people a chance to read and critique it.

The objective of the management presentation is to permit management to decide on the next step to take for the development of the information system, to give their full support and approval to the chosen direction, and to commit money and other needed resources. Management will make one of these six decisions: develop an in-house system, modify the current information system, purchase a software package, purchase a package and develop an in-house system, perform additional systems analysis work, or stop all further work. The implications of these decisions are described in more detail here.

1. *Develop an in-house system*. This decision means your next step is to begin the systems design phase for the new information system.

2. *Modify the current information system*. This decision means your next step is to begin the systems design phase for the modified information system.

3. *Purchase a software package*. For this decision, management's next step is to negotiate a contract with the software vendor. If the package will be used with

no modifications, then your next step is to begin planning the systems implementation and evaluation phase. If you must make modifications to the package, then your next step is to begin the systems design phase. If the vendor must make package modifications, then your next step is to begin the systems development phase to plan the testing of the modifications.

4. *Purchase a package and develop an in-house system*. Making this decision implies that a package will satisfy a portion of the information system's requirements and that an in-house system will handle the remaining requirements. Management would negotiate the software contract, while you begin the systems design phase for the in-house system and begin package installation planning activities.

5. *Perform additional systems analysis work*. Management might make this decision for several reasons. For example, management might want you to further investigate certain alternatives, or to explore alternatives that were not examined, or to reduce the scope because of cost constraints, or to expand the scope because of new developments. Whatever the reason might be, your next steps are to plan and complete the additional work and to schedule a follow-up management presentation.

6. *Stop all further work*. This decision could be made because of your recommendation, because of a shift in priorities, because of costs, or because of a number of other reasons. Your departmental management's next step is to assign you to work on another information system after you have completed any remaining tasks for the systems analysis phase.

Because the participants in the management presentation received a copy of the system requirements document well before the presentation, they should be familiar with it. Therefore, you do not need to present all the information contained in that document. Instead, your management presentation should be organized by the following five parts:

1. Start with a brief overview of the purpose and primary objectives of the information system project.
2. Summarize the primary viable alternatives. For each alternative, tell what it is, what it will cost, and what its relative tradeoffs are.
3. Present your recommended alternative solution, giving the reasons why you and the selection team chose this alternative.
4. Allow a period of time for discussion and for questions and answers.
5. Obtain a decision from management, or at least obtain agreement concerning what should be done next.

■ Change control

The system requirements document contains the detailed requirements for the new information system. This document serves as a contract between the systems developers and the end users. The end users must be sure that their requirements are faithfully represented in the document and that an information system developed to meet these requirements will be acceptable to them. The systems developers must be confident that the requirements are accurate and complete and that they will be successful if they develop a well-performing information system that satisfies the requirements. All cost projections, schedules, and plans for further developmental work are based on the information system's requirements, as specified in the system requirements document.

If the requirements change for any reason during the remaining phases of the systems development life cycle, then costs, schedules, and plans might have to change as well. Minor changes to requirements have a marginal effect. Major changes to requirements have a significant effect — a major reduction of requirements lowers costs and accelerates the schedule, whereas a major addition of requirements increases costs and lengthens the schedule. Another consideration is the later in the systems development life cycle a major addition or change is made to the requirements, the greater the impact to costs, schedules, and plans. Major changes requested after the systems design has been completed and the programs have been completed, for example, have a much greater impact than if the changes were requested before the design began.

A good analogy to the impact of change on an information system is the impact of change when constructing a new house. The builder and the customer sign a contract for a specific house on a specific site at a given cost, schedule, and level of quality. The builder will construct the house according to the agreed upon requirements. If the customer requests a minor change, such as a change only to the color of the master bedroom carpet before the carpet is purchased, then there should be no impact. If the customer requests a major change, such as the addition of a glass-enclosed porch or the elimination of one bathroom, then there will be a significant impact to costs and schedules. If the customer makes the request before construction has started, then the impact to costs and schedules is much less than if the excavation, framing, and interior wall work have already been completed. The quality of the finished house also might be more uncertain if framing and walls have to be torn down and rebuilt.

To counteract the impact to costs, schedules, and plans caused by changes to the requirements, many companies freeze the requirements. To **freeze the requirements** means that the approved system requirements document is a fixed document that cannot be changed. If you freeze the requirements, then you maximize the chance for the successful delivery of an information system that satisfies the requirements within the agreed upon projected costs and schedules.

Change to the information system's requirements, however, is inevitable. Changes might be needed because requirements were overlooked or misinterpreted. Changes might be needed for external reasons; examples include the government imposing a new business tax, a customer such as General Motors dictating new requirements on their suppliers, and a need to offer customer services similar to that of a competitor. Changes might be required for internal reasons; examples include the sudden acquisition of new computer equipment, the changes required by a newly hired group of top-level executives, and new strategies imposed because of major changes in company direction.

One disadvantage of freezing the requirements is you run the risk of delivering an information system that is useless to the end users. If, for example, changes that are critical for an acceptable information system solution are not included, and if the end users are dissatisfied with the delivered solution and refuse to use it, then you have failed — no matter how well the information system satisfies the original requirements.

The wisest approach for you to follow, therefore, is to allow change to occur, but to manage and control the change. **Change control** is the process of managing and controlling the requested changes in requirements for an information system. Some people refer to the current requirements as the information system's configuration, and the process of managing the different configurations caused by requested changes as **configuration management**. We will discuss the details of change control in Chapter 11.

Prototyping and the fourth-generation environment

Even the simplest information system is complicated enough that a systems analyst might easily overlook or misinterpret the end users' requirements. The end users are comfortable interacting with the information system, and they know what they need to get their jobs done. The end users, therefore, serve an important function when they review and verify the accuracy and completeness of the system requirements document. One major drawback for the end users in their review is the system requirements document itself; the document is not a real information system. The system requirements document is only a paper model of the system. Paper models, regardless of how well done, are subject to interpretation and are difficult to verify. Even the use of data flow diagrams and other graphics do not completely overcome this problem. This does not mean that paper models are useless. What this does mean is that you must be aware of difficulties with a paper model and use alternative tools and approaches, if possible, to supplement the paper model.

Prototyping is one such alternative approach that is used to overcome the problem of completely and accurately developing verifiable requirements. A **prototype** is an early and rapidly constructed, working version of an information system that exhibits the essential features of the target information system. The process of creating the prototype is called **prototyping**. The prototyping process resembles techniques used in the engineering world, where, for example, a less expensive working model is created to eliminate the bugs before the final product is designed and produced.

■ Prototyping software tools

What makes prototyping possible is the use of modern software tools that are integrated, have powerful features, are easy to use, and are nonprocedural. With a **nonprocedural tool** you specify the problem that has to be solved but not how to solve it. In contrast, with a **procedural tool** you must specify the detailed steps, or procedures, to solve the given problem. Examples of procedural tools are programming languages such as BASIC, Pascal, and COBOL.

The modern software tools used in prototyping an information system are a data dictionary, a relational database management system, a report writer, a query language, a screen generator, a program generator, and a fourth-generation language. Combined, these tools comprise what is termed the **fourth-generation environment**. Figure 5-7 illustrates the fourth-generation environment and the software tools used in this environment.

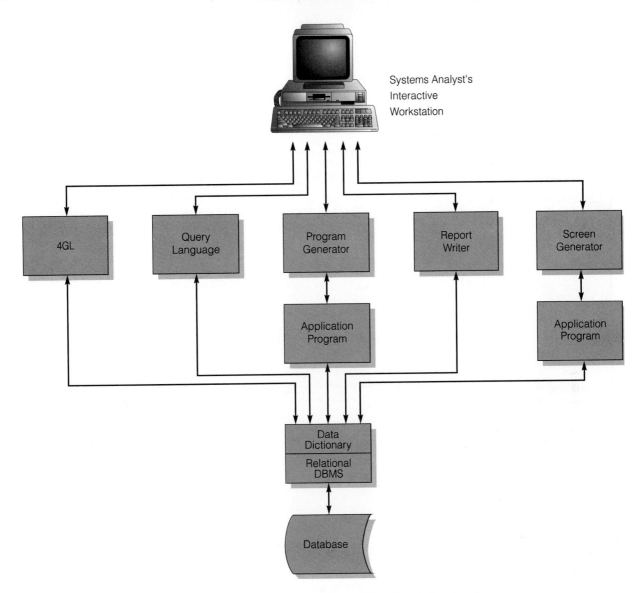

Figure 5-7 *The fourth-generation environment and its software tool components.*

Central to the fourth-generation environment is a database, a relational database management system (DBMS), and a data dictionary. A **database** is the repository of all data and relationships among the data for the information system. A **relational database management system** is a software package designed to manipulate data in a database on behalf of all the end users. We define the data for our information system in the data dictionary, and the data is stored in the database, which is managed by the database management system. We will discuss the details of databases and database management systems in Chapter 9.

A **report writer** is a nonprocedural language for producing formatted reports from data in a database. In most cases, the report generated by the report writer is printed on paper, but the report can also be output to a terminal screen or to a disk file. A report writer is sometimes called a **report generator**. Figure 5-8 on the next page illustrates a simple report writer request and the report it produces.

A **query language** is a nonprocedural language for retrieving data from a database. The retrieved information typically is displayed on a screen but may also be printed on paper or output to a disk file. A query language request and the output it generates might look similar to the report writer example in Figure 5-8.

```
PRINT SALES REP, CUSTOMER NAME, CUSTOMER #, BALANCE
PRINT GRAND TOTAL RESERVE (CURRENCY)
    MATCH ON REP NUMBER
    IN ORDER BY ASCENDING SALES REP, CUSTOMER NAME
    ALL TOTALS FOR BALANCE
    COUNT BY SALES REP
    CALCULATE RESERVE = 2.5% *BALANCE
    TITLE "CLIENT LIST BY SALES REPRESENTATIVE"
```

```
11/28/97          CLIENT LIST BY SALES REPRESENTATIVE          PAGE 1


                                          CUSTOMER          CURRENT
  SALES REP          CUSTOMER NAME          NUMBER          BALANCE
  June Heinman       Don Charles             311            $200.10
                     Mary Chen               522              49.50
                     Al Nelson               405             201.75

  SALES REP TOTAL:    3                                     $451.35

  Sam Markowitz      Sally Adams             124             418.75
                     Dan Martini             412             908.75
                     Hector Mendez           622             575.50

  SALES REP TOTAL:    3                                   $1,903.00

  Mary Rathbone      Joe Daniels             567             201.20
                     Tom Nguyen              315             320.75
                     Judy Roberts            587              57.75
                     Ann Samuels             256              10.75

  SALES REP TOTAL:    4                                      $590.45

  GRAND TOTALS:                                           $2,944.80

        RESERVE           $73.62
```

Figure 5-8 *A sample report writer request and the report it produces.*

A query language is similar in many ways to a report writer. The main objective of a report writer, however, is to produce a printed report, whereas that of a query language is to display retrieved information on a display screen. Consequently, report writers tend to be more compatible with batch processing, and query languages are more online processing oriented. Report writers tend to have more sophisticated output-formatting capabilities, whereas query languages are built for rapid response.

A **screen generator** is an interactive software tool that generates an application program used for creating and maintaining display and data entry formats for screen forms. The screen generator allows you to define how the screen is to be **painted**, which refers to how captions are displayed on the screen and how color and other visual attributes are handled. The screen generator lets you define the placement of variable data that the end user is to enter or that is to be displayed. Through its interaction with the data dictionary, the generated program performs verification of values entered by the end user. Table lookups, calculations, interaction with the DBMS, and a user exit facility are other functions handled by the generated program. **Screen painter, screen mapper**, and **form generator** are three other common names used for a screen generator.

A **program generator** is a software tool that generates a second- or third-generation language program. The objective of a program generator is to allow a programmer or systems analyst to more productively create and maintain programs written in traditional languages. The generated program is called an application program.

A **fourth-generation language (4GL)** is a modern programming language that has both procedural and nonprocedural features. Thus, 4GLs allow you to write computer programs much faster and more accurately than is the case with traditional programming languages, while providing similar features and power.

■ Prototyping during systems analysis

You can use prototyping during the systems analysis phase. Prototyping would be used in parallel with fact-finding during requirements determination. As you collect facts about the information system, you construct the prototype (Figure 5-9). You initially attempt to construct a prototype that you feel satisfies end user requirements. You can do this rapidly by using the productive software tools. This initial prototype is given to the end users, who actively use the prototype to assess how well it satisfies their needs. The end users are encouraged to be highly critical of the prototype and to suggest changes and improvements. You continue developing the prototype in an iterative fashion by repeatedly refining it and releasing it back to the end users until they are completely satisfied with it. When prototyping is used, the end users must spend considerably more time and be more actively involved in the systems analysis phase. Finding the time to devote to prototyping could be a problem for the end users, unless they can be freed from their normal activities. Because prototyping increases the effort required for the systems analysis phase, costs will be higher for this phase. These costs, however, are usually offset by lower costs for subsequent systems development life cycle phases.

The software tools used during prototyping produce a functioning system that is inefficient compared to systems developed with traditional programming languages; these inefficiencies include slower computer processing speeds and slower online response times. Also, because your

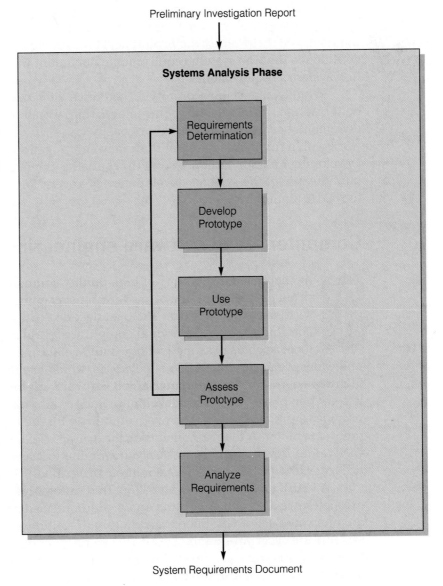

Figure 5-9 The steps followed when prototyping during the systems analysis phase.

primary objective during prototype development is to quickly react to the essential, observable processing of the information system, the finished prototype lacks security requirements, exception and error handling procedures, and other critically required functions. You most likely made many implementation compromises in developing the prototype that would have to be reconsidered and done differently if the prototype were to serve as the basis for the new information system.

If the new information system does not demand a high level of performance, then the prototype might serve as the basis for the finished information system. You would continue to improve and extend the prototype until it satisfied all end user requirements and functioned in an acceptable manner in your computer environment. The end effect of the prototyping process would be to significantly reduce the time and cost spent developing the information system. This reduction would occur because you would be bypassing separate systems design and development phases in the systems development life cycle by combining them with the systems analysis phase.

If the information system demands a performance level higher than can be obtained from the fourth-generation software tools, then the prototype serves as the definition of the end users' requirements. In this case, you would proceed through the remaining phases of the systems development life cycle in the normal way and develop the new information system using traditional third-generation programming languages. In effect, you throw away the prototype. However, you have gained something valuable: confidence that the system requirements document will truly represent the new information system's requirements.

When you develop a prototype, you have an actual information system that might better define the end users' requirements than would the system requirements document, because people can more easily visualize what they will be getting when they work with a functioning system than they can by reading a written document. Developing an information system that satisfies the needs of the end users is the ultimate aim of the systems development life cycle, and prototyping is a very effective tool in attaining this goal.

Computer-aided software engineering (CASE)

The increased availability of high-quality computer-aided software engineering products has been one of the four most exciting advances for information systems developers over the past decade — the other exciting advances are low-cost, high-powered personal computers; graphical, highly intelligent software tools, such as drawing packages and relational database management systems; and widespread communications networks, which are the foundation of the information highways of tomorrow. **Computer-aided software engineering (CASE)** is the computer automation of the process of developing and maintaining information systems. CASE provides systems analysts and programmers with the software tools they need to do their jobs better. A diagramming tool, for example, allows systems analysts to draw and verify data flow diagrams, and a programming tool assists programmers in conducting accuracy and performance tests on their programs.

A **CASE tool** is a software product that automates a specific systems life cycle task; examples are a screen generator and a computerized data dictionary. A **CASE toolkit** is an integrated set of CASE tools that automates a phase, or a portion of a phase, of the systems life cycle; an example is a software product that integrates the creation of data flow diagrams, data dictionary entries, and process descriptions for the systems analysis phase. A **CASE workbench** is an integrated set of CASE toolkits that automates multiple phases of the systems life cycle; an example is a software product that automates the logical and physical design process and automatically generates executable programs. Systems developers today commonly use individual CASE tools, but the newer CASE toolkits and workbenches hold the greatest promise for improvements in the information systems field.

■ Categories of CASE tools

The development and maintenance of an information system consists of a wide range of tasks. The range of CASE tools is almost equally wide. CASE tool categories include diagramming tools, prototyping tools, a central repository, data design tools, programming tools, project management tools, and maintenance tools.

A **diagramming tool** lets you draw a diagram such as a data flow diagram, store the drawing away, and then modify the drawing at a later time. Diagramming tools are available for manipulating data flow diagrams and most other popular diagramming techniques. Diagramming tools are available, for example, that support systems flowcharts and state-transition diagrams (discussed later in this chapter) and entity-relationship diagrams (discussed in Chapter 9).

Figure 5-10 shows an actual data flow diagram drawn on a personal computer screen using Intersolv's Excelerator workbench; the icons used to draw and manipulate the DFD are shown along the upper left of the screen. Typical manipulations you can do on the screen include: placing, moving, and deleting symbols; connecting symbols; naming each symbol and data flow; printing the diagram on paper or to a disk file; changing the on-screen zoom level; linking documentation to the data dictionary; and exploding a process to a lower level DFD. Similar icons are available with other vendors' products and for other diagramming techniques.

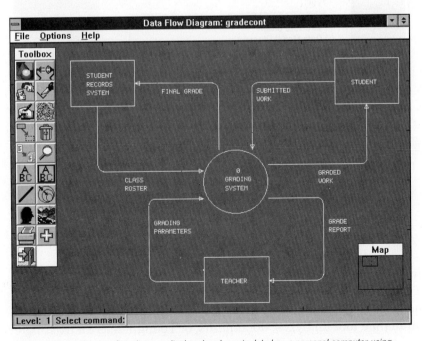

Figure 5-10   *A data flow diagram displayed and manipulated on a personal computer using Intersolv's Excelerator workbench.*

Prototyping tools include the report writers, query languages, screen generators, and fourth-generation languages that we discussed in the previous section.

A **central repository** is a data dictionary that stores, updates, analyzes, and reports on the information for one or more integrated CASE tools. If, for example, you had a diagramming tool for developing data flow diagrams integrated with a central repository, then all information pertaining to the data flow diagrams that you develop would be stored in the central repository. You could then have the toolkit analyze a set of DFDs for balance and print a report of this analysis. Or, you could have the toolkit analyze the same set of DFDs and print a report of any DFD symbols or flows not yet entered in the repository.

The greater the number of tools integrated into the toolkit or workbench central repository, the greater the analysis and reporting capabilities. Figure 5-11 shows the Excelerator Diagram Editor menu, which lists the numerous diagramming tools that are integrated with the central repository. From the main menu, you can then use the Screens & Reports menu choice to prototype your information system and the Analysis menu choice to balance and verify your diagrams against each other and with the central repository.

A **data design tool** assists you in the logical and physical modeling of files and databases.

A **programming tool** assists you in the development of computer programs. Examples include testing tools, program debuggers, and code generators. A **code generator** creates program code from program design specifications.

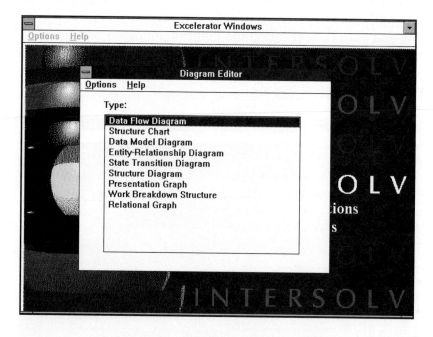

Figure 5-11 *The Excelerator Diagram Editor menu.*

A **project management tool** assists you in the planning, tracking, controlling, and reporting of information system projects. We will discuss the specific types of tasks supported by these tools in Chapter 11.

A **maintenance tool** analyzes, documents, or reengineers an existing computer program. All preceding CASE tools are examples of **forward engineering tools**, which support you as you go forward, phase by phase, through the systems development life cycle. A **reverse engineering tool** converts program code into design specifications. A **reengineering toolkit** combines reverse and forward engineering to an existing computer program to produce an improved version of the program. A reengineering toolkit first converts the existing program to its design specifications. Then, the toolkit analyzes the design specifications and reports the analysis to you so you can make any fine-tuning decisions. When the specifications are acceptable to you, a code generator produces the new, improved version of the program.

CASE tools also are classified as either front-end or back-end products, according to when they are used during the systems life cycle. A **front-end tool**, which is also called an **upper-CASE tool**, is used during the preliminary investigation, systems analysis, or systems design phases. A **back-end tool**, which is also called a **lower-CASE tool**, is used during the systems development or systems implementation and evaluation phases or during systems operation. If all your information systems run on personal computers, then it is likely that all your tools will also run on personal computers. If you have some information systems on either minicomputers or mainframes, then the front-end tools typically will be used on personal computers, whereas the back-end products will run on minicomputers or mainframes.

Figure 5-12 lists some of the major CASE products on the market today. A complete inventory of CASE tools would be numbered in the hundreds. Each year, new CASE products reach the market, with some older products no longer being sold.

Vendor	CASE Product
Anderson Consulting	Foundation
Bachman Information Systems	Bachman/Analyst
Cadre Technologies Inc.	Ensemble
Cincom Systems Inc.	AD/Advantage
Evergreen CASE Tools Inc.	EasyCASE System Designer
Future Tech Systems Inc.	Envision
IntelliCorp	Kappa Family of Software
Intersolv Inc.	Excelerator
KnowledgeWare	Application Development Workbench
Mark V Systems Ltd.	ObjectMaker Analysis and Design Tool
Oracle Corp.	Oracle Designer
Popkin Software & Systems Inc.	System Architect
R&O Inc.	Rochade
SES Inc.	SES/objectbench
Sterling Software Applications	Answer: Architect
StructSoft Inc.	TurboCASE
Sybase Inc.	Deft
Texas Instruments	Information Engineering Facility
Visible Systems Corp.	Visible Analyst Workbench

Figure 5-12   *Some of the major CASE products and their vendors.*

■ Advantages and disadvantages of CASE

CASE technology provides numerous advantages over nonautomated methods of development and maintenance. One advantage is improved productivity, because by automating paper-and-pencil tasks, these tools take less time to accomplish the same tasks. Automating tedious, clerical tasks is a second advantage; this has positive morale and motivating influences on systems developers. Another advantage of using CASE is the standardization and consistency the tools enforce among the systems developers; this improves productivity because everyone can more easily follow other people's work. A final advantage is that CASE tools improve the accuracy, consistency, and overall quality of the work product produced.

Although the *advantages of CASE far outweigh the disadvantages,* you should keep in mind a few *potential disadvantages.* The cost of the hardware and software to support CASE can be considered an initial disadvantage. Most CASE products require the more powerful personal computers, and the price of each CASE tool, toolkit, and workbench ranges from hundreds to thousands of dollars per workstation. The tradeoff is improved productivity, quality, and completeness; this translates into a long-term cost savings.

A second potential disadvantage is the current lack of CASE standards, which is not a problem if you use the same CASE products far into the future. If you want to switch at some future point to a competing product, however, you will probably have problems transferring the completed work under your current product to the newer product.

A third potential disadvantage is you might have to change the way you develop and maintain information systems. Each product has a particular approach, or methodology, you must follow. If you cannot find a product that supports your current approach and you want to use a CASE product, then you are going to have to change your current approach.

A final disadvantage is although CASE technology replaces paper and pencil and tedious clerical work, the technology does not replace the thinking of a systems developer. The systems analyst and the programmer must still make intelligent decisions and work smart. Management and the uninformed, however, might not have this point of view; they must often be educated about the proper role of CASE. You might overhear someone say, for example, "Good, now we don't have to teach our new systems analysts how to create data flow diagrams; we can just have them learn how to work with the new CASE toolkit." What's wrong with this statement? What's wrong is that the systems analyst must still learn how to create data flow diagrams properly. Learning the *how* is independent of using the tool, whether the tool be paper and pencil or a computer.

Object-oriented systems analysis

The object-oriented approach to the systems development process has emerged in recent years. Object-oriented programming languages (C++ and Smalltalk are two examples) were the first to evolve, followed by object-oriented techniques for analysis and for design. Object-oriented databases are the subject of extensive research and development, and several are currently available in the marketplace.

The primary emphasis in the object-oriented approach is on the data instead of procedures; that is, a system is seen as a collection of objects. An **object** is a unit of data, along with the actions that can affect that data. A PRODUCT object, for example, would consist of data relevant to a product (name, description, unit price, and so on) along with the actions that can take place on product data (add a product, change a price, and so on).

In the object-oriented approach, objects are defined from the specific to the general, as common characteristics are recognized and abstracted. We might, for example, have identified the objects HOURLY-EMPLOYEE and SALARIED-EMPLOYEE, which together encompass all the employees of the organization and the actions that affect them. We could then abstract those data items and actions common to both, define a new object called EMPLOYEE, and then define both HOURLY-EMPLOYEE and SALARIED-EMPLOYEE as subclasses of EMPLOYEE. Because of **inheritance**, an essential concept of the object-oriented approach, a subclass object inherits all the characteristics of the object upon which it is based. When we later recognize that the object CLIENT has data items and actions in common with the object EMPLOYEE, we would define a new object called PERSON with the common traits; EMPLOYEE and CLIENT would then be defined as subclasses of the object PERSON.

During object-oriented analysis, the systems analyst identifies all the objects in the system and determines the relationships among those objects. Analysis then becomes essentially a bottom-up process of abstracting objects into higher-level object classes. Procedure definition and specification of data structures is deferred until the design phase. This, proponents of the object-oriented approach argue, promotes increased flexibility in the developing design.

Object definitions are stored in an object library and can be accessed and used by other systems. Similarly, module libraries of object-related code are available for reuse by other systems. The reusability of objects and code is cited as a major advantage of the object-oriented approach.

Alternative graphical tools

D ata flow diagrams are an integral part of structured analysis; DFDs show the logical model of an information system and are suitable for physical modeling during the subsequent systems design phase. Data flow diagrams, however, are not the only graphical tool useful in the development of information systems. Hundreds of other graphical tools have enjoyed popularity in the past, and some of these tools are still used by a number of systems developers. In addition, each year several new graphical tools are devised, publicized, and gain their share of supporters. Some tools have narrow use during a certain phase of systems development, while other tools have wider application. Of these alternative graphical tools, the two most frequently used during systems analysis are systems flowcharts and state-transition diagrams.

■ Systems flowcharts

Systems flowcharts have been used since the early days of information systems development. A **systems flowchart** graphically illustrates the major processes, inputs, and outputs of an information system. Systems flowcharts have several symbols used to represent different media, such as disks, tapes, documents, terminal inputs, and terminal outputs. Consequently, systems flowcharts are used primarily for the physical modeling of an information system.

A systems flowchart for the handling of customer receipts in an order system is shown in Figure 5-13. Lines with arrowheads indicate the flow of data, just as they do with data flow diagrams. The flow of data generally goes from top to bottom and left to right, and systems flowcharts depict the sequence of processing steps along these data flow lines.

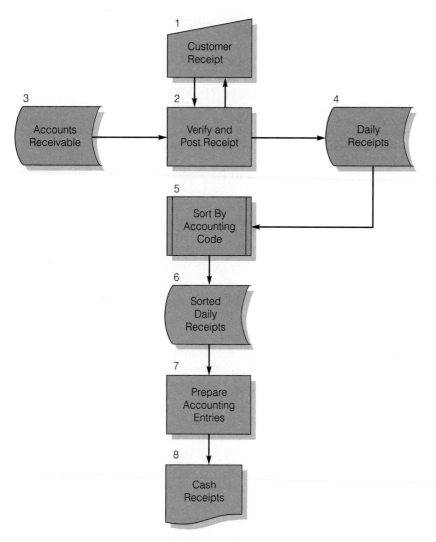

Each symbol's shape indicates its purpose. We have numbered the symbols for our discussion here, but such numbers do not usually appear in a systems flowchart. The symbols in Figure 5-13 that represent data or files stored in specific physical media are symbols 1, 3, 4, 6, and 8. Symbol 1 is a terminal or workstation symbol; symbols 3, 4, and 6 are disk symbols; and symbol 8 is a document or report symbol.

The other three symbols, 2, 5, and 7, signify major processes that transform the data or files into another form. Symbols 2 and 7 are process symbols that represent programs, and symbol 5 is a predefined process symbol that represents a system utility program.

Figure 5-13, therefore, pictures three major processing steps that are completed in the following sequence. The first step (symbol 2) verifies terminal-entered customer receipts (symbol 1) by reading from the accounts receivable file (symbol 3), reports back to the terminal on the validity of the receipt, and posts the valid receipts to the daily receipts file (symbol 4). The second step (symbol 5) sorts the daily receipts into accounting code sequence and creates the sorted daily receipts file (symbol 6). The third step (symbol 7) reads the sorted daily receipts and consolidates information to produce the cash receipts report (symbol 8).

Figure 5-13 *A systems flowchart for the handling of customer payments in an order system.*

Systems flowcharts are easy to construct and easy to understand. Many systems analysts continue to use systems flowcharts effectively. The increasing use of data flow diagrams for logical and physical modeling has led, however, to a steady decline in the use of systems flowcharts in recent years.

■ State-transition diagrams

One criticism of data flow diagrams is that they do not allow the systems analyst to graphically show the controls and time-dependent nature of real-time systems. A **real-time system** is a system that processes data it receives from its environment rapidly enough to cause change to that same environment. Examples of real-time systems are operating systems, missile control systems, patient monitoring systems, microprocessor-controlled thermostats, microwave ovens, and ATMs. Some people equate **online**

transaction processing systems with real-time systems; but online transaction processing systems interact with people, whereas real-time systems interact with both people and an environment. Examples of online transaction processing systems are airline reservation systems and banking systems.

Real-time systems react to events that occur by changing the state of the system. The events are either changes to environmental conditions or externally triggered signals. Examples of changes to environmental conditions are a change in room temperature sensed by a thermostat and a change in a patient's heart rate sensed by patient monitoring equipment. Examples of externally triggered signals are a person setting the cooking time on a microwave oven and a computer operator entering a terminal command to an operating system to initiate a program.

A **state-transition diagram (STD)** is a graphic tool for showing the events, states, and time-dependent behavior of a real-time system. Figure 5-14 shows a state-transition diagram for a microwave oven. The lines with arrowheads show the events that occur, and the boxes show the different states of the system. For example, the microwave oven sits idle until the *time entered* event occurs. The oven then waits for the *power setting entered* event, followed by a wait for the *start pushed*

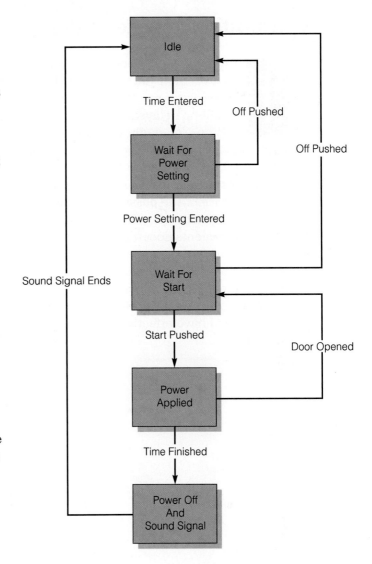

Figure 5-14   *A state-transition diagram for a microwave oven.*

event. In any of these cases, the oven will return to its idle state if the *off pushed* event occurs. The *start pushed* event initiates the power applied state. If the *door opened* event occurs, the oven returns to its wait for start state; otherwise, the oven continues applying power until the *time finished* event occurs. At this time, the power goes off, a sound is signaled, and then the oven returns to an idle state.

You can create a state-transition diagram as the partitioned, lower-level diagram for a process symbol on a data flow diagram. In this way, data flow diagrams and state-transition diagrams can be used together to logically model a real-time system.

Transition to systems design

I f management decides that an in-house developed system is the proper direction to take, then you would next begin the third systems development life cycle phase: systems design. You might immediately begin systems design or you might be delayed for days, or weeks, or even months before starting systems design. You might also be assigned to the systems design phase, even though you participated in neither the preliminary investigation nor the systems analysis phases. Finally, though you worked on the systems analysis phase, other systems analysts might take over the systems design phase from you.

Because of the possible time delay before systems design begins and the potential change in project team members, the creation of a complete, accurate, and readable system requirements document is critical. This document presents the requirements of the new information system and is the starting point for initiating the systems design phase. Errors, omissions, ambiguities, and other problems with the system requirements document will negatively impact the quality and completeness of the systems design. You must be positive, therefore, that you have conducted a thorough and accurate systems analysis and have effectively communicated this analysis in the system requirements document.

CHAPTER CASE STUDY

James Tool Company — Completing the Systems Analysis Phase and Considering Alternative Tools

Systems analyst Don Mard and programmer/analyst Howard Coswell have completed the logical model of the payroll system for James Tool Company. Meanwhile, the information systems department has recently purchased and installed Excelerator, a CASE workbench that supports logical and physical modeling. Mard and Coswell were sent to a one-week workshop to learn the package. After returning from the workshop, Mard and Coswell decided to enter the logical model for the payroll system into the Excelerator package. They thought the time spent now would pay for itself on later phases of the project. Three of the DFDs that Mard and Coswell created with Excelerator are shown in Figures 5-15 through 5-17 on pages 5.32 and 5.33. These DFDs are similar to the ones that they had previously drawn by hand and that were shown at the end of Chapter 4.

In the next month, Mard and Coswell looked at alternatives and spent their time evaluating the various alternatives. Based on their evaluation, they determined that the best software solution would be the purchase of a payroll package. Unfortunately, the union processing was unique enough that none of the favored software packages would handle the union requirements.

The systems analysts consolidated the logical model, the alternative evaluations, cost and time estimates, and all other information into the system requirements document for the payroll system. The document was printed and distributed, and an executive presentation was scheduled for the end of the following week. Mard and Coswell had worked closely with their management and with the end users and had received their approvals on individual portions of the document as it was being prepared; thus, they did not need to schedule any other presentations prior to the management presentation.

Coswell gave the management presentation. He recommended that James Tool Company purchase the payroll package sold by Lennox Software Solutions and that union processing be developed in-house to interact with the payroll package. After Mard and Coswell had satisfactorily answered several questions, management concurred with their recommendation. The next step would be for management to negotiate a contract with Lennox Software Solutions and for Mard and Coswell to begin the systems design for union processing.

Summary

In this chapter, we completed our coverage of the systems analysis phase by studying its concluding activities: the evaluation of alternatives, the preparation of the system requirements document, and the management presentation.

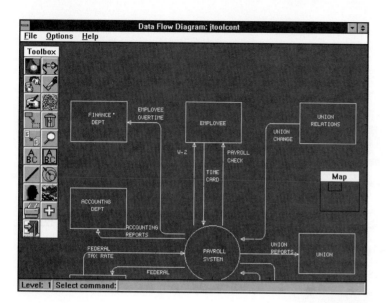

Figure 5-15a *The top portion of the context diagram DFD for James Tool Company's payroll system as viewed using Excelerator's close-up zoom mode.*

Figure 5-15b *The bottom portion of the context diagram DFD for James Tool Company's payroll system as viewed using Excelerator's close-up zoom mode*

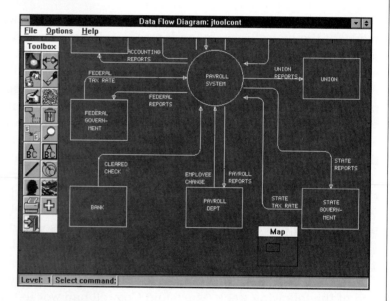

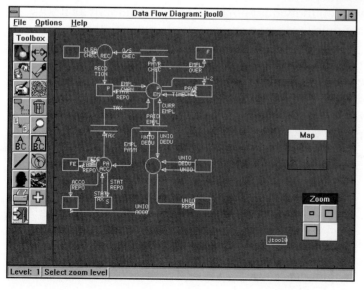

Figure 5-16a *The diagram 0 DFD for James Tool Company's payroll system as viewed using Excelerator's layout zoom mode.*

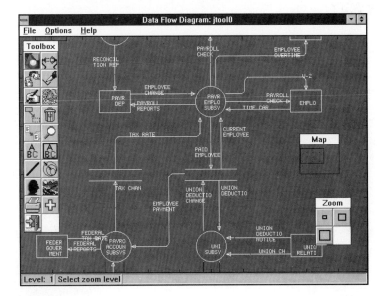

Figure 5-16b   The diagram 0 DFD for James Tool Company's payroll system as viewed using Excelerator's medium zoom mode.

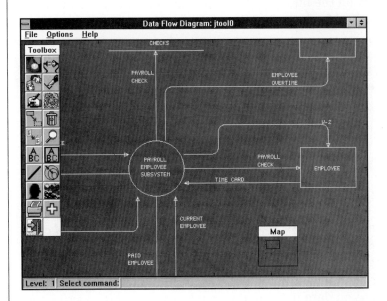

Figure 5-16c   The diagram 0 DFD for James Tool Company's payroll system as viewed using Excelerator's close-up zoom mode.

Figure 5-17   Diagram 4 DFD, UNION SUBSYSTEM, for James Tool Company's payroll system as viewed using Excelerator's medium zoom mode.

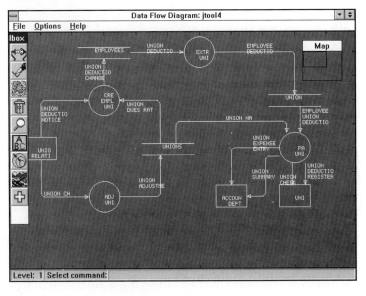

The most important software alternatives are developing an in-house system, buying a software package, and buying a customized software package. Compared to developing an in-house system, purchasing a commercial software package is an appealing alternative, because generally a package costs less, takes less time, has fewer errors, has a proven track record, requires fewer systems developers, and is frequently upgraded. In-house development must be pursued whenever requirements or constraints dictate that a software package would be inadequate, but a customized software package could also be an appropriate alternative in these situations.

The procurement of both software packages and hardware follow a similar selection process: evaluate needs, identify possible solutions, evaluate these solutions, make the purchase, and install the product. In addition to the three principle software alternatives, you might have to consider outsourcing and end user computing as possible information system solutions.

The system requirements document is the end product that you produce at the conclusion of the systems analysis phase. This document details all requirements and constraints, recommends the best information system solution, and provides cost and time estimates for future development work. The system requirements document is the basis for the management presentation. Based on your findings and recommendations, management decides on the next steps to pursue for the information system's development. If further work on the information system is warranted, instituting a change control procedure to manage the inevitable changes to the requirements is an important step to take at this point.

We also examined prototyping, the fourth-generation environment, computer-aided software engineering (CASE), and object-oriented systems analysis. Prototyping is helpful in accurately determining the information system requirements. By using powerful software tools, you can construct a limited, working version of the information system. The resulting prototype is either discarded or used as the basis for the new information system. The fourth-generation environment software tools used in prototyping are a data dictionary, a relational database management system, a report writer, a query language, a screen generator, a program generator, and a fourth-generation language.

Computer-aided software engineering (CASE) is the computer automation of the process of developing and maintaining information systems. CASE workbench products consist of CASE toolkits, which are sets of CASE tools that automate a specific systems life cycle task. Hundreds of commonly used CASE products are available that support information system development from the start of the systems life cycle to the end. The many advantages of CASE outweigh the disadvantages, and the trend is for rapid growth in CASE product use.

Object-oriented systems analysis focuses on data instead of procedures and views a system as a collection of objects and the relationships among the objects. Each object is a unit of data, along with the actions that can affect the data. Objects are defined from the specific to the general, and a subclass object inherits all the characteristics of the object upon which it is based. Object definitions are stored in an object library and can be accessed and used by other systems.

We also discussed systems flowcharts, which graphically show the physical model of an information system, and state-transition diagrams, which graphically show the events, states, and time-dependent behavior of real-time systems.

Review Questions

1. Explain the difference between horizontal application software and vertical application software.

2. What is the most common reason for a company to choose to develop its own information system? Give two other reasons that a company chooses the in-house approach.

3. Discuss four advantages of buying a software package.

4. Describe two ways that a software vendor can customize its package.

5. What problems can a company encounter when it uses a customized software package?

6. What is an RFP, and how does it differ from an RFQ?

7. Explain where you would investigate to identify potential software vendors.

8. What is the purpose of a benchmark test?

9. Explain the difference between a software license and a maintenance agreement.

10. Is the use of outsourcing increasing or declining, and why?

11. Define a turnkey system.

12. What information is typically placed in the functional requirements section of the system requirements document?

13. To what different groups of people do you give presentations at the end of the systems analysis phase?

14. What are the six different decisions management could reach at the end of the systems analysis phase, and what would be the next steps taken in each of these cases?

15. Give three reasons why change to the requirements of an information system is inevitable.

16. What is configuration management?

17. What is a prototype?

18. What are the prototyping software tools?

19. What is a 4GL?

20. What is CASE?

21. How do CASE tools, toolkits, and workbenches differ?

22. List and describe five different categories of CASE tools.

23. Define reengineering and describe its steps.

24. Give three advantages of using a CASE tool.

25. What is an object?

26. What is the purpose of a systems flowchart? Is its use increasing or declining, and why?

27. What is a real-time system? Give two examples of real-time systems.

28. Give a definition for a state-transition diagram.

Discussion Questions

1. When discussing computer-aided software engineering (CASE) in this chapter, we said, "The development and maintenance of an information system consists of a wide range of tasks. The range of CASE tools is almost equally wide." This statement implies that some development and maintenance tasks cannot be automated. Is this statement correct, or should the word almost be deleted from the second sentence? If the statement is true, then what are the tasks that cannot be automated?

2. For the past twenty years, some experts have been saying that COBOL is an antiquated, nonstructured language and have been predicting that modern, structured third- and fourth-generation languages would rapidly replace it. Due to the many hundreds of billions of dollars invested in existing COBOL programs, however, COBOL remains the most widely used language for business information systems development. What are your views about the future of COBOL as a primary business information system language? Are there any technological

developments that make it more reasonable to believe that COBOL's use will decline more and more in the future?

3. Visit the data center at your school or at a local company and investigate the use of CASE tools. Present to your class what tools are being used. How satisfied are the systems developers and management with the results of their use of CASE?

4. Select a specific type of horizontal application software to investigate. Visit local libraries and computer stores to determine what software packages are available. Describe the common features of these packages and the features that distinguish one product from another.

5. Visit the data center at your school or at a local company and investigate the use of the object-oriented approach to systems development. Present to your class what object-oriented methodology and programming language are being used. What has the data center staff found to be the major benefits and difficulties of the object-oriented approach?

6. COBOL-85 is the latest standard version of this widely-used programming language. Research which major features are being proposed for the next COBOL standard. Which of these features are characteristic of object-oriented programming languages?

MINICASE STUDIES

Cutting Edge Incorporated

Cutting Edge Incorporated is a company engaged in the development of computer-aided design software packages. Michele Kellogg is employed at Cutting Edge as a product manager and is the key end user for a new package being developed for sale to the furniture industry. Santiago Benitez is the lead systems analyst for this effort, which is now one month into the systems design phase that began October 6. The completion and first installation of the package is scheduled for August 1 of the following year.

On November 6, Kellogg received a change request from the vice president of development; a new functional capability needed to be added to the package. She requested that Benitez analyze this change to determine its impact to the project.

Kellogg and Benitez reviewed the results of the analysis at a meeting on November 15. Adding the new requirements to the package at this time would increase the developmental costs by $28,000 and would add one month to the schedule. Benitez evaluated a second alternative, which is to continue to develop the package without the requested changes and to incorporate the changes into the package as part of a follow-up release. This second alternative would take three months and $66,000 to accomplish.

Questions

1. Because the project is in the systems design phase and no programming has been started, why would incorporating the requested change add one month and $28,000 to the project?

2. Why would it take two extra months and $38,000 more if the changes were done after package development has been completed?

3. Suppose you were Michele Kellogg and had to recommend action on the change request. What would be the factors you would consider in making your recommendation? What would be your recommendation?

Ridgeway Company

The Ridgeway Company requirements were described in a Chapter 4 minicase. The following assignments are based on those same requirements.

Questions

1. If you have a CASE diagramming tool available for preparing data flow diagrams, use the tool to create the entire set of data flow diagrams for the Ridgeway Company's billing system.

2. If you have access to prototyping software tools, prototype the monthly statement and the daily sales report.

Genealogy System

The genealogy system requirements were described in a Chapter 4 minicase. The following assignments are based on those same requirements.

Questions

1. If you have a CASE diagramming tool available for preparing data flow diagrams, use the tool to create the entire set of data flow diagrams for the genealogy system.

2. If you have access to prototyping software tools, prototype the family report and the descendents report.

STUDENT CASE STUDY 5

Western Dental Clinic — Completing the Systems Analysis Phase and Considering Alternative Tools

Introduction

The Western Dental Clinic requirements that Jim Archer gathered were described at the end of Chapter 4. The following student assignments are based on those same requirements.

Student Assignments

1. If you have a CASE diagramming tool available for preparing data flow diagrams, use the tool to create the context diagram, diagram 0, and the lower-level diagrams for the Western Dental Clinic system. If the CASE diagramming tool is integrated with a data dictionary, use the tool to document all data stores and the data elements for these data stores.

2. If you have access to software tools for prototyping, prototype two of the Western Dental Clinic reports.

3. Write the management summary and information systems background portions of the system requirements document for the Western Dental Clinic system.

PHASE 3

Systems Design

6.4 CHAPTER 6: OUTPUT DESIGN

Systems de

■ Logical d

The logic
relation
all th
an

CHAPTER

Output Design

Objectives

You will have mastered the material in this chapter when you can:

- Explain the differences between logical and physical design
- List and describe the major activities of the systems design phase
- Discuss the goals and guidelines for systems design
- Define and describe the different classifications of output reports
- Design and size a printed report
- Design a screen report
- Explain what methods are used for output control

Introduction

This is the first of five chapters devoted to the third phase of the systems development life cycle: systems design. During the systems design phase, we design an information system that satisfies the requirements that were specified in the system requirements document during the systems analysis phase.

We begin this chapter with an overview of systems design and then follow with general guidelines and tips for designing information systems. Next, we discuss design techniques and strategies for the output component of an information system; specifically, we examine design techniques and strategies for printed reports, screen output, and other systems outputs. We conclude the chapter with a discussion of the critical topic of output control and an examination of automated output design tools.

...sign overview

...esign and physical design

The **...al design** of an information system defines the logical or conceptual ...ships among the components of the information system. A logical design defines ...e input available to the system, all the outputs that must be produced by the system, ...ll all the processes that must be performed to meet the defined system requirements *...dependent of how they will be physically accomplished*. That is, a logical design does *not* address the actual methods of implementation. Part of the logical design for a customer information system, for example, would describe all the customer data items that must be input to the system, specify that the customer data be sorted in customer number order, and describe all the information to be output in customer number order to a customer status report. The physical process of inputting customer data, the physical method used to sort that data, the physical process of creating the report, and the exact format of the report are *not* of concern to the logical design. Because it defines the necessary, or *essential*, requirements of an information system, we also refer to the logical design as the **essential model** of an information system.

In contrast, the **physical design** of an information system is concerned with the actual physical implementation of the logical design. The physical design of an information system is built on the system's logical design and describes the actual implementation of all the components of the information system. In a customer information system, for example, the physical design describes the actual processes of inputting, verifying, and storing the data, the physical layout of the file on disk, the sorting procedure, the precise format of the report, and so on.

Another way to describe the differences between logical and physical design is to say that logical design is concerned with *what* is required, whereas physical design is concerned with *how* the requirements are satisfied. For a logical design, you determine what data will be input to the system, what processes must be performed, what information will be output, and what constraints must be met. The physical design describes how the data is input, how it is stored and processed, how the output is produced, and how the constraints are met.

The logical design of an information system is completed during the systems analysis phase. During that second phase of the systems development life cycle, you investigate, determine, analyze, organize, and document all the logical input, processing, and output requirements and the constraints of the information system. The third phase of the SDLC, systems design, is when you complete the physical design of the information system.

■ Phase iterations

The phases in the systems development life cycle are sometimes said to be iterative. Many information systems professionals say that you iterate between analysis and design, repeating and refining, until an effective physical design is developed. Planned iteration between phases is *not* a wise strategy. A systems analyst should never expect to return to a previous phase. Such a mind-set all too easily leads to the attitude, "I can do an incomplete job during this phase because I'll be iterating back through it again anyway."

During the systems design phase you might have to return to a previous phase only in certain circumstances. You would need to return to fact-finding, for example, if you discovered that a required fact was overlooked, if the end users have new or revised facts to offer, or if legal or governmental rules change. You might also have to return to requirements analysis if design tradeoffs and adjustments make a reassessment of the analyzed system necessary. The possibility for phase iteration, however, is not an excuse for sloppy or incomplete work in the first place.

During the systems design phase a good mental attitude to have is to picture yourself locked in a room away from all end user contact with just the system requirements document available to provide facts about the information system. This design scenario forces you to conduct your systems analysis carefully and completely.

■ Systems design activities

In Chapter 1, we defined an information system and showed a simple figure illustrating the components of an information system. We are now ready to refine that definition. Figure 6-1 again illustrates the information system components of data, data stores, people, procedures, hardware, software, and information. In addition, we now show the processing components interacting with one another. These interrelationships are significant to the design process.

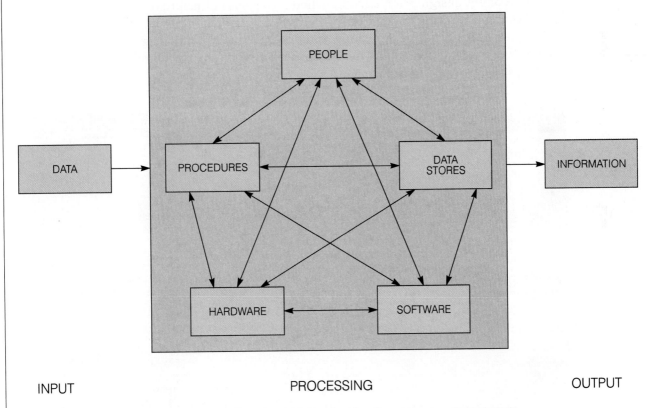

INPUT　　　　　　　　　　　　PROCESSING　　　　　　　　　　　　OUTPUT

Figure 6-1 Information system model illustrating interactions among processing components.

Because the components of an information system are so interdependent, you first must thoroughly understand the entire logical design before beginning the physical design of any one component. As the first step in systems design, therefore, you should review the system requirements document prepared at the end of the systems analysis phase. Two common situations make such a review absolutely necessary. First, the systems analyst or analysts assigned to systems design might not have participated in the systems analysis; this is especially common in large organizations. Second, weeks or months might have passed between the conclusion of systems analysis and the start of systems design; even a systems analyst involved in both phases might have worked on other projects in the interim.

Once you have reviewed the system requirements, you are ready to begin the actual design process. With such an interdependence of components, you might think that there is no good place to start. Or you might think that the design process could begin equally well with any one of the components. Is there a logical method of attack, a best way to progress through the systems design process?

Of all the components of an information system, the output requirements best define the system. The system outputs tell you what the information system must produce and, thus, are often said to *drive* the system definition. You will usually be most effective at systems design, therefore, if you begin with output design.

Because the components of an information system interact with one another, the design process is not a series of well-defined, nonoverlapping steps; that is, you cannot completely finish output design before you begin to design one of the other information system components. The decisions you make in your output design affect the design of other components, and vice versa. In general, the design process begins with the output, progresses to input, then data stores (files and databases), systems processing, and software. Component design is not accomplished as a series of isolated steps, however; you will find yourself working concurrently on more than one component.

As the final systems design steps, you prepare the system design specification report and present your results. These steps and all the other systems design activities are listed and described in Figure 6-2.

Step	Activity	Description
1	Review the system requirements	Become thoroughly familiar with the complete logical design.
2	Design the system	
	■ Design the systems output	Design the physical layout for each systems output and define the physical disposition and handling of the output.
	■ Design the systems input	Determine how the data will be input to the system, design source documents for capturing the data, design the input data records, and design audit trails and system security measures.
	■ Design the systems files and databases	Design the systems data stores by considering organization, access, storage, and usage requirements.
	■ Design the systems processing	Design the processing that will be accomplished by systems software and utilities, as well as any processing steps that will be performed by people.
	■ Design the software	Design the program software
3	Present the systems design	Create the system design specification document, in which you detail the complete proposed systems design, the anticipated benefits of the system, and the estimated development and implementation costs of the design. Also give presentations of the results of this phase.

Figure 6-2 Design phase activites.

General guidelines for systems design

The goal of the systems design effort is to design an information system that will be effective, reliable, and maintainable. To be effective, the system must satisfy the defined requirements and meet the specified constraints. But a system that is not used cannot be effective. Even more importantly then, an effective system is one that the end users accept and actually use.

The reliability of an information system relates to how the system reacts to errors, whether they are input data errors, processing errors, hardware failures, or human mistakes. One approach to reliability is to prevent all errors from even occurring. This is a very expensive, complex approach that is most likely doomed to failure. No system can be completely foolproof! A more realistic approach for system reliability is for the system to plan for errors, detect them when they first occur, and allow for their correction.

An information system has maintainability if it is simple, flexible, and easy to modify. No matter how well you have analyzed, designed, and implemented a system, the system will have to be modified. Modifications will be necessary to correct errors in the system, to adapt the system to changing end user requirements, or to enhance the system to add capabilities or to take advantage of changing technology. Your systems design must be flexible enough to accommodate future modifications.

■ Design tips

The following tips will help you design effective, reliable, and maintainable information systems. To make them easier to use, we have classified these tips by end user considerations, data considerations, and processing considerations (Figure 6-3).

Systems Design Tips

End User Considerations

- Consider points where end users interact with the system
- Anticipate future end user needs

Data Considerations

- Enter data where and when it occurs
- Verify data when it is input
- Use automated data-entry methods whenever possible
- Control access for data entry
- Report every instance of entry and change to data
- Enter data only once
- Avoid duplicating data in data stores

Processing Considerations

- Choose the simple solution
- Create independent modules that perform a single function

Figure 6-3 Design tips grouped by end user, data, and processing classifications.

End user considerations You will be faced with many decisions during systems design. At nearly every step of the way, you will have at least two, and often more, viable choices. The one factor that should weigh most heavily in your decision is the effect on the end user. Always keep in mind that you are designing the system for the end user.

Carefully consider any point where the end user will be interacting with the system. Input processes should be well documented, easy to follow, natural to use, and forgiving of end user errors. Outputs should be attractive, easy to understand, and present the appropriate level of detail. **User interfaces**, the mechanisms by which the end user requests specific systems actions and receives responses, must be especially clear and well documented.

Try to anticipate future end user needs. Consider, for example, the one-character employee category code stored in an employee file. The code currently has two valid values: an F indicates a full-time employee, and a P indicates a part-time employee. Depending on the code value, either FULL-TIME or PART-TIME will be printed on the employee detail lines of several different reports. Those two caption values could be programmed, or **hardcoded**, into the report programs. Designing a table file of category codes and captions to be accessed by report programs might be a better choice. The hardcoded solution is more straightforward. But if the company ever added another employee category code, such as an S for job-sharing, a programmer would have to change all the report programs. By designing for the table file, only the file would have to be updated; no report programs that read that file would require updating. This example demonstrates a pure design decision. As long as the number of different category codes remains unchanged, the choice you make will be undetectable by the end user. Pure design decisions such as this do not require end user approval.

Suppose that an end user wants a proposed customer accounting system to provide a screen display of all customers whose balance exceeds $5000. How should you design this feature?

The selection statement in the program that will produce the display could be hardcoded to check customer balances against 5000. This approach is certainly a straightforward, simple solution that exactly meets the end user's specifications. This approach is also an easy solution from the end user's viewpoint; no unnecessary keystrokes or commands are required to produce the specified display. However, if someday the end user needed a display of only those customers whose balance exceeds $7500, the existing system could not provide the desired response. To accommodate this new request, the program would have to be changed, the system retested, and the documentation rewritten.

On the other hand, the program could be designed to produce a report of all customers whose balance exceeds some specific amount input by the end user. Then, every time the end user wants to see the display of balances that exceed $5000, he or she would have to enter the value 5000. This solution requires the end user to work harder to produce the specified display and also adds the potential for keying errors if, for example, he or she typed 4000 instead of 5000. If the end user needed a display of all balances in excess of some other figure, however, that display could be produced without changing the system.

Sometimes a compromise is possible. In this particular example, you could design the program to compare balances against a variable input amount with a displayed default input amount of 5000. If a $5000 cut-off is appropriate, then the end user would press only the ENTER key; for other cut-off figures, the end user would have to enter the desired amount.

The best solution in this situation is probably the one preferred by the end user. Your role is to develop and explain the alternatives, along with their advantages and disadvantages, so the end user can decide among them. ∎

Data Considerations Designing the system for the end user is your primary consideration when you make decisions during systems design. Whenever the end user can be satisfied equally by two or more design approaches, you should then choose the approach that best conforms to the following data-related design tips.

Data should enter the system where and when it occurs, because unnecessary delays can lead to lost or incorrect data. For example, data about shipments received should be entered by employees in the receiving department when the shipments arrive; data about new orders should be entered by sales department personnel when the order is taken.

Data should be verified when it is input. If an erroneous data value is input, the error should be recognized and flagged immediately. The system should allow corrections to errors at any time. Some errors are most easily corrected at entry time while the original source documents are at hand or the customer is on the phone, for example. Other errors might require investigation to determine the correct data value or the cause of the error; therefore, the end users must also be able to correct errors at a later time.

Use automated methods of data entry whenever possible. Receiving department employees in many companies, for example, use hand-held scanners to capture data about merchandise received. Automated data-entry methods such as these reduce input errors and improve employee productivity.

Access for data entry should be controlled, and every instance of entering or changing critical data values should be reported. Most dollar fields and many volume fields are considered to be critical data. Examples of critical volumes include the number of parts scrapped, the number of medical prescriptions dispensed, and the number of insurance premium payments received. Reports that trace the entry and changing of critical data values are called **audit trails** and are essential outputs from an information system.

Data should be entered into an information system only once. Once data has been input correctly, an end user should not have to re-input the data. If data input to the fixed asset system is also needed for the general ledger system, for example, you should design a programmed interface between the two systems so the fixed asset system data can be passed automatically to the general ledger system.

Avoid duplicating data retained in data stores. The address of the supplying vendor, for example, should not be stored with every part in an inventory system file. The address of a vendor who supplies 100 different parts would be repeated 100 times in the data file, which is an unnecessary waste of file storage space. If the vendor's address ever changed, all those 100 part records would have to be changed, which would potentially be a lengthy and costly process. Unnecessary data duplication can also produce inconsistencies. If those 100 stored addresses for the vendor are not identical, how would you know which version is correct?

Processing considerations In addition to considering the end user and the system data in your systems design decisions, you should also take into account the following processing considerations.

Aim for processing simplicity. If you have a choice of two methods, one straightforward and one more sophisticated and complex, choose the simpler solution.

Create independent modules that perform a single function. Such modules are easier to understand, not only when they are being designed, but also when they are written, implemented, and maintained. Independent single-function modules also contribute to greater system operational flexibility. Modifications and enhancements can often be isolated to a single module; therefore, such changes can be made, tested, and documented more easily.

■ Tradeoffs

You will discover that the design tips just presented are often in conflict. In the design process, you must constantly analyze alternatives and weigh tradeoffs. To make a system easier to use, for example, you might have to make the programming requirements more complex. In making a system more flexible, you might make it more difficult to maintain. To satisfy one end user's requirements, you might have to compromise another end user's satisfaction. Measures you take to reduce implementation costs might result in higher operational costs.

Most design tradeoff decisions that you will face can be reduced to the basic conflict of quality versus cost — increasing the quality tends to cause higher costs, while limiting costs tends to cause lowered quality. No simple rule can be applied to such decisions. Each tradeoff must be considered individually, and you must reach a decision that is acceptable to the end users, the information systems staff, and management.

Output design introduction

The primary output media for an information system are printers and screens, but several other media are used to output information (Figure 6-4). The choice of output media is determined during systems analysis and affects your methods and strategies during systems design. Printed output, or **hard copy**, can be produced reasonably fast at a relatively low cost. Some printers can produce more than one copy of the output in a single operation by using multiple-part paper. Printed output can be referenced repeatedly, stored, and saved. For certain uses, such as for documents that must be distributed to employees, customers, or suppliers, or for **turnaround documents**, which are documents that are output from an information system and then later input back into that same system or some other system, printed output is still the predominant output choice. A telephone or other utility bill, for example, is printed by the utility's billing system. When you return the billing statement with your payment, the statement is input through a scanning device into the utility's accounts receivable system to record that the bill has been paid.

Output Device	Description
Printer	Produces text and graphics on paper
Screen	Displays text and graphics on a monitor
Plotter	Produces hard-copy graphic output
Computer Output Microfilm (COM)	Records reduced-size information on sheet film called microfiche or on roll microfilm
Voice	Conveys information to the end user from the computer in the form of speech
Specialized device	Produces output for specialized applications; examples include point-of-sale terminals and ATMs

Figure 6-4 *A summary of the most common output devices.*

Printed output, or **hard copy**, can be produced reasonably fast at a relatively low cost. Some printers can produce more than one copy of the output in a single operation by using multiple-part paper. Printed output can be referenced repeatedly, stored, and saved. For certain uses, such as for documents that must be distributed to employees, customers, or suppliers, or for **turnaround documents**, which are documents that are output from an information system and then later input back into that same system or some other system, printed output is still the predominant output choice. A telephone or other utility bill, for example, is printed by the utility's billing system. When you return the billing statement with your payment, the statement is input through a scanning device into the utility's accounts receivable system to record that the bill has been paid.

Printed output, however, is not without its disadvantages. Costs are associated with the purchase, storage, and eventual disposal of printer paper. Even at best, an end user will experience a delay between the request for and delivery of printed information. Printed information might also be outdated soon after it is generated. An inventory status report, for example, is correct only until a single item is added to or removed from the inventory.

The **screen**, also called the **monitor**, **CRT (cathode ray tube)**, or **VDT (video display terminal)**, is another important output device. On most screens, the output display area is 80 or more characters wide and 24 or more lines deep. Graphic output can also be produced on a screen. Output that is displayed on a screen is called **soft copy**.

Screen output is the most popular output medium because most end users have easy access to monitors; in many organizations, terminals or microcomputers (both having monitors) are installed in most or all offices and other company locations. The greatest advantage of screen output is its timeliness, because the display can reflect the current status of the information. For example, consider an on-line inventory database that is updated every time an item is added to or removed from inventory. A screen display generated on demand reflects actual up-to-the-minute inventory status. The information can also be displayed on a screen more rapidly than it can be printed and distributed. Of course, screen output is appropriate only when hard-copy output is not necessary.

Sometimes the output from one information system becomes input to another information system; that second information system can be either internal or external to the organization. Many companies, for example, send W-2 Wage and Tax Statement records to the IRS on magnetic tape or disk or transmit the records electronically. In recent years, selected tax preparation firms have transmitted data from an individual's tax forms directly to the IRS. Payment information that is output from a company's accounts receivable system is input to the company's general ledger system. The output from a budgeting system might be input to a generalized graphics system. Magnetic tapes, disks, diskettes, and electronic transmission are the media and methods most often used as interfaces between information systems.

Many specialized media are also used for output. Today's cash registers, or **point-of-sale terminals**, are actually computer terminals capable of printing credit card charge slips and detailed register receipts and creating inventory update records. Automated Teller Machines (ATMs) process bank transactions and print deposit slips and cash withdrawal receipts. Computer terminals record and print lottery tickets. Driver's licenses are printed on special-purpose printers. Programmable television sets, VCRs, and microwave ovens produce visual output displays. Output can also be directed to fax or e-mail transmission.

We will now discuss specific considerations for the systems design of outputs from an information system. We first examine the design of printed reports, then screen output, and finally other information system outputs.

Designing printed reports

Reports are classified by their content and by their distribution. The classification by content includes detail, exception, and summary reports, whereas the classification by distribution includes internal and external reports.

■ Reports classified by content

Detail reports   In a **detail report**, one or more lines of output, which are termed **detail lines**, are produced for each record processed. All the fields in the record do not have to be printed, nor do the fields have to be printed in the sequence in which they appear on the record. Some information from every record, however, is printed in a detail report. Figure 6-5 shows a very simple detail report of employee hours for a chain of retail shops. Notice that one detail line is output for each employee. Employee paychecks, which show multiple output lines for each record processed, are another example of a detail report.

```
03/17/97                    EMPLOYEE HOURS                      PAGE 1
                  WEEK ENDING DATE:  03/15/97


   SHOP        EMPLOYEE                    REGULAR   OVERTIME  TOTAL
  NUMBER         NAME          POSITION     HOURS     HOURS    HOURS
  ------------------------------------------------------------------

     8      Andres, Marguertie   Clerk       20.0       0.0    20.0
     8      Bogema, Michelle     Clerk       12.5       0.0    12.5
     8      Davenport, Kim       Asst Mgr    40.0       5.0    45.0
     8      Lemka, Susan         Clerk       32.7       0.0    32.7
     8      Linquist, Linda      Clerk       16.0       0.0    16.0
     8      Ramirez, Rudy        Manager     40.0       8.5    48.5
     8      Ullery, Ruth         Clerk       20.0       0.0    20.0
    11      Byrum, Cheri         Clerk       15.0       0.0    15.0
    11      Byrum, Mary          Clerk       15.0       0.0    15.0
    11      Deal, JoAnn          Clerk        4.8       0.0     4.8
    11      Gadzinski, Barbara   Manager     40.0      10.0    50.0
    11      Huyhn, Loc           Clerk       20.0       0.0    20.0
    11      Schuller, Monica     Clerk       10.0       0.0    10.0
    11      Stites, Carol        Clerk       40.0      12.0    52.0
    11      Thompson, Mark Kay   Asst Mgr    40.0       1.5    41.5
    17      De Martini, Jennifer Clerk       40.0       8.4    48.4
    17      Haff, Lisa           Manager     40.0       0.0    40.0
    17      Rittenbery, Sandra   Clerk       40.0      11.0    51.0
    17      Wyer, Elizabeth      Clerk       20.0       0.0    20.0
    17      Zeigler, Cecille     Clerk       32.0       0.0    32.0
```

Figure 6-5 *A simple detail report. One line of output is printed for each employee.*

Detail reports should include appropriate totals for numeric fields. End users need totals for control purposes and for balancing the computer-generated reports with the accounting records. In the report in Figure 6-5, for example, grand totals of regular hours, overtime hours, and total hours for all the employees should be calculated and printed. In addition, subtotals of those fields for each shop are appropriate. Figure 6-6 shows this same detail report but with subtotal and grand total lines added. In this example, the shop number field is called a **control field**, which is a field that controls the output. Notice that the detail lines are printed in shop number sequence; thus, shop number is said to control, or order, the output. When the value of a control field changes, a **control break** is said to have occurred. Special action occurs when there is a control break. Most often, the action includes printing subtotals. The detail report shown in Figure 6-6 is, therefore, called a **control-break report**.

```
03/17/97                 EMPLOYEE HOURS                    PAGE 1
                    WEEK ENDING DATE:  03/15/97

     SHOP         EMPLOYEE                   REGULAR   OVERTIME  TOTAL
    NUMBER          NAME        POSITION      HOURS     HOURS    HOURS

       8      Andres, Marguertie  Clerk        20.0      0.0     20.0
       8      Bogema, Michelle    Clerk        12.5      0.0     12.5
       8      Davenport, Kim      Asst Mgr     40.0      5.0     45.0
       8      Lemka, Susan        Clerk        32.7      0.0     32.7
       8      Linquist, Linda     Clerk        16.0      0.0     16.0
       8      Ramirez, Rudy       Manager      40.0      8.5     48.5
       8      Ullery, Ruth        Clerk        20.0      0.0     20.0
                                               -----     -----    -----
                   SHOP 8 TOTALS:             181.2     13.5    194.7

      11      Byrum, Cheri        Clerk        15.0      0.0     15.0
      11      Byrum, Mary         Clerk        15.0      0.0     15.0
      11      Deal, JoAnn         Clerk         4.8      0.0      4.8
      11      Gadzinski, Barbara  Manager      40.0     10.0     50.0
      11      Huyhn, Loc          Clerk        20.0      0.0     20.0
      11      Schuller, Monica    Clerk        10.0      0.0     10.0
      11      Stites, Carol       Clerk        40.0     12.0     52.0
      11      Thompson, Mark Kay  Asst Mgr     40.0      1.5     41.5
                                               -----     -----    -----
                  SHOP 11 TOTALS:             184.8     23.5    208.3

      17      De Martini, Jennifer Clerk       40.0      8.4     48.4
      17      Haff, Lisa          Manager      40.0      0.0     40.0
      17      Rittenbery, Sandra  Clerk        40.0     11.0     51.0
      17      Wyer, Elizabeth     Clerk        20.0      0.0     20.0
      17      Zeigler, Cecille    Clerk        32.0      0.0     32.0
                                               -----     -----    -----
                  SHOP 17 TOTALS:             172.0     19.4    191.4
                                               =====     =====    =====

                   GRAND TOTALS:              538.0     56.4    594.4
```

Figure 6-6 A detail report with control breaks. Subtotals and grand totals of appropriate numeric fields are printed.

A detail report can be quite voluminous. Consider, for example, a detail report of all parts in inventory for a large wholesale firm. If the firm stocks 3000 parts, then 3000 detail lines would be printed; the report would span more than fifty printed pages. An end user who uses the report to track parts in low supply would have to wade through 3000 detail lines in order to find the critical parts. In this case, a report which listed only the parts in low supply would be easier to work with; such a report is called an exception report.

Exception reports An **exception** report shows only those records that satisfy a specific, exceptional condition. An exception report is appropriate when the end user has no need to know all the detail used to produce the report. Exception reports are especially useful when the end user must take action only if a particular condition exists. A delinquency report that lists only those customers whose accounts are past due, and an error report that lists data entered incorrectly are typical exception report applications. Another common example is a report of only those employees who have worked overtime. Figure 6-7 shows such an exception report for our retail shop example.

```
03/17/97                    OVERTIME REPORT                    PAGE 1
                    WEEK ENDING DATE:  03/15/97


       SHOP                      EMPLOYEE            OVERTIME
       NUMBER     POSITION         NAME                HOURS
       - - - - - - - - - - - - - - - - - - - - - - - - - - - - - -
         8        Asst Mgr     Davenport, Kim           5.0
                  Manager      Ramirez, Rudy            8.5
                                                       -----
                                          SHOP TOTAL:  13.5

         11       Manager      Gadzinski, Barbara       10.0
                  Clerk        Stites, Carol            12.0
                  Asst Mgr     Thompson, Mary Kay        1.5
                                                       -----
                                          SHOP TOTAL:  23.5

         17       Clerk        De Martini, Jennifer      8.4
                  Clerk        Rittenbery, Sandra       11.0
                                                       -----
                                          SHOP TOTAL:  19.4
                                                       -----

                                                       -----
                                         GRAND TOTAL:  56.4
```

Figure 6-7 *An exception report. Only those employees who have worked overtime are included in the report.*

Summary reports Upper level managers are often concerned only with totals and do not need or want to see all the supporting detail. In these cases, a summary report is appropriate. In a **summary report**, only totals are printed. The marketing vice president, for example, might need to know the total sales for the period for each sales representative but would not want a detail report listing every sale each sales representative has made. Similarly, the personnel manager might need to know the total regular and overtime hours worked by employees in each shop but would not be interested in the number of hours each individual employee worked. For the personnel manager, a summary report, such as the one shown in Figure 6-8, is most useful. In general, the higher in the organization a report is directed, the more condensed and summarized the report should be.

■ Reports classified by distribution

In addition to classifying reports by the level of detail shown, we can classify a report by where it is distributed.

Internal reports **Internal reports** are distributed and used within the organization and are rarely seen by anyone who is not an employee of the organization. The reports shown previously in Figures 6-6 through 6-8 are all internal reports.

```
03/17/97              EMPLOYEE HOURS SUMMARY              PAGE 1
                   WEEK ENDING DATE:  03/15/97

                 SHOP    REGULAR   OVERTIME   TOTAL
                NUMBER    HOURS      HOURS     HOURS
                --------------------------------------
                   8      181.2      13.5     194.7

                  11      184.8      23.5     208.3

                  17      172.0      19.4     191.4
                         -------    ------    ------
                TOTALS:   538.0      56.4     594.4
```

Figure 6-8 A summary report. Only the subtotal and grand total lines are included in the report.

When you design an internal report, you are concerned about producing a useful report at a low cost. Internal reports are usually printed on **stock paper**, which is blank, single-ply, standard-sized, continuous-form paper. Not only is stock paper less expensive than other types of printer paper, it also does not require an operator's time to stop the printer to load and align special paper.

External reports **External reports** are received and used by people outside the organization. Statements, invoices, governmental tax reports, company checks, employee paychecks, and mailing labels are commonly produced external reports.

External reports are usually prepared on **specialty forms**, which include all types of printing paper other than stock paper; that is, any printer paper that is a size other than standard size, is not single-ply, is preprinted with information of some type, or any combination of these characteristics is considered a specialty form. Specialty forms are more expensive than stock paper. Also, an additional cost is associated with using any type of specialty form: the time required to load and unload the form in the printer. Every time specialty paper is used, a computer operator must stop the printer, remove the stock paper, insert and align the specialty forms, and restart the printer. When the printing is completed, an operator must reverse the entire process to reload the printer with stock paper. Multiple-part paper also requires an additional step to physically separate the various plies after printing. All these activities require an operator's time, and, thus, cost money.

Because external reports are distributed outside the organization, it is important to the organization's public image that such reports be attractive and appear official and professional. Invoices produced on special invoice forms that are preprinted with the company's logo and other information look more official than would those printed on plain paper; the preprinted invoice form makes the company appear more permanent and professional. Most organizations believe that the benefits of using special preprinted invoice forms outweigh all the associated costs. Figure 6-9 shows a typical preprinted invoice form.

Sometimes the external recipient places a requirement on the format and paper used for the report. Bank checks, such as the sample paycheck shown in Figure 6-10, must conform to banking industry standards, for example. Many governmental reports must be produced on specialty forms designed for specific purposes.

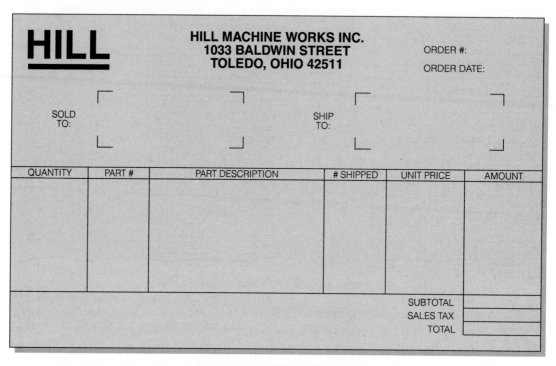

Figure 6-9 A sample preprinted invoice.

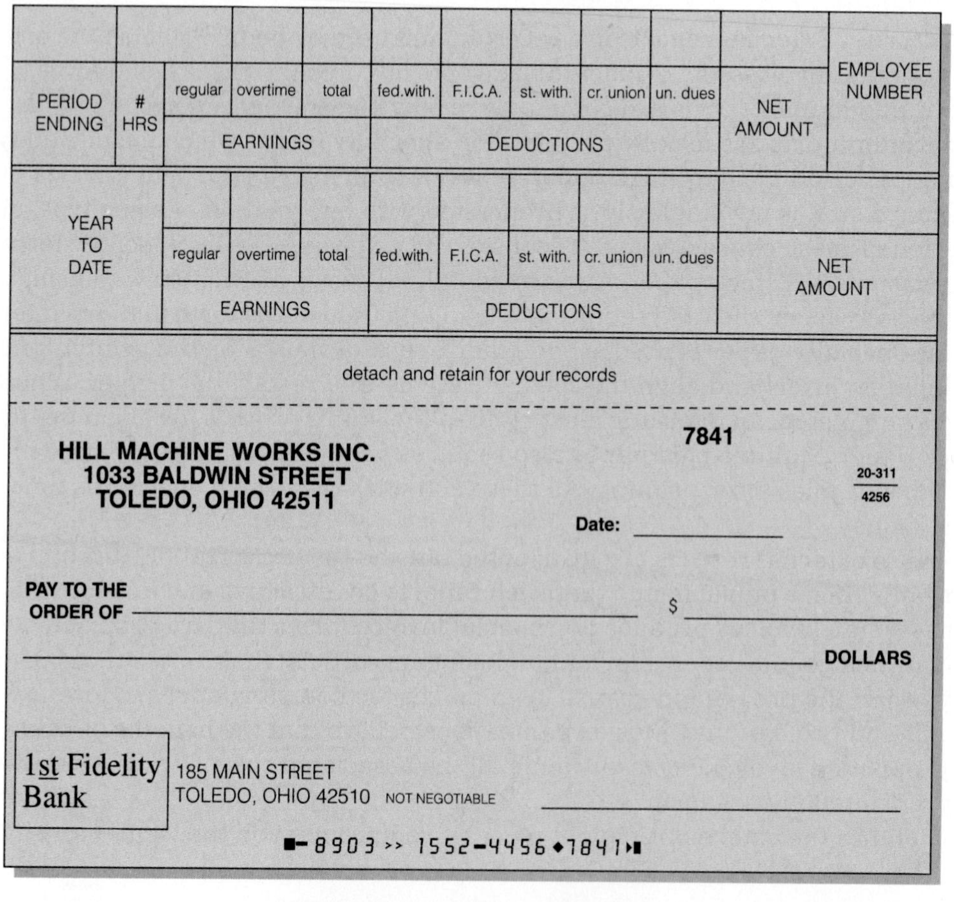

Figure 6-10 A sample preprinted paycheck.

Mailing labels are often computer-printed on special mailing label forms. These forms are continuous sheets to which the gummed mailing labels are attached. From one to four labels may appear across a sheet. Some organizations use special labels that are preprinted with the company logo and other information, as shown in Figure 6-11; other organizations use simple, blank mailing labels. In either case, there are costs associated with purchasing and printing such mailing labels; these costs, however, are more than offset by the benefits of their appearance, ease of use, accuracy, and minimal clerical involvement.

Figure 6-11 *A sample preprinted mailing label form. This form is called a 2-up form, because there are two labels across the form.*

Multiple-part paper is considered to be a specialty form because it is not the paper normally loaded in the printer, and, therefore, has an associated load/unload cost. Some types of multiple-part paper are otherwise standard; that is, the paper is standard-sized and blank. This paper, although technically a specialty form, is used primarily for making multiple copies of internal reports.

■ Report design considerations

To design the actual physical format of a printed report, you use a printer spacing chart, such as the one shown in Figure 6-12. **Printer spacing charts** provide a standardized method for visually documenting a report format; programmers use them when writing the program to produce the report.

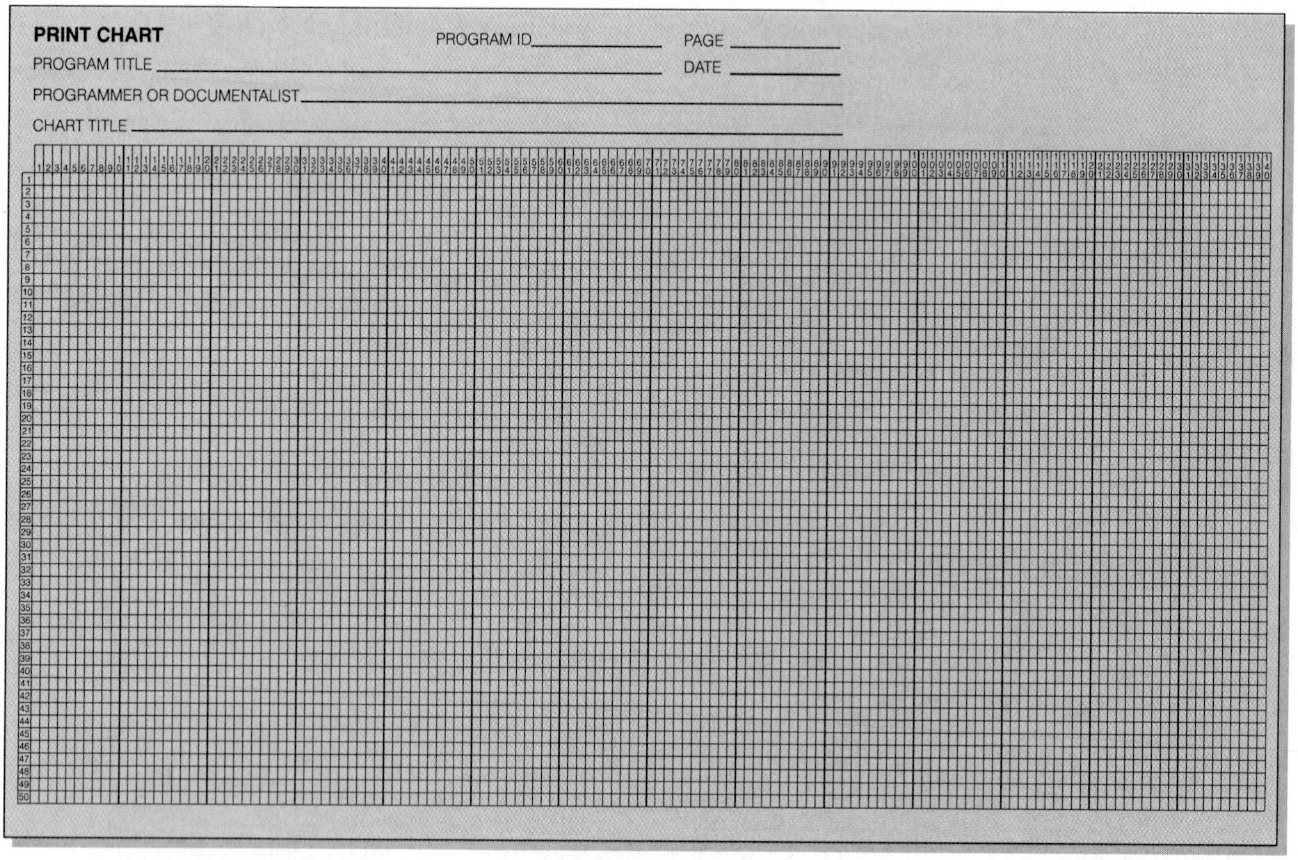

PRINT CHART

PROGRAM ID_____ PAGE _____

PROGRAM TITLE _____ DATE _____

PROGRAMMER OR DOCUMENTALIST_____

CHART TITLE _____

Figure 6-12 A printer spacing chart.

A printer spacing chart is marked off into rows and columns to represent the available lines and print positions, respectively, on a single page of printer paper. Most high-speed printers provide up to 132 print positions per line. Therefore, printer spacing charts include at least that many positions. Some printers, however, allow more or fewer print positions per line and more or fewer lines per page. It is important to know the characteristics of the printer that will be used to produce the report so that you design the report within the printer limits.

To design a report, you select the print positions on the printer spacing chart where a specific field will be printed. Then, you indicate the presence of the field in those positions by marking the corresponding boxes with appropriate indicators. You specify constant or unchanging information, such as titles and headings, by entering them on the printer spacing chart exactly as they will appear on the printed page. In Figure 6-13, the constant headings LAST NAME, FIRST NAME, AGE, and BIRTH DATE appear on the first print line.

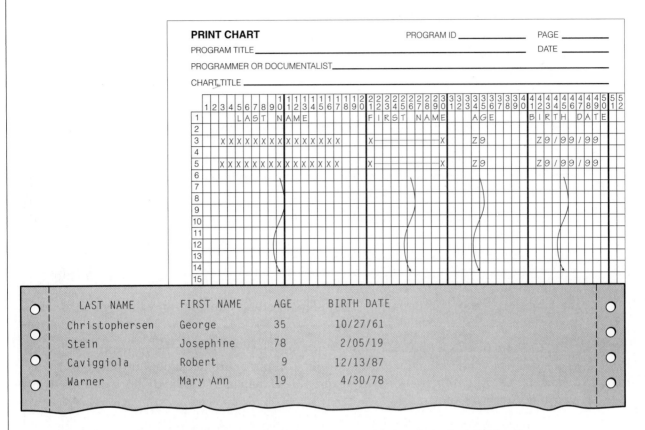

Figure 6-13 *A printer spacing chart and report sample with both constant and variable information.*

You indicate print positions for variable, or changing, information by writing in a format specifier. You most often use COBOL or BASIC format specifications because they provide an excellent means for documenting output printing requirements and maximum field sizes. The third and fifth lines on the printer spacing chart in Figure 6-13 illustrate variable output specifications for the detail lines on the report. The first output field on line 3 is the last name, which is a 15-character field. The format specification for that field is shown simply as XXXXXXXXXXXXXXX. The second output field, first name, is a 10-character field. Its format specification could have been written as XXXXXXXXXX; however, you may also write long alphanumeric formats by marking the first and last positions with an X and connecting the Xs with a line. Hence, you can indicate XXXXXXXXXX as X————X.

The third field to be printed on the detail line is age, a 2-digit field. In Figure 6-13, you can see the format is written as Z9 to indicate that any leading zero in the age is to be suppressed. The fourth field is birth date, which is a 6-digit field. Here the format you want is Z9/99/99.

Notice that the specification for the fifth line is identical to that for the third line. The detail line specification was repeated to indicate the desired line spacing. Because the fourth line was left blank, you are telling the programmer that the output detail lines are to be double-spaced. If single-spacing was intended, the two detail line specifications would appear on consecutive lines.

The wavy vertical lines drawn under each output field on the fifth line of the printer spacing chart in Figure 6-13 indicate that detail line output is to continue, using the same format. Thus, a third detail line with the same format specifications would be printed on line 7 of the report, a fourth on line 9, and so on.

Remember always to show the first and second detail lines on a printer spacing chart to explicitly illustrate line spacing; you should also show the last detail line on the chart, especially when other output, such as totals, will follow that last detail line. For reports that will span multiple pages, you should prepare a printer spacing chart for subsequent pages, if they are in any way different from the first report page.

Stock paper reports You should follow several principles when designing a stock paper report. Some of these principles are functional, serving to make the report easier to use. Other principles relate to aesthetics, or how the report looks. Both functional and aesthetic principles are important; together they help make a stock paper report readable and usable.

Page heading lines. Because stock paper is blank, the program that produces the report must generate all the necessary title and heading lines. Every page of a stock paper report should include the report title, the page number, and the date the report was produced; if the report will be produced more than once a day, the time should also appear on each page. This page heading information uniquely identifies the report. If the pages of a report get separated, the page heading information will be valuable for correctly reassembling the report.

Column heading lines. Column headings identify the data items printed on detail lines; every printed field must be identified. Column headings should be short and descriptive. Avoid abbreviations, however, unless they are standard abbreviations whose meanings are well known.

Column heading alignment. Figure 6-14 shows several column heading alignment options. Example 1, with left-justified column headings, is generally unsatisfactory for numeric fields; the amount 1.25, for example, would print entirely to the right of the AMOUNT heading. Example 2, with right-justified headings, is generally unsatisfactory for alphanumeric fields; none of the nonblank characters in a short name would print under any part of the NAME heading. Centering headings over maximum field widths, as shown in Example 3, is not ideal when many of the actual values are smaller (shorter) than maximum. Most report designers prefer Example 4, centering headings over average field widths, or Example 5, left-justifying headings over alphanumeric fields and right-justifying over numeric fields. Some designers use a combination of the two techniques by centering headings for alphanumeric fields over average field widths, right-justifying headings over shorter numeric fields, and centering headings over average widths for larger numeric fields.

Spacing between columns. Columns of information should not be printed too close to one another; a crowded report is difficult to read. Neither should you allow too much blank space between columns; large gaps make it difficult for the eye to follow along a line. Placing two or three positions between columns (or column headings) is adequate without being excessive.

Example 1: Column headings are left-justified over maximum field widths.

Example 2: Column headings are right-justified over maximum field widths.

Example 3: Column headings are centered over maximum field widths.

Example 4: Column headings are centered over average field widths.

Example 5: Column headings are left-justified over alphanumeric fields and right-justified over numeric fields.

```
NAME                                    NUMBER      AMOUNT
XXXXXXXXXXXXXXXXXXXXXXXX                 ZZZ9     ZZZ,ZZ9.99


                                NAME   NUMBER      AMOUNT
XXXXXXXXXXXXXXXXXXXXXXXX                 ZZZ9     ZZZ,ZZ9.99


             NAME                      NUMBER      AMOUNT
XXXXXXXXXXXXXXXXXXXXXXXX                 ZZZ9     ZZZ,ZZ9.99


          NAME                         NUMBER      AMOUNT
XXXXXXXXXXXXXXXXXXXXXXXX                 ZZZ9     ZZZ,ZZ9.99


NAME                                   NUMBER      AMOUNT
XXXXXXXXXXXXXXXXXXXXXXXX                 ZZZ9     ZZZ,ZZ9.99
```

Figure 6-14 Column heading alignment options.

TRADE OFF

Sometimes not enough print positions are available across the printer page for the optimal design of a printed report. Is there one best solution for designing layouts for these too-wide reports?

When there are adequate positions to print all the detail values, but only enough room for overly abbreviated, cryptic column headings, you can print a legend at the bottom of each page that explains the column headings. This solution, which typically requires that two or three lines of every page be reserved for the legend, does not significantly add to the total report size.

When there is adequate width for the detail values, but not enough room for subtotal or grand total lines, you can print the subtotals and totals on two or more lines. For example, consider an item report that includes sales figures for each of twelve months on every detail line. There is just enough room on a detail line to fit the three-digit monthly sales detail values. How should you print the monthly item class subtotals and the grand totals, each of which could be as large as five digits? You could use the entire page width and as many lines as you need to present the subtotals (or totals), captioning each field individually, such as JAN TOTAL: ZZ,ZZ9, FEB TOTAL: ZZ,ZZ9, and so on (Figure 6-15a on the next page). Or, you could use two lines for the subtotals and totals, printing the values for the odd-numbered months on one line and the values for the even-num-

bered months on a second line (Figure 6-15b on page 6.23).

In the situations just described, the space problem actually involved only heading or footing lines. What do you do when there are not enough positions on one line to print all the detail values? Unfortunately, there is no simple solution for this situation. One possible solution (Figure 6-16a on page 6.23) is to split the report into two or more versions: each report version would include only as many detail values as would fit on a single line; every detail value would appear on at least one version of the report. The advantage of this solution is that each report version can be attractive and readable. If the report has multiple end users, perhaps a report version can be tailored for each end user. This solution, however, might be unacceptable to an end user who needs most or all of the information; that end user would have to shuffle through multiple report listings to find all the information for one item. Another potential disadvantage of this solution arises because those fields that uniquely identify a detail line must be repeated on every report version; when the identifying fields are lengthy and leave little room for printing other detail values, several report versions might be required just to print all the other detail fields. The resulting total print volume could, therefore, be excessive.

A second potential solution (Figure 6-16b on page 6.23) is to print all the information in a single report, using two or more single-spaced print lines for each detail. This solution requires that you stack column headings for all the detail lines at the top of each page, and, to aid readability, you must print a blank line between each detail set. The advantage of this solution is that a single report contains all the information needed by any end user. The primary disadvantage of this solution is that it is very difficult to design a multiline report that will not confuse an end user. There is one technique you can use for multiline reports that can help reduce confusion and improve readability — whenever possible, stack alphanumeric fields over numeric fields and vice versa. This reduces ambiguity about which field belongs to which column heading printed above it.

A third solution (Figure 6-16c on page 6.24), which also produces a single report, is possible when all the nonidentifying field values will fit on a single line. In that case, a single set of column headings for the nonidentifying fields is printed. Two single-spaced print lines are utilized for each detail. On the first of these lines, the identifying fields are printed with left captions, such as ITEM#: XXXXX   ITEM DESCRIPTION: XXXXXXXXXXXXXXXXXXXX. The rest of the detail values are printed on the second line, aligned under their column headings. To separate detail sets, there must be a blank line between each set. This solution, like the other multiline solution previously described, has the advantage of producing a single report with all the necessary information. Furthermore, unlike the previous solution, the resulting report is rarely confusing or ambiguous. If all the nonidentifying field values do not fit on a single line, however, this solution will not work. When that is the case, you might correct the problem by moving one or more nonidentifying fields (alphanumeric fields work best) to the first print line.

Each of these three solutions has advantages and disadvantages. When you have a report with too much detail for one print line, you should probably try all three design solutions and then determine which solution requires the least printer time and paper and is the most readable by end users. Only by offering the end user a choice can you be certain that the best report design is selected. ■

```
01/15/97                         ITEM SALES ANALYSIS                                    PAGE 1

                          UNIT  SELLING - - - - - - - - - - - MONTHLY SALES - - - - - - - - - - - -  YEARLY
ITEM# ITEM DESCRIPTION    COST   PRICE  JAN FEB MAR APR MAY JUN JUL AUG SEP OCT NOV DEC   TOTAL

218CW CHROME WIDGET              1.23   8.95  241 134 198 180 187 294 295 159 268 352 378 400    3,086
227DS DOUBLE-TWISTED ANGLE STOPPER 11.20 34.80  0  80 270 512 717 732 882 890 735 913 901 879    7,511
       .         .              .         .
       .         .              .         .
297PB PLASTIC BASE                .87   5.98  812 801 813 860 501 981 992 879 899 888 940 979   10,345

     ITEM CLASS SUBTOTALS:   JAN TOTAL: 21,916   APR TOTAL: 24,003   JUL TOTAL: 25,027   OCT TOTAL: 25,897
                             FEB TOTAL: 22,113   MAY TOTAL: 20,880   AUG TOTAL: 23,632   NOV TOTAL: 25,371
                             MAR TOTAL: 24,291   JUN TOTAL: 24,765   SEP TOTAL: 24,111   DEC TOTAL: 24,669

                                                                              YEARLY TOTAL: 286,675
```

Figure 6-15a *A report designed with subtotals and captions printed on multiple lines.*

```
01/15/97                          ITEM SALES ANALYSIS                          PAGE 1

                         UNIT  SELLING - - - - - - - - - - - MONTHLY SALES - - - - - - - - - -  YEARLY
ITEM# ITEM DESCRIPTION     COST  PRICE  JAN FEB MAR APR MAY JUN JUL AUG SEP OCT NOV DEC   TOTAL

218CW CHROME WIDGET        1.23   8.95  241 134 198 180 187 294 295 159 268 352 378 400   3,086
227DS DOUBLE-TWISTED ANGLE STOPPER 11.20 34.80  0  80 270 512 717 732 882 890 735 913 901 879   7,511
             .                          .           .           .           .
             .                          .           .           .           .
             .                          .           .           .           .
297PB PLASTIC BASE          .87   5.98  812 801 813 860 501 981 992 879 899 888 940 979  10,345

         ITEM CLASS SUBTOTALS:       21,916   24,291   20,880   25,027   24,111   25,371  286,675
                                     22,113   24,003   24,765   23,632   25,897   24,669
```

Figure 6-15b *A report designed with subtotals printed on alternating lines without captions.*

```
01/15/97                          ITEM SALES ANALYSIS                          PAGE 1

                         UNIT  SELLING - - - - - - - - - - - MONTHLY SALES - - - - - - - - - -  YEARLY
ITEM# ITEM DESCRIPTION     COST  PRICE  JAN FEB MAR APR MAY JUN JUL AUG SEP OCT NOV DEC   TOTAL

218CW CHROME WIDGET        1.23   8.95  241 134 198 180 187 294 295 159 268 352 378 400   3,086
227DS DOUBLE-TWISTED ANGLE STOPPER 11.20 34.80  0  80 270 512 717 732 882 890 735 913 901 879   7,511
```

```
01/15/97                    ITEM SALES ANALYSIS                   PAGE 1

                         QTY ON    QTY        QTY      QTY ON  UNIT  SELLING
ITEM# ITEM DESCRIPTION     HAND  ALLOCATED  AVAILABLE  ORDER   COST   PRICE

218CW CHROME WIDGET        183       4        179       300   1.23    8.95
227DS DOUBLE-TWISTED ANGLE STOPPER 322  121    201       500  11.20   34.80
```

Figure 6-16a *A report split into two reports because the detail values cannot fit on one print line.*

```
01/15/97                          ITEM SALES ANALYSIS                          PAGE 1

                         UNIT  SELLING
ITEM# ITEM DESCRIPTION     COST  PRICE

  QTY ON    QTY        QTY      QTY ON                 - - - - - - - MONTHLY SALES - - - - - - -  YEARLY
   HAND  ALLOCATED  AVAILABLE  ORDER          JAN FEB MAR APR MAY JUN JUL AUG SEP OCT NOV DEC   TOTAL

218CW CHROME WIDGET        1.23   8.95  241 134 198 180 187 294 295 159 268 352 378 400   3,086
    183       4        179       300
227DS DOUBLE-TWISTED ANGLE STOPPER 11.20 34.80  0  80 270 512 717 732 882 890 735 913 901 879   7,511
    322      121       201       500
```

Figure 6-16b *A report using two lines for each detail with stacked column headings.*

```
01/15/97                        ITEM SALES ANALYSIS                        PAGE 1

 QTY ON    QTY        QTY    QTY ON UNIT SELLING - - - - - - - - - - - MONTHLY SALES - - - - - - - - - - -   YEARLY
   HAND ALLOCATED AVAILABLE  ORDER COST  PRICE  JAN FEB MAR APR MAY JUN JUL AUG SEP OCT NOV DEC   TOTAL
- - - - - - - - - - - - - - - - - - - - - - - - - - - - - - - - - - - - - - - - - - - - - - - - - - - - - - - -
ITEM#:  218CW  ITEM DESCRIPTION:  CHROME WIDGET
    183        4         179    300  1.23   8.95  241 134 198 180 187 294 295 159 268 352 378 400   3,086

ITEM#:  227DS  ITEM DESCRIPTION:  DOUBLE-TWISTED ANGLE STOPPER
    322      121         201    500 11.20  34.80    0  80 270 512 717 732 882 890 735 913 901 879   7,511
```

Figure 6-16c A report using two lines for each detail with captions used for the first line and
a single set of column headings used for the second line.

Order of data items on detail lines. Reports are generally read from left to right and from top to bottom. The order of the items from left to right on a detail line, therefore, should be logical. If one or more fields serve to uniquely identify the detail line, those fields are normally presented first. Logically related items should be grouped. For the report in Figure 6-17, detail lines are output in order by name within shop number, so we have printed the shop number in the leftmost column, followed by the name. Employee position is logically tied to employee name, so we printed employee position next to the name. Finally, the three hours fields are logically related, so they are presented together.

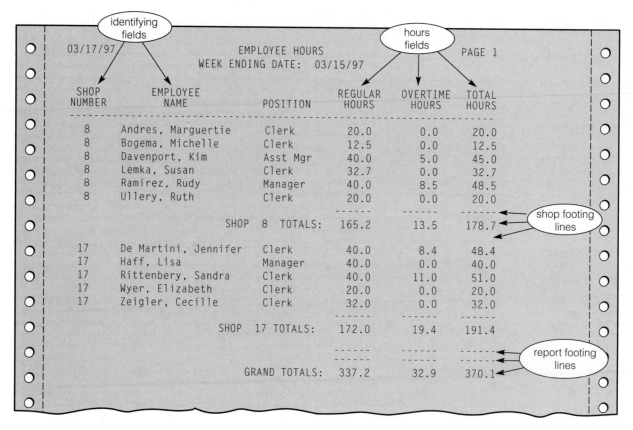

Figure 6-17 A detail report with control breaks. Subtotals and grand totals of
appropriate numeric fields are printed.

Grouping detail lines. If the detail lines are grouped in a meaningful way, such as in a control-break report, the groupings should be visually highlighted in some manner. You might print a special subheading above the first detail line in a group, or you might print a footing after the last detail line in a group. For the report in Figure 6-17, there are three footing lines for each shop. In the first footing line, three sets of hyphens appear under each of the three hours fields; these hyphen sets resemble the lines placed under a column to be totaled, and thus serve as a visual clue to the information printed below them. In the second footing line, the group totals for those three hours fields are printed; to further identify the line as a group total line, the words SHOP nn TOTALS: are also printed. The third group footing line is simply a blank line that serves to visually separate a group from the group that follows it.

Report footing. Every stock paper report that will span more than one page should have a report footing to identify the end of the report. A report footing, together with consecutive page numbers on every page, assures report users that they have a complete report copy. A report footing may include field totals when appropriate, as shown in the report in Figure 6-17. Or the report footing can be as simple as a line saying END OF REPORT.

Improving a report design. The Employee Hours Report in Figure 6-17 has met each of the considerations we have discussed so far, but the report could still be improved. Unnecessary detail information clutters the page, forcing report readers to search for meaningful or special information. Can you see any unnecessary detail that could be eliminated? If the usual situation is that an employee does not work overtime, then nonzero overtime hours should somehow stand out; we can easily accomplish this by not printing the 0.0 when overtime hours are zero. Repeating the same shop number for all employees of a single shop is also unnecessary; the shop number needs to be printed only for the first detail in a group. Finally, most of the employees in a shop are clerks; the managers and assistant managers would stand out more if we did not print Clerk for all the clerks. In Figure 6-18 on the next page, we have made these three changes. The name and position columns were also exchanged to eliminate a large gap between names of clerks and their hours.

Documenting a report design. Figure 6-19 on the next page shows the final printer spacing chart for the report shown in Figure 6-18 on the next page. The detailed analysis document that was prepared during the systems analysis phase and that served as the basis for this report is shown in Figure 6-20 on page 6.27. After a report design is finished and approved, you must document the design details. The final version of the documentation form for this report with the addition of design details is shown in Figure 6-21 on page 6.28.

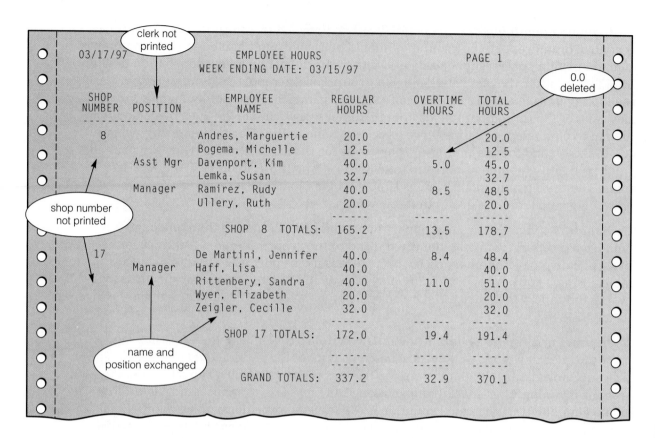

Figure 6-18 *An improved version of the report shown in Figure 6-17 on page 6.24.*

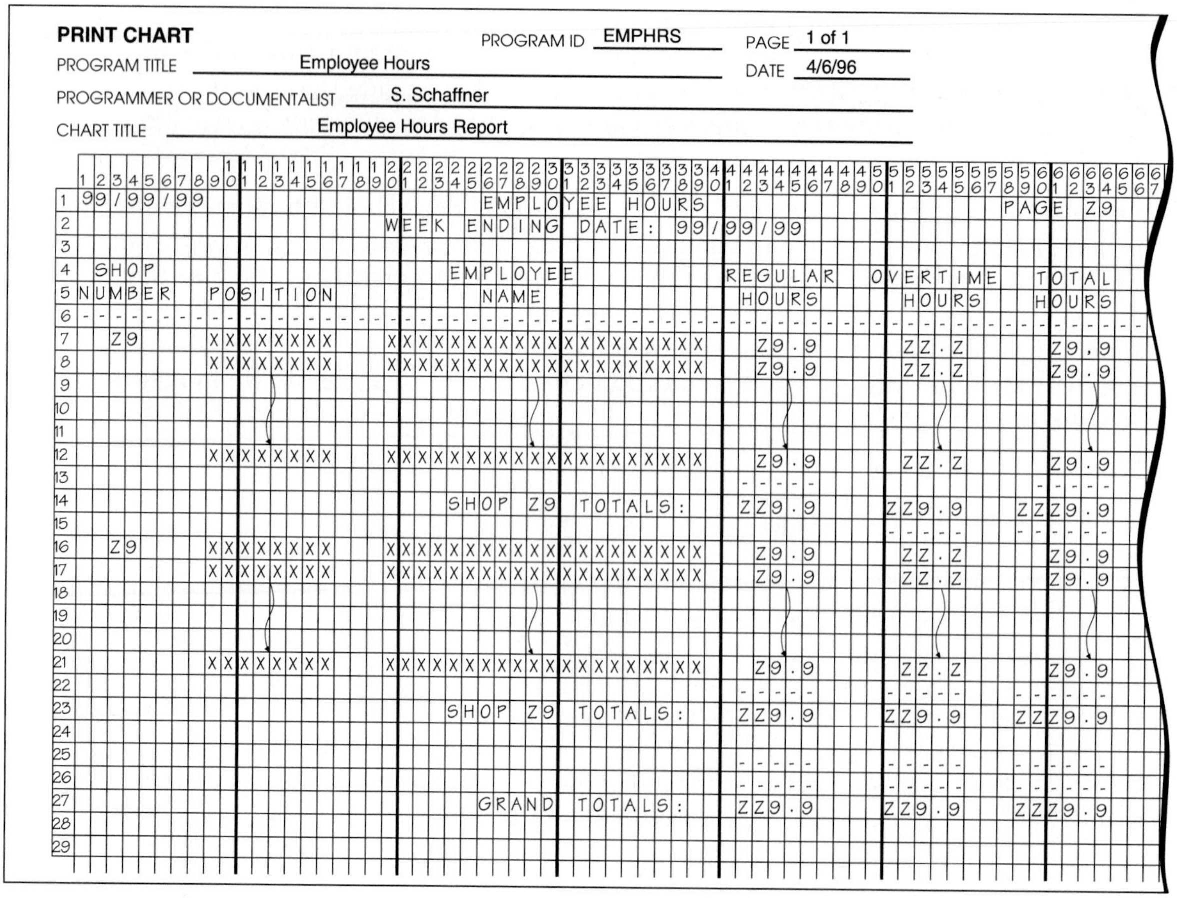

Figure 6-19 *The printer spacing chart for the report shown in Figure 6-18.*

SYSTEM DOCUMENTATION

NAME OF SYSTEM	DATE	PAGE 1 OF 1
Payroll	February 23,1997	

ANALYST	PURPOSE OF DOCUMENTATION
S. Schaffner	Report Analysis-Employee Hours Report

FIELD	FIELD TYPE	FIELD LENGTH
Shop Number	Numeric	2
Employee Position	Alphanumeric	8
Employee Name	Alphanumeric	20
Regular Hours	Numeric	3 (1 decimal position)
Overtime Hours	Numeric	3 (1 decimal position)
Total Hours	Numeric	3 (1 decimal position)

COMMENTS

    Week ending date is printed at the top of the report.
    Detail lines are in order by employee name within shop number.
    Shop totals for regular, overtime and total hours are printed.
    Grand totals for regular, overtime, and totals are printed.

FREQUENCY

    One copy of the report is printed weekly, reporting on the employee hours for the previous week.

DISTRIBUTION

    The report is to be delivered to the director of personnel.

Figure 6-20 The original Report Analysis Form for the Employee Hours Report.

Consistency among reports. When several stock paper reports are produced by a single information system, the reports should be stylistically consistent. For example, date and page number should appear in the same place on all the reports from a system. If one report prints the page number in the upper right-hand corner of each page, while another prints it centered at the bottom of each page, the end user would have to search for page numbers. One report in a system using #, another NO, and a third NUM to abbreviate the word number in headings is inconsistent and unnecessarily confusing. If one system report prints inventory location fields as floor number followed by bin number, then printing bin number followed by floor number on another report in the system is inviting confusion.

SYSTEM DOCUMENTATION

NAME OF SYSTEM	DATE	PAGE 1 OF 1
Payroll	April 3, 1997	

ANALYST	PURPOSE OF DOCUMENTATION
S. Schaffner	Report Analysis-Employee Hours Report

FIELD	FIELD TYPE	FIELD LENGTH
Shop Number	Numeric	2
Employee Position	Alphanumeric	8
Employee Name	Alphanumeric	20
Regular Hours	Numeric	3 (1 decimal position)
Overtime Hours	Numeric	3 (1 decimal position)
Total Hours	Numeric	3 (1 decimal position)

COMMENTS

Week ending date is printed at the top of the report.
Detail lines are in order by employee name within shop number.
Shop totals for regular, overtime, and total hours are printed, identified by Shop Number.
Grand totals for regular, overtime, and total hours are printed.

Shop Number is printed only for the first employee detail line for a shop and for the
    first employee detail line on a page.

Employee Position is printed only for nonclerks. If Employee Position is equal to "Clerk   ",
    eight blank characters are printed.

Only nonzero Overtime Hours are printed. If Overtime Hours is equal to 0.0, four blank
    characters are printed.

The report is printed on single-ply, standard white stock paper

FREQUENCY
    The report is printed weekly on the first working day of the week or before 10:00 a.m. on
        the second working day of the week.

DISTRIBUTION
    The report is to be delivered to the director of personnel no later than 11:00 a.m. of the
        second working day of each week.

ATTACHMENTS
    Printer spacing chart and mock-up report are attached.

Figure 6-21 *The final Report Analysis Form for the Employee Hours Report.*

Specialty form reports   Many of the design principles for stock paper reports also apply to specialty form reports. In fact, designing reports to be produced on multiple-part paper that is otherwise standard is exactly like designing a stock paper report. For reports produced on preprinted or special-sized forms, you need to apply some additional and some different design considerations. For example, unchanging title or heading information is usually not printed. That information either has been preprinted, as in bank checks, invoices, and customized mailing labels, or is not necessary, as in blank mailing labels.

Specialty form output consists of detail lines and, in some cases, subtotal and total lines. You can use a printer spacing chart to indicate the format and positioning of output fields on specialty forms, just as for stock paper reports. You would first draw the outline of the form on the chart, then place the preprinted information, if any, in the proper positions. You then indicate the variable information to be printed on the chart in the same manner as you do for stock paper reports. For example, Figure 6-22 shows a printer spacing chart for the preprinted invoice shown in Figure 6-9 on page 6.16. A systems analyst drew the form outline and then filled in the logo, title, and heading information, exactly as they appear on the form. Variable output indicators, in the form of format specifications, were then placed on the chart in the appropriate positions.

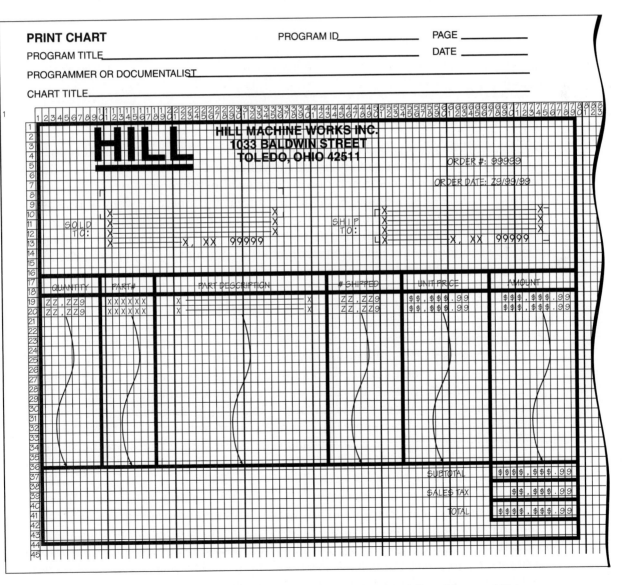

Figure 6-22 The printer spacing chart for the preprinted invoices shown in Figure 6-9 on page 6.16.

In the Figure 6-22 example, the systems analyst was working with a preprinted form that had already been designed. This will be the case if you are designing reports for standard forms, such as bank checks, government forms, and so on. You could also have a predesigned preprinted form when you are enhancing or replacing an existing information system; preprinted forms used in the original system might also be usable in the new system. Sometimes, however, you will be designing a new preprinted form at the same time as you are designing the variable output layout.

Many of the functional and aesthetic design principles described for stock paper reports also apply to designing preprinted forms. You should label all fields with identifiers that are short but descriptive. You should avoid the use of nonstandard abbreviations. Allow adequate, but not excessive, spacing between columns for readability. The placement and order of printed fields should be logical. Clearly identify totals.

When you are designing a preprinted form, you will want to work closely with representatives from the forms vendor or printer. The representatives can provide valuable advice on paper sizes, type styles and sizes, paper and ink colors, field placement, and so on. Your goal is to design a form that is attractive, readable, and useful without being excessively expensive. In some cases, the forms printer might offer a standard form that is appropriate. You might be able to use a standard invoice form, for example, on which your company logo can be printed; such a form is likely to be less expensive than a completely customized form.

■ Report volume calculations

During the systems analysis phase, you estimated the size of every printed report. Systems analysts and management use these volume calculations to decide if additional printers must be purchased. In addition, estimates of print volume are necessary for efficient and realistic scheduling of print operations, for timely delivery of finished reports, and for accurate estimations of paper and storage requirements. The more accurate those volume estimations, the better. When you have completely designed a report, you can then more accurately estimate the length of the report and the time it takes to print the report.

As an example, consider the report in Figure 6-18 on page 6.26. Assume that this company has a total of 380 employees in six shops. The stock paper used on the printer that will produce the report has 66 lines per page. Six of those lines are reserved for top and bottom margins, leaving room for 60 printed lines per page. In this report, every page begins with six lines of heading information. This leaves 54 lines per page available for printing employee detail lines, shop footing lines, and grand total footing lines.

Because there are 380 employees, we will print 380 detail lines. Each of the six shops has three footing lines, for a total of 18 shop footing lines. Finally, the grand total requires an additional three lines. The complete report will include 401 detail and total lines. At 54 lines per page, the report would require 7.4 pages. Therefore, our final estimate for the paper requirements for this weekly report is eight printer pages a week.

We can also estimate how long it will take to print the report. Assume that the report is to be printed on a line printer with a maximum output rate of 2400 lines per minute. The printer, however, will not always be printing at top speed; the time required to eject to a new page is just one of the factors that reduces effective printer speed. Assume that the printer's effective speed has been estimated at 2000 lines per minute. Our report includes 380 detail lines, 12 *printed* shop footing lines, 3 grand total lines, and 40 *printed* page and heading lines. That totals to 435 lines that are actually printed. Notice that blank lines are not included in this calculation. Finally, we calculate that printing 435 lines at 2000 lines per minute requires 0. 2175 minutes, or approximately 13 seconds to print. Our best estimate for the report print time, therefore, is approximately 13 seconds. Both calculations for this report are detailed in Figure 6-23.

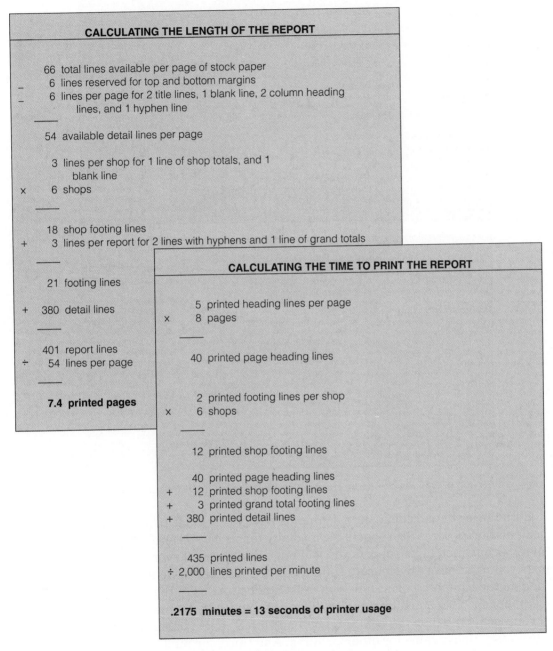

CALCULATING THE LENGTH OF THE REPORT

```
     66  total lines available per page of stock paper
  −   6  lines reserved for top and bottom margins
  −   6  lines per page for 2 title lines, 1 blank line, 2 column heading
            lines, and 1 hyphen line
     ────
     54  available detail lines per page

      3  lines per shop for 1 line of shop totals, and 1
            blank line
  ×   6  shops
     ────
     18  shop footing lines
  +   3  lines per report for 2 lines with hyphens and 1 line of grand totals
     ────
     21  footing lines

  + 380  detail lines
     ────
    401  report lines
  ÷  54  lines per page
     ────
    7.4  printed pages
```

CALCULATING THE TIME TO PRINT THE REPORT

```
      5  printed heading lines per page
  ×   8  pages
     ────
     40  printed page heading lines

      2  printed footing lines per shop
  ×   6  shops
     ────
     12  printed shop footing lines

     40  printed page heading lines
  +  12  printed shop footing lines
  +   3  printed grand total footing lines
  + 380  printed detail lines
     ────
    435  printed lines
  ÷ 2,000  lines printed per minute
     ────
  .2175  minutes = 13 seconds of printer usage
```

Figure 6-23 *Report volume calculations for the report shown in Figure 6-18 on page 6.26, assuming 380 employees in 6 shops.*

Be aware that these volume calculations are still, at best, ballpark estimates. Because one or more of the figures you use in the calculations are approximations, the result is only an approximation. We would not expect this example report to print in exactly 13 seconds. Actual print time might be somewhat lower or higher.

The paper requirements and printer time calculations for a much larger report are shown in Figure 6-24 on the next page. This example dramatically demonstrates the value of volume estimates. Imagine the problems the first time the report was printed if no one had anticipated that it would print for nearly 19 hours and use 13 boxes of paper!

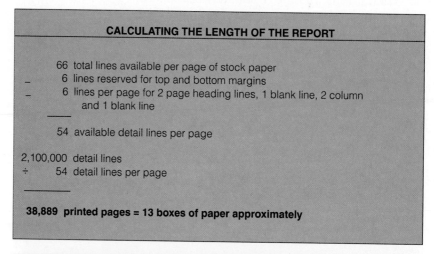

CALCULATING THE LENGTH OF THE REPORT

66	total lines available per page of stock paper
− 6	lines reserved for top and bottom margins
− 6	lines per page for 2 page heading lines, 1 blank line, 2 column and 1 blank line
54	available detail lines per page
2,100,000	detail lines
÷ 54	detail lines per page

38,889 printed pages = 13 boxes of paper approximately

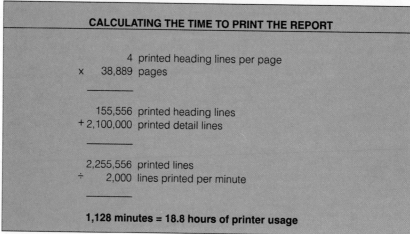

CALCULATING THE TIME TO PRINT THE REPORT

4	printed heading lines per page
× 38,889	pages
155,556	printed heading lines
+ 2,100,000	printed detail lines
2,255,556	printed lines
÷ 2,000	lines printed per minute

1,128 minutes = 18.8 hours of printer usage

Figure 6-24 Report volume calculations for a monthly report of 2,100,000 customer accounts.

Both these volume calculation examples were for reports printed on stock paper. The calculation process for reports on specialty forms can differ in three respects. First, for many preprinted form reports you will not completely fill every page; for such reports you must have an accurate estimate of the number of detail lines per page. Second, to the estimated print time you must add estimates of the time to load the specialty forms before printing and to unload the specialty forms after printing; this total represents the time the printer is tied up with a report using any specialty form and therefore unavailable for other printing. And third, for multiple-part paper, you must indicate the time necessary to separate the plies.

Consider, for example, the invoices printed once each day on the specialty form shown in Figure 6-9 on page 6.16 and Figure 6-22 on page 6.29. Assume that from past invoice volume figures you have determined that an average of 400 invoices must be printed each day and that the average invoice includes 7.2 different items or detail lines. Figure 6-25 shows the details of the resulting report volume calculations.

CALCULATING THE LENGTH OF THE REPORT

400 invoices printed per average day = 400 pages per day

CALCULATING THE TIME TO PRINT A REPORT

	1	order number line per invoice
+	1	order date line per invoice
+	4	address lines per invoice
+	7.2	detail lines per average invoice
+	1	subtotal line
+	1	sales tax line
+	1	total line

	16.2	printed lines per invoice
×	400	invoices per day

6,480	printed lines per day
2,000	lines printed per minute

	3.24	minutes of actual printing time
+	3.50	minutes to load invoice forms
+	3.00	minutes to remove invoice forms and load stock paper

9.74	**minutes of printer usage**

Figure 6-25 *Report volume calculations for daily printing of 400 invoices, using the preprinted invoice forms of Figure 6-9 on page 6.16.*

Let's reconsider the report shown in Figure 6-18 on page 6.26 as a second example and assume that the report is to be printed on 3-ply paper instead of stock paper. All the calculations shown in Figure 6-23 on page 6.31 still apply; the number of pages required would not change, nor would the actual printing time. But the printer would be unavailable for other printing during the time it takes to load and unload the multiple-part paper, so those times must be added to the printer usage time. In addition, the time required to separate the three copies must be noted. These times have been added to the volume calculations and are shown in Figure 6-26 on the next page.

CALCULATING THE LENGTH OF THE REPORT

   66 total lines available per page of stock paper
-   6 lines reserved for top and bottom margins
-   6 lines per page for 2 title lines, 1 blank line, 2 column heading lines, and 1 hyphen line
_____

   54 available detail lines per page

    3 lines per shop for 1 line with hyphens, 1 line of shop totals, and
×   6 shops
_____

   18 shop footing lines
+   3 lines per report for 2 lines with hyphens and 1 line of grand totals
_____

   21 footing lines
+ 380 detail lines
_____

 401 report lines
÷ 54 lines per page
_____

7.4 printed pages

CALCULATING THE TIME TO PRINT THE REPORT

    5 printed heading lines per page
×   8 pages
_____

  40 printed page heading lines

    2 printed footing lines per shop
×   6 shops
_____

  12 printed shop footing lines

  40 printed page heading lines
+ 12 printed shop footing lines
+   3 printed grand total footing lines
+ 380 printed detail lines
_____

  435 printed lines
÷ 2,000 lines printed per minute
_____

 .2175 minutes of printing time
+ 3.0000 minutes to load 3-ply paper
+ 3.0000 minutes to remove 3-ply paper and load stock paper
_____

6.2175 minutes of printer usage

TIME NEEDED FOR ADDITIONAL OPERATIONS

1.2 minutes to separate the 3-ply paper

Figure 6-26 *Report volume calculations for the report shown in Figure 6-18, assuming 380 employees in 6 shops and using 3-ply paper.*

■ Report approvals

The end users must approve every report design. Designing all the reports before you seek approval on any one of them is not a good strategy. If you designed some unacceptable feature into several reports, you would have to redesign all the affected reports. A much wiser practice is to submit each report design for approval as it is completed. The end users find it easier to consider one report at a time, instead of being overwhelmed with many report designs all at once.

You should find the printer spacing charts useful for the report design process and for documenting the final design layout. In general, however, printer spacing charts should not be shown to the end users. Unless the end users are familiar with such charts, they are likely to be confused by the editing symbols and other programming conventions. You should instead prepare a **mock-up report**, or **prototype**, which is a printed report simulation you create with made-up field values to illustrate how the actual printed report will look. Report mock-ups are typically one or two pages long and include enough records to demonstrate all the report design features. The reports shown in Figures 6-5 (page 6.12), 6-6 (page 6.13), 6-7 (page 6.14), 6-8 (page 6.15), 6-17 (page 6.24), and 6-18 (page 6.26) are mock-up reports. You might use a word processor or a report generator for creating mock-up reports.

If the end user requests a change to the proposed report design, you should redesign the layout, prepare a new printer spacing chart and mock-up report, and resubmit the design. You should repeat this process until the end user is completely satisfied with the report design. When the end user is completely satisfied, some organizations require that the end user sign and date the mock-up report to designate approval; other organizations require an approval memo from the end user.

Designing screen output

Screen output is very important to business organizations. Today, most people in an organization have ready access to a VDT or personal computer; you find computer workstations everywhere from shop floors and loading docks to executive offices. Screen output offers several advantages over printed output. Most importantly, screen output is timely. An end user can view a report within moments of requesting it, and that output can reflect up-to-the-minute information. Screen output can also be produced at the very location where it is needed. In addition, screen output can be selective. A shop floor supervisor, for example, might need to know the current inventory status of three specific items; with an appropriately designed online system, the information on those three items, and only those items, can be requested and viewed.

■ Screen design considerations

Many of the design principles we have discussed for printed output design also apply to screen output design. For example, screens should be uncluttered and visually attractive. You should present information logically and consistently and identify all variable output items.

Screen output has one requirement not found with printed reports: you should provide instructions on the screen to the end users about how to use the display. At the very least, you must tell them how to end the display. In many cases, several optional actions, each of which must be specified on the screen, will be available to the end users.

Typically, either the top or the bottom screen display line is reserved for option instructions. Some screens have considerable information presented, leaving no room for instructions; these cases will be covered when we discuss input design in Chapter 7.

In addition, you will often have a need to communicate messages to the end user. If the end user pressed an erroneous key, for example, you might want to print an error message on the screen. The bottommost of the remaining available screen lines is often reserved for these messages, which effectively limits the available screen space for displaying variable information to an approximate 80 column by 22 line area. Alternatively, error messages can be displayed in a box that appears in the middle of the screen display.

Systems analysts often use a special screen display layout form, such as the one illustrated in Figure 6-27, for screen design. There are 80 columns and 24 lines on the form, matching the 80 x 24 limits of most standard screens. If you are designing for a screen that allows more columns or lines of output, or if screen display layout forms are not available, you can simply rule off the appropriate screen limits on a printer spacing chart.

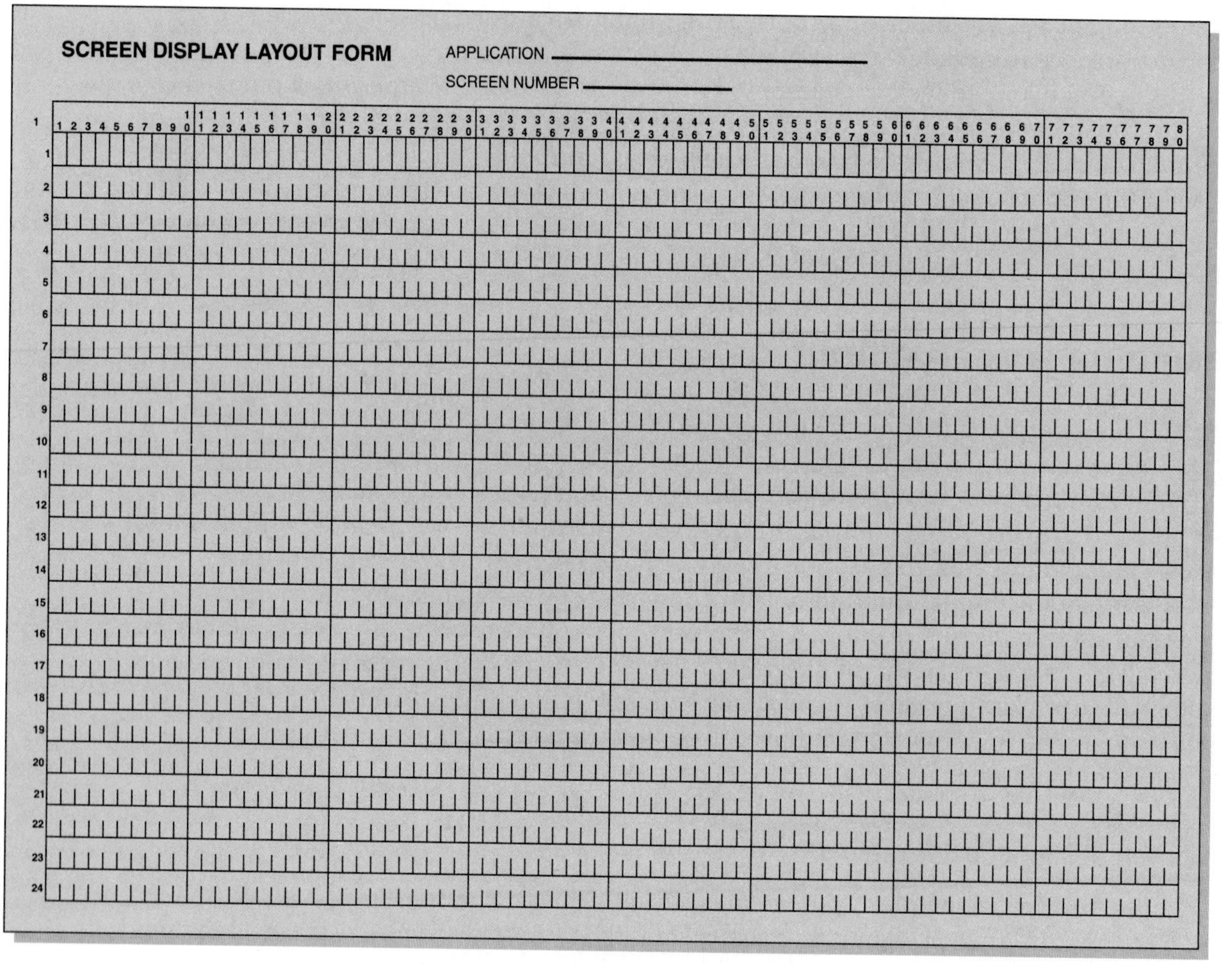

Figure 6-27 A sample screen display layout form.

■ Character output

A complete screen report is shown in Figure 6-28. This screen display is very similar to the printed version of the report, which is also shown in Figure 6-28. If you compare the

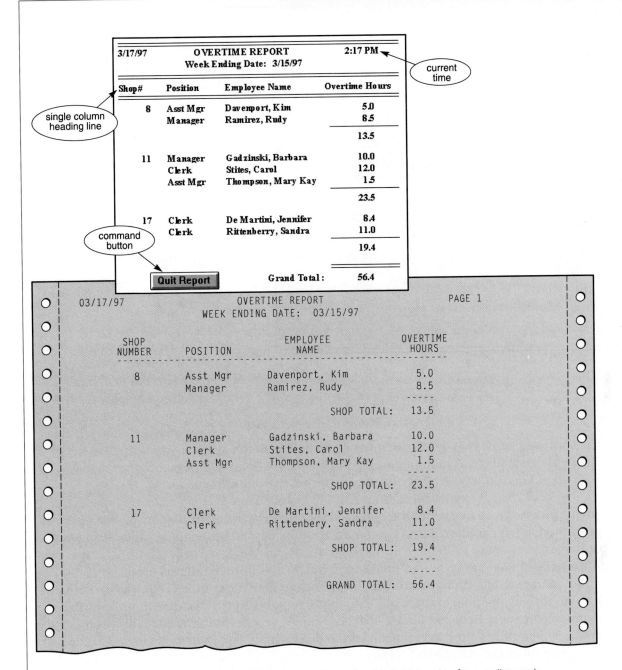

Figure 6-28 *A screen version and a printed report version of an exception report.*

report and the screen, however, you will notice several differences. First, the current time is displayed in the upper right-hand corner of the screen. Second, to conserve lines, the column headings on the screen occupy only a single line. Because a screen is smaller than a printed page, you might have to adjust formats or eliminate information in order to fit the information to be displayed within the screen limits. In this case, the report body was small enough to fit on a single screen; reformatting the column headings was the only significant change necessary to fit the entire report on the screen. In other cases, you might have to generate multiple screens to display the same information that can appear on a single printed page. The third difference between the two output versions is the command button at the bottom of the screen. In this case, only one action is available: when the end user has finished viewing the report, pointing to the *Quit Report* button and clicking the mouse button clears the screen and ends the program.

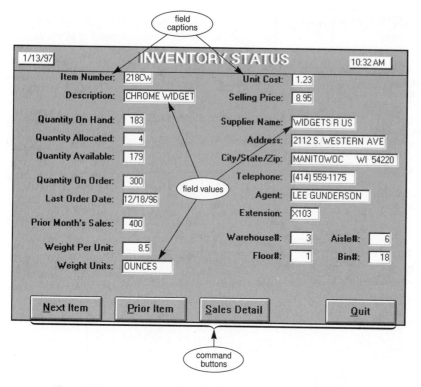

Figure 6-29 *A sample screen report showing all data for a single inventory item.*

Single-screen reports, such as the one in Figure 6-28, are not typical. The report shown in Figure 6-18 on page 6.26, for example, would fit across the screen, but it is too long to fit on a single screen. In the most likely screen treatment for this report, information for only one shop would appear on any one screen; the complete report would use as many screens as there are shops. You could then provide options that allow the end user to move from one shop display to another.

Often, an entire screen is needed to display information for a single record or entity. Figure 6-29 on the next page shows a screen display for a single inventory item. Notice that this screen layout is very different from any you have seen for printed reports. The field captions appear to the left of the fields instead of in column heading lines, and the fields are presented vertically instead of horizontally. Why is this very different presentation used?

A columnar format with column headings is the most logical, efficient (space-saving), and easy-to-understand format when you are printing or displaying multiple values for each field caption. But a columnar layout is not the best choice when displaying information relating to a single entity. Figure 6-30 illustrates several different screen presentations of field captions and fields. In Example 1, column headings are used; in the other examples, left captions are used. Notice that all five examples require five screen lines to display the information, but Example 1 requires more columns to present the same information. Because screen space is limited, a presentation that requires less space is generally better. When you want to display only one field value for each caption, left captions are preferable.

Examples 2 through 5 in Figure 6-30 illustrate different ways of aligning left captions and field values. Many people find Example 5, with captions right-justified and field values left-justified, the easiest to read. This is the presentation method used in Figure 6-29.

Notice the command buttons at the bottom of Figure 6-29. The end user is given four options: to terminate the program, to display the values for the previous or the following inventory item, or to display the prior year's sales detail for the current item. On the sales detail screen (not illustrated), there would be a similar command button for returning the display to the inventory status screen for the item. Two different screens were needed because all the status and sales information for one item would not fit on a single screen. When there are multiple screens for a single item, you must provide a way for the end user to move from one screen to another.

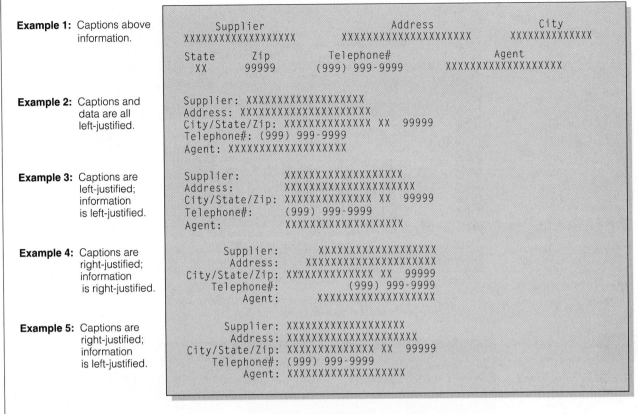

Example 1: Captions above information.

Example 2: Captions and data are all left-justified.

Example 3: Captions are left-justified; information is left-justified.

Example 4: Captions are right-justified; information is right-justified.

Example 5: Captions are right-justified; information is left-justified.

Figure 6-30 *Screen presentation options.*

■ Graphical output

So far we have discussed displaying character information on a screen, but many screens also can display information presented graphically. For example, consider the screen shown in Figure 6-31. The top part of this display includes some of the character information that was displayed in Figure 6-29. On the bottom part of the screen, a table of units sold by month by store is displayed. This table presents the data clearly, but a graphical presentation of this information might be more effective. A new command button is included: when the end user clicks the *Graph* command button, a graphical display appears.

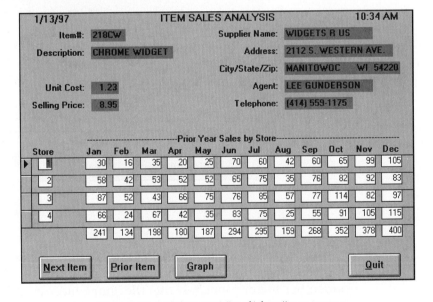

Figure 6-31 *A tabular presentation of information on a screen.*

Figures 6-32 and 6-33 on the next page show two possible graphs for this application. Figure 6-32 is a bar chart of the sales figures for each store in each month of the prior year. Notice the legend that tells which symbol stands for which store. Figure 6-33 is a connected line graph of total sales for all stores in each month of the previous year. Included on both screens is a *Table* command button to return to the table display screen of Figure 6-31.

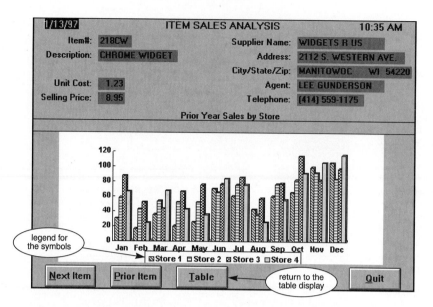

Figure 6-32 *A bar chart presentation of the sales information in Figure 6-31 on the previous page.*

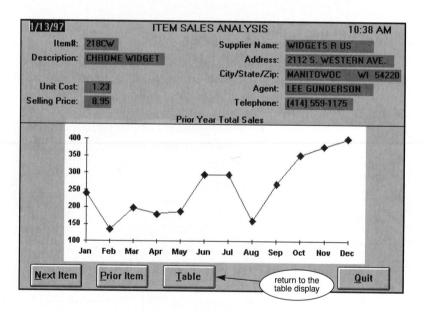

Figure 6-33 *A connected line graph of the total sales information in Figure 6-31 on the previous page.*

Many graphic display forms are possible, including pie charts, maps, bar charts, step charts, scatter diagrams, and curves. Whatever the type of graphical display, remember to appropriately title the chart, indicate and label any scales you use, and include a legend to explain the meaning of special shapes or characters.

■ Special video effects

You can add special video effects to all types of screen displays. On most screens, whether monochromatic or color, the available effects include high brightness, blinking, and reverse video. Color effects are also available for color monitors. Special effects, when used appropriately and in moderation, can enhance a screen display, but they are not a shortcut or replacement for good screen design. You must first develop a basic screen design that is logical, usable, and attractive. Then, you might consider adding special effects to supplement or enhance that design.

Designing other outputs

■ Tapes, disks, and diskettes

Often, information that is output from one system is utilized as input to another system. To accomplish the information transfer, the first system could print a report of the information, which some person would then use to create input to the second system; this method, however, is awkward, time consuming, and prone to error. In an integrated business environment, the information transfer is accomplished automatically: the necessary information is output from the first system on tape or disk, which is then directly input to the second system.

If you are developing a new accounts receivable system, for example, the system outputs might include a disk or tape file that is to be input to the organization's general ledger system. Some information from a system you are developing might possibly be input to a generalized graphics system or a spreadsheet system. Or, your organization might have a mailing label printing system, to which you need to input a file of names and addresses. In all these examples, the required format for the output disk/tape file is already defined by the input format requirements of the existing system. Your design process, therefore, consists of documenting the information that will be output in the predefined format and calculating the output volumes. The volume calculations for tape and disk output files are the same as those for data stores and will be discussed in Chapter 9.

The format would not be predefined for output tape and disk files such as archive files, transaction history files, and error files. For such files, you will have to design appropriate, efficient file layouts. The file design considerations for system data stores, which will be discussed in detail in Chapters 8 and 9, are equally appropriate for such output files; therefore, we will not discuss any specifics for output tape and disk file design at this point.

■ Other output media

For output directed to most other media, the output format and contents depend on the device and its requirements. Output directed to a plotter, for example, consists of a series of commands presented in the exact format required by the particular plotter being used. Similarly, output directed to an audio device must match that device's specific format requirements. As with predefined tape and disk output formats, your design process for such outputs primarily consists of documenting the exact information that will be output in the required format.

COM (computer output microfilm) output most often consists of report page images. To design for COM output, you would first design, size, and document the report as you would any printed report. Report page images are then input to the COM machine, which handles the production of the report onto the COM medium.

Output control

T he topic of output control encompasses all measures necessary to ensure that output information is correct, complete, and secure. The importance of output controls cannot be overemphasized.

Output must be correct and complete to be of value. If data integrity is lost during processing or output, the problems must be recognizable and recognized so that they can be corrected. You should take several measures to help ensure the correctness and completeness of output. Every report should be appropriately titled and should include the date the report was prepared and the period covered by the report. Report pages should be numbered consecutively, and the end of the report should be explicitly identified. Control totals and record counts should be printed and then reconciled against input totals and counts. On a random basis, reports should be selected for a thorough check of correctness and completeness.

Some special measures specifically apply to output error reports and procedures. End users should periodically review error reports to verify that errors are appropriately identified. You should print error control totals and record counts that can then be reconciled with the output totals produced after the errors have been corrected and re-input. You could create an independent error file that is periodically examined for records that were never corrected and re-input.

Output security is concerned with protecting the privacy rights of individuals and organizations, as well as protecting the company's proprietary data from theft or unauthorized access. Output security measures include the following: ensuring that only the required number of report copies are produced; ensuring that reports are distributed only to authorized personnel; keeping sensitive reports in secure areas; clearly labeling all pages of confidential reports as such; and burning or shredding sensitive, out-of-date reports, output from aborted runs, and used carbons. Specialty output forms such as blank check forms require special security treatment; they should be stored in a secure location and regularly inventoried to check for missing forms. Check signature stamps should be stored in a secure location physically removed from the forms storage location. In most organizations, the responsibility for many of the security control measures we have just mentioned are placed with the information systems department. As a systems analyst, you can help by providing complete documentation of proper report production and distribution procedures.

Automated design tools

C ommercial software tools can help you productively design output reports and screen displays. Many database management system (DBMS), fourth-generation language (4GL), and CASE products include online report and screen generator features.

With a typical **report generator**, you respond to prompts or use function keys to provide the constant information for the report (report titles, headings, and footings), and specify a print position for each. You select variable fields to be printed from the data dictionary and specify where each is to be located; the report generator uses the field sizes, edit masks, and captions from the data dictionary to lay out detail lines and column headings. You can decide to move fields you have previously positioned at any time in the process. When you are satisfied with the report layout you have designed, the report generator outputs a report definition that is essentially equivalent to a printer spacing chart. You can also input made-up field values to a report generator to create a mock-up report; mock-up reports created by a report generator are often called **report prototypes**. Some report generators can also create a program that will actually produce the report. Such programs often are not as efficient as those written by programmers. For reports that are small or printed only occasionally, however, the generated program might end up as the one used in the information system.

A **screen generator** is similar to a report generator. With a screen generator, you can create screen display definitions that are equivalent to screen display layout forms, screen mock-ups — often called **screen prototypes** — and programs to produce the display.

Report and screen generators ensure consistency with the data dictionary. These generators also relieve you from some tedious design tasks, such as counting field lengths, centering information, and filling form boxes. You can usually create and document an output design more rapidly by using a generator, but using such generators does not guarantee *good* designs. You still must know and apply all the principles of effective report and screen design.

Completing an effective and accurate output design for an information system is an excellent first step in systems design. You must continue with effective and accurate systems designs for all information system inputs, which we will discuss in Chapter 7, all information system files and databases, which we will discuss in Chapters 8 and 9, and all information system software, which we will discuss in Chapter 10. Combining effective and accurate designs for all these components of an information system will help ensure a quality information system development.

James Tool Company — Output Design

Having completed the systems analysis phase, Don Mard and Howard Coswell began their design activities on the payroll information system project. While James Tool Company's management negotiated with Lennox Software Solutions for purchase of their payroll package, Mard and Coswell began to design the union system. Because most payroll requirements would be handled by the payroll package, Mard and Coswell spent only a few hours studying the system requirements document and reacquainting themselves with the union processing requirements.

Fortunately, the negotiations with Lennox Software Solutions were completed rapidly to everyone's satisfaction, and by the end of the week, Don Mard turned his complete attention to the payroll package. A newly hired systems analyst, Kimberly Wallace, was assigned to work with Mard full-time on developmental activities for the package. Coswell concentrated his time on the systems design of the union system and its interaction with the payroll package.

Coswell's first systems design step was to design the outputs from the union system. Three output reports are the Union Deduction Register, the checks to the unions, and the Union Payment Summary. The fourth and final output is the union expense entry that is to be output as a disk file for input to the accounting system. The standard James Tool Company check is to be used for making the union payments. Also, the output entry to the accounting system has been specified by the accounting department in the standard format for all entries input to the accounting system. In essence, the output design for the union check and the union expense entry was complete.

Coswell then prepared a design for the Union Deduction Register. Because the unions were pleased with the current report, which is shown in Figure 6-34, Coswell made minimal design changes to the report. He made changes to conform to the standards for report page headings at James Tool Company, added a control heading for the union name and number, and added a control footing of the total for the reporting period's union dues. This total figure would be matched against the amount of the union checks to be sure they were in balance before distribution to the unions. After completing the printer spacing chart, Coswell prepared the mock-up report shown in Figure 6-35.

JAMES TOOL COMPANY
UNION DEDUCTION REGISTER

UNION _____ Machinists _____   PAGE ___ 1 ___
LOCAL NUMBER _____ 328 _____   PERIOD ___ 03/16/97 - 04/15/97 ___

EMPLOYEE NAME	SOCIAL SECURITY NUMBER	WEEK ENDING DATE	WEEKLY EARNINGS	UNION DUES	TOTAL UNION DUES THIS PERIOD
Avcollie, David Lee	261-24-9021	3/23	361.90	1.50	
		3/30	352.00	1.50	
		4/06	352.00	1.50	
		4/13	352.00	1.50	
		4/20	352.00	.60	6.60
Bombeck, Estelle Louise	....	3/23	......	1.50	
		....	....	....	

Figure 6-34 Sample of the current Union Deduction Register.

```
2/07/97                    JAMES TOOL COMPANY                      PAGE 1
                        UNION DEDUCTION REGISTER
                        PERIOD: 1/06/97--2/02/97


UNION: Machinists Local 328              UNION NUMBER: 1

                         SOCIAL     WEEK                        TOTAL
                         SECURITY   ENDING   WEEKLY    UNION    UNION DUES
EMPLOYEE NAME            NUMBER     DATE     EARNINGS  DUES     THIS PERIOD
===========             ========   =======  ========  =====    ===========
Avcollie, David Lee     261-24-9021  1/10   361.90    1.50
                                     1/17   352.00    1.50
                                     1/24   352.00    1.50
                                     1/31   352.00    1.50     6.00

Bombeck, Estelle Louise 388-99-4326  1/12   420.00    1.50
                                     1/19   420.00    1.50
                                     1/26   420.00    1.50
                                     2/06   420.00    1.50     6.00

Timmers, Belinda Sue    902-33-9829  1/26   291.20    1.50
                                     2/02   364.00    1.50     3.00

            TOTAL UNION CHECK AMOUNT:                          15.00
```

Figure 6-35 Sample Union Deduction Register for the new union subsystem at James Tool Company.

Coswell next prepared the report analysis form for the Union Deduction Register (Figure 6-36). Coswell took the report analysis form and mock-up sample with him to a meeting with Delbert Donovan, the director of union relations. Donovan agreed with all the report changes and approved the report design.

SYSTEM DOCUMENTATION

NAME OF SYSTEM	DATE	PAGE 1 OF 1
Payroll	April 3, 1997	

ANALYST	PURPOSE OF DOCUMENTATION
Howard Coswell	Report Analysis-Union Deduction Register

FIELD	FIELD TYPE	FIELD LENGTH
Employee Name	Alphanumeric	25
SSN	Numeric	9
Week Ending Date	Numeric	8
Weekly Earnings	Numeric	6 (2 decimal positions)
Union Dues	Numeric	4 (2 decimal positions)

COMMENTS

Report printing date, company name, and page number print on first line.
Period reporting start and end dates print on third line.

Union name and number print in a control heading. Start a new page for each new union.

Print only month and day portion of week ending date.

Print union dues total for each employee and each union.

FREQUENCY

The report is printed once every four weeks per the production schedule.

DISTRIBUTION

One copy of the report is printed, separated by union, and forwarded to the unions with their check by noon on Friday for the four-week period just ended.

ATTACHMENTS

Mock-up report is attached.

Figure 6-36 *The Report Analysis Form for the Union Deduction Register at James Tool Company.*

The Union Payment Summary is to be a new report to serve as a control report. The union check amounts should balance with the union expense entries output to the accounting system. The accounting department would use this report to verify these other outputs and to balance against the union dues totals printed on the payroll system's Payroll Register report.

A mock-up design of the Union Payment Summary report made by Coswell is shown in Figure 6-37. Although the report is a simple summary report, it is still important for Coswell to review the design with the end user and obtain design approval. Consequently, Coswell met with Dale Klish, the director of accounting, to review the proposed design with him. Klish was very pleased with the new report and felt it would also be acceptable to the internal company auditor and to the outside auditors. Klish gave his approval of the report design, subject to the approval of the auditors. Klish volunteered to meet with the auditors by the end of the week.

```
                    JAMES TOOL COMPANY              PAGE 1
                    UNION PAYMENT SUMMARY

                 PAYMENT DATE: 2/07/97


        UNION                              CHECK AMOUNT
        -----                              ------------
        -----                              ------------

    1 Machinists Local 328                     15.00

    2 Electricians Local 74                    72.00

    3 Plumbers Union                           54.00

    4 Teamsters Local 811                     528.00


        TOTAL UNION PAYMENTS:                 669.00
```

Figure 6-37   *Sample Union Payment Summary for the new union subsystem at James Tool Company.*

Coswell was now finished with the union system's output design and turned his attention to the design of the other components of the union information system.

Summary

In this chapter, we began our study of the systems design phase. The purpose of systems design is to create a physical design that satisfies the logical design requirements defined during the systems analysis phase. The three major activities in systems design are reviewing the system requirements document, designing the system components, and presenting the completed design. The process of designing system components usually begins with the output but does not proceed as a series of independent, nonoverlapping activities.

Printed output reports can be classified in two ways. We can classify an output report as a detail, exception, or summary report, and as an internal or external report. We then covered printed report design principles for both stock paper and specialty form reports and explained how to perform report volume calculations. We discussed screen output design, considering both character and graphical output.

Next, we addressed the topic of output control and discussed various measures you can take to achieve adequate control of output. Finally, we discussed report and screen generators, which are automated tools useful to the output design process.

Review Questions

1. What is a physical information system design? What is a logical information system design? During which life cycle phases are they created?

2. Discuss why you agree or disagree with the following statement: During the systems design phase, the systems analyst creates and refines the logical and physical designs, iterating between them.

3. What is the first activity of the systems design process? Why?

4. What does it mean when we say that an information system is effective? Reliable? Maintainable?

5. Discuss the advantages and disadvantages of printed output.

6. What is a detail report?

7. What is a control-break report? Define the terms control field and control break.

8. What is an exception report? When is an exception report appropriate?

9. What is a summary report? When is a summary report appropriate?

10. What is an internal report? An external report? In what ways do their design considerations differ?

11. Define the terms specialty form and preprinted form. Are they synonymous?

12. When using a printer spacing chart or screen display layout form, how do you indicate constant fields? Variable fields? How do you indicate line spacing?

13. What is a mock-up report? For what purpose is it used?

14. What additional information must be provided on a screen display that need not be present on a printed report of the same data?

15. List three or more special video effects, and describe how they might be used to improve the end user interface.

Discussion Questions

1. A systems analyst has designed the report layout (Figure 6-38) as shown on the next page. Identify the flaws in the report design and suggest specific improvements.

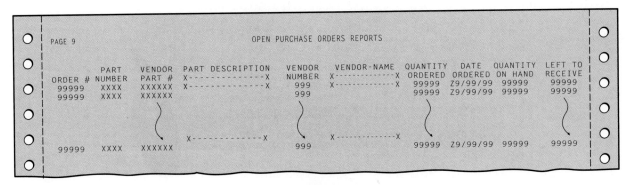

Figure 6-38

2. Some systems analysts argue, "You must give end users what they ask for. If they want long reports with reams of data, then that is what you give them. Otherwise, end users will be unhappy and feel that the systems analyst is trying to tell them how to do their jobs." Others say, "The systems analyst should dictate to the end user what information can be obtained from the information system. If you listen to end users, you'll never get anywhere, because they don't really know what they want and don't understand information systems." What do you think of these arguments? Why?

3. Obtain copies of one or more computer output documents, such as computer-printed invoices, bills, or a student grade report. Assess the functionality and aesthetics of each document, and try to identify at least one possible improvement for each.

Carl's Corvettes

Carl Dekker owns a sales and service shop that deals only with Corvettes. About one year ago, Carl purchased a computer system to keep track of customers, sales, and service appointments. In addition to the main computer in his own office, which he shares with his assistant Linda, Carl installed a terminal at the service desk. Throughout the year, Carl and Linda have entered service data for every job that was performed. Appointment records contain appointment number, date, customer name, and automobile registration number. Every appointment has one or more task records. Each task record contains the following information:

Appointment number	5 numeric digits
Mechanic	15 alphanumeric characters
Task code	4 numeric digits
Task description	20 alphanumeric characters
Standard task time	3 numeric digits
Actual task time	3 numeric digits

Carl would like to have a report of his mechanics' services for the past three months. The report should list for each mechanic all the tasks performed by that mechanic, listed in date order. For each task, Carl wants to see the code, description, date, standard time, actual time, and the percent by which the actual task time was over (under) standard task time. He wants a total line for each mechanic, giving the total number of tasks and the percent that the total of the mechanic's actual task times is over (under) the total of the standard task times. He also wants a grand total line, giving similar totals for the entire service operation. In an average month, the four mechanics at Carl's Corvettes work on a total of 120 appointments, each appointment averaging 2.35 tasks.

Questions

1. Design the report on a printer spacing chart.
2. Perform volume calculations for the report you designed. Assume the report will be printed on stock paper by a character printer that effectively prints 150 lines per minute.

Carl would also like a screen display for the appointment scheduler's use. For any specified task, he wants to see the task code, description, standard task time, the ten most recent (or all, if there are fewer than ten) actual times achieved for that task along with the assigned mechanic, and the average actual time of the displayed tasks.

Question

3. Design a screen display for the appointment scheduler.

G. H. Ames & Company

The Marketing Department at G. H. Ames & Company has requested a new report in their Sales Analysis System. They want a biweekly report, showing the following information for the most recent two-week period for each of the company's 62 sales representatives: sales representative name (20 characters), number of sales calls, number of orders taken, total of the order amounts, and total miles driven. For each sales call, they would like to see the name (25 characters) and city (15 characters) of the customer visited, the date of the visit, the date of the previous visit (if any) to that same customer, and the amount of the order (if any) resulting from that visit. Each sales representative visits 38 customers in an average two-week period; a visit produces an order about 60% of the time. The average order total is $1200; $9999.99 is a reasonable maximum single order value. The information for each sales representative should start on a new page.

Questions

1. Design the requested report on a printer spacing chart. Prepare a mock-up for one page of your designed report.
2. Perform volume calculations for the report you designed. Assume the report will be printed on stock paper on a line printer that effectively prints 300 lines per minute.
3. Prepare a report analysis (similar to Figure 6-21 on page 6.28) for the report you designed.

Ridgeway Company

Thomas McGee, vice president of operations for the Ridgeway Company, has the responsibility of running the Blue Waters Country Club. He recently requested three new reports to be produced by the club's billing system:

1. A report listing all the month's sales for the pro shop, restaurant, and bar, printed in order by date within facility.
2. A report listing the total of the sales for the month for members with purchases, printed in member number order.
3. A report listing all members who made no purchases during the month, printed in member number order.

The following information is available on a billing record:

Field	Description
Charge date	8 numeric digits, YYYYMMDD form
Charge amount	6 numeric digits, including 2 decimal positions
Charge location code	1 numeric digit: 1=restaurant, 2=bar, 3=pro shop
Charge description	25 characters
Member number	4 numeric digits
Member last name	18 characters
Member first name	15 characters

Questions

1. Design a format for each of the three management reports using printer spacing charts. Include any control totals you feel are appropriate.
2. Explain how the control totals included in your report designs should be calculated, and how McGee should use them.

STUDENT CASE STUDY 6

Western Dental Clinic — Output Design

Introduction

The associates at Western Dental Clinic approved Jim Archer's recommendations for a new computer system. Archer's next step was to develop the design for the new information system. He began with the design of the dental system's outputs. The outputs needed are:

- A daily appointment list for each provider
- A daily call list
- A weekly provider report
- A monthly preprinted statement for selected patients
- Mailing labels twice a month

Student Assignments

1. Design the daily appointment list using a printer spacing chart, a mock-up report, and a report analysis form.
2. Design the daily call list using a printer spacing chart, a mock-up report, and a report analysis form.
3. Design the weekly provider report using a printer spacing chart, a mock-up report, and a report analysis form.
4. The monthly statement will be a new preprinted form that you must design. Prepare a printer spacing chart and a report analysis form for your design of this preprinted form.
5. Design the daily call list, but assume that the call list will be a screen output instead of a printed report. Explain what the advantages and disadvantages of this approach would be.
6. What output controls are needed for the dental system?
7. Insurance processing must be included in the Western Dental Clinic system. For the weekly insurance company report and the monthly insurance aged trial balance, prepare printer spacing charts and mock-up reports.
8. Because insurance processing is now included, are there additional output controls that are needed for the dental system? If so, what are these additional output controls?

CHAPTER 7

Input Design

Objectives

You will have mastered the material in this chapter when you can:

- Discuss the objectives of systems input design
- Explain the differences among data capture, data entry, and data input
- Explain the differences between batch and online input
- List and describe the different types of data validation checks
- Discuss effective source document design
- Design input records
- Discuss guidelines for effective screen design
- Describe and design data entry screens, process control screens, graphical user interfaces, and help screens
- Discuss input control techniques

Introduction

Have you ever heard the saying, *Garbage in, garbage out*, or GIGO, for short? Although it is an oversimplification, it is basically true. The quality of the output from an information system is directly related to the quality of its input. Input design encompasses all the activities that help to ensure the quality of the systems input.

In recent years, many of the most exciting developments in computer technology have involved computer input devices. Long gone are the days when the punched card was the only means of inputting computer data. Today's systems analysts can choose from an amazing array of input media (Figure 7-1 on the next page) and methods.

Input Device	Description
Keyboard	Most commonly used input device. Can operate in either online or key-to-storage modes.
Terminal	Input device that may be dumb (video display screen and keyboard only) or intelligent (screen, keyboard, and independent storage and processing capabilities).
Mouse	Small input device used to move the cursor on a screen and select options.
Touch screen	Screen that lets users interface with the computer by touching the screen.
Touch-tone telephone	Telephone that lets users press the buttons on it to make transactions such as electronic funds transfers, shop-at-home service purchases, and call-in school registration.
Graphic input device	Device such as a light pen, digitizer, or graphic tablet that translates graphic data into a form that can be processed by a computer.
Voice input device	Device that lets users enter data and issue commands into a computer by spoken words.
MICR reader	Used primarily in the banking industry to read the magnetic ink characters printed on checks.
Scanner/optical recognition devices	A variety of devices that read printed codes, characters, or images.
Data collection device	Portable terminal used for on-site data entry in extreme environments such as warehouses, shop floors, and shipping docks.

Figure 7-1 *A summary of the most common types of input devices.*

The latest trend in input device technology is toward more direct data entry to minimize or even eliminate the need for human entry or interaction. For example, auto-mated teller machines (ATMs), time clocks, and hand-held scanners read magnetic data strips affixed to bank cards, employee badges, or library books, respectively. Hospitals now imprint a bar code on patient identification bracelets and use portable scanners when gathering data on patient treatment and medication. Retail stores use portable bar code scanners to log new inventory shipments and to gather current inventory data within the store. Cash registers at retail stores are now generally replaced by point-of-sale (POS) terminals that operate online to a central computer system transmitting and receiving inventory data. POS terminals combine the following input and output devices: a keyboard or keypad; a visual display screen for the operator; a visual display screen for the customer; a wand reader or bar code scanner; a magnetic credit and debit card scanner; a narrow printer for producing customer receipts; and a small internal printer for producing receipt journals. Many grocery store POS terminals also have scales and coupon printers incorporated into the system.

During input design, a systems analyst must determine the appropriate methods and techniques for best delivering the data supplied by various input devices to the information system under development. In this chapter, we discuss the systems design of the input to an information system. We begin with an explanation of the objectives and activities of input design. Then, we discuss online and batch input methods, data input guidelines, and data validation techniques. Next, we examine design techniques for source documents, input records, input screens in general, data entry screens, menu and prompt process control screens, graphical user interfaces, and help screens. We conclude the chapter with a discussion of input control techniques and automated input design tools.

Input design objects

nput design includes the development of procedures and specifications for all aspects of data capture, data entry, and data input. **Data capture** refers to the identification and recording of source data. **Data entry** is the process of converting source data into a computer-readable form. During **data input**, the computer-readable source data is actually input to the information system.

The input design process for a given information system includes the following six activities:

1. Design or modify source documents for data capture
2. Determine how data will be entered and input
3. Design input data records
4. Design data entry screens
5. Design user interface screens
6. Design audit trails and system security measures

The first listed activity, which involves source document design, is concerned with data capture. Appropriate data entry and data input methods are also determined early in the input design process. Then, depending on the data entry and input methods to be used, you will design input data records, or data entry and user interface screens, or both. The final listed activity concerns input control. You do not, however, wait to consider input control until after everything else is done. You must consider input control measures throughout the entire systems input design process.

The goal of all input design activities is to enable the information system users to provide high-quality data to the system in an efficient manner. The following objectives will help you meet that goal:

- Utilize appropriate input media and methods
- Develop efficient input procedures
- Reduce input volume
- Reduce input errors

Utilize appropriate input media and methods

Perhaps the most obvious input design decisions you must make involve the selection of input entry methods and media. Input methods are classified as either batch or online. Current trends are toward online input methods, in which data entry is performed online, interactively with the computer. Often, the data capture process is also online, using a direct input medium such as a magnetic data strip scanner. Online data entry offers several advantages. The data can be validated as it is input. The data is available for processing sooner. If the data is also captured online, the need for human interaction is minimized, resulting in faster and more accurate input.

With batch methods, data entry is performed periodically (hourly, daily, weekly) for a collection, or batch, of source data. Although the data capture process might involve a direct input medium, most often the data is recorded on forms, keyed by a data entry clerk, and then input in batches.

Online input methods might appear to be the best choice because of the many advantages of online data capture and data entry, but this is not always the case. Online input methods involving human interaction execute more slowly than do batch input methods, are usually more expensive than batch methods, and typically must be performed during normal working hours when computer demand might be at its highest. Some inputs do not require immediate processing, so that batch-gathering delays are not important. Other inputs occur naturally in batches. A mail-order distributor, for example, receives both orders and payments in batches when the mail arrives. Also, when microcomputers are used for data entry, data is often transmitted, or **uploaded**, to a central computer in files or batches for input to an information system. When the entry is done on a central computer and the information system processing is performed on a microcomputer, files or batches are transmitted, or **downloaded**, from the central computer to the microcomputer.

■ Develop efficient input procedures

Efficient input procedures consist only of necessary steps performed in a logical order. Just one seemingly innocuous but unnecessary step can add significant time to the input process. The data capture procedures for an order, for example, might require one person to collect and date stamp all orders and a second person to log and number the orders. The time spent transferring the documents from one step to the next might amount to only a few seconds per transaction; but if thousands of transactions are processed every month, the total time could be significant.

As you develop your input design, you must recognize points in the input process where delays could occur. A good input design avoids potential bottlenecks. For example, if one specific person must approve all orders before they are released for data entry, that approval process might create a bottleneck. To determine the likelihood of a problem, you must have information about that person's schedule, availability, and other responsibilities. You need realistic estimates of order volumes as well. If a bottleneck seems likely, then data capture procedures must be changed: perhaps a second person could share approval responsibility; or perhaps approvals should be required only for exceptional orders.

Most input bottlenecks occur at the data entry stage. Designing efficient and easy-to-use source documents, capturing data at its source, reducing input volume, and streamlining data entry procedures are among the measures that can reduce the likelihood of data entry bottlenecks.

■ Reduce input volume

To reduce input volume, you must reduce the number and size of data item values that must be input for each transaction or entity. Both data capture and data entry require the efforts of people. When you reduce data volume, you reduce labor costs. You also reduce the amount of time required to get the data into the system. The sooner the data is in the system, the sooner the system can produce useful results. Also, the number of errors in a given set of data is related to its volume; that is, as data volume increases, the probable number of errors also increases. By reducing data volume, you reduce the number of errors that must be subsequently detected and corrected.

The following four guidelines help to reduce input data volume.

1. ***Input necessary data only.*** Do not input every available item of data. If a data item is not needed by the system, don't input it. A completed order form, for example, often contains the name, initials, or number of the clerk who took the telephoned order. If that data is neither relevant nor necessary, it should not be input to the order system.

2. ***Do not input data that can be retrieved from system files or calculated from other data.*** Variable data and identification data must, of course, be input. For our order system example, identification data such as customer number and ordered item numbers, must be input. Variable data, such as the quantity of each item ordered, must also be input. Because the customer number is input, the customer name and address can be retrieved from the customer master file. The item numbers are also entered, so that the item descriptions and current item prices can be retrieved from the item master file. The extended price can be calculated by multiplying the input quantity by the retrieved item price, the gross total can be calculated by summing all the extended prices, and the sales tax and order total amount can be calculated. Consequently, customer name and address, item descriptions and prices, extended prices, gross totals, sales tax, and order totals should not be input.

3. ***Do not input constant data.*** If orders are input in batches and if all the orders in one batch always have the same order date, then it is not necessary to enter an order date with every order in that batch; the order date needs to be entered only once: before or with the first order in a batch. Additionally, if orders are entered online as they are received, then the order date can be retrieved from the computer system date and, therefore, need not be input at all.

4. ***Use codes.*** When we discussed codes and coding schemes in Chapter 3, you learned that codes are usually shorter than the data they represent. One advantage of using codes, then, is reduced data entry time. In our order example, customer number and item number are actually codes. The requested order shipping method is an example of another data item that could be appropriately coded.

You might be wondering why we are discussing data volume reduction, when the determination of which data items to input was completed in the prior phase. The reason is that during systems design you determine when and how the data items are input, and so the guidelines just described must also be applied in this phase. For example, the system requirements document might specify that item description must be input to the system, but during systems design you would decide when to enter an item description and when to retrieve the item description from a system file.

In our discussion on reducing input volume, we mentioned that you should input only necessary data. As an example, we considered an order form source document containing both a customer name and a customer number. We noted that because a customer name could be retrieved from system master files based on the input customer number, it was not necessary to input the customer name. Is it wise *never* to require that a customer name (or any other retrievable data) be input? Doesn't the customer name provide a type of check against the customer number?

If data entry is performed online, you can retrieve and display a customer name immediately after the operator enters a customer number. The operator can then visually verify the customer name.

If the displayed name does not match the name on the source document, then something is obviously wrong. The operator can immediately reject that source document and set it aside for investigation and correction. A good online data entry program will allow the operator to avoid entering a record for the suspect document. If more source documents must be entered, the operator should be able simply to change the displayed customer number to that for the next source document and then continue. When using online data entry, therefore, you do not have to require entry of a retrievable data item, such as a customer name.

What if you use batch input methods? With batch input methods, data is verified when it is input, not while it is being entered. What if the customer number on the source document is wrong but happens to match another customer's number? If the customer name has not been entered, how would this error be detected? Unfortunately, the error might not become evident until the wrong customer received the shipment, an order confirmation, or a bill. We do need some way to check the validity of a batch-input customer number. For batch input, customer name could qualify as necessary data that you must enter.

Does entering and inputting the customer name solve all the problems or create others? When you add characters to the input record length, you increase data entry time and costs, data storage requirements and costs, and data input time and costs. In addition, you introduce the possibility of rejecting good records as well as bad ones during the input process. If the input customer name is JONES, TOM and the stored customer name is JONES, THOMAS M., then the record will be rejected. Similarly, MARTINELLI AND SONS does not match

MARTINELLI & SONS. Perhaps by requiring customer name on input, you have merely incurred more costs while creating a different set of problems.

This problem is typically handled in one or both of the following ways. First, batch source documents can be checked before being released for data entry. One or more people assigned that responsibility would verify customer numbers and correct all erroneous numbers appearing on source documents. These individuals might also be responsible for correcting any customer name variations. Second, only some part of the customer name could be entered, to help avoid false rejections. For example, if only the first three characters of a customer name were input, then the two records just cited would not be erroneously rejected. By using both methods, you can avoid most customer number errors or at least correctly detect them during input. ■

■ Reduce input errors

Reducing the number of errors in the input data will certainly add to the quality of the data. All the efforts we have discussed previously to reduce input data volume will help reduce errors. The customer name cannot be misspelled if it is not entered. Similarly, an outdated item price cannot be used mistakenly if item price is retrieved instead of input.

Good input design can also help reduce errors. As we will see when we discuss source documents, a document's layout, captions, and instructions can be designed to make the data capture and data entry processes easier and more error-free. Well-designed screen layouts also help reduce error rates.

Even with the best input designs and procedures, input errors will occur. The final defense against erroneous data entering the system is catching and correcting the errors as they are input. Data should be validated as soon as possible (during online data entry or batch data input), and detected errors should be corrected. At least eight types of validation checks can be applied to data.

1. **Sequence checks** are used when the data must be input in some predetermined sequence. If orders must be input in order-number sequence, for example, then an out-of-sequence order number indicates an error. If transactions must be input in date order, then a transaction with an out-of-sequence date would trigger an error.

2. **Existence checks** are used for data items that must be input. If a data item must be entered and if a blank value is not valid for the item, the existence check would determine that a data item with no input value is incorrect.

3. **Class checks** test that a data item fits the required data class; that is, a numeric field must be numeric, and an alphabetic field can contain only the characters A-Z, a-z, or blanks.

4. **Range checks** test data item values against absolute minimum and maximum values. The hours worked by an employee in one week, for example, must fall within the range of zero to 168 hours, because there are 168 hours in a week. When the validation check involves a minimum or a maximum, but not both, it is often called a **limit check**. Checking that a payment amount is greater than zero is a limit check.

5. **Reasonableness checks** point out values that are suspicious or unreasonable, but not necessarily wrong. For example, input payment values of $.05 and $5,000,000.00 both pass a simple limit check for a payment value greater than zero, and yet both values might be erroneous; a reasonableness check can catch such unusual values. Similarly, an hours-worked value of 160 passes a zero to 168 range check; but that value is an unlikely one that should be rechecked.

6. **Validity checks** are used for data items that have a finite number of valid values. If an inventory system has twenty valid item classes, for example, then any input item class that does not match one of those twenty item classes is erroneous. Verifying that an order's customer number matches a number on the customer master file is a validity check; so too is verifying that the customer number input while adding new a customer does not match a number already on the customer master file.

7. **Combination checks** are performed on two or more fields to ensure that they are consistent or reasonable when considered together. Even though all the fields involved in a combination check might have passed all their individual validation checks, the combination of the field values might be erroneous. For example, if an order input for thirty units of a particular item has an input discount rate applicable only for purchases of 100 or more units, the combination is invalid; either the input order quantity or the input discount rate is erroneous.

8. **Batch controls** are totals used to verify batch input. Batch controls might include both record counts and numeric field totals. For example, a clerk could manually calculate the total number of orders, the sum of the customer numbers, and the sum of all the order quantities for the order forms in a batch. When the order batch is input, the computer program would calculate the same three totals, and the clerk could compare the totals to the corresponding manual batch control totals. If any of the totals do not match, then an error must have occurred during data entry or data input of that batch. Unlike the other validation checks we have discussed, batch control checks cannot pinpoint erroneous fields. When the sum of the input customer numbers does not match the batch control total, you know only that one or more customer numbers in that batch were incorrectly entered, or that one or more orders were not input. Notice also that control totals are not necessarily meaningful numbers. A **hash total** is a meaningless, but useful, total used for control purposes; the sum of the customer numbers is an example of a hash total.

Source document design

Paper documents are still commonly used in all aspects of business for collecting, circulating, and storing information. In this section, we examine **source documents**, those forms that elicit and capture data for input to an information system, serve as an authorization or trigger for input action, and provide a record of original input data.

During systems input design, you will have the opportunity to design new source documents or modify existing source documents. You will want to design documents that fulfill their purpose and are easy to fill out, easy to use, attractive, and no more expensive than necessary.

You have probably struggled to fill out many forms that were less than ideal. You often do not have enough room to print the requested information, or you are not sure exactly what information is being requested or in what format, or you have to look over the entire form to find the sections you are supposed to complete. All of these are symptoms of poor form layout, which you will want to avoid when you design source documents.

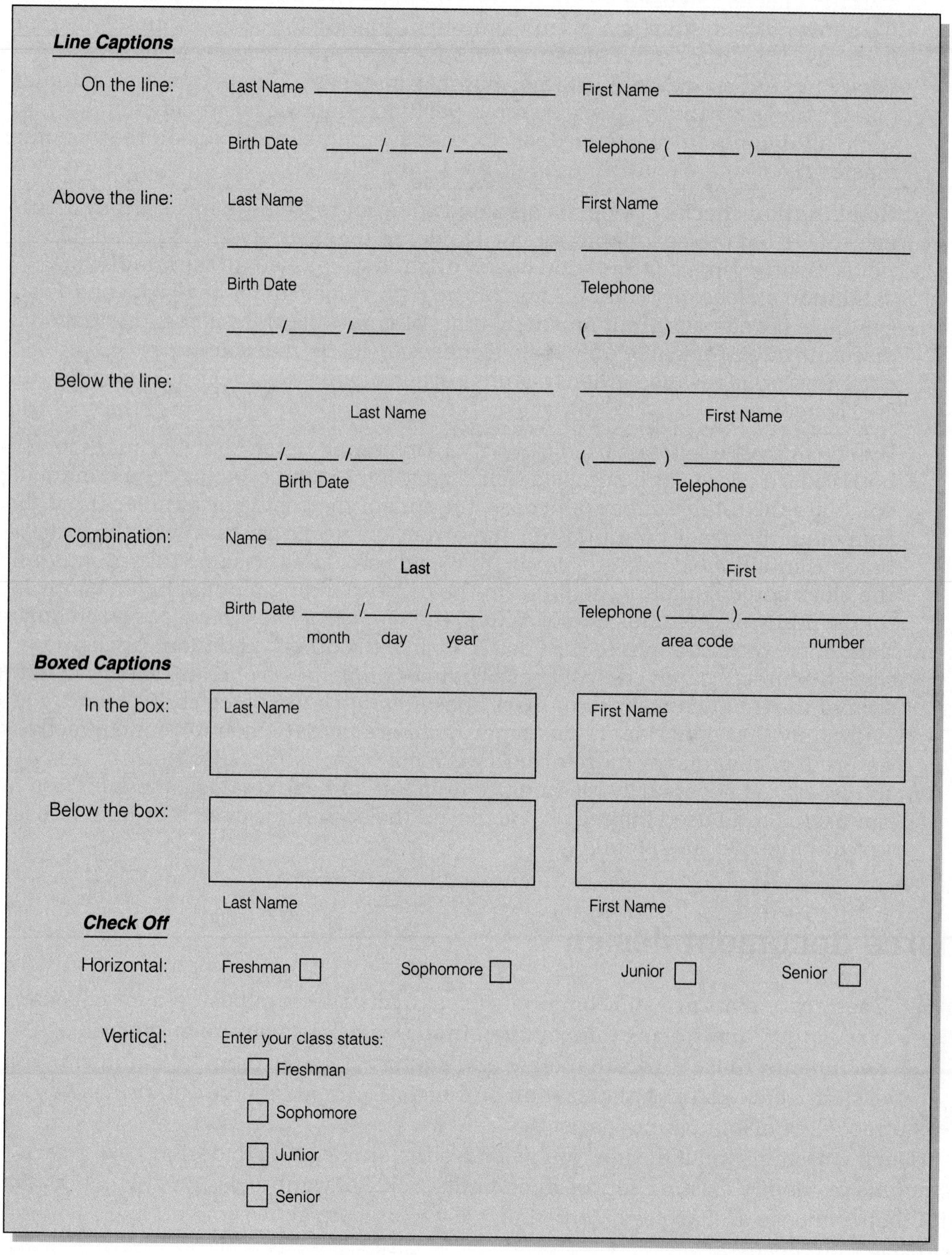

Figure 7-2 *Common source document caption techniques.*

A good layout makes it easy to accurately complete a form. You must provide enough space, both vertical and horizontal, for entering the requested data. If form completers will use a typewriter or computer printer, the lines to be filled should be a multiple of one-sixth of an inch apart; most typewriters and printers print six lines per inch. If the form will be handwritten, lines to be filled should be at least one-quarter of an inch apart. Lines that are one-third of an inch apart work well for both machine-printed and handwritten entry. The entry line itself should be long enough to hold the data to be entered. Normally one inch of space should be provided for every five or six characters that must be entered, but if the form will always be used with a typewriter or printer, then one inch for every ten characters is sufficient.

The position in which variable data is to be entered can be indicated by a blank line or a box. In either case, each item to be completed must be clearly identified with a descriptive caption. Figure 7-2 details optional positioning techniques for both line and box captions. For forms that might be completed with a typewriter, avoid captions that appear below the entry space, because they might not be visible when the typewriter is positioned on the line or in the box. Also shown in Figure 7-2 are two presentation methods for check-off boxes, which are used when the form completer must indicate one of a finite number of choices.

The order of appearance of logical groups of information on a form is important. The majority of source documents include most, if not all, of the zones shown in Figure 7-3. The heading zone typically includes the company name or logo and the title and number of the form. Codes, identification information, numbers, and dates used for storing completed forms are entered in the control zone. The instruction zone includes form completion directions. The body zone usually takes up at least half the form and includes captions and areas for entering variable data. If totals are applicable, they appear in the totals zone. Finally, the authorization zone contains required signatures and usage directives.

The layout of the zones shown in Figure 7-3 is typical. Notice how the flow of information on the form proceeds from left to right and top to bottom, matching the way people naturally read documents. Within a zone, especially the body zone, the flow should also progress from left to right, top to bottom. This makes the form easier to use not only for the form completer, but also for the data entry operators who work from completed forms to generate computer input.

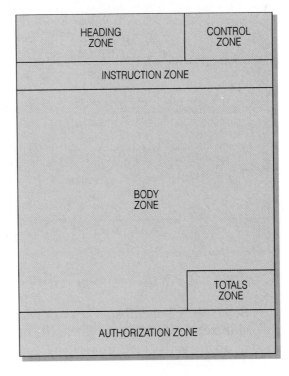

Figure 7-3 *Source document zones.*

Several source documents are shown in Figures 7-4 through 7-8. Although zoning is more obvious in some forms than in others, notice that each of these forms has been designed to be processed from left to right, top to bottom.

To reduce form printing and storage costs, source documents are usually designed in a standard size, such as 3"x 5", 5"x 7", 8"x 10", or 8 1/2"x 11". The appropriate paper type is usually dictated by the type of treatment the form will receive. Forms that will be handled by many people or used in harsh environments should be printed on stronger (heavier) paper. When multiple copies of a completed form are needed, multiple-part forms can be designed, often using different paper colors for each copy. For example, the license application in Figure 7-4 also serves as a receipt. This form is a two-part form; the top white copy is returned to the applicant and the bottom yellow copy is retained to serve as the source document.

Figure 7-4 *Sample source document for a dog license application and receipt.*

Some source documents are external documents seen and used by people outside the organization. As was true with external reports, external source documents must present an attractive and professional appearance. Appearance is less critical for internal source documents, such as the employee expense voucher shown in Figure 7-6 on page 7.12.

BAXTER COMMUNITY COLLEGE

REGISTRATION FORM

Student Number _____ Semester/ Year _____

Last Name _____ First Name _____ Initial ___ Local Telephone Number _____ Date _____

Street Address _____ City _____ State ___ Zip ___

Subj.	Course Number	Section (A, A1, 01)	Cr	Days	Times	Room	Bldg.

Total Credits = _____

Date Received / Initial _____ Advisor Approval _____ Date _____

Figure 7-5 Sample source document for student registration form.

Although you should try to design source documents that are not unnecessarily expensive, the cost to produce a form is not the most important consideration. The expenses associated with using any form are usually much higher than the printing expense—as much as twenty times higher according to some estimates. The typical form has many users, including the person who completes the form, the person who checks it, the person who authorizes or approves it, and the person who uses the form for data entry. Processing a poorly designed, inexpensively produced form can produce excessively high labor costs. Thus, the functionality of a form is a more critical consideration than is its cost.

Input record design

Batch data is input to a computer system in groups, or batches. During the data entry process, batch data must be placed in a temporary file; that temporary file then becomes the input file during the actual data input process. You can use a word processor or a data dictionary to document the formats of the batch input records you design. You can also use an **input record layout chart** to describe the format of all records in a batch input file. Whichever documentation method you use, these record layouts are used by programmers during systems development; if the data will be keyed by data entry clerks during systems operation, they could use the same record layout documentation.

Figure 7-9 on page 7.15 illustrates a typical input record layout chart. Notice that you can define up to three different input records on one chart page. Many source documents have repeating field sets. The expense voucher in Figure 7-6 on the next page, for example, provides space for data related to up to eight expenses. A completed video rental form (Figure 7-8 on page 7.14) can have data for up to six different videos. For such source documents, you will typically design one record to contain all the nonrepeating data, and a second record that will repeat as often as necessary to include all the repeating data fields.

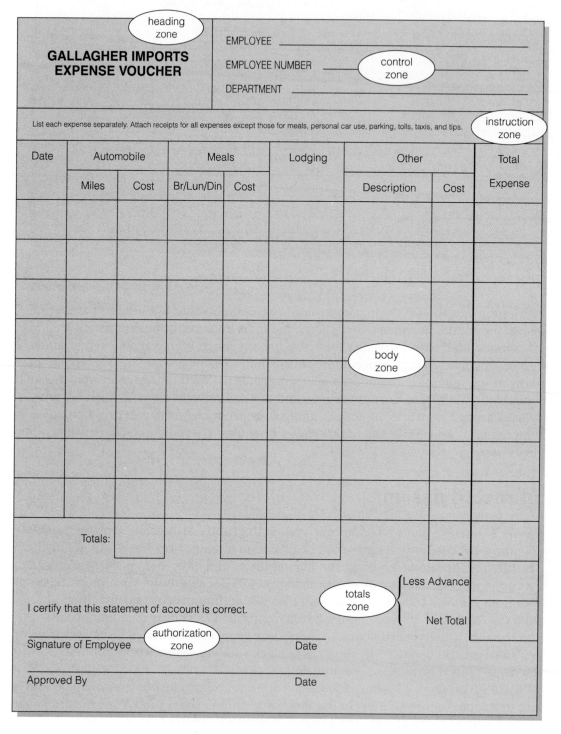

Figure 7-6 *Sample source document for an employee expense voucher form.*

BATES VIDEO CLUB — MEMBERSHIP APPLICATION

Print the following information:

Name		
Address		
City	State	Zip Code
Home Phone	Work Phone	

Security: Check the applicable box

```
        VISA [ ]     Card#_____

   MasterCard [ ]

American Express [ ]

       Other [ ]     Expiration Date_____
```

I agree to the following video club membership terms:

1. I may keep no rented video for longer than seven (7) days.
2. I may have no more than ten (10) rented videos at any one time.
3. If I fail to comply with the above terms, I understand that I will be obligated to return all rented videos at once, and that my video club membership may then be terminated.

Signed_____ **Date**_____

For office use only:

Accepted: [ ]   Member Number: [   ] Date: [   ]
Rejected: [ ]

Figure 7-7 Sample source document for a video club membership application.

BATES VIDEO CLUB — VIDEO RENTAL FORM

Member Number_____ Date_____

Title	ID#	Rental Fee	Date Returned

Total Rental Amount:_____

I agree to return the above rented videos within seven (7) days.

Signed: _____

Figure 7-8 *Sample source document for a video club rental form.*

Figure 7-9 documents the record layouts for the student registration form illustrated in Figure 7-5 on page 7.11. Figure 7-10 on page 7.16 is a system documentation form presenting the same information. We have defined layouts for two types of records. On both records, the first field is a one-character code to indicate the type of record; this record-type code will be needed during the input process. The first record type is a student record, which includes the necessary data from the top of the form. Notice that we have specified that only the first four characters of the name will be input; the telephone number, date, and address fields will not be input at all, because they are all retrievable items. The second record type is a course record, which draws data from the table on the form. Only the first three fields of the table are included in the course record. The fourth field, number of credits, can be retrieved. The computer registration system has no need for the last four fields, so they will not be input to the system. This registration form is actually a three-part form: the student keeps one copy, the advisor gets the second copy, and the third copy is used as the source document for data entry. Those last four fields, which specify the meeting times and location for the courses, appear on the form only for the convenience of the student.

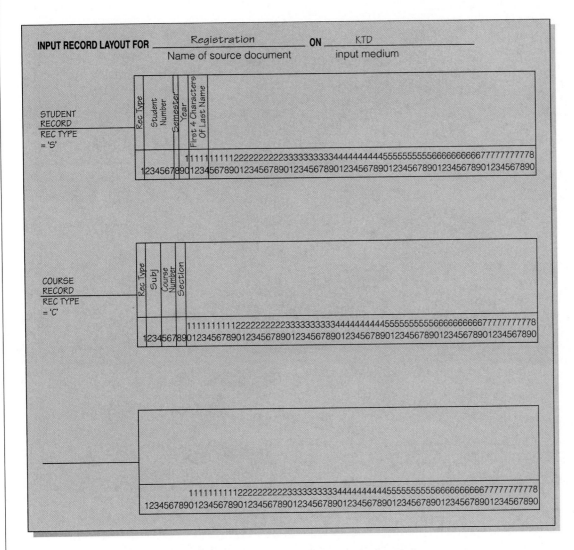

Figure 7-9 *Input record layouts for the student registration form.*

SYSTEM DOCUMENTATION

NAME OF SYSTEM	DATE	PAGE 1 OF 1
REGISTRATION	2/17/97	

ANALYST	PURPOSE OF DOCUMENTATION
M. Friedman	Registration Input Record Layouts

STUDENT RECORD — One record is created for each registration form

FIELD	TYPE	POSITIONS	COMMENTS
REC TYPE	A	1	= "S" for a student record
STUDENT NUMBER	N	2-7	
SEMESTER	A	8	= "F" for Fall, "W" for Winter, "S" for Summer
YEAR	N	9-10	Last two digits of the year
NAME	X	11-14	Only the first four characters of the Last Name are entered

COURSE RECORDS — One record is created for each course on the form

FIELD	TYPE	POSITIONS	COMMENTS
REC TYPE	A	1	= "C" for a course record
SUBJ	A	2-4	Standard department abbreviation
COURSE NUMBER	N	5-7	
SECTION	X	8-9	Left-justified

Figure 7-10 Input record documentation for the student registration form.

Figure 7-11 depicts a completed registration form. A data entry clerk working from this form would create six records: one student record and five course records. The information flow for data entry is also shown in that same figure. Notice that records and fields are entered in the order they appear, across and down the form. This design is no coincidence; the record layouts were designed from the source document to make the data entry process as straightforward as possible.

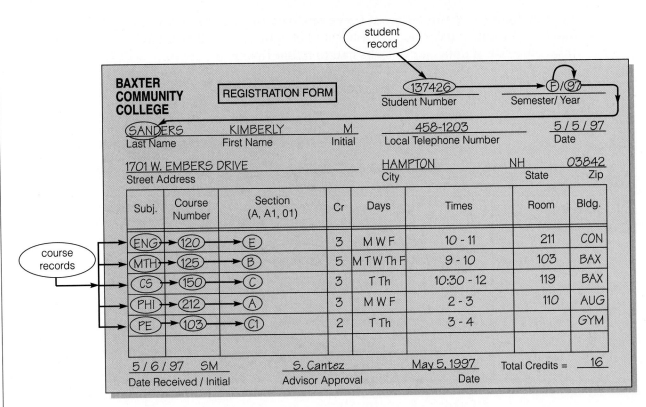

Figure 7-11 *Data entry information flow for the student registration form.*

In Figure 7-12, two different flows, one bad and one good, are shown for a hypothetical form layout. You can see the job would be much more difficult, time-consuming, and prone to error if data entry clerks had to follow the illogical flow.

ILLOGICAL INFORMATION FLOW:

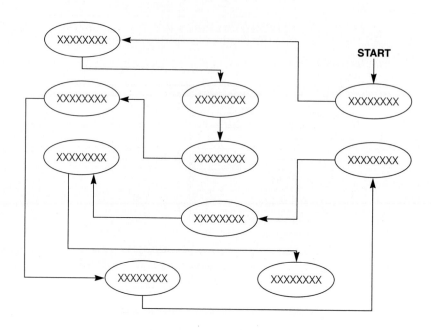

LOGICAL INFORMATION FLOW:

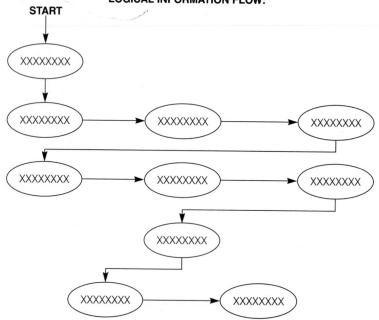

Figure 7-12 *The information flow shown in the top diagram is awkward and confusing. Source document information flow should be straightforward and logical like that shown in the bottom diagram.*

Screen design

We first considered screen design in Chapter 6, when we discussed output screen displays. We will now complete our coverage of screen design by discussing design principles for data entry screens and all types of user interface screens.

All screen displays serve the same two general purposes: to present information and to assist the operator using the system. As you might expect, many of the design guidelines we discussed for output screens are also applicable to data entry and user interface screens. These guidelines are, therefore, worth reconsidering.

1. All screen displays should be attractive and uncrowded.

2. The information on a single screen should be displayed in a meaningful, logical order.

3. Screen presentations should be consistent; that is, screen titles, messages, and instructions should all appear in the same general locations on all types of screen displays. Terminology should also be consistent. Don't use delete in some cases, cancel in others, and erase in still other cases to mean the same action. Similarly, be consistent in use of the terms Enter, Return, CR, or Carriage Return.

4. All messages, including error messages, should be explicit, understandable, and politely stated; avoid messages that are cute, cryptic, or insulting. Error messages such as *WRONG! You goofed!* and *Error DE4-163* are not particularly helpful and might even antagonize or frustrate operators. *Enter a number between 1 and 5* or *Customer number must be numeric* are examples of much better error messages.

5. Messages should remain on the screen long enough to be read. You could display a message for a specific length of time, say ten seconds, before erasing it, but if the operator is distracted during those ten seconds, he or she would miss the message. On the other hand, if the operator is familiar with the system and the message, ten seconds can seem like forever. It is better to give the operator control by displaying a message until the operator takes some action; then the message should be erased.

6. Special video effects should be used sparingly. Color, blinking, high brightness, reverse video, and sound effects all can help attract the operator's attention; but the overuse of such effects distracts rather than focuses an operator's attention.

7. Feedback is important. Error messages provide appropriate negative feedback, but reassuring positive feedback is also helpful. After an option is selected, the system often must perform some type of processing (file reading or writing, record sorting, and so on) before it can generate the display that results from that option. If a processing delay will be longer than a few seconds, you should give some positive, explicit indication of that valid option selection. For especially lengthy delays, you can help the operator by displaying the anticipated length of the delay and counting down the time remaining.

8. As was true for output screen designs, all input screen design layouts should be documented on a screen display layout form for later use by programmers. You should also obtain approval for your screen designs as they are developed. Do not wait until you have finished all the screens before presenting any one screen design to the end user. If you have followed the other guidelines, all your screen designs conform to some consistent presentation method. If an end user doesn't like one screen, you will likely also have to rework all the other screen designs you have developed.

Do not show the screen display layout form to end users. Prepare mock-up screen displays instead, because you want to simulate as well as possible what the end users will actually see. The ideal screen mock-up is a prototype with which end users can actually interact.

■ Data entry screen design

Form-filling is the traditional technique for online screen data entry. In **form-filling**, a complete form is first displayed on the screen; the operator then fills in the form by entering data, field by field. Figure 7-13 shows a simple data entry screen form; the operator has already entered the first field value and is in the process of entering the second field value, as you can tell by the position of the cursor and by the text displayed in the message line. Let's use this figure as an example, while we consider fourteen guidelines for data entry screen design.

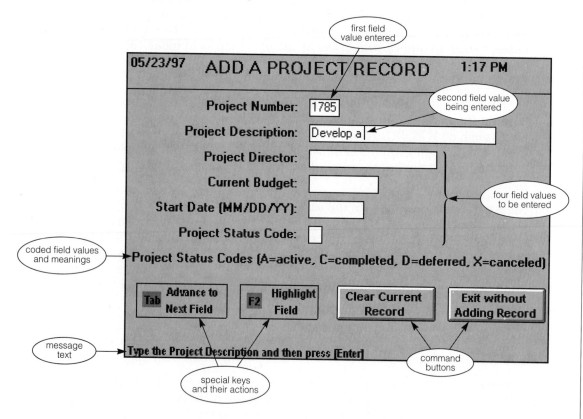

Figure 7-13 *A simple data entry screen. The operator is in the process of entering a project description.*

1. Restrict operator access to only those areas on the screen where data is to be entered. When the screen in Figure 7-13 is first displayed, the cursor should be positioned in the first entry location for project number. After the operator has entered a project number, the cursor should move to the first entry location for the next field in the form. A screen user should not be able to position the cursor, either accidentally or intentionally, so as to type over any part of the form display text.

2. Caption every field to be entered, and explicitly indicate the locations for all field entries. Field entry indications should demonstrate the required or maximum field size. In Figure 7-13, the white boxes are used to indicate the location

and maximum length of each field to be entered. Other methods often used to indicate field entry locations are to use underscores or to use special symbols, such as Project Number: < >. You can also use a combination of these two methods, as in: Project Number: <_____>.

3. If a field must be entered in some specific format, display that format. In Figure 7-13, the start date is to be entered in month/day/year order, as opposed to year/month/day or some other order. The caption for that field includes a reminder of the required format.

4. For consistency, require an ending keystroke for every field that is entered. The ENTER key is most often used to signal the end of a field entry. Unfortunately, many existing data entry screen programs require the operator to type an ending keystroke only when the entered field is less than the maximum length; full-length entries automatically cause the cursor to advance to the start of the next field. This can be confusing to operators, who might have to stop to look at the screen to decide whether they should press the ENTER key.

5. Do not require screen users to enter special characters, such as currency signs in dollar fields or slashes in date fields. To enter a project start date of November 24, 1997, the operator should have to enter only 112497. After the entry has been completed, the program can redisplay the input in the standard form, as 11/24/97.

6. Do not require screen users to type leading zeroes for numeric fields or trailing spaces for alphanumeric fields. For example, if the project number is 45, the operator should be able simply to type 45 instead of 0045 before pressing the ENTER key. Similarly, entering 11793 for a date should be allowed; that date should be interpreted and redisplayed as 01/17/93. Notice that an exception occurs when entering a date such as October 5, 1997. The operator must type the leading zero for the day. That date is correctly entered as 100597; 10597 would be interpreted as January 5, 1997.

7. Do not require that decimal points always be typed. To enter a value of $98.76, 98.76 is the appropriate entry form. But if the value is $98.00, the data entry operator should be allowed to enter only 98, without the decimal point and trailing zeroes.

8. For a field that has a standard value, display that value as a default. If the default value is appropriate, the screen user simply types the designated ending keystroke; if the default value is not appropriate, the user enters another value. A default value can also be used when the value for a field is likely to be constant for several successive records or throughout the data entry session. For example, transactions are often entered in date order. The date from the first transaction can be used as a default until a new date is entered, at which time this date becomes the default value.

9. For coded fields with only a few valid values, display those valid values and their meanings. In Figure 7-13, the valid values and meanings for the Project Status Code are displayed on the data entry screen.

10. Provide a means for leaving the data entry screen at any time without creating an input record. In Figure 7-13, the *Exit without Adding Record* command button is designated for this purpose. This feature is especially useful for clean, trouble-free exits when someone has accidentally accessed the data entry screen. In case the data entry screen user makes several mistakes and wants to restart at the beginning of the form, you should also provide a way to do this; the *Clear Current Record* command button serves this function in Figure 7-13.

11. After the form has been completely filled in and validated, give the data entry screen user a final opportunity to examine and accept or reject the complete set of data before it is committed for input. Typically, the user is asked to respond to a prompt such as *Add this record? (Y/N)*. If the answer is Y, a record with the values displayed on the screen is added to the system, the entry fields are cleared (except for default values), and the cursor is positioned in the first field ready for entry of another set of data. The answer would be N if the user notices that one or more fields are incorrectly entered. The user then must be allowed to move from field to field to correct the errors. After passing the last form field, the prompt appears again.

12. Provide a means for moving from field to field on the form. This feature allows screen users to enter fields in any order they choose. It is especially useful for correcting entry errors before the data is committed for input. For example, in Figure 7-13 on page 7.20 the TAB key is used to move from field to field.

13. If the operator will be working from a source document during data entry, you should design the screen form layout to match it. If student registration data is to be entered online, for example, the data entry screen might look like Figure 7-14. Notice the similarities between this screen and the registration form shown in Figure 7-5 on page 7.11. The data entry information flow that you saw in Figure 7-11 on page 7.17 is equally appropriate for this data entry screen except that no part of the name is actually entered; instead, the entire student name, as well as the telephone and address fields, will be retrieved based on the entered student number. The date displayed on the screen is the current system date (to record the date the data was input). In the lower part of the screen, the displayed credits are also retrieved values.

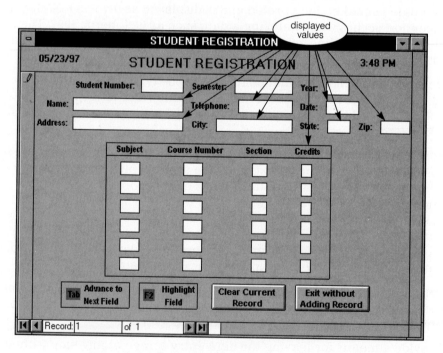

Figure 7-14 *A data entry screen for the student registration form.*

14. Allow the operator to add, change, delete, and view records. Screens very similar to the one shown in Figure 7-13 on page 7.20 could be used for changing, deleting, and viewing project records. In all three cases, after the screen user has entered a project number, the appropriate project record is accessed and the current values for all fields are displayed. On a data entry screen for record changes, the user would then move through the form, changing field

values where appropriate. The user would then have to respond Y to *Apply these changes? (Y/N)* before the entered changes actually took effect. On a data entry screen for record deletions, the prompt *Delete this record? (Y/N)* would appear after the field values are displayed; the record would be deleted only if the screen user answers Y. For viewing a data record, the field values are displayed until the user either types a special key, answers Y to an appropriate prompt, or clicks a special command button.

Alternatively, one screen could be used to allow the operator to perform all four functions of add, change, delete, and view. You could provide special keys or command buttons to start the add process, to confirm a delete, and so on.

At what point during online data entry should data fields be validated? Should all appropriate field checks be applied as soon as a field is entered, or should you wait until all fields are input before validating any one of them?

Sometimes the system environment makes the decision for you. Interactive interface systems, such as CICS in IBM-mainframe environments, for example, often impose specific design strategies. In a centralized, multiuser environment, considerations such as transmission times and transaction processing delays often add design constraints. In such environments, the data entry process usually operates significantly faster if all fields are first entered and transmitted before any validation is performed.

When the operating environment does permit a realistic choice, which is the better practice? Some fields are best validated when first entered, especially those fields that provide unique identification or that are the basis for retrieval or calculation of other displayed fields. For example, when the student number is entered on the student registration screen, you might want to immediately verify that the student number is valid and, if so, retrieve and display the student name, address, and telephone number. Some fields cannot be immediately validated. A field involved in a combination check, for example, cannot be completely validated until all fields involved in that check have been entered. How should you handle the other fields: those that do not fit into either of these two categories? Should you validate them as they are entered or wait until all fields are entered?

If you validate immediately, operators are asked to enter a corrected value while their attention is still on the given field in the source document; they won't have to scan through the source document looking for the field. If the error resulted from simple mistyping, the value can be retyped or corrected and the

data entry process continued. If the data as recorded on the source document is incorrect, the operator can note the error on the document, set it aside for checking and correction, and then either move on to another source document or quit the data entry process. Either way, the operator has not wasted time entering all the fields for a source document that will eventually be rejected.

Interrupting the data entry process for every error, however, does interrupt the operator's concentration. Many operators prefer to enter all source document fields without interruption and then correct the fields as necessary. If the operator somehow missed the signal that a field error occurred, he or she would enter the next data field at the prompt for the earlier, erroneous field. By the time the errors are noticed, time has been wasted entering data at the wrong prompts.

Waiting to validate until after all the fields have been entered avoids the problems cited in the previous paragraph, but potential problems exist with this technique, too. One of the data entry screen design guidelines suggests providing a means for moving from field to field on the form. While we expect that the operator will usually enter fields in form order, in some cases the operator might want to enter fields in another order. How can you be sure at what point you should start validating fields? If you validate whenever the operator passes the last entry field, you might validate fields the operator has not yet entered, thus wasting processing and operator time.

When you have a choice for validation timing, there is no one right, always best, practice. You should probably present two or more operating screen mock-ups of the data entry screen to the people who will be using it and let them choose the method they prefer. One final word of caution: using different validation techniques for data entry screens in the same information system is not a good idea. Inconsistent treatments can cause needless operator confusion. ■

■ Process control screen design

In many information systems, some or all of the system processing is designed to execute in an online mode in response to requests entered by end users. For such online systems, you must design appropriate input screens for entering the end user processing requests. These screen displays are called process control screens, or dialogue screens.

Two processing control methods are commonly used: menu input and prompted input. In the following paragraphs, we will examine design principles for each of these methods, and then we will briefly consider how they could be used together.

Menu screens A menu screen displays a list of processing options and allows the end user to select one of the options. An option might be selected by entering an option number; or, keyboard function keys, cursor movement keys, mice, light pens, or touch screens can be used. Figure 7-15 shows a menu for a simple online system for project tracking. Selecting option 1 leads the user to the data entry screen we saw in

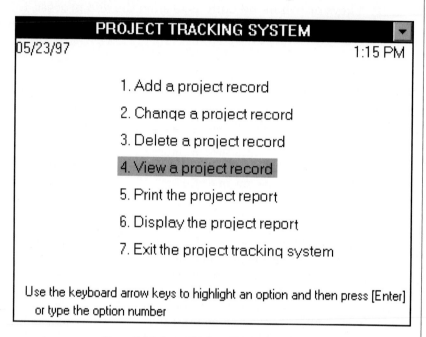

Figure 7-15 on page 7.20. Options 2, 3, and 4 lead to the change, delete, and view screens we briefly discussed in the last section. Selecting options 5 or 6 causes the project report to be either printed or displayed on the screen. Finally, option 7 allows the user to exit the project tracking system. This project tracking system is called a menu-driven system, because it uses one or more menus for process control.

Most online information systems are much more complex than our simple project tracking example and, therefore, have many more processing options. Presenting more than ten options on a single menu screen can result in a display that is crowded and confusing, however. When there are many options, you should present the options in a series of menus, arranged in a logical hierarchy. The first menu presented when an end user accesses the system is called the main menu, or top-level menu. The main menu presents several broad classifications of processing choices. Some or all of the main menu choices can lead to other menus, called submenus, with more specific processing choices. In more complex systems, submenus might exist under submenus. Eventually, every path in the menu selection hierarchy leads to some specific system process.

The menu hierarchy for an online, menu-driven grading system is shown in Figure 7-16. The main menu options are shown in the left-hand column of the figure. Each of the main menu options 1-6 leads to a submenu. The options for each of those six submenus are shown in the right-hand column of the figure. Each submenu option leads to a specific system process. Notice that each submenu has an option to return to the main menu. If such a menu option is not provided, then a standard function key or other control key must be specified for this purpose. The ability to return to the main menu is a necessary feature for navigating through the menu hierarchy.

Figure 7-15 *A menu for the project tracking system.*

MAIN MENU

1. Student Score Processing

STUDENT SCORE PROCESSING MENU

1. Add a set of scores
2. Edit a set of scores
9. Return to Main Menu

2. Class List Processing

CLASS LIST PROCESSING MENU

1. Add a new class list
2. Edit a class list
9. Return to Main Menu

3. Report Processing

REPORT PROCESSING MENU

1. Print reports without dropped scores
2. Print reports with dropped scores
3. Print a score data entry form
9. Return to Main Menu

4. History Processing

HISTORY PROCESSING MENU

1. Add a class to the history file
2. Search for a specific student
9. Return to Main Menu

5. Class Setup Processing

CLASS SETUP PROCESSING MENU

1. Add/Edit grading scale
2. Add/Edit score descriptions
3. Add/Edit maximum scores
4. Edit a student's final grade
9. Return to Main Menu

6. System Configuration

CONFIGURE SYSTEM MENU

1. Configure entire system
2. Configure monitor and colors
3. Configure printer
4. Configure disk drive
9. Return to Main Menu

9. Exit System

Figure 7-16 *Menu hierarchy for the student grading system.*

The various screen displays in a menu-driven system are often assigned a number based on their hierarchical position. The main menu is always screen 0. Screens on the next level are numbered to match the main menu option to reach them. For example, in the Figure 7-16 menu hierarchy, the student score processing menu is screen 1.0, the class list processing menu is screen 2.0, and so on. The data entry screen for adding a set of scores is screen 1.1; this number reflects the fact that an end user must specify option 1 on the main menu and then option 1 on the 1.0 screen to reach that data entry screen. Similarly, the data entry screen for changing, or editing, a set of scores is screen 1.2, and the data entry screen for editing a student's final grade is screen 5.4. For complex menu-driven systems with several menu levels, 2.3.1.4 and 1.7.3.1 might both be valid screen numbers. This screen numbering system is useful for documentation purposes.

The menu method of process control has several advantages. First, menus are easy to understand. Selecting options from a restaurant menu is something we all have done. If you decide you are hungry for seafood, you look at the seafood submenu. If you then decide on Lobster Newburg, you have to consider yet another submenu for your choices of salad, soup, vegetable, and so on. Selecting processing options from a screen menu display is comparable to selecting items from a restaurant menu. With menus, end users do not have to memorize all the available processing options; they merely have to be able to recognize the desired option from a short list of options.

Multiple-level menus can be confusing, especially if they are not structured in a hierarchy that makes sense to the end user. For that reason, your menu hierarchy must reflect groupings that are logical from the end user's point of view, even if that hierarchy does not match logical processing relationships.

For experienced end users, using multiple-level menus might become tedious. For example, screen number 1.3.4 might be an often-used data entry screen in an online information system. To reach that particular data entry screen, the end user would have to work through three menu screens, selecting option 1 from the main menu, option 3 from the first submenu, and option 4 from the submenu's submenu. An impatient end user might resent the many menu screens and delays necessary to get to the desired process. You can head off this problem by providing shortcuts. In this case, if you allowed an end user to enter an option choice of 1.3.4 at the main menu, you could then skip all the intermediate screens and immediately display the desired data entry screen. Always try to provide such menu navigation shortcuts for multiple-level menu systems. End users who do not want to use the shortcut feature can step through the menu hierarchy in the standard manner, but those end users who know where they want to go can choose to use the shortcut.

Prompt screens   With prompted input process control methods, the end user types something in response to a prompt that appears on the screen. One prompt with which you are familiar is the computer system's own prompt, such as > or C:>, for example. To respond to a computer system's prompt, end users type actual computer system commands, such as the command to execute a data entry program or a menu program. Command language processors can also be used for process control. End users respond to a command language prompt by typing a command in the required syntax. SQL (Structured Query Language), pronounced *sequel*, is one such commercially available command language processor. In response to a SQL prompt, an end user can type an INSERT command to create a new data record, for example. In the following paragraphs, we will discuss other types of prompted input: responses to prompts that are displayed on screens generated by the information system itself.

With menu screens, a full-screen menu display is first presented; when the end user enters a single option, a new full-screen display of some type is presented; thus, menu screens normally involve full-screen displays. In contrast, a prompt screen display is initially an almost completely blank screen with a single displayed prompt. When the end user responds to the first prompt, usually a second prompt displays, appearing below the first prompt and response. The typical prompt screen display is scrolled; that is, when the screen is full, the line at the top of the screen disappears and all other screen lines move up one line, making the last screen line available for the next end user response. Usually, several of the most recent prompts and their responses are visible on a prompt screen. They might not be visible, however, if the most recent prompt response produced a data listing on the screen. In that case, the screen might be filled with the end of the data listing and the new prompt that follows it.

One type of prompted input is the **question/answer screen**, in which the prompts include actual questions, and end user responses take the form of answers to the questions. Figures 7-17a and 7-17b show two question/answer screens as they might appear after several questions have been asked and answered. To make using question/answer screens easier for the end user, you can provide an expected or typical response as a default value. A default answer NO is shown for the last question in Figure 7-17a. To accept the displayed default value, the end user merely presses the ENTER key; or he or she can choose to type any response over the displayed default value. In Figure 7-17b, the end user has typed ADD in response to the first question, and REGISTRATION in response to the follow-up question. As soon as the end user presses the ENTER key, the data entry screen shown in Figure 7-17c displays on the screen.

Question/answer screens can be an acceptable alternative to menus for process control, especially if sophisticated and flexible question/answer sequences are developed. Keep in mind, however, that in general such question/answer sequences work well only for casual, unsophisticated end users. Experienced system users often find the question/answer dialogue tiresome.

```
Do you wish to add, edit, delete, display, or print records?
>PRINT
Which report do you want printed?
>CLOSED CLASSES
         Printing...
Do you want another report?
>YES
Which report do you want printed?
OPEN CLASSES
         Printing...
Do you want another report?
>NO
```

Figure 7-17a *A question/answer screen sequence.*

```
Do you wish to add, edit, delete, display, or print records?
>ADD
What source document will be used to add the records?
>REGISTRATION
```

Figure 7-17b *A question/answer screen sequence.*

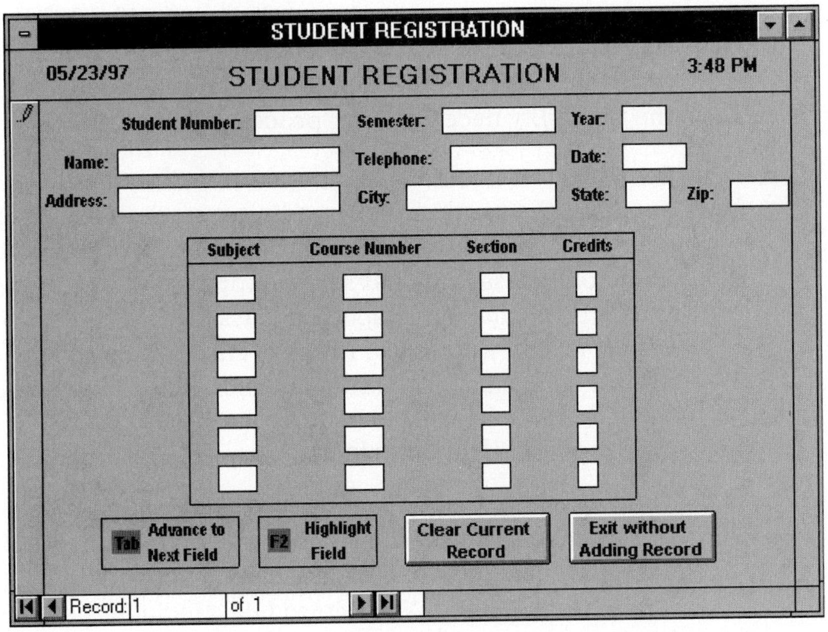

Figure 7-17c *This data entry screen for a student registration appears in response to Figure 7-17b.*

A second type of prompted input utilizes a command language integrated with the information system. Figure 7-18 is a command language prompt screen after several commands have been entered; the illustrated command sequence is comparable to the two screens shown in Figures 7-17a and 7-17b on the previous page. Some command languages are called **natural languages**, because the end user types commands or requests in normal, natural English sentences. The technology for natural language processors is not yet what it should be, and so they are not extensively used today. Perhaps in the near future such natural language processors will be commonplace.

```
>PRINT CLOSCLSS
        Printing Complete
>PRINT OPENCLSS
        Printing Complete
>ENTERREG▊
```

Figure 7-18 A command language prompt screen after several commands have been entered.

```
..Print the closed classes report
        PRINTING COMPLETED

..Print the open classes report
        PRINTING COMPLETED

..Let me add registration records ▊
```

Figure 7-19   A natural language prompt screen.

Figure 7-19 simulates a prompted natural language interchange between an end user and an information system.

With command language prompts, the end user is in control of the accessible system processes, instead of at the mercy of a rigid menu system or question/answer series. All but the very simplest of command languages require extensive end user training. Unfortunately, the easier a command language is to use, the more likely it is to lack the flexibility necessary for process control.

Combination screens   Menu input and prompted input are often used in combination. For example, the menu-driven grading system shown in Figure 7-16 on page 7.25 also uses prompt screens for some input. One such prompt screen asks the end user to enter the name of a class file. That screen appears after he or she specifies any processing option that is performed on a specific class, such as adding or editing a set of scores and adding or editing a class list. In those cases, the appropriate data entry screen is displayed after a valid class file name has been entered on the class file prompt screen.

■ Graphical User Interfaces

The most recent evolution in screen design involves graphical user interfaces. A **graphical user interface (GUI)** uses windows, menu bars, pull-down and pop-up menus, and graphical pictures (called **icons**) with which the end user communicates with the application system. Well-known GUIs include the Apple Macintosh interface, Microsoft Windows, IBM's OS/2, and NeXTSTEP. In a Microsoft Windows environment, for example, an end user might use a mouse to double-click an icon in order to select a particular application system for execution. Typically, the user interface for that application system would utilize a GUI that is entirely consistent with that of Microsoft Windows; that is, all windows, menus, option selection techniques, and so on, would have a similar appearance in all Microsoft Windows applications. Because GUIs are used for data entry as well as for process control, the fourteen guidelines for traditional data entry screen design discussed previously in this chapter are equally applicable to GUI designs.

With GUIs, there is no sharp differentiation between process control screens and data entry screens. Instead, windows within a single screen are displayed, changed, or erased as necessary in response to user selections;

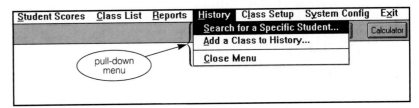

Figure 7-20 *A GUI menu bar and toolbar for the student grading system.*

such windows might contain processing options, data entry options, or both.

Figure 7-20 shows a GUI version of the main menu for the student grading system. The main menu options, such as Student Scores and Class List, are displayed across the top of the screen. This type of display, in which menu choices are presented horizontally across the top of the screen, is called a **menu bar**. A second bar, called a toolbar, appears under the menu bar. The **toolbar** contains icons representing common commands that the end user can select by clicking the mouse button. These commands might be navigation shortcuts for the application system or might trigger other systems to execute, as is the case for the toolbar icons shown in Figure 7-20. An end user could click the *E-mail* toolbar button, for example, to read his or her electronic mail; exiting the e-mail application system would return the end user to the student grading system main menu screen.

To select a main menu option, the end user positions the mouse pointer over the desired menu choice and then clicks the mouse button. Alternatively, the end user can use the keyboard to select a main menu option by pressing the letter key that is underscored for the desired main menu option. In Figure 7-21, for example, the end user has selected the History processing option by clicking *History* on the menu bar or pressing *H* on the keyboard. The subsidiary options for history processing are then displayed in a **pull-down menu**, which is a submenu that appears beneath a selected menu option. The end user then uses the mouse or keyboard to select a pull-down menu option.

Figure 7-21 *A pull-down menu for the student grading system.*

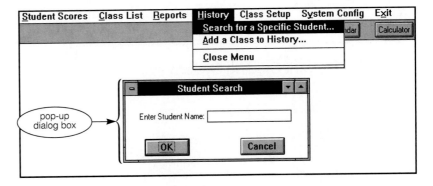

Figure 7-22 *A pop-up dialog box.*

In Figure 7-22, a pop-up dialog box requesting the entry of a student name has appeared. A **pop-up window** is one that temporarily appears, superimposed over the other windows on the screen.

```
┌─ Dialog box controls ──────────────────┐
│ ┌─ Text box ──────┐  ┌─ Toggle button ─┐ │
│ │ Employee Name   │  │   [Vested]      │ │
│ │ [_____]  │  │                 │ │
│ └─────────────────┘  └─────────────────┘ │
│ ┌─ List box ──────┐                       │
│ │ Asst Mgr    [▲] │  ┌─ Drop-down list box ─┐│
│ │ Clerk           │  │ Machinists Union [▼] ││
│ │ Manager     [▼] │  └───────────────────────┘│
│ └─────────────────┘                       │
│ ┌─ Option buttons ┐  ┌─ Check boxes ────┐ │
│ │ ◉ Non-exempt    │  │ ▨ Optional dental plan│
│ │ ○ Exempt        │  │ ⊠ Family coverage │ │
│ └─────────────────┘  └───────────────────┘ │
│ ┌─ Command buttons ┐ ┌─ Spin bar ──────┐ │
│ │ [Update] [Cancel]│ │ Exemptions: 1 [▲▼]│
│ └──────────────────┘ └─────────────────┘ │
└─────────────────────────────────────────┘
```

Figure 7-23 *Common controls for dialog boxes.*

A **dialog box** is a window display used to request information about a task to be performed or to supply needed information. Figure 7-23 illustrates eight different GUI techniques used for entering information or choosing options.

- A **text box** is used for entering alphanumeric data.
- A **toggle button** is either on or off; clicking the button switches the selected status.
- A **list box** displays a list of choices; if there are more choices than can fit in the box, a **scroll bar** like the one shown at the right of the list box allows the user to move quickly through the display of all the list choices.
- A **drop-down list box** appears initially as a rectangular box with the current selection displayed; when the user selects the arrow in the square box at the right, a list of the available choices appears.
- **Option buttons** (also called **radio buttons**) represent mutually exclusive options; only one option may be selected at a time, with the selected option containing a black dot.
- A **check box** next to an option means that the option can be selected or not; selection is indicated by an X in the box. Unlike option buttons, any number of check box options may be selected.
- **Command buttons** initiate an immediate action; a command button followed by an ellipsis (...) opens another dialog box.
- Finally, a **spin bar** changes a number; clicking the up arrow at the right increases the number, while the down arrow decreases the number.

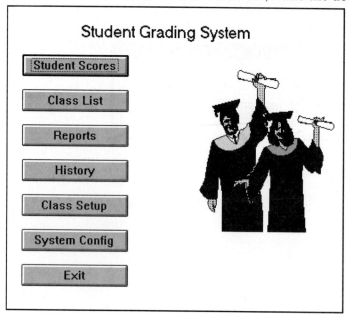

Figure 7-24 *A switchboard for the student grading system.*

As shown in Figure 7-24, the switchboard is an alternative to process control menus like those shown in Figure 7-15 on page 7.24 and Figure 7-20 on page 7.29. A **switchboard** is a form-like window, containing command buttons that represent the options available to an end user. The command buttons can contain words like those in Figure 7-24 or they can contain icons. Some application systems, especially those that are large and complex, might use switchboards, menus, and toolbars. However, most systems rely on one or, at most, two of these visual tools.

No matter what visual tools are used, the most significant advantage of a GUI is the ease and speed with which an end user can learn to use the system. Many packaged application systems now utilize a

GUI. Some companies are now using GUIs for their own internally-produced application systems. Because the advantage of ease of learning and use is compromised if an end user must interact with several different, inconsistent GUIs, all such application systems within a particular organization should be developed using a single GUI design strategy. Application systems designed in such a similar way are commonly described as having the same look and feel.

■ Help screen design

Even with the best of online input processing designs, end users might occasionally require additional assistance or information. Online **help screens** display a window or screenful of text that explains concepts, procedures, menu choices, function keys, formats, and so on.

End users typically request help in one of two ways: by pressing a special key (usually one of the function keys) or by clicking a command button, toolbar button, or menu option designated for that purpose. Many information systems use both techniques.

Help information is typically presented in two different ways. With **context-sensitive help**, the information system presents information relevant to what the end user was doing when help was requested. Figure 7-25 is an example of a help screen that might appear if an end user requested help while entering the semester field of the data entry screen of Figure 7-14 on page 7.22. Notice that the help screen describes the data field and its format and lists all valid field values with their meanings. Clicking the *Close* command button returns the end user to the point from which help was requested. In this case, the help screen would be erased, the data entry screen would again be displayed, the student number that had already been entered would be redisplayed, and the pointer would be positioned in the semester entry position.

With the other technique for presenting help information, a help switchboard or menu is displayed whenever an end user requests help. By making appropriate choices throughout the help screen hierarchy, the end user eventually reaches a text screen with the information needed. Figure 7-26 illustrates the main help switchboard for the grading system.

Both techniques just described can be useful, and they can be used in combination. Many information systems provide both context-sensitive and menu-driven help.

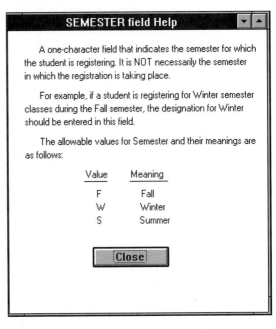

Figure 7-25 *A context-sensitive help screen for a student registration entry.*

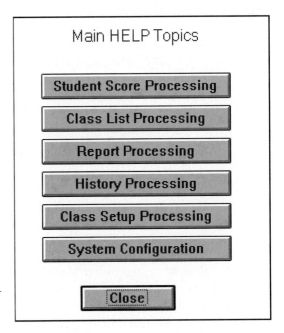

Figure 7-26 *A main help switchboard for the grading system.*

All the guidelines we discussed for designing process control menu and switchboard screens are also relevant when you design help *menu* screens. The following guidelines will help you design help *text* screens.

1. Provide a direct route for the end user to return to the point where help was requested.
2. Title every help screen to identify the help text that follows.
3. Write the help text in easy-to-understand, everyday language.
4. Present attractive screens. Help screens should not be too crowded; a blank line between paragraphs makes it easier to read the information.
5. Provide examples whenever appropriate.

Input control

Input control encompasses all measures necessary to ensure that input data is correct, complete, and secure. As we stated earlier in this chapter, this topic cannot be treated as a mere afterthought. You must consider input control throughout all aspects of your systems input design.

We have already discussed many of the measures you can take to ensure that input data is correct and complete. Effective source document design promotes both correctness and completeness. For batch input, critical source document fields can be prechecked during data capture, and batch control totals can be used during data input. During either online data entry or batch data input, you can validate all data fields. Your online data entry program can simply refuse to accept invalid field values; your batch data input program should write all rejected records to a log file, which then must be periodically checked for rejected records that have not been corrected and reinput.

Every piece of information that leaves the information system should be traceable back to the input data that produced it. This means that you must provide an audit trail, recording the source of all data and the date it was input. An audit trail must do more than simply record the original entry of data. If someone signs on to the system, accesses a record, changes a field value, and then signs off the system, all those activities must also be noted in the audit trail file and report.

Source document handling procedures must be developed and followed to help ensure that data is not lost before it is ever input. All source documents that arise from outside the organization should be logged when they are received. Whenever source documents are passed between departments, that transfer should also be logged.

To prevent duplicate data from entering the system, a source document should be stamped or otherwise marked as it goes through a data entry process.

Data security is concerned with protecting the data from loss or damage and with recovering the data when it is lost. Once the data they contain has been entered, source documents should be stored in a safe location for some specified length of time. Audit trail files and reports should also be stored and saved. Then, if a data file is damaged, you can reconstruct the lost data. Data security also involves protecting data from unauthorized access. System sign-on procedures should be developed to help prevent unauthorized individuals from accessing the system. Data files should be given **passwords**; especially sensitive data can be **encrypted**, or coded, so that it cannot be read except by special decoding software.

As was true for the output control measures we discussed in Chapter 6, the responsibility for many of the input control measures we have covered are placed with the information systems department. As a systems analyst, you can play a significant role in providing effective input control.

Automated design tools

I n Chapter 6 on output design, we discussed the screen and form generator software provided with many DBMS, 4GL, and CASE products. A screen or form generator can be useful during input design as well. The screen display definitions you develop using a screen or form generator can serve the same documentation purposes as screen display layout forms. Screen prototypes can also serve as screen mock-ups. As before, such screen or form generators can ensure consistency with the data dictionary, as well as relieve you from some of the more tedious design tasks.

Screen or form generators that create programs to produce the screen can be especially useful. For data entry screens, those created programs often can include many of the field validation checks documented in the data dictionary. The generated program can, therefore, be used by end users or operators to simulate a reasonably realistic data entry session. A hierarchy of menu screens, switchboard screens, or a mixture of the two can also be simulated with a program created by a screen or form generator. Such generated menu screen programs are often used in the actual information system implementation.

CHAPTER CASE STUDY

James Tool Company — Input Design

Don Mard and Kimberly Wallace, systems analysts at James Tool Company, were starting a three-day workshop with Lennox Software Solutions at James Tool Company headquarters. This workshop began their training and the training of the end users on the detailed processing and functions of this vendor's payroll package. The payroll package from Lennox Software Solutions was scheduled to arrive the next week, so Mard and Wallace were happy that the payroll system effort was going so smoothly.

Meanwhile, programmer/analyst Howard Coswell began to design the inputs to the union system. Coswell needed to design four inputs. Two of these inputs were new forms: a Union Change Form and an Employee Union Dues Authorization Form. The other two inputs would be two new data entry screens to correspond to the new forms; these screens would allow for the processing of union and employee union dues changes.

Coswell started with the Union Change Form. Because the only critical values needed on this form were the union name and number and the weekly dues amount, he designed the simple form shown in Figure 7-27. Coswell felt that this one form could be used for adding new unions, changing dues amounts and union names for existing unions, and deleting unions that might no longer represent the employees of James Tool Company. These three actions would be accomplished by having the submitter of the form simply check off the type of change. Finally, he added a place on the form that could be signed by the director of union relations, who would submit the form and authorize union changes.

Next, Coswell needed to design a data entry screen to handle the data from the Union Change Form. Because the James Tool Company had screen design standards, Coswell easily and quickly developed the data entry screen shown in Figure 7-28. Coswell decided that the screen could be more useful if it could also be used to view data on the existing unions. By entering the appropriate action code for add, change, delete, or view, the operator could handle any situation that arose concerning the maintenance of unions.

Rather than obtain end user approval of the Union Change Form and the corresponding screen design at this point, Coswell continued with the design of the Employee Union Dues Authorization Form. Coswell reasoned that it would be more effective to review the entire input package at one time, because all the inputs would need to be approved by the same end users.

The Employee Union Dues Authorization Form would be a much more complicated form than the Union Change Form, because it has more required data and signatures. After a couple hours' work, Coswell had designed the form shown in Figure 7-29 on the next page. He divided this form into three sections: the top section completed by the employee, the middle section signed by the union secretary, and the bottom portion completed by the director of union relations.

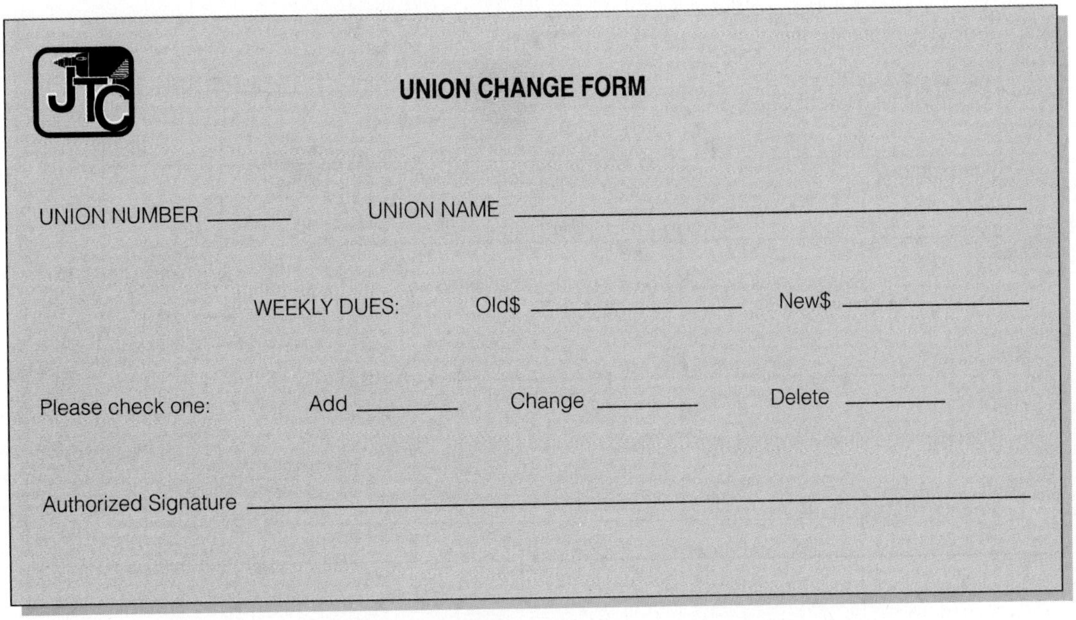
UNION CHANGE FORM

UNION NUMBER ______ UNION NAME ______________________

WEEKLY DUES: Old$ ____________ New$ ____________

Please check one: Add ______ Change ______ Delete ______

Authorized Signature ______________________________

Figure 7-27 *The Union Change Form for the new union system at James Tool Company.*

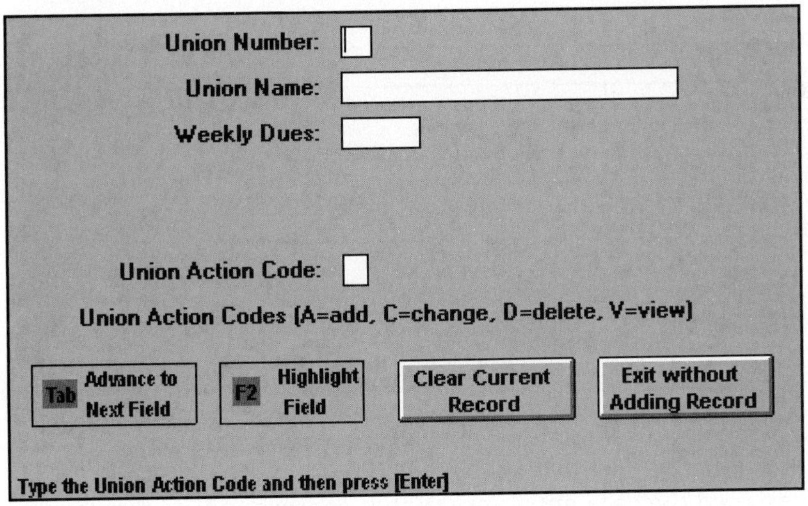

Figure 7-28 *The new data entry screen to add, change, delete, and view unions at James Tool Company.*

Figure 7-29 The Employee Union Dues Authorization Form for the new union system at James Tool Company.

Coswell next designed the data entry screen that corresponds to this form (Figure 7-30). Coswell designed this screen to be consistent with the other union system screen he had already designed. Once again, the one screen could be used to add, change, delete, or view data — in this case, employee union dues deduction data.

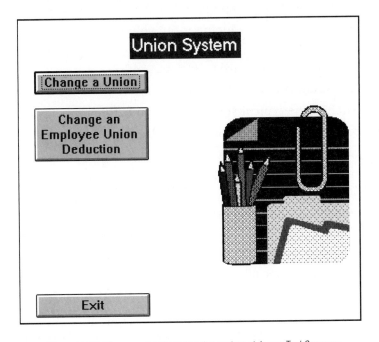

Social Security Number:	- -	Employee Name:	
Union Number:		Union Name:	
Effective Date:	/ /	Weekly Dues:	

Union Action Code: ☐

Union Action Codes (A=add, C=change, D=delete, V=view)

| Tab /Advance to Next Field | F2 Highlight Field | Clear Current Record | Exit without Adding Record |

Type the Union Action Code and then press [Enter]

Figure 7-30 *The data entry screen to add, change, delete, and view employee union deductions for the new union system at James Tool Company.*

Coswell realized he needed a menu screen to link these two data entry screens, so he designed the screen shown in Figure 7-31. Having completed all the inputs for the union system, Coswell met with Delbert Donovan, director of union relations, and Jim McKeen, director of the payroll department. This meeting was fruitful, and both Donovan and McKeen enthusiastically approved the new input designs.

Union System

Change a Union

Change an Employee Union Deduction

Exit

Figure 7-31 *The menu for the new union system at James Tool Company.*

Summary

In this chapter, we continued our study of the systems design phase by discussing the design of systems input. With today's technology, a wide variety of input media is available, including VDTs, optical, voice, and magnetic recognition devices, special purpose terminals, and graphical input devices.

Input design objectives include utilizing appropriate input media and methods, developing efficient input procedures, reducing input volume, and reducing input errors. Relevant to these objectives is understanding the differences between data capture, entry, and input: data capture involves identifying and recording source data; data entry involves converting source data into a computer-readable form; and data input involves the actual inputting of data to the information system. To help reduce input errors, data is validated by one or more checks of sequence, existence, range and limit, reasonableness, validity, combination, and batch control.

We covered source document design considerations, followed by input record design for batch input data. We then turned our attention to all types of input screen design. Form-filling screens are the traditional technique for online data entry. Both menu-driven and prompted-input process control screens enable end users to access and request online information system processes. Graphical User Interfaces (GUIs) represent the latest evolution in screen design; a GUI combines the functions of data entry and process control by utilizing the latest developments in graphical and windowing capabilities. Online help screens provide context-sensitive or menu-driven assistance to system users.

Finally, we discussed input control and examined the use of automated design tools in the systems input design process.

Review Questions

1. What is uploading? What is downloading?

2. Explain the differences between data capture, data entry, and data input.

3. List and briefly discuss four ways of reducing input volume.

4. Briefly discuss each of the data validation checks mentioned in this chapter. Is data validation performed during data capture, data entry, or data input?

5. What is a control total? What is a hash total?

6. What is included in each of the typical source document zones?

7. Briefly discuss the design guidelines applicable to all types of input screens.

8. Discuss the design guidelines for online data entry.

9. Describe two different prompted input techniques.

10. What does it mean when we say that an information system is menu-driven? For what purpose other than process control can menus be used?

11. What is a GUI? How does a GUI approach differ from the traditional approach? Consider data entry screens and process control screens in your answer.

12. Briefly describe the different types of screens and screen controls that can be used in a GUI for inputting information.

13. What is meant by context-sensitive help?

14. What is meant by input data security? List and briefly discuss several different input data security measures.

Discussion Questions

1. Some systems analysts maintain that when converting from a manual system to a computer system, the computer system should be designed to use existing source documents. They point out that if new source documents are designed, data entry operators must be retrained and the probability of errors in the preparation of input data is much higher. If the system is designed around currently existing source documents, then there is less chance for error in the capture and entering of the data. Costs will also be less, because the analyst will not have to spend time designing new forms, new forms will not have to be printed, and training will not be necessary. Other systems analysts argue that the function of the systems analyst is to determine if more effective source documents can be designed, and if so, to design them. They claim that any of the costs associated with new source documents will eventually be offset by savings resulting from increased efficiency. Which position do you support? Why?

2. At Baxter Community College, whenever a faculty member contacts the Records Office for a student's address or telephone number, a clerk accesses the online student information system to retrieve the data stored for that student. Faculty members complain that the addresses and telephone numbers they are given are often outdated.

   When students first enroll at Baxter, their current address and telephone number are entered into the student information system. If a student ever changes his or her address and/or telephone number, he or she is expected to pick up a change-of-address form at the Records Office, fill it out, and turn it in; in practice, few students ever bother to submit such forms.

   The registration form (Figure 7-5 on page 7.11) includes spaces for current address and telephone number. Those fields are ignored during the data entry of the registration forms, which is accomplished using the Figure 7-14 screen on page 7.22. After all the registration forms have been entered, they are filed and stored. When time permits, a Records Office clerk goes through all the registration forms one by one, entering corrected addresses and telephone numbers when appropriate, so that final grade reports sent at the end of the semester are correctly addressed. This lengthy process is necessary because change-of-address forms are rarely submitted.

   Faculty members have requested that address and telephone corrections be entered as the registration forms are entered, so that the student information system always has current data. Records Office personnel argue that they are already swamped with work during registration, and the current practice is the best they can do. Do you have any suggestions for resolving this problem?

3. Obtain copies of one or more actual source documents used to capture data. (Possible documents include credit card charge slips, application forms, tax forms, and so on.) Comment on the form's design, considering aspects of layout, spacing, zoning, and appearance. Discuss how well the document would serve as the basis of an online data entry form.

MINICASE STUDIES

Bates Video Club

The Bates Video Club has hired you to design two online data entry screens for them.

Questions

1. Design a data entry screen for entering new members, using the source document illustrated in Figure 7-7 on page 7.13. Assume that name and address are both 30-character fields, city is a 25-character field, credit card numbers can contain up to 16 digits, and member number is a 5-digit number.

2. You were not consulted when the membership application form in Figure 7-7 on page 7.13 was originally designed. Do you have any criticisms on its design? How would you suggest that it be improved? Justify your suggestions.

3. Design a data entry screen for entering video rentals, using the source document shown in Figure 7-8 on page 7.14. Assume that titles can contain up to 40 characters, ID# is a 5-digit field, and any single rental fee will not exceed $99.99. Designate which, if any, of the fields on this screen will be retrieved and displayed instead of entered.

4. Do you have any suggestions for improving the video rental form? Justify your suggestions.

Carl's Corvettes

Carl Dekker, owner of Carl's Corvettes, has recently begun computerizing his customer, sales, and service recordkeeping. In a Chapter 6 minicase, we listed the contents of appointment and task records and described the Mechanic's Service Record report and the appointment scheduler's Task History display.

Questions

1. Design a data entry screen for creating new customer records. The customer file records designed by Carl include the following fields:

Customer Name	40 alphanumeric characters
Address	30 alphanumeric characters
City	15 alphanumeric characters
State	2 alphanumeric characters
Zip Code	5 numeric digits
Home Phone Number	7 numeric digits
Work Phone Number	7 numeric digits

And for each Corvette owned by the customer (maximum of 3):

Registration Number	17 alphanumeric characters
Year	4 numeric digits
Color	10 alphanumeric characters

2. Design a data entry screen for adding a new task code record, which contains task code, task description, and standard time.

3. Design one data entry screen for adding a new appointment record and its associated task records. Assume a maximum of ten tasks per appointment.

4. Outline a menu system for controlling the processing for Carl's Corvettes. Provide options for adding, changing, deleting, or viewing either customer records, task code records, or appointment records, printing lists of all current customers and tasks, displaying task histories, and printing the Mechanic's Service Record report. Design all necessary prompt screens.

STUDENT CASE STUDY

Western Dental Clinic — Input Design

Introduction

After completing the output design for the dental system at Western Dental Clinic, Jim Archer turned his attention to the design of the system's input.

Student Assignments

1. Determine the data required for a new patient. Design an input source document that will be used to capture this data.

2. Design a data entry screen to handle the entry of data for a new patient.

3. Besides the data entry screens required for a new patient, what other data entry screens are required? Design data entry screens for each.

4. What input controls are needed for the dental system? Write a report to the associates of Western Dental Clinic, describing the input controls you recommend.

CHAPTER 8

File Concepts

Objectives

You will have mastered the material in this chapter when you can:

- Define the terms field, logical record, and physical record, and explain the relationships among them
- Describe the six general types of information system data files
- Define and distinguish between primary keys, candidate keys, foreign keys, and secondary keys
- Explain the differences between sequential and random access, and describe the processing situations for which each is appropriate
- Discuss the advantages and disadvantages of the different media used for file storage
- Describe the processes for accessing and updating a file with sequential organization
- Describe the processes for accessing and updating a file with direct organization, and explain key addressing, hashing, and hashing collision management
- Describe the processes for accessing and updating a file with indexed organization, describe the differences between indexed random and indexed sequential, and discuss data file management for files with indexed sequential organization
- Compare the advantages and disadvantages of the various file organizations

Introduction

his is the first of two chapters devoted to the design of files and databases for information systems. We begin this chapter with a review of file terminology and concepts. Then, we examine the different types of system files. After discussing file access methods, we review the various media used for system files and databases. Finally, we examine each type of file organization, and then discuss the advantages and disadvantages of each.

Terminology and concepts

n your previous programming courses, you probably created and accessed many files, so you are already familiar with most, if not all, of the terminology and concepts that relate to files. This and the next chapter are based on a basic understanding of system files, so let's take time first to review file terminology and concepts.

■ File components

The smallest amount of data that can be stored is the bit. Bits are grouped into bytes (or characters). Collections of bytes form a **field**. A field is an individual element of data or a fact about a person, place, thing, or event. Every instance, or occurrence, of a field has some specific value. For example, customer number is a field. One instance of customer number might have the value 123; another occurrence of that field might have the value 647. A field is also called a **data element** or a **data item**.

A **logical record** is a collection of fields related to a single person, place, thing, or event. Logical records correspond to the way that both people and application programs view sets of fields. For example, a customer record is a logical record consisting of fields that relate to a customer. One instance of a logical customer record contains a specific value for customer number, a value for customer name, a value for credit limit, and so on, all relating to a single customer. Most often when people simply say **record**, they mean logical record. Whenever an application program executes a read command, the operating system supplies one logical record to the program. Similarly, whenever an application program executes a write command, the operating system accepts one logical record from the program.

A **physical record**, also known as a **block**, is the smallest unit of data that is accessed by the operating system and transferred between memory and a specific file. The operating system reads or writes one physical record, or block, at a time. When the operating system reads a physical record, it transfers that physical record from the file to a **buffer**, which is a block-sized segment of computer memory. Similarly, when the operating system writes a physical record, all the data in the buffer is written to the file.

A physical record consists of one or more logical records; the **blocking factor** is the number of logical records in one physical record. If the blocking factor is some value other than one, then every execution of an application program read or write command does not result in the physical action of reading and writing; sometimes, the read or write command requires only a transfer of data from one memory location to another. The physical action of reading and writing takes time; by blocking several logical records into a single physical record, a systems analyst reduces the number of physical file accesses required for reading and writing and, thus, speeds up application program execution. You could save the most time by making a file's blocking factor equal to the number of records in the file; but the amount of computer memory available for the buffer is limited. Rarely will an entire file fit into available memory; therefore, a file usually consists of many physical records.

A **file** is a collection of logical records and contains data about an information system entity. An **entity** is a person, place, thing, or event for which data is collected. For example, PRODUCT is an entity in an inventory system. The product file contains data about that entity; each logical record holds data about one instance of the PRODUCT entity.

The relationships among fields, logical records, blocks (physical records), and files are shown in Figure 8-1.

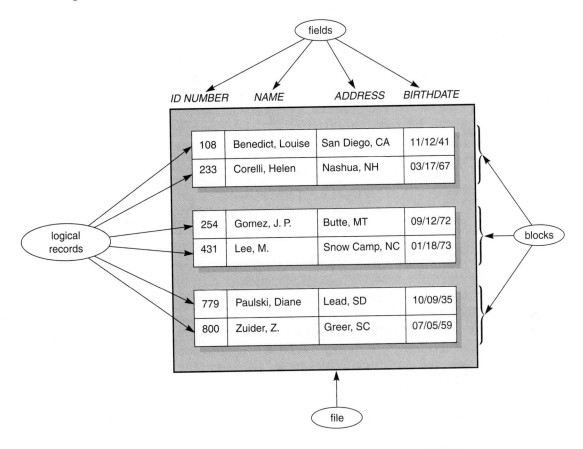

Figure 8-1 *A file consists of blocks, which consist of logical records, which consist of related fields.*

■ Types of files

An information system uses one or more of each of the following types of files: master files, table files, transaction files, work files, security files, and history files.

Master files   A **master file** is a relatively permanent file relating to a standard entity in the information system. Some fields within a master file logical record might be updated periodically, but the number of logical records in a master file changes less frequently. For example, consider a product master file containing one logical record for each product the company sells. The quantity-on-hand field in each record might change daily, but the number of product master file records does not change from day to day. A logical record would be added to or deleted from the product master file only when the company begins offering a new product or discontinues an old product. Examples of master files include customers, sales representatives, students, employees, patients, warehouses, fixed assets, requisitions, reservations, and general ledger accounts.

Table files   A **table file** contains reference data used by information system processes. Like master files, table files are relatively permanent; but unlike master files, table files are not updated by the standard, periodic system processes. Only special table update programs change the data values in a table file. Examples of table files include tax tables, postage rate tables, and department code tables.

Transaction files   A **transaction file** contains records that reflect the day-to-day activities of an organization. A transaction file is an input file that is used to update a master file; once this is done, the transaction file has served its purpose. Unless they are saved for security or backup reasons, transaction files are temporary files. Examples of transaction files include orders, new employees, patient releases, cash receipts, commissions, and customer payments.

Work files   A **work file** is a temporary file created by an information system for a single task. Most often a work file is created by one process in the information system and used by another process within the same system. Work files are also called **scratch files** and **temporary files**. Some work files contain copies of master file records; others contain transaction file record copies; still others contain records created for some other purpose. Example of work files include sorted files and **report files**, which are temporary files to hold output reports until they are actually printed.

Security files   A **security file** is a file that is created and saved for backup/recovery purposes. Audit-trail files are security files, as are backup copies of master, table, and transaction files. New security backup files must be created periodically to replace old, outdated security files.

History files   A **history file** is a file copy created and saved for historical or archiving reasons. New history files, unlike new security files, do not replace the old files; usually both the old and new history files are saved.

In some organizations, inactive master file records are periodically deleted from a master file and added to a special file that is a type of history file. For example, the record for a student who has not registered for any course in the last two semesters might be deleted from the active student master file and added to a file containing the data records of inactive students. That inactive student file is a type of history file because it contains historical data. Unlike the file-copy type of history file, the inactive student file might be used for processing much like a master file is used, as the basis for file queries or periodic reports. If an inactive student returns to school, his or her data record would be deleted from the inactive student file and added back to the active student master file.

■ Key fields

Some fields within a record serve as key fields. There are four types of key fields: primary keys, candidate keys, foreign keys, and secondary keys. We first defined primary keys in the data dictionary discussion in Chapter 4. At that time, you learned that you should identify all primary keys in your data dictionary logical record entries. Likewise, you should identify all candidate keys, all foreign keys, and all secondary keys in the data dictionary. In the paragraphs that follow, we will expand upon our original definition of a primary key and then examine candidate, foreign, and secondary keys.

Primary keys   A **primary key** is the field or combination of fields in a master file or table file that *minimally and uniquely* identifies a particular entity. In our customer file example, the customer number field is the primary key. No two customer records have the same value for customer number; any particular value for customer number appears in at most one logical record, so we see that customer number satisfies the uniqueness criterion for a primary key. We could say the same thing for the combination of customer number and address; those two fields taken together also uniquely identify one particular customer. Could the combination of customer number and address, therefore, be designated as the primary key? The answer is no, because that combination is not minimal; something less, namely customer number alone, can do the job as well. Could customer name be designated as the primary key? The answer is maybe — if your company has a rule that no two customers can have the same name. Because such an unusual rule is seldom enacted, then customer name does not satisfy the uniqueness criterion and cannot be the primary key. A primary key should also not change; because a customer name might change, this is an added reason to reject customer name as the primary key.

Why did we say or *combination of fields* in our definition of a primary key? One of the files in a typical student records system is the registration file, which contains one record for every student registered in every course in a specific semester. If you are taking three courses this semester, your student number would appear in three different records in that file. If twenty students are registered for a particular course, that course would appear in twenty different records in that file. What is the primary key for the registration file? Neither student number nor course identification code uniquely identifies one record, so neither field alone can be the primary key. The primary key must be the combination of student number and course identification code; the combination of the two fields uniquely and minimally identifies a particular registration file record.

Figure 8-2 on the next page illustrates four different record designs, each with sample data records. The first three record types have single-field primary keys: student number, advisor number, and course ID, respectively. For GRADE records, the primary key is the combination of student number and course ID. Verify that the designated primary keys minimally and uniquely identify a particular record in each case.

Candidate keys   Sometimes you do have a choice of two or more fields or field combinations for the primary key. For example, if every product has a unique description, then either the product number or the product description could be designated as the primary key of the product file. Any field that could serve as the primary key is called a **candidate key**. Only one of the candidate keys is designated as the primary key; typically, you select the field that is smallest and easiest with which to work. A **nonkey field** is any field that is not a candidate key.

All the primary keys illustrated in Figure 8-2 are also candidate keys. Two additional candidate keys have also been noted in that figure: Social Security number in the ADVISOR records and course description in the COURSE records.

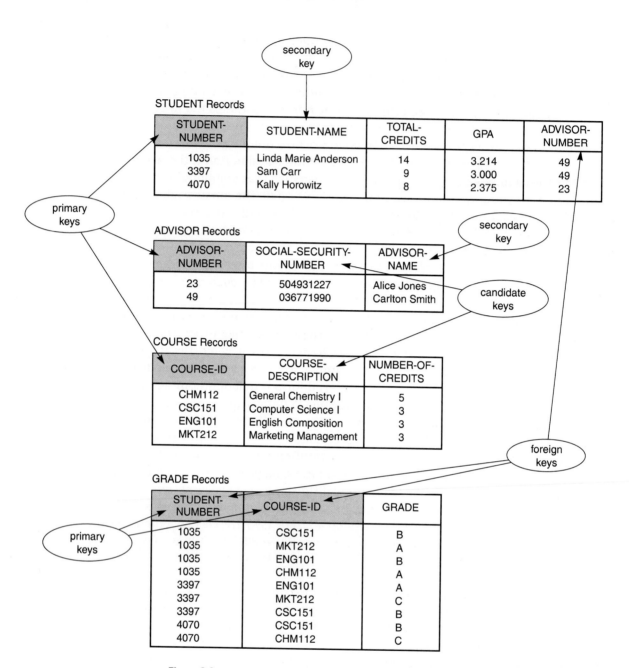

Figure 8-2 *Primary keys, candidate keys, foreign keys, and secondary keys.*

Foreign keys   A **foreign key** is a field or combination of fields in a file that must match a primary key value in some other file, thereby establishing a relationship between the two files. Foreign keys are found in all types of files. In a customer master file record, for example, the sales representative number, or sales rep number for short, must match a sales rep number in the sales rep master file. Similarly, the customer number in an order transaction file record must match a customer number in the customer master file. Notice that occurrences of foreign keys in a file need not be unique. A particular sales rep number can appear several times in the customer file, once for each customer represented by that sales rep. Likewise, a particular customer number might appear several times in the order file if that customer placed more than one order in the transaction file period.

In Figure 8-2, the advisor number in the STUDENT records is a foreign key, because it must match one of the advisor numbers in the ADVISOR records. The two fields that together comprise the primary key for the GRADE records are also both foreign keys: the student number must match a student number in the STUDENT records, and the course ID must match one of the course IDs in the COURSE records.

Secondary keys   A **secondary key** is a field or combination of fields that will be the basis for a retrieval. Secondary key values need not be unique; most often there are many file records with a given secondary key value. For example, if you need to access only those customers with a given credit limit for some particular process, then credit limit is a secondary key. The insurance code field in the employee file would be a secondary key, if, during some process, you need to retrieve only those employees who subscribe to a particular insurance plan.

The need for a secondary key often arises simply because a file is allowed to have only one primary key. For a customer file, you would probably designate customer number as the primary key; this field is unique, and is, therefore, the appropriate primary key for most customer file processing. Sometimes an end user needs to access the customer file, knowing only the customer name. If you have designated customer name as a secondary key for the customer file, then access by customer name is possible.

In Figure 8-2, student name and advisor name have been identified as likely secondary keys. Other fields could also be secondary keys, depending on end user needs. For example, to find all dean's list students, access by GPA would be useful; GPA, therefore, might be a secondary key. If the advisor number field in the STUDENT records is designated as a secondary key, it would be possible to access all the students with some particular advisor.

■ Data storage

Data can be stored in five basic data storage formats: EBCDIC, ASCII, packed decimal, binary, and floating point. Floating point, which is an inexact representation of a numeric value, is used primarily in scientific applications. Business systems analysts are most concerned with the other four.

EBCDIC, which stands for Extended Binary Coded Decimal Interchange Code, is the method of data storage used on most mainframe computers. **ASCII**, which is an acronym for American Standard Code for Information Interchange, is used on some mainframe computers and on most microcomputers and minicomputers. In EBCDIC and ASCII, each letter, symbol, and digit is assigned a unique one-byte code. For example, to store AB in EBCDIC or ASCII requires two bytes of storage; the number 123 requires three bytes; 1.23 and -123 each require four bytes.

If you are storing alphabetic or alphanumeric data, then EBCDIC or ASCII (whichever is available on your computer) is the only choice. Numeric data can be stored in EBCDIC or ASCII, but most operating systems cannot perform arithmetic operations on EBCDIC or ASCII fields. Numbers must first be converted to another form before they can be used in any numeric comparison or computation.

In **packed decimal** numeric data storage, each digit occupies one half-byte. To compute the storage space needed for a packed decimal field, you add the maximum number of digits in the field plus one for a sign (whether or not the field actually has a sign) and divide by two; if there is a remainder, you round up to the next integer to get a whole number of bytes. The packed decimal version of -123, therefore, requires two bytes; the first byte contains the 1 and 2, and the second byte contains the 3 and the -. To store the numeric value -1.23 also requires two bytes; the decimal point does not add to the storage requirements, because you define in the program where the decimal point should be located, and the generated program code handles the decimal point placement automatically.

Packed decimal storage offers several significant advantages. First, it saves storage space. Also, reading and writing data occurs more rapidly because packed decimal data requires only about one-half as much storage as ASCII or EBCDIC. Packed decimal data is already in a form acceptable for computations; the operating system does not need to convert a packed decimal number to another form for arithmetic and then convert the result back for storage. Thus, arithmetic processing also proceeds more rapidly.

Because of these advantages, packed decimal format is a good choice for numeric fields in master and table files. For transaction and work files, however, storing numeric fields in EBCDIC or ASCII is probably better. Numeric fields in that form can be easily read in simple file dumps, and the additional space requirements are not significant, because transaction and work files are generally temporary in nature.

A **binary** format can be used to store numeric integer fields. On most computers, you can specify binary field storage lengths of two bytes (a halfword), four bytes (a fullword), or even eight bytes (a doubleword). A halfword can store integer values between -32768 and +32767; you can store integer values as large as four billion in a binary fullword.

For all but the smallest integers, a binary format requires less storage space than a packed decimal format. The potential savings in storage space and transmission times with binary data is even greater than for packed decimal. However, most computer systems would need to convert a binary field to a packed decimal form for computations, and a binary format is not appropriate for decimal values.

What is the best way to store a date field? Most end users find that inputting dates in MMDDYY or MM/DD/YY form is convenient, and generally they prefer to see dates output in the MM/DD/YY format. Should you, therefore, store a date in a MMDDYY form?

For years, inputting and storing only two digits for the year has not caused problems, but we must reconsider this practice as we near the end of a century. Certainly it makes sense now to store a year as four digits. Years so stored can be printed and displayed as either two or four digits, whichever the end users prefer. If the end users prefer to input only two-digit years, programs could assign a century; rules for determining the appropriate century would have to be established on a field-by-field basis; birth dates, for example, would be treated differently from sales forecast dates.

If a date need never be sorted, compared to another date, or used in a calculation, the date could be stored in a MMDDYYYY form, possibly in a binary or packed decimal format. Dates in the MMDDYYYY form can be sorted and compared, but only if you break the year apart from the month and day and treat the date field as two or three separate fields.

A date stored as YYYYMMDD can be sorted and used as is in comparisons. If a date in that form tests larger than a second date in that same form, then the first date is later than the second. For example, 19970815 is greater than 19970131, just as August 15, 1997 is later than January 31, 1997.

What if dates must be used in calculations? For example, if a manufacturing order is placed on June 23 and will take three weeks to complete, on what date will the order be finished? If a customer payment due on December 28 is not paid until the following February 7, exactly how late is the payment and how much interest is owed? Julian dates and absolute dates are easier to use in such calculations.

A standard **Julian date** is a five-digit number in which the first two digits represent the year and the last three represent the day of the year. Thus, the Julian date form of January 1, 1997 is 97001, while June 23 of that same year is 97174. Julian dates are commonly used in business applications; in some cases, end users might even prefer Julian dates to

MM/DD/YY dates in output reports and displays. An extended Julian date is a seven-digit number in which the first four digits represent the year. Thus, the extended Julian date for June 23, 1997 is 1997174; and three weeks later is 1997195 (1997174 + 21). Julian dates work well for calculations with dates that fall in the same year; extra work is required, however, to add five weeks to December 3 or to calculate the number of days between December 28 and the following February 7.

An **absolute date** is the total number of days from some specific base date. To calculate the number of days between two absolute dates, you simply subtract one from the other. For example, if you use a base date of January 1, 1900, then December 28, 1997 has an absolute date of 35,791; the absolute date for February 7, 1998 is 35,832, which is 41 days later than December 28, 1997. Figure 8-3 explains the calculation of absolute dates.

If a date is to be used in a calculation, should you store the date in an extended Julian or absolute form instead of as YYYYMMDD? If you do, then the date must be converted once to be stored and might have to be converted to another form every time it is displayed or printed. Absolute dates must always be converted to another form for display or printing; in some cases, Julian dates are acceptable for display and printing in their stored form. On the other hand, if you store the date in a YYYYMMDD form, you do not have to convert it to another form to store, print, or display it, but every time the date is used in a calculation, extra processing steps are required. Which method is better?

The answer depends on how the specific date will be used. You must consider how often the date will be used in a calculation versus how often it will be printed or displayed. ∎

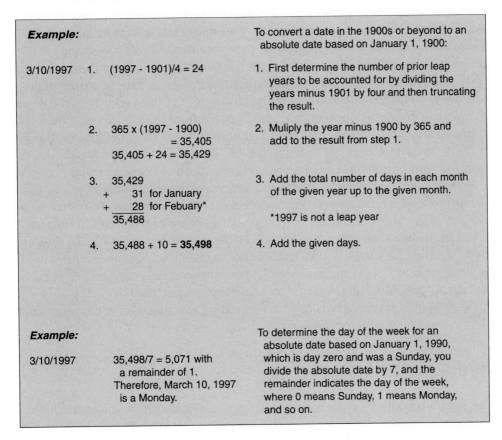

Figure 8-3 Calculations for determining an absolute date and the day of the week.

Access methods

For each file to be included in the information system, you must consider the accessing requirements to decide on the file medium and organization to use. File organization concerns the way the logical records in a file are stored. **File access** concerns how the system's programs access (read and write) the file records: sequentially or randomly. You must use a file's accessing requirements to determine an appropriate file medium and file organization, so let's consider the two file access methods first.

A program using the **sequential access** method to process a file starts by reading or writing a particular logical record (usually the first record in the file), and then proceeds to read or write one record after another, in sequence, until done. That is, to sequentially access the third record in the file, the program must read the first, second, *and* third records; if the eighth record must then be accessed, the program must first read the fourth through the seventh records before reading that eighth record.

With the **random access** method, a program can access any logical record in the file without having to read all the preceding records; that is, the program can access records in any random order. Your needs might require the program to read the sixtieth file record, then the second, and then the twentieth, for example. Random access is sometimes called **direct access,** because a program can go directly to any desired record. Random access is comparable to how you might use a record album or CD, whereas sequential access is comparable to how you must use a cassette tape.

Randomly accessing all the records in a file takes much longer than sequentially accessing the entire file. For that reason, sequential access is usually appropriate when a program needs to look at a relatively high percentage of the records in a file; random access is more appropriate when only a small percentage of the file records will be processed in one execution of the program. For example, consider a program that will use a transaction file to update records in a master file. You would obviously process the transaction file sequentially because all the transaction file records will be read. To decide if the master file should be processed sequentially or randomly, you need accurate estimates of transaction frequencies and resulting master file activity. If you determine that a large percentage of the master file records will need to be accessed, then you would probably choose to sequentially process the master file. In that case, the transaction file must be sorted so the transaction records appear in master file order. When deciding how to access the master file, you are weighing the time to sort the transaction file against the total time spent accessing the master file.

Typically, sequential access is used for batch processing and reporting, while random access is used for online processing.

File media summary

The media usually used for system files are magnetic tape, magnetic disks and diskettes, mass storage devices, and optical disks. We will now briefly discuss the advantages and disadvantages of each of these media.

Magnetic tape is a reliable, inexpensive, standard, and transportable medium for data storage, but magnetic tape has a significant disadvantage. All the other file media we mentioned allow for either random or sequential access; tape files can be accessed only sequentially. For that reason, magnetic tape is rarely used for master files. Magnetic tape could be used for a table file small enough to be stored in memory during program execution, but storing a small table file on some other medium is usually easier and less expensive than dedicating an entire tape to that table file. Magnetic tape could be used for transaction and work files and is usually considered the best medium for security and history files.

Magnetic disk and diskettes, optical disks, and mass storage devices allow both random and sequential access for the reading and writing of file records. Magnetic tape is probably still less expensive, byte for byte, than these devices, but this will change as the storage capacities of disks, diskettes, and mass storage devices increase and their costs decrease. **Diskettes**, which are also called **floppy disks** or **floppies**, are relatively inexpensive, portable and mailable, and easy to store. Diskettes can be used on both microcomputers and mainframe computers, but diskette files created under one operating system usually cannot be read by a different operating system.

Magnetic disks, which are also called **hard disks** or **direct access storage devices (DASDs)**, are storage media most commonly used for all computers from microcomputers or personal computers to supercomputers. The storage capacities, access and transfer speeds, and other physical characteristics of different magnetic disks vary greatly, depending on the manufacturer and type of disk, but these differences are all handled by the operating system; application program logic for accessing magnetic disk files is standardized.

Optical disks, which are also called **CD-ROMs (Compact Disk Read Only Memory)**, represent the very latest technology in storage media. Information is stored on an optical disk by burning microscopic holes on its surface with a laser; a laser is also used to read an optical disk. A massive amount of data can be stored on a single optical disk, and, as optical disk technology advances, storage capacities are increasing. Optical disk access is very rapid, and the stored information can be read repeatedly without any degradation of the disk. One significant disadvantage with standard optical disks is that once information is written on an optical disk, the information cannot be modified. Optical disks are often called **WORM devices**, for *write once, read many*. Standard optical disks are practical, therefore, only for files that are rarely or never updated. **Rewritable optical disks** are now available that allow you to update data many times—just like magnetic disks. These rewritable optical disks are expensive, but their costs should continue to decline in the coming years.

As their name suggests, **mass storage devices** offer massive storage capability. A mass storage device consists of a library of storage media and an automated retrieval/access device. Although some mass storage devices use diskettes, the typical unit uses cartridge tapes. When access to a particular file is requested, the device selects the appropriate cartridge from the library and transfers the file to magnetic disk; when the program is finished with the file, the device copies the file back onto the tape cartridge and returns the cartridge to the library; all this is accomplished without any human intervention. The application program logic for accessing mass storage device files is exactly the same as that for magnetic disk files. Such devices, therefore, provide the random access capability of disk while using the less expensive tape cartridges or diskettes for file storage. Mass storage devices are too expensive for all but the very largest organizations, and the access process, although rapid, is too slow for most online applications.

File organization

ile organization refers to the physical structure of a file on disk or other storage medium. The three file organization techniques available are sequential, direct, and indexed.

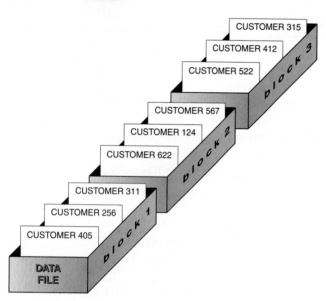

Figure 8-4 Sequential organization showing record arrival sequence (a pile) in a blocked file with a blocking factor of three.

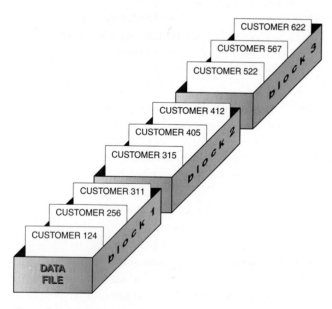

Figure 8-5 Sequential organization with records in sequence by primary key in a blocked file with a blocking factor of three.

■ Sequential organization

When a program creates a file using **sequential organization**, the records are stored in physical sequence as they occur during processing. Two different types of sequential organization are possible. If records are stored in no special sequence except chronological (that is, time occurrence or arrival sequence), the file is called a **pile**. Figure 8-4 shows a customer file organized as a pile with a blocking factor of three. Notice that the records are not in order by customer number, nor are they in order by any other field. An unsorted batch transaction file is often a simple pile.

With the second type of sequential organization, records are created and, thus, stored in primary key order. Figure 8-5 shows a customer file with this type of sequential organization.

Only sequential access can be used with a sequentially organized file; random access is not possible. When you sequentially access a sequential file, if one specific record needs to be retrieved from the file, you must first retrieve all the records physically preceding that record. Thus, sequential organization is not suited for an online environment where random access is necessary.

The word sequential describes both a type of file access and a type of file organization. In this book, we will clearly identify which meaning of the word we are using.

When updating a sequentially organized file, records can be added to the end of the file; if changes must be made to an existing record, that record can be updated and rewritten to the same physical location. If a new record must be inserted somewhere in the middle of the file, the entire file must be recopied to a new physical location with the new record properly positioned. Physically deleting an existing record also requires that the file be recopied to a new physical location; the deleted record would not be output to the new version of the file. Figure 8-6 demonstrates the addition and deletion process: customer records 256 and 522 from Figure 8-5 have been deleted; customer record 600 has been added.

■ Direct organization

With **direct organization**, a record is stored and retrieved at an address based on a formula applied to the value of the record's primary key. If the primary key is alphanumeric, it must be converted to a number before it can be used in the formula. Two different types of direct organization are possible: one using key-addressing techniques and the other using hashing techniques.

Key-addressing techniques   With **key-addressing techniques,** the formula is applied to the primary key field and results in a *unique* **relative record number**. Figure 8-7 shows a very simple example of this technique. For this example, the nine customer records have been given the customer numbers 1 through 9. Each record is stored at the relative record number equal to its key. To retrieve the record for customer number 8, a program simply reads the record whose relative record number is 8. The formula in this example is to use the primary key field value without any change.

Figure 8-8 on the next page shows a second key-addressing example. In this case, an actual formula of (customer number - 3) / 2 is used. (We assume for this case that customer numbers are all odd numbers greater than or equal to 5.) For customer number 19, you subtract 3 from the customer number value and divide the resulting value of 16 by 2 giving 8 as the relative record number to be used. Again each primary key value results in a unique relative record number used for file access. Notice that it takes just one file access to store or to retrieve a specific record. Speed of file access is a distinct advantage of the key-addressing technique for direct organization.

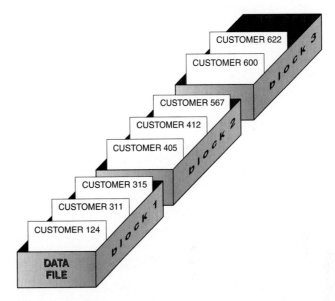

Figure 8-6 *The file in Figure 8-5 after the records for customers 256 and 522 have been deleted and the record for customer 600 has been added.*

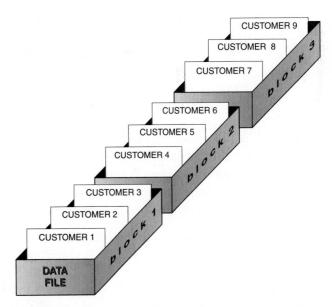

Figure 8-7 *Direct organization using a key-addressing technique in which the relative record number equals the customer number.*

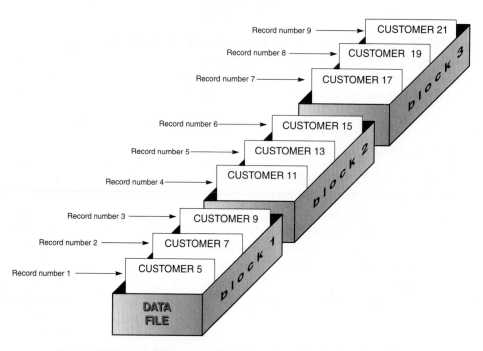

Figure 8-8 *Direct organization using a key-addressing technique in which the relative record number is calculated from the formula (customer number - 3) /2.*

In these two examples, the primary key values have a pattern that maps the records to file storage locations without any wasted space. Such a perfect pattern is usually impossible to establish. Our original customer file example is more typical of situations you will encounter in actual practice. The customer file shown in Figure 8-9 is stored by using the customer number value for the relative record number. As with the first two key-addressing examples, only one access is required to retrieve a given record. Notice, however, that only nine out of the first 622 available record storage locations are used. The unused storage locations, called **gaps**, must be reserved, even though they are not being used. Typically, you must trade off wasted storage space against speed of access when using the key-addressing technique.

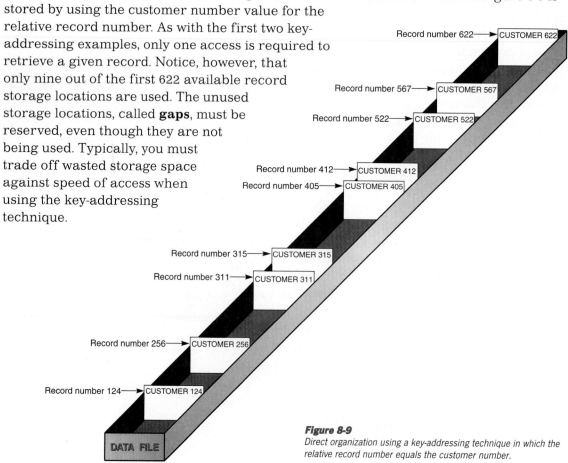

Figure 8-9
Direct organization using a key-addressing technique in which the relative record number equals the customer number.

Unless you have a primary key that can be mapped compactly to relative record numbers, the key-addressing technique is not a wise choice for direct organization. Although it provides for immediate access, it can leave too many gaps that waste storage space.

Hashing techniques **Hashing techniques** are similar to key-addressing techniques in that a formula is applied to the primary key of a record, resulting in a value used as the address for storing and retrieving that record. The difference is that hashing does not guarantee a unique storage address. The formula might give the same value for two or more records. Because this would obviously cause problems, why would you want to use a hashing technique? The reason is to utilize storage efficiently while providing for rapid random access for online processing. However, fast random access is possible only if you can minimize the effects of duplicate results from the formula you use.

Hashing techniques are sometimes called **randomizing techniques**. The formula used to transform the primary key into a record address is also known as a **hashing algorithm**, a **hashing routine**, a **randomizing routine**, or simply a **hash function**. The hash function is chosen so that the records are spread as evenly as possible throughout the file, but the stored records typically end up being stored in no particular sequence.

Let's use a hash function, for example, that adds the first digit of a customer number to the last two digits. Figure 8-10 shows the results of using this formula with our original customer file. The nine customer records are mapped into 72 storage locations, a considerable improvement over the 622 locations required by the key-addressing technique used in Figure 8-9. But what happens if a record with a customer number of 553 is to be added to the file? It should be stored using a relative record number of 58, but the customer 256 record is already stored there. You now have two records that need to be stored in the same disk location. When two or more records have the same hash function value, you have a **collision**. The records involved in a collision (the customer 256 and 553 records in our example) are called **synonyms**, because they share the same hash function value. Before we discuss different methods of managing the collision problem, let's review two hashing techniques that are frequently used.

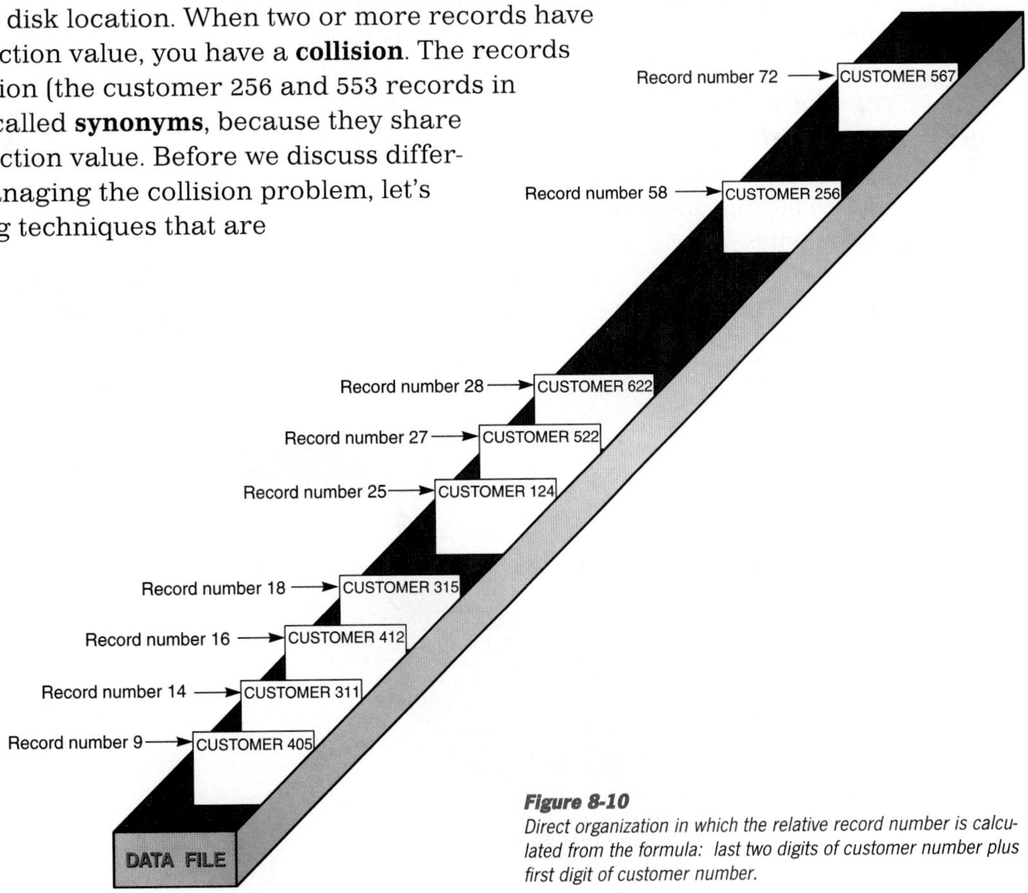

Record number 72 ⟶ CUSTOMER 567

Record number 58 ⟶ CUSTOMER 256

Record number 28 ⟶ CUSTOMER 622

Record number 27 ⟶ CUSTOMER 522

Record number 25 ⟶ CUSTOMER 124

Record number 18 ⟶ CUSTOMER 315

Record number 16 ⟶ CUSTOMER 412

Record number 14 ⟶ CUSTOMER 311

Record number 9 ⟶ CUSTOMER 405

DATA FILE

Figure 8-10
Direct organization in which the relative record number is calculated from the formula: last two digits of customer number plus first digit of customer number.

1. *Folding hashing technique.* The hash function used in Figure 8-10 is an example of the **folding method**. To use this method, you take the primary key value, divide its digits into two or more groups, and add these groups of digits together. The resulting sum is used as the address. In effect, you take a somewhat large primary key value and transform it into a smaller number. This is true of all hashing techniques where you are dealing with large primary key values, such as Social Security numbers and bank account numbers. Your objective is to map each primary key value into a small address space while minimizing the collision problem. Notice that none of the original nine records in Figure 8-10 has a current synonym; however, you are utilizing only 12.5% (9/72) of the available space. This percentage is referred to as the **packing density**, or **load factor**, of the file.

2. *Division-remainder hashing technique.* The **division-remainder method** uses a formula where the primary key value is divided by a fixed, preselected number, and the remainder of this division is used for the record address. Research has proven that the number selected for the division should be a prime number and that this method is one of the very best hashing techniques. Because the remainder could be zero, we will add one to the remainder to get the relative record number in the following examples.

Figure 8-11 shows division-remainder hashing for the same customer file records using a divisor of 29. The customer 412 record, for example, is stored at relative record 7: 412 divided by 29 is 14 with a remainder of 6; adding one to that remainder gives relative record number 7. In this example, the nine customer records fit into 29 storage locations, a 31% packing density.

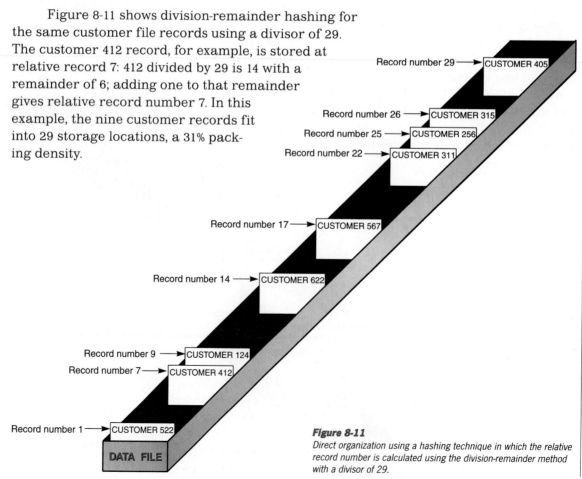

Figure 8-11
Direct organization using a hashing technique in which the relative record number is calculated using the division-remainder method with a divisor of 29.

Even though Figure 8-11 has no collisions, you cannot guarantee you will not have any in the future. For example, if you try to add the record whose customer number is 625, you would calculate a relative record number of 17. The customer 567 record is a synonym for this new record, so collision results.

Collision management   No matter how well you choose your hashing algorithm, you must face the likelihood of collisions and their management. A variety of techniques are used to minimize the occurrence of collision and to minimize the effects of collision when it does occur.

You could design a hash function to generate a block number instead of a relative record number. In Figure 8-12, seven blocks have been allocated, and each block can store three customer records. The division-remainder method is used with a divisor of 7, and you again add 1 to the result to obtain an address, in this case a block number. The customer 315 and 567 records both hash to block 1, but both records can be stored in that block. Hence, you have minimized the effects of collision, because a collision does not necessarily cause a problem.

If you enlarge the size of each block to hold more records, then the effect of collision is further reduced. The file in Figure 8-12 has a packing density of 42% (9/21, the maximum number of records that can be stored). If you enlarge each block to hold four records and keep the number of blocks and the hash function the same, the packing density reduces to 32% (9/28). So the more you try to eliminate collision by relying strictly on larger block sizes, the less efficiently you utilize storage space.

Although utilizing block addressing minimizes collision effects, it does not completely eliminate the collision problem. You still need a method for adding a record that hashes to a block that is full and for later retrieving that same record. We will look at two collision handling techniques: the linear search method and the overflow area method.

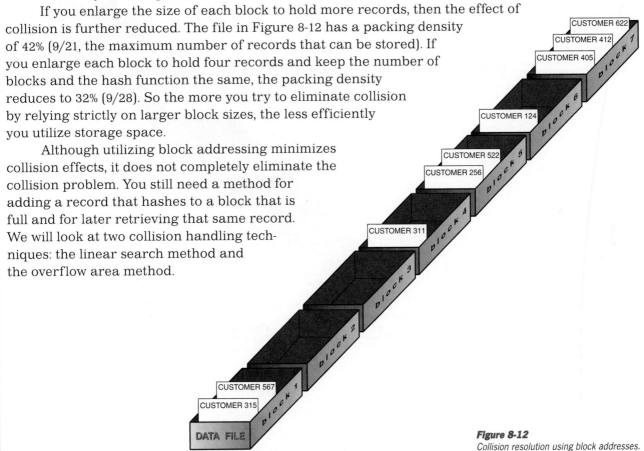

Figure 8-12
Collision resolution using block addresses.

1. *Linear search method.* With this method, if you find that a block is full when attempting to add a new record to it, you place the record in the first available record slot in the following blocks.

    For example, suppose you need to add two new records to those shown in Figure 8-12. These records are for customer numbers 623 and 630, both of which hash to block 1. The customer 623 record is placed into block 1 because there is room for one more record; and the customer 630 record is placed into block 2, the next block with an available record slot. Figure 8-13 shows the result of these two record additions. How would you later retrieve the customer 630 record? Applying the division-remainder hash function to 630 gives you a remainder of zero, so you would retrieve block 1. But when you find that the customer 630 record is not located there, you would linearly search the following blocks until the record is found.

The advantage of the linear search method is that records that hash to the same address are stored in a cluster — in the same block or nearby blocks. What happens when so many other records have hashed to the first three blocks that the customer 630 record must be stored in block 4? Four file accesses would be required to find a location for this new record, and the potential need for multiple accesses is even greater for large files with high packing densities. You might have to search through thousands of blocks before you can store or retrieve a desired record or find that such a record does not exist. The access advantages of direct organization have definitely been compromised when you have to search large portions of a file sequentially.

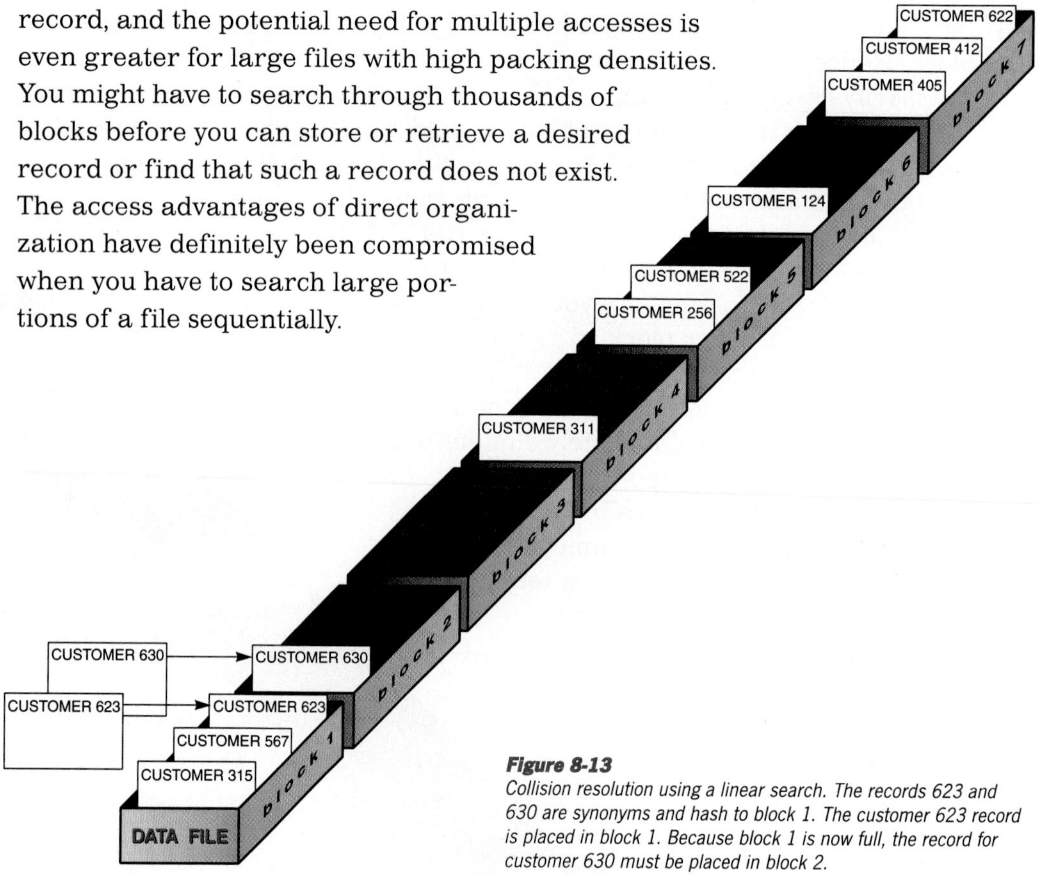

Figure 8-13
Collision resolution using a linear search. The records 623 and 630 are synonyms and hash to block 1. The customer 623 record is placed in block 1. Because block 1 is now full, the record for customer 630 must be placed in block 2.

2. *Overflow area method.* This method for collision management avoids the problems encountered with the linear search method. This second method uses an **overflow area**, which is a separate part of the file reserved for storing records that cannot be placed in the exact block specified by the hash function. Figure 8-14 shows the use of overflow blocks. The data file now contains nine blocks: the seven original blocks are termed the **prime area**, and blocks 8 and 9 constitute the overflow area. Rather than store the customer 630 record in block 2, as you did with the linear search method, this record is stored in block 8, in the first available record slot in the overflow area. When you later need to retrieve the customer 630 record, you would employ the division-

remainder hash function, resulting in a value of 1 for the block. After retrieving block 1 and learning that the customer 630 record is not located there, you would then retrieve the first overflow block (block 8) and locate the record.

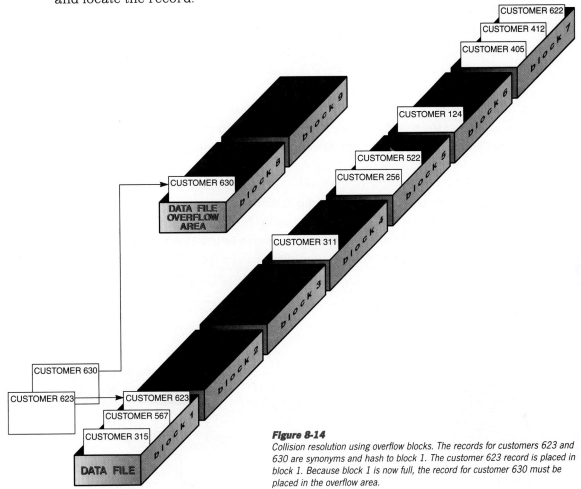

Figure 8-14
Collision resolution using overflow blocks. The records for customers 623 and 630 are synonyms and hash to block 1. The customer 623 record is placed in block 1. Because block 1 is now full, the record for customer 630 must be placed in the overflow area.

With the specific files shown in Figure 8-13 and Figure 8-14, exactly two accesses are required to retrieve the customer 630 record. In general, however, the linear search and overflow area methods are not equally efficient. The overflow area approach proves to be more efficient in the long run. When collision occurs with the linear search method, the record is placed in the closest nearby block, which potentially will cause collision for a future record that hashes to that same block. Also, searching through a smaller overflow area is faster than searching through the prime area, where records that properly hash to a given block are intermingled with records placed in that block because of collision management.

The efficiency of both the linear search method and the overflow method can be improved through the use of a **pointer chain** (also known as a **synonym chain** or a **collision chain**). When using a pointer chain, each block includes one additional field, called a pointer, that indicates whether collision has occurred on that block. In Figure 8-15 on the next page, blocks 2 through 6 have a pointer value of zero, meaning that no collision has occurred in these blocks. Blocks 1 and 7 have pointer values of 8, meaning that collision has occurred in both blocks; in both cases, the synonym records have been stored in block 8 in the overflow area. The use of a pointer chain helps to minimize the number of blocks that must be searched when collision occurs.

The precise performance of a given hashing technique in a given application depends on a number of factors. Among these factors are:

- The characteristics of the primary key used as the basis for the hash function
- The hash function chosen
- The collision management technique chosen
- The block size selected; larger block sizes tend to reduce the likelihood that a record will need to be placed outside its proper block
- The packing density; with higher packing densities, a record will more frequently need to be placed outside its proper block. Experts claim that the packing density should be no higher than 80%. On the downside, very low packing densities result in greater waste of storage, so that 40% to 80% is the typical range for effective packing density.

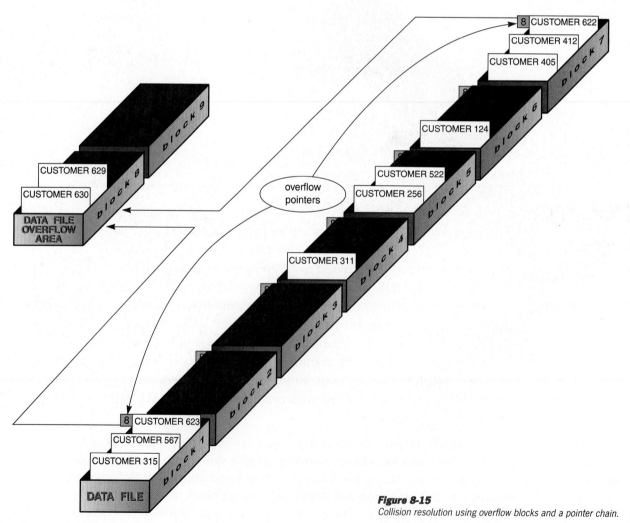

Figure 8-15
Collision resolution using overflow blocks and a pointer chain.

■ Indexed organization

For all types of file organization, the logical records are stored in a file termed the data file. With **indexed organization**, you also have a separate **index file**, or simply **index**. Each index file record contains a key value and the data file address for the record with that key value. We say that the data file is *indexed by* the index file.

Indexed random organization   When the data file records of an indexed file are not stored in any significant sequence, the organization is called **indexed random organization**, or **indexed nonsequential organization**. An example of indexed random organization is shown in Figure 8-16. The nine records of the customer file are stored in random order in the data file, and the index has one record, or entry, for each of the nine data file records. Each index record contains a customer number, which is the primary key, and the data file block number, where the record having that key value is stored.

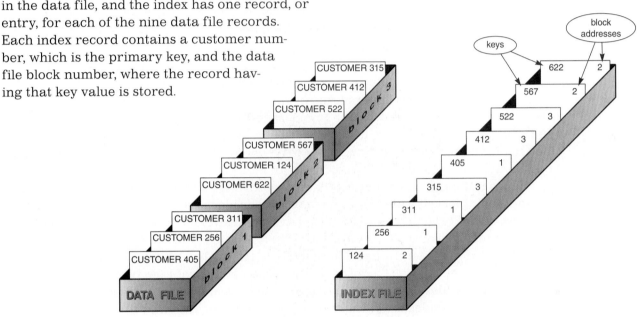

Figure 8-16 *Indexed random organization.*

The index file obviously requires additional storage space, and creating and maintaining an index file requires additional processing. What can the index do for you that justifies this additional storage and processing? One use for the index is the sequential retrieval of data file records. Although the logical records in the data file in Figure 8-16 are not stored in any meaningful order, the index records are stored in primary key sequence. By retrieving customer records in the order specified by the index, you will actually be accessing them in customer number sequence. Thus, the index provides for sequential retrieval of random data file records; but because the logical records are not in sequence, there must be one index record for each logical record in a file with indexed random organization.

The index is even more useful when you want to randomly access a specific record. To retrieve the customer 522 record in Figure 8-16, you could sequentially access data file blocks until you locate that record in the third block; three data file accesses would be required. If you use the index instead, you would sequentially access and search the index until you locate the desired key; then, you would access the data file once to retrieve the block containing the desired record. If each index record required an access, seven index accesses would be needed to find the record for customer 522 and then one data file access to read the third block. Eight file accesses versus three file accesses might not appear to be an improvement, but the overall search time is actually substantially less. One reason that total time is less when using the index concerns the relative sizes of data file records and index records. Data file records are normally quite large; in many applications, each logical record is hundreds or thousands of bytes in size. On the other hand, each index record is very small. In typical cases the address is four bytes, so adding the primary key length of three bytes in our example gives a record size of only seven bytes. A program can read these small index file records significantly faster than the larger data file records.

Because index file records are small, usually you would fit many index records into one index file block. In Figure 8-16, the nine index records constitute one block, so actually only one index file access is required to read the entire index into memory. To randomly access the 522 customer record of Figure 8-16 would actually require at most two accesses: one access of the index file (if the index is not already in memory), a sequential memory search of the index block, and then one access of the data file. With larger index blocks, faster search methods, such as a binary search, can be used to further reduce the search time to a very small fraction of a second.

As the number of data file records grows, the number of records in the index grows at the same rate. Index search time also increases, but this time is still significantly less than the time necessary to sequentially search through the data file. When the index grows to a point where it can no longer fit into memory, you can treat the index as if it were a data file and create an index to the index.

Figure 8-17 shows the process of indexing an index. The level 2 index file is our original index, now blocked with four index records per block. The level 1 index file is the new index to that original index. You now have a two-level index, or what is often called a **multilevel index**. Because the key values in the level 2 index are in sequence, you need only one record in the level 1 index for each block in the level 2 index. Typically the highest valued key in each level 2 index block is stored in the level 1 index. The level 1 index is termed a **sparse index,** because it does not contain an entry for each record in the file it indexes. The level 2 index is a **dense index,** because it has one entry for each record in the data file.

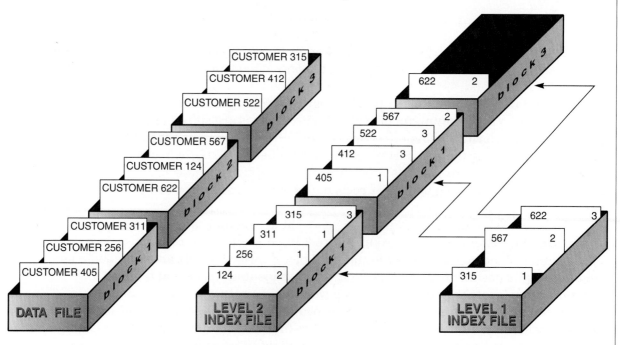

Figure 8-17 *Indexed random organization using a two-level index.*

To randomly access the data file of Figure 8-17, a program first reads the level 1 index into memory. Then, for each record to be randomly accessed, the program would search the level 1 index with no file access required, retrieve the proper level 2 index block, search that level 2 index block in memory, and finally, retrieve the data file block containing the record you need. This means that you need only two accesses or file retrievals to randomly retrieve a logical record. Because the example data file has only nine records and three blocks, two accesses might not seem like a significant savings. To fully appreciate the benefits of using an index for random access, picture a data file and low-level index requiring thousands of blocks of file storage. If necessary, the indexing structure can expand to many more levels than we have shown.

An additional advantage of indexed random organization is that a program does not need to access the data file if all you want to know is if a logical record having a specific primary key value exists. This question can be answered by restricting the search to the index. If the primary key is found in the index, you know the record exists; if the key is not in the index, you know it does not exist.

A final advantage of indexed random organization is the data file records do not need to be in sequence. When records are added, they can simply be added to the end of the file. Maintaining the data file is, therefore, quite straightforward. The programming to handle the indexes, however, can become complicated. Fortunately, indexed organization is a standard feature on most computers, which means that index management is the responsibility of the operating system file access routines and not the responsibility of the programmer.

Indexed sequential organization **Indexed sequential organization** means that indexed organization is being used and the data file records are in primary key sequence. In Figure 8-18, the customer records are in sequence by the primary key of customer number. The index looks much like the one for the indexed random organization of Figure 8-16. Do you need a dense index with one index record for each data file record? No, you do not. Because the data file records are in sequence, you really need only one index record for each data file block.

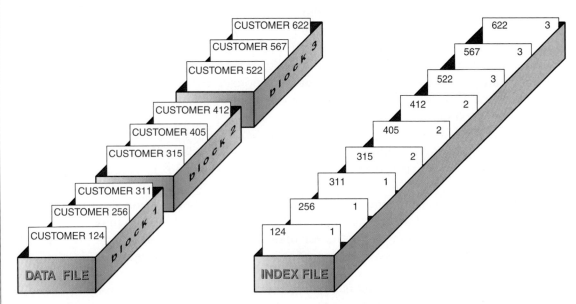

Figure 8-18 *Indexed sequential organization with a dense index.*

The index, therefore, can be reduced in size and stored as a sparse index (Figure 8-19). Most operating systems use sparse indexes with indexed sequential organization. By using indexed sequential organization with a sparse index, the index file is smaller, search times are faster, and you need fewer index levels for very large data files. On the other hand, you can no longer determine the existence of a specific primary key value by searching only through the index as you could with indexed random organization; one additional access, an access of a data file block, is required to answer this question. Because fewer index blocks and levels are required, actual practice shows that fewer disk accesses are necessary. Overall, indexed sequential organization is even more efficient than indexed random organization.

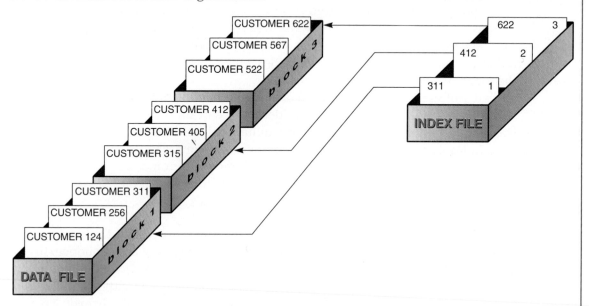

Figure 8-19 *Indexed sequential organization with a sparse index.*

Because indexed sequential takes less space and performs better than indexed random, why would you ever want to use indexed random organization? The reason is that you can index a data file by more than one field. In addition to the primary index, you can have a number of **secondary indexes** built on other data file fields. Because the data file is in one sequence only, indexed sequential organization can be used only for the primary key index. All secondary indexes must use indexed random organization or some other structure for relating a secondary key value to the record or records containing that particular value.

If you need to sequentially retrieve records from an indexed sequential file by its primary key, you do not need to use the index. Because the data file is in primary key sequence, you simply retrieve data file blocks in order. The index is used for random access retrieval only.

What happens to the primary key sequence of the data file when you attempt to add a new logical record to a block that is full? Where does the system insert the record, and what happens to the index? To answer these questions, we need to look into the data file management alternatives available under indexed sequential organization.

Indexed sequential organization data file management   One method for managing data file insertions under indexed sequential organization is through the use of an overflow area and a pointer chain, which were both discussed with direct organization. Suppose you need to add the customer 350 record to the example shown in Figure 8-19. Because all data file blocks are full, a record must be placed in an overflow block. As Figure 8-20 illustrates, a separate overflow area has been added, as well as two new fields in each data file block. One of the new fields is an overflow location pointer that links a data file block to the next logical record, which is located in the overflow area. The overflow location pointer consists of an overflow block number and relative record number within that block. The 4 1 for block 2 means that the next logical record can be found in the overflow area in the relative record position 1 of block 4. The other new field represents the highest key value associated with the given data file block that is stored in the overflow area. For block 2, that key value is 412. Note that the new customer 350 record was positioned in proper sequence in block 2, and the customer 412 record is the one that has been relocated to the overflow area. In the figure, the dashes (– –) for data file blocks 1 and 3 represent the fact that overflow has not occurred for these blocks. Finally, this logical record insertion has resulted in no change to the index file.

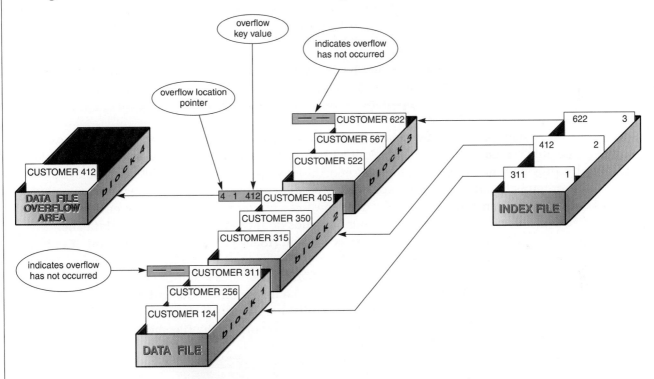

Figure 8-20 *Indexed sequential organization using an overflow area with a pointer chain after adding the customer 350 record.*

When the customer 410 record is now added, it must be stored in the overflow area, as shown in Figure 8-21 on the next page. Because this record precedes the customer 412 record already in the overflow area, the block 2 location pointer must be changed to indicate where the customer 410 record is located. Within the overflow area, a pointer, chaining the customer 410 record to the customer 412 record, is also necessary. The records in the overflow area are kept in arrival sequence, not logical sequence, and thus, pointer chaining is required for the overflow area. The pointer associated with the customer 412 record in the overflow area would be dashes (– –), indicating that that record is the end of the chain.

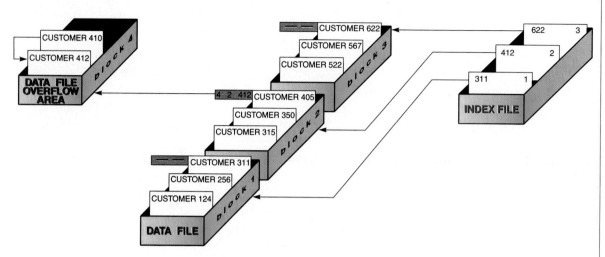

Figure 8-21 *Indexed sequential organization using an overflow area with a pointer chain after the customer 350 and 410 records have been added.*

As you can guess, performance worsens as more records are added to the overflow area and the pointer chains become longer. Periodically, an indexed sequential file must be reorganized to place all the records in the data file in correct logical sequence; the index file is then reconstructed.

When the overflow area technique is used with indexed sequential organization, usually the data file is initially built with gaps in each block; that is, each data file block is only partially filled with logical records, leaving empty record slots for use by future additions to the file. These gaps are called **distributed free space**. The use of distributed free space reduces the need for overflow area chaining; but it does not entirely eliminate the problem, and the lower packing densities do increase the size of the data file.

IBM's **indexed sequential access method (ISAM)** is one implementation of indexed sequential organization. ISAM uses the overflow area technique on a somewhat more complicated basis that relies on the physical characteristics of the magnetic disk used.

A second method for managing data file insertions under indexed sequential organization is through the use of the **block splitting** technique. As an example of this technique, we will again add the customer 350 record to the file shown in Figure 8-19 on

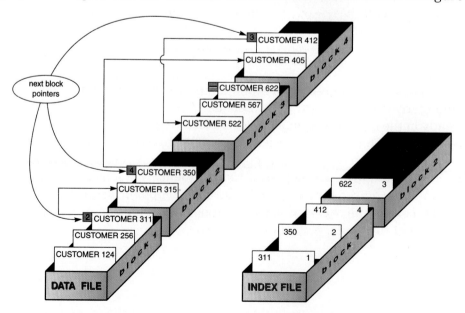

Figure 8-22 *Indexed sequential organization using block splitting after adding the customer 350 record.*

page 8.24. Block 2 is where this new record should be stored, but there is no room left in block 2. The next available empty block, block 4, is used; and the customer 350 record, along with the three records in block 2, are divided between the two blocks. The index is changed to reflect the change in the data file. The result is shown in Figure 8-22. We have split the contents of the full block into two blocks, and, thus, block splitting is the name given to this technique.

Adding the customer 410 record presents no difficulty. As shown in Figure 8-23, this record is simply stored in block 4, which has room for one additional record. Now block 4 is full. It might seem that you would be splitting blocks quite frequently using this technique. This is not the case; we have kept our examples small to illustrate concepts. In practice, you would store a larger number of logical records in each block. If you stored twenty customer records in each block, then when you split the contents of a full block into two blocks, you would have enough room to accommodate ten more records in each of the two blocks.

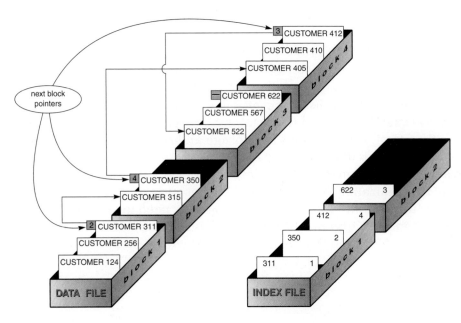

Figure 8-23 *Indexed sequential organization using block splitting after the customer 350 and 410 records have been added.*

Notice that the data file records in Figures 8-22 and Figure 8-23 are no longer physically stored in sequence. How can the data file be sequentially accessed? Typically one additional field is stored in each data file block that serves as a pointer to the next logical block in sequence. This pointer field is shown in Figures 8-22 and 8-23 as the *next block pointer*, and arrows have been drawn to indicate the correct data file block sequence. When the file is sequentially processed, the operating system uses the next block pointers to determine the order for accessing data file blocks.

Distributed free space can be used with the block splitting technique when the indexed file is first created to delay the need for redistributing records. IBM's **virtual storage access method (VSAM)** uses both distributed free space and the block splitting technique to manage its implementation of indexed sequential organization.

File organization advantages and disadvantages

Files with sequential organization require the least amount of file storage space, because only the logical records themselves need to be stored. No additional physical structure fields are needed, so the file is as compact as possible, but sequentially organized files can be accessed only sequentially.

Direct file organization provides the fastest random access but is inappropriate for sequential access. For determining record locations, key-addressing techniques are the most efficient, because they require only one file access to store or retrieve a specific record. Key-addressing techniques, however, are impractical in most situations because of the low packing densities and large amounts of storage space required. Hashing techniques provide a reasonable tradeoff between very fast access and efficient use of file storage space, but because of collisions, direct files using a hash function require more than one access to store or retrieve a given record. After some number of record addition collisions, the performance of hashed direct files can begin to degrade; in some cases, it is then necessary to reorganize the file with a new hash function, blocking factor, and/or collision management technique.

Indexed organization provides an efficient means of both sequentially and randomly accessing records. However, random record retrieval with indexed files is not as fast as the best forms of direct file retrieval and extra file storage space is required to store the index and additional pointers.

Indexed sequential organization is usually preferable to indexed random organization. The performance of indexed sequential files begins to suffer, however, after a number of record additions that require the use of pointer chains for storage and retrieval. Thus, indexed sequential files must be reorganized (recreated) periodically.

If all the programs in the information system need to access a file sequentially, then it is best if that file has sequential organization. If all the programs need to access the file randomly, then direct organization is the appropriate choice. If some programs need to access the file sequentially and others randomly, then indexed organization is a good compromise. If future program file accessing needs are uncertain, indexed organization is a safe choice.

CHAPTER CASE STUDY 8

James Tool Company — File Concepts

James Tool Company received the payroll package they had purchased from Lennox Software Solutions. Systems analysts Don Mard and Kimberly Wallace, working with senior computer operator Sarah Muralski, were busy installing and checking out the package.

Programmer/analyst Howard Coswell, meanwhile, began to consider the files for the union system. Using the data flow diagram prepared during the systems analysis phase, Coswell identified two potential union system files: the data store for unions and the data store for union deductions. The data dictionary record definitions entered by Mard for those two data stores are shown in Figure 8-24 below and on the next page; the data dictionary entries for the data elements in the unions data store are shown in Figure 8-25 on the next two pages.

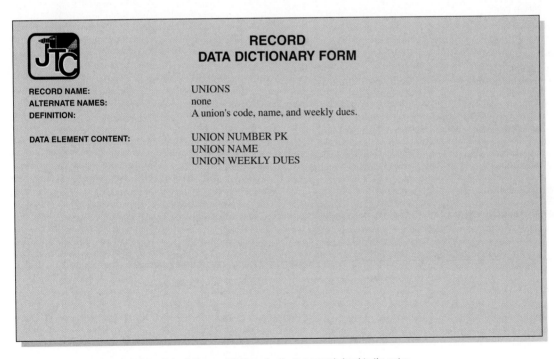

RECORD
DATA DICTIONARY FORM

RECORD NAME: UNIONS
ALTERNATE NAMES: none
DEFINITION: A union's code, name, and weekly dues.

DATA ELEMENT CONTENT: UNION NUMBER PK
                        UNION NAME
                        UNION WEEKLY DUES

Figure 8-24   Data dictionary definitions for the two records local to the union
system: unions and union deductions.

RECORD
DATA DICTIONARY FORM

RECORD NAME: UNION DEDUCTIONS
ALTERNATE NAMES: UNION DUES DEDUCTION
DEFINITION: A detailed recording of an employee's union dues deductions.

DATA ELEMENT CONTENT:

                              SSN
                              EMPLOYEE NAME
                              UNION NUMBER
                              WEEK ENDING DATE
                              WEEKLY EARNINGS
                              UNION DUES

Figure 8-24 (continued)

DATA ELEMENT
DATA DICTIONARY FORM

DATA ELEMENT NAME: UNION NUMBER
ALTERNATE NAMES: none

TYPE AND LENGTH: 1 A
OUTPUT FORMAT: X
DEFAULT VALUE: none
PROMPT / COLUMN HEADER: UNION NUMBER
SOURCE: Union Relations Department
SECURITY: Union Relations Department (update)

RESPONSIBLE END USER: Union Relations Department

ACCEPTABLE VALUES: any one-character unique value
OTHER VALIDATION: none

DERIVATION FORMULA: none

DESCRIPTION AND COMMENTS: A one-character code that identifies each union. Must be a unique value.

Figure 8-25 Data dictionary definitions for the three data elements in the unions record.

DATA ELEMENT
DATA DICTIONARY FORM

DATA ELEMENT NAME:	UNION WEEKLY DUES
ALTERNATE NAMES:	UNION DUES, EMPLOYEE UNION DUES
TYPE AND LENGTH:	4 N, 2 decimal
OUTPUT FORMAT:	Z9.99
DEFAULT VALUE:	none
PROMPT / COLUMN HEADER:	UNION DUES
SOURCE:	Union Relations Department
SECURITY:	Union Relations Department (update)
RESPONSIBLE END USER:	Union Relations Department
ACCEPTABLE VALUES:	any number
OTHER VALIDATION:	none
DERIVATION FORMULA:	none
DESCRIPTION AND COMMENTS:	The weekly dues for an employee who belongs to a particular union.

DATA ELEMENT
DATA DICTIONARY FORM

DATA ELEMENT NAME:	UNION NAME
ALTERNATE NAMES:	none
TYPE AND LENGTH:	25A
OUTPUT FORMAT:	X(25)
DEFAULT VALUE:	none
PROMPT / COLUMN HEADER:	UNION NAME
SOURCE:	Union Relations Department
SECURITY:	none
RESPONSIBLE END USER:	Union Relations Department
ACCEPTABLE VALUES:	any 25-character name
OTHER VALIDATION:	none
DERIVATION FORMULA:	none
DESCRIPTION AND COMMENTS:	

Figure 8-25   *(continued)*

Coswell first considered a union file to correspond to the unions data store. The union file would be a master file in the union system. Two of the three data elements in a union file record, namely union number and union name, are alphanumeric fields requiring one and twenty-five storage bytes, respectively. Because union weekly dues is a numeric field, however, several storage format choices are possible. Coswell decided to store union weekly dues in a packed decimal format; he calculated that three bytes would be necessary to store the maximum union weekly dues value. One record of the union file would therefore require 1 + 25 + 3 = 29 bytes of storage.

Records in the union file would be added, changed, deleted, or viewed using the Modify/View Unions data entry screen Coswell had already designed. Union file records would also be accessed (but not updated) whenever the Employee Union Deduction data entry screen was used to add, change, delete, or view employees' union affiliations. Because the union file would be used for online processing, rapid access of records would be important. Coswell knew the very fastest access would be a memory access. Because James Tool Company presently has only four unions, the total space required to store the entire union file in memory would not be significant. Even if the number of unions were to double, memory space would not be a problem. Coswell then decided the union file should be a simple sequential file — to be read into memory in its entirety whenever the Union System Menu is first invoked. Then, as they are needed, the appropriate records can be located using a memory search. If any union record was updated during the session, the union file would be rewritten in its entirety when the union system was exited.

Coswell mentioned his planned union file organization to Mard the next time they met. Mard said, "You might be right that a sequential organization would be the fastest solution. But did you consider that union records are rarely updated? Most often, if the Modify/View Union screen is used, only one union record will be involved. It might be faster to directly read and then rewrite only one record than to sequentially read and rewrite all the records. Also, employees don't change union affiliations all that often, so most of the time only one, or maybe two, union records will be needed when the Employee Union Deduction screen is being used. Is it faster to read one or two records directly than it is to read four records sequentially?"

Coswell checked with Delbert Donovan, director of union relations, and Jim McKeen, director of the payroll department, to find out how many union records they would need to access in a typical online session of the union system. He learned that Mard's evaluation of the union file activity level was correct. After investigating access speeds for direct and sequential files, Coswell decided to make the union file a direct file, using a key-addressing technique to directly convert union number to relative record number; the two processes that will use the union file would then directly access the union file record(s) as needed. Figure 8-26 shows the updated data dictionary entries for the unions data store and the union weekly dues data element, reflecting Coswell's design decisions.

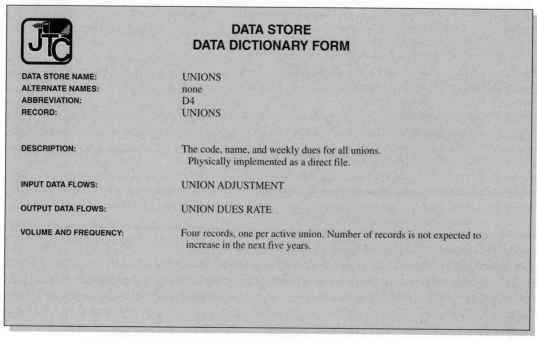

DATA STORE
DATA DICTIONARY FORM

DATA STORE NAME:	UNIONS
ALTERNATE NAMES:	none
ABBREVIATION:	D4
RECORD:	UNIONS

DESCRIPTION: The code, name, and weekly dues for all unions.
Physically implemented as a direct file.

INPUT DATA FLOWS: UNION ADJUSTMENT

OUTPUT DATA FLOWS: UNION DUES RATE

VOLUME AND FREQUENCY: Four records, one per active union. Number of records is not expected to increase in the next five years.

Figure 8-26 The updated data dictionary entries for the unions data store and the union weekly dues data element.

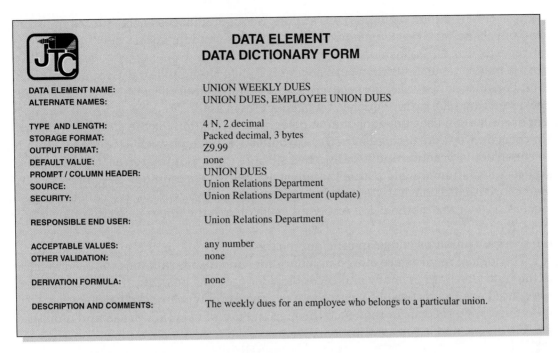

Figure 8-26 *(continued)*

Next, Coswell considered the union deductions data store. A union deduction file, corresponding to that data store, would be a work file. Once each week, a new union deduction file would be created by the Extract Union Deduction process, which would write one record for every employee with a union deduction. Every four weeks, the four most recent union deduction files would be merged and sorted before being used in the Pay Union Dues process; the four files could then be deleted when the Pay Union Dues process was completed and the output verified. Because each union deduction file would be created and used sequentially, Coswell decided that a sequential organization was the logical choice for the union deductions file.

Four of the data elements in the union deduction file are numeric fields: SSN, a nine-digit field, could be most efficiently stored as a four-byte binary fullword; week-ending date, an eight-digit field of YYYYMMDD form, could also be stored (and would sort correctly) as a four-byte binary fullword; weekly earnings, which includes six numeric digits, could be stored as a four-byte packed decimal field; union dues could be stored in the same format as union weekly dues, as a three-byte packed decimal field. Having made those decisions, Coswell had completed the union system file design.

Summary

A file consists of physical records, or blocks, that contain one or more logical records; the number of logical records in each physical record is termed the blocking factor. Typical information system file types include master files, table files, work files, transaction files, history files, and security files.

A logical record is composed of fields, some of which might be designated as key fields. The primary key of a file is the field or field combination that uniquely and minimally identifies a particular logical record. A foreign key is a field or field combination that must match the primary key of some other file. A secondary key is a field or field combination used as the basis for sorting or retrieving file records. Both alphanumeric and numeric fields can be stored in an EBCDIC or ASCII format; numeric fields can also be stored as packed decimal or binary numbers.

File access can be either sequential or random. Sequential access necessitates the storage and retrieval of records in a predetermined order, whereas random access permits the storage and retrieval of records in a direct fashion.

The three major file organizations are sequential, direct, and indexed. Sequential organization permits sequential access only. Records within a data file with sequential organization can be unordered (the pile) or in sequence by primary key value.

Direct organization uses an algorithm to determine a location for the storage and later retrieval of records. Key-addressing techniques produce a unique physical storage location but are difficult to construct in practice and usually leave storage gaps that waste disk storage. Hashing techniques use a hash function algorithm that does not guarantee a unique disk storage location. When two or more records hash to the same storage location, the records are called synonyms, and collision occurs. Two of the methods for resolving collision are the linear search and overflow methods.

Indexed organization provides an efficient means for both sequentially and randomly accessing records. The logical records are stored in a data file, and a separate index is used to locate records in the data file. Both primary and secondary indexes are possible. Indexed random and indexed sequential are two different forms of this organization type. Indexed sequential organization must keep records in sequence through the use of overflow areas and pointer chains, distributed free space, and block splitting.

Review Questions

1. Explain the difference between a logical record and a physical record.
2. What is blocking? Explain the tradeoffs associated with large blocking factors.
3. List and briefly describe the six types of information system files. Indicate which are relatively permanent files and which are usually temporary files.
4. Define these terms: primary key, candidate key, secondary key, and foreign key. Which of these, if any, is what we call a nonkey field?
5. Consider a student master file with record fields for student name, student number, address, sex, major, credits earned, and GPA. Identify the possible candidate keys, the likely primary key, a probable foreign key, and a potential secondary key. Justify your choices.
6. How many bytes are required to store a four-digit signed integer in EBCDIC or ASCII? In packed decimal? In binary?
7. What are the advantages of packed decimal data storage?
8. What are the advantages and disadvantages of binary data storage?
9. What is a Julian date? What is an absolute date? How would March 1, 1996, be represented in each form?
10. What are the three general classifications of file organization?
11. What is a pile?
12. What is the difference between key-addressing and hashing?
13. Describe two different hash function techniques.
14. How is a pointer chain used with collision management?
15. What is the difference between a sparse index and a dense index?
16. Describe the use of distributed free space with the block splitting technique.
17. If a file with direct organization has twenty-five blocks, each of which can store five records, what is the packing density if seventy-five records are stored?

Discussion Questions

1. In the section on access methods, the statement *randomly accessing all the records in a file takes much longer than sequentially accessing the entire file* appears. Explain why this statement is true.

2. A hash function using the division-remainder method and a divisor of 37 is used to store records into a direct file with thirty-seven blocks, each block containing up to three records. You create the file with records with these key values: 75, 112, 130, 149, 186, 195, and 225. To which block does each of these keys hash? Does collision occur? If so, does the collision create a problem?

3. You have a data file of ten records with primary key values of 5, 10, 20, 25, 30, 50, 60, 70, 80, and 90. Construct an indexed sequential file for these records with a two-level index, storing two data records and three index records per block. Add one record that requires block splitting, and show the changes caused by its addition.

4. A mail-order company recently acquired an 800 number for customer inquiries. At the same time, the order and customer master files were reorganized as direct files for rapid access by the customer service operators. The system performed well the first several weeks of operation. But recently, accessing a specific order on the order file has been taking longer. What could be the cause of the access delays?

5. *Magnetic tape is obsolete. Given the availability of direct-access devices with large data storage capabilities and rapid access speeds, there is no reason for a modern data processing installation to use magnetic tape devices with limited processing capabilities and slow access speeds.* Do you agree with this statement? Why or why not?

MINICASE STUDIES

8

Ridgeway Company

The Ridgeway Company requirements were described in a Chapter 4 minicase study. The following assignments are based on the work you did for that minicase. Assume that each data store you identified will be a file in the Ridgeway Company billing system.

Questions

1. For each file, determine the file type (master file, transaction file, and so on), and identify all key fields.
2. For each file, determine the appropriate file organization, and specify the access method for every process using the file.
3. For every numeric data element that you identified, specify an appropriate storage format.

Genealogy System

The genealogy system requirements were described in a Chapter 4 minicase study. The following assignments are based on the work you did for that minicase. Assume that each data store you identified will be a file in the genealogy system.

Questions

1. For each file, determine the file type (master file, transaction file, and so on), and identify all key fields.
2. For each file, determine the appropriate file organization, and specify the access method for every process using the file.

STUDENT CASE STUDY 8

Western Dental Clinic — File Concepts

Introduction

After completing the output and input designs for the dental system at Western Dental Clinic, Jim Archer turned his attention to the system's files. He began by assuming that each data store identified in the data flow diagrams previously prepared would be a file in the system.

Student Assignments

1. Determine the appropriate file organization for each file in the system and specify the access method for every process using the file.
2. For each file, determine an appropriate storage format for every numeric data item in the file.

CHAPTER 9

File and Database Design

Objectives

You will have mastered the material in this chapter when you can:

- Describe an entity-relationship diagram, and draw and describe the symbols used in constructing it
- Define and recognize the three basic types of entity relationships
- Explain the differences between data flow diagrams and entity-relationship diagrams, and describe how you use one to create the other
- Draw a complete entity-relationship diagram to satisfy an information system's data storage requirements
- Define first, second, and third normal form, and discuss the advantages of each
- Transform an unnormalized set of record designs into a set of equivalent record designs in third normal form
- List the components of a database management system
- Describe each of the database models
- Compare the advantages and disadvantages of the database approach versus the file processing environment
- Estimate the size and storage requirements for a file
- Discuss file and database control measures

Introduction

Many of your file and database design efforts are actually completed during the systems analysis phase. During systems analysis, you identify and describe all the data elements in the information system, create data flow diagrams, designate data stores, assign the data elements to those data stores, and normalize the data store designs. During the systems design phase, you evaluate and refine your data store designs.

Even though many file and database activities are completed during systems analysis instead of during systems design, we present all the information related to file and database design in this chapter. First, we explain how to create entity-relationship diagrams and how to translate those diagrams into file designs. Next, we discuss normalization, which is the process of identifying and eliminating potential problems in your record design, and present a methodology for converting record designs into third normal form. Then, we turn our attention to general database concepts and database design. First, we discuss the components of a database management system and then follow with an examination of four database models. Then, we present the advantages and disadvantages for each model as well as for the database approach in general. After summarizing the steps to follow when designing files and databases, we conclude the chapter with a discussion of file and database control.

Entity-relationship diagrams

We have previously defined an entity as a person, place, thing, or event for which data is collected. A **relationship** is a logical association between entities. A relationship exists between the entities PRODUCT and WAREHOUSE, for example, because products are stored in warehouses. A logical relationship is based on the nature of the entities involved and the environment in which they exist. The logical relationships between entities in an information system are graphically represented in an **entity-relationship diagram (ERD)**.

Figure 9-1 shows the basic format of an ERD for two related entities. Each entity is represented as a rectangle; a diamond, which represents the relationship, connects the entities. Entity rectangles are labeled with singular nouns; relationship diamonds are labeled with active verbs.

Experts in drawing ERDs would interpret Figure 9-2 in two ways: *a doctor treats a patient*, using the active voice, and *a patient is treated by a doctor*, using the passive voice. These two interpretations are equally legitimate, although many people prefer the active voice interpretation.

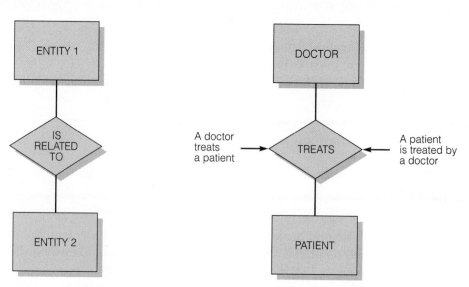

Figure 9-1 *A basic entity-relationship diagram.*

Figure 9-2 *In an entity-relationship diagram, entities are labeled with singular nouns, and relationships are labeled with verbs. The ERD is interpreted as simple English sentences.*

Unlike data flow diagrams and systems flowcharts, entity-relationship diagrams do not depict data or information flows. An ERD has no arrowheads. One of the entities must necessarily be positioned above or to the left of the other entity, but this does not imply a superior/inferior relationship between the entities or a flow from the first entity to the second entity.

Three types of relationships can exist between entities. A **one-to-one relationship**, abbreviated as **1:1**, exists when there is exactly one of the second entity for each of the first entity. ERDs for several possible 1:1 entity relationships are shown in Figure 9-3. A 1 is placed alongside each of the two lines connecting a rectangle to the diamond to indicate the 1:1 relationship.

A **one-to-many relationship**, abbreviated as **1:M**, exists when one occurrence of the first entity can be related to many occurrences of the second entity, but each occurrence of the second entity can be associated with only one occurrence of the first entity. For example, the relationship between DEPARTMENT and EMPLOYEE is typically one-to-many: one department can have many employees, but each employee is assigned only to one department. In some organizations, an employee can be assigned to more than one department; in such organizations, the relationship between DEPARTMENT and EMPLOYEE would not be 1:M. You must understand the actual environment in which the entities exist when you analyze entity relationships. Several possible 1:M entity-relationship diagrams are shown in Figure 9-4. The line connecting the MANY entity to the relationship is labeled with an M, whereas a 1 labels the other connecting line.

How many is many? The first 1:M relationship in Figure 9-4 states, *an individual owns an automobile*. One automobile is owned by, or registered to, exactly one individual. But a particular individual might own twenty automobiles, or one, or even none. Thus, many can mean any number, including zero.

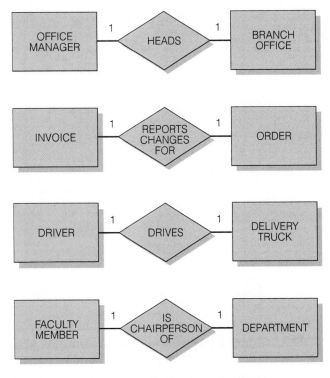

Figure 9-3 *One-to-one (1:1) relationships.*

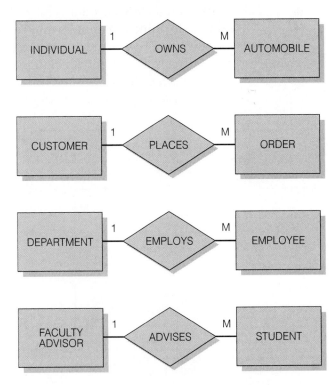

Figure 9-4 *One-to-many (1:M) relationships.*

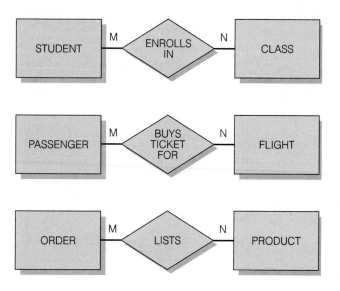

A **many-to-many relationship**, abbreviated **M:N**, exists when one occurrence of the first entity can be related to many occurrences of the second entity, and one occurrence of the second entity can be related to many occurrences of the first entity. The relationship between STUDENT and CLASS, for example, is many-to-many: one student can take many classes, and one class can have many students enrolled in it. Figure 9-5 shows several M:N entity-relationships. One of the lines connecting an entity to the relationship is labeled with an M, whereas an N labels the connection between the other entity and the relationship.

Figure 9-5 *Many-to-many (M:N) relationships.*

In a complete entity-relationship diagram, all the system entities and all the relationships between these entities are illustrated. In Figure 9-6, a more complete ERD relates SALES REP, CUSTOMER, ORDER, WAREHOUSE, and PRODUCT. The relationship between SALES REP and CUSTOMER in this example is one-to-many, which is typical; in some organizations, however, a customer might be served by more than one sales rep in a many-to-many relationship. The relationship between WAREHOUSE and PRODUCT in the figure is many-to-many; that relationship would be one-to-many in another organization if all instances of one product are always stored in a particular warehouse.

Many CASE products support the drawing of entity-relationship diagrams. Although a CASE product cannot analyze an information system's requirements and determine the entities and relationships for you, the process of drawing and modifying ERDs is much less tedious with an automated ERD tool.

To create an entity-relationship diagram for a system, you must first identify the system entities. Because an entity is something for which data is collected, the best approach is to start with the data stores that you have already identified in your data flow diagrams — let each data store represent an entity. Then, look at these entities two at a time. For each pair of entities, ask the question, *Are these entities related?* and if they are, *How are they related?* Add each identified relationship to the developing system ERD. As you progress, you might even think of some system entities and relationships you had not initially identified; add these new entities and relationships to your system ERD.

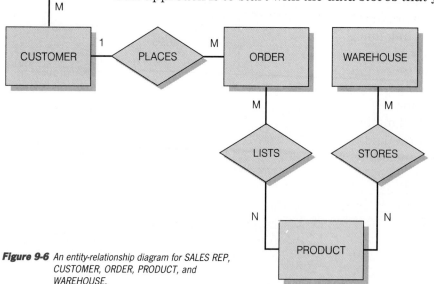

Figure 9-6 *An entity-relationship diagram for SALES REP, CUSTOMER, ORDER, PRODUCT, and WAREHOUSE.*

Don't worry if you sense that you have somehow missed one or more entities or relationships. You will be normalizing your entity records, and one possible result of the normalization process is the identification of previously unrecognized system entities.

Normalization

Normalization is a process by which you identify and correct inherent problems and complexities in your record designs. You start with a collection of record designs and, through normalization, you produce a new collection of records equivalent to the original (that is, containing the same data) but as free of potential processing problems as possible. The normalization process involves three types of normal forms: first normal form, second normal form, and third normal form. These three normal forms constitute a progression in which a record that is in first normal form is better than one that is unnormalized; a record that is in second normal form is better yet; and a record that is in third normal form is best.

■ First normal form

A record is in **first normal form (1NF)** if it does not contain a repeating group. A **repeating group** is a set of one or more data items that can occur a variable number of times in a record. As an example, we will consider a record of order and product information that contains the order number, order date, and as many repetitions of product number, product description, and number ordered as appropriate. For this example, assume that all the data relevant to both products and orders has been accounted for in this one record design. Three sample data records for this record design are shown in Figure 9-7.

RECORD #	ORDER-NUM	ORDER-DATE	PRODUCT-NUM	PRODUCT-DESC	NUM-ORDERED
1	40311	03111997	304	All-purpose gadget	7
			633	Trangam	1
			684	Super gismo	4
2	40312	03111997	128	Steel widget	12
			304	All-purpose gadget	3
3	40313	03121997	304	All-purpose gadget	144

Figure 9-7 Unnormalized ORDER records.

A standard way to present this record layout is:

ORDER (ORDER-NUM, ORDER-DATE, (PRODUCT-NUM, PRODUCT-DESC, NUM-ORDERED))

The field ORDER-NUM is underlined to indicate it is the primary key. The fields PRODUCT-NUM, PRODUCT-DESC, and NUM-ORDERED are enclosed in an extra set of parentheses to indicate they are fields within a repeating group. If a customer ordered three different products in one order, then the set PRODUCT-NUM, PRODUCT-DESC, and NUM-ORDERED would be repeated three times in the corresponding record; the first sample ORDER record in Figure 9-7 on the previous page includes three such repetitions.

To convert an **unnormalized record**, which is a record that contains one or more repeating groups, to a record in 1NF, you remove the repeating group and expand the primary key to include the key of the repeating group. The 1NF form of the ORDER record would be:

ORDER (<u>ORDER-NUM</u>, ORDER-DATE, <u>PRODUCT-NUM</u>, PRODUCT-DESC, NUM-ORDERED)

The 1NF form of our sample records is shown in Figure 9-8. The primary key of the 1NF records cannot be the ORDER-NUM field, because multiple records can have the same value for ORDER-NUM. Similarly, PRODUCT-NUM cannot be the primary key. We need a combination of ORDER-NUM and PRODUCT-NUM to uniquely identify a single record. Therefore, those two fields together constitute the primary key.

RECORD #	<u>ORDER-NUM</u>	ORDER-DATE	<u>PRODUCT-NUM</u>	PRODUCT-DESC	NUM-ORDERED
1	40311	03111997	304	All-purpose gadget	7
2	40311	03111997	633	Trangam	1
3	40311	03111997	684	Super gismo	4
4	40312	03111997	128	Steel widget	12
5	40312	03111997	304	All-purpose gadget	3
6	40313	03121997	304	All-purpose gadget	144

Figure 9-8 *1 NF ORDER records.*

One field in one occurrence of an unnormalized record with repeating groups can have multiple values; for example, the field PRODUCT-NUM has three values in the first sample record of Figure 9-7 on the previous page and two values in the second sample record. But all the fields in a 1NF record occurrence have only one value. Thus, by eliminating the repeating group in this first normalization step, you simplify the record design.

■ Second normal form

To understand second normal form, you must first understand the concept of functional dependence. The field Q is said to be **dependent** on the field R if a value for R determines a single value for Q. For example, an order date is dependent on an order number; for a particular order number, there is only one value for the order date. In contrast, the product description is not dependent on the order number; for a particular order number, it might be possible to associate several product descriptions, one for each product ordered.

A record design is in **second normal form (2NF)** if it is in 1NF and if all fields that are not part of the primary key are dependent on the entire primary key. If any field in a 1NF record depends on only one of the fields in a combination primary key, then the record is *not* in 2NF. A 1NF record with a primary key that is a single field is automatically in 2NF.

`ORDER (`<u>`ORDER-NUM`</u>`, ORDER-DATE, `<u>`PRODUCT-NUM`</u>`, PRODUCT-DESC, NUM-ORDERED)`

The primary key is the combination, or **concatenation**, of the order number and the product number. The NUM-ORDERED field depends on the entire primary key; that is, for a number ordered value of 7 to be meaningful, you need to know the product number *and* the order number to which it relates. However, the ORDER-DATE field depends only on the order number, which is only a part of the primary key; similarly, the PRODUCT-DESC field depends only on the product number. Therefore, this record design is not in 2NF.

What are the potential problems with this non-2NF design? Four categories of problems exist. First, consider the work that is necessary to change a particular product's description. If you need to change the description for product number 304 in Figure 9-8, you must change the product description field in every record in which product number 304 appears. Thus, updating can be a cumbersome and lengthy process.

Second, non-2NF records can contain inconsistent data. Nothing about the non-2NF design prohibits product number 304 from having two different product descriptions in two different records; in fact, if product number 304 appeared in thirty order records, thirty different product descriptions could potentially exist for this product number.

The third problem with non-2NF designs concerns additions. How would you add a new product and its description? Because the primary key includes both the order number and the product number, you need values for both fields to add a record. What value do you use for the order number when you want to add a new product that has not yet been ordered by any customer? Your only choice is to make up a dummy order number, and then replace it with a real order number once the product is actually ordered. Certainly this is an awkward, unacceptable solution.

The fourth problem concerns deletions. If all the related records are deleted once an order is filled and paid for, what happens if you delete the only record that contained product number 633? The information about that product number and its description is lost.

There is a standard procedure for converting a record design from 1NF to 2NF. First, for each field in the primary key you create a separate record. Then, you create additional separate records for all combinations of the primary key fields taken two at a time, three at a time, and so on, until you finally create a record with the entire original primary key. Designate the field or fields in each of the new records as the primary key for that record. For our example non-2NF record, you would begin by creating these three partial records:

`(`<u>`ORDER-NUM`</u>`,`
`(`<u>`PRODUCT-NUM`</u>`,`
`(`<u>`ORDER-NUM`</u>`, `<u>`PRODUCT-NUM`</u>`,`

Next, place each of the remaining fields with its appropriate primary key, the minimal key upon which it depends. When you have finished placing all the fields, remove any record that has had no additional field placed into it. The remaining records are the 2NF version of your original record design. For our example record, this process would yield:

```
ORDER (ORDER-NUM, ORDER-DATE)
PRODUCT (PRODUCT-NUM, PRODUCT-DESC)
ORDER-LINE (ORDER-NUM, PRODUCT-NUM, NUM-ORDERED)
```

Instead of one non-2NF record design, you now have three records that are all in 2NF. These records should be given new, descriptive names, such as ORDER, PRODUCT, and ORDER-LINE, respectively. The 2NF versions of our sample records are shown in Figure 9-9.

ORDER RECORDS

RECORD #	ORDER-NUM	ORDER-DATE
1	40311	03111997
2	40312	03111997
2	40313	03121997

PRODUCT RECORDS

RECORD #	PRODUCT-NUM	PRODUCT-DESC
1	128	Steel widget
2	304	All-purpose gadget
3	633	Trangam
4	684	Super gismo

ORDER-LINE RECORDS

RECORD #	ORDER-NUM	PRODUCT-NUM	NUM-ORDERED
1	40311	304	7
2	40311	633	1
3	40311	684	4
4	40312	128	12
5	40312	304	3
6	40313	304	144

Figure 9-9 2NF ORDER records, PRODUCT records, and ORDER-LINE records.

Has the 2NF design eliminated all four identified potential problems? To change a product description, you need to change only one PRODUCT record. Having multiple, inconsistent values for the product description for a particular product is impossible, because that product's description appears in only one location. To add a new product and its description, you simply create a new PRODUCT record; creating a dummy order record is not necessary. When you remove the last ORDER-LINE record for a particular product number, you do not lose that product number and its description; the PRODUCT record would still exist. The four potential problems have therefore been eliminated, and the three 2NF record designs are superior to both the original unnormalized record and the 1NF record design.

Third normal form

Consider the following CUSTOMER record design.

CUSTOMER (<u>CUSTOMER-NUM</u>, CUSTOMER-NAME, ADDRESS, SALES-REP-NUM, SALES-REP-NAME)

This record is in 1NF because the record has no repeating groups. We also know that the record is in 2NF because the primary key is a single field. But this design still has four potential problems similar to the four problems described for non-2NF designs. Changing the name of a sales rep requires changing every record in which that sales rep appears. Nothing about the design prohibits a particular sales rep from having different names in different records. To add a new sales rep who has not yet been assigned to any customers (assuming we do not already have a separate sales rep master file), we must create a dummy customer record. Finally, if we were to delete all the records of the customers of sales rep number 22, we would lose that sales rep number and name. These potential problems are caused because the record design is not in 3NF.

A record design is in **third normal form (3NF)** if it is in 2NF and if no nonkey field is dependent on another nonkey field. (Recall that a nonkey field is a field that is not a candidate key for the primary key.) Our CUSTOMER record example is not in 3NF because one nonkey field, SALES-REP-NAME, depends on another nonkey field, SALES-REP-NUM.

To convert to 3NF, remove all fields from the 2NF record that depend on another nonkey field and place them into a new record with the other field as the primary key. For our CUSTOMER record, you would remove SALES-REP-NAME and place it into a new record with SALES-REP-NUM as its primary key. Therefore, the third normal form is:

CUSTOMER (<u>CUSTOMER-NUM</u>, CUSTOMER-NAME, ADDRESS, SALES-REP-NUM)
SALES-REP (<u>SALES-REP-NUM</u>, SALES-REP-NAME)

By converting the one CUSTOMER record design to 3NF, you have created two record designs: CUSTOMER and SALES-REP. Sample records for the 2NF design and the 3NF version of the same data are shown in Figure 9-10 on the next page.

CUSTOMER IN 2NF

RECORD #	CUSTOMER-NUM	CUSTOMER-NAME	ADDRESS	SALES-REP-NUM	SALES-REP-NAME
1	108	Benedict, Louise	San Diego, CA	41	Kaplan, James
2	233	Corelli, Helen	Nashua, NH	22	McBride, Jon
3	254	Gomez, J.P.	Butte, MT	38	Stein, Ellen
4	431	Lee, M.	Snow Camp,NC	74	Roman, Harold
5	779	Paulski, Diane	Lead, SD	38	Stein, Ellen
6	800	Zuider, Z	Greer, SC	74	Roman, Harold

CUSTOMER IN 3NF

RECORD #	CUSTOMER-NUM	CUSTOMER-NAME	ADDRESS	SALES-REP-NUM
1	108	Benedict, Louise	San Diego, CA	41
2	233	Corelli, Helen	Nashua, NH	22
3	254	Gomez, J. P.	Butte, MT	38
4	431	Lee, M.	Snow Camp, NC	74
5	779	Paulski, Diane	Lead, SD	38
6	800	Zuider, Z.	Greer, SC	74

SALES-REP IN 3NF

RECORD #	SALES REP-NUM	SALES REP-NAME
1	22	McBride, Jon
2	38	Stein, Ellen
3	41	Kaplan, James
4	74	Roman, Harold

Figure 9-10 *2NF and 3NF record designs for CUSTOMER and SALES-REP data.*

■ A complete normalization example

To illustrate the normalizing of records for an entire system, we will consider a system with three identified entities: ADVISOR, COURSE, and STUDENT. Figure 9-11 shows the initial ERD for that system.

The initial design of the record for the STUDENT entity includes the student number, student name, total credits taken, grade point average (GPA), advisor number and advisor name, and, for every course the student has taken, the course number, course description, and grade received. Three sample STUDENT records are shown in Figure 9-12.

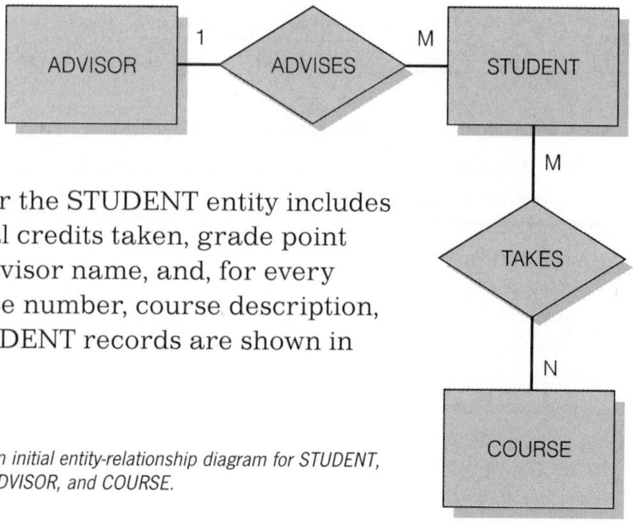

Figure 9-11 *An initial entity-relationship diagram for STUDENT, ADVISOR, and COURSE.*

STUDENT

STUDENT-NUMBER	STUDENT-NAME	TOTAL-CREDITS	GPA	ADVISOR-NUMBER	ADVISOR-NAME	COURSE-NUMBER	COURSE-DESC	GRADE
1035	Linda	17	3.647	49	Smith	CSC151	Computer Science I	B
						MKT212	Marketing Mangement	A
						ENG101	English Composition	B
						CHM112	General Chemistry I	A
						BUS105	Introduction to Business	A
3397	Sam	9	3.000	49	Smith	ENG101	English Composition	A
						MKT212	Marketing Management	C
						CSC151	Computer Science I	B
4070	Kelly	14	2.214	23	Jones	CSC151	Computer Science I	B
						CHM112	General Chemistry I	C
						ENG101	English Composition	C
						BUS105	Introduction to Business	C

Figure 9-12 *Unnormalized STUDENT records.*

This STUDENT record design can be written as:

STUDENT (STUDENT-NUMBER, STUDENT-NAME, TOTAL-CREDITS, GPA, ADVISOR-NUMBER, ADVISOR-NAME, (COURSE-NUMBER, COURSE-DESC, GRADE))

The record designs for the ADVISOR and COURSE entities are:

ADVISOR (ADVISOR-NUMBER, ADVISOR-NAME)
COURSE (COURSE-NUMBER, COURSE-DESC, NUM-CREDITS)

The ADVISOR and COURSE records are already in 3NF. Because it contains a repeating group, the STUDENT record, however, is unnormalized. To convert the STUDENT record to 1NF, you expand the primary key to include the key of the repeating group and then remove the repetition from the repeating group, producing:

STUDENT (STUDENT-NUMBER, STUDENT-NAME, TOTAL-CREDITS, GPA, ADVISOR-NUMBER, ADVISOR-NAME, COURSE-NUMBER, COURSE-DESC, GRADE)

The 1NF version of the sample STUDENT data is shown in Figure 9-13 on the next page. Do any of the fields in the 1NF STUDENT record depend on only a portion of the primary key? The student name, total credits, GPA, advisor number, and advisor name all relate only to the student number; they have no relationship whatsoever with the course number. The course description depends on the course number but not on the student number. Only the GRADE field depends on the entire primary key.

STUDENT

STUDENT-NUMBER	STUDENT-NAME	TOTAL-CREDITS	GPA	ADVISOR-NUMBER	ADVISOR-NAME	COURSE-NUMBER	COURSE-DESC	GRADE
1035	Linda	17	3.647	49	Smith	CSC151	Computer Science I	B
1035	Linda	17	3.647	49	Smith	MKT212	Marketing Management	A
1035	Linda	17	3.647	49	Smith	ENG101	English Composition	B
1035	Linda	17	3.647	49	Smith	CHM112	General Chemistry I	A
1035	Linda	17	3.647	49	Smith	BUS105	Introduction to Business	A
3397	Sam	9	3.000	49	Smith	ENG101	English Composition	A
3397	Sam	9	3.000	49	Smith	MKT212	Marketing Management	C
3397	Sam	9	3.000	49	Smith	CSC151	Computer Science I	B
4070	Kelly	14	2.214	23	Jones	CSC151	Computer Science I	B
4070	Kelly	14	2.214	23	Jones	CHM112	General Chemistry I	C
4070	Kelly	14	2.214	23	Jones	ENG101	English Composition	C
4070	Kelly	14	2.214	23	Jones	BUS105	Introduction to Business	C

Figure 9-13 *1NF STUDENT records.*

Creating records for each field and combination of fields in the primary key, and then placing the other fields with their appropriate key produces the following record designs:

```
STUDENT (STUDENT-NUMBER, STUDENT-NAME, TOTAL-CREDITS, GPA,
   ADVISOR-NUMBER, ADVISOR-NAME)
COURSE-X (COURSE-NUMBER, COURSE-DESC)
GRADE (STUDENT-NUMBER, COURSE-NUMBER, GRADE)
```

The original STUDENT record has now been expanded to three records, all of which are in 2NF. One of these three records, COURSE-X, has the same primary key as our original COURSE record. At any time during normalization, whenever you have two or more records with identical primary keys, you should merge them into a single record that includes all fields from all the records. In this case, the new COURSE-X record has no field that was not already in the original COURSE record design, so we will keep our original COURSE record and discard the COURSE-X record.

The 2NF STUDENT, COURSE, and GRADE records for the sample data are shown in Figure 9-14. Are all three records in 3NF? COURSE and GRADE are in 3NF. STUDENT is not, however, because the ADVISOR-NAME field depends on the advisor number, which is not part of the STUDENT primary key. To convert STUDENT to 3NF, you remove the ADVISOR-NAME field from the STUDENT record and place it into a new record with ADVISOR-NUMBER as its primary key; in this case, the new record would duplicate your original ADVISOR record, so no new record is needed.

The 3NF versions of the sample data for STUDENT, ADVISOR, COURSE, and GRADE are shown in Figure 9-15 on page 9.14.

Our final 3NF design for all the entity records is:

```
STUDENT (STUDENT-NUMBER, STUDENT-NAME, TOTAL-CREDITS, GPA,
   ADVISOR-NUMBER)
ADVISOR (ADVISOR-NUMBER, ADVISOR-NAME)
COURSE (COURSE-NUMBER, COURSE-DESC, NUM-CREDITS)
GRADE (STUDENT-NUMBER, COURSE-NUMBER, GRADE)
```

STUDENT

STUDENT-NUMBER	STUDENT-NAME	TOTAL-CREDITS	GPA	ADVISOR-NUMBER	ADVISOR-NAME
1035	Linda	17	3.647	49	Smith
3397	Sam	9	3.000	49	Smith
4070	Kelly	14	2.214	23	Jones

COURSE

COURSE-NUMBER	COURSE-DESC	NUM-CREDITS
BUS105	Introduction to Business	3
CHM112	General Chemistry I	5
CSC151	Computer Science I	3
ENG101	English Composition	3
MKT212	Marketing Management	3

GRADE

STUDENT-NUMBER	COURSE-NUMBER	GRADE
1035	CSC151	B
1035	MKT212	A
1035	ENG101	B
1035	CHM112	A
1035	BUS105	A
3397	ENG101	A
3397	MKT212	C
3397	CSC151	B
4070	CSC151	B
4070	CHM112	C
4070	ENG101	C
4070	BUS105	C

Figure 9-14 *2NF STUDENT, COURSE, and GRADE records.*

STUDENT

STUDENT-NUMBER	STUDENT-NAME	TOTAL-CREDITS	GPA	ADVISOR-NUMBER
1035	Linda	17	3.647	49
3397	Sam	9	3.000	49
4070	Kelly	14	2.214	23

ADVISOR

ADVISOR-NUMBER	ADVISOR-NAME
23	Jones
49	Smith

COURSE

COURSE-NUMBER	COURSE-DESC	NUM-CREDITS
BUS105	Introduction to Business	3
CHM112	General Chemistry I	5
CSC151	Computer Science I	3
ENG101	English Composition	3
MKT212	Marketing Management	3

GRADE

STUDENT-NUMBER	COURSE-NUMBER	GRADE
1035	CSC151	B
1035	MKT212	A
1035	ENG101	B
1035	CHM112	A
1035	BUS105	A
3397	ENG101	A
3397	MKT212	C
3397	CSC151	B
4070	CSC151	B
4070	CHM112	C
4070	ENG101	C
4070	BUS105	C

Figure 9-15 *3NF STUDENT, ADVISOR, COURSE, and GRADE records.*

We now have four identified entities: STUDENT, ADVISOR, COURSE, and GRADE. Figure 9-16 shows the corrected, more complete ERD. Compare Figure 9-16 to Figure 9-11 on page 9.10, which was drawn before we had identified GRADE as an entity. Notice that the many-to-many relationship between STUDENT and COURSE has been converted to two one-to-many relationships, one between STUDENT and GRADE and the other between COURSE and GRADE. This is always a result of normalization: many-to-many relationships are decomposed into two or more one-to-many relationships.

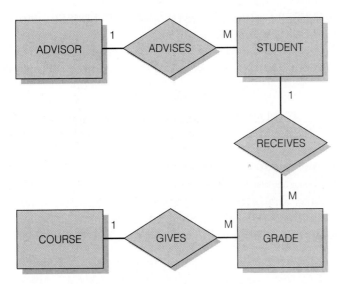

Figure 9-16 *The entity-relationship diagram for STUDENT, ADVISOR, and COURSE after normalization. The entity GRADE was identified during the normalization process.*

Have the example non-3NF record designs we have presented seemed unnatural and unlikely? In fact, most of these designs were contrived to better illustrate normalization concepts. Many systems analysts find normalization so natural and logical that their initial designs are in 3NF. Still, even if you usually design in 3NF automatically, you need to understand the criteria for first, second, and third normal form. In the real world, record designs are much more complex than the samples presented in this chapter; you will need to verify that even long, complicated record designs are truly in 3NF.

■ Higher normal forms

Generally speaking, your goal is to develop a series of record designs that are in third normal form. But third-normal form is not the highest of the normal forms. Consider a record design with a primary key that is the concatenation of three fields:

RECORD (A, B, C, D, . . .)

If field A is associated with a collection of values for B *independent* of the values for C, there is said to be a **multivalued dependence** of field B on field A. In that case, potential update problems similar to those discussed for second and third normal form exist. Fourth normal form avoids these potential problems. A record is said to be in **fourth normal form (4NF)** if it is in 3NF and there are no multivalued dependencies. Note that it is not the case that any record with three fields in the primary key has a problem. It is the *independence* of the primary key field values that causes some records with three-part primary keys to be non-4NF.

Fortunately, there is an easy way to avoid creating non-4NF records. Such records arise when you begin the design process with a non-normalized record with more than one repeating group. A simple extension to our rule for converting to first normal form will guarantee that the 3NF records you eventually create are also in 4NF. When you convert a record with multiple repeating groups into first normal form, you must place each separate repeating group into a separate record. For example, assume that a student can declare more than one major and has an advisor for each declared major. We might start our design with the following unnormalized record:

STUDENT (<u>STUDENT-NUMBER</u>, (MAJOR-CODE, ADVISOR-NUMBER, ADVISOR-NAME), (COURSE-NUMBER, COURSE-DESC, GRADE))

To convert this record to 1NF, we would create *two* new records, one for each repeating group:

STUDENT-MAJOR (<u>STUDENT-NUMBER</u>, <u>MAJOR-CODE</u>, ADVISOR-NUMBER, ADVISOR-NAME)
STUDENT-COURSE (<u>STUDENT-NUMBER</u>, <u>COURSE-NUMBER</u>, COURSE-DESC, GRADE)

We would now continue to convert these two relations to 2NF and 3NF as before. The resulting record designs would then automatically be in 4NF.

Even higher normal forms have been defined, including fifth normal form (5NF) and domain-key normal form (DK/NF). These normal forms are the subject of much research, but as of now, are of little value to the practical design process.

Should record designs always be converted to third normal form? Are there ever good reasons for backing off from a 3NF design?

Consider this record design:

SUPPLIER (<u>SUPPLIER-NUMBER</u>, SUPPLIER-NAME, ADDRESS, CITY, STATE, ZIP-CODE, . . .)

Knowing the zip code, you can certainly determine the associated city and state. To convert this record design to a true 3NF, you would shift the city and state fields to another record with zip code as the primary key. While this is a legitimate action, doing so is overkill. Would you ever need to change the city or state associated with zip code 70933? Would you ever need to store the fact that zip code 36062 corresponds to Petrey, Alabama, if your company has no suppliers with that zip code? Would it matter that by deleting the only supplier with zip code 45405, you would lose the knowledge that 45405 is one of the zip codes for Dayton, Ohio? The answer to each of these questions is no. Leaving this particular record design in its non-3NF form is certainly more natural. Even with the non-3NF design, you are unlikely to encounter the types of update problems previously discussed.

A second reason for using non-3NF record designs is to improve system performance, although doing so might introduce redundancy or potential update problems. Consider these two record designs:

ORDER-LINE (<u>ORDER-NUM</u>, <u>PRODUCT-NUM</u>, PRODUCT-DESC, NUM-ORDERED, QUOTED-PRICE)
PRODUCT (<u>PRODUCT-NUM</u>, PRODUCT-DESC, UNITS-ON-HAND, . . .)

The PRODUCT-DESC field depends only on PRODUCT-NUM, so the first record is not in 2NF and therefore not in 3NF. Because the PRODUCT record also includes PRODUCT-DESC, simply removing PRODUCT-DESC from the ORDER-LINE record would produce a design that is in 3NF. The resulting 3NF design would not only eliminate redundancy and potential update problems, but would also save storage space.

There is an advantage, however, to the design as it is presented. To print detailed customer invoices and other reports, for example, you do not have to access a PRODUCT record simply to retrieve the description. By using the non-3NF design, you might eliminate the need to access PRODUCT records for many of the processing steps involving ORDER-LINE records. Those processes then will be simpler and will execute more rapidly. You must weigh the advantages of this increased efficiency against the disadvantages associated with non-3NF records. ∎

Database

I n a typical file processing environment, each end user department has its own information system, and each information system has its own collection of files. Two potential problems might occur with this environment. First, **data redundancy**, in which data common to two or more information systems is duplicated in multiple files, is possible. Data redundancy obviously results in using extra storage space. In addition, maintaining all instances of redundant data requires that updates to that data must be duplicated for input and processing by all the involved information systems; the potential for inconsistent data exists if updates are not universally applied. For example, consider an organization with independent payroll and personnel systems, as shown in Figure 9-17. The employee master file and personnel master file probably have many data items in common, including employee names and numbers, department numbers, and positions. When an employee is transferred to a new department, that change must be input to both the payroll and personnel systems; if the change is applied to only one of the systems, resulting in inconsistent employee information in the two systems, we have a **data integrity**, or data quality, problem.

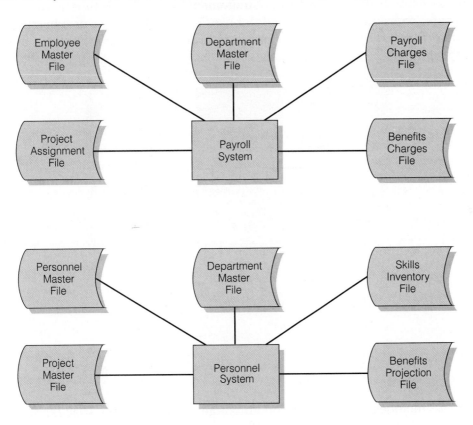

Figure 9-17 *The typical file processing environment. Every information system has its own master data files.*

The second problem with the typical file processing environment concerns management decision support. A top-level manager might need to relate information from more than one end user department; this requires accessing independent information systems, which might be an awkward and inefficient process at best.

Database technology presents a solution to these problems. We define a **database** as a structure that can store data relating to multiple entities, as well as relationships among those entities. Some definitions of a database include the word **self-describing**, meaning that a database contains within it a description of itself; thus, a database is a logically complete structure that does not rely on a separate structure for information about itself. Another word often used in database definitions is **integrated**, which means that a database contains and supports relationships. A phrase that appears in many database definitions is **controlled redundancy**, which means that data is not unnecessarily duplicated. A final word often used in the definition of a database is **shared**, which simply means that two or more end users can simultaneously access the database.

■ Database management systems

In a file processing environment, data files are designed to fit individual applications. In contrast, in a database environment, the application systems are built around the database. Figure 9-18 shows a database environment with a single database serving five separate information systems. Notice that the interaction between information systems and the database is not direct. A **database management system (DBMS)** is a software system used to create, access, and control the database. The DBMS serves as a bridge, or interface, between the database and the application programs, systems analysts, and end users of the database.

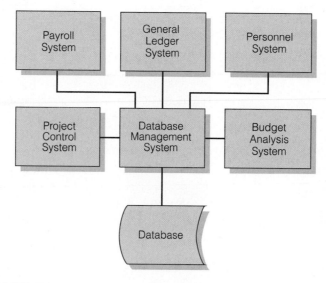

Figure 9-18 *The database environment in which multiple information systems access a single, integrated database.*

A DBMS includes a data definition language, a data manipulation language, a query language, a data dictionary, and utility services.

Data definition language   A **data definition language (DDL)** is used to describe the structure of the database. The complete definition of the database, which includes descriptions of all fields, records, and relationships, is called the **schema**. You also use the DDL to define one or more subschemas for the database. A **subschema** is a view of the database used by one or more programs or end users. A subschema defines only those portions of the database that a particular program or end user needs or is allowed to access. For example, to protect individual privacy, you would not want to allow just any program or end user to retrieve an employee's pay rate. To restrict access to the pay rate field, you would define the field in only the appropriate subschemas; any end user or program using a subschema lacking the pay rate field would be unable to access that field. Subschemas are also used to restrict the type of access allowed. For example, a subschema that includes the pay rate field might allow both retrieval and update of the field, or that subschema might restrict access of the field to retrieval only.

Data manipulation language   A **data manipulation language (DML)** provides the commands necessary for storing, retrieving, updating, and deleting database records. DML commands can be embedded in applications programs written in **host languages**, which are procedural programming languages such as COBOL, BASIC, and PL/1.

Query language   A **query language** is a nonprocedural language used to access a database. A **nonprocedural language** is one in which you specify a task to be done without specifying how the task is to be accomplished. Many different types of query languages are used today. With some query languages, the user enters complete commands; many of these query languages are said to be **natural languages**, meaning that the commands resemble ordinary English statements. Some query languages use question and answer dialogues. With a **Query-By-Example (QBE)** language, the user describes the desired database access by specifying an example. The most widely-used query language is **SQL (Structured Query Language)**, which is available on most platforms and has powerful capabilities beyond those implied by its name. All types of query languages are designed to be simple to learn and use, so the end users can access the database themselves.

In many microcomputer DBMSs, a single language serves as the DML, DDL, and query language. For example, SQL is a language available with some microcomputer DBMSs, and it has DML, DDL, and query capabilities.

Data dictionary   The **data dictionary** in a DBMS is the central storehouse of information about the database. The schema and all subschemas are stored in the data dictionary.

Utility services   Most DBMSs include the necessary support for interactive processing, database security, backup and recovery, transaction journaling, data integrity, and shared update. To say that a DBMS supports **shared update** means that two or more people can simultaneously access and update the database.

Most DBMSs also provide several utility services to assist in the general maintenance of the database. These services typically include utilities for creating a database, changing the structure of the database, gathering and reporting patterns of database usage, and detecting and reporting database structure irregularities.

■ Database models

The four basic models for database organization are hierarchical, network, relational, and object-oriented. The hierarchical model is the oldest of these models. Next came the network model and then the relational model. The object-oriented model is the newest of the four. Hierarchical and network model databases are mainly found on mainframes. The relational database model is the dominant model used on microcomputers, while the object-oriented model appears mostly on minicomputers. All new DBMSs over the past few years have been either relational or object-oriented DBMSs. Due to its underlying philosophy and its relative newness, aspects of the object-oriented model will influence future DBMS development. Each of the four basic models is represented by several commercially available database management systems (Figure 9-19).

DBMS Type	DBMS Product	Vendor
Hierarchical	IMS	IBM
Network	CA-IDMS	Computer Associates
Network	IMAGE	Hewlett-Packard
Object-Oriented	GemStone	Servio Corp.
Object-Oriented	IDB Object Database	Persistent Data System
Object-Oriented	Objectivity/DB	Objectivity, Inc.
Object-Oriented	ObjectStore	Object Design, Inc.
Object-Oriented	Ontos DB	Ontos, Inc.
Object-Oriented	OpenODB	Hewlett-Packard
Object-Oriented	UniSQL/X	UniSQL, Inc.
Object-Oriented	Versant Object DBMS	Versant Object Technology Corp.
Relational	Access	Microsoft Corp.
Relational	Approach	Lotus Development Corp.
Relational	CA-dBFast	Computer Associates
Relational	dBASE	Borland International Corp.
Relational	DB2	IBM
Relational	FileMaker Pro	Claris Corp.
Relational	FoxPro	Microsoft Corp.
Relational	Ingres	Ingres Corp.
Relational	Oracle	Oracle Corp.
Relational	Paradox	Borland International Corp.
Relational	PowerBuilder	Powersoft
Relational	SQLBase	Gupta Corp.
Relational	SQL Server	Microsoft Corp.
Relational	Superbase	Software Publishing Corp.
Relational	Supra	Cincom Systems, Inc.
Relational	Sybase SQL Server	Sybase, Inc.

Figure 9-19 Some commercially available DBMS products for the four basic database models.

Hierarchical databases   In a **hierarchical database**, data is organized in a series as in a family tree or organization chart. Like a family tree, the hierarchical database has branches made up of parent records and child records. A parent record can have multiple child records, but each child record can have only one physical parent. The parent record at the top of the hierarchy is called the root record. Figure 9-20 shows a hierarchical database for departments, faculty, students, and majors. DEPARTMENT is the parent of two types of records: FACULTY and MAJOR. FACULTY is the parent of STUDENT. Notice that a dotted line instead of a solid line connects MAJOR and STUDENT. MAJOR cannot be a parent to a STUDENT record, because STUDENT already has FACULTY as a physical parent. There are, however, a number of ways to get around this restriction to establish an effective relationship between students and their majors; with one technique, MAJOR is defined as a logical as opposed to a physical parent.

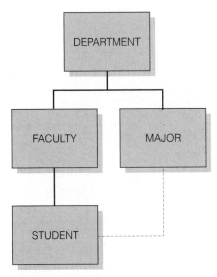

Figure 9-20 *A hierarchical database for DEPARTMENT, FACULTY, STUDENT, and MAJOR records.*

Relationships in a hierarchical database are defined by the parent/child associations. The DBMS follows pointers from the root down, up, and along the branches of the hierarchy in a process called **navigation** to access records and to determine relationships. Most commonly, the navigation order progresses from top to bottom and from left to right in a path called a **preorder traversal**. The order of record access for one occurrence of a DEPARTMENT record with all its descendants is shown in Figure 9-21 on the next two pages. To find the name of a particular student's advisor, you would execute a program command to find that STUDENT record. The DBMS would retrieve records starting from the root until it retrieved the desired STUDENT record; at that point, the ADVISOR record that had been most recently read would be the parent ADVISOR record. To determine all the students that a particular faculty member advises, you would execute a command to find that FACULTY record and then issue a series of commands to find all the STUDENT records associated with that FACULTY record.

The hierarchical model has a number of disadvantages. First, a child record occurrence *must* have a parent; in the database shown in Figure 9-20, a student without an assigned faculty advisor cannot be stored unless a dummy advisor record is created. Second, modifications to the structure of one or more record types requires reorganizing and rebuilding the database and changing and recompiling all affected application programs. We have previously mentioned a third disadvantage of hierarchical databases: special measures must be taken to get around the restriction that a child can have only one physical parent. Finally, the hierarchical data model is conceptually complex; the programs that interact with a hierarchical DBMS can be quite complicated and difficult to understand.

For application systems whose relationships form a hierarchical structure, the performance of hierarchical database systems is better than that provided by current relational and object-oriented systems and no worse than that provided by the network model. Other advantages of the hierarchical model relate to the fact that IBM's Information Management System (IMS) is the most notable of the commercial DBMSs that utilize hierarchical databases. IBM's continued support of this data model means that organizations can depend on future improvements to IMS and help in resolving current IMS problems. Also, there is a large base of current, knowledgeable IMS users, many of whom have formed organizations to address common problems and needs.

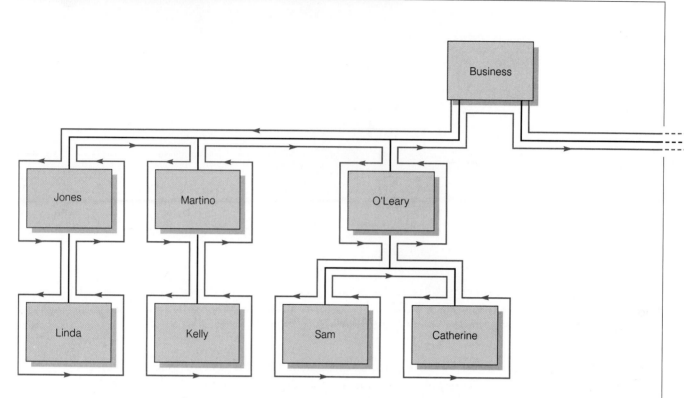

Figure 9-21 *A representation of the navigation of a hierarchical database for one occurrence of the DEPARTMENT-FACULTY-STUDENT-MAJOR hierarchical structure. The directed line indicates the DBMS preorder transversal path.*

Network databases The **network database model** is based on the concept of a **network**, which is a collection of records and one-to-many relationships. The majority of existing network DBMSs conform to a standard established by the CODASYL (COnference on DAta SYstems Languages) organization.

The terms record and field are used in the network model exactly as they are in the standard file processing environment. Relationships are implemented with a construction called a **set**. For example, the one-to-many relationship between FACULTY and STUDENT would be represented by the set ADVISES. One occurrence of ADVISES would include one faculty member and all the students advised by that faculty member. In this example, the FACULTY record is called the **owner** record, and the STUDENT records are called **member** records.

In the network model, a record can be a member of multiple sets; there is no restriction comparable to the hierarchical model's restriction of one physical parent per child. Figure 9-22 illustrates the network implementation of the database for DEPARTMENT, FACULTY, STUDENT, and MAJOR records.

A particular occurrence of a member record type can exist without an owner record in a network database. A student who has no assigned advisor, for example, can still be stored in the database; that record would simply not be represented in any occurrence of the set ADVISES.

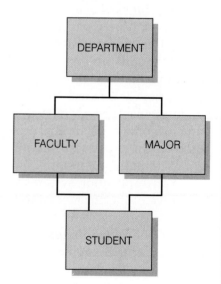

Figure 9-22 *A network database for DEPARTMENT, FACULTY, STUDENT, and MAJOR records.*

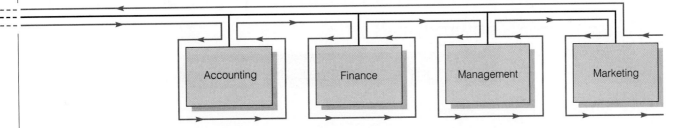

Figure 9-21 (continued)

A network DBMS navigates the database by following
pointer chains. Each set occurrence has a *first* pointer in the
owner record to one of the member records, and a *next*
pointer to another member record in each of the member
records; the next pointer for the last member record in a set
points back to the owner record, thus, forming a complete,
closed chain of pointers for the set occurrence (Figure 9-23).
You can optionally store *owner* pointers from each member
record to the owner record, *last* pointers from the owner
record to the last member record in the set, and *prior* pointers in each member record.

To determine the advisor for a particular student, you
would first execute a program command to find the
STUDENT record and then execute a command to find the
owner within the ADVISES set. To find all the students a particular faculty member advises, you would first execute a
command to find that FACULTY record, then execute a command to find the first member record in the ADVISES set,
and then execute a series of commands to find the
remaining member records within that set.

Network model DBMSs, and specifically CODASYL
DBMSs, have been commercially available since the late
1960s; many proven, successful database systems follow this
model. Unlike hierarchical databases, there are no limitations on the types of data relationships that can be represented in the network model. The performance of network
DBMSs is also better than that of most currently available relational and object-oriented
models and is no worse than hierarchical DBMSs.

The network model shares several of the disadvantages cited for the hierarchical
model. Making changes to the database structure requires rebuilding of the database
and recompilation of affected programs. Similar to the hierarchical database model,
programs that interact with a network DBMS are typically quite complex.

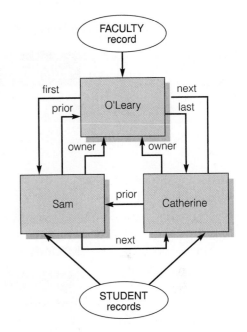

Figure 9-23 A representation of first, next, owner, last, and prior pointers for the one occurrence of an ADVISES set in a network database.

Relational databases In a **relational database**, data is organized in two-dimensional tables called **relations**. Each row in a table is called a **tuple** and each column is called an **attribute**. You can think of a relation or table as a file, tuples or rows as records, and attributes or columns as fields. Figure 9-24 shows four tables from a relational database, one for each of the four relations of DEPARTMENT, FACULTY, MAJOR, and STUDENT.

DEPARTMENT

DEPARTMENT NUMBER	DEPARTMENT NAME	CHAIRPERSON NUMBER
103	Business	35
285	Chemistry	93
297	Computer Science	06
414	Mathematics	49

FACULTY

FACULTY NUMBER	FACULTY NAME	DEPARTMENT NUMBER
06	Kolhapur	297
18	Jones	103
23	Smith	297
35	Martino	103
49	Paulson	414
87	O'Leary	103
93	Hoffman	285

MAJOR

MAJOR	MAJOR DESCRIPTION	DEPARTMENT NUMBER
ACC	Accounting	103
FIN	Finance	103
IS	Information Systems	297
MGT	Management	103
MKT	Marketing	103
SE	Software Engineering	297

STUDENT

STUDENT NUMBER	STUDENT NAME	TOTAL CREDITS	GPA	MAJOR	ADVISOR NUMBER
1035	Linda	17	3.647	MKT	18
3397	Sam	46	2.400	ACC	87
4070	Juan	35	3.000	IS	23
5166	Catherine	117	2.877	FIN	87
8892	Kelly	93	2.214	ACC	35

Figure 9-24 A relational database with DEPARTMENT, FACULTY, MAJOR, and STUDENT tables.

In a relational database, a relationship is accomplished by matching an attribute appearing in more than one table; the columns containing that attribute might have the same name, although that is not necessary. For example, in Figure 9-24 the relationship between the faculty members and their departments is achieved by matching a department number in the FACULTY table to a department number in the DEPARTMENT table. DEPARTMENT NUMBER is the primary key of the DEPARTMENT table and a foreign key in the FACULTY table; thus, we say that relational databases use foreign keys to form relationships. Similarly, by matching an advisor number in the STUDENT table to a faculty number in the FACULTY table, the relationship between students and their advisors is achieved.

To find the name of the advisor for a particular student, the DBMS locates that student in the STUDENT table and then, using the advisor number, locates the appropriate row in the ADVISOR table. To find all the students for a particular advisor, the DBMS finds all the rows in the STUDENT table with that advisor number.

An important advantage of a relational database is its conceptual simplicity. Even computer illiterate individuals can easily grasp the concepts of data tables and the mechanics of relationships. Adding a new column to a table or deleting an existing column is a simple matter. You merely define the new column; you do not have to redefine or restructure the entire database to add or remove table columns. Defining a completely new table or removing an old table is equally simple. Thus, you can establish new relationships at any time. This flexibility is another significant advantage of relational databases. The relational data model is the focus of much database research today. Therefore, significant advances in database technology are likely to occur with this model.

Object-oriented databases   In the last several years, a new approach to the system development process has emerged: the object-oriented approach. In answer to this new approach to system development, object-oriented DBMSs are now available. Many of these current DBMSs are actually hybrids that combine object-oriented features within the framework of the relational model.

Key concepts of object-oriented systems include objects, methods, messages, and inheritance. An **object** is a unit of data along with the actions that can affect that data. A CUSTOMER object, for example, would consist of the data relevant to customers (number, name, address, credit limit, and so on) along with the actions that can take place on customer data (add a customer, change a credit limit, and so on). The actions defined for an object are called **methods**. Methods are defined during the data definition process. (In contrast, in the traditional non-object-oriented approach, actions are created as part of data manipulation instead of data definition.) In the object-oriented approach, therefore, the emphasis is on the data instead of on processes.

A **message** is a request to execute a method. As part of sending a message, you must send the required data. For example, to add a customer, you would send a message that included all the data items for the new customer. The process is similar to the process of calling a subroutine in a standard programming language.

To illustrate the concept of inheritance, we will again consider our database involving departments, faculty, students and majors (Figure 9-24). We could begin by defining an object called PERSON, which would consist of all data relevant to a person, such as identifying number, name, home address, home telephone number, and so on. In addition, we would define for the PERSON object all appropriate person-related actions, such as adding or deleting a person from the database. This object definition would then be placed in the DBMS object library, which would contain reusable objects and code, available to anyone using that DBMS.

We can now use that library definition to define FACULTY as a subclass of the PERSON object. Because of **inheritance**, a subclass inherits all the characteristics of the object upon which it is based. Thus, FACULTY automatically includes all the same data and all the same actions previously defined for PERSON — those data items and actions do not have to be redefined when we create FACULTY. In addition, we can define additional properties for a subclass. For FACULTY, for example, we would need to add data items (and only those data items) specifically relevant to faculty members, such as job title, department number, office number, and office telephone number. Similarly, we would need to add actions specific to faculty members, such as changing the job title.

The advantage of the reusability of objects in the object library becomes more evident when we add students to our database definition. A student is also a person, so we can now define STUDENT as another subclass of PERSON. Once again, all the same data and actions previously defined for PERSON are now automatically characteristics of STUDENT. We now need define only those data items and actions specifically relevant to a student (such as the data items total credits and GPA, and the action of calculating GPA).

Figure 9-25 shows an object-oriented definition of our Figure 9-24 database on page 9.24 (not including the actions). The FACULTY and STUDENT objects are both based on a PERSON object; the first lines in the specifications of FACULTY and STUDENT accomplish this definition. The second and third lines in the STUDENT object define the two additional data items in our database that are relevant to students: total credits and GPA.

PERSON OBJECT

Number:	ID number
Name:	Name

DEPARTMENT OBJECT

Deptnum:	Department number
Deptname:	Department name
FACULTY:	FACULTY OBJECT; MV

        (all the faculty members within a given department)

MAJOR:	MAJOR OBJECT; MV

        (all the majors for a given department)

FACULTY OBJECT

PERSON:	PERSON OBJECT
STUDENT:	STUDENT OBJECT; MV

        (all advisees of a given faculty member)

DEPARTMENT:	DEPARTMENT OBJECT; SUBSET [Deptnum]

        (the department to which the faculty member belongs

STUDENT OBJECT

PERSON:	PERSON OBJECT
Totcred:	Total credits
GPA:	GPA
MAJOR:	MAJOR OBJECT; SUBSET [Majcode]

        (the student's major)

FACULTY:	FACULTY OBJECT; SUBSET [Number, Name]

        (the name and number of the student's faculty advisor)

MAJOR OBJECT

Majcode:	Major code
Majdesc:	Major description
STUDENT:	STUDENT OBJECT; MV

        (all students with a given major)

DEPARTMENT:	DEPARTMENT; SUBSET [Deptnum]

        (the department to which the major belongs)

Figure 9-25 An object-oriented representation of a database for DEPARTMENT, FACULTY, STUDENT, and MAJOR.

Relationships are accomplished by including related objects within each other's object definitions. For example, the DEPARTMENT definition includes the FACULTY object, with an "MV," indicating that the relationship is multivalued; that is, a single occurrence of a DEPARTMENT object can contain multiple occurrences of the FACULTY object, one for each faculty member assigned to that department. Conversely, the FACULTY definition includes the DEPARTMENT object. This definition does not include an "MV," however, because the relationship is not multivalued in this direction — a particular faculty member is assigned only to one department. In this case, we have included only one data item (department number) from the DEPARTMENT object in the FACULTY object; we could have included department name if end users would always need to know the department name as well for a particular faculty member.

The relationships between departments and the majors they offer, between students and their faculty advisors, and between students and their majors are also implemented by including the appropriate objects within one another. It is important to understand that these object definitions do *not* imply that the data is physically stored in this fashion. Rather, an object definition specifies the way that an object *appears* to the end user.

Proponents of the object-oriented approach believe that it offers significant advantages because of its emphasis on data instead of processes, and that the use of an object library reduces system development and maintenance time and costs. Object-oriented DBMSs play a central role in achieving these advantages.

Advantages of the database approach

he database approach offers a number of advantages over the file processing environment, especially when a powerful, full-functioned DBMS is used.

1. *Economy of scale.* Concentrating the data in one location allows for the possibility of smaller numbers of larger and more powerful computers, which can result in an economy of scale. The same economy of scale might be realized by the concentration of technical expertise. Furthermore, because many end users are sharing the database, any improvement in the database will potentially benefit many different end users. In general, economy of scale means that the collective cost of several combined operations might be less than the sum of the costs of the individual operations. Database processing makes this type of combination possible.

2. *Sharing of data.* An organization's data can be shared among all authorized end users, allowing end users acceËs to more of the data. Integrating data from more than one application is easier; thus, more information can be produced in an organization from the same amount of data. Even for an individual end user, the flexibility furnished by the DBMS to locate and access data in a number of different ways aids in satisfying new information and processing needs.

3. *Balancing conflicting requirements.* In order for the database approach to function adequately, there must be a person or group within the organization in charge of the database itself. This body is often called **Database Administration (DBA)**. By keeping the overall needs of the organization in mind, DBA can structure the database to the benefit of the entire organization, not just a single end user group. Although this means an individual group might be less well served than it might have been if it had its own isolated system, the overall organization will benefit.

4. *Enforcement of standards.* DBA can ensure that standards for data names, usages, formats, and documentation are followed uniformly throughout the organization.

5. *Controlled redundancy.* Because the data is stored in a single database, data items need not be duplicated in separate files for isolated application systems. Because some duplication of database data items might be introduced to improve performance, we say the database approach allows you to control redundancy rather than eliminate it. Data consistency follows from eliminating unnecessary redundancy.

6. *Security.* DBA can define authorization procedures to ensure that only legitimate end users access the database and can allow different end users to have different types of access to the same data. Most DBMSs provide sophisticated security support.

7. *Increased programmer productivity.* Because programmers accessing a database do not have to worry about the mundane data manipulation activities, as they would when accessing files, they can be more productive. Studies have shown that on average programmers will be two to four times more productive; that is, a new application can be developed in one-quarter to one-half the time it would take if it were a file-oriented application. When using fourth-generation languages built around database management systems, the productivity increases can be even more dramatic: twentyfold increases in productivity are not uncommon.

8. *Data independence.* Programs that interact with a DBMS are relatively independent of the actual data in the database. Many changes that might be made to the structure of the data do not require changes to existing application programs. This characteristic, called **data independence**, enables DBA to freely make changes to the database structure in order to improve performance or to meet changing requirements.

Disadvantages of the database approach

he list of database advantages is impressive. You would never expect to receive so many benefits, however, without incurring costs of some type. The database approach has the following disadvantages:

1. *Size.* To support all the complex functions it provides to end users, a database management system must by its very nature be a large program occupying megabytes of disk space, as well as a substantial amount of internal memory.

2. *Complexity.* A DBMS is a very complex product. Programmers and systems analysts must understand the features of the DBMS to take full advantage of it, and they have a great deal to learn. When designing a new system that will use a DBMS, a systems analyst will make many design choices. Unfortunately, a few incorrect choices can spell disaster for the whole project.

3. *Cost.* A good DBMS is an expensive product. By the time a DBMS is purchased for a major mainframe system, the total price can easily run into the $100,000 to $400,000 range. Microcomputer DBMSs can cost hundreds or thousands of dollars per workstation.

4. *Additional hardware requirements.* The size and complexity of a DBMS requires greater hardware resources than would be necessary without the DBMS. If the hardware resources are not increased when a DBMS is purchased, the end users of the computer system might suffer a severe degradation in performance.

5. *Higher impact of a failure.* The procedures for security, backup, and recovery are not only more complicated in a database environment but are also more critical. A large portion of the organization's data is concentrated into a single database; thus, a failure of any DBMS component has a more far-reaching effect than in a nondatabase environment.

6. *Performance compromises.* Although using the database approach might be best for an organization as a whole, some individual end users might be less well served. An isolated conventional-file information system specifically designed to meet the needs of a single end user group might be more straightforward and less expensive to design and implement than a database application and also might be easier and faster to use.

When the database approach was first developed, many eager supporters envisioned integrating all of an organization's data and applications into a single database system that would serve everyone. Unfortunately, this vision has generally proved to be impractical in the real world. Even those organizations committed to the database approach most often have several independent databases, along with several file-based information systems instead of one massive database system.

Why does this vision usually fail to transfer to reality? The list of disadvantages furnishes some clues. A single database containing all the organization's data might be so big, so complex, or so costly that it would be overwhelming to develop and use. A single database might even need to be so large that it is operationally impossible to implement using existing DBMSs and hardware.

To develop one single database, the organization's existing information systems must be rewritten or converted. Such an effort usually requires a massive commitment of personnel, time, and money; many organizations have difficulty finding the necessary resources to complete the process. The development of reverse engineering CASE tools, which were described in Chapter 5, might ease this process.

Designing files and databases

he following four analysis and design steps constitute a systematic method for the creation of file and database designs. To illustrate the steps, we will use as an example a microcomputer information system for an independent video rental store.

1. *Create the initial ERD.* Identify all the data stores in your data flow diagrams as system entities, and create a rough draft of a complete entity-relationship diagram (ERD) for the system. Analyze each relationship to determine if it is 1:1, 1:M, or M:N. Figure 9-26 shows the initial ERD for the entities MEMBER and VIDEO in the video rental system.

```
MEMBER (MEMBER-NUMBER, NAME, ADDRESS, CITY, STATE, ZIP, HOME-PHONE,
    WORK-PHONE, CREDIT-CARD-CODE, CREDIT-CARD-NUMBER, (VIDEO-ID, TITLE,
    DATE-RENTED, DATE RETURNED))
(VIDEO (VIDEO-ID, TITLE)
```

Figure 9-26 The initial entity-relationship diagram and unnormalized record designs for the video rental systems.

2. *Assign all data elements to entities.* Verify that every data element in the data dictionary is associated with an entity; assign any unassigned data element to the entity to which it logically relates. For the video rental system, the initial record designs with all the system data elements are listed beneath the ERD in Figure 9-26.

3. *Normalize entities and create the final ERD.* Normalize all record designs, taking care to identify all primary, secondary, and foreign keys. Generate the final entity-relationship diagram, which will include any new entities identified during normalization. Figure 9-27 shows the final ERD and the normalized records for the video rental system. Notice that a new entity, RENTAL, was identified during normalization and that the M:N relationship between the two original entities was simplified into two 1:M relationships.

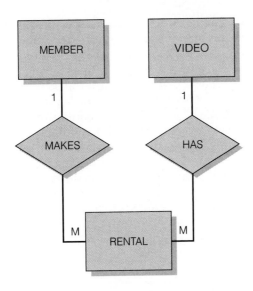

```
MEMBER (MEMBER-NUMBER, NAME, ADDRESS, CITY, STATE, ZIP, HOME-PHONE,
   WORK-PHONE, CREDIT-CARD-CODE, CREDIT-CARD-NUMBER)
(VIDEO (VIDEO-ID, TITLE)
RENTAL (MEMBER-NUMBER, VIDEO-ID, DATE-RENTED, DATE RETURNED)
```

Figure 9-27 *The final entity-relationship diagram and normalized record designs for the video rental system.*

4. *Verify all data dictionary entries.* Verify that the data dictionary entries for all data stores, records, and data elements are completely and correctly documented.

In the past, systems analysts often performed an additional step between steps 3 and 4 just described for their nondatabase applications: they would consider denormalizing record designs and combining two or more entities into a single file. Combining entities can reduce the number of files that programs must access and, therefore, in theory, can enable programs to execute faster. How does a systems analyst determine entities that might be combined advantageously? What are the disadvantages of combining multiple entities into one file?

Certainly it makes sense to combine only closely related entities; you would want to avoid illogical combinations. Your system ERD is the best source for identifying related entities. Combining data stores only if they participate in many of the same processes also makes sense; otherwise you would save nothing by combining them. Your DFDs indicate which data stores are used in which processes. A third guideline for combining entities relates to their **volatility**, which is the degree to which you add, change, and delete records for the entity. Generally you should consider combining entities only if they are equally volatile. If data element values in one of the entities change very often while the elements of the other rarely change, the entities are probably not good candidates for combining — the update process for the more volatile entity will take much more time because the double-entity file is so much larger.

What can you gain by combining two or more entities into a single file? As an example, consider order data. During the normalization process earlier in this chapter, we separated ORDER and ORDER-LINE, recognizing each as an entity and designing a record for each. These two entities are logically related and equally volatile. Most of the system processing that involves one entity also involves the other, including adding or updating orders, generating invoices and other reports, and responding to order queries. The ORDER and ORDER-LINE entities, therefore, seem to be good candidates for combining into a single file. Updating and accessing the single file might be convenient, fast, and more efficient than dealing with two files.

What might you lose by combining those two entities into a single file? Because the number of order lines per order will vary, the combined file must have variable-length records; reading the combined file is more complicated than reading the two files with fixed-length records would be. More importantly, some types of file queries become much more complex. Consider the inventory manager who needs information for a particular product, such as *How many units of this product are required to fill the outstanding orders?* Using the combined file is much more difficult, because you have lost the ability to access order-line data directly by product. For some types of processing, accessing the combined file is slow, inconvenient, and less efficient.

Accurately estimating the positive and negative performance effects of combining entities can be difficult. Many systems analysts believe it is safer not to combine entities during the systems design phase. It is much easier at some later time to combine entities that can advantageously be combined than it is to try to separate entities that should not have been combined. In addition, as computer processing speeds become faster, computer processing costs become lower, and personnel costs become higher. Keeping your file designs as normalized, as simple, and as clean as possible makes sense. The current trend is to denormalize cautiously, most often only after testing the completed information system and then only if doing so will improve intolerable system performance. ■

Calculating file sizes and volumes

One of the final steps in the physical design of a file is estimating the file size. You need accurate estimates of file sizes to verify that adequate physical storage capacity is available for the system files or to determine how much additional storage capacity must be provided. You should plan for reasonable growth when sizing a file. For example, if your company has 1,000 customers today and the customer base is expected to increase by 6% every year, then in three years you would expect to have 1,191 customers; therefore, you might use 1,200 instead of 1,000 for the number of customer records. If you wanted to provide instead for five years' growth, you could use an estimate of 1,350 records in your calculations.

■ Sizing diskette files

The number of bytes that can be stored on a diskette depends on the diskette type, the capabilities of the disk drive being used, and the specifications of the software used to format the diskette. The approximate capacities of 5 1/4" diskettes are typically either 180,000, 360,000, or 1,200,000 bytes; the approximate capacities of 3 1/2" diskettes are typically either 720,000, 1,440,000, or 2,800,000 bytes of data.

For a file of 1,500 records, each of which contains 139 bytes, you will need 208,500 (1500 * 139) bytes of storage. If the file will be stored on a 3 1/2" diskette with a 360,000-byte capacity, it will occupy approximately 60% (208,500/360,000) of the available diskette storage capacity.

■ Sizing tape files

Typical recording densities for magnetic tapes are 800, 1,600, 3,200, and 6,250 bytes per inch. To allow space for stopping and starting the tape between blocks, an unused area called an **interblock gap** exists between each block on the tape; typical interblock gaps are from 0.3 to 0.6 inches in length. You must know the recording density and the size of the interblock gap before you can accurately estimate the size of a file to be stored on tape.

Figure 9-28 details the storage requirements calculation for a tape file of 20,000 records, each containing 275 bytes of data. For calculation A, the records are unblocked; a blocking factor of 20 was used for calculation B; and a blocking factor of 40 was used for calculation C. Notice the dramatic difference in the sizes of the unblocked file and the file with a blocking factor of 20: the unblocked file requires nearly eight times as much tape. The additional decrease in file size for a blocking factor of 40 is much less dramatic.

TYPE CHARACTERISTICS:

2400	Foot reel of tape (28,800 inches)
6250	Bytes/inch recording density
0.5	Inch interblock gaps

FILE CHARACTERISTICS:

20,000	Records
275	Bytes/record

A. Unblocked records

$$275/6250 = 0.044 \text{ inches for one record}$$
$$20,000 \times (0.044 + 0.5) = 10,880 \text{ inches for the file}$$
$$10,880/28,800 = 38\% \text{ of one tape is required to store the file}$$

B. Blocking factor of 20

$$(275 \times 20)/6250 = 0.88 \text{ inches for one block}$$
$$20,000/20 = 1000 \text{ blocks in the file}$$
$$1000 \times (0.88 + 0.5) = 1380 \text{ inches for the file}$$
$$1380/28,800 = \text{less than } 5\% \text{ of one tape to store the file}$$

C. Blocking factor of 40

$$(275 \times 40)/6250 = 1.76 \text{ inches for one block}$$
$$20,000/40 = 500 \text{ blocks in the file}$$
$$500 \times (1.76 + 0.5) = 1130 \text{ inches for the file}$$
$$1130/28,800 = \text{less than } 4\% \text{ of one tape to store the file}$$

Figure 9-28 *Calculations of tape file storage requirements using unblocked records and blocking factors of 20 and 40 records.*

■ Sizing Disk Files

The volume calculations for disk files are more complex than those for tapes or diskettes. For the typical disk, one or more blocks must be written on a single disk track; blocks cannot span across tracks. Each disk track, therefore, contains a whole number of blocks, and any leftover track space is wasted. Keyed files, which include both direct files and indexed files, require several additional bytes for each record for direct addressing. Because the storage capacities and characteristics of disks vary greatly, most disk manufacturers supply charts or programs for determining optimum file blocking factors, based on the record length and the presence or lack of record keys.

For the calculations presented in Figure 9-29 on the next page, we have assumed a typical disk capacity and have used the appropriate blocking factor determined for that disk for the given record size and file type. Figure 9-29 includes calculations of disk storage requirements for a sequential file, a direct file with 100% packing density, a hashed direct file with 65% packing density, an indexed sequential file, and an indexed random file. The basic calculations do not differ significantly for the five examples; but for direct and indexed files, you must consider packing density and make provisions for overflow areas. You must also estimate the size of the index for indexed files. If you will have any secondary indexes, these index files must also be sized.

FILE CHARACTERISTICS: 2000   Records
                             175   Bytes/record

A. Sequential file

For a file without keys, we determine that we should use a blocking factor of 24, which permits us to store 3 blocks per track.

2000/24 = 84 blocks in the file

84/3 = 28 tracks to store the file

B. Direct file – 100% packing density

For a file with keys, we determine that we should use a blocking factor of 23, which permits us to store 3 blocks per track.

If the primary key values range from 1 to 2000, relative record number can be equal to the key value, producing a 100% packing density.

2000/23 = 87 blocks

87/3 = 29 tracks to sort the file

C. Direct file – 65% packing density

If we will use a hashing function and want a 65% packing density, we must allow space for 2000/65%=3077 records.

3077/23 = 134 blocks in the file

134/3 = 45 tracks to store the file

D. Indexed sequential file

As for the direct file in B above, we will have 23 records per block.

2000/23 = 87 blocks in the file

To allow for an overflow area, we decide to provide space for 120 blocks.

120/3 = 40 tracks to store the file

We must also store the index file. We will have a sparse index with only one index entry for each block. If each index record contains 12 bytes, the entire index field can be contained in a single block that will fit within a single track.

E. Indexed random file

As for the above keyed files, we will have 23 records per block.

2000/23 = 87 blocks in the file

87/3 = 29 tracks to store the file

We must also store the index file, which will be a dense index with one entry for each data record. We determine that we will use a blocking factor of 315 for the 12-byte index records, which allow us to store 4 index blocks per track.

2000/315 = 7 blocks in the index file

7/4 = 2 tracks to store the index

Figure 9-29 *Calculations of disk file storage requirements.*

File and database control

File and database control encompasses all measures necessary to ensure that stored data is correct, complete, and secure. File and database control is not completely independent of input and output control. Input control includes measures for ensuring the correctness and completeness of the data before it is stored in a file or database, as well as the creation of audit trail files that report accesses and changes to data files or databases; output control measures help ensure that the stored data is secure from unauthorized access and output. In the following paragraphs, we will discuss additional control measures for protecting the data stored in your files and databases.

Most database management systems provide extensive control and security features, including passwording, encryption, subschemas, audit trails, and backup and recovery procedures. Your responsibility as systems analyst is to ensure that these features are used. For traditional file systems, however, you will have to design and implement the necessary file control measures.

Limiting access to files and databases is the most common measure for protecting stored data. Only those end users who furnish an appropriate access code should be allowed to access a file or database. Different privileges can be associated with different access codes, so some end users can be denied access to certain data, others can be limited to a read-only access, still others might be allowed to both read and update the data, and only a very few end users are allowed full privileges to read, write, update, and delete data. For sensitive data, additional access codes can be established at the record or field level. Stored data can also be encrypted, so the data can be interpreted only by special decoding software; data would be decrypted for legitimate users, but anyone who manages to circumvent the system programs to access the file or database would be unable to decipher the data.

All system files and databases must be regularly backed up, and the backup file copies must be retained for a period of time. In the event of a file catastrophe, recovery procedures can be used to restore the file or database to the state it was in at the point of the last backup. Audit trail files, which record details of all accesses and changes to the file or database, are then used to recover changes made since the last backup file was created.

You can also include **audit fields**, which are special fields within data records to provide additional control or security information. Such typical audit fields include the date the record was created, the person who created the record, the date the record was last modified, the person who last modified the record, and the number of times the record has been accessed.

We discuss additional information system controls in the next chapter when we examine the systems design of software, which will complete our coverage of the systems design phase. Also in that chapter, we will discuss the activities that conclude the systems design phase.

CHAPTER CASE STUDY 9

James Tool Company — File and Database Design

At his next meeting with Don Mard and Kimberly Wallace, Howard Coswell presented his file and record designs for the union and union deduction files. They briefly considered making the union system a database application but then rejected the idea. They all believed the union system was simple and straightforward; potential database advantages, such as data sharing, shared update, and data independence, were not really relevant to the union system.

Wallace then asked to see the entity-relationship diagram for the union system. Coswell suddenly realized that he had completely forgotten to create an ERD and to normalize his record designs. He immediately sat down at a microcomputer and launched Excelerator, the CASE workbench used at James Tool Company. His first ERD, shown in Figure 9-30, included only two entities, UNION and UNION DEDUCTION, and the one-to-many relationship between them. "It doesn't feel right, and it shouldn't be that simple," Mard argued. Coswell suggested adding the EMPLOYEE entity to the diagram because the union deductions are related to employees, and the others agreed.

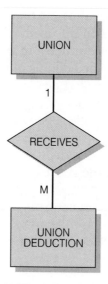

Figure 9-30 The initial version of the entity-relationship diagram for the union system at James Tool Company.

The second version of the union system ERD is shown in Figure 9-31.

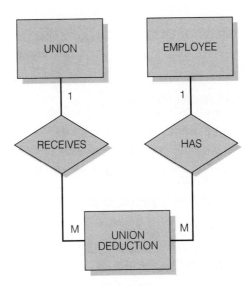

Figure 9-31 *The final version of the entity-relationship diagram for the union system at James Tool Company.*

Coswell then considered the UNION file record, which he wrote down in this form:

```
UNION (UNION-NUMBER, UNION-NAME, UNION-WEEKLY-DUES)
```

"This record is obviously in 1NF, because it has no repeating groups," Coswell observed. "It's obviously in 2NF as well, because it has a single field as the primary key. And I'm sure it's in 3NF, because both the union name and the union weekly dues depend on the union number. So this design is okay." Mard and Wallace agreed.

Coswell then wrote out the UNION-DEDUCTION file record:

```
UNION-DEDUCTION (SSN, EMPLOYEE-NAME, UNION-NUMBER, UNION-DUES, WEEK-ENDING-DATE,
   WEEKLY-EARNINGS)
```

"How can I normalize this record?" Coswell asked. "It's a sequential file, not a keyed file, so there is no primary key." Wallace said, "Of course it has a primary key. In any one union deduction file, there is at most one record per employee, so the primary key is either SSN or employee name." "Yes, but then what about the one merged and sorted version of the four union deduction files? Most of the time, there would be four records for each employee," Coswell pointed out. Mard suggested that they consider the combination of SSN and the week-ending date as the primary key; together those two fields would define a unique record in all cases. So Coswell underlined those two fields, producing:

UNION-DEDUCTION (<u>SSN</u>, EMPLOYEE-NAME, UNION-NUMBER, UNION-DUES, <u>WEEK-ENDING-DATE</u>, WEEKLY-EARNINGS)

Wallace observed that the UNION-DEDUCTION record was in 1NF but not in 2NF, because all the fields did not depend on the entire primary key. After some thought, Coswell rewrote the original record design as three records:

EMPLOYEE (<u>SSN</u>, EMPLOYEE-NAME, UNION-NUMBER)
UNION (<u>UNION-NUMBER</u>, UNION-DUES)
EARNINGS (<u>SSN</u>, <u>WEEK-ENDING-DATE</u>, WEEKLY-EARNINGS)

"Wait — that's not right. What if the union weekly dues were increased during the four-week period? The actual union dues withheld depends on date, as well as union number," Coswell realized. He again rewrote the record designs, producing:

EMPLOYEE (<u>SSN</u>, EMPLOYEE-NAME, UNION-NUMBER)
UNION (<u>UNION-NUMBER</u>, <u>WEEK-ENDING-DATE</u>, UNION-DUES)
EARNINGS (<u>SSN</u>, <u>WEEK-ENDING-DATE</u>, WEEKLY-EARNINGS)

After a few moments, Mard offered his opinion. "An employee could change from one union to another at any time. So an employee's union number also depends on the week-ending date." Coswell then moved UNION-NUMBER from the first to the third record, producing:

EMPLOYEE (<u>SSN</u>, EMPLOYEE-NAME)
UNION (<u>UNION-NUMBER</u>, <u>WEEK-ENDING-DATE</u>, UNION-DUES)
EARNINGS (<u>SSN</u>, <u>WEEK-ENDING-DATE</u>, WEEKLY-EARNINGS, UNION-NUMBER)

Wallace then suggested that an employee's name also depended on week-ending date — a person could change his or her name at any time. Coswell suggested that a union employee who started work in the middle of the week would not have to pay an entire week's dues, so the amount of union dues withheld could vary from union member to union member. Deciding that both an employee name and an employee's deducted union dues depended on the combination of SSN and WEEK-ENDING-DATE, Coswell wrote out this record design:

UNION-DEDUCTION (<u>SSN</u>, <u>WEEK-ENDING-DATE</u>, WEEKLY-EARNINGS, UNION-NUMBER, EMPLOYEE-NAME, UNION-DUES)

"We're right back where we started from!" complained Coswell. "Yes, but now we know we have a good record design. If we hadn't gone through all of this, we could never be positive that all potential problems with the design had been anticipated and eliminated," Mard pointed out. All three analysts finally agreed that the session had been worthwhile.

Summary

An entity-relationship diagram (ERD) is a pictorial representation of all the system entities and the relationships between those entities. ERDs do not depict data flows and processing steps; that information is presented in data flow diagrams. The entities in your initial ERD correspond to the data stores in your completed DFDs. Three basic relationship types are represented in an ERD: one-to-one relationships, one-to-many relationships, and many-to-many relationships.

Normalization is the process of identifying and correcting potential problems in record designs. A first normal form (1NF) record has no repeating groups. A record is in second normal form (2NF) if it is in 1NF and has no field dependent on only part of the primary key. A record is in third normal form (3NF) if it is in 2NF and if no field in the record depends on a nonkey field. A methodology was presented for converting unnormalized record designs to third normal form.

A file contains data relating to a single entity. In contrast, a database stores data for multiple entities, as well as the relationships among those entities. A database management system (DBMS) serves as the interface between the database and the programs and people that use it. Commercial DBMSs typically include a data definition language (DDL), a data manipulation language (DML), a query language, a data dictionary, and utility services for database support and maintenance.

There are four basic database models. The hierarchical model stores entities as a hierarchy or family tree. A parent record type can have many children, but a child record type can have only one physical parent. In the network database model, entities are stored in a network of owner and member record types; a record type can be the owner of multiple member record types and also the member of multiple owners. Each owner-member relationship is defined as a set. Although their implementation can be quite complex, both the hierarchical and network models are represented by many commercial DBMSs that perform rapidly and successfully.

The relational model is the simplest conceptually, and is the object of much current database research. Data is stored in two-dimensional tables called relations; the table rows are called tuples and the columns are called attributes. Relationships are formed by matching attributes from different tables. Many commercial DBMSs support the relational database model, especially microcomputer DBMSs.

Object-oriented model databases are a very recent development. Data items and the actions (called methods) that can affect those data items are defined as objects. A method is activated by sending a message. New object definitions can be based on previously defined, stored objects; by the property of inheritance, the new object inherits all the characteristics of the object upon which it is based. Relationships in the object-oriented model are implemented by including related objects in each other's object definitions.

The database approach offers the advantages of economy of scale, data sharing among end user groups, effective balancing and resolution of conflicting end user requirements, enforcement of standards, controlled redundancy, effective security, flexibility and responsiveness, increased programmer productivity, and data independence. Databases, however, are often very large, complex, and expensive, and might require the purchase of additional hardware. Although the database approach might be good for the organization as a whole, some end users might be less well served than they would be otherwise with their own independent file-based system. Having a database is also like placing all your eggs in one basket — if the database ever fails, the impact of that failure will be felt throughout the organization.

The process for file and database design includes these steps: create an initial system ERD, assign all data elements to an entity, normalize all record designs, and complete the data dictionary entries for files, records, and data elements. All designed files should be sized to estimate the amount of diskette, tape, or disk storage they will require.

File and database control measures include limiting access to the data, data encryption, backup and recovery procedures, audit trails, and internal audit fields.

Review Questions

1. What are entity-relationship diagrams? How are they used?
2. What symbol is used for an entity in an entity-relationship diagram? What symbol is used for a relationship?

3. What are the three basic types of relationships between entities? What is the abbreviation for each of these basic relationship types?

4. In a one-to-many relationship, for one occurrence of the one entity, what is the minimum number of occurrences of the many entity?

5. What is the criterion for a record design to be in first normal form?

6. How do you convert an unnormalized record design to 1NF?

7. What are the criteria for a record design to be in second normal form?

8. How do you convert a non-2NF record design to 2NF?

9. What are the criteria for a record design to be in third normal form?

10. How do you convert a non-3NF record design to 3NF?

11. What is a DBMS? Briefly describe the five components of a DBMS.

12. What is a DBMS schema? What is a subschema? What purposes does a subschema serve?

13. How are relationships defined or created in the hierarchical database model? In the network model? In the relational model? In the object-oriented model?

14. Name the database model in which each of the following terms is used: object, child, member, owner, message, parent, method, relation, root, set, tuple, inheritance.

15. What are the specific disadvantages associated with the hierarchical database model? Which of these disadvantages are shared by the network database model?

16. What are the specific advantages and disadvantages of the network database model?

17. List and briefly discuss the advantages of the database approach.

18. List and briefly discuss the disadvantages of the database approach.

19. List and briefly describe the four steps for developing, evaluating, and refining record designs.

20. What information is needed to size a diskette file?

21. What information is needed to size a tape file?

22. How does the size calculation for an indexed file differ from that for a sequential file?

23. What is an audit field? List five typical audit fields.

Discussion Questions

1. In this chapter's discussion of third normal form, a 2NF customer record design was converted to two 3NF records. Verify that the four potential problems identified for non-3NF records have been eliminated in the 3NF design.

2. The final step in the standard procedure for converting a record design from 1NF to 2NF is, "When you have finished placing all the fields, you then remove any record that has had no additional field placed into it. The remaining records are the 2NF version of your original record design." Exceptions exist, however, where you do want to retain a record that has had no additional fields placed into it. Consider, for instance, that the 1NF STUDENT records in Figure 9-13 on page 9.12 do not contain a GRADE field because the design is for *current* courses instead of completed courses. In that case, the 2NF GRADE record in Figure 9-14 on page 9.13 would have no additional fields placed into it; the record would consist of only the primary key of STUDENT-NUMBER and COURSE-NUMBER. Yet the GRADE record must be retained (with a different, more descriptive name). Explain why the GRADE record must be retained.

3. A systems analyst developing a database application system created a secret subschema allowing full access privileges to all data fields, including several sensitive, private data items. The systems analyst intends to use the subschema only if there are later problems with the implemented system, in order to immediately act and thoroughly investigate any data irregularities. What do you think of the systems analyst's action? Should this have been prevented from occurring? How?

4. Figure 9-24 on page 9.24 showed some sample data for the application system with the four entities of DEPARTMENT, FACULTY, MAJOR, and STUDENT. Assume that this system will be implemented as a nondatabase, standard file-based system. Are the entities DEPARTMENT and MAJOR potential candidates for combining into a single data file? What would the one record for the combined file look like? Is that record in 1NF? Is it in 2NF? Is it in 3NF? What might you gain by combining the entities? What might you lose? Would you recommend combining those two entities?

MINICASE STUDIES

Cutting Edge Incorporated

Cutting Edge Incorporated is a company engaged in the development of computer-aided design software packages. The management of Cutting Edge has requested the development of a project tracking system to accumulate and report data on projects, employees, and departments. Tracy Ripstein, the systems analyst assigned to the project, has developed this initial record design:

```
(PROJECT-NUMBER, PROJECT-NAME, START-DATE, PROJECT-STATUS, (EMPLOYEE-NUMBER,
   EMPLOYEE-NAME, DEPARTMENT-NUMBER, DEPARTMENT-NAME, JOB-TITLE, PROJECT-HOURS))
```

Tracy believes the only system entities are PROJECT, DEPARTMENT, and EMPLOYEE; but because she is also assigned to two other projects, she has not yet had the time to consider the relationships among those system entities or to normalize the record design.

Questions

1. Draw an initial entity-relationship diagram for the system, using the entities Tracy has identified. State any assumptions you must make about the Cutting Edge organization to determine the types of the relationships. (*Hint*: Tracy's situation provides a clue for one of the assumptions you must make.)
2. Convert the record design to third normal form.
3. Draw a final entity-relationship diagram for the system.

LePan Airlines

LePan Airlines is a small, commercial airline company operating in three northeastern states. LePan is in the process of computerizing its passenger reservation system. The following data items have been identified: flight number, flight date, origination town, destination town, departure time, arrival time, passenger name, booking agent number, booking agent name, and seat number. For example, flight number 303, which is scheduled every Tuesday and Thursday, leaves Augusta, Maine, at 9:23 a.m. and arrives in Nashua, New Hampshire, at 10:17 a.m. All seats are preassigned. For simplicity, assume that a given passenger always uses the same booking agent.

Questions

1. Draw the entity-relationship diagram for the system.
2. Create third normal form records for the system.

Ridgeway Company

The Ridgeway Company requirements were described in a Chapter 4 minicase study. The following assignments are based on the work you did for that minicase.

Questions

1. Create an initial entity-relationship diagram for the Ridgeway Company billing system.
2. Normalize your record designs.
3. If you identified any new entities during normalization, create a final entity-relationship diagram for the system.

Genealogy System

The genealogy system requirements were described in a Chapter 4 minicase study. The following assignments are based on the work you did for that minicase.

Questions

1. Create an initial entity-relationship diagram for the genealogy system.
2. Normalize your record designs.
3. If you identified any new entities during normalization, create a final entity-relationship diagram for the system.

STUDENT CASE STUDY 9

Western Dental Clinic — File and Database Design

Introduction

Jim Archer decided to implement the dental system for Western Dental Clinic as a standard file-based system and was now ready to complete his file designs.

Student Assignments

1. Create an initial entity-relationship diagram for the Western Dental Clinic system.
2. Normalize your record designs.
3. If you identified any new entities during normalization, create a final entity-relationship diagram for the system.
4. Size the patient, insurance company, and provider files.
5. What file controls would you recommend for the dental system?

CHAPTER 10

Software Design and Completing the Systems Design Phase

Objectives

You will have mastered the material in this chapter when you can:

- Discuss the characteristics, advantages, and disadvantages of batch and online processing, centralized and distributed processing, and single-user and multiuser processing
- Distinguish between client/server computing and distributed processing
- Discuss the major processing functions of data input and validating, updating, sorting, and reporting, and describe how these functions differ by processing environment
- Describe the standard backup and recovery methods for batch and online processing systems
- Explain how to determine which programs are required for an information system
- Discuss the differences between traditional development and object-oriented development
- Define the contents of the system design specification, and explain the purpose of this document

Introduction

Recall that we define an information system as the interacting collection of data, people, procedures, data stores, hardware, software, and information required to accomplish an organized set of functions. Designing an effective information system requires the proper integration of each system component with each of the other components. We have previously examined systems design strategies for data, information, and data stores in other chapters, and we have integrated systems design considerations for people, procedures, and hardware throughout all the systems design chapters (Figure 10-1 on the next page).

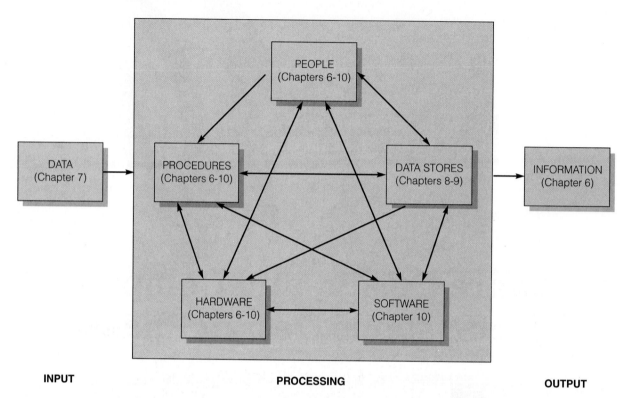

INPUT   PROCESSING   OUTPUT

Figure 10-1 *Information system model components and the chapters that discuss systems design for each component.*

In this chapter, we discuss the processing methods that influence software design, the major processing and support functions that we must accommodate in our software design, and software design itself. We conclude the chapter by describing the completion of the systems design phase: the preparation of the system design specification document and the presentations of the systems design to management and to information systems department personnel.

Processing methods

Each information system functions in a specific environment or uses a specific platform. An **environment**, or **platform**, is the combination of hardware and systems software that is used for the developed information system. One information system, for example, might function only in a PC and DOS environment, whereas another information system might require a DEC and UNIX platform.

The environment influences the software design process and strategies. The requirements for an information system typically dictate the environment, but in some companies the environment is fixed and the requirements must be modified to fit the environment. Different processing methods are possible within each environment. We will discuss online, batch, centralized, distributed, single-user, and multiuser processing methods.

■ Online processing

An **online processing** system is an information system in which transactions are processed when and where they occur and which allows output directly to end users. The end users work at their own personal computer or are connected from their personal computers to a central computer. **Online transaction processing** and **interactive processing** are other terms for online processing.

The diagram shown in Figure 10-2 provides a general picture of an online processing system. For example, an end user enters a transaction using a **workstation**, which is either a personal computer or terminal, and the online processing system verifies the transaction values and allows the end user to interactively correct errors. The online processing system then stores the transaction in the appropriate database or online file. An **online file** is a file with direct or indexed organization that allows random access.

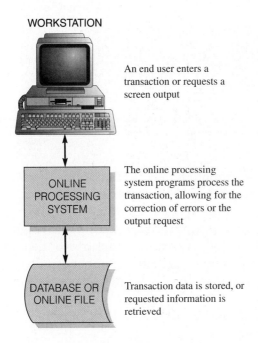

WORKSTATION

An end user enters a transaction or requests a screen output

ONLINE PROCESSING SYSTEM

The online processing system programs process the transaction, allowing for the correction of errors or the output request

DATABASE OR ONLINE FILE

Transaction data is stored, or requested information is retrieved

Figure 10-2 *The direct interaction of an online processing system with the end user and stored data.*

Two separate processes for a bank savings online processing system are shown in Figure 10-3 on the next page. The first process illustrates the sequence of steps used by the online processing system to process a customer deposit. When a customer makes a deposit, the bank clerk enters on the workstation the customer's bank account number and deposit amount (step 1). The bank savings system program accesses the savings account master, using the bank account number as the primary key, to verify the bank account number and to retrieve the customer's savings account record (step 2). Next, the program verifies that the deposit amount is numeric and within an acceptable range (step 3). If the program detects an actual or potential data entry error, the program notifies the bank clerk, who then corrects the error and resubmits the transaction. When the bank clerk has correctly entered both the bank account number and deposit amount, the program stores the transaction in the savings transaction history file or database and updates the customer's savings account balance in the savings account master file or database (step 4), reports the successful completion of the transaction posting to the bank clerk, and prints the deposit slip (step 5).

BANK SAVINGS SYSTEM
DEPOSIT PROCESS - PROCESS 1

BANK EMPLOYEE

Step 1: Bank clerk enters deposit transaction data:
Bank account number
Deposit amount

BANK SAVINGS SYSTEM

Step 2: Retrieves savings account record
Step 3: Verifies values
Step 4: Stores data
Step 5: Reports successful completion to bank clerk and prints the deposit slip

Data stored in
• Savings account master
• Savings transaction history

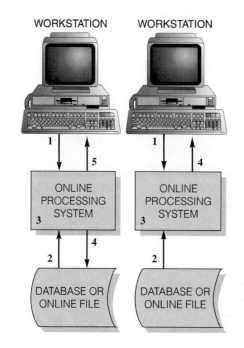

BANK SAVINGS SYSTEM
QUERY PROCESS - PROCESS 2

BANK EMPLOYEE

Step 1: Bank clerk submits a query to request a customer's savings account balance by entering:
Bank account number

BANK SAVINGS SYSTEM

Step 2: Retrieves current account balance
Step 3: Verifies bank account number
Step 4: Displays balance on bank clerk's screen

Data retrieved from
• Savings account master

Figure 10-3 *An example of two processes in a bank savings online processing banking system: the processing of a customer deposit, and the processing of a request to display a customer's current account balance.*

The second process shown in Figure 10-3 illustrates the sequence of steps used by the bank savings online processing system to process a bank clerk's query request to display a customer's current savings account balance. After the clerk enters the request (step 1), the bank savings system program accesses the savings account master, using the bank account number as the primary key, to retrieve the customer's savings account record (step 2) and to verify the bank account number (step 3). Then, the program displays the customer's current savings account balance on the bank clerk's workstation (step 4).

Based on these examples, you can see that the principal characteristics of an online processing system are:

■ Transactions are completely processed when and where they occur.
■ End users directly interact with the information system programs.
■ Random access is required. A database or files with direct or indexed organization, therefore, must be used.
■ The information system must be continuously available whenever end users require processing of their transactions and requests for information.

■ Batch Processing

A **batch processing** system is an information system in which data is collected and, at some later time, all the data that has been gathered is processed as a group, or *batch*. Batch processing was used extensively when computers were first used in businesses during the 1950s and 1960s. Frequently, source documents containing the data were brought to a central location where the data was punched on cards or stored on magnetic tape. All the data, in one single group, or batch, was then read into the computer for processing.

Today, batch processing is still the best way to implement some applications. Applications that require periodic processing of a large number of records are good possibilities for batch processing. Payroll applications that issue paychecks periodically, such as every other week, normally operate using a batch method of processing. Other users of batch processing include utility companies, which must send out thousands of bills each month, and credit card companies, which process thousands of charges and payments each month.

As shown in the example of a credit card system in Figure 10-4, the following steps take place when a group of credit card receipt transactions are batch processed.

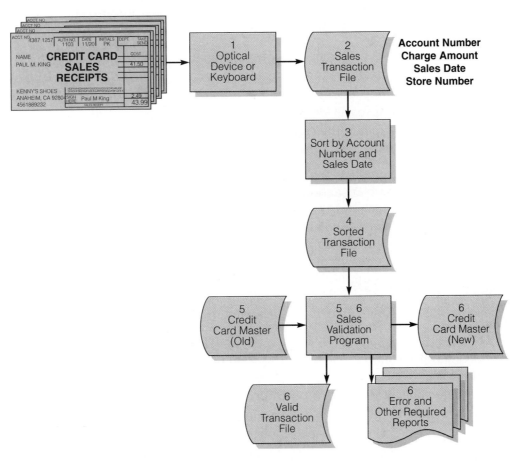

Figure 10-4 *An example of credit card sales receipts processing in a batch processing credit card system.*

1. Customers use credit cards to purchase items from stores. For each purchase, a store clerk completes a sales receipt, which becomes the sales transaction source document. A store employee forwards the sales receipt to the data entry section of the information systems department at the bank or company processing the credit card purchases. Data entry clerks process the credit card sales receipts in batches through optical scanning equipment or make entries manually.

2. The credit card sales transactions are stored in a computer-readable sales transaction file on disk.

3. When all the sales receipts received that day have been entered, the sales transaction file on disk is sorted into sales date within account number sequence. This sort is necessary if the credit card master file is sequentially organized, so the sales transactions are in the same sequence as the customer records on the credit card master file.

4. The sort step produces the sorted transaction file, which contains all sales transactions in the desired sequence.

5. The sales validation program processes one sorted transaction record at a time by matching the transaction account number against the account number on the credit card master.

6. Errors detected by the sales validation program are written to an error report, which the data entry clerks later use to correct and resubmit the rejected sales transactions. The sales validation program also writes valid transactions to the valid transaction file, uses these valid transactions to update the customer's current balance before writing the new credit card master, and might produce other required reports.

The point of this example is that the input records are all batched into a single input transaction file. The transactions are then processed as a group, updating the credit card master. At some later time, other programs in the credit card system process all credit card master records and all valid transactions as batches to produce account statements and other outputs. In applications of this type, hundreds or thousands of records are processed in one run of the program. Batch processing is the appropriate processing method for this application because human intervention is not required for most of the steps.

Based on this example, the principal characteristics of a batch processing system are:

- Transactions are collected and processed in a group at specified intervals.
- Computer operators execute batch programs according to a predetermined schedule without end user involvement. Batch programs can run during regular business hours, at night, or on weekends.
- Batch programs can access files and databases either sequentially or randomly. In the example shown in Figure 10-4 on the previous page, the credit card master file is processed sequentially, but this need not be the case.

■ Combined online and batch processing

Online and batch processing can be combined in a single application. Combined processing is shown in Figure 10-5, which illustrates the processing of sales transactions in a retail store. The following steps occur during the processing.

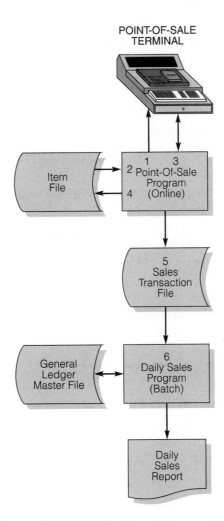

Figure 10-5 *This example illustrates both online and batch processing performed for sales transactions in a retail store. Inventory balances are updated online, but the preparation of the sales report and the update of the general ledger master file are completed using batch processing at the end of the day.*

1. *Online processing.* The store clerk enters the details of the sale on a point-of-sale terminal. The sales data includes the item number of a purchased item and the quantity purchased.

2. *Online processing.* The program retrieves the record corresponding to the item number entered by the clerk. The three important data elements in the retrieved record are the unit price for the item, the quantity of the item in inventory, and a short description of the item.

3. *Online processing.* The program reduces the quantity in the item record by the quantity purchased, giving the new inventory quantity. The program also multiplies the quantity purchased by the unit price to determine the total sales amount. The total sales amount and the short description for the item are sent to the point-of-sale terminal, which prints these values on the sales receipt.

4. *Online processing.* The program then writes the updated item record back into the item file.

5. *Online processing.* The program adds a record to the sales transaction file. The sales transaction file contains a record for each sale that is made during the day at the store. These sales transaction records will be used at the end of the day in batch processing.

6. *Batch processing.* After the store is closed and all transactions have been completed, the sales transaction file is input to a program that produces the daily sales report and updates sales data in the general ledger master file.

This application illustrates both online processing and batch processing of data generated from a single transaction. When the sales clerk enters the sale on the point-of-sale terminal and the program responds with the total sales amount and the short item description, online processing has occurred. As soon as the sales clerk entered the data, the program processed the data by performing the calculations, updating the item file, and producing output on the point-of-sale terminal. At the same time, input data for batch processing was created when the program wrote a record to the sales transaction file. When these collected transactions were used to produce the daily sales report and to update the general ledger master file, batch processing occurred. Producing the daily sales report and updating the general ledger master file before all the sales transactions for the day had been completed would make little sense. Thus, batch processing is the appropriate method to use to accomplish these two functions. Online processing is the appropriate method for the sales and item record processing because each sale must be processed as it occurs.

■ Online and batch processing advantages and disadvantages

Online processing systems have two primary advantages over batch processing systems. First, because data is entered and validated as it occurs, the stored data is available sooner in a more accurate form. The second advantage follows from the first: the stored data is up-to-date at all times.

The online processing environment, however, is typically more expensive than a batch environment, when you consider the combined costs of the required hardware and the complicated systems software. Additionally, backup and recovery for online processing is more difficult, and the effects of computer system outages are more visible and disruptive to the end users.

In actual practice, most information systems use a combination of online processing to handle normal business transactions and end user queries and batch processing to produce regularly scheduled repetitive reporting.

■ Centralized and distributed processing

Centralized processing occurs when a company's computer resources are located in one central location. In the early days of computers, a company commonly placed all hardware, data entry personnel, and other computer resources in a single location. All source documents within the organization were sent to the central location for data entry, computer processing, and output report generation. The reports were then sent in printed form to designated recipients at various locations within the company. This extreme form of centralized processing is not often used today.

A more popular form of centralized processing today consists of centralizing all computer functions with the exception of data entry, which is performed in multiple locations within the organization. Entering data from various locations in an organization is called **distributed data entry**. Quite often, the data entry takes place at the site where the data is generated — for example, sales orders are entered by the sales department. Data entered using distributed data entry under centralized processing is typically processed in an online processing mode with multiple remote workstations connected by data communications to the central computer; this type of processing is called **teleprocessing**. The nationwide hotel and airline reservation systems and banking ATMs are examples of teleprocessing systems.

The increased use of powerful, low-cost personal computers and minicomputers has led to less reliance on centralized processing and greater use of distributed processing. **Distributed processing** is processing that occurs on computers at multiple locations that are connected by a data communications network. A data communications **network** is a collection of terminals, computers, and other equipment that use communication channels to share data. Networks can be classified as either local area networks or wide area networks. The use of distributed processing and networks allows an organization to place its computing power in optimal physical locations to meet the information processing needs of its end users, as well as those of the entire organization.

Wide Area Networks (WANs) and Local Area Networks (LANs) A **wide area network (WAN)** is a communications network that is geographic in scope (as opposed to local) and uses phone lines, microwaves, satellites, fiber optics, or a combination of these communication channels. A **local area network (LAN)** is a privately owned communications network that covers a limited geographic area, such as an office, a building, or a group of buildings. The LAN consists of a communication channel, such as a cable, that connects either a series of computer terminals together with a minicomputer or, more commonly, a group of personal computers to one another. Very sophisticated LANs might connect a variety of office devices, such as word processing equipment, computer terminals, video equipment, and personal computers.

Two common applications of networks are hardware resource sharing and information resource sharing. **Hardware resource sharing** allows each workstation in the network to access and use devices that would be too expensive to provide for each workstation or would not be justified for each workstation because of only occasional use. For example, when a number of personal computers are used on the network, each computer might need to periodically use a laser printer. One laser printer could be purchased and made a part of the network. Whenever a computer user needed the laser printer, the printer could be accessed over the network.

Figure 10-6 on the next page shows a simple local area network, consisting of four personal computers linked together by a cable. Three of the personal computers (computer 1 in the sales and marketing department, computer 2 in the accounting department, and computer 3 in the personnel department) are available at all times. Computer 4 is used as a **network control unit**, or **server**, which is a computer that is dedicated to handling the communication needs of the other computers in the network. Computers that are used as servers usually have high-capacity hard disks and have faster processing speeds than the other computers in the network. The users of this LAN have connected the laser printer to the server. All computers on the LAN, including the server, can use the laser printer.

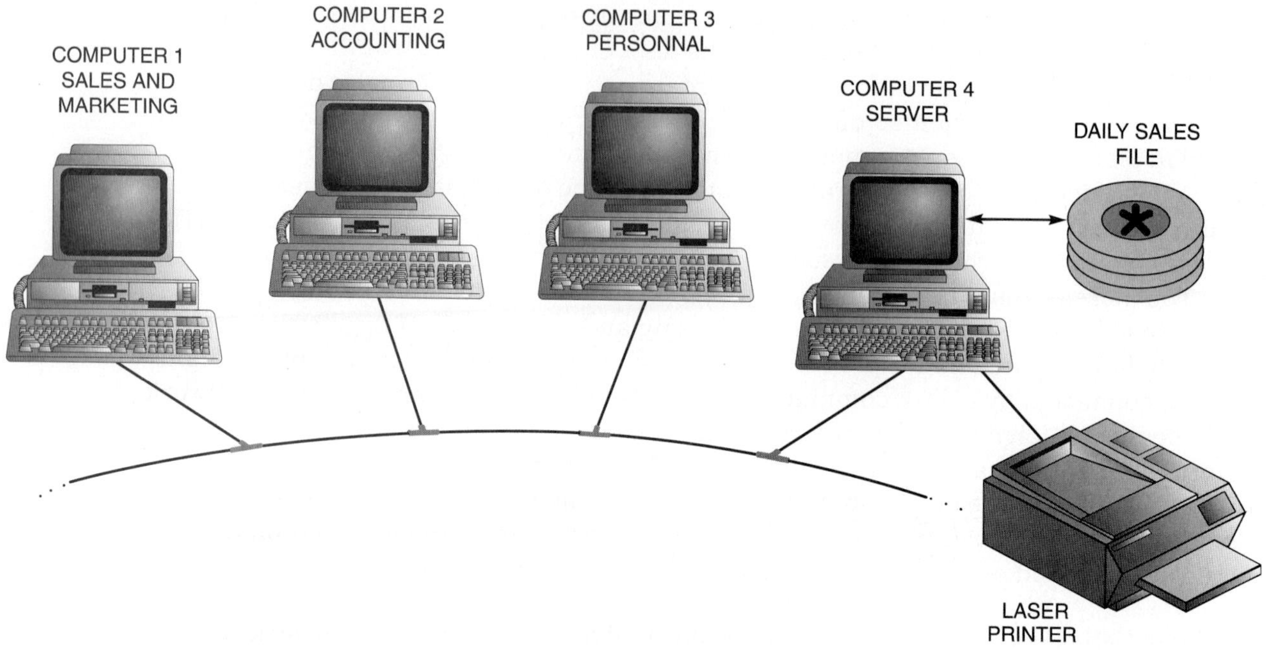

COMPUTER 1
SALES AND
MARKETING

COMPUTER 2
ACCOUNTING

COMPUTER 3
PERSONNAL

COMPUTER 4
SERVER

DAILY SALES
FILE

LASER
PRINTER

Figure 10-6 *A local area network (LAN) consists of multiple workstations connected to one another. The LAN allows end users to share hardware and information. This is an example of a bus network.*

Information resource sharing allows anyone using a workstation on a network to access data stored on any computer in the network. In actual practice, hardware resource sharing and information resource sharing are often combined. The daily sales file shown in Figure 10-6, for example, could be stored on the server's hard disk. Anyone on the network who needs access to the sales records could use this information resource. The capability to access and store data on common auxiliary storage is an important feature of networks. Much current work by vendors of database management systems is concerned with the development of distributed database management systems that can manage distributed databases. **Distributed databases** are databases stored on computers at several sites on a computer network and from which the end users can access data at any site in the network.

Software that is used by two or more end users is another resource that is often shared on a network. For example, if all the end users need access to word processing software, the software can be stored on the server's hard disk and accessed by all the end users as needed. Having the software stored on each computer would be more expensive. Keep in mind, however, that the licensing agreements from many software companies do not permit the purchase of a single software package for use by all the computers in a network. Instead, many software vendors now sell network versions of their packages; you must obtain a special agreement, called a **site license**, that permits you to store the commercial software package on a server's hard disk and allows many end users to access the package.

Communication networks for LANs and WANs are usually configured, or arranged, in one or a combination of three patterns; each of the patterns is called a **topology**. These three configurations are the bus, star, and ring networks.

Bus network   When a **bus network** is used, all devices in the network are connected to and share a single communication channel. Information is transmitted in either direction from any one workstation to another. Any message can be directed to a specific device. An advantage of the bus network is that devices can be attached or detached from the network at any point without disturbing the rest of the network. In addition, if one workstation on the network fails, the other end users of the network are not necessarily affected. Figure 10-6 shows a simple bus network.

Star network   A **star network** contains a central computer and one or more workstations connected to it, forming a star (Figure 10-7). A star network configuration is often used when the central computer contains all the data required to process the input from the workstations; an airline reservation system is an example of a star network. If queries are being processed in a star network, all the data to answer the queries would be contained in the database stored on the central computer.

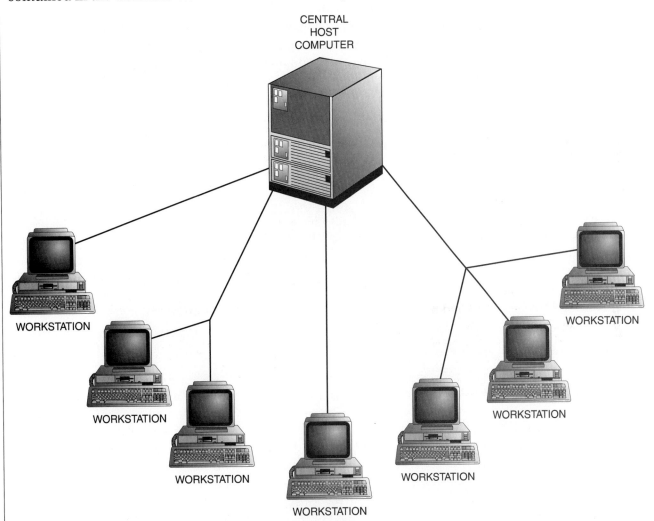

Figure 10-7 *A star network contains a single, centralized host computer with which all the workstations in the network communicate.*

A star network can be relatively efficient, and you can maintain close control over the data processed on the network. The star network's major disadvantage is that the entire network is dependent on the central computer and its associated hardware and software. If any of these central components fail, the entire network is disabled. In most large star networks, therefore, backup systems are available in case the primary system fails.

Frequently, data for an information system is predominately processed at one of the remote workstations or on the central host computer, but some data is needed periodically at one of the other locations. The data files needed in these cases either can be uploaded from a workstation to the central computer or downloaded from the central computer to a workstation.

Ring network   A **ring network** does not use a centralized host computer; instead, it uses a series of computers that communicate with one another (Figure 10-8). A ring network can be useful when all the processing is done at local sites, not at a central site. Computers could be located, for example, in three departments: accounting, personnel, and shipping and receiving. The computers in each of these departments could perform the processing required for their individual departments. On occasion, however, the computer in the shipping and receiving department could communicate with the computer in the accounting department to update data stored on the accounting department computer. Ring networks have not been extensively implemented for data communications systems that are used for WANs; instead, ring networks are more frequently used for LANs.

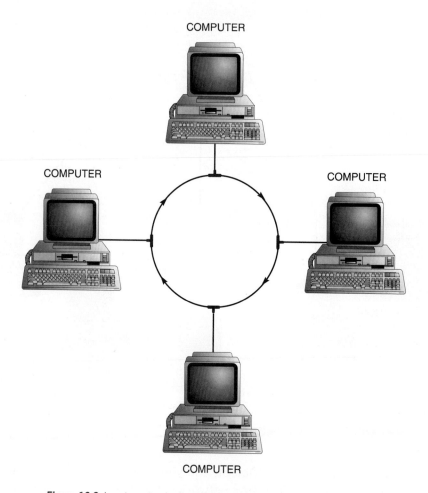

Figure 10-8 *In a ring network, all computers are connected in a continuous loop. Data flows around the ring in one direction only.*

■ Client/server architecture

Client/server computing takes distributed processing one step further. With client/server computing, or more simply **client/server**, processing is distributed among a network of client workstations (PCs) and one or more servers, which can be PCs or mini-computers. (A mainframe could be used as a server, but this is rare.) Client/server differs from simple distributed processing in that the client, not the server, controls the processing and determines which computer (client or server) will perform actual processing. To an end user sitting at a client PC, the client/server architecture is nearly invisible; instead, the end user feels as if he or she is working on a extremely powerful, extremely fast PC. The development of more powerful PCs, networks (both LANs and WANs), graphical user interfaces (GUIs), and distributed databases has made client/server possible and practical.

Because PCs have become increasingly powerful, while simultaneously becoming less expensive, client/server computing enables companies to **downsize**, or transfer applications from expensive mainframes to less expensive client/server platforms. Client/server offers several additional advantages over mainframe architecture. By utilizing graphical user interfaces (GUIs), which are not available with mainframe applications, end user interfaces can be easier to learn and simpler to use. In addition, the actual data storage is moved closer to the end users, enabling data to be accessed and utilized more rapidly.

One practical application of client/server is electronic data interchange. As first defined in Chapter 1, **electronic data interchange (EDI)** is the computer-to-computer transfer of data between companies. Note that EDI is *not* facsimile transmission (fax); instead, it is a standardized transmission of data that must be encoded by the sending computer and subsequently recognized and interpreted by the receiving computer. EDI is most often used in the areas of purchasing and payment processing. For example, if both a company and its supplier use EDI, the company's ordering system might automatically determine when an order is necessary and then submit an order by sending a computer message to the supplier via EDI (Figure 10-9 on the next page, steps 1 through 5). The supplier's client/server would receive and interpret the order (Figure 10-9 on the next page, steps 6 through 8), and then automatically feed that order to its order-entry application system (step 9). The order-entry application system would then process the order and issue appropriate directives to the shipping system, inventory system, and customer invoicing and billing system (steps 10 through 12), all of which are linked to the supplier's client/server. The invoicing and billing system could then use EDI to return an invoice to the ordering company; similarly, the shipping application system could also utilize EDI to send a shipping notice informing the company of the expected delivery date (steps 13 through 16). The ordering company would receive and interpret the invoice and the shipping notice, which would trigger appropriate update information to the company's receiving system (steps 17 through 20). All of this can be accomplished, in theory, without ever creating an actual printed order, invoice, or shipping notice, thus leading to what is called the "paperless office."

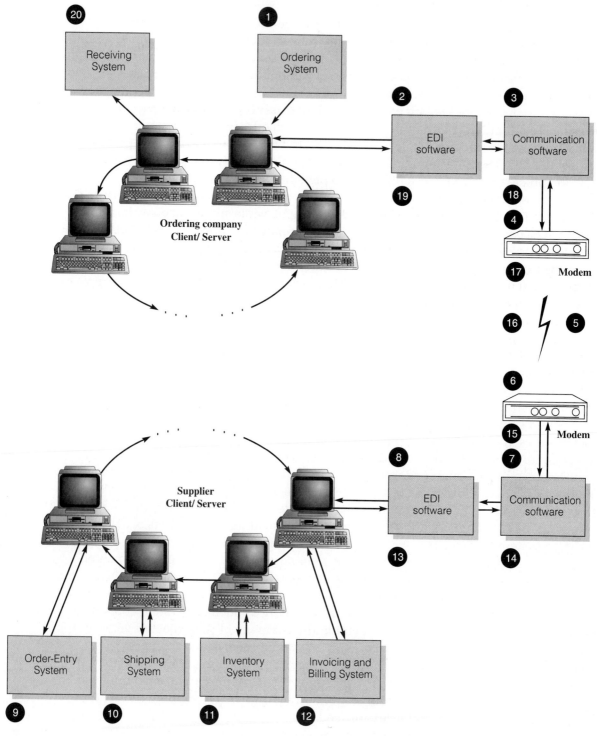

Figure 10-9 *An example of the use of electronic data interchange (EDI) for transferring data between two companies. The ordering company's client/server automatically transmits orders to the supplier. The supplier's client/server automatically processes the order and transmits confirmation information back to the ordering company.*

■ Single-user and multiuser processing

Some applications are **single-user processing** systems, which are information systems designed to be used by one individual at a time on a given computer. A word processor and a departmental budget system developed for a manager are two examples of single-user applications. Most single-user processing systems execute under the control of **single program operating systems**, which are operating systems that allow only a single end user to run a single program at one time. Today, many personal computers use this type of operating system; DOS is an example of a single program operating system.

Some operating systems allow a single user to run two or more programs or tasks at the same time. These operating systems are called **multitasking operating systems**; Microsoft Windows is an example of a multitasking operating system.

Other applications are developed for multiuser processing. A **multiuser processing system** is an information system designed to be used by one end user on a computer at the same time as other individuals are using the same information system or other information systems on the same computer. Multiuser processing systems execute under the control of **multiprogramming operating systems**, which are operating systems that allow more than one program to be run at the same time. IBM's MVS/XA is an example of a multiprogramming operating system.

Some software design considerations are different for single-user processing and for multiuser processing. Online data entry verification, for example, can be done a field at a time for single-user processing; however, it is typically done a screen at a time for multiuser processing because of the need to minimize data communications time delays.

Suppose you have implemented one program that allows instructors to enter grades for their classes. The program has been designed to execute in an online, single-user processing mode on a personal computer with a hard disk on which the program and the master file are stored. An instructor enters a command to start the program and then a menu appears. Depending on the menu choice he or she selected, the program displays either a data entry screen on which grade data can be entered or a display screen showing previously entered grades.

You are now asked to make the program work on a mainframe computer using online, multiuser processing; the program and master file will be stored on the mainframe computer. How easy is this task? Depending on the design decisions you made during your development of the program for the personal computer, accomplishing this task could range from relatively difficult to very difficult.

What are some of the design decisions that might influence the difficulty of the task? First, you might have used a programming language that is not supported on the mainframe computer. If you used a language such as Pascal or Modula-2, for example, the mainframe computer might not have a language compiler available to support that language. If programming language unavailability is a problem, you would have to rewrite the program in a different programming language. Even if the mainframe computer does have the appropriate language compiler, the syntax of the two language versions is most likely different, and you would at least have to modify the program for syntax reasons.

A second issue concerns the two different online environments. On the personal computer, the program you developed controls all interaction with an instructor. On the mainframe computer, a teleprocessing monitor would control this interaction. A **teleprocessing (TP) monitor** is a systems software product that controls a host computer's terminal communications and all the application programs executed by the terminal users. A teleprocessing monitor permits only certain programming languages, so language selection is influenced by the specific teleprocessing monitor being used. Further, each teleprocessing monitor dictates how programs must be designed and how many functions each program can perform. Because of the teleprocessing monitor, you might have to write one program to handle the menu interaction, a second program for the data entry of grades, and a third program for the display of grades.

A third issue concerns how grades will be stored on the mainframe computer. Will there be one grade master file for all instructors, or will each instructor have his or her own grade master file? Again, the specific teleprocessing monitor will influence this decision — in most cases, a single grade master file would be shared by all instructors. This decision leads to another issue, which is how to secure each instructor's grades from being accessed and updated by other instructors. You might need to add

an instructor identification code to the grade master file in order to segregate each instructor's grades. The teleprocessing monitor would control the concurrent multiple-user access and update to the grade master file, but you might also need to consider this in your design.

The few issues we have described demonstrate that the environment has a great impact on the decisions you make during design. Changing a program to work properly in a different environment is not usually a trivial task. ■

Major processing functions

When designing the software for an information system, you must be sure to account for all the processing functions that are documented in the system requirements document. These processing functions interact with the input data, the data stores, and the output information. Although each information system has its own unique requirements, all information systems have these four basic processing functions: data input and validating, updating, sorting, and reporting.

■ Data input and validating

For online processing systems, the same program handles the data entry, the data input, and the validation functions for a given transaction (Figure 10-3 on page 10.4) because values are input, validated and corrected as the transaction is entered. An online banking system, for example, might have one program to handle the data entry, data input, and validation of deposits, a second program to handle these functions for withdrawals, a third program to handle these functions for loan payments, and so on. Some online banking systems, however, have one large program that handles the data entry, data input, and validation functions for all the different possible types of transactions. Other banking systems exist that fit between these two extremes.

Batch processing systems also might have one program for each type of transaction, one program for all transactions, or fall somewhere in between these two extremes. Data entry and validation for batch processing systems, however, differs from online processing systems in two ways.

First, the data entry function for batch processing systems is done separately from the data input and validation functions. A payroll data entry program and a separate payroll validation program are shown as an example in Figure 10-10. Second, the batch processing system must have some means for handling transactions that were entered with errors. With some information systems, the valid transactions are processed immediately, while the error transactions are reported on a transaction error report. The data entry clerks use the transaction error report at a later time as a basis for reentering corrected versions of the error transactions for subsequent reprocessing. This reprocessing of the error transactions will typically occur whenever time is not a critical factor or where partial processing will suffice for this portion of the information system. A magazine subscription system processing address changes is an example of an application where partial processing might be acceptable.

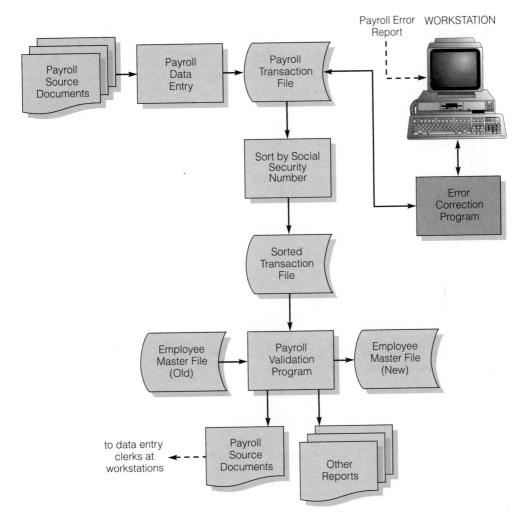

Figure 10-10 *An error correction program used to make corrections to a transaction file. The same employee master file used previously would again be input, along with the corrected payroll transaction file, to the payroll validation program.*

With some information systems, however, *all* transactions must be correct before any additional processing can occur. A payroll system, for instance, typically requires that all transactions be correct prior to processing the weekly payroll. Two fundamental problems with reentering the error transactions for time-critical applications are that more errors might be made during the correction cycle and the productivity level of the data entry clerks is lowered.

A second method for handling corrections is to add a program that allows corrections to the payroll transaction file. Figure 10-10 shows the use of an error correction program to handle corrections to errors. The data entry clerks use the payroll error report and interact with the error correction program to enter corrections to the payroll transaction file. The corrected payroll transaction file is then sorted once again and reprocessed through the payroll validation program, which inputs the same employee master file that had been previously used. Although this method is a relatively easy way to make the corrections, sorting, reading, and validating the entire transaction file a second time is a major disadvantage. With small transaction files, this additional processing might not be a significant problem; however, excessive processing time might be consumed for large-sized transaction files.

A more common method for handling corrections is to have the payroll validation program create a file containing all the error transactions, as shown in Figure 10-11. A file that contains error transactions awaiting correction is frequently called a **suspense file**. The error correction program allows corrections only to the suspense file, which is then sorted and processed through the payroll validation program. The previously correct transactions are not reprocessed because they have already updated the employee master file. Consequently, the recently created new version of the payroll master file serves as the input payroll master file to this correction-cycle processing of the payroll validation program.

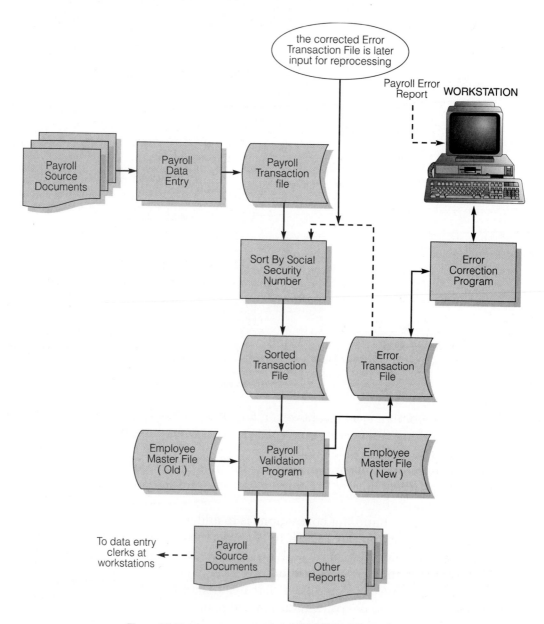

Figure 10-11 *An error correction program used to make corrections to a transaction file. The employee master file output previously would become the new input to the payroll validation program.*

One other consideration for online and batch programs that validate input data is the frequent need for these programs to randomly access other master or table files.

This need exists whenever the validity of a input value is based on its correctness as a foreign key to a master or table file. The payroll validation program in Figure 10-11, for example, might need to access a department table file if the correctness of the employee's department number is based on the existence of a record in the department table file having that same department number. Large applications might have several master and table files randomly accessed for validation purposes.

■ Updating

Updating, or **file maintenance**, is the process of adding and changing records to and deleting records from a master file or a table file. The contrast between online and batch updating is shown in Figure 10-12.

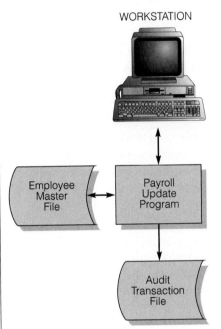

A. Online Update Progrm with Random Access

An online update program randomly updates a master file as shown in Figure 10-12A. Furthermore, data entry, data input, validation, and update functions are usually all handled by the update program. Because it is critical to record the modifi-cations that occur to master files, an online update program outputs an audit transaction file, which identifies master file modifications and which can be input to a batch report program that produces an audit transaction report.

Some batch update programs update a master file sequentially. Figure 10-12B shows a batch payroll update program. This program reads a sorted transaction file and the current employee master file with both files in the same sequence by

B. Batch Update Program With Sequential Access

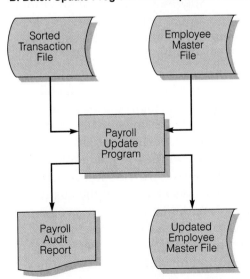

C. Batch Update Program With Random Access

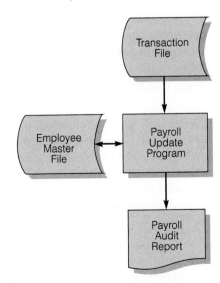

Figure 10-12 *The contrast in processing strategies between an online update program and batch update programs. Both sequential and random access methods of batch updating are shown.*

the primary key of the master file. Output by the batch payroll update program are a payroll audit report, which identifies the master file modifications, and an updated employee master file.

Transactions to add and change master file records result in the batch update program writing new and changed records to the updated master file. Transactions to delete master file records result in the batch update program not writing these deleted records from the current master file to the updated master file. A master file record without a matching transaction is written as is to the updated master file. A batch update program also frequently performs validation (and, thus, would output an error report), but the data entry and data input functions are performed prior to the execution of the batch update program.

A batch update program can also update a master file randomly, as shown in Figure 10-12C on the previous page. A batch update performed randomly does not require the transaction file to be sorted, but sorting the file might result in more efficient processing.

Some online and batch update programs logically delete records from master files instead of physically deleting records. **Logical deletion** is the use of a special master file field or flag whose value identifies whether the record should be treated as if it had been deleted. Logical deletions are used whenever the file organization does not permit physical deletions; some implementations of direct and indexed organizations, for example, do not actually physically delete records. Logical deletions are also used whenever records cannot be deleted immediately. Payroll systems, for instance, need to retain employee records on file until year-end processing in order to produce year-end reports for former employees who worked at some point during the year. Finally, logical deletions are often used to allow for the potential reactivation of deleted records; in these cases, a special transaction containing the primary key and a special reactivation code is used to *undelete* a logically deleted record. Reentering and validating a physically deleted record is less efficient than simply using such a reactivation transaction. Records that are logically deleted are usually physically deleted at some predefined frequency. Employee records in a payroll system that were logically deleted during the year, for example, are physically deleted at the start of the new year.

Some update programs, usually batch processing programs, do not require the use of a transaction file. The year-ending version of an employee master file, for example, is used as the basis for all the year-end payroll reporting. A special payroll program inputs this version of the employee master file and creates an updated employee master file, which becomes the initial employee master file for the new calendar year. The special payroll program removes the records of former employees and initializes accumulation fields without the use of a transaction file.

Some transactions require that the update program modify more than one master file. Figure 10-13 shows an example of multiple-file updating. The input to the example update program consists of a sorted transaction file, the customer master file, and the customer invoice file. The customer master file contains all the permanent data about the customer, such as the name, address, credit status, and year-to-date payments. The customer invoice file contains all the unpaid invoices. The sorted transaction records contain data that can randomly update both the customer master file and the customer invoice file. For example, when an invoice is paid by the customer, the update program removes the invoice from the customer invoice file. In addition, since a payment has been received from the customer, the update program updates the year-to-date payments field in the customer master file. Multiple-file updating is not unusual, and you might occasionally have to design programs that update even three or more files.

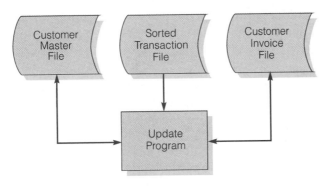

Figure 10-13 *An example of multiple-file updating where both the customer master file and the customer invoice file are updated by the same update program.*

■ Sorting

In many companies, one-third or more of the computer processing consists of sorting file and database records. We have already discussed the need to sort transaction files prior to the execution of a batch update program. Most of the sorting that occurs, however, is for the production of reports; master files and other files are sorted so the records in these files are in the sequence needed for the reports. To produce a payroll report in sequence by employee name within department, for instance, the employee master file that is in Social Security number sequence would need to be sorted by the employee name within department sequence required by the report. Each computer environment usually has sort utility programs available, so a systems analyst needs only to define the files to be sorted and the sequence in which the records are to be sorted.

■ Reporting

The reporting of output information is a major function of both batch and online processing systems. A systems analyst must design programs to generate all predefined printed reports in the information system. Predefined online queries must also be designed — either by the design of programs to handle the queries or through the design of script files that can be processed through a query language utility processor.

Processing support functions

Errors and problems will occur, even for the most precisely developed information system. Hardware failures, systems software errors, end user and operator mistakes, and power outages are just a few examples of the problems that can occur with an operational information system.

As part of the systems design, you must anticipate these future problems and plan ways to recover from them. We have already discussed the need to include in the systems design data validation, audit trails, security measures, and other control features to help ensure that data is correctly entered and processed under normal processing conditions. You must provide additional means, however, to allow for continued processing of an information system when the data in files and databases is destroyed or damaged, or when processing is interrupted before it's completed. Two critical factors you must consider are that data from files and databases must not be permanently lost or damaged, and processing within an information system must be restarted properly after problems have been corrected. We will examine four processing support functions that address these two critical factors. These processing support functions are backup and recovery, file retention, restart, and start-up processing.

■ Backup and recovery

Backup refers to making copies of data files so that if data is lost or destroyed, a timely **recovery** can be made and processing can continue.

Batch processing presents few backup and recovery problems. The transaction file and the previous version of the master file are saved as backup files in case the new master file is damaged or the execution of the update program is abnormally interrupted. Any problems that occur can be corrected simply by reexecuting the update program with the transaction file and the previous master file as inputs. Making a backup copy of the new master file is also useful if the master file is damaged after it has been created by the update program.

Backups should be made as soon as possible, usually immediately after the master file has been updated. A master file that is updated daily should be backed up daily, whereas a master file that is updated monthly needs to be backed up monthly. Backups on personal computers are made to diskette or magnetic tape, and mainframe and minicomputer backups are usually made to magnetic tape or magnetic cartridge.

Online processing presents greater backup and recovery problems than does batch processing. Figure 10-14 shows the backup and recovery steps for online processing. Backup copies of master files generally can be made only when the online system is inactive; that is, at those times when the end users are not interacting with the online system. Because these inactive times usually occur overnight and on weekends, the most recent backup would probably be many hours old if the master file is damaged during online processing. Transactions processed since the backup is created, therefore, must be captured as they are entered and reprocessed automatically, or else the end users would be forced to manually reenter these transactions. Most online systems software control programs that interact with application update programs provide a feature to *remember* transactions by saving images of the modified master file records on special files called log files or journal files. A **log file**, or **journal file**, contains copies of each modified master file record both before and after modification. If a master file is damaged, the current backup is used to recover, or **restore**, the master file. Then, a special systems software transaction recovery program processes the log file to bring the master file forward to its state at the time the damage occurred. The total recovery time could take an hour or more for master files with large numbers of records and a great deal of transactional activity. Automatically recovering the master file, however, is more accurate and less time consuming than if the end users had to reenter their transactions manually.

■ File retention

File retention refers to the length of time a file needs to be retained before the space it occupies can be used for another purpose. For a backup file placed on diskette, for example, file retention specifies how long the backup file must be kept on the diskette before the diskette can be used for storing other files.

Online Backup

Step 1: Make a nightly backup of the on line master file.

Step 2: Create the log file during on line processing.

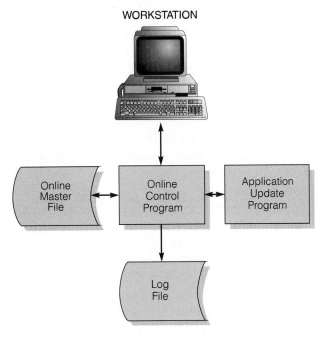

Online Recovery

Step 1: Use the most recent nightly backup file to restore the online master file.

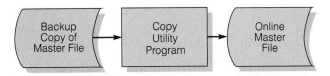

Step 2: Reprocess the day's transactions from the current log file.

Figure 10-14 *The backup and recovery steps in an online processing environment. Backup consists of making a backup copy of the master file and creating a log file during online processing. Recovery consists of restoring the online master file from the backup copy and processing the day's transactions from the log file.*

Online master and table files are permanent files, so their file retention is limited only by the life of the information system. File retention for transaction files, backup files, and master files updated through sequential batch processing is determined by a combination of processing and legal requirements. Processing requirements dictate that file retention be sufficient to permit the recovery of all master file data if the master file is damaged. Many companies retain sequentially organized master files that are updated during batch processing for three generations; that is, for three updating cycles. This three-cycle concept is called the grandparent, parent, and child strategy. The *grandparent* file represents the oldest master file retained, the *parent* file represents the second oldest file, and the *child* file represents the current master file. Retaining these three files and the transactions that were used to update the files is usually adequate backup retention; the current file can be recreated by rerunning the processing that changed the parent file to the child file or by rerunning the two previous cycles.

Legal requirements dictate how long critical processing data must be retained to conform to government and regulatory laws and rules and to substantiate financial transactions. If a government rule specifies that a record of all payments to the company be kept for three years and these records are kept in a payment file on disk, then your design must accommodate the retention of the records for at least three years. Designing a payment history file or retaining monthly backup copies of the payment file for three years are two common ways of satisfying such a government rule.

One other file retention consideration concerns the issue of lost reports. Many companies print and distribute dozens of reports from a central location during a processing day, and some of the reports might not reach their destinations for several days if they have to be mailed to remote locations. What happens if a report is lost? If the report is small and easily recreated, then the report program can be rerun to produce a second copy of the report for distribution. If the report is lengthy or impossible to recreate because the files or database used to produce the report have already changed, then a different solution is required. One common solution is to initially output the report to a disk or tape file. Then, a utility step prints the report from the file, and the file is retained for a sufficient number of days to allow for the receipt of the report. If the report is lost, then the report can be reprinted from the retained file. When the report is received or the retention period has lapsed, the file is deleted.

■ Restart

When an error occurs while a program is executing, the first step is to correct the error. If a disk master file is destroyed due to physical damage to the disk, for example, then the first step is to replace the disk and recover the master file from the latest backup. After the correction is made, the program must be restarted. Part of your systems design must include specifications of how programs should be restarted, depending on where the error occurred.

Restarting online processing systems is relatively simple. For single-user processing systems on personal computers, the end user reenters the transactions that had been processed since the latest backup. For multiuser processing systems, the log file is processed to the point of interruption.

If you need to restart a batch processing program that runs a relatively short time, say less than one hour, you would rerun the program from its beginning. If the batch processing program runs for a longer period of time, then you should consider the use of checkpoints. A **checkpoint** is a point within the processing of a program where all the important program status indicators are saved to disk. These indicators include the records being processed, the contents of main memory, and all other information necessary to restart the program from that point. The indication that a checkpoint is to be taken is given by special instructions in the program itself. After the checkpoint is taken, the program resumes normal processing. Checkpoints would occur periodically while the program executes; for example, every thirty minutes. If the checkpointed program needs to be restarted, the program does not need to be completely rerun. The program instead can be restarted at the last checkpoint taken before the error occurred. The computer operator simply gives the proper instructions to the operating system, and the restart takes place automatically.

Because the printing of special outputs, such as paychecks and invoices, might be interrupted due to a power failure or a printer problem, you should design restart procedures for the printing of these special outputs. Reprinting from the beginning again would be a waste of time and money for those outputs that were correctly printed before the interruption occurred. One method of restarting the printing is for the print program to request that the computer operator enter check numbers for the last check printed correctly and the next check that will be printed. The program then would bypass all employees whose paychecks were already correctly printed and resume paycheck printing with the next employee.

■ Start-up processing

In addition to the design of the software programs and other processing for the information system once it is in operation, you must design any required start-up processing. **Start-up** processing is the special processing that occurs in making the transition from the current information system to the new information system. The primary requirement is the creation of the new system master files from existing data.

If the current information system is a manual system, then using the new system's normal input processing methods to construct the master files might be possible. If this is not possible or if the current system is also computerized, then you might have to design special programs to convert the existing data. We will discuss the issue of start-up processing and special conversion programs at greater length when we discuss the systems implementation and evaluation phase in Chapter 13.

Software design

Software design consists of two distinct levels. The first level of software design is the systems analyst's responsibility and consists of determining which programs are required and what each program will do. The second level of software design is the programmer's responsibility and consists of designing exactly how each program will accomplish what it must do. The first level of software design is completed during the systems design phase, whereas the second level of software design is done during the systems development phase. We will discuss the first level now and the second level in Chapter 12, which examines programming, testing, and documentation.

■ Programs required

During the systems design phase, you must partition the information system's software functions into programs. Your company might have standards that dictate some aspects of this partitioning effort. Your starting point, however, is to review all the process descriptions developed during the systems analysis phase and extract those processes that must be handled by application software programs.

No definitive rules can answer the question of how best to partition the information system software requirements into programs. We can, however, provide the following general guidelines that will help you to determine what programs are needed.

One update program for each master and table file. In general, each master and table file needs its own update program to allow maintenance against that file. Let's consider our earlier multiple-file updating example, where we had one batch update program that input a sorted transaction file to randomly update both a customer master file and a customer invoice file. We would also have a second program to update only the customer master file and a third program to update only the customer invoice file. If we assume that these two update programs are online programs, then the three needed update programs are shown in Figure 10-15.

As shown in this example, one program might update two files or, in certain situations, even more than two files. Such exceptions to the guidelines — that each master and table file have its own update program — would be clearly specified in the process descriptions.

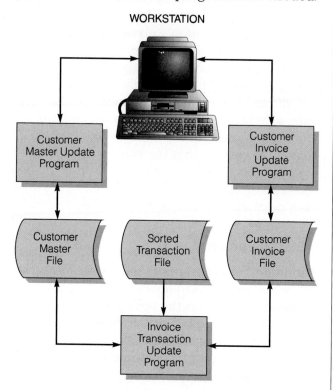

Figure 10-15 *Each master file has its own update program that handles additions, changes, and deletions of records in the file. In this example, a third update program maintains records in both master files.*

One validation program for each update program that does not handle its own validation. All transactions must be validated, so you need to be sure that no update programs are supplied with nonvalidated transactions. Because most online update programs handle their own validation, batch update programs are usually the ones you need to review carefully in applying this guideline.

One report program for each report. In general, a single report program produces a single report. Before applying this guideline, determine if a nonreport program, such as an update program or a validation program, should produce the report; if so, then you do not need to design a separate report program to produce the report.

You can then reduce the number of report programs by considering which reports are produced on the same frequency against the same file or files. Suppose that an invoice system has two reports that are printed in invoice number sequence and are produced daily during nightly report processing. If both reports input only the customer invoice file, then you should consider designing one report program to produce both reports. Two separate report programs would each have to read the entire customer invoice file, whereas a single report program would read the file only once. More efficient and cost-effective processing results with one report program in this situation.

One or more menu programs for online processing control. Online processing systems that have a menu-driven interface require programs to display the menus and to initiate appropriate programs for further processing. The number of menu programs is usually a function of the online processing environment and information systems department standards, so you should be guided in your decisions by them.

Programs required to perform special processing. As you design the update, validation, report, and menu programs, you should place the process descriptions from the system requirements document with the programs that will handle those processes. If you have remaining process descriptions, then you might need to design additional programs. Many master files, for example, have accumulation fields, such as month-to-date and year-to-date dollar accumulations. An employee master file, as a specific example, has monthly, quarterly, and yearly accumulations for taxes, earnings, and deductions. One or more programs are needed to initialize these accumulation fields at the beginning of a month, quarter, and year. A special initialization program usually is designed to perform the required initializations. Most information systems have a number of special processing situations that require special programs not covered under the previous guidelines.

■ Program documentation

After deciding which programs are required, what documentation do you need for each program? Figure 10-16 on the next page presents sample program documentation for an Employee Hours Report in a payroll system. As shown in this figure, you must provide the following information for each program.

1. *Program identification.* Each program usually has two means of identification: an English version program name and a computer program name. One program that prints a payroll register and another program that updates an inventory master file might have English version names of *payroll register program* and *inventory update program*, respectively. The computer program name is the name of the program on your computer system and is usually determined by standards developed by the information systems department. The computer program name for the inventory update program, for example, might be INVUPD or IN205. If INVUPD was chosen as the name and the program was implemented on a personal computer under DOS, then the actual name for the executable version of the program would be INVUPD.EXE and the source code version of the program might be INVUPD. PAS for a Pascal program or INVUPD. COB for a COBOL program.

2. *Purpose of the program.* A brief one- or two-sentence description of the program's purpose.

3. *Files.* Each of the files that is input to the program, output by the program, printed by the program, and updated by the program must be identified by name. Use the data dictionary name for the file; the data dictionary describes the detailed contents of the file. Refer to printer spacing charts, screen layouts, and source documents used by the program.

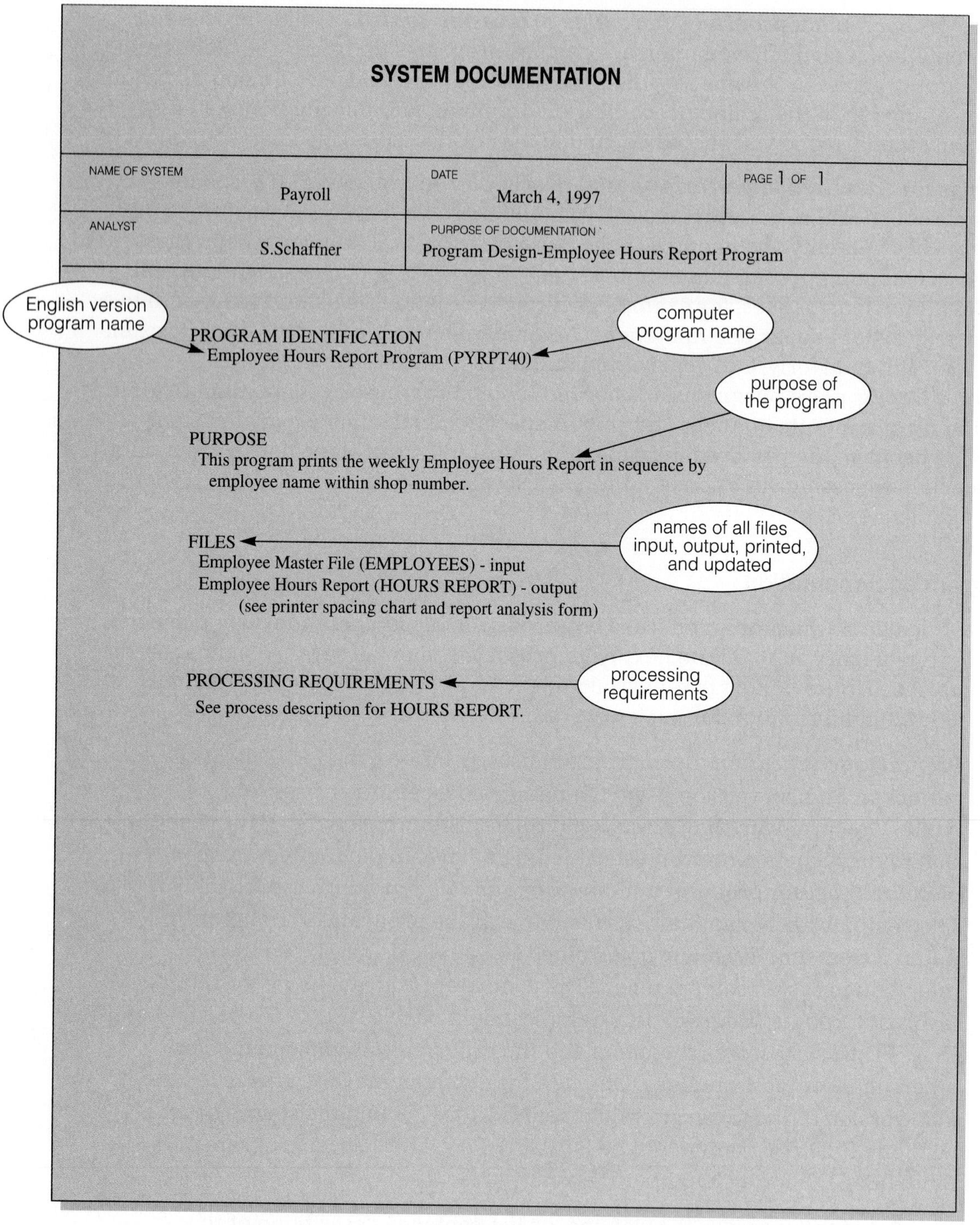

SYSTEM DOCUMENTATION

NAME OF SYSTEM	DATE	PAGE 1 OF 1
Payroll	March 4, 1997	

ANALYST	PURPOSE OF DOCUMENTATION
S.Schaffner	Program Design-Employee Hours Report Program

(English version program name)

PROGRAM IDENTIFICATION
Employee Hours Report Program (PYRPT40)

(computer program name)

(purpose of the program)

PURPOSE
This program prints the weekly Employee Hours Report in sequence by
employee name within shop number.

FILES
Employee Master File (EMPLOYEES) - input
Employee Hours Report (HOURS REPORT) - output
(see printer spacing chart and report analysis form)

(names of all files input, output, printed, and updated)

PROCESSING REQUIREMENTS
See process description for HOURS REPORT.

(processing requirements)

Figure 10-16 *Program documentation for the Employee Hours Report Program.*

4. *Processing requirements.* The process descriptions that the program must handle
were developed during the systems analysis phase and represent the program's
processing requirements. Any added requirements determined during the systems
design phase must be added to these process descriptions in the data dictionary.

Object-oriented design

We learned in Chapter 5 that there is a significant difference between the traditional approach and the object-oriented approach to the systems analysis phase. During the traditional systems analysis phase, a systems analyst focuses on data flows and procedures, using CASE tools or other graphical tools to assist in the top-down modeling and functional decomposition of those data flows and procedures. The object-oriented analysis phase, in contrast, utilizes a bottom-up approach that places emphasis on data rather than data flows. It is during the design phase of the object-oriented approach that traditional tools, such as data flow diagrams (DFDs) and entity-relationship diagrams (ERDs), are most useful.

During the object-oriented design phase, the systems analyst designs methods to implement objects. Because an object consists of data and all the actions that affect that data, each method can be independently designed and even independently prototyped and tested.

The line separating object-oriented systems analysis and object-oriented systems design is not as clear-cut as it is in traditional systems development life cycle; that is, in the object-oriented approach, the last stages of systems analysis overlap with the first stages of systems design. Similarly, the last stages of object-oriented systems design often overlap with the first stages of implementation, especially when prototyping is utilized or when the same object-oriented language environment is used for both design and implementation.

Systems design completion

The preparation of the system design specifications and the presentations to management and to information systems personnel are the final activities that complete the systems design phase. Prior to the presentations, you also need to be sure you have obtained the support and approvals from the information systems department's management and technical staff and from the end users on all the design features that specifically affect them.

■ System design specification

The **system design specification** is a document that presents the complete systems design for the new information system, along with detailed costs, staffing, and scheduling for completing the next SDLC phase, systems development. The system design specification is also called the **technical design specification** and the **detailed design specification**.

The system design specification serves as the baseline from which systems development will begin and against which the operational system will be measured in terms of its technical performance. Unlike the system requirements document, which is written in the language of the end users, the system design specification must be written in language oriented toward programmers, because programmers will use the system design specification as the basis for the programming work they do during the systems development phase. Portions of the system requirements document will be repeated in the system design specification — process descriptions, data dictionary entries, and data flow diagrams, for example, will appear in both documents.

The system design specification will be dozens or hundreds of pages in length, so you must format and organize it so it is easy to read and reference. You should, therefore, have a cover page, a detailed table of contents, an index, a glossary of terms, and all the pages numbered in sequence.

The contents of the system design specification varies, depending on company standards and the complexity of the information system. Most system design specifications have a structure similar to that shown in Figure 10-17.

SYSTEM DESIGN SPECIFICATION

1. Management Summary

2. System Components Details
   a. Program Design
   b. Output Design
   c. Input Design
   d. File and Database Design
   e. Support Processing Design

3. Environmental Requirements

4. Implementation Requirements

5. Time and Cost Estimates

6. Appendices (as needed)

Figure 10-17 *The organization of a System Design Specification.*

1. *Management Summary.* This is a concise summary of the critical points contained in the rest of the document. The Management Summary outlines the developmental efforts to date, provides a current status of the project, summarizes the to-date project costs and projected costs for the remaining project phases, reviews the overall benefits of the new information system, presents the systems development phase schedule, and highlights any issues that need to be addressed by management. If significant problems occurred during the systems design phase — for example, actual phase costs were substantially higher than were originally estimated — the problems should be discussed and explained.

2. *System Components Details.* This section contains the complete systems design for the new information system. You would include the complete systems design for all programs, outputs, inputs, and files and databases. You should include in this section source documents, printer spacing charts, screen layouts, DFDs, and all other documentation that represents the systems design. You should also include the design requirements for all support processing, such as backup and recovery, file retention, and restart processing. If the purchase of a software package is part of the solution, then you must be sure to include any

interface information required between the package and the information system you are developing. If you use a CASE design tool, you can print design diagrams and most other design documentation directly from the CASE tool.

3. *Environmental Requirements*. Here you provide the constraints under which the information system must operate. In this section, you document the operating constraints, hardware and systems software constraints, and security requirements. Operating constraints include volumes, sizes, and frequencies, and timing considerations, such as reporting deadlines, online response times, and processing schedules.

4. *Implementation Requirements*. You specify start-up processing requirements, user training plans, and software test plans in this section.

5. *Time and Cost Estimates*. In this section, you provide detailed schedules, estimates, and staffing requirements for the systems development phase and revised projections for the remainder of the systems development life cycle. You also present the total costs expended to date for the project and compare these costs with the prior estimates.

6. *Appendices*. Supplemental material can be included, as needed, in appendices at the end of the system design specification. Copies of important documents from the first three phases, a copy of the change request procedure, and copies of government regulations are examples of the information you might want to include in appendices.

■ Approvals

End users must review and approve all report and output screen designs, menu and data entry screen designs, source documents, manual processing, and other parts of the systems design with which they will eventually interact. The review and approval process is a continuous process during the systems design phase. When you complete the design for a report or a group of reports that will be used by an end user, for example, you should meet with him or her to review the designed material or prototypes, adjust the design if necessary to satisfy the end user's requirements, and obtain written approval of the design.

Securing approvals from the end users throughout the systems design phase ensures that you do not have a major task of collecting approvals at the end of the phase, keeps the end users involved with the information system's development, and gives you the feedback you need to give you confidence that you are staying on target with your efforts. Some portions of the system design specification, such as the program documentation, will be of no interest to the end users. Whatever portions of the systems design specification that do affect the end users, however, should meet with their approval prior to the presentation you conduct at the end of the systems design phase.

Information systems department personnel also need to review and approve those portions of the system design specification that will affect them. Information systems department management, for example, is concerned with staffing and cost requirements, hardware and systems software requirements, and the effects on the operating environment of adding the new information system. The programming staff will want to feel confident they will be able to develop the programs from the system design specifications and be able to maintain and enhance the information system once it is implemented. The operations group will be interested in program scheduling, report distribution and frequency, additional loads to online processing systems, and any new equipment they might have to support. Other personnel within the department will have other concerns about the new information system. In all these cases, the best approach is to keep the appropriate personnel involved throughout the systems design phase to keep them informed, to obtain their recommendations in areas that affect their jobs, and to secure approvals.

When you complete the system design specification, you will distribute the document to the key end users, information systems department personnel, and company management. You should distribute the document one week or more before any scheduled presentations to allow the recipients sufficient time to review the material in the document.

■ Technical and management presentations

You will usually give two or three presentations at the end of the systems design phase. The first presentation, which at times you do not need to give, is an internal departmental presentation to the systems analysts, programmers, computer operators, and technical support staff who will be involved in future project phases or who will have to support the system when it becomes operational. This presentation gives you the opportunity to explain the information system to these people, to answer questions they have, to react to their concerns and criticisms, to potentially adjust the systems design based on these concerns and criticisms, and to secure their approval of the systems design. Because of the interests of the audience, this presentation is a technically oriented presentation.

You give the second presentation to the top management of the information systems department and the end users. Your objectives are the same as for the first presentation, with your primary objective being to obtain the support and approval of these people for the systems design. This presentation is not a technical presentation; instead, it is aimed at end user interactions with the system and with management's interests in costs, schedules, staffing, and impacts to the production environment.

The final presentation is given to company management. By the time you give this presentation, you should have obtained all prior approvals from previous presentations, and you should have the support of the end users and the information systems department. As was the case with the systems analysis phase presentation to management, the objective of the management presentation at the end of the systems design phase is for management to decide on the next step to be taken for the development of the information system, to give its full support and approval to the direction it has chosen, and to commit money and other needed resources.

Based on the presentation and all the data submitted, management might reach one of three decisions: proceed on to the systems development phase, perform additional work on the systems design phase, or terminate the project. The next chapter begins our discussion of the next SDLC phase: systems development.

CHAPTER CASE STUDY 10

James Tool Company — Software Design and Completing the Systems Design Phase

Programmer/analyst Howard Coswell had completed the output, input, and file designs for the new union system at James Tool Company. While working on these portions of the systems design, Coswell met with the management of the payroll and union relations departments to discuss the processing environment for the union system. Coswell and the management from payroll and union relations agreed that the union system would use both online and batch processing on the personal computer located in the union relations department. The union system would also need to interface with the new payroll package from Lennox Software Solutions on the mainframe computer by uploading and downloading files. Coswell next met with his management and also secured their approval for this approach.

■ Mainframe processing

Coswell then started the design of the programs for the union system. His first step was to meet with Kimberly Wallace, one of the systems analysts working on the installation of the payroll package. They discussed how the payroll package handled deductions and what the best method would be for interfacing the payroll and union systems.

The method they designed is shown in Figure 10-18 on the next page. The payroll is run once a week, updating the employee master file with pay and deduction information for the current payroll period. They would write a special union deduction extract program, therefore, to run on the mainframe computer and to use the updated employee master file in creating the union deduction file. The union deduction file would be downloaded to the personal computer in the union relations department.

Changes to an employee's union deduction are initiated in the union relations department and need to be communicated to the payroll package. The payroll package allows deduction changes to be made either online or in batch. Because Coswell planned to have the union relations department enter deduction changes on its personal computer, Coswell and Wallace agreed that using the batch employee maintenance program would be the most accurate and productive approach to transfer these changes to the mainframe. A union deduction change file would be created in the union relations department and then uploaded to the mainframe computer in a format acceptable to the payroll package. The employee maintenance program would then batch process these transactions to randomly update the employee master file.

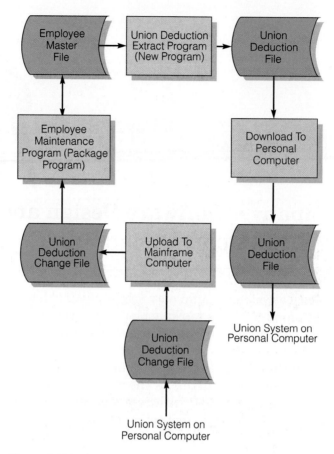

Figure 10-18 *Mainframe processing for the union system at James Tool Company.*

The Employee Union Dues Authorization Forms would be used by the union relations department to enter deduction changes on their computer; these forms would then be forwarded to the payroll department. If any validation errors in the union deductions occurred during the update of the employee master file by the batch employee maintenance program, the payroll clerks would use the Employee Union Dues Authorization Forms to enter the corrections online to the employee master file.

No changes would need to be made to the payroll package. The union deduction extract program would be the only new mainframe program required to support the union system.

■ Personal computer online processing

Coswell next turned his attention to designing the online processing needed for the union system within the union relations department and quickly sketched the diagram shown in Figure 10-19. Two online programs would handle the union system requirements.

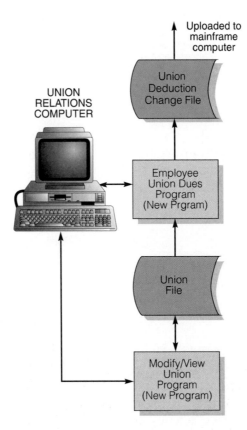

Figure 10-19 Personal computer online processing for the union system at James Tool Company.

Modifications to unions would be processed by the modify/view union program. This program would handle the validation of union data and updates to the union file. Updates would consist of adding new unions, changing existing union data, and deleting unions. The program would also display union data on the screen when requested by the end user.

A second online program would process employee union dues changes. Data about employees joining unions, changing unions, and leaving unions would be entered and validated on the union relations computer; valid data would be output to the union deduction change file, which would be uploaded weekly to the payroll system on the mainframe computer.

■ Personal computer batch processing

Finally, Coswell designed the batch processing flow on the computer within the union relations department for the union system (Figure 10-20 on the next page). Each weekly payroll run would create a union deduction file, which would be downloaded to the union relations computer. Once every four weeks, the four most recent union deduction files would be merged and sorted into employee name within union number sequence.

The pay union dues program would input the sorted union deduction file and create four outputs: three reports and one disk file. The reports are the Union Deduction Register, the Union Payment Summary, and one check to each of the unions. The disk file is the union expense entry file, which would be uploaded to the mainframe computer and processed by the company's accounting system.

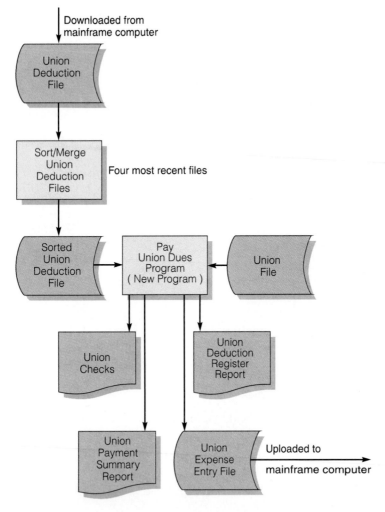

Figure 10-20 *Personal computer batch processing for the union system at James Tool Company.*

UNION SYSTEM ▾
05/23/97   1:15 PM
1. Change a union
2. Change an employee union deduction
3. Pay union dues
4. Print union checks
5. Print union deduction register
6. Print union payment summary
7. Delete union deduction files
8. Exit the union system
Use the keyboard arrow keys to highlight an option and then press [Enter] or type the option number

Figure 10-21 *The revised menu for the union system at James Tool Company.*

■ Personal computer overall control

Because the staff of the union relations department would control their own online and batch processing, Coswell had to be sure that the union system would be as automated as possible. He decided that batch files would handle the uploading and downloading of files and the merging and sorting of the union deduction files.

Coswell determined that the union system menu, which he had designed earlier during the input design, should be expanded to control the features not handled by batch files (Figure 10-21). Coswell added options three through seven to the menu. Once every four weeks, the union relations department would use the first four of these five new options to control the running of the pay union dues program and the printing of the three reports this program creates. After all outputs were verified and approved, the fifth new option, which is choice 7 on the menu, would delete the four union deduction files.

Coswell then consolidated the three diagrams he had drawn into one systems flowchart (Figure 10-22). A total of four new programs would be needed. The union deduction extract program would be a batch program on the mainframe computer. On the union relations computer, the employee union dues program and the modify/view union program would be online programs, while the pay union dues program would be a batch program.

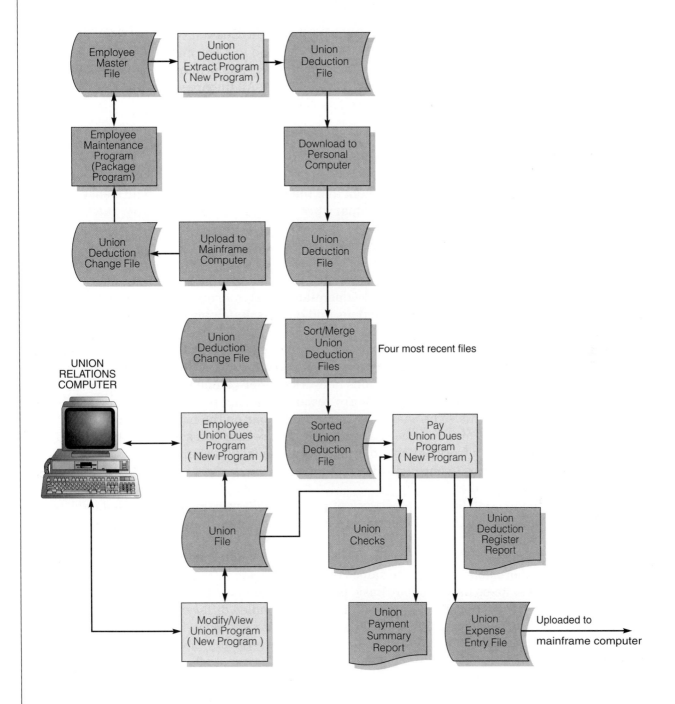

Figure 10-22 *The complete union system at James Tool Company.*

■ Completing the systems design phase

Coswell completed the program design by writing the program documentation and by designing the backup and recovery, file retention, restart procedures, and start-up procedures. He then consolidated the output, input, file, and program designs into the system design specification for the union system.

After writing the draft of the entire specification document, Coswell reviewed the entire design with Kimberly Wallace and Don Mard. After they agreed to a few minor adjustments, Coswell modified the document. The system design specification was printed and distributed, and they scheduled presentations for the end of the following week. All the presentations went well, and management approved the systems development phase for the union system.

Summary

The hardware and systems software environment and the methods of processing influence the software design for an information system. The primary processing methods are online, batch, centralized, distributed, single-user, and multiuser.

End users directly interact with online systems, which continuously process end users' transactions when and where they occur and update files and databases randomly. In contrast, batch systems process transactions in groups, execute according to a predetermined schedule, and access files and databases either randomly or sequentially. Most information systems use online processing to handle normal business transactions and queries. Batch processing is used to generate regularly scheduled reports.

Centralized processing places computer resources in one location, whereas distributed processing locates computer resources in multiple locations and connects these resources using data communications networks. Communications networks either can be LANs, local area networks, or WANs, wide area networks. Hardware resource sharing permits hardware devices, such as printers and hard disks, to be shared by the workstations on the network, and information resource sharing allows information to be shared. Networks are also categorized by their configurations: bus networks connect workstations to a single communication channel in a line, star networks connect workstations to one central computer, and ring networks connect workstations to a single communication channel in a ring.

Client/server computing involves a network of powerful PCs utilizing a distributed database and graphical user interfaces. Using client/server enables companies to downsize and to utilize electronic data interchange.

Single-user systems are used by one person at a time on a single computer, whereas multiuser systems have two or more people using the same computer.

All information systems have the four basic processing functions of data input and validating, updating, sorting, and reporting. Each of these functions is handled differently based on the processing methods you use. Each information system must also anticipate problems through the implementation of support functions that support backup and recovery, file retention, restart, and start-up processing.

Although each information system has unique requirements, a system must have programs to update files and databases, validate input data, produce reports, control online interaction, and handle special processing situations. Program documentation is an extension of other systems analysis and design documentation and specifies the program's identification, purpose, files, and processing requirements.

The system design specification presents the complete systems design for an information system and is the basis for the presentations that complete the systems design phase. Following the presentations, the project either proceeds on to the systems development phase, requires additional systems design work, or is terminated.

Review Questions

1. What is a platform? Give two examples.
2. What is an online processing system, what are two other names for online processing, and what is an online file?
3. Give four characteristics of an online processing system.
4. What is a batch processing system?
5. Give three characteristics of a batch processing system.
6. Are most information systems online, batch, or combined online and batch processing systems? Why?
7. What is centralized processing?
8. What is distributed processing?
9. What is the difference between a LAN and a WAN?
10. What is a distributed database?
11. What are hardware resource sharing and information resource sharing?
12. Name and describe three different network topologies.
13. What is client/server? How does it differ from simple distributed processing?
14. What is electronic data interchange?
15. What is multiuser processing? Describe three design issues that might be resolved differently when you implement an information system under multiuser versus single-user processing.
16. Name the four major processing functions.
17. What is a logical deletion? Give three reasons for using logical deletions.
18. Describe how backup and recovery differs between batch and online processing systems.
19. Explain the terms grandparent, parent, and child files.
20. What is a log file? What is another name for a log file?
21. What two types of requirements do you use to determine a file's retention period?
22. What is a checkpoint?
23. What is start-up processing?
24. What information is usually placed in the system components details section of the system design specification?
25. To what different groups of people might you have to give a presentation at the end of the systems design phase?

Discussion Questions

1. Some authorities feel that standards must be imposed on the information systems profession, including programming standards, documentation standards, and design standards. These authorities argue, "Millions of dollars and thousands of hours of time are wasted in retraining whenever individuals change jobs because every installation is different. Standards would eliminate this problem." Other authorities argue, "Standards stifle creativity. We will never progress as a profession if all people in information systems are required to follow prescribed standards. Standards imply a *best way* — we haven't found the *best way* yet in information systems.

Information systems is much too young as a profession to begin to impose standards." What is your opinion?

2. An executive from one of the leading accounting firms in the country recently remarked, "It is virtually impossible for accountants in our firm to properly audit any large-scale computerized financial or inventory system. For one thing, most systems are not designed for any type of efficient auditing and, even if they are, the multitude of data that can be processed on a large computer would take hundreds of workyears to audit the system." What do you think of this executive's opinion?

3. After spending eleven months on the first three phases of the SDLC of a major information systems project, you are scheduled to give the final management presentation for the systems design phase in two days. You, as the systems analyst in charge of the project, have just been informed of a major new hardware announcement. Upon investigation, you know that this new product will result in substantial improvement both in cost and effectiveness of the new system. The new product, however, will require a substantial redesign of the system and will require at least three months of additional effort to redesign the system using the latest hardware. What would you do, and why?

4. One senior executive states, "When a presentation is made to management relative to a new systems design, I prefer to have a written report only; no oral presentation is necessary. I want the facts. The costs, the time to implement, and the resulting benefits are easily recorded in a written form. On the basis of the facts, I'll make a decision as to whether the system is to be implemented. Systems analysts don't get paid to make management-level decisions, and that's exactly what they try to do when they try to sell a system in an oral presentation. I've seen too many systems implemented because smooth-talking systems analysts have convinced management that a system is an absolute necessity when the recorded facts just don't justify it." Do you agree with this point of view? Justify your position.

5. Howard Coswell documented the backup and recovery and file retention procedures for the union system, but these procedures were not explained in the James Tool Company chapter case study. What should these procedures be?

6. For the James Tool Company chapter case study, a union might negotiate a union weekly dues change for all employees belonging to the union. Based on the design Coswell presented, the union relations department would have to enter a change for every employee in the union. Are there more productive ways to handle these changes? Describe them.

7. Visit the data center at your school or at a local company and investigate the use of client/server computing and electronic data interchange (EDI). Present to your class the ways in which EDI is being used. What has the data center staff found to be the major benefits and difficulties of client/server and EDI?

Naugatuck Industrial Supply Company

Naugatuck Industrial Supply Company (NISC) distributes maintenance tools and supplies, cleaning materials, and general-purpose equipment to companies in the Naugatuck River Valley region. NISC has had a minicomputer for the past six years; the information systems on the minicomputer run both batch and online processing in a multiuser environment. NISC also has seven personal computers that run single-user programs and are connected to the minicomputer in a star configuration. When interacting with the minicomputer, the personal computers both download and upload data and act as terminals to the end users for online processing against the central files and programs stored on the minicomputer.

The information systems department has been concerned about the difficulties of backup and recovery on the minicomputer because recovery of the online system takes at least two hours, during which time the end users do not have access. One of the two hours is spent restoring the master files from backup files, and the rest of the time is spent reprocessing transactions from the log file. The systems analysts and operations management are studying various alternatives to reduce the recovery time.

NISC is developing a new online purchase order system on the minicomputer. The purchase order system will have two master files: a purchase order master and a vendor master. The systems analyst for this project has proposed a new method for updating these two master files. Transactions will be entered and validated online, as is the case with all current online systems. Rather than directly update the master files at this point, however, the online program will store the valid transactions in a file on disk. Then, during nightly batch processing, the transactions will be processed to update the two master files.

Questions

1. What are the advantages of this deferred method of updating?
2. What additional processing must the online validation program perform under this approach?
3. What are the potential problems with this approach?
4. Draw a diagram illustrating the backup and recovery processing that would be used for this system.

Ridgeway Company

The Ridgeway Company requirements were described in a Chapter 4 minicase study. The following assignments are based on the work you did for that minicase.

Questions

1. Determine the programs required for the billing system. Prepare program documentation for each program by specifying the program's name, purpose, files used, and processing requirements.

2. Document the backup and recovery requirements for all files in the system.

Genealogy System

The genealogy system requirements were described in a Chapter 4 minicase study. The following assignments are based on the work you did for that minicase.

Questions

1. Determine the programs required for the genealogy system. Prepare program documentation for each program by specifying the program's name, purpose, files used, and processing requirements.

2. Document the backup and recovery requirements for all files in the system.

Western Dental Clinic — Software Design and Completing the Systems Design Phase

Introduction

Jim Archer has completed the output, input, and file designs for the dental system at Western Dental Clinic. The associates at the clinic have accepted Archer's recommendation to install four personal computers on a local area network; one of the four personal computers would function as a server with a high-capacity hard disk. Both a laser printer and a dot matrix printer would be accessible by any of the four personal computers on the network. Jim Archer next began the design of the system's application software.

Student Assignments

1. Determine the programs required for the dental system. Prepare program documentation for each program by specifying the program's name, purpose, files used, and processing requirements.

2. Prepare a diagram (either a systems flowchart or another diagramming method recommended by your instructor) of all the programs and files in the system.

3. Document the backup and recovery requirements for all the files in the system.

4. Document the file retention periods for all the files used in the system.

5. Document the restart procedures that will be used in the system.

6. Document the start-up procedures that will be used for the dental system.

7. Prepare the system design specification for the dental system. This document should include:
   a. a management summary
   b. the system components details for all output, input, files, programs, and support processing
   c. environmental requirements
   d. implementation requirements
   e. time and cost estimates

PHASE 4

Systems Development

CHAPTER 11

Project Management and Costs

Objectives

You will have mastered the material in this chapter when you can:

- Define the role of the project manager and identify the major functions of project management
- Explain the project planning process and how project activities and events are identified
- Discuss the estimating process for project activities
- Estimate programming times using one of three estimation techniques
- Describe the scheduling process
- Create Gantt charts and PERT/CPM networks, and explain their uses
- Explain the objectives of project monitoring and control
- Discuss the evaluation and reporting of project progress
- Describe the steps in a software change-control procedure
- Identify and discuss the various cost and benefit classifications
- Perform cost-benefit analyses

Introduction

This chapter examines project management, cost estimation, and control for information systems projects. We discuss planning, estimating, scheduling, monitoring, control, reporting, and the use of project management software. We describe how Gantt charts and PERT/CPM are used for scheduling and monitoring projects and how software change-control procedures help manage changes to project requirements. Finally, we discuss several techniques for determining, estimating, and evaluating the costs and benefits for an information systems project.

Project management

Project management is the ongoing process of directing and coordinating all the steps in the development of an information system. Effective project management is necessary throughout the entire systems development life cycle, not just during the systems development phase; by placing project management at this point in the text, we do not mean to imply that project management is relevant only during systems development. Research and studies devoted to the project management of information systems have traditionally concentrated on the systems development phase. Systems development is often the longest and most costly of the SDLC phases; thus, the need for effective project management is most often recognized during systems development. Also, project management is easiest, both for study and in actual practice, during the systems development phase. This phase is the most predictable of the SDLC phases because necessary end products have been completely defined in detail before the start of the phase and because systems development activities involve little interaction with people outside the information systems department.

■ Project management overview

The goal of project management is to produce an information system that is acceptable to its end users and that is developed within the specified time frame and budget. The acceptability, deadline, and budget criteria must all be met for a project to be considered completely successful. Failing to meet any one of these three criteria usually indicates a failure, at least in part, in project management. Even though outside factors might contribute significantly to project failure, the role of project management is to recognize such factors and to eliminate or minimize their negative effects.

The job of a **project manager** is to manage a project to develop an information system. The project manager is usually a member of the information systems department, typically a senior systems analyst. For very large projects, the project manager might be an actual manager in the information systems department. Smaller projects might be managed by a programmer/analyst or even, in rare cases, a programmer. The project manager might also be called the **project leader** or, when appropriate, the **lead analyst** or the **chief programmer**.

Most information system projects also have a project coordinator. The **project coordinator** handles the administrative and procedural responsibilities for the developing information system. This person also negotiates between end users when they have conflicting requirements and makes the final ruling on all requests for change to the system requirements document after the requirements have been frozen.

The project coordinator is usually a manager or an end user who is familiar with the information system's requirements and who can effectively arbitrate disagreements and make decisions. The project manager and project coordinator positions are typically filled by two different people, although occasionally one person does fill both roles, especially in smaller companies.

■ General management functions

In business today, the generally recognized management functions are planning, staffing, organizing, directing, and controlling. These five functions apply to all types of managers in all kinds of situations; an information system project manager is no exception. A project manager's planning activities include identifying and planning project tasks and estimating project times and costs. Staffing activities include selecting the project team and assigning specific tasks to team members. Organizing activities include structuring and scheduling the project work. Monitoring the progress of the project team and guiding, supervising, and coordinating the team's workload are part of a project manager's directing activities. Finally, control activities include monitoring and reporting on project progress, evaluating results, and taking corrective action, when necessary, to keep the project on target. We will next examine these project management activities in more detail.

Project planning

Project planning takes place at both the *beginning and end* of every SDLC phase. End-of-phase planning is necessary for formulating estimates of costs, manpower requirements, and schedules for all subsequent phases; these estimates, which are included in the documents prepared at the end of each phase, are used by management to decide on future action.

Planning is necessary at the beginning of each phase to determine all the specific activities to be accomplished during that phase. An **activity**, or **task**, is any project-related work requiring the use of project resources (personnel, time, or money) or any external effort that impacts the project. Examples of internal activities are conducting an interview, designing a report layout, and selecting equipment for purchase, whereas awaiting the delivery of purchased equipment is an example of an external activity. An activity is the smallest unit of work over which the project manager desires control. Activities should be relatively small and manageable. If the project team must code five programs, for example, you should define one activity for each program for a total of five activities rather than define one activity for the coding of all five programs.

An **event** is a project milestone representing the beginning or end of an activity. Each activity has two related events: one event represents the activity's beginning, and the other event represents the activity's completion. Some events signal the end of one activity and the start of another activity. Figure 11-1 on the next page shows the relationships between activities and events for the work associated with creating and analyzing a questionnaire. All events must be concrete and recognizable so you can verify with complete certainty that an event has occurred. Delivery of purchased equipment, beginning report design, obtaining user approval for report specifications, completing user training, and completing the tabulation of returned questionnaires are good examples of events. Completing 50% of a program's testing is not a good event definition, because you will not know exactly when you reach that milestone.

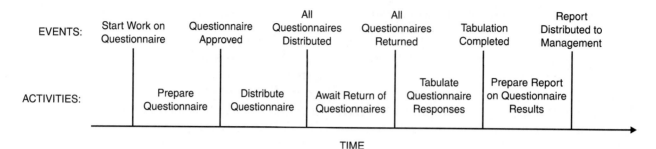

Figure 11-1 *A sequence of activities and the events that indicate each activity's beginning and end.*

The project manager defines a project's activities and events and estimates the time and cost necessary to complete each activity. The project manager then schedules and assigns the activities to specific members of the project team. During the project phase, the project manager coordinates activities, monitors events, and evaluates and reports on the progress of these activities and events.

Project estimating

D etermining realistic time estimates for project activities is one of the most difficult of a project manager's duties. The project manager must consider many factors that can affect time requirements.

One of the most important of these factors is the size of the project, because the relationship between a project's size and its required development resources is not proportional. If Project B is twice the undertaking as Project A, for example, it will take much more than twice as many resources to develop Project B. Let's assume that Project A has two systems analysts assigned to develop a single-department information system for three end users and that Project B has four systems analysts assigned to develop a second information system for two departments with three end users in each department. Let's also assume that the second information system has twice as many programs, reports, files, data elements, calculations, and so on. Why would Project B typically take much more than twice as many resources as Project A even though Project B is exactly twice the size of Project A? Looking at just three facets of the project resource requirements will illustrate the point. First, more systems analysts means more time must be spent in communication among team members. Each of the four analysts on Project B must communicate with each of the other three analysts, for a total of six interactions; the two analysts on Project A need to communicate only with each other. Second, individual project products from Project B must be submitted to twice as many people as those from Project A; the more end users who must approve a particular product, such as a report design, the greater the probability that at least one end user will request changes to the product. Third, if Project B has six programs and Project A has only three programs, then Project B has five times as many potential program interfaces (Figure 11-2) and, thus, is likely to have more than twice as many actual program interfaces.

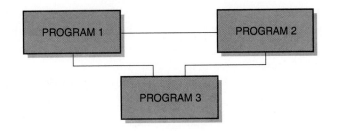

3 programs have 3 potential interfaces

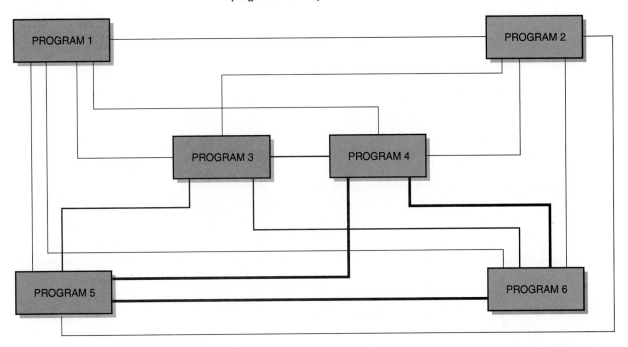

6 programs have 15 potential interfaces

Figure 11-2 *A project with three programs has three potential program interfaces, whereas a project with six programs has fifteen potential program interfaces.*

The graph in Figure 11-3 shows the relationship between project resources and project size. If doubling the project size exactly doubled the required project resources, then plotting resources against size would produce the dashed line in the figure. The actual resource curve lies entirely above the dashed line, illustrating that as project size increases, required project resources increase even more rapidly.

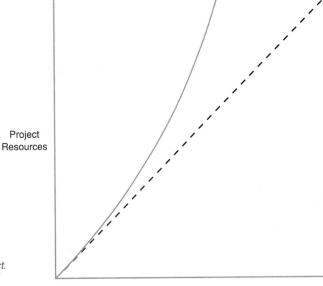

Figure 11-3 *The relationship between project size and project. Larger projects require even greater amounts of time, money, and personnel.*

The attributes of individual project team members also affect time requirements. A team member with less experience, knowledge, education, maturity, and imagination requires more time to complete a project activity than does a more knowledgeable and experienced team member.

Other examples of factors that can affect project time requirements include the attitudes and availability of end users, the level of upper management commitment, and the priority of the project compared to the priority of other projects in progress within the organization.

Time estimates are usually expressed in **person-days**, which are the number of days required for a person to complete an activity. Preparing time estimates in terms of person-days presents another difficulty for the project manager. If one person requires twenty days to perform a particular task, it is usually not true that two people could do it in ten days or that four people could do it in five days. If a task can be perfectly partitioned and if the participants would require no communication, then the product of time and number of people might be a constant; mowing lawns and stuffing envelopes are possible examples of such partitionable tasks. For most systems analysis and programming tasks, however, *time and people are not interchangeable*. If one systems analyst requires two hours to interview an end user, for example, two systems analysts would most likely also require two hours for the same interview rather than the one hour if time and people were interchangeable.

Most of the research done on estimating techniques concerns programming activities during the systems development phase. Project managers typically use one of three methods (or a combination of these methods) to estimate programming times. These methods are the quantitative method, the experience method, and the constraint method.

■ Quantitative method

The quantitative method uses tables and formulas to determine an estimate of required programming time for a single program. The tables for one such method are shown in Figure 11-4. With this particular method, the number and types of the files, the functions performed by the program, and the programmer's experience are assigned weighting points from the tables. These three weighting points are then factored together and divided by a general productivity factor to produce a person-days estimate of programming time required. The actual steps are detailed in the example shown in Figure 11-5.

Table 1
Files and Their Characteristics

FILE TYPE	POINTS
Sequential Tape or Disk File	0.5
Indexed or Direct Disk File	1.0
Database File	2.0
Printer Report, one line per detail	0.5
Printer Report, multiple lines per detail	1.0
Screen Display, single screen	1.0
Screen Display, multiple screens	3.0

Table 2
Program Functions

PROGRAM FUNCTION	POINTS
Validate	1.0
Complex Calculations	1.0
Update Files	2.0

Table 3
Programmer Experience

POSITION	POINTS
Programmer/Analyst or Senior Programmer	0.5
Programmer	1.0
Programmer Trainee	3.0

Figure 11-4 *Tables for estimating programming time using a quantitative method.*

Task: Write, text, and document a program that will read and validate a sequential file of transaction records, update an indexed master file, and generate a master file update report and a report of transactions errors. The program will be developed by a programmer with two years of programming experience. Only 70% of the programmer's total available time will be spent productively working on the program.

1. Using Table 1, determine the points based on the files used by the program.

Sequential transaction file	0.5
Indexed master file	1.0
Simple output update report	0.5
Simple output error report	0.5
Total:	2.5

2. Using Table 2, determine the points based on the program's functions.

Validate input transactions	1.0
Update master file	2.0
Total:	3.0

3. Using Table 3, determine the points based on the programmer's experience.

Programmer position	1.0

4. Calculate total program points by adding the points based on the files used (step 1) to the points based on the program's functions (step 2).

    $$2.5 + 3.0 \quad = 5.5$$

5. Multiply the total program points (step 4) by the programmer's experience (step 3).

    $$5.5 \times 1.0 \quad = 5.5$$

6. Determine the estimated person-days by dividing the result of step 5 by the productivity factor.

    $$5.5/.70 \quad = 7.8 \text{ person-days}$$

Figure 11-5 *An example of estimating programming time using a quantitative method.*

We must consider a general productivity factor in our estimates, because a programmer does not productively spend all eight hours of every eight-hour workday on project assignments. Meetings and project reviews, other interactions with people, training, computer unavailability and downtime, vacations, holidays, and sick days all reduce the time available for productive work such as programming. In addition, personnel turnover and team member inactivity due to the imperfect fit of project activities to project personnel result in loss of productive time. We must consider all such time losses when estimating. With the technique used in the example shown in Figure 11-5, lost productivity is accounted for in the estimated general productivity factor. A productivity factor of 70%, for example, indicates that the project manager expects a programmer to be involved in actual productive programming work only 5.6 hours, on average, in each eight-hour workday. Productivity factors vary by company, so you must use the productivity factor that is standard for your company.

■ Experience method

With the experience method, the project manager develops project estimates based on the resources used for a similar, previously developed information system. The assumption underlying the experience method is that like tasks require like resources.

The experience method works best for small- to medium-sized projects when the two information systems are alike in size, basic content, and operating environment; minor differences in algorithms or routines are generally inconsequential. This method does not work quite as well for larger systems; the more the number of variable factors in the project, such as the number of programs, files, or team members, the greater the possibility of complications that will require additional resources.

Trying to apply experience from projects developed for a completely different environment is not advisable. For example, for the first project in a new environment, such as a newly purchased database management system, you have no previous experience to use as a basis for your estimate. Many organizations develop a pilot system to gain technical and estimating experience in a new environment. A **pilot system** is a small, noncritical information system that is completely developed to serve as a basis for understanding a new environment. A pilot system is, therefore, a practice system; often, the system is discarded once it has served the purpose of providing experience.

■ Constraint method

With the constraint method, one or more of the resources of time, dollars, or personnel are specified and fixed; the project manager agrees to complete the project within the given constraint. Once the constraints, and thus the estimate, have been agreed upon, the end user and the project manager define a set of information system requirements that can be completed within the estimate. With the quantitative and experience methods, the project requirements are fixed and the estimates reflect the resources necessary to satisfy the requirements. In contrast, the constraint method holds one or more of time, dollars, and personnel fixed and then adjusts the requirements to fit the resources allocated.

Project scheduling

The project scheduling functions of the project manager include determining the order in which activities will be performed, setting start and end times for each activity, and assigning specific tasks to team members.

The first step in determining the order for performing activities is to identify all activity dependencies. To say that an activity is **dependent** means that the activity cannot be started until one or more of the other activities have been completed. You cannot tabulate questionnaires, for example, until the questionnaires have been developed, tested, approved, distributed, and returned. Similarly, you cannot begin a system test before the programs have been written. After the project manager identifies all activity dependencies, he or she can then arrange the activities into logical sequences, representing the order in which the activities can be performed.

Once the activity order is determined, the project manager sets start and end times for the activities. The start time for a particular activity depends on the end times for all the preceding activities; an activity can start no earlier than the latest of the ending times of all activities upon which it depends. The end time for a particular activity can be no earlier than its start time plus the estimated duration estimate for that activity.

While scheduling activities, the project manager must also consider personnel assignments. He or she cannot have more activities occurring simultaneously than people are available to perform those activities. Also, any one person should not be overscheduled. At the same time, the available personnel should not be underutilized. A team member with nothing to do must still be paid, and personnel morale can suffer when periods of boring inactivity alternate with periods of intense effort.

For all these reasons, personnel assignments cannot be treated independently from activity scheduling. The estimating and scheduling processes are often iterative; a project manager must work back and forth between activity estimates, personnel assignments, and the activity schedule until a satisfactory, workable schedule is developed. You can see that project estimating and scheduling can be very complex for all but the smallest of projects.

Scheduling tools

everal graphical planning aids can assist a project manager in the scheduling process. We will examine two of these tools: Gantt charts and PERT/CPM.

■ Gantt charts

Gantt charts were formulated by Henry L. Gantt in 1917 to control the production of war materials. A **Gantt chart** is a horizontal bar chart that graphically illustrates a schedule. As shown in the Figure 11-6 Gantt chart, time is represented by the horizontal axis and activities are listed vertically, typically in order by their start dates. The positioning of the bar for a particular activity shows the start and end of the activity; the length of a bar, therefore, indicates the duration of the activity.

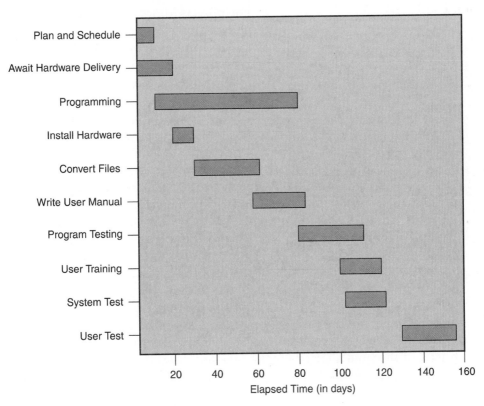

Figure 11-6 A Gantt chart for the systems development phase of a typical project.

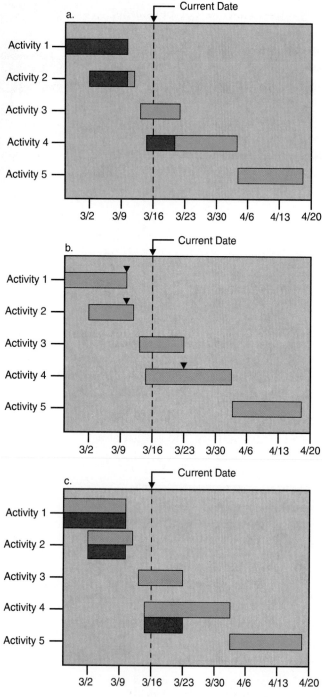

Figure 11-7 *Three ways to illustrate project status on a Gantt chart. All three charts indicate the activity 1 has been completed, that activity 2 is approximately 80% complete and is behind schedule, that activity 3 has not yet begun and is also behind schedule, and that activity 4 is ahead of schedule.*

Medium-sized projects can have dozens of activities, and very large projects can have hundreds, or even thousands, of activities. Thus, a detailed Gantt chart might possibly be too large and too unwieldy to be useful. In such cases, project managers often combine related activities for Gantt charting; an activity on a Gantt chart might actually represent many separate, but related, activities. Figure 11-6 shows, for example, a Gantt chart for the activities in the systems development phase of a typical project. The activities in this Gantt chart labeled Programming, Write User Manual, and Program Testing are actually activity groups, each representing more than one specific activity. For larger projects, project managers often create multiple Gantt charts: a master Gantt chart illustrates the major project activities and activity groups; individual Gantt charts, one for each team member or one for each activity group, for example, represent the assigned activities.

For project phases that have been scheduled but not yet started, the time axis is usually shown as elapsed time from a zero point, as shown in Figure 11-6 on the previous page. For phases in progress, actual dates are shown along the horizontal axis (Figure 11-7).

A Gantt chart is useful for tracking and reporting progress, as well as for graphically displaying a schedule. Progress can be indicated on a Gantt chart in several ways. Bars, or parts of bars, can be darkened to illustrate completed activities (Figure 11-7a), or arrowheads can be used to indicate the completed proportion of a started activity (Figure 11-7b), or the actual progress on an activity can be shown with a second bar drawn below the schedule bar for that activity (Figure 11-7c). In all cases, a vertical line, typically either bold or dashed, indicates the reporting date. Notice that on all three charts activity progress is shown by indicating the proportion of the activity that has actually been completed, *not* the proportion of the allotted time for the activity that has passed. Activity 2 in Figure 11-7, for example, is shown to be approximately 80% complete, even though 100% of the time allotted for the task has passed. Similarly, activity 4 is shown to be 37% complete, even though we are only about 5% of the way through the allotted time for the task.

Gantt charts are often used to report progress because they present an easily understood picture of project status. Gantt charts, however, are not an ideal tool for project control. One problem with Gantt charts is that they do not indicate activity dependencies; looking at just a Gantt chart, you cannot determine the impact on the entire project caused by a single activity that is behind schedule. Also, the number of hours or days required to complete an activity cannot be deduced from a Gantt chart. The length of a bar indicates only the time span allotted for completing an activity; it does not indicate the number of people assigned nor the total person-hours or person-days, although a project manager could write the estimates inside the bars. For these two reasons, you cannot determine how far ahead or behind schedule a project is just by looking at its Gantt chart.

■ PERT/CPM

The **Program Evaluation Review Technique (PERT)** was developed by the Navy Special Projects Office in the 1950s to control the development of the Polaris submarine missile program. At approximately the same time, the **Critical Path Method (CPM)** was developed by private industry to meet similar project management needs. The important distinctions between the two methods have disappeared over time, so today the technique is generally called **PERT/CPM**.

PERT/CPM charting conventions   In a PERT/CPM chart, project activities and events are graphically presented as a network of vectors and nodes, respectively. As shown in Figure 11-8a, event nodes are usually drawn as circles, but rectangles may also be used. An activity vector, or line with a single arrowhead, connects one node to another. Vectors on a PERT/CPM chart are comparable to bars on a Gantt chart with one important difference: the length of the vector is not necessarily proportional to the duration of the activity it represents.

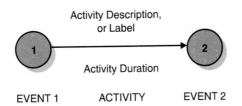

Figure 11-8a *A PERT/CPM circle, or node, represents an event; that vector connecting two events represents an activity. A node is identified by a number. An activity vector is identified with a description of the activity or with a single-letter label explained in an accompanying table. The estimated duration of the activity appears below the activity line.*

Figure 11-8a shows two events connected by an activity. Event 1 marks the beginning of the activity, and event 2 represents the end of that same activity. In a complete PERT/CPM chart, most events represent the end of one activity and the beginning of another. Events in a PERT/CPM chart are identified by unique numbers placed inside the nodes. You can label an activity with a short description appearing above the vector; alternatively, you can identify each activity with a letter or code that is explained in an accompanying table. The estimated duration of an activity appears below the vector.

The activity connecting events 3 and 4 in Figure 11-8b on the next page is a dummy activity, which is indicated by a dashed vector. A **dummy activity** is used in a PERT/CPM chart to indicate only an event dependency; dummy activities do not require the use of resources or the passage of time. The dummy activity connecting events 3 and 4 tells us that event 4 cannot occur until event 3 has occurred. For example, event 3 could represent completing program design and event 4 could represent beginning the preparation of the end-of-phase presentation.

EVENT 3   DUMMY ACTIVITY   EVENT 4

Figure 11-8b A PERT/CPM dummy activity is indicated by a dashed vector. Dummy activities, which require no time and use no resources, indicate event dependencies; in the example, event 4 cannot occur until event 3 has occurred. Dummy activities are never labeled with a description or time duration.

    Activities can be scheduled serially or in parallel. Figure 11-9a shows three serial, or dependent, activities: event 2, which represents the completion of activity A, must occur before activity B is begun; and event 3, which represents the completion of activity B, must occur before activity C can be started. In Figure 11-9b, D and E are parallel activities that can occur simultaneously. The durations of activities D and E need not be the same. Activity D might represent conducting interviews over a two-week period of time, for example, whereas activity E might represent developing a questionnaire in a single day. Notice that activity F is dependent on both activities D and E; activity F cannot begin until both events 6 and 7 have occurred. The dummy activity between events 6 and 7 effectively reconnects the parallel activities into a single path leading to activity F.

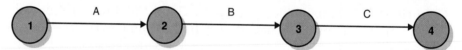

Figure 11-9a Activities A, B, and C are serial activities. Activity A must be completed before activity B can begin. Similarly, activity B must be completed before C can begin.

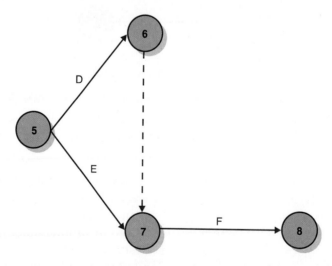

Figure 11-9b Activities D and E are parallel activities that can occur simultaneously. Both D and E must be completed before activity F can begin. The dummy activity connecting events 6 and 7 is necessary to indicate that event 6, which represents the completion of activity D, must occur before activity F can begin.

Figures 11-10a and 11-10b show a Gantt chart and a PERT/CPM chart for the same systems development phase of a project. The Gantt chart includes ten activities, some of which actually represent groups of related activities. To make the PERT/CPM chart relatively simple and directly comparable to the Gantt chart, we have included the same ten activities in the PERT/CPM chart. This is not realistic, however. In an actual PERT/CPM chart, each individual activity would be represented, and all activity dependencies would, therefore, be explicitly illustrated. In a more realistic version of the Figure 11-10b PERT/CPM chart, the programming activity, for example, would be a combination of several parallel and serial *write program* X activities.

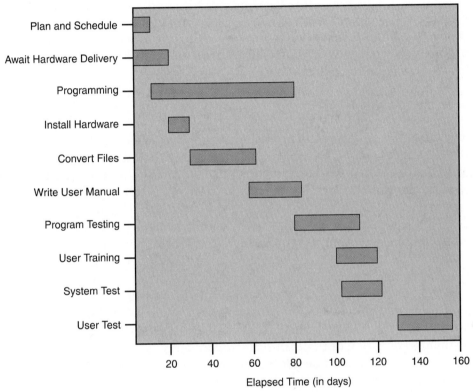

Figure 11-10a *A Gantt chart for the systems development phase of a typical project.*

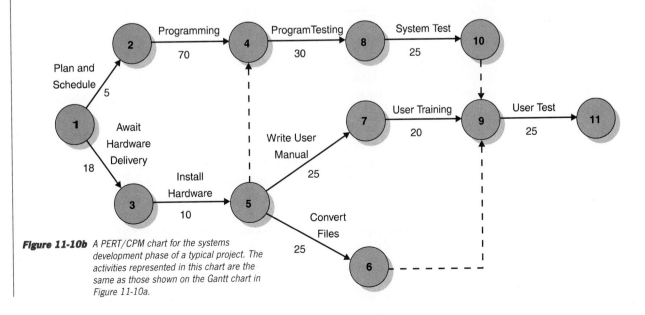

Figure 11-10b *A PERT/CPM chart for the systems development phase of a typical project. The activities represented in this chart are the same as those shown on the Gantt chart in Figure 11-10a.*

In addition to the ten activities, the PERT/CPM chart in Figure 11-10b on the previous page includes eleven events. Three dummy activities, used to reconnect parallel paths at appropriate events, are also shown in the PERT/CPM chart.

Activity duration   Traditional PERT techniques use a formula for calculating estimated activity duration. The project manager first determines three time estimates for each activity: an optimistic estimate (O), a most likely estimate (M), and a pessimistic estimate (P). The expected activity duration is then calculated as:

$$(O + 4M + P) / 6$$

For example, the project manager might estimate that a file-conversion activity could be completed in as few as twenty days or could take as many as thirty-four days, but is most likely to require twenty-four days. Using the formula, the expected activity duration is 25 days from the calculation:

$$(20 + 4 \times 24 + 34) / 6 = 25$$

Earliest completion times   After the project manager creates a PERT/CPM network for a project and assigns durations to each activity, he or she then determines the duration of the project. The first step is to determine the **earliest completion time (ECT)** for each event, which is the minimum amount of time necessary to complete all activities that precede the event. We will use Figure 11-11 to illustrate this step. (Figure 11-11 shows the same PERT/CPM chart as does Figure 11-10b on the previous page. The number in the left half of each enlarged event node is the event number. Ignore for now the two numbers in the right half of each event node.) You calculate earliest completion times from left to right across the PERT/CPM chart. The first event, event 1 in the figure, is given an ECT of zero. Working across the chart, the ECT for event 2 is 5, because the expected duration of the *Plan and Schedule* activity is 5 days. Similarly, the ECT for event 3 is 18. The ECT for event 5 is 28, which is the sum of the ECT for the preceding event 3 plus the estimated duration of the *Install Hardware* activity. In the simplest cases, the ECT for an event is determined by adding the duration of the immediately preceding activity to the ECT of the immediately preceding event.

How do you calculate the ECT for an event with more than one immediately preceding event? Such an event would be one into which dummy activities lead; each of the preceding activities, which consist of one actual and one or more dummy activities, represents a path to the event. The ECT for such an event is the *largest* of the earliest completion times for each possible path to the event. In Figure 11-11, dummy activities lead to both events 4 and 9. Let's consider event 4. One of the paths leading to event 4 is 1-2-4 (meaning event 1, followed by event 2, followed by event 4); the earliest completion time for this path is 75 (5 + 70) days. The other path leading to event 4 is 1-3-5-4; the earliest completion time for this path is 28 (18 + 10 + 0) days. Because event 4 cannot occur until all preceding events have occurred, the ECT for event 4 is the larger of 75 and 28, which is 75 days. We can now state a general rule for determining ECTs: the earliest completion time for an event is the largest of the sums determined by adding the duration of an immediately preceding activity to the ECT of its immediately preceding event.

When you have determined ECTs for all the nodes in the PERT/CPM network, the ECT of the last node is the expected project duration. Because the ECT for event 11 in Figure 11-11 is 155 days, this systems development phase is expected to take 155 days to complete.

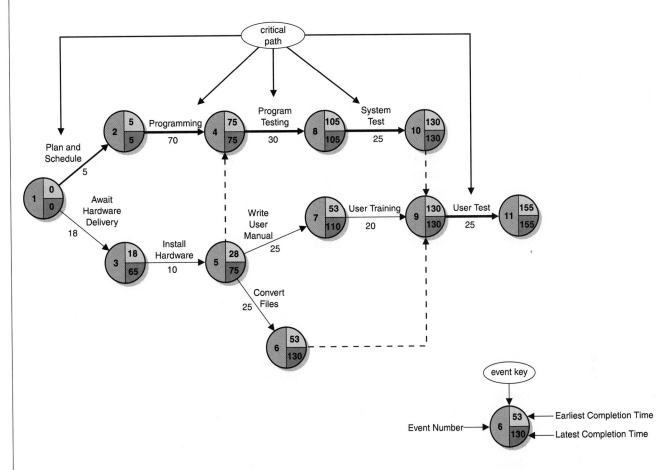

Figure 11-11 *The PERT/CPM chart of Figure 11-10b on page 11.15 has been enhanced to show earliest completion times, latest completion times, and the critical path.*

Latest completion times You must also determine the latest completion time for each event. The **latest completion time (LCT)** for an event is the latest time at which the event can occur without delaying the project. To determine LCTs, you work backward through the PERT/CPM chart, starting from the rightmost, or last, node. The LCT of the last node is always the same as its ECT. For all other events, the LCT is the smallest difference between the LCT of an immediately following event and the duration of the activities connecting the two nodes.

We will again use the PERT/CPM chart of Figure 11-11 to illustrate the calculations. The LCT of the last event, event 11, is set equal to its ECT, which is 155 days. The LCT for event 9 is 130 days, which is calculated by subtracting the 25 days for the *User Test* activity from 155 days. Events 6 and 10 are both connected to event 9 by dummy activities, which have no duration; therefore, the LCT is also 130 days for both events 6 and 10. Continuing to work backward, the LCT for event 7 is 110 days (130 - 20), the LCT for event 8 is 105 days (130 - 25), and the LCT for event 4 is 75 days (105 - 30).

What is the LCT for event 5? Event 5 leads to three other events. The differences between those following event LCTs and the connecting activity durations are 75 (75 days - 0 for event 4), 85 (110 days - 25 for event 7), and 105 (130 days - 25 for event 6). Thus, the LCT for event 5 is 75 days, the smallest of 75, 85, and 105.

In Figure 11-11 on the previous page, ECTs and LCTs have been added to the PERT/CPM chart. Each node now contains three numbers. The number appearing in the left half of a node is its unique event identification number. The upper number in the right half of a node is the ECT for the event; the number in the lower right is the event's LCT.

The **slack time** for an event is the amount of time by which an event can be late without delaying the project; the slack time for a particular event is the difference between its LCT and ECT. Looking at Figure 11-11, we see that the slack time for event 6 is 77 days (130 - 53). That means that the *Convert Files* activity could be as many as 77 days behind schedule without necessarily delaying the project schedule or affecting the project completion date.

Critical path   There will always be at least one complete path through a PERT/CPM network for which every node has equal ECTs and LCTs. In Figure 11-11, the ECTs and LCTs are equal for every event in the path 1-2-4-8-10-9-11; that path, called the critical path, has been highlighted in the figure. A **critical path** is a series of events and activities with no slack time. If any activity along the critical path falls behind schedule, the entire project schedule is similarly delayed. The critical path includes, as its name implies, all the activities and events most critical to the project schedule.

Comparing Gantt charts and PERT/CPM   One significant advantage of PERT/CPM charts is that, unlike Gantt charts, all individual activities and activity dependencies are explicitly illustrated. Most project managers, therefore, find PERT/CPM charts very helpful for project scheduling. PERT/CPM charts are also useful for monitoring and controlling projects. As a project proceeds, the project manager can closely monitor the activities along the critical path and can easily evaluate the effects of any activity that is behind schedule, whether it is on or off the critical path. PERT/CPM charts are inferior to Gantt charts for reporting purposes, however; the PERT/CPM chart for even a small project can be rather complicated, and the picture presented by a PERT/CPM chart is not as immediately clear as is a Gantt chart.

PERT/CPM and Gantt charts are not mutually exclusive techniques. Project managers often use both techniques, thereby gaining the advantages of each. Neither Gantt charts nor PERT/CPM, however, adequately address personnel scheduling and **resource leveling**, which is the process that a project manager uses to ensure that no team members are either underutilized or overscheduled.

Project monitoring and control

Project phase planning, estimating, and scheduling are completed before the project phase work actually begins. Once the project phase has begun, the project manager becomes a leader and the traditional management functions of directing and controlling come into play.

Directing project team personnel includes motivating, evaluating, rewarding, advising, appraising, correcting, guiding, and so on. Directing information systems personnel on an information system development project is not significantly different from directing any other personnel in any other type of work. The necessary skills and guidelines are discussed and described in all basic management textbooks, so we need not discuss them here.

Monitoring and control includes setting standards and ensuring that they are followed, keeping track of the activities and progress of team members, comparing actual progress against the plan, and verifying project milestones. To help insure the correctness, quality, and adherence to standards of the work produced by members of a project team, many project managers institute structured walk-throughs. A **structured walk-through** is a review of a project team member's work that is performed by other members of the team. Generally, systems analysts review the work of other systems analysts, and programmers review the work of other programmers. Occasionally, a project manager who is a systems analyst or programmer will participate in structured walk-throughs, but only in the role of systems analyst or programmer. Members of information systems department management, however, rarely attend structured walk-throughs. Thus, a structured walk-through is sometimes called a **peer review**. Structured walk-throughs can take place throughout the systems development life cycle; often, they are termed requirements reviews, design reviews, code reviews, or testing reviews, depending on the SDLC phase in which they occur.

Setting a schedule is one thing; following the schedule is another. Few plans are executed without encountering at least some problems or delays. By monitoring and controlling a project, the project manager strives to have enough knowledge to anticipate problems, prevent their occurrence, if possible, or at least minimize their impact, identify potential solutions, and select the best solution.

The better the original plan and schedule, the easier the job for the project manager to monitor and control the project. If concrete, verifiable milestones have been established, then the project manager has a simple task to determine if and when milestones are achieved. If sufficient milestones have been defined so that checkpoints occur frequently, then no problem can go undetected for long.

A project manager who uses PERT/CPM to schedule a project can use that same PERT/CPM network to monitor and control the project. As the project progresses, the project manager revises the PERT/CPM network to record actual times for completed activities and revised estimated times, if any, for activities not yet completed. A project manager will often focus his or her monitoring and control efforts on the activities along the critical path. Problems and delays along the critical path have the greatest potential for delaying or jeopardizing the project. Other activities, however, cannot be ignored. If some activity off the critical path takes too long, the path containing that activity could then become the new critical path.

Project reporting

embers of a project team must regularly report their progress to the project manager, and the project manager must regularly report project status and progress to the end users and management. For a project manager, therefore, project reporting involves both receiving and distributing status information.

■ Project status meetings

Most project managers elect to have regularly scheduled status meetings that all project team members attend. At these meetings, typically held weekly, each team member reviews the work accomplished to date and reports any potential or actual problems or schedule delays. Although the total team time spent reporting status might be less if the project manager met with each team member individually, most project managers believe that having all the team members involved in status meetings is worthwhile; team members can better appreciate how their work fits into the big picture if they are involved in team status meetings.

Even with team status meetings, the project manager should not expect team members to recognize all the potential problems at the first hint of trouble. One reason is that project team members do not know the project schedule as thoroughly as the project manager who developed it. Project team members also might not fully appreciate the interdependencies among the various activities. A final reason is the difficulty in assessing the progress of incomplete activities. Progress is often simply reported as a percentage of the allotted time; that is, if an activity is scheduled to take four weeks, and if after one week you ask the person assigned the activity how much of the activity has been completed, he or she will almost always report 25%. He or she might not recognize until the deadline is imminent that the activity will not meet its schedule.

Activities are rarely completed significantly ahead of schedule due to human nature. If an activity is scheduled to take four weeks, a person will probably take approximately four weeks to complete the activity even if that time allotment is excessive. For all these reasons, when receiving progress reports from team members, the project manager must attempt to evaluate and assess actual progress.

■ Project status reports

The project manager must regularly report to his or her immediate supervisor, the end user departments, and top-level management. Although a progress report might be given verbally to an immediate supervisor, the reports to the end users and upper management are usually written. Also, as mentioned earlier in the chapter, Gantt charts are often used in progress reports to pictorially illustrate project status.

Determining when a potential problem becomes an actual problem can be difficult. At what point should you inform management about potential project problems, such as cost overruns, schedule delays, and technical problems?

At one extreme is the overcautious project manager who alerts management to every potential snag and every slight delay. The danger with this tactic is that management might see the manager as the child who cried wolf and, consequently, dismiss or ignore potentially serious situations.

At the other extreme is the project manager who tries to handle all situations single-handedly and who does not alert management until a problem is serious. The very real danger with this approach is that management might not learn about a problem until there is little or nothing it can do to resolve the problem.

A project manager's best course of action lies somewhere between the two extremes, but probably closer to the first. If you are unsure of the consequences of a developing situation, you should err on the side of caution and warn management about the possibility of a problem. When you report the situation to management, you should also describe what you are doing to handle and monitor the situation. If you believe the situation is beyond your control, you might suggest actions that management could take to resolve the situation. Although management prefers that all projects be carried out perfectly and that no last-minute surprises surface, problems do occur on most projects. Be sure that you alert management early enough to any problem that jeopardizes the project or that requires management intervention. ■

Project management software

P ERT/CPM and other project management tools once required the power and memory of large mainframe computers. Today, many project management software systems are available for use on microcomputers.

Project management software can assist the project manager in almost all phases of management, including planning, estimating, scheduling, monitoring, and reporting. Although single-purpose software is available, more useful are the interactive project management systems that integrate multiple tools; the features most often included in such systems are PERT/CPM, Gantt charts, resource scheduling, resource leveling, project calendars, cost tracking, and cost-benefit analysis — all of which can be output automatically by the software as printed reports, screen displays, or graphical plots. Most CASE software packages also include a project management module with some of these same kinds of tools.

Figure 11-12 shows a PERT/CPM screen display produced by Microsoft Project, a typical microcomputer project management software package. The activities represented in Figure 11-12 are exactly the same as those used in Figure 11-10 on page 11.15 and Figure 11-11 on page 11.17. You will notice some significant differences in the resulting PERT/CPM chart, however. In traditional PERT/CPM charts, recall that events are shown as nodes and activities are shown as vectors. In contrast, all project management software PERT/CPM charts show activities as nodes; vectors serve to connect the paths between activity nodes and to indicate *activity* dependencies. Events, as such, are not explicitly indicated; therefore, dummy activities (indicated in traditional PERT/CPM charts as dashed vectors) to indicate *event* dependencies are not necessary.

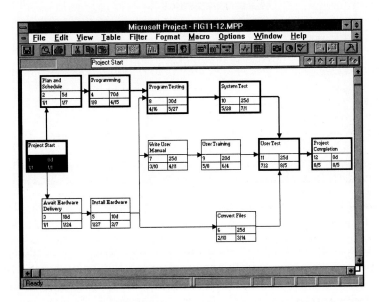

Figure 11-12 *A Microsoft Project version of the PERT/CPM chart. Activities are depicted as rectangular nodes, which contain the activity description, activity number, duration, start date, and end date. Activities along the critical path are shown with thicker borders.*

The traditional PERT/CPM chart shown in Figure 11-10b on page 11.15 and Figure 11-11 on page 11.17 included ten solid vectors, representing ten actual activities. In Figure 11-12, those same ten activities are shown as nodes 2 through 11.

Two additional activity nodes have been added to the PERT/CPM chart in Figure 11-12: node 1, which represents the start of the project, and node 12, which represents the end of the project. Those two nodes, which are essentially dummy activities with zero activity durations, serve to mark a single beginning point and a single end point for the project.

The activity nodes in Figure 11-12 are rectangular instead of circular; this is typical of PERT/CPM charts produced by project management software packages. Each node contains the activity description, the unique activity identification number, the activity duration, the start date (scheduled or actual), and the end date (scheduled or actual). The critical path is indicated by thicker borders outlining critical path activity nodes; in addition, the vectors along the critical path are also thicker.

Figure 11-13 is a screen display of a Gantt chart produced by Microsoft Project. This chart is essentially identical to the Gantt chart shown in Figure 11-10a on page 11.15. One minor difference is that the Gantt chart in Figure 11-10a showed elapsed time in days, whereas Figure 11-13 shows elapsed time in weeks. The only significant difference relates to the two additional activities (*Project Start* and *Project Completion*) that appear on the Figure 11-13 chart. Because both of these are dummy activities with zero duration, they are indicated on the Gantt chart by diamonds instead of rectangles.

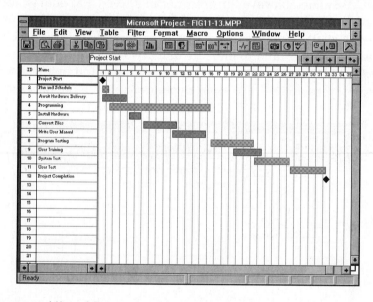

Figure 11-13 *A Microsoft Project version of the Gantt chart for the project depicted in Figure 11-12 on the previous page.*

Earlier in this chapter, we discussed the fact that project schedules, activity estimates, and personnel assignments are all interrelated; as a result, planning and estimating must be an iterative process. One significant advantage of integrated interactive project management software is that it allows the project manager to rapidly iterate among schedules, estimates, and resource assignments to develop a workable schedule.

Figure 11-14 lists some of the major project management products on the market today. Each year, new project management software products reach the market, while some older products are no longer sold.

PROJECT MANAGEMENT PRODUCT	VENDOR
Artemis Prestige	Lucas Management Systems
Flow Mark	IBM
Hyper Analyst	Bachman Information Systems, Inc.
MicroMan II Project	Poc-It Management Services, Inc.
MicroPlanner	Micro Planning International, Inc.
Project	Microsoft Corp.
Project Planner	Primavera Systems, Inc.
Project Scheduler	Scitor Corp.
Project Visualization System	Intelligenceware, Inc.
Project Workbench	Applied Business Technology Corp.
SAS System	SAS Institute, Inc.
SuperProject	Computer Associates International, Inc.
Texim Project	Welcom Software Technology
Time Line	Symantec Corp.

Figure 11-14 Some of the major project management software products and their vendors.

Software change control

Software change control, also called **configuration management**, is the process of managing and controlling requested changes to the system requirements document after the requirements have been accepted and frozen. As we discussed in Chapter 5, changes to an information system's requirements are inevitable; effective change control is, therefore, necessary for the successful development of an information system. The project coordinator instead of the project manager has the primary responsibility for change control, because requests for change most often are initiated by someone outside the information systems department.

One component of a change control process is a procedure for handling requests for change. The change control procedure must be formal enough so all changes are addressed, while non-bureaucratic enough so valid, required changes are handled promptly with minimal paperwork and impact to the project's progress. A procedure for processing requests for changes to an information system's requirements consists of the following four steps: complete a change request form, take initial action on the request, analyze the impact of the requested change, and determine the disposition of the requested change.

1. *Complete a change request form.* The person requesting the change completes a System Requirements Change Request form similar to the one shown in Figure 11-15 on the next page. On the form the requester describes in detail the changes he or she needs and the justification for the changes. The requester attaches helpful documents and pertinent information, such as new calculations, copies of government regulations, and memos from executives specifying new strategies and directions.

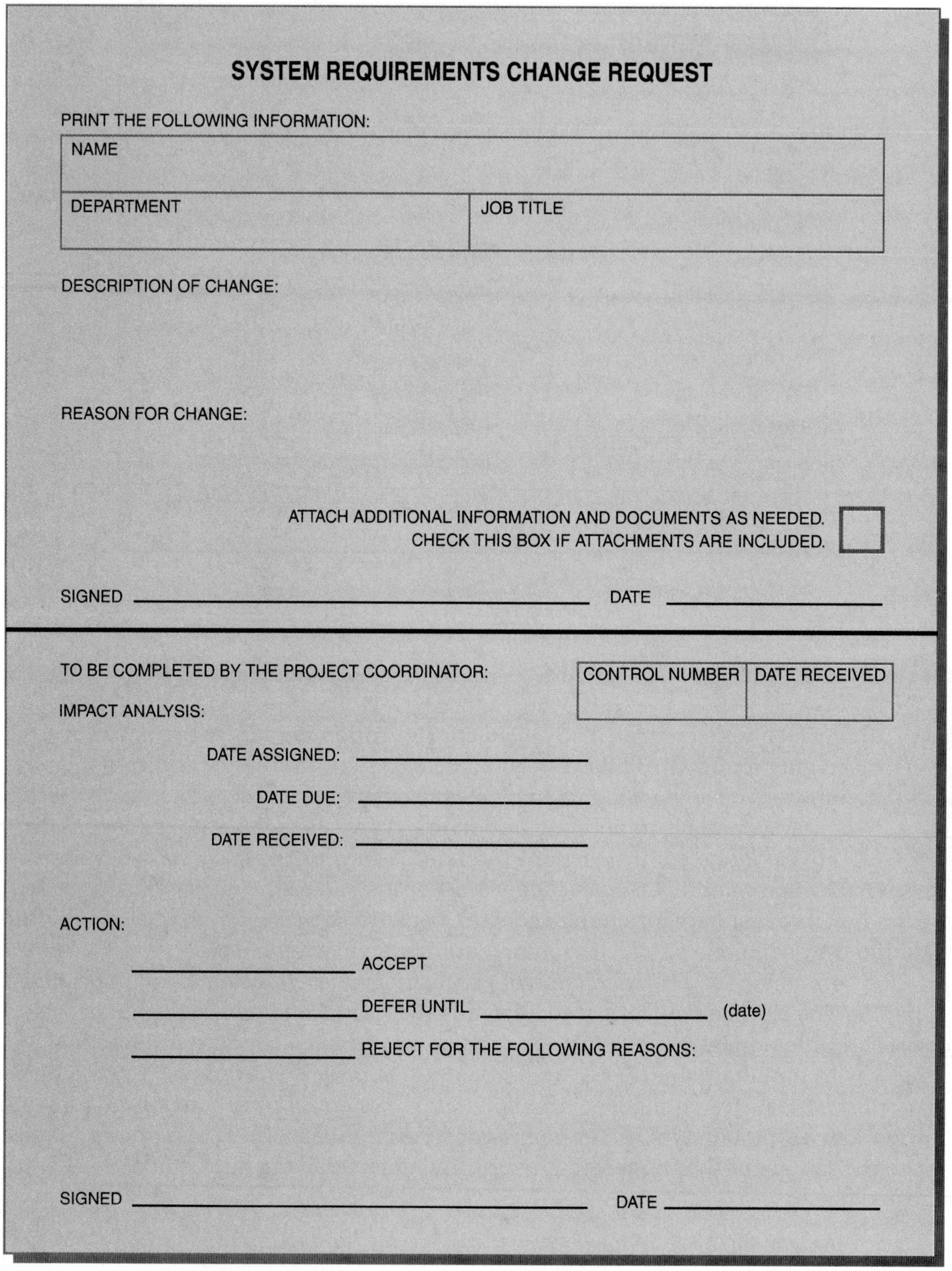

SYSTEM REQUIREMENTS CHANGE REQUEST

PRINT THE FOLLOWING INFORMATION:

NAME	
DEPARTMENT	JOB TITLE

DESCRIPTION OF CHANGE:

REASON FOR CHANGE:

ATTACH ADDITIONAL INFORMATION AND DOCUMENTS AS NEEDED.
CHECK THIS BOX IF ATTACHMENTS ARE INCLUDED. ☐

SIGNED _____ DATE _____

TO BE COMPLETED BY THE PROJECT COORDINATOR:

CONTROL NUMBER	DATE RECEIVED

IMPACT ANALYSIS:

DATE ASSIGNED: _____

DATE DUE: _____

DATE RECEIVED: _____

ACTION:

_____ ACCEPT

_____ DEFER UNTIL _____ (date)

_____ REJECT FOR THE FOLLOWING REASONS:

SIGNED _____ DATE _____

Figure 11-15 *A sample System Requirements Change Request form.*

2. *Take initial action on the request.* The project coordinator fills in a sequential control number and the date on the change request form, reviews the specific change, and determines if the change should be deferred to a later date, rejected for specific reasons, or investigated further. If the request is deferred or rejected, the project coordinator sends a copy of the request back to the requester. If the change is to be

investigated further, the request is then reviewed for impact by the project manager or a systems analyst.

3. *Analyze the impact of the requested change.* The project manager or a systems analyst must review the request and determine the impact of incorporating the change into the information system's requirements. The manager or analyst then prepares an impact analysis that describes the effect of the change on the information system's requirements and on costs and schedules. The analysis should address the impact of incorporating the change immediately versus incorporating the change after the currently configured information system has been implemented.

4. *Determine the disposition of the requested change.* Based on the impact analysis and the project coordinator's perspective, the change may be accepted and incorporated into the information system's requirements, deferred, or rejected. In each of these three cases, the project coordinator informs the requester of the action taken.

Why projects fail

An information system project is said to have failed if the resulting information system does not meet the end users' needs, if the costs exceed the budget, or if the deadline is not met. What are the typical causes of these different kinds of failures?

When the final information system is not acceptable to the end users, the likely causes include: unidentified requirements, inadequately defined scope, or imprecise targets, all of which result from shortcuts or sloppy work during systems analysis; poor design choices; insufficient testing or inadequate testing procedures; lack of appropriate change control; and unrealistic end user expectations.

Cost overruns most often result from unrealistic estimates that either were simply too optimistic or were based on incomplete definitions of work to be done, from poor monitoring of progress and inadequate reaction to early signs of problems, or from schedule delays due to unanticipated factors.

Overdue or late completion of projects most often results from a failure to recognize activity interdependencies, from confusing effort with progress, from poor monitoring and control of progress, from personality conflicts among the team members, or from turnover of project personnel.

In general, the failure of an information system is due to a failure in project management. If the project manager fails to properly plan, staff, organize, supervise, communicate, motivate, evaluate, direct, *and* control, then the project is certain to fail. Even when a project failure is in part the result of factors outside the project manager's control, then the project manager has failed if those factors were not recognized as soon as possible and handled appropriately.

When the project manager first recognizes that a project is in trouble, behind schedule, or out of control, what options are available? In general, the available alternatives fall into one of four classifications: trimming the project requirements, adding to the project resources, delaying the project deadline, and improving the quality of the project management.

Sometimes when a project experiences schedule delays or cost overruns, the information system can still be delivered on time and within budget if several less critical requirements are trimmed. In that case, the information system as originally delivered will satisfy only the most necessary requirements. The additional features can be added later, as a part of a maintenance/enhancement project; or, multiple releases of the system can be planned, each release adding more functionality to the information system.

If a project is in trouble because of a lack of resources or organizational support, management might be willing to give the project a *privileged* status that can result in faster turnaround times for computer executions, clerical support, end user attention, and management decisions. If there is more project work to do than people to do it, adding more people to the project team might help. Adding staff will, however, reduce the time necessary to complete the work only if the work to be done can be divided into separate tasks on which different people can work. If the project is jeopardized because the current team members are not adequately experienced or proficient in the required technology, you might consider supplementing the project team with expert temporary help, such as consultants, contract programmers or analysts, or service bureau personnel. Keep in mind, however, that adding new staff means that more time is required for training and for team member interactions and communication. At some point, adding more people to a project will actually increase the time necessary to complete the project! Adding new staff also means adding to the costs, with the potential for going over the budgeted project costs.

The action most often taken when a project is behind schedule is to add more time to the schedule. This is an alternative only if the original target date is not an absolute deadline that must be met and if extending the target date will not incur unacceptably excessive costs.

When a project is in trouble for whatever reason, the project manager must try to improve the quality of his or her project management to get the project back under control and to keep it under control. The project manager must monitor more closely all future activities to prevent a recurrence of the problem. ∎

Cost considerations

Throughout the entire systems development life cycle, project managers and systems analysts must be concerned with costs. Estimates of projected costs and benefits must be determined at the end of each SDLC phase as input to the end-of-phase management decision. Each end-of-phase report must also include an accounting of all the project costs incurred to that point. Understanding the nature of costs enables you more accurately to meet two requirements: estimating anticipated costs and identifying actual costs.

■ Cost classifications

Costs can be classified as tangible or intangible, direct or indirect, and fixed or variable. **Tangible costs** are costs for which you can determine a specific dollar amount. Examples of tangible costs include employee salaries, hardware and software purchases, and office supplies. In contrast, **intangible costs** are costs whose dollar amount cannot be accurately determined. The costs of customer dissatisfaction, lowered employee morale, and reduced information availability are examples of intangible costs. Most of the costs associated with the development of an information system are tangible costs.

Direct costs are costs that can be directly associated with the development of a specific information system. Examples of direct costs include the salaries of project team members and the purchase of hardware to be used only with the new system. In contrast, **indirect costs** cannot be specifically attributed to the development of a particular information system. The salaries of computer operators, the monthly rental for a copy machine, and the costs of air conditioning and insurance are all examples of indirect costs. Indirect costs are also called **overhead expenses**.

Fixed costs are costs that are relatively constant and that do not depend on a level of activity or effort. Many fixed costs recur regularly, such as employee salaries and hardware rental charges; other fixed costs are one-time-only costs, such as software purchases. **Variable costs** are costs that vary in proportion to a level of activity. The costs of computer printer paper and other computer supplies, and the costs of employee overtime wages are examples of variable costs.

■ Information systems department chargeout methods

As an information system is being developed, the information systems department incurs costs that can be directly attributed to the developing system. The salaries of project team members and the purchase of hardware, software, and supplies to be used with only the new system are examples of direct development costs. After a new information system goes into operation, some direct costs might also be incurred; system-specific hardware and software lease charges and supplies are examples of direct operational costs. When you determine the costs associated with a proposed or developing new system, you will usually find such direct costs to be relatively easy to identify and predict.

Many costs incurred within the information systems department cannot be directly attributed to a specific information system or end user group. These indirect information systems department costs can include general hardware and software purchase or lease expenses; facility maintenance expenses, such as air conditioning, heating, security, rent, and insurance; general supplies; and the salaries of operations, technical support, and information center personnel.

A **chargeout method** is a technique used to bill the end users for the indirect costs of running the information systems department. Depending on the particular chargeout method you use in your organization, estimating and determining indirect costs can be relatively easy or quite difficult. Most organizations use one of four chargeout methods: no charge, a fixed charge, a variable charge based on resource usage, or a variable charge based on volumes.

1. *No charge.* Some organizations treat indirect information systems department costs as a necessary cost of doing business. The services of the information systems department are seen as benefiting the entire organization. Thus, the costs are treated the same way as all other general organizational costs and are not charged to any other departments. In this case, the information systems department is a **cost center**, which is not expected to make a profit or break even. In a few organizations, an information systems department that is considered a cost center does not charge out even its direct costs.

2. *Fixed charge.* The indirect information systems costs are divided among all the other departments in the organization, each of which is assessed a fixed monthly charge. The monthly charge might be the same for all departments, or the charge might be based on a relatively constant factor, such as department size or the number of information systems. In either case, a particular department's charges do not vary from month

to month. For this method, all indirect costs are charged out, and the information systems department is considered to be a profit center. A **profit center** is a department that is expected to make a profit or, at worst, break even.

3. *Variable charge based on resource usage.* **Resource allocation** is the charging of indirect costs based on the resources used by an information system. The allocation might be based on connect time, CPU time, the number of disk accesses, the number of tape mounts, the number of lines printed, total disk space used, or a combination of these or other factors. **Connect time** is the total time that elapses while an information system executes on a computer, and **CPU time** is the time that an information system is actually executing and, therefore, using the central processing unit.

   The amount a particular department is charged will vary from month to month, depending not only on that department's resource usage, but also on the total resource usage. The information systems department is considered to be a profit center when an organization uses the resource allocation method.

4. *Variable charge based on volumes.* The indirect information systems department costs are allocated to other departments based on user-oriented volumes, such as the number of transactions processed or the number of master file records. As is true with resource allocation, a department's share of the costs will vary from month to month, depending on both its own volumes and the total organizational volumes. Here, too, the information systems department is considered to be a profit center.

Benefit considerations

Recognizing and understanding the various classifications of benefits is helpful when you want to identify all the benefits of an information systems project. Like costs, benefits can be classified as tangible or intangible, fixed or variable, and direct or indirect. Another useful benefit classification relates to the source of the benefit: positive benefits versus cost-avoidance benefits. **Positive benefits** are those that increase revenues, improve services to customers or employees, or otherwise contribute to the organization or its image as a direct result of the performance of the information system. Examples of positive benefits include improved information availability, greater flexibility, faster service to customers, higher employee morale, increased sales, support for new products or capabilities, and better inventory management.

Frequently, an information systems project is initiated in order to eliminate the high costs of a current operation. The new system is expected to provide significant **cost-avoidance benefits**. Examples of cost-avoidance benefits include reduced clerical cost and reduced overtime wages. In general, a new information system will achieve cost-avoidance benefits equal to all the operating costs of the system that it replaces.

Cost-avoidance benefits are as important and as real as positive benefits. You must consider both types of benefits when you perform cost-benefit analyses.

Cost-benefit analysis

Cost-benefit analysis is the process of comparing the anticipated costs of an information system to its anticipated benefits. Cost-benefit analyses are performed *throughout* the systems development life cycle to determine the economic feasibility of an information system project, to determine if a particular project solution is economically viable, and to compare and rank alternative viable solutions. Many strategies exist for cost-benefit analyses, but we will discuss only three of the most common: payback analysis, return on investment analysis, and present value analysis.

■ Payback analysis

When you plot the costs associated with an information system year by year over its entire potential lifetime, you typically produce a curve shaped like the one shown in Figure 11-16. The curve is high at the beginning, reflecting all the costs associated with developing the system. When the system becomes operational, the costs rapidly decrease at first and then remain relatively low for some number of years. Eventually, as the system requires more and more maintenance, costs begin to increase rapidly. The years between the beginning of systems operation and a point when operational costs are rapidly increasing are called the **economically useful life** of the system.

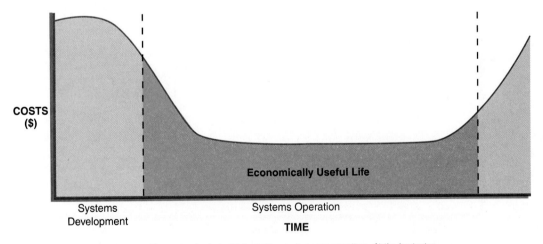

COSTS ($)

Economically Useful Life

Systems Development

Systems Operation

TIME

Figure 11-16 *The costs of a typical information system vary over time. At the beginning, system costs are high due to the high development costs. Costs are then lower during systems operation. System maintenance costs will eventually begin to increase until the system at some point reaches the end of its economically useful life. The area between the two dashed lines represents the economically useful life of the information system.*

When you plot the benefits provided by an information system against time, the resulting curve typically resembles the one seen in Figure 11-17 on the next page. Benefits begin to appear shortly after the system becomes operational, increase rapidly for a time, and then level off.

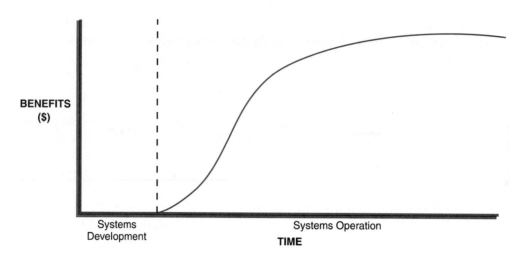

Figure 11-17 *The benefits provided by an information system vary with time. No benefits are realized before the system becomes operational. Once it is operational, benefits typically increase rapidly at first, and then level off.*

To perform payback analysis, you determine the **payback period**, which is the amount of time that passes before the accumulated benefits of an information system equal the accumulated costs of developing and operating that system. In Figure 11-18, we have plotted the cost and benefit curves on the same graph; the dashed line indicates the payback period. Notice that the payback period does not correspond to the point when *current* benefits equal *current* costs, which occurs where the two curves cross. The payback period relates to *accumulated* costs and benefits. (Mathematically, the payback period corresponds to that time for which the areas under the two curves are equal.)

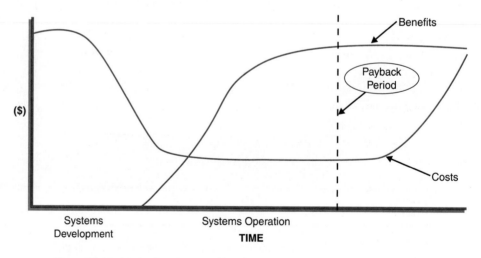

Figure 11-18 *A system's cost curve and benefit curve plotted on the same graph. The dashed line indicates the payback period, when the accumulated benefits equal the accumulated costs.*

Figure 11-19 shows two cost-benefit tables. The tables detail the anticipated annual costs, cumulative costs, annual benefits, and cumulative benefits for two information systems projects. Year 0 (zero) corresponds to the year in which systems development begins. The development of Project A takes less than one year, and, thus, some benefits are realized in year 0; the systems development for Project B requires more than one year, so the benefits do not begin until some time in year 1.

PROJECT A:

YEAR	COSTS	CUMULATIVE COSTS	BENEFITS	CUMULATIVE BENEFITS
0	60,000	60,000	3,000	3,000
1	17,000	77,000	28,000	31,000
2	18,500	95,500	31,000	62,000
3	19,200	114,700	34,000	96,000
4	21,000	135,700	36,000	132,000
5	22,000	157,700	39,000	171,000
6	23,300	181,000	42,000	213,000

Payback period is approximately 4.2 years

PROJECT B:

YEAR	COSTS	CUMULATIVE COSTS	BENEFITS	CUMULATIVE BENEFITS
0	80,000	80,000	-----	-----
1	40,000	120,000	6,000	6,000
2	25,000	145,000	26,000	32,000
3	22,000	167,000	54,000	86,000
4	24,000	191,000	70,000	156,000
5	26,500	217,500	82,000	238,000
6	30,000	247,500	92,000	330,000

Payback period is approximately 4.7 years

Figure 11-19 *Payback analysis for two information systems projects.*

At the end of year 4 for Project A, the cumulative costs are $135,700, which slightly exceeds the $132,000 cumulative benefits through that year. By the end of year 5, however, the $171,000 cumulative benefits far exceed the cumulative costs, which are $157,700. At some point in time, between the end of year 4 and the end of year 5, closer to the beginning of year 5, the accumulated costs and benefits were equal. The payback period for Project A is, therefore, approximately 4.2 years. By a similar process, the payback period for Project B is determined to be approximately 4.7 years.

Payback analysis is often criticized because it places all the emphasis on the earlier costs and benefits, ignoring all the benefits received after the payback period. Even if the benefits for Project B in year 6 were as incredibly high as $500,000, the payback period for that project would still be 4.7 years. In defense of payback analysis, the earlier cost and benefit predictions are more certain than are later predictions; in general, the further into the future you must extend your projections, the more uncertain the values. Payback analysis, then, could be said to use the best of your cost and benefit estimates.

Payback analysis is rarely used to compare or rank projects because later benefits are ignored. You would never decide that Project A is better than Project B simply because the payback period for A is less than that for B; considering all the costs and all the benefits when comparing projects makes more sense.

Payback analysis does have it usefulness, however. Many business organizations establish a minimum payback period for projects to be undertaken. If company policy requires a project to begin paying for itself within five years, for example, then both the projects in Figure 11-19 on the previous page would be considered economically feasible; neither project would meet a three-year payback criterion, however.

■ Return on investment analysis

Return on investment (ROI) is a percentage rate that measures profitability by relating the estimated total net benefits (return) received from a project to the estimated total costs (investment) of the project. ROI is calculated as follows:

```
ROI = (total benefits - total costs) / total costs
```

Return on investment analysis considers the costs and benefits for a longer time span than does payback analysis. In theory, you could compute the ROI of a proposed information system for the entire expected life of the system or at least for its useful economic life. In practice, however, the total costs and benefits for a somewhat shorter period of time, typically five to seven years, are used in an ROI calculation, thus using only the more certain future cost and benefit estimates.

The tables in Figure 11-19 on the previous page included cost and benefit predictions through six years of operation for each of two systems, which might or might not represent the entire economically useful life of those systems. In Figure 11-20, an ROI for six years of operation is calculated for each information system. The ROI for Project A is 17.7%; the ROI for Project B is 33.3%.

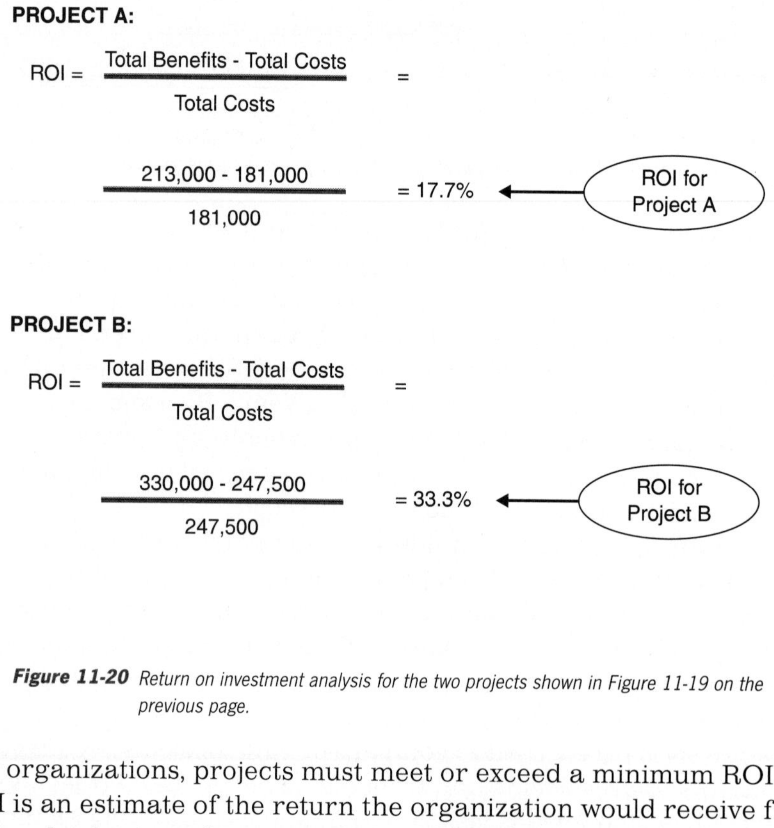

PROJECT A:

$$ROI = \frac{\text{Total Benefits - Total Costs}}{\text{Total Costs}} =$$

$$\frac{213,000 - 181,000}{181,000} = 17.7\% \longleftarrow \text{ROI for Project A}$$

PROJECT B:

$$ROI = \frac{\text{Total Benefits - Total Costs}}{\text{Total Costs}} =$$

$$\frac{330,000 - 247,500}{247,500} = 33.3\% \longleftarrow \text{ROI for Project B}$$

Figure 11-20 *Return on investment analysis for the two projects shown in Figure 11-19 on the previous page.*

In many organizations, projects must meet or exceed a minimum ROI. This minimum ROI is an estimate of the return the organization would receive from investing its money in standard external opportunities, such as stocks and treasury bills. If company policy requires a minimum ROI of 15%, for example, then both Projects A and B would meet the criterion.

You can also use ROIs for ranking projects. If Projects A and B represent two different proposed solutions for a single information systems project, then the solution represented by Project B would be considered better than the Project A solution. If Projects A and B represent two different information systems projects, and if the organization has sufficient resources to do only one of the two projects, then Project B would be considered the better choice.

Critics of return on investment analysis raise two points. First, an ROI is only an *average* rate of return for the total period. The annual return rates can vary considerably. Two projects with equal ROIs might not be equally desirable if the benefits of one occur significantly earlier than the benefits of the other; in other words, return on investment analysis, unlike payback analysis, ignores the timing of the costs and benefits. The second criticism of return on investment analysis, one that applies to payback analysis as well, is that ROI ignores the time value of money, which is the basis for the last strategy for cost-benefit analysis that we will examine.

■ Present value analysis

A dollar today is worth more than a dollar one year from now. If you have $1 today, you could invest that dollar and receive interest on it, and, thus, have more than $1 a year from now. For example, if you received 8% interest for the year, after one year you have $1.08; in that case, $1 today is worth $1.08 a year from now. At that same interest rate, $1 a year from now is worth somewhat less than 93 cents today, because that 93 cents could be invested at 8% and grow to $1 in a year. Thus, money one year from now is worth less than the same amount today. This phenomenon is known as the **time value of money**, and it forms the basis for present value analysis.

The **present value** of a future dollar is the amount of money that, when invested today at some specified interest rate, would grow to exactly one dollar at that point in the future. That specified interest rate is called the **discount rate**, or **opportunity cost**. In present value analysis, an organization uses a discount rate that represents an acceptable return on its investments, which is one that equals the return available from other investments, such as stocks, bonds, or money market accounts.

The present value (PV) of a dollar n years from now at a discount rate of i is calculated by the following formula:

$$PV = 1 / (1 + i)^n$$

Thus the present value of $1 one year from now at 8% is:

$$PV = 1 / (1 + .08)^1 = \$0.926$$

Similarly, the present value of $1 five years from now at 12% is:

$$PV = 1 / (1 + .12)^5 = \$0.567$$

As an aid for present value analysis, present value factors for various interest rates and various numbers of years are calculated and printed in tables called present value tables. Figure 11-21 on the next page shows a portion of a present value table; values for ten years and five discount rates are included. You can find tables that cover more discount rates for longer periods in most accounting and finance textbooks. To use a present value table, you locate the value in the column representing the appropriate discount rate and in the row for the appropriate number of years. To determine the present value of $1 at 12% for five years, for example, you look down the column headed by 12% until you reach the row representing 5 years; the table value is 0.567, which is exactly the same value we just calculated. To determine the present value of three thousand dollars, five years in the future at a discount rate of 12%, you simply multiply the present value factor from the table by the dollar amount; that is, $PV = \$3,000 \times 0.567 = \$1,701$.

PERIODS	6%	8%	10%	12%	14%
1	0.943	0.926	0.909	0.893	0.877
2	0.890	0.857	0.826	0.797	0.769
3	0.840	0.794	0.751	0.712	0.675
4	0.792	0.735	0.683	0.636	0.592
5	0.747	0.681	0.621	0.567	0.519
6	0.705	0.630	0.564	0.507	0.456
7	0.665	0.583	0.513	0.452	0.400
8	0.627	0.540	0.467	0.404	0.351
9	0.592	0.500	0.424	0.361	0.308
10	0.558	0.463	0.386	0.322	0.270

Figure 11-21 *Portion of a present value table. Values in the table are calculated as $1/(1+i)^n$ where i = interest rate and n = number of periods.*

To perform present value analysis on a project, you first multiply each of the projected annual benefits and costs by the appropriate present value factor; then, you sum all the benefit present values and also all the cost present values. You then calculate the **net present value** of the project, which is the total present value of the benefits minus the total present value of the costs. Figure 11-22 shows the calculation of net present value for each of our two example projects.

Any project with a positive net present value is an economically worthwhile undertaking; if the net present value is positive, then investing in the project results in a larger monetary return than could be achieved by annually investing and reinvesting amounts of money equivalent to the annual costs at an interest rate equal to the discount rate. Both of the example projects of Figure 11-22 have positive net present values and are, therefore, economically worthwhile.

PROJECT A: **PRESENT VALUE ANALYSIS**

	Year 0	Year 1	Year 2	Year 3	Year 4	Year 5	Year 6	Total
Benefits:	3,000	28,000	31,000	34,000	36,000	39,000	42,000	
Present Value Factor (12%):	1.000	0.893	0.797	0.712	0.636	0.567	0.507	
Present Value:	3,000	25,004	24,707	24,208	22,896	22,113	21,294	143,222
Costs:	60,000	17,000	18,500	19,200	21,000	22,000	23,300	
Present Value Factor (12%):	1,000	0.893	0.797	0.712	0.636	0.567	0.507	
Present Value:	60,000	15,181	14,745	13,670	13,356	12,474	11,813	141,239
Net Present Value:							net present value of Project A ➔	$1,983

Figure 11-22 *Present value analysis for the two information systems projects shown in Figure 11-19 on page 11.31.*

PROJECT B: **PRESENT VALUE ANALYSIS**

	Year 0	Year 1	Year 2	Year 3	Year 4	Year 5	Year 6	Total
Benefits:	—	6,000	26,000	54,000	70,000	82,000	92,000	
Present Value Factor (12%):	—	0.893	0.797	0.712	0.636	0.567	0.507	
Present Value:	—	5,358	20,722	38,448	44,520	46,494	46,644	202,186
Costs:	80,000	40,000	25,000	22,000	24,000	26,500	30,000	
Present Value Factor (12%):	1.000	0.893	0.797	0.712	0.636	0.567	0.507	
Present Value:	80,000	35,720	19,925	15,664	15,264	15,026	15,210	196,809
Net Present Value:						net present value of Project B	→	$5,377

Figure 11-22 (continued)

Net present values are also appropriate for comparing and ranking projects. The project with the highest net present value is the best investment. In the Figure 11-22 example, Project B is a better investment than Project A because it has a higher net present value.

All the criticisms applied to payback analysis and return on investment analysis are answered by present value analysis. Present value analysis considers all the costs and benefits, not just the earlier values. At the same time, the timing of costs and benefits is taken into account by the present value factors; the factors are larger for the earlier years, therefore giving more weight to earlier costs and benefits. Similarly, those earlier estimates, about which you are more certain, weigh more heavily than do the later, less certain estimates. Finally, present value analysis is based on and does consider the time value of money.

CHAPTER CASE STUDY 11

James Tool Company — Project Management and Costs

Howard Coswell, a programmer/analyst at James Tool Company, has been working on a union system that will interface with and supplement the payroll package recently purchased from Lennox Software Solutions. The systems flowchart Coswell has prepared for the union system is shown in Figure 11-23.

Coswell has completed the design of the union system, so he can now begin planning for the systems development phase. Coswell knows that he must determine programming time estimates for all the union system programs as one of his first steps in phase planning. The union system will require four new programs: a union deduction extract program, an employee union dues program, a modify/view union program, and a pay union dues program. The union deduction extract program will execute on the mainframe computer; the other three programs will run on the personal computer in the union relations department.

Coswell has never prepared time estimates. Consequently, when he encounters Clyde Harland in the hallway, Coswell asks for advice on determining estimates. Harland, the manager of systems and programming at James Tool Company, gives Coswell a copy of the department's documentation of a quantitative method for determining programming time estimates. That method, which is based on program files, program functions, and programmer experience, is similar to the method we described in this chapter. Harland suggests that Coswell use that method to determine estimates for each of the programs. Then, Harland offers to check his history files for programming times for comparable systems and suggests that they meet the following afternoon to discuss the time estimates.

Because he does not know who will be doing the actual programming, Coswell decides to develop two estimates for each of the programs. One estimate will represent the time for a programmer/analyst or senior analyst to complete the task; the second estimate, which is double the first, will represent the time necessary for a programmer to write the program.

The union deduction extract program will read the employee master database file and create the sequential union deduction file. Coswell's calculation of programming time estimates for this program is shown in Figure 11-204 on page 11.38.

The employee union dues program will process employee union dues changes in an online mode. One data entry screen will allow the end users to enter data about employees joining, changing, or leaving unions. To validate the data, the employee union dues program must access the union file, which is a direct file. Valid employee union dues changes are then output to a sequential union deduction change file, which is uploaded weekly to the payroll system on the mainframe computer. Figure 11-25 on page 11.38 shows Coswell's calculation of the two programming time estimates for the employee union dues program.

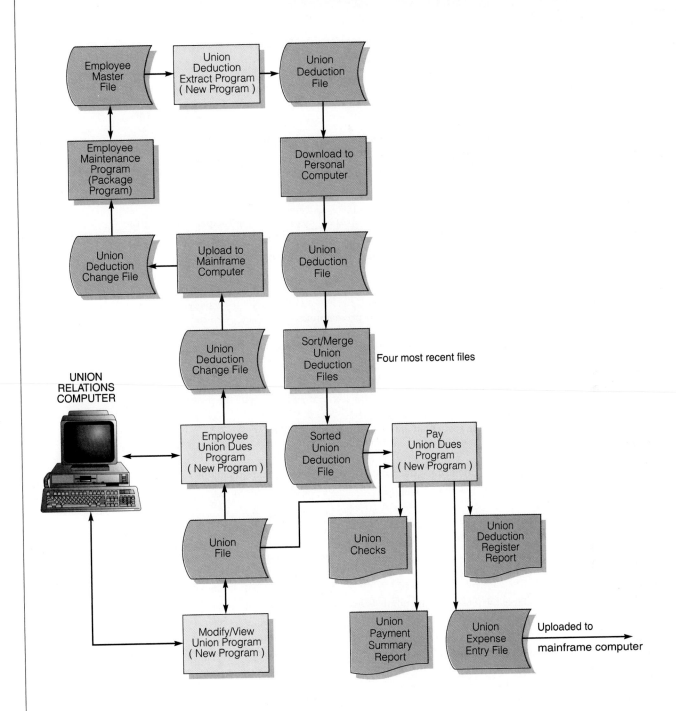

Figure 11-23 The systems flowchart for the James Tool Company union system.

1. Using Table 1, determine the points based on the files used by the program.

Access the employee master database file	2.0
Create the sequential union deduction file	0.5
Total:	2.5

2. Using Table 2, determine the points based on the program's functions.

Total:	0.0

3. Using Table 3, determine the points based on the programmer's experience.

Programmer position	1.0

4. Calculate total program points by adding the points based on the files used (step 1) to the points based on the program's functions (step 2).

$$2.5 + 0.0 \ = 2.5$$

5. Multiply the total program points (step 4) by the programmer's experience (step 3).

$$2.5 \times 1.0 \ = 2.5$$

6. Determine the estimated person-days by dividing the result of step 5 by the productivity factor of 60%.

2.5/.60	= 4.2 person-days
Programmer estimate	= 4.2 days
Programmer/analyst or senior programmer estimate	= 2.1 days

Figure 11-24 *Time estimate calculations for the union deduction extract program.*

1. Using Table 1, determine the points based on the files used by the program.

Access the direct union file	1.0
Create the sequential union deduction change file	0.5
Display one data entry screen	1.0
Total:	2.5

2. Using Table 2, determine the points based on the program's functions.

Validate union dues changes	1.0
Total:	1.0

3. Using Table 3, determine the points based on the programmer's experience.

Programmer position	1.0

4. Calculate total program points by adding the points based on the files used (step 1) to the points based on the program's functions (step 2).

$$2.5 + 1.0 \ = 3.5$$

5. Multiply the total program points (step 4) by the programmer's experience (step 3).

$$3.5 \times 1.0 \ = 3.5$$

6. Determine the estimated person-days by dividing the result of step 5 by the productivity factor of 60%.

3.5/.60	= 5.8 person-days
Programmer estimate	= 5.8 days
Programmer/analyst or senior programmer estimate	= 2.9 days

Figure 11-25 *Time estimate calculations for the employee union dues program.*

The modify/view union program, which will also execute online, validates union data entered by end users and updates the union file. A single data entry screen is used for adding a new union, changing existing union data, deleting a union, and viewing union data. The time estimate calculations for programming the modify/view union program are shown in Figure 11-26.

1. Using Table 1, determine the points based on the files used by the program.

    Access the direct union file   1.0
    Display one data entry screen   <u>1.0</u>
                                       Total: 2.0

2. Using Table 2, determine the points based on the program's functions.

    Validate union dues changes   1.0
    Update the union file   <u>2.0</u>
                                       Total: 3.0

3. Using Table 3, determine the points based on the programmer's experience.

    Programmer position   1.0

4. Calculate total program points by adding the points based on the files used (step 1) to the points based on the program's functions (step 2).

    2.0 + 3.0   = 5.0

5. Multiply the total program points (step 4) by the programmer's experience (step 3).

    5.0 x 1.0   = 5.0

6. Determine the estimated person-days by dividing the result of step 5 by the productivity factor of 60%.

    5.0/.60   = 8.3 person-days

    Programmer estimate   = 8.3 days
    Programmer/analyst or senior programmer estimate   = 4.2 days

Figure 11-26 *Time estimate calculations for the modify/view union program.*

The pay union dues program will be a batch program that reads the union file and a merged and sorted sequential union deduction file and creates four outputs: three reports and one disk file. Two of the reports, the union deduction register and the union payment summary, are simple reports with one output line per detail. Outputting the union checks, however, is slightly more complicated because each check includes multiple lines. The output disk file is the sequential union expense entry file. Time estimate calculations for the pay union dues program are shown in Figure 11-27.

1. Using Table 1, determine the points based on the files used by the program.

    Access the sequential union deduction file   0.5
    Access the direct union file   1.0
    Create the union deduction register report   0.5
    Create the union payment summary report   0.5
    Create the union dues checks (multiple lines)   1.0
    Create the sequential union expense entry file   <u>0.5</u>
                                       Total: 4.0

2. Using Table 2, determine the points based on the program's functions.

                                       Total: 0.0

3. Using Table 3, determine the points based on the programmer's experience.

    Programmer position   1.0

4. Calculate total program points by adding the points based on the files used (step 1) to the points based on the program's functions (step 2).

    4.0 + 0.0   = 4.0

5. Multiply the total program points (step 4) by the programmer's experience (step 3).

    4.0 x 1.0   = 4.0

6. Determine the estimated person-days by dividing the result of step 5 by the productivity factor of 60%.

    4.0/.60   = 6.7 person-days

    Programmer estimate   = 6.7 days
    Programmer/analyst or senior programmer estimate   = 3.4 days

Figure 11-27 *Time estimate calculations for the pay union dues program.*

While checking his work, Howard Coswell realized that he had completely forgotten about the program to control all the union processing on the union relations department's personal computer. That program will present a single process-control screen and will, depending on the option the end user chooses, shift control to one of the other three local programs, direct the actual printing of a previously created report, delete all the union deduction files, or exit. Coswell then calculated time estimates for the union system control program; these estimates are shown in Figure 11-28.

1. Using Table 1, determine the points based on the files used by the program.
   Display one menu option screen   1.0
                                                      Total: 1.0

2. Using Table 2, determine the points based on the program's functions.
                                                      Total: 0.0

3. Using Table 3, determine the points based on the programmer's experience.
   Programmer position   1.0

4. Calculate total program points by adding the points based on the files used (step 1) to the points based on the program's functions (step 2).
                                         1.0 + 0.0   = 1.0

5. Multiply the total program points (step 4) by the programmer's experience (step 3).
                                         1.0 x 1.0   = 1.0

6. Determine the estimated person-days by dividing the result of step 5 by the productivity factor of 60%.
                                         1.0/.60   = 1.7 person-days

   Programmer estimate   = 1.7 days
   Programmer/analyst or senior programmer estimate   = 0.8 days

Figure 11-28 *Time estimate calculations for the union system control program.*

Coswell now has the time estimates for each of the five union system programs. He is very curious to learn how these calculated time estimates compare to actual times for similar programs. The following afternoon, Harland meets with Coswell and tells him that his search for actual time data from similar systems has been successful. "But first," Harland says, "show me the estimates you've come up with."

"I calculated an estimate of four days for a programmer to write the mainframe extraction program," Coswell replies. "Do you have data for a similar program?"

Harland points out that the new payroll system has an operating environment completely different from those they have previously encountered at James Tool Company. "Basing estimates on experience we have gained in totally different environments is never a good idea, so we cannot use any of my historical data for this program's estimate," Harland explains. "You'll have to base your final estimate on the calculations you've made. But I do have one suggestion. Writing the first program in a new environment can be tricky. Unanticipated complications have a way of popping up. I recommend that you increase your estimates for the extraction program, just to be safe."

"The rest of the programs, however, will operate in an environment we are familiar with, using direct and sequential files on a personal computer," Harland continues. "What estimates do you have for the next program?"

Coswell reports that his estimate for the employee union dues program is 6 programmer days. Harland finds three comparable programs from the past; these programs had required 4.5, 4.8, and 5 days to complete. "Your calculated estimate is definitely in the same ballpark," says Harland. "And let me anticipate and answer your next question: whenever you have actual experience for a similar program, system, and environment, it is best to base your estimates on that experience rather than use general-purpose formulas."

Coswell and Harland continue the process of comparing actual times to the estimates calculated for the other three programs. In two of the cases, the historical data leads Coswell to increase his estimates; in the third case, historical experience suggests an estimate slightly less than the calculated estimate. Coswell's final programming time estimates for all five programs are summarized in Figure 11-29.

Programming Time Estimates

PROGRAM	SENIOR PROGRAMMER, PROGRAMMER/ANALYST	PROGRAMMER
Union Deduction Extract Program	3.0 days	6.0 days
Employee Union Dues Program	2.5 days	5.0 days
Modify/View Union Program	5.0 days	10.0 days
Pay Union Dues Program	3.0 days	6.0 days
Union System Control Program	1.0 days	2.0 days

Figure 11-29 *The final programming time estimates for the James Tool Company union system.*

Summary

This chapter covered two major topics: project management and the determination and evaluation of project costs and benefits.

Project management, the goal of which is to produce an acceptable information system within a specified time and budget, is a process that continues throughout the systems development life cycle. Most project management duties fall to the project manager, who is the member of the information systems department responsible for coordinating that department's development projects. The project manager's major duties include planning, estimating, scheduling, monitoring and controlling, and reporting.

Project planning takes place at both the beginning and the end of every project phase. At the beginning of a phase, the project manager identifies all the necessary phase activities, along with the events that mark the start or completion of the activities. The project manager then estimates the time that will be required to complete each activity; activity time can depend on the project size, the abilities of the person performing the activity, end user and management commitment, and project priority. One of three methods is often used for estimating programming activities: a quantitative method that considers program files, program functions, and programmer experience; the experience method, which considers actual times required for similar activities; or the constraint method, which varies the project requirements to fit a fixed limit on time, money, or personnel.

The first step in project scheduling is to determine activity dependencies; once this is done, the project manager can determine the order for performing activities and can establish start and end times for the activities. Because project scheduling is not independent of activity time estimates and personnel assignments, the project manager must often iterate between these functions until he or she develops a satisfactory schedule.

Project managers use Gantt charts, which are bar charts of activities versus time, to graphically illustrate project schedules and activity progress. PERT/CPM charts graphically represent activities and events as a network. PERT/CPM charts explicitly illustrate activity dependencies and can be used to determine earliest and latest completion times and slack times for each event, from which the critical path can be determined. PERT/CPM charts are more useful than Gantt charts for monitoring progress, but Gantt charts are better for reporting progress to management and end users.

Project monitoring and control includes ensuring the quality of the work performed, checking activity progress, and comparing progress against the plan by verifying the completion of events. Structured walk-throughs, in which project team members review each other's work, help ensure that the team's work is consistent, correct, and of high quality.

Most project managers hold weekly project status meetings with all team members attending. Project managers must also regularly report progress and problems to their supervisors, the end users, and upper management.

Project managers can choose from a wide variety of helpful project management software packages. Such packages usually include Gantt charting, PERT/CPM techniques, personnel scheduling, resource leveling, cost tracking, and cost-benefit analyses.

The project coordinator handles project administration and serves as a liaison between the end users and the information systems department. One of the project coordinator's major responsibilities is software change control, or configuration management, which involves managing and controlling change to the information system's requirements. The four components of a typical change control procedure are the completion of a formal request for change; an initial determination on the request; an analysis, if necessary, of the impact of the requested change; and a final decision on the request.

Costs can be classified as tangible or intangible, direct or indirect, and fixed or variable. The same classifications apply to benefits; in addition, benefits can be classified as either positive benefits, resulting directly from the new information system, or as cost-avoidance benefits, which result from replacing the old system.

Indirect information systems department costs are often charged to other departments with a chargeout method that assesses either a fixed monthly charge or a variable charge computed on the basis of resource usage or volumes; those information systems departments that operate as cost centers do not charge out their indirect costs.

Cost-benefit analysis is the process of comparing the expected costs of an information system to its expected benefits. We considered three techniques for performing a cost-benefit analysis. To perform payback analysis, you determine the payback period, which is the time that must pass before the accumulated benefits of a system equal the accumulated costs. With return on investment analysis, you compute an ROI, which is equal to the net benefits divided by the total cost. Payback analysis ignores all costs and benefits that occur after the payback period, whereas return on investment analysis completely ignores the timing of costs and benefits. Both techniques ignore the time value of money. The third cost-benefit technique we considered was present value analysis. The present value of a future amount is the money you would need to invest today to achieve that future amount in the given period of time. The net present value of a project is the difference between the sum of the present values of its benefits and the sum of the present values of its costs. Present value analysis is widely used because it is based on the time value of money; present value analysis, unlike payback or return on investment analysis, does consider all costs and benefits while simultaneously giving more weight to the earlier costs and benefits.

Review Questions

1. What three criteria must be met for an information systems project to be considered successful?

2. What is the role of the project coordinator?

3. What is an activity? What is an event? How are they related?

4. What three techniques are used to estimate programming times? Briefly describe each. Which of these are applicable for nonprogramming tasks?

5. What is a pilot system?

6. Describe a Gantt chart. For what purposes is a Gantt chart most useful?

7. How may a completed activity be indicated on a Gantt chart?

8. In a PERT/CPM chart, what is a dummy activity? What purpose does it serve?

9. How might expected activity duration be calculated in a traditional PERT system?

10. How is the earliest completion time for an event determined?

11. How is the latest completion time for an event determined?

12. What is slack time?

13. How is a critical path determined? What is the significance of a critical path?

14. What is the purpose of a structured walk-through?

15. By what other name is change control also known?

16. In what ways might costs be classified? Briefly describe each classification.

17. What is a chargeout method? What are the four most commonly used chargeout methods?

18. What is a payback period?

19. What is ROI and what formula is used to calculate it?

Discussion Questions

1. An estimate is needed for the time necessary to create a program that will update a direct master file, using a tape file of transactions. The program will also access a sequential table file and an indexed master file. Three reports will be generated: a detailed transaction activity report, a transaction error report, and an exception report; only the transaction activity report will require more than one print line per detail. Assuming that you estimate the general productivity factor to be 67%, how many days would you estimate for a programmer to create the program?

   After checking your records from previous projects for which you were the project manager, you learn that a programmer required twenty days to complete a comparable program. Would this information cause you to change your estimate? Why or why not? What if the previous program had taken only seven days to complete?

2. The annual budget for the information systems department has just been increased. If you were the director of information systems, would you use the additional funds to hire one senior programmer or two programmer trainees? Support your position.

3. Members of the information systems department management staff rarely attend a structured walk-through. Why do you think this is so?

4. Visit a local computer store (or if that is not possible, look through computer magazines for advertisements or product comparison articles) to gather information about three project management software packages. For each, determine which of these features are supported: Gantt charts; PERT or PERT/CPM; critical path determination; customized calendars; scheduling in hourly, daily, or weekly increments; resource leveling; and cost tracking and reporting. What other features does each provide? Compare the three packages as to the maximum number of activities, the maximum number of resources (team members), and the maximum schedule duration each allows.

MINICASE STUDIES

Gallagher Imports

Julie Hippen, a systems analyst at Gallagher Imports, is serving as project leader for the development of a sales information system. Julie is currently scheduling the activities for one of the developmental phases and has identified eleven activities. She has also determined the activity dependencies and has estimated the time necessary to complete each activity. The eleven activities are listed, along with the events that precede and follow each activity and the expected duration of each activity, in the following table.

ACTIVITY	PRECEDING EVENT	FOLLOWING EVENT	DURATION
A	1	2	10
B	2	3	45
C	2	4	20
D	4	5	20
E	4	6	15
F	3	7	20
G	3, 5	8	30
H	6	9	50
I	8	10	15
J	7, 10	11	10
K	9, 11	12	10

Figure 11-30

Questions

1. Create a PERT/CPM chart for the identified activities and events.
2. Calculate the earliest completion times, latest completion times, and slack times for each event.
3. Identify the critical path.
4. Create a Gantt chart to illustrate the scheduled activities. Assume that each activity is scheduled to start and end as early as possible.

G. H. Ames & Company

The marketing department at G. H. Ames & Company has recently recognized the need to strengthen and intensify their sales forecasting efforts in order to more accurately predict staffing and production requirements and future inventory needs. They have requested that the information systems department either design and implement an in-house computerized forecasting system or assist in locating and installing an appropriate forecasting software package. Neal Killian, a systems analyst, has been assigned to the project.

Neal has located a software package, ForeKast, that would meet the marketing department's needs and has developed related cost and benefit estimates for the next five years. He has also developed five-year cost estimates for designing and implementing an in-house forecasting system. Those estimates are summarized in the following table.

YEAR	FOREKAST SYSTEM COSTS	IN-HOUSE SYSTEM COSTS	BENEFITS
0	28,000	25,000	4,000
1	5,000	4,000	8,000
2	5,500	5,500	9,000
3	7,500	6,800	10,000
4	6,200	7,500	12,000
5	6,750	8,700	15,000

Figure 11-31

Questions

1. Determine the payback period for each alternative. If G. H. Ames & Company requires that all projects begin paying for themselves within four years, would either, neither, or both of these alternatives be acceptable?

2. Calculate a return on investment for each alternative. If the company requires a minimum ROI of 10%, would either, neither, or both of these alternatives be acceptable?

3. Calculate the net present value of each alternative, using a discount rate of 10%. Do either, neither, or both of these alternatives have an acceptable net present value?

4. Neal isn't certain that he considered *all* the relevant costs and benefits. Please help him by listing all the costs and benefits that he should consider when weighing these two alternatives. Be as specific as possible.

Ridgeway Company

When the Ridgeway Company management first requested a computerized billing system for its country club, the systems analysts gathered the following cost and volume data:

I. The country club currently has 2,000 full members and 1,000 social members. The number of full members is expected to increase by fifty members per year for each of the next several years. The number of social memberships is expected to increase by 10% each year for the next several years.

II. Currently, the average member (full or social) has fifteen charges in a month. That average is expected to increase to eighteen charges per month the next year, and then level off at twenty transactions per month for the following years.

III. Costs associated with the current system:

   A. For each 8,000 transactions/month increase over current volume, an additional accounting clerk must be hired. The starting salary for an accounting clerk is $14,000, which is not expected to change in the near future. Benefits require an additional annual expenditure equal to 25% of salary.

   B. Employee salary raises average 5% per year.

   C. When any new person is hired, a one-time $1,000 cost is incurred. For each two new people hired, additional office space must be provided at a one-time cost of $40,000.

   D. Miscellaneous supplies average $5.00 per member per year.

IV. Costs associated with the proposed system:

   A. A one-time cost of $170,000 would be incurred for the development of the system and site preparation.

   B. One microcomputer and three POS registers would be purchased for use with the new system. The total cost of $20,000 would be depreciated equally over the first five years of operation. (*Hint:* The $20,000 is not part of the developmental costs; instead, the $4,000/year depreciation expense is treated as an annual fixed cost.)

   C. Computer cost is estimated at $50/hour. Processing the monthly transactions and preparing the statements and other reports is estimated to take one hour per 10,000 transactions, or fraction thereof.

   D. One data entry clerk will be hired when the system goes into operation at a salary of $14,000.

   E. Miscellaneous supplies will cost $5,000 the first year and will increase 10% each year.

Questions

1. Assume that the proposed system could be developed this year and would become operational, replacing the current system, at the beginning of next year. Prepare a table for the current year and the next five years. Compute the membership totals and monthly transaction volumes for each year in the table. Detail all the estimated costs associated with operating the current system for the next five years. Determine the estimated developmental and operational costs for the proposed system for this year and for the next five years.

2. Compute the payback period for the proposed system.

3. Compute the return on investment for the proposed system for five years of systems operation.

4. Compute the net present value of the proposed system at the end of the fifth year of operation. Assume a discount rate of 14%.

STUDENT CASE STUDY 11

Western Dental Clinic — Project Management and Costs

Introduction

Jim Archer, the consultant hired by Western Dental Clinic to computerize their office systems, is ready to begin the systems development phase. The associates and office staff of Western Dental are, like typical end users, impatient and eager to begin using their new system. Archer knows that the programs, and thus the entire project, would be completed quicker if more people were involved in the programming. Besides, programming is not the best use of Archer's talents, skills, and time, so he would like to share the programming load with others. Archer also would like to get opinions, criticisms, and suggestions on his design from other computer professionals, even though the systems design is already complete. For all these reasons, Archer plans to subcontract part of the programming workload.

Archer calls two programmers he has worked with in the past, and whose work he respects, to determine if they are available. The first, Lee Gimble, has just completed another large assignment and is now available to work for up to forty hours a week. Dana Hubbard, the second contract programmer, is currently working part-time on another assignment, but could work up to twenty hours a week on the Western project. Archer is also working on other projects and he can spend at most thirty hours a week on the Western Dental programming activities.

Jim Archer must now develop a schedule and determine task assignments for himself, Gimble, and Hubbard. He must consider the following factors:

- Each program will be written by only one person.

- Any program written by one of the two programmers must be reviewed by Archer. Archer must schedule an amount of his time equal to 10% of the programmer's estimated programming time for a program review. He will do the reviews alone; that is, he requires no programmer time for the reviews.

- The menu program for process control ties the entire system together. That program should be the first assignment for one of the three people.

- A report program cannot be started until all the update programs for all the files it accesses have been completed and, if necessary, reviewed by Archer.

- Except for the restrictions in the previous two factors, the programs are independent and can be written in any order.

- Archer, Gimble, and Hubbard are paid only for the time they actually work. Scheduling any of the three people for less than the maximum available time imposes no penalty, except that the programming work might take longer than necessary.

- Archer must also develop a user manual. He estimates that writing the manual will require forty hours of his time, of which he can do up to about twenty hours before all the programs have been completed. He can use that twenty hours to fill any of his available but otherwise unassigned time during the programming phase. Archer cannot complete the remaining user manual work, however, until after all the programs have been written and reviewed.

Student Assignments

1. Using the quantitative method described in this chapter, determine time estimates for every program that must be written. Use a programmer/analyst skill level for Archer and a programmer skill level for Gimble and Hubbard in your estimates. Assume a productivity factor of 100%. Multiply each estimate by 8 to get an estimate in person-hours.

2. Develop a schedule for completing all the programming, review, and user manual tasks in the least amount of elapsed time. Your week-by-week schedule should show each person's hours and activities.

CHAPTER 12

Programming, Testing, and Documentation

Objectives

You will have mastered the material in this chapter when you can:

- Describe the activities you complete during the systems development phase
- Discuss the role of a systems analyst during program development
- Describe the different types of documentation you must prepare
- Explain the different phases of testing

Introduction

Systems development is the systems development life cycle phase during which the information systems department creates, documents, and tests new application software programs. If a software package is to be used as the new information system, the programs already exist; but you still must test the system, and you might also have to prepare documentation to supplement the package's documentation.

During the systems development phase, programmers code, test, and document individual programs; the systems analyst oversees these activities. In addition, both programmers and systems analysts must test the entire information system and must prepare documentation for the system, the operations group, and the end users. We assume that you are already familiar with the details of program design, coding, testing, and documentation from your introductory programming courses. Thus, in this chapter we focus our discussion of the systems development phase on the responsibilities of the systems analyst.

Program development

rogram development is the process of creating the programs needed to satisfy an information system's processing requirements. Program development consists of the following five steps: review the program documentation, design the program, code the program, test the program, and complete the program documentation (Figure 12-1).

Figure 12-1 *The five steps of program development.*

■ Review the program documentation

A programmer's first step in the program development cycle is to review the program documentation that was prepared during previous SDLC phases. The program documentation consists of data flow diagrams, process descriptions, screen layouts, report layouts, source documents, and data dictionary entries. This documentation helps programmers understand the work that needs to be done by the program. To clear up any misunderstandings with the program requirements, programmers usually have one or more meetings with the systems analysts who designed the software during the systems design phase. Recall that the software design is completed by systems analysts during the systems design phase. This is the first level of program design; the systems analysts determine which programs are required and what each program will do.

If a programmer believes some aspect of the program design, such as a screen layout, should be changed, he or she must discuss the change with the systems analyst. If the programmer and systems analyst agree on the change and if the change affects the end user (as is the case with a screen layout change), then the systems analyst must review the change with the end user and obtain the end user's approval of the change. The systems analyst would then change the system design specifications to reflect the authorized design change. No change to the program design should be made without recording the change in the system design specifications. The systems analyst and the end users, through the system design specifications, have specified *what* programs are required and *what* is to be done by each program. The programmer's job is to determine *how* a program will be structured to satisfy the specified requirements.

■ Design the program

After reviewing the program documentation, a programmer designs the program. The program design completed by a programmer during systems development is the second level of program design. During this second level of program design, a programmer decides exactly how the program will accomplish what it must do by developing a logical solution to the programming problem. The logical solution, or logic, for a program is a step-by-step solution to a programming problem. The programmer typically uses one of several program design tools to aid in logic development; **structure charts**, or **hierarchy charts** (Figure 12-2), **program flowcharts** (Figure 12-3 on page 12.4), and **pseudocode** (Figure 12-4 on page 12.5) are examples of such program design tools. This second level of program development is usually completed by the programmer. Systems analysts do not normally participate in this second level of program design; some companies, however, have their systems analysts, instead of their programmers, prepare the program design.

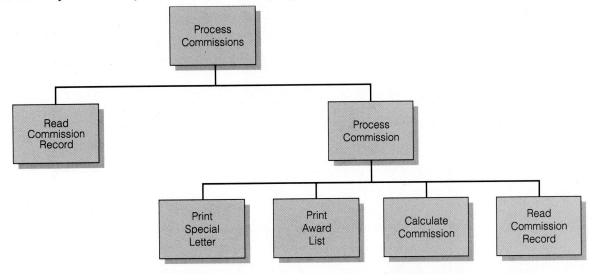

Figure 12-2 *A structure chart graphically illustrates the relationship of individual program modules.*

■ Code the program

Coding the program is the process of writing the program instructions that implement the program design specifications. If a programmer has prepared a thorough program design, the coding process is greatly simplified and can sometimes be a one-for-one translation of the design step into the coding step. For small programs, the coding for the entire program is done by a single programmer; for very large programs, however, the various program routines might be subdivided into individual modules, and two or more programmers could be assigned the task of developing the code for a single program.

Each company establishes standards, specifying which programming languages a programmer can use and the specific coding standards for each language. COBOL, RPG, Visual BASIC, Ada, and C++ are examples of commonly used programming languages. The trend, however, is toward greater use of software tools, such as report writers, screen generators, program generators, fourth-generation languages, and other CASE tools that generate actual program code directly from program design specifications.

■ Test the program

A programmer must thoroughly test a program to ensure it functions correctly before the program processes actual data and produces information on which people will rely. A programmer would perform several different types of tests on an individual program.

A programmer first compiles the program to identify **syntax errors**, which are language violations caused by typing mistakes, inconsistencies in the program, and language grammar errors. The programmer corrects the program to eliminate these syntax errors until he or she obtains a **clean compilation**, which is a compilation without any errors.

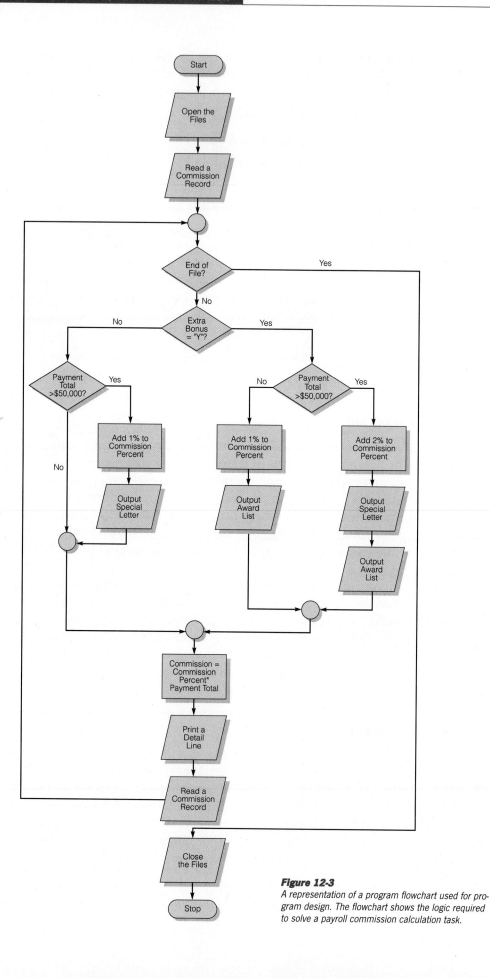

Figure 12-3
A representation of a program flowchart used for program design. The flowchart shows the logic required to solve a payroll commission calculation task.

```
Open the files
Read a COMMISSION record
Do until end of file
        If EXTRA BONUS equals Y
                If PAYMENT TOTAL is greater than $50,000
                        Add 2% to COMMISSION PERCENT
                        Output SPECIAL LETTER
                        Output AWARD LIST
                    Else
                        Add 1% to COMMISSION PERCENT
                        Output AWARD LIST
                ENDIF
            Else
                If PAYMENT TOTAL is greater than $50,000
                        Add 1% to COMMISSION PERCENT
                        Output SPECIAL LETTER
                ENDIF
        ENDIF
        Calculate COMMISSION = COMMISSION PERCENT times PAYMENT TOTAL
        Print a detail line
        Read a COMMISSION record
ENDDO
Close the files
End the program
```

Figure 12-4 *This pseudocode is another way of documenting the logic shown in the program flowchart in Figure 12-3.*

Next, the programmer might desk check the program. **Desk checking** is the process of reading the program and mentally reviewing its logic. Desk checking is a simple process that can be performed by the programmer who wrote the program or by other programmers. The disadvantage of desk checking is that detecting other than obvious errors is difficult.

Many organizations require a more formal type of desk checking called a **structured walkthrough**, or **code review**, of the program. Other programmers on the team and the systems analyst who designed the program usually participate in the code review. The objectives of the code review are to detect errors, to ensure adherence to standards, and to verify that the program satisfies the requirements it was designed to accomplish.

Finally, a programmer tests the program. The testing of an individual program is called **unit testing**. The objective of unit testing is to identify and eliminate both **execution errors**, which are errors that cause the program to abnormally terminate, and **logic errors**, which are errors in the accuracy and completeness of a program's processing. **Test data** should contain both correct data and erroneous data that the program must identify and properly handle. The test data should test the limits within the program; for a field that allows a range of values, for example, the test data should contain minimum and maximum values for that field plus values outside the acceptable range. To assist in program testing, programmers might use CASE tools, such as **online debuggers**, which allow you to interactively determine the location and potential causes of program errors, and **code analyzers**, which assess the quality of the program's logical flow, to aid in the unit testing process.

To obtain an independent and unbiased test of the program, someone other than the programmer who wrote the program usually creates the test data and reviews the test results. Systems analysts frequently create the test data during the systems design phase as part of an overall test plan. A **test plan** provides all details of the testing that are to occur during the systems development phase. Regardless of who creates the test data, however, the project manager or a designated systems analyst should review all the final test results. Some organizations also require the end users to approve the final unit test results.

■ Document the program

Accurate and complete program documentation is essential for the successful operation and maintenance of the information system. Program documentation helps the next programmer who, six months or one year later, might be asked to make a correction or change to the program. Quality documentation can substantially reduce the amount of time that the new programmer will have to spend learning enough about the program to know how best to make the change.

Documentation

Documentation is the written material that explains what the information system does and how people interact with the system. Without complete and accurate documentation, the end users and information systems department personnel would neither know the capabilities of the system nor how best to work with the system. The four components of documentation are program documentation, system documentation, operations documentation, and end user documentation.

■ Program documentation

Developing the program documentation is an ongoing activity during systems development that begins with the systems analysis phase and that is completed after the program is successfully tested and ready for implementation. Systems analysts prepare most of the program documentation, such as process descriptions and report layouts, during the early SDLC phases. The programmers prepare the remaining program documentation during the systems development phase by including comments within the programs and printed copies of each program in the complete documentation package. A systems analyst usually verifies that the internal program documentation is complete and accurate.

■ System documentation

System documentation describes the features of an information system and explains how these features are implemented. The systems analyst prepares most of the system documentation during the systems analysis and design phases. The system documentation contains, for example, all data dictionary entries, data flow diagrams, screen layouts, source documents, and the systems request form that originally initiated the development effort.

During the systems development phase, a systems analyst must review the system documentation and verify that it completely and accurately represents the information system being developed. Inaccuracies and modifications required due to program development changes must be incorporated into the system documentation before the end of the systems development phase. If the design or content of a screen or report is modified during systems development, for example, the systems analyst must change the system documentation to reflect this modification. Programmers and systems analysts who maintain the information system rely on complete and accurate system documentation to guide them when and if they make changes to the system.

■ Operations documentation

If the information system will operate in a minicomputer or mainframe environment, the systems analyst must prepare operations documentation for the operations group within the information systems department. The **operations group** is in charge of the centralized computers, the data communications equipment, and centralized peripheral devices, such as printers and optical scanners. This group also schedules the execution of batch jobs, distributes printed output, and serves as the first line of contact when the end users have problems with their operational information systems.

Operations documentation tells the operations group how and when to run the programs for an information system. A program run sheet is a commonly required operations document that explains how and when to run a program. The **program run sheet** contains all the information needed by the operations group for processing the program data and for distributing output information. A typical program run sheet shown in Figure 12-5 on the next page provides the following information:

1. Program, job, systems analyst, programmer, and system identification
2. Scheduling information, such as run frequency and deadlines
3. Input files and where they originate, and output files and their destinations
4. Report distribution
5. Special forms required and special comments
6. Restart procedures
7. Error and informational messages to operators, and the required operator responses
8. Special instructions, such as security requirements and special operator tasks

Operations documentation must be clear and concise, as shown in Figure 12-5 on the next page. Each computer operator might handle hundreds of jobs each day, so an operator must know exactly what to do without having to read pages of documentation and instructions. Today, most systems analysts agree that the operations documentation should be online, where the computer operator can easily and rapidly view exactly what he or she must do.

Each installation usually has specific, standard requirements for operations documentation. You should review the operations documentation with the operations group as early as possible during the systems development phase, because the operations group must approve the documentation before accepting responsibility for the system. If you keep the operations group involved and informed and solicit their requirements during early phases of the SDLC, it will be easier for you to give the operations group the documentation they need and to obtain their approval.

■ End user documentation

End users need documentation to assist them in both their initial learning and their ongoing use of the information system. The systems analysts and programmers are responsible for preparing the documentation. At a minimum, end users need documentation on these aspects of the information system:

- System overview, highlighting the major features of the system
- Source document content, preparation, processing, and samples
- Menu and data entry screen options, contents, and processing instructions
- Output report calculations, frequencies of printing, distribution, and samples
- Security and control considerations

PROGRAM RUN SHEET

PROGRAM NAME ① Print Employee Paychecks	JOB NAME ① PAY110	ANALYST ① T. Simaz	PROGRAMMER ① L. Cohen
SYSTEM NAME ① Payroll	FREQUENCY ② Weekly	DEADLINE ② Tuesday 4:00 p.m.	DATE PREPARED 11/12/97

INPUT / OUTPUT INSTRUCTIONS

DEVICE	USE	FILE DESCRIPTION	SOURCE/DESTINATION	COMMENTS
Tape	I	Payroll Master	Library	Latest generation
Console	I	Starting Check Number	Payroll Dept	Payroll Mgr supplies
Disk	O	Check Recon Trans.	To Job PAY115	
Printer	O	Employee Paychecks	To Payroll Dept	Paycheck stock forms
Printer	O	Check Control Numbers	To Payroll Dept	
③	③	③	③ ④	⑤

RESTART INSTRUCTIONS ⑥

    If program aborts, correct the problem and restart from beginning of job.
    If checks are damaged during printing, retain the damaged checks and forward
       to the payroll manager. Also see Special Instructions below.

MESSAGES ⑦

    INCORRECT STARTING CHECK NUMBER - Action: reenter starting check number.
    WRONG MASTER FILE - Action: mount correct payroll master and restart job.
    LOAD PAYCHECKS - Action: load paycheck stock forms into printer.

SPECIAL INSTRUCTIONS ⑧

    1. Keep track of all starting and ending preprinted check numbers used.
       These numbers will be input to payroll job PAY115.
    2. All checks must be given to the payroll manager after the program has
       completed and the checks have printed.

Figure 12-5 *Sample program run sheet with instructions to the operations group for a program to print employee paychecks.*

- Responsibility for specific processing requirements
- Deadlines for time-critical processing
- Procedures and policies for requesting changes and for reporting problems
- Examples of exceptions and error situations

The documentation usually consists of both written and online documentation. The written documentation is customarily called a **user manual**. A sample page is shown in Figure 12-6.

PROJECT CONTROL SYSTEM

05/23/97	ADD A PROJECT RECORD	1:17 PM

Project Number: 1785

Project Description: Develop a

Project Director:

Current Budget:

Start Date (MM/DD/YY):

Project Status Code:

Project Status Codes (A=active, C=completed, D=deferred, X=canceled)

Tab /Advance to Next Field	F2 Highlight Field	Clear Current Record	Exit without Adding Record

Type the Project Description and then press [Enter]

ADDING A PROJECT RECORD

1. Enter the 4-digit project number and press TAB.
   • The system will verify that this number does not duplicate an existing project number.
   • If the project number already exists, the message DUPLICATE PROJECT NUMBER — PLEASE RE-ENTER appears, and the cursor moves to the beginning of the project number field for you to enter the correct project number.
   • If the project number is correct, the cursor moves to the beginning of the project description field.
2. Enter up to 35 characters for a project description and press TAB.
3. Enter up to 25 characters for the name of the project director and press TAB.

Figure 12-6 *A sample page from a user manual. The instructions describe the procedure for adding a new project record to the system.*

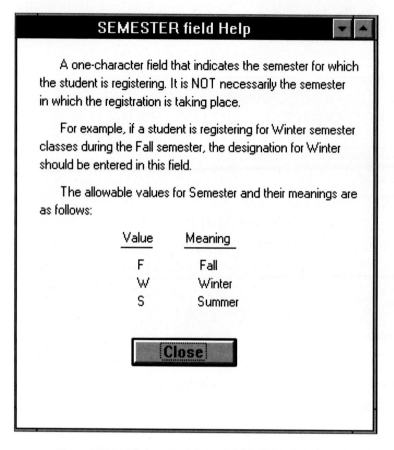

SEMESTER field Help

A one-character field that indicates the semester for which the student is registering. It is NOT necessarily the semester in which the registration is taking place.

For example, if a student is registering for Winter semester classes during the Fall semester, the designation for Winter should be entered in this field.

The allowable values for Semester and their meanings are as follows:

Value	Meaning
F	Fall
W	Winter
S	Summer

Close

Figure 12-7 A context-sensitive help screen for student registration entry.

Systems analysts are usually responsible for preparing the user manual, but many organizations require that the end users also participate in preparing it. Some organizations make the end users completely responsible for user manual preparation; they do this with the objective that by writing the manual, the end users will fully understand the information system and will include appropriate end user terminology in the user manual.

Although a user manual is a necessary and helpful form of end user documen-tation, most information systems today also contain online documentation. In most cases, systems analysts and programmers must develop the online documentation. Two typical types of online documentation are help screens and tutorials. In Figure 12-7, we see a sample help screen like we first discussed in Chapter 7. A **tutorial** is a series of online lessons designed to train an end user to use the system; we will discuss tutorials in more detail in Chapter 13.

Testing

rogrammers are responsible for unit testing the individual programs they develop. After the programmers have tested each program, then the programs within the system that depend on one another must be tested together, and f   lly the entire system must be tested, as shown in Figure 12-8.

■ Link testing

Testing two or more programs together that depend on one another is called **link testing**, **string testing**, **series testing**, or **integration testing**. For example, suppose you have an information system with a transaction validation program and a separate master file update program. The output from the validation program must be properly formatted and must contain the correct data to be input to the update program. Testing each of these two programs independently does not guarantee that the file passed between the two programs is correct. Only by performing a link test for this pair of programs could you be confident that the programs work together correctly. In Figure 12-8, we show link testing the interfaces from program 1 to program 2, from program 2 to programs 3 and 4, and from program 4 to programs 5 and 6.

Another reason for link testing programs in a minicomputer or mainframe environment is to ensure that the job streams are correct. A **job stream** is the series of job control statements necessary to invoke the proper programs to be processed, to define the files and databases to be created and processed, and to designate the storage devices that are to be used for the files and databases. If files or databases are defined incorrectly or programs are called improperly, the information system will not work the way in which it was intended; the testing of the job stream, therefore, is as important as the testing of the programs within the system.

Systems analysts usually develop the data they use in link testing. As is the case with all forms of testing, the link test data must consider both normal and unusual situations — passing a file with a dozen records between two programs, followed by passing a file with zero records, which might be a more unusual situation, is an example of the proper link testing of both normal and unusual conditions.

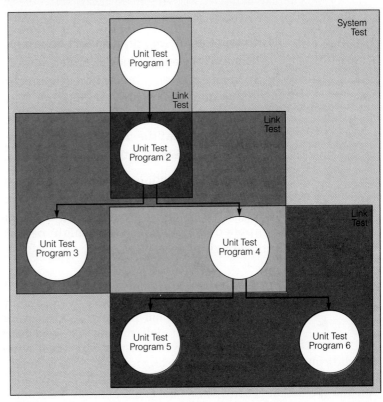

Figure 12-8 Testing a system starts with unit tests of individual programs, proceeds to link tests of groups of programs, and ends with system tests of the entire system.

Small amounts of test data that simulate actual and extreme conditions are appropriate during link testing. You are primarily testing the interfaces between programs at this point, not the programs themselves. You should assume that the programmers have thoroughly checked out all programs individually and that the project manager or a systems analyst has approved the unit test results. A program should not move to the link test stage unless it has passed all of its unit tests.

■ System testing

After you complete link testing, you must run through a series of system tests. A **system test** is a test of the entire information system using live data supplied by the end users, in an attempt to exercise all processing situations under typical conditions (Figure 12-8). During a system test, the end users prepare source documents, enter data, and select reports for output, while the operations group attempts to run the information system in compliance with the operations documentation. All processing options, output information, and other components of the information system are verified by the end users and the project team of systems analysts and programmers to ensure the system functions correctly. Unit and link testing might be bypassed for a software package, so that a system test could serve as the first test of a purchased software package. You should system test a software package as carefully as you would an in-house developed system. The major objectives of system testing are:

- To perform a final test of all programs against the design specifications
- To ensure that the operations group has adequate documentation and instructions to operate the system properly, process the incoming data, and distribute outgoing information from the system
- To guarantee that the end users can successfully interact with the system

- To test the backup and restart capabilities of the information system to be sure they are adequate under actual processing conditions
- To verify that all information system components are correctly integrated so data and information flow smoothly among departments and through the computer within predicted time requirements
- To confirm that the information system can handle normal production volumes of data in a timely and responsive manner

Successful completion of system testing is the key factor to end user and management acceptance of the developed information system, which is why the final system tests are frequently called **acceptance tests**. The term acceptance test, however, is usually applied to system tests that might be performed during the systems implementation and evaluation phase.

System testing can verify that you have developed a reliable information system. In many cases, however, determining when to end system testing can be a difficult task. Because system testing is one of the last major steps before the systems implementation and evaluation phase, you and the end users are eager to complete the project and might be under pressure to terminate system testing prematurely. Pressure could also result if actual costs are exceeding estimated costs or if you have fallen behind schedule. The pressure might also be imposed by management, who wants you to finish the project and start the next critical project, or by an external organization, such as a credit bureau that wants you to start supplying it with new information as quickly as possible. Thus, you might declare that system testing has been completed even though important tests have been skipped or incompletely verified. If you terminate system testing prematurely, however, you might fail to detect a significant error in the system until the system is actually in produc-tion, when the consequences are potentially disastrous.

On the other hand, very few information systems are completely error free. Each system test typically uncovers another set of errors and problems. Some end users prefer to withhold their approvals until all the system tests are perfect, because additional corrections are usually impossible during systems development once the end users have approved the tests. Certainly, errors that compromise the integrity and security of the system must be corrected immediately; but minor errors, such as an incorrectly titled screen, could be corrected as maintenance changes after the system is implemented. Categorizing an error as minor versus serious and obtaining agreement between a systems analyst and the end users on that categorization, however, might be difficult in some cases.

Trying to balance the need to finish system testing with the need for perfection in the information system you develop is not an easy task. Even when you have preestablished criteria that define the acceptable level of system testing, you might encounter situations that are not covered by the criteria. Determining when system testing is completed is best left to the judgment of the project coordinator, who might have previous experience making this type of decision. ■

Management approval

After system testing is completed and the end users are satisfied with the new information system, you must present the results of the systems development phase to management. Your presentation to management should highlight the system test results, the status of all the required documentation, and the opinions of the end users regarding the quality and acceptability of the new system. You must also provide detailed schedules, estimates, and staffing requirements for the systems implementation and evaluation phase, report on the total costs expended to date for the project, and compare these costs with the prior estimates. If the system has performed adequately during system testing and the end users enthusiastically support the new system, then management will usually approve the systems development phase and direct you to proceed to the systems implementation and evaluation phase, which is the subject of the next chapter.

CHAPTER CASE STUDY 12

James Tool Company — Systems Development

Management and the payroll end users at James Tool Company had decided that the new payroll package from Lennox Software Solutions should be implemented before any additional work was done on the new union system. Systems analysts Don Mard and Kimberly Wallace and programmer/analyst Howard Coswell formed the project team that completed the implementation of the new payroll package on the mainframe computer at James Tool Company. Two payroll cycles had been successfully completed, and the end users have expressed satisfaction with the system's features, screens and reports, and ease of use.

The success of the payroll system implementation allowed Coswell to resume development of the union system. He had previously completed the systems design phase, so he was now ready to begin the systems development phase. Coswell needed to develop five programs: the union deduction extract program, the employee union dues program, the modify/view union program, the pay union dues program, and the union control program. The first program would execute on the mainframe computer, while the other four programs would execute on the personal computer in the union relations department (Figure 12-9 on the next page).

Because all programmers, programmer/analysts, and other systems analysts at James Tool Company were busy on other projects, Coswell would be developing the union system by himself. He had estimated a total of fourteen days for the development of the five programs; this estimate included the time needed to design, program, unit test, and document the programs. In addition, Coswell had estimated eight more days for link and system testing, for completing the union system documentation, and for receiving management approval of the systems development phase.

■ Mainframe program development

Coswell's first step was to meet with Kimberly Wallace to discuss the design of the union deduction extract program; this program executes on the mainframe computer to create the union deduction file after each weekly payroll has been run. Coswell had planned to write the program in COBOL, which was the programming language used for all the programs in the payroll package. Wallace and Coswell, however, now had considerable experience with the payroll package and decided that Coswell should write the program using the payroll package's report writer utility program. Coswell and Wallace agreed that the program would take less time to develop and would be easier to maintain if the report writer were used.

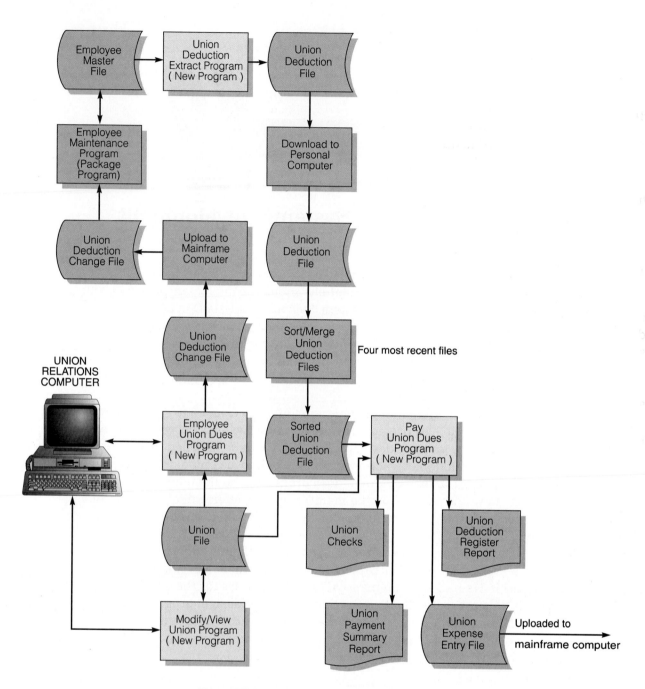

Figure 12-9 *The complete union system at James Tool Company*

Coswell studied the report writer documentation, prepared the report writer commands, unit tested the program against the test files that he, Wallace, and Mard had created, and verified the test results in less than one day. Coswell then created the procedures for downloading the union deduction files to the personal computer in the union relations department, tested these downloading procedures, and updated the documentation for the union system. Because Coswell had finished developing the union deduction program in two days, he was now one day ahead of schedule.

■ Personal computer program development

Coswell next began developing the four programs for the personal computer in the union relations department. He decided to use a CASE screen generator for the three online programs: the employee union dues program, the modify/view union program, and the union system control program. He had planned to take eight and one half days to complete these programs, but using the screen generator reduced the total program development time to six and one half days, putting him now three days ahead of schedule.

For the final program, the batch pay union dues program, Coswell decided to use a microcomputer COBOL compiler that he had previously used for other projects. The pay union dues program turned out to be more complicated to program and test than he had projected, and Coswell spent four and one half days developing the program instead of the two and one half days he had planned. He was now one day ahead of schedule.

■ Completing the systems development phase

Coswell next developed the uploading procedures for the union deduction change file, tested these uploading procedures, and link tested the union system programs. He found no serious problems during the link testing and easily corrected and retested the few minor errors that occurred. The system testing with the end users from the payroll and union relations departments also was successfully completed. The link and system testing required three days to complete.

Coswell had been preparing the user documentation and instructions and updating the system and operations documentation in parallel with his program activities, so he needed just two days to finish all the documentation. He then reviewed the documentation with Mard and Wallace, the end users, and the operations group and obtained their approvals on all aspects of the work he had done. Coswell reviewed the union system development in meetings with information systems management and company management. He then received management approval to proceed with the next SDLC phase: systems implementation and evaluation.

Summary

The systems development phase consists of program development and the documentation and testing of a new information system. During program development, programmers review the program documentation from the systems design phase, complete the program designs, code the programs, test the programs, and complete the program documentation.

During the systems development phase, systems analysts complete the system documentation and prepare operations and end user documentation. Operations documentation provides instructions and information to the operations group for the proper running of the programs in the information system; a program run sheet is an example of one type of operations documentation that you might prepare. End user documentation supplies instructions and information to the end users for their interaction with an information system; user manuals, help screens, and tutorials are examples of end user documentation.

Desk checking, code reviews, and unit testing are typical of the types of tests that programmers conduct during program development. In addition, you must link test programs that depend on one another and system test the entire system. The end users participate in system testing, which serves as the final major activity of the systems development phase prior to your presentation to management. If management approves the results of this phase, you would next begin the systems implementation and evaluation phase.

Review Questions

1. What five steps does a programmer complete during program development?
2. Give three examples of program design tools.
3. What types of tests might a programmer conduct in the testing of an individual program?
4. What is a program run sheet, and what information does the program run sheet supply to the operations group?
5. What types of information do you need to provide in the end user documentation?
6. What is link testing? What are other names commonly used for link testing?
7. Who participates in system testing?
8. What are the major objectives of system testing?

Discussion Questions

1. A systems analyst recently asserted, "Link testing is a waste of time. If each program has been adequately tested and if program specifications are prepared properly, link testing is not needed. Only system testing is required to check out the system procedures." Do you agree or disagree? Justify your position.
2. The end users normally use live data during system testing. Are there circumstances where simulated data is preferable to live data? What are these circumstances?

MINICASE STUDIES 12

Green Pastures Limited

Management at Green Pastures has decided to replace Kirby Ellington, who had developed the company's new billing information system. Kirby had used the C programming language in developing the programs for this system and had prepared neither operations nor end user documentation for the system. After billing statements had been mailed to all their customers, Green Pastures discovered that all the billing statements were wrong; they reissued all the statements manually.

You are hired by Green Pastures to replace Kirby, and your first assignment is to get the new billing system working correctly. Kirby's last day at Green Pastures coincides with your first day on the job, and you will be able to meet with him for two hours in the morning and one hour in the afternoon.

Questions

1. What specific information would you attempt to obtain from Kirby during your meetings with him? In addition to an interview with Kirby, what other fact-finding techniques would you use to learn more about the billing system? Why?

2. What are your options for completing the billing system, and what are the most important factors you should consider in recommending the appropriate course of action?

Ridgeway Company

The Ridgeway Company requirements were described in a Chapter 4 minicase study. The following assignments are based on the work you did for that minicase.

Questions

1. Design the testing that will be required for the billing system. You should consider program, link, and system testing in your test plan.

2. Design the test data that will be used for the testing of the billing system. You should include data for all tests that will be performed on the system in all phases of testing.

STUDENT CASE STUDY

Western Dental Clinic — Systems Development

Introduction

Jim Archer has completed the systems design for the dental system at Western Dental Clinic. The associates at the clinic have approved Archer's system design specification, and Archer has developed a systems development phase plan. Archer has hired two programmers, Dana Hubbard and Lee Gimble, who have worked with Archer in the past, to assist him with the programming and testing of the dental system.

Student Assignments

1. Design the testing that will be required for the dental system. You should consider program, link, and system testing in your test plan.
2. Design the test data that you will use for testing the dental system. You should include data for all tests that will be performed on the system in all phases of testing.
3. Prepare documentation for Western Dental Clinic that will explain when each program will be executed and, for each program, what inputs and outputs are required.

PHASE 5

Systems Implementation and Evaluation

CHAPTER 13

Systems Implementation and Evaluation

Objectives

You will have mastered the material in this chapter when you can:

- Explain the reasons for having separate operational and test computer environments
- Determine who should receive training on a new information system, discuss who might perform the training, and explain how that training might be accomplished
- Compare the contents and purposes of training manuals versus online tutorials
- Describe the activities of the file-conversion process
- List four system changeover methods, and discuss the advantages and disadvantages of each method
- Explain the purposes of a post-implementation evaluation, discuss who might perform the evaluation, and describe what is evaluated
- Describe the contents of the final report to management

Introduction

In this chapter, we discuss the activities of the systems implementation and evaluation phase. The activities in this final phase of the systems development life cycle are common to all information systems projects from newly developed in-house systems to purchased packages used without modification.

When the systems implementation and evaluation phase begins, all the software and hardware for the new information system is complete and available. As the first step in this phase, you prepare a production environment and transfer the programs and procedures for the new information system into that environment. In the second activity of this phase, you are involved in the training of the end users, operations personnel, and other people who will interact with the new information system. After all the training has been completed, you perform the actual conversion effort, which includes file conversion and system changeover. The last two activities of the systems implementation and evaluation phase are the post-implementation evaluation and the final report to management.

Operational and test environments

The hardware and software environment for actual system operation is called the **operational environment**, or the **production environment**. The environment used by programmers to develop new programs and to maintain existing programs is called the **test environment**. Virtually all mainframe and minicomputer installations require separate operational and test environments.

Although the implementation mechanics are different, the reasons for separate environments are equally applicable for microcomputer systems.

Access to the procedures, programs, and files in the operational environment is strictly controlled. With just two exceptions, only authorized end users should be able to access the operational environment. The two exceptions are when program or procedure corrections or file reconstructions are required to recover from problems and when authorized modifications or enhancements to the information system are applied. In all other instances, neither systems analysts nor programmers should have access to the production environment. In many computer installations, a single operational environment is used for all production information systems; in other installations, an operational environment is created for each production system.

The test environment for an information system contains copies of all the system's programs and procedures, as well as all the test data files. During systems operation, whenever you make program or procedure modifications to the system, those modifications must first be completely tested in the test environment. Next, the end users review and approve the test results and documentation updates. Only then are the modified programs or procedures transferred into the production environment. Figure 13-1 shows the relationship between the operational and test environments.

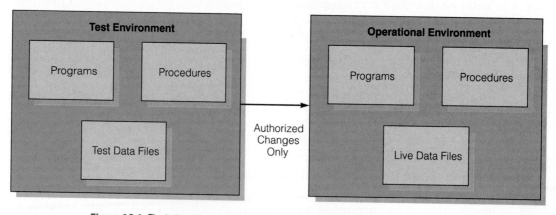

Figure 13-1 *The test environment versus the operational environment.*

One of your first activities in the systems implementation and evaluation phase is to create an operational environment for the new information system, if one does not already exist. All the programs and procedures that have been developed for the new system are then transferred into the operational environment.

Mainframe and minicomputer information systems also require job control language (JCL) to control system operations. In many installations, the production JCL is written by project team members and then checked for efficiency and conformation to standards by the information systems department technical support group; in other installations, the production JCL is actually written by the members of the technical support group or the operations group. In either case, the production JCL is placed in the operational environment along with the production programs and procedures.

Nearly every computer installation has at least one horror story to tell about a seemingly innocent program change that was introduced into the production system without first being adequately tested. After any system modification, you should repeat the same acceptance tests that you applied when the system was first developed. By establishing two separate environments, restricting access to the operational environment, and thoroughly testing the entire system in the test environment after every program change or modification, you help to ensure that the production system will continue to operate and serve the end users.

Training

Training is another activity you must undertake early in the systems implementation and evaluation phase. The planning for training, however, actually begins at the end of the systems development phase. If the information system solution includes the purchase of software or hardware, then vendor-supplied training is one of the features you should investigate or request in the RFPs (requests for proposal) or RFQs (requests for quotation). During the systems development phase, you prepare user and operations documentation that, while not a substitute for training, does serve as a necessary supplement to the training process.

All people who will interact with or use the new system must understand their roles in the operation of the system. One of your first steps in the implementation and evaluation phase, therefore, is to specifically identify all the individuals who should receive training and to determine what training is appropriate for each. The types of training that will be required depend on the new information system and how it will operate. You might have to train clerks and data entry personnel, for example, on the preparation or use of source documents. Computer operators will require training on system procedures and on any new hardware. If the new system will operate on microcomputers, you might first have to train end users to operate the equipment. The end users will definitely require training specific to the application, including capturing data, accessing the system, entering, correcting, and querying data, initiating system operations, and requesting and interpreting system output. Finally, managers who will use output from the system to make decisions need to understand the source, meaning, and limitations of that output information.

After you have identified who needs what kind of training, you must determine who will perform the actual training. One valuable source of training is vendors. Most hardware and software vendors offer training programs for the equipment and systems they sell. Many vendor training courses are offered free of charge with the purchase of hardware or software, but some vendors do charge a fee for training sessions. The courses are usually conducted at the vendor site by experienced trainers and provide valuable hands-on experience.

If a large number of people must be trained, you might arrange for vendor classes to be held at your own location, although vendors almost always charge a fee for such in-house training. You might also arrange for an independent professional training firm to provide in-house hardware or software training. In-house training offers several potential advantages: employees incur no travel expenses; employees are on-site and able to respond to job emergencies that require their immediate attention; and training can take place in the actual environment in which the system will operate. Two of these advantages, however, can also become disadvantages. Employees who are constantly being distracted by telephone calls and other job duties might not get all they can out of a training session. Using the organization's computer facilities for training sessions can disrupt normal computer operations; when normal operations cannot be interrupted, the amount of actual hands-on training might have to be severely limited.

For training on an information system that you have developed within the organization, professional outside trainers are not a choice. The information systems department and the end user departments must share the responsibility for developing and conducting in-house training programs on internally developed software. If your information systems department includes an information center, that group would train end users on microcomputer use; the information center might also be able to assist with application system training. If your organization has a media or graphic arts group, they can assist in the preparation of training materials, such as videotapes or films, or programmed instructional material.

When you develop a training program, you should keep in mind the following guidelines.

Train people in groups. Group training is a more efficient use of your time and of the training facilities. In addition, group training is usually more effective, because trainees can learn from the questions and problems of other trainees.

Develop separate training programs for distinct employee groups. A training program should be appropriate to the job interests and skills of the participants. The information required by computer operations personnel is different from the information required by end users, for example. Whenever possible, you should avoid intermingling computer-sophisticated end users with novice end users in a single training program; the necessary breadth and depth of the training will differ for the two groups, and someone is sure to be frustrated in a single program that attempts to meet everyone's needs.

Provide for learning by hearing, seeing, and doing. Some people learn best from lectures, discussions, and question-and-answer sessions. Others learn best from viewing demonstrations or from reading documentation and other material. Most people learn best from actual hands-on experience. You should provide for all three types of learning.

Prepare a training manual or a tutorial. A typical training manual outline is shown in Figure 13-2. The Introduction describes the information system and its features. The Getting Started section contains basic introductory information, such as how to turn on a microcomputer or terminal, how to insert a diskette, and so on. The Lessons section contains step-by-step instructions for using all the features of the information system.

Figure 13-3 shows a sample first lesson for a microcomputer-based project tracking system. The first page of lesson two for that same system is shown in Figure 13-4 on page 13.8.

Training Manual
1. Introduction
2. The Information System
a. Getting Started
b. Lessons
3. Reference Manual
4. Appendices
a. Error Messages
b. Codes
5. Index

Figure 13-2 *Typical organization for a training manual.*

LESSON
ONE

ENTERING AND EXITING THE SYSTEM

1. Start your computer as described in the previous section.
2. Double-click the Special Information Systems group icon to open the Special Information Systems group window.

The screen should now look like this:

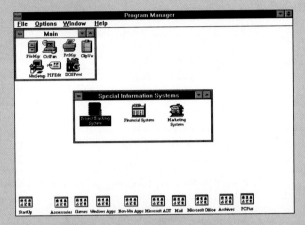

3. Double-click the Project Tracking System Icon In the Special Information Systems group window.

A new screen display containing the Project Tracking System main menu will appear. The menu screen will look like this:

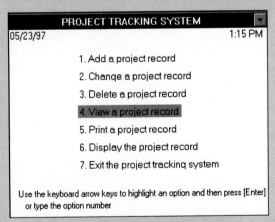

(The actual date and actual time will appear at the upper left and upper right corners of your screen display.)

4. The option number to exit the system is 7. Type a 7 now to exit the system.

After successfully exiting from the Project Tracking System, the screen shown at the top of this page will again appear.

Figure 13-3 *Sample training manual lesson.*

LESSON
TWO

ADDING A NEW PROJECT

1. Start your computer and launch the project tracking system as before. The menu option for adding a new project record is 1. Type a 1 now and the "ADD A PROJECT RECORD" display will now appear on your screen.

05/23/97   ADD A PROJECT RECORD   1:17 PM

Project Number: ☐

Project Description: _____

Project Director: _____

Current Budget: _____

Start Date (MM/DD/YY): _____

Project Status Code: ☐

Project Status Codes (A=active, C=completed, D=deferred, X=canceled)

| Tab /Advance to Next Field | F2 Highlight Field | Clear Current Record | Exit without Adding Record |

Type the Project Description and then press [Enter]

---

2. Type 1785 as the project number and then press the Enter key. The cursor will move to the next line. Type the following data, pressing the Enter key after typing the last letter or digit of each data item.

Materials Tracking System
Carolyn Appleton
8000
112497
A

The screen should now look like this:

05/23/97   ADD A PROJECT RECORD   1:17 PM

Project Number: 1785

Project Description: Materials Tracking System

Project Director: Carolyn Appleton

Current Budget: 8,000

Start Date (MM/DD/YY): 11/24/97

Project Status Code: A

Project Status Codes (A=active, C=completed, D=deferred, X=canceled)

| Tab /Advance to Next Field | F2 Highlight Field | Clear Current Record | Exit without Adding Record |

Type the Project Description and then press [Enter]

Compare your screen to the above display.

If your screen looks like the above display (except for the date and time in the upper corners), press the Enter Key.

Sample training manual lesson.

The Reference Manual section summarizes all options and commands; after becoming somewhat familiar with the information system, an end user could use the Reference Manual section to quickly find an answer to a question or problem. The meaning of and appropriate responses to all the system's error messages are included in the

Error Messages section. All codes used by the system are listed and explained in the Codes section.

A **tutorial** is a series of online or workbook lessons that an end user accesses on a microcomputer or terminal. Tutorial lessons are usually quite similar in structure to the sample training manual lessons shown in Figure 13-3 on page 13.7 and Figure 13-4. Most often, a tutorial is used for training end users on a microcomputer-based system, whereas training manuals are more often used for systems that operate on mainframes or minicomputers; this is not, however, a necessary distinction. A training program that uses both training manuals and tutorials might be appropriate for some information systems.

Use previous trainees. After one group of end users has been trained on the information system, that group can assist in the training of other end users. End users share common interests and viewpoints and, often, a common language. As a result, end users can often learn more rapidly and easily from other end users.

After all the training sessions have been completed, many organizations conduct an additional system or acceptance test as a final training experience. This last system test serves as a dress rehearsal for the end users and computer operations personnel; the systems analysts observe the process but do not participate in it. All the system procedures, including those special procedures that are executed only at the beginning or end of a month, quarter, or year, are included in this final system test. As questions or problems arise, the participants consult the documentation or each other to determine appropriate answers or actions. This extra system test provides valuable experience to all the participants. Perhaps even more importantly, a final system test can instill feelings of confidence and comfort for everyone involved with the new information system before that system actually goes live.

File conversion

After you have established the new information system's production environment and people have been trained on the new system, you can begin the actual conversion effort. **Conversion** refers to those activities necessary to transfer operations from the old information system to the new system. The conversion effort includes two major activities: file conversion and system changeover. File conversion is the subject of this section; system changeover is discussed in the following section.

During **file conversion**, all the existing system data is loaded into the new information system's master and table files or into a database. File conversion is typically a long and costly process, requiring the extensive efforts of the end users, as well as the information systems project team.

When a new system is replacing an older computerized system, you can automate much of the file conversion effort. If the old system had exporting capabilities, that system's data could be **exported**, or output in either a standard format, such as ASCII, or in a format acceptable to the new system. If the exported files are not in a form that can be input directly to the new system, special programs developed during the systems development phase would then be executed to convert those output files into the required format. If the old system did not have export capabilities, you would have developed programs during the systems development phase to extract data from the old system's master and table files and simultaneously convert the data to the format required for the new system's files or database. The data files would then be **imported**, or input into the new system.

Even if the file conversion can be automated in part, most often the new information system requires at least some data items not present in the old system files. To complete the file conversion effort, therefore, the end users must then input values for these new data items. If the new system supports online data entry, the end users can access the normal file update processes of the new information system to enter values for the additional data items. If the new system is a batch system, the end users must code the necessary additional data items onto appropriate source documents, which then must be processed by data entry personnel. In either case, if a lot of data entry is required, you might need to hire temporary help and borrow terminals or microcomputers from other departments of the organization to shorten the elapsed time for data entry.

The file conversion effort is even more severe when the new information system is replacing a manual system. In that case, *all* the new system's master and table file or database data must be entered manually, again either by online data entry or by source document preparation followed by batch data entry.

You might be tempted to bypass or relax all the system, input, and output controls to speed up the file conversion process. This is *not* a good idea; data is highly vulnerable during an intensive conversion effort. All system control measures must be in place and in operation during file conversion to protect files or databases from unauthorized access and to help prevent the input of erroneous values.

Even with the most careful of file conversion efforts using the most thorough input controls, invariably some incorrect data will enter the system and some essential data will be missed. One additional, lengthy step is therefore required in the file conversion process: the end users must verify all the data input to the new system, correct every incorrect data item, and input every missing data item. The normal reports and displays output by the new system can help the end user in this verification effort.

System changeover

System changeover is the process of putting the new information system into production and retiring the old system. System changeover can be either a rapid or slow process, depending on which of the four changeover methods you use. The four changeover methods are direct cutover, parallel operation, pilot operation, and phased changeover. The changeover from the old to the new system is instantaneous when the direct cutover method is used; the changeover occurs over some length of time in a parallel operation mode; two additional changeover options, phased changeover and pilot operation, are compromises between direct cutover and parallel operation. Figure 13-5 illustrates these four changeover methods.

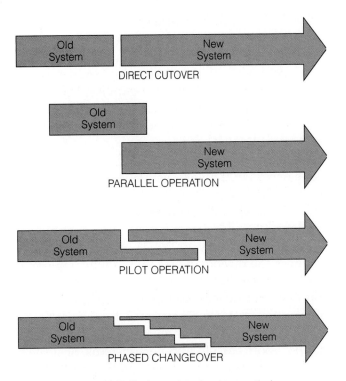

Figure 13-5 *The four system changeover methods.*

One or more of the changeover methods might not be a viable choice for implementing a particular information system. Each of the changeover methods has its advantages and disadvantages, especially in the areas of cost and risk; the relative cost and risk levels of the four changeover methods are summarized in Figure 13-6.

Changeover Method	Risk	Cost
Direct Cutover	High	Low
Parallel Operation	Low	High
Pilot Operation	Medium	Medium
Phased Changeover	Medium	Medium

Figure 13-6 *The relative risks and costs of the four changeover methods.*

As a systems analyst, your role is to consider the particular information system to be implemented, weigh the advantages and disadvantages of each of the four changeover methods, and recommend an appropriate changeover method. The actual decision on the changeover method you use is then made either by management or by the end users.

■ Direct cutover

With the **direct cutover** method, the change from the old system to the new system occurs instantaneously. One day the old system is used; the next day the new system is in operation and the old system is discontinued. The direct cutover method is usually the least expensive of all the changeover methods. The old information system is stopped the moment the new system is implemented, so at any one point in time only one system is incurring operational costs and requiring operational support.

Regardless of how thoroughly and carefully you have conducted the testing and training processes, some problems will inevitably arise when an information system is first put into operation. Problems can result from data situations that were not tested or not even anticipated, or from end user or operator errors; an information system can also encounter difficulties because live data typically occurs in significantly larger volumes than test data. Although initial implementation problems are a concern for all four changeover methods, they are most significant for the direct cutover method. Detecting minor or subtle errors in the new system is more difficult with direct cutover, because the end users cannot verify current output from the new system by comparing it to current output from the old system. Some major errors could even cause a system process to terminate abnormally; with direct cutover, you cannot easily revert to the old system if the new system fails completely.

You would likely choose the direct cutover method for implementing purchased software systems where the possibility of total system failure is considered to be minimal. For information systems developed in-house, you most often use direct cutover only for noncritical information systems. Sometimes, however, the direct cutover method is your only choice for even critical information systems. For example, if the operating environment cannot support both the old and new systems, or if the old and new systems are completely incompatible, then only the direct cutover method is viable.

Timing the implementation can be critical when you use the direct cutover method. Most information systems are somewhat cyclical, running in cycles of a week, month, quarter, or year. As an extreme example, consider a payroll system. If certain employees are paid every week, then the payroll system operates on a weekly cycle. If other employees are paid twice a month, then the payroll system also operates on a semimonthly cycle. A payroll system also operates on a monthly cycle for those reports that are generated once each month. Certain types of tax statements must be prepared every quarter, so a payroll system also operates on a quarterly cycle. Many other tax statements and reports must be generated at the end of each year, so the payroll system also operates on a yearly cycle.

When a cyclical information system is implemented in the middle of any cycle, the processing for the end of that cycle will require information generated by both the old and the new systems. To minimize the need to manually draw data from two different systems, the end users usually choose to cutover to a new cyclical information system at the beginning of a quarter, calendar year, or fiscal year.

■ Parallel operation

With the **parallel operation** changeover method, both the old and the new information systems are in full operation for some period of time. As data is generated and collected during the parallel period, it is input to both systems. The output generated by the new system is compared to the equivalent output from the old system. When everyone is satisfied that the new system is operating correctly, the old system is stopped.

The most obvious advantage of the parallel operation method is the minimization of risk. It is not a catastrophe if the new system does not work correctly, or even if it does not work at all, because the old system is still in operation and serving as the primary system. It is much easier for you and the end users to verify that the new system is working properly under parallel operation than it is with a direct cutover, because many of the outputs from the old and new systems can be matched and checked.

The parallel operation method has, however, a number of significant disadvantages. It is the most costly of all the changeover methods. Because both the old and the new systems are in full operation, all the costs for both systems are incurred during the parallel period. The end users have extra work to do to support both systems; sometimes you must employ temporary help to assist them with the extra workload. If the old system is a computerized system, then running both systems might place a burden on the operating environment; all the users of the organization's computer facilities might suffer delays or degraded service during the parallel period. Parallel operation might not completely test the new system if some end users ignore the new system, using only the old system as long as it is available; in that case, the intended parallel operation changeover actually becomes a direct cutover that occurs when the parallel period ends.

Parallel operation may not be a viable implementation choice for some information systems. If the operating environment cannot support the workloads of both systems, then parallel operation is impossible. Parallel operation is also inappropriate when the old and new systems are incompatible. If the new system is being developed to support a change in the way the organization operates, for example, then the new system does not parallel the old system; in that case, parallel operation would be meaningless.

■ Pilot operation

With the **pilot operation** changeover method, you first implement the new system for only a subset of the organization. A new sales reporting system, for example, might be implemented first in only one branch office, or in the branch offices located in only one region. Similarly, a new payroll system might be implemented first for the employees in only one department. A software house might first release a new system or system revision to only a small number of clients. In those examples, the branch office, region, department, or client that first uses the new system is called a **pilot site**. During the pilot operation of the new system, the old system continues to operate for the entire organization, including the pilot site; thus, pilot operation is a kind of semiparallel operation. After the system has been proven to operate successfully in the pilot site, it is then implemented in the rest of the organization, most often using the direct cutover method. Pilot operation, therefore, is a combination of the direct cutover and parallel operation methods.

By restricting the initial implementation to the pilot site, you limit the area that can be negatively affected by new system's errors and failures; thus, the risk is less with the pilot operation method than with the direct cutover method. Operating both the old and new systems only for the pilot site is less expensive than a parallel operation for the entire organization. Even if you complete the final implementation using the parallel operation method instead of a direct cutover, the final parallel period can be much shorter if the system has already achieved successful pilot site operation. The cost of pilot operation is, therefore, less than the cost of the full parallel operation method.

■ Phased changeover

With a **phased changeover**, you implement the new system in pieces, or modules. Instead of implementing a new manufacturing system all at once, for example, you might first implement the purchasing subsystem, then the production control subsystem, then the shop floor control subsystem, and so on. You can implement each individual subsystem, or module, using any of the other three changeover methods.

Phased changeover and pilot operation are often confused. Both methods combine direct cutover and parallel operations to reduce risk and costs. With phased changeover, however, you give some part of the system to everyone; contrast this with pilot operation, where you give the entire system to only some people.

One advantage of phased changeover is that the risks associated with errors or failures are often limited to just the one module being implemented. If, for instance, the new production control subsystem fails to operate properly, that failure might not impact the new, previously implemented purchasing subsystem or the old, yet to be replaced shop floor control subsystem. Even if those other subsystems are affected by a failure in the new production control subsystem, you have the advantage of knowing in which subsystem the problem lies and can more easily find and correct the problem.

Phased changeover is usually less costly than a full parallel operation of the total system. Even if you use a parallel operation method to implement each of the modules, only one module is implemented at any one time. Thus, the peak demands are lighter on the end users and the operational environment. Phased changeover is inappropriate, however, if the system cannot be easily separated into logical modules.

Post-implementation evaluation

Once the new system is completely operational, it is easy to believe that the project effort is done. Two important activities remain, however, before you have truly completed the project. One of these activities is the post-implementation evaluation, which is the topic of this section. The other activity, the final report to management, is the subject of the following section.

In a **post-implementation evaluation**, the quality of an information system and its developmental effort is assessed. A post-implementation evaluation verifies that the new information system meets specified requirements, complies with end user objectives, and achieves anticipated benefits. In addition, by providing feedback to the development team, a post-implementation evaluation also helps improve information systems development practices for future projects.

In a post-implementation evaluation, you can and should examine all aspects of the systems development effort and the developed information system. Typical evaluation criteria include the accuracy, completeness, and timeliness of information output by the system, end user satisfaction, quality of the system/end user interfaces, adequacy of system controls and security measures, hardware efficiency and platform performance, quality of database implementation, performance of the information systems team, quality and completeness of all the documentation, quality and effectiveness of the end user training, and accuracy of the cost and benefits estimates and developmental schedules.

You can use the same fact-finding techniques in a post-implementation evaluation that we examined earlier in the text for determining system requirements. As the evaluator, you should:

- Interview members of management and key end users
- Observe the end users and computer operations personnel actually working with the new information system
- Read all the documentation and training materials
- Examine all source documents, output reports, and screen displays
- Use questionnaires to gather information and opinions from a large number of end users

Figure 13-7 shows the first page of a sample User Evaluation Form that surveys end users' opinions about the new information system.

USER EVALUATION FORM

System:	Evaluator:	Date:

Please evaluate the information system project by circling the one number for each factor that best represents your assessment.

	Poor		Average			Good
SYSTEM OUTPUT						
1. Accuracy of information............	1	2	3	4	5	6
2. Completeness of information........	1	2	3	4	5	6
3. Ease of use........................	1	2	3	4	5	6
4. Timeliness of information..........	1	2	3	4	5	6
USER INTERFACE						
5. Clarity of instructions...........	1	2	3	4	5	6
6. Quality of help messages..........	1	2	3	4	5	6
7. Ease of use........................	1	2	3	4	5	6
8. Appropriateness of options........	1	2	3	4	5	6
9. Clarity of error messages.........	1	2	3	4	5	6
10. Prevention of input errors........	1	2	3	4	5	6
INFORMATION SYSTEMS STAFF						
11. Cooperation.......................	1	2	3	4	5	6
12. Availability......................	1	2	3	4	5	6
13. Knowledge.........................	1	2	3	4	5	6
14. Reporting of progress.............	1	2	3	4	5	6
15. Communication skills..............	1	2	3	4	5	6
TRAINING						
16. Completeness......................	1	2	3	4	5	6
17. Appropriateness...................	1	2	3	4	5	6
18. Schedule..........................	1	2	3	4	5	6

Figure 13-7 Sample User Evaluation Form.

A post-implementation evaluation is more effective if it is conducted by objective, disinterested people who were not directly involved in the systems development effort. Some organizations have an internal audit department whose members evaluate the work performed in all other departments in the organization; other organizations hire outside auditors or evaluators. Usually, however, the end users and information systems department personnel perform the post-implementation evaluation. In fact, very often the same people who developed the system then perform the post-implementation evaluation; although this is not ideal, a system evaluation performed by the development team is better than no evaluation at all.

When should the post-implementation evaluation take place? Is it better to perform the evaluation after the new system has been in operation for one month, or six months, or one year, or even longer?

Details of the developmental effort can be forgotten if too much time elapses before the evaluation team performs the post-implementation evaluation. After several months or a year or two, for instance, the end users might not be able to remember the source for their knowledge of a system function; the source could have been from their training, from the user documentation, or through experimentation with the system. The end users might also forget their impressions of information systems team members and what these members did that was especially helpful. One purpose of the post-implementation evaluation is to improve the quality of the efforts of the information systems department, including interaction with the end users, training, and documentation. Consequently, the evaluation team should perform the evaluation while the end users can still recall specific incidents, successes, problems, and suggestions for improvement.

On the other hand, the post-implementation evaluation is also concerned with assessing the quality of the new system. If the evaluation team performs the evaluation too soon after implementation, the end users will not have had enough time to thoroughly use the system and all its features, to appreciate the system's strengths, and to recognize the system's weaknesses or failings. For this reason, many experts recommend beginning the post-implementation evaluation six to nine months after system implementation.

In actual practice, the evaluation team would typically perform a post-implementation evaluation between one and three months after implementation, or even just before implementation. Although this may not be the best time for the evaluation, practical considerations come into play. Because the same people who worked on the systems development very often perform the evaluation, the evaluation must be completed before those information systems personnel can be assigned to other projects. ■

Ideally, conducting post-implementation evaluations would be a standard practice for all information systems projects. Unfortunately, this is not the case. In some organizations very few, if any, projects are subjected to a careful final evaluation. The reasons for skipping the post-implementation evaluation are numerous: the end users are eager to get on with their own work; the information systems personnel must be reassigned to other priority projects; no other qualified personnel are available to perform the evaluation; and, most importantly, management does not appreciate the significant benefits that can be gained in return for the costs of a post-implementation evaluation.

Final report to management

t the end of each of the systems development life cycle phases, you produce a report to management. The last phase, systems implementation and evaluation, is no exception. The final report to management includes the following:

- Final versions of all system documentation
- Any future modifications and enhancements to the system that have already been identified
- A recap of all the systems development costs and schedules in the final report
- A comparison of actual costs and schedules to original estimates
- The post-implementation evaluation, if it has been completed

Thus, the final report to management signals the end of the systems development life cycle and the start of systems operation. In the next chapter, we will examine the role of a systems analyst during systems operation so that you know the effects of the decisions you make and the work you perform during the development of an information system.

CHAPTER CASE STUDY 13

James Tool Company — Systems Implementation and Evaluation

After a successful period of parallel processing, the payroll package purchased by James Tool Company from Lennox Software Solutions had been implemented. As specified by the schedule developed by James Tool management and the payroll department, implementation of the union system was now ready to begin.

As the first step in implementing the union system, programmer/analyst Howard Coswell installed the microcomputer portion of the union system on the personal computer in the union relations department. Coswell then met with Delbert Donovan, the director of union relations, and Dean Rosen, a union relations department clerk, for a half-day training session. The session went very well; Donovan and Rosen were very pleased with the union system and both were confident of their future roles. As their final training exercise, Donovan and Rosen successfully created the union file using the modify/view union program, thus completing all the necessary file-conversion effort for the union system.

Meanwhile, payroll department employees were still preparing the required union reports and checks manually, much as they always had; the only difference was that now they were using union deduction data produced by the new payroll system. To eliminate the manual effort and resulting overtime as soon as possible, Jim McKeen, director of payroll, had requested a direct cutover to the new union system; Coswell, Donovan, and management had agreed. Coswell made preparations to place the union system into operation at the beginning of the next four-week union cycle.

Coswell loaded the union deduction extract program into the mainframe payroll operational environment. He also added the necessary commands to the payroll system JCL to accomplish two things. First, the union deduction change file would be uploaded and input to the payroll system's employee maintenance program. Second, the union deduction extract program would be executed during every payroll cycle, creating a union deduction file that would be downloaded to the union relations microcomputer.

The direct cutover to the union system occurred without major problems, and the entire union system performed accurately and properly. After the union system had been operational for four weeks and had successfully produced the first batch of union checks and reports, Coswell prepared a final report to management. Coswell also wrote a memo to accompany the report. This memo, which is shown in Figure 13-8, was sent to Arnold Henderson, vice president of finance, whose request for system services had initiated the payroll system and union system projects. With the distribution of the final report to management, the development effort for the union system was completed.

MEMORANDUM

DATE: September 15, 1997
TO: Arnold Henderson
CC: Delbert Donovan, David Greene, Jim McKeen
FROM: Howard Coswell
SUBJECT: Union System

On September 9, 1996, the information systems department recieved your request for systems services to investigate problems with the payroll system. That investigation led to the purchase and implementation of the payroll system from Lennox Software Solutions and the development of the union system.

The union system was implemented on August 15, 1997. As of today, the system has been in operation for more than four weeks. One complete cycle of union reporting and check writing has been completed without problems. The payroll department, union relations department, and the union leaders have all expressed satisfaction with the new union system.

As shown in the attached schedule and budget final report, the union system was implemented exactly on schedule with total development costs $2,390.00 under budget.

Figure 13-8 *The memo accompanying the final report to management for the union system for the James Tool Company.*

Summary

The systems implementation and evaluation phase, which is the final phase of the systems development life cycle, includes six major activities. In the first activity in this phase, you establish an operational, or production, environment for the new information system that is completely separate from the test environment. The operational environment, which contains all the programs, procedures, and live data files for the information system, is accessible only by authorized end users; once the operational environment is established, members of the information systems department can access that environment only to apply authorized corrections, modifications, and enhancements. The test environment, in which the project team has been developing and testing the new system, continues to exist even after the operational environment is established; all future changes to the information system must be verified using the test data files in the test environment before the changes are applied to the operational environment.

All the people who will interact with the new information system must receive training that is appropriate to their roles and skills. Sometimes, much of the training can be provided by software or hardware vendors or by professional training organizations; often, however, the responsibility for training falls on the members of the information systems department. If you must develop a training program, remember the following guidelines: train people in groups; utilize people already trained to help train others; develop separate programs for distinct employee groups; and provide for learning by hearing, seeing, and doing, with lectures and discussions, demonstrations and documentation, and training manuals or tutorials.

The file-conversion effort is often a lengthy, complicated process. During file conversion, all master and table data for the new information system is loaded into files or a database and is verified by the end users using the file maintenance processes and outputs of the new information system. If the system being replaced is a computerized system, some of the file-conversion effort can be performed by special programs that read the old system's master and table files and then output appropriate data in the form the new system requires.

System changeover is the process of putting the new information system into operation and retiring the old system. We considered four changeover methods: direct cutover, parallel operation, pilot operation, and phased changeover. With direct cutover, the old system is stopped and the new system is started simultaneously; direct cutover is the least expensive and most risky of the changeover methods. With parallel operation, the end users operate both the old and new information systems for some period of time; parallel operation is the most expensive and least risky of the changeover methods. Pilot operation and phased changeover represent compromises between direct cutover and parallel operation; both are less risky than direct cutover and less costly than parallel operation. With pilot operation, a subset of the organization uses the new system for a period of time, while the old system continues to operate for the entire organization; after the system is proven for the pilot site, it is implemented for the rest of the organization. With the phased changeover approach, you implement the system for the entire organization a module at a time until the entire system is in operation.

A post-implementation evaluation assesses and reports on the quality of the new information system and of the work done by the project team. Although it is best if the post-implementation evaluation is performed by people who were not involved in the systems development effort, often the members of the project team perform the evaluation.

The final report to management includes all the final system documentation, describes all the future system enhancements that have already been identified, and details all the project costs. The distribution of the final report represents the end of the information systems department's development effort and the beginning of the end users' responsibility for the new information system.

Review Questions

1. What is the purpose of an operational environment?
2. By what other name is an operational environment known?
3. What types of personnel must receive training before a new information system is implemented?
4. What is typically included in a training manual? How is a tutorial different from a training manual?
5. Is file security more or less important during file conversion than during subsequent system operation?
6. List four system changeover methods.
7. Which of the system changeover methods is typically the most costly? Why?
8. Which of the system changeover methods is typically the most risky? Why?
9. What does it mean to say that an information system is cyclical?
10. How does phased changeover differ from pilot operation?
11. Who should perform a post-implementation evaluation? Who typically does perform the evaluation?
12. List four investigative techniques that can be used when performing a post-implementation evaluation.
13. What information is usually included in the final report to management?

Discussion Questions

1. Obtain and evaluate an online tutorial or reference manual lesson for some software product. Are the instructions and lesson steps clear? Are the illustrations appropriate and helpful? What level of computer sophistication does the lesson assume the user already has? If the lesson requires some prior computer knowledge, are novice users told where to find supplementary information? What specific suggestions do you have for improving the lesson?
2. Prepare a tutorial to train someone in the use of a specific device or appliance, such as a lawn mower, microwave oven, or VCR.
3. Prepare a one-page questionnaire to be distributed to computer operators for a post-implementation evaluation of a recently implemented information system. Include at least twelve questions, with at least two questions in each of the general categories for which you consider it important to receive feedback from operational personnel.

Hoober Industries

You are the project manager for the development of a new mainframe information system that will operate on a weekly cycle at Hoober Industries. The new information system will be implemented using the direct cutover method and will ideally start operation on a Monday.

Before the system changeover can take place, two activities must be completed: first, you must train twenty-two end users, four computer operators, and three managers; second, the end users must complete the file-conversion process. File conversion can begin as soon as at least one computer operator and one end user have been trained. You estimate that each training session will take two complete days and that no more than eight people can be involved in any one training session. You have developed three different types of training sessions, one for the end users, one for the managers, and one for the computer operators. Assume that all four computer operators could attend the same training session and that the session could be held during regular hours on two consecutive weekdays.

Each end user can spend at most twenty hours of a forty-hour week in training or file conversion; the remaining twenty hours are required for other job duties.

You have estimated that the file-conversion effort will require a total of twenty-one end user person-weeks, of which nineteen person-weeks will be spent entering and verifying constant data. The remaining two person-weeks are required for entering and verifying current balance data; this task can only be accomplished during a single weekend just before the cutover. The computer center is operational and is staffed by an operator throughout the weekend. A maximum of 100 overtime hours has been approved for the end users for the file-conversion effort.

Question

1. Prepare a training and file-conversion schedule that will result in the earliest possible implementation while minimizing the amount of overtime required.

Ridgeway Company

The Ridgeway Company requirements for the new billing system for the Blue Waters Country Club were first described in a Chapter 4 minicase study; subsequent minicase studies in Chapters 8, 9, and 10 addressed the design of files and programs for the system. The following assignments are based on the work you have done on those minicase studies.

Questions

1. Identify the specific groups of people who will require training on the new system. For each group, describe the type of training you would recommend and list the topics you would cover.

2. Recommend a changeover method for the new billing system, and justify your recommendation. If your recommendation is for phased changeover, specify the order in which you would implement modules; if your recommendation is for pilot operation, specify the department or area you would select as the pilot site.

3. Develop a file-conversion plan: specify which data items in which files must be entered during the file-conversion process; suggest an order in which the data could be entered; indicate those data items for which the timing of the data entry is most critical.

STUDENT CASE STUDY 13

Western Dental Clinic — Systems Implementation and Evaluation

Introduction

All the programs and procedures for the new computerized office information system for Western Dental Clinic have been prepared, tested, and approved; eight microcomputers have been purchased and have been installed and networked in the clinic offices. Jim Archer, the consultant hired by Western Dental to develop the system, is now ready to begin systems implementation.

Student Assignments

1. Identify the specific groups of people who will require training on the new system. Describe the type and level of training you would recommend for each group.

2. Recommend a changeover method for the new Western Dental Clinic office system, and justify your recommendation. If your recommendation is for either phased changeover or pilot operation, specify the order in which you would implement modules or the department you would select as the pilot site.

3. Develop a file-conversion plan: specify which data items in which files must be entered during the file-conversion process; suggest an order in which the data could be entered; indicate those data items for which the timing of the data entry is most critical.

CHAPTER 14

Systems Operation

Objectives

You will have mastered the material in this chapter when you can:

- Discuss the sources and purposes of the three different types of maintenance
- Describe a standard maintenance procedure
- Explain how and why the procedure is different under some circumstances for corrective maintenance
- Discuss the role of configuration management in systems operation
- Describe the process of capacity planning, and discuss the workload and performance measurements used in capacity planning
- Recognize the signs of information system obsolescence

Introduction

Work on an information system does not end when the system is implemented. In most organizations, at least 50% of information systems department staff time is spent working on existing, operational information systems; in some organizations, the information systems department staff might spend as much as 80% of their time working on operational systems. Changes to operational information systems reflect organizational growth and change, which are natural and usually positive processes. Even very high quality information systems require modification during their systems operation. In fact, the better the system, the more likely the system will be used extensively, and the higher the enthusiasm of its end users; that enthusiasm often generates new ideas for enhancing or expanding the information system.

We begin this chapter with a general discussion of information system maintenance. Then, we consider each of the three standard classifications of maintenance: corrective, adaptive, and perfective. Next, we describe issues of systems operation management, including the maintenance team, configuration management, and maintenance release methods. Then, we consider the performance of operating information systems, followed by a discussion of CASE maintenance tools. We conclude the chapter by examining system obsolescence and discussing how to recognize when an information system is no longer economically useful.

Information system maintenance

The **systems operation** phase of an information system begins when a system is implemented and ends when the system is no longer used, either because the services provided by the system are no longer needed or because a replacement system has been implemented. For example, the end of systems operation for an inventory control system for an appliance repair firm might occur with any of the following events: the firm sells all its inventory and begins purchasing parts on an as-needed basis from a local distributor; the firm outsources its inventory control operations to an outside company; the firm develops and implements a new inventory control system; or the firm purchases and implements an inventory control software package.

Information systems departments often call systems operation the **maintenance phase** because maintenance is what they spend most of their time doing during this phase. The end users, however, view their systems as operating and useful systems, not merely as sources of maintenance activity. Systems operation is, therefore, the preferred term.

Maintenance includes all the activities associated with changing any program, procedure, or documentation for an operational information system to keep the system operating correctly, to adapt the system to meet the changing requirements of the system's end users, or to make the system operate more efficiently. These three objectives are met by corrective, adaptive, and perfective maintenance, respectively; that is, you perform corrective maintenance to correct errors in an information system; you perform adaptive maintenance to add features to the system to satisfy new end user requirements; and you perform perfective maintenance to improve the system's efficiency.

In Chapter 11, we considered the total costs of an information system over its entire life span, including systems operation. Figure 14-1 shows a typical curve of information system costs versus time for only the systems operation phase. Some of the costs incurred during systems operation are operational expenses, such as supplies, equipment rental, and software lease expenses; these operational expenses are usually either relatively constant or gradually increasing over time. The area under the dashed line in Figure 14-1 represents that portion of the total operating costs that is attributable to operational expenses. The remainder of the systems operation costs is associated with maintenance; the area under the cost curve but above the dashed line in Figure 14-1 represents the system maintenance costs.

As shown in Figure 14-1, systems operation costs incurred by maintenance activities vary over time. Maintenance costs are typically high immediately after implementation, when errors and omissions in the initial system are detected, investigated, and corrected. After most initial system errors have been corrected, maintenance costs remain relatively low during a period in which maintenance primarily consists of minor adaptive maintenance. After a time, both adaptive and perfective maintenance activity and costs increase, because significant system changes are needed to meet changing organizational and operating environments. Near the end of an information system's useful life, maintenance costs increase rapidly, due not only to new adaptive and perfective maintenance activity, but also to the effort necessary to correct errors introduced into the system by previous maintenance. The table in Figure 14-2 shows the typical patterns of occurrence for each of the three standard classifications of maintenance activities over an information system's operational life span.

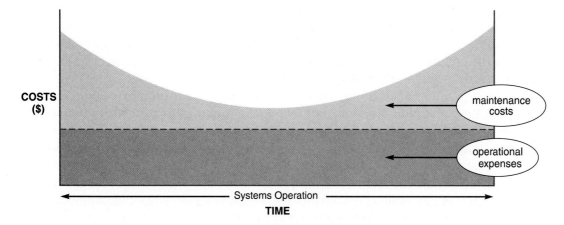

COSTS ($)

Systems Operation
TIME

Figure 14-1 *The total costs associated with an information system during systems operation include both operational expenses and maintenance costs. Operational expenses are relatively constant, whereas maintenance costs vary over time.*

	Immediately After Implementation	Early Operational Life	Middle Operational Life	Later Operational Life
Corrective Maintenance	High	Low	Low	High
Adaptive Maintenance (Minor Enhancements)	None	Medium	Medium	Medium
Adaptive Maintenance (Major Enhancements)	None	None	Medium to High	Medium to High
Perfective Maintenance	Low	Low to Medium	Medium	Low

Figure 14-2 *Typical information system maintenance patterns depend on the type of maintenance, as well as the age of the system.*

Sometimes the word maintenance is used to refer to only what we call corrective maintenance, and the word enhancement is used to refer to what we call adaptive maintenance and perfective maintenance. An **enhancement** is a feature or capability added to an operational information system, or a change made to a system to improve its efficiency or maintainability. In this chapter, we use the word maintenance in its broader sense to include enhancements as well as corrective maintenance.

■ Corrective maintenance

Corrective maintenance involves the diagnosis and correction of errors in an operational information system. If a program abnormally terminates or produces incorrect results, or if the end user documentation or operations documentation is erroneous, you must perform corrective maintenance.

Corrective maintenance is often necessary not only for errors present in the original version of the information system, but also for new errors introduced with maintenance changes. Careful development of the original system can reduce or eliminate initial errors; similarly, careful analysis, design, and testing of all types of maintenance changes will help reduce the chances of introducing new errors into the system. An ideal maintenance procedure, therefore, is a logical progression of investigation, analysis, design, development, and testing steps that are all performed *before* the implementation of a change.

You cannot always take these steps in their logical order for corrective maintenance because errors vary in their severity, and, therefore, the procedures for handling the different types of errors also vary. You follow the organization's standard maintenance procedure for minor errors, such as an incorrect report title, an inappropriate data element output format, or a documentation error. For a typical standard maintenance procedure, an end user submits a systems request, which is then evaluated, prioritized, and scheduled by the systems review committee. Eventually, a maintenance team, consisting of one or more systems analysts or programmers, analyzes the problem and designs, tests, documents, and implements a correction. Figure 14-3 shows a sample systems request for the correction of a relatively minor error in an operational information system.

For more severe errors, such as an incorrect output control total or missing master file records, an end user must still submit a systems request along with supporting evidence, such as file listings, reports, or screen display prints. The prioritizing and scheduling steps are typically bypassed for severe errors, and a maintenance team immediately begins analyzing the problem and designing, testing, documenting, and implementing a correction. Severe errors often occur because the systems developers did not anticipate or test for specific situations or data combinations. As part of your maintenance efforts, therefore, you will often have to add new data records to the system's test data files to ensure that the data does completely test the system.

For errors that cause total system failure, you perform the steps in the maintenance procedure in a very different order. When a system failure is detected, a reactive process known as fire fighting takes place. When **fire fighting**, the maintenance team bypasses the initial maintenance steps and attempts to devise and implement an immediate correction, or **fix**. Meanwhile, a formal systems request is prepared either by an end user, an operations clerk, or a member of the information systems department; that systems request is added to the maintenance records for the information system to keep those records complete. Only after the system is again operational or the critical problem has been fixed does the maintenance team carefully analyze the problem and design a permanent correction. The test data files are then supplemented, if appropriate. Then, the changed information system is thoroughly tested, the change is documented, and, if a better correction was developed, the new correction is implemented.

REQUEST FOR INFORMATION SYSTEMS SERVICES

		Request for:
DATE:	November 6, 1997	[x] MODIFICATION
SUBMITTED BY:	Marilyn Keefer	OF EXISTING
TITLE:	Director	SYSTEM
DEPARTMENT:	Marketing	
PHONE:	X1429	[ ] NEW SYSTEM

DESCRIPTION OF REQUESTED SYSTEMS SERVICE:
(Attach Additional documents as necessary)

On October's Advertising Performance report, an expense
value of $108,500 did not print correctly. Instead,
it was shown as 8,500. The expense category subtotal
and the grand total were both correct, however.

I have attached a copy of the two report pages that include
all the output for that particular expense category.

(To be completed by the Information Systems Department)

DATE:

ACTION:

Figure 14-3 *A systems request for the correction of an error.*

■ Adaptive maintenance

Adaptive maintenance involves changing or adding new features, capabilities, or functions to an operational information system. The need for adaptive maintenance usually arises from business environment changes, such as a new product offering, an inventory reorganization, a change in the way fixed assets are depreciated, a new legal reporting requirement, or the need to interface with another, newly developed information system.

The procedure for adaptive maintenance is much like the procedure for minor corrective maintenance. An end user submits a systems request; the request is evaluated and prioritized; and then a maintenance team analyzes the requirements and designs, tests, documents, and implements the enhancement. Although the procedures for the two types of maintenance are similar, the amount of information systems department resources required for the adaptive maintenance effort is usually much greater than that required for minor corrective maintenance.

An adaptive maintenance effort can actually be described as a *mini-SDLC*. All the activities and tools we described in Chapters 2 through 13 for new development projects are equally applicable to adaptive maintenance. Adaptive maintenance projects, however, are usually smaller in scope and require less time and fewer personnel than new development. The additional constraint that the enhancement must work within the existing information system, however, means that adaptive maintenance is very often more difficult than new development.

■ Perfective maintenance

Perfective maintenance involves changing an operational information system to make it more efficient, more reliable, or more maintainable. Several examples of specific perfective maintenance projects are listed in Figure 14-4.

Perfective Maintenance Projects

- Rewrite a program in a more efficient language
- Reengineer or restructure a program
- Install a new operation system or compiler
- Change user interface to a GUI
- Change a data structure
- Change storage devices
- Change blocking factors
- Store intermediate results
- Eliminate temporary work files
- Eliminate loops
- Eliminate or reorganize calls to external modules
- Simplify calculations

Figure 14-4 *Examples of typical perfective maintenance projects to improve an information system's efficiency, reliability, or maintainability.*

Although the end users normally initiate requests for corrective and adaptive maintenance, people in the information systems department usually initiate specific suggestions for perfective maintenance projects. In some cases, however, end user complaints about worsening system performance can result in a perfective maintenance project.

During systems operation, the way the end users interact with the system and the frequencies or patterns of system input data can change. As a result, an information system might not operate as efficiently as it did originally or as efficiently as possible. **Fine-tuning**, which is one kind of perfective maintenance, is the process of adapting an information system to changing patterns of usage.

Operational information systems not performing as well as they once did are potential candidates for perfective maintenance. If a system's end users complain about the system's performance, or if systems operation statistics indicate that an information system is taking considerably longer to execute, you should investigate the cause of the performance problem. In many cases, a perfective maintenance project can reduce execution times by increasing system efficiency.

You can also undertake perfective maintenance to improve system reliability by preventing potential system errors or failures or by lessening the chance that future maintenance of any type will cause problems. You might, for example, rewrite a section of a program when you recognize that the program logic would be deficient in some situations; in this case, your perfective maintenance eliminates a possible future error.

Making an information system more maintainable is closely related to improving its reliability. When a system is more maintainable, not only are future maintenance projects easier and less costly, but they are also less risky. You might, for example, reorganize and rewrite a long, complex program to improve its maintainability. The perfective maintenance you perform on a program today will make it easier to correctly determine where and how to make future maintenance changes to that program.

One perfective maintenance technique becoming more popular is automated reengineering. A **reengineering tool** is a CASE tool that analyzes a program and, with some human assistance and input, rewrites the program; for example, you can use a reengineering tool to translate a program from one language to another or to transform a program from one database implementation to another. A **restructuring tool** is a closely related CASE product that analyzes and rewrites a program into an equivalent form.

Programs with a large number of past maintenance changes are often very good candidates for rewriting or for automated reengineering or restructuring. The more a program changes, the more likely it is to become inefficient, more difficult to change, and more vulnerable to errors. Keeping detailed records of all maintenance activities can help you identify those programs with a high adaptive or corrective maintenance history.

Perfective maintenance is usually performed infrequently, even though performing it is often advisable and economically worthwhile. In some cases, the reason for infrequent perfective maintenance is that very few perfective maintenance projects are identified and proposed. Organizations with limited resources often consider new development, adaptive maintenance, and corrective maintenance to be more important than perfective maintenance. New, high-priority projects are continually requested, and so the low priority perfective maintenance projects rarely reach the top of the project queue. When worthwhile perfective maintenance proposals cannot be budgeted or scheduled as separate projects, combining some perfective maintenance work with other maintenance projects might be possible. If a significant new function must be added to a program, for example, you might be able to integrate some perfective maintenance for that program into the adaptive maintenance project.

Perfective maintenance is usually most cost effective and most appropriate in the mid-years of an information system's operational life. During early systems operation, perfective maintenance is often unnecessary. Late in systems operation, perfective maintenance, although often necessary, is not cost effective. Most of the benefits of perfective maintenance are future benefits; they cannot be fully realized if the information system will soon be discontinued or replaced.

Systems operation management

The systems operation phase, as with all other phases in the life of an information system, requires effective management. Systems operation management includes creating a group of people called a **maintenance team** who follows an established **configuration management** process to complete maintenance projects; these maintenance projects result in a number of **maintenance releases** of the information system. In the following sections, we define and examine each of these three components of systems operation management.

■ The maintenance team

A maintenance project is performed by a maintenance team consisting of one or more systems analysts and one or more programmers from the applications group in the information systems department. All systems analysts, whether they are working on maintenance projects or on new development, should possess the traits we first discussed in Chapter 1. These traits include a knowledge of computer concepts, tools, and techniques; an understanding of business concepts; interactive people skills; communication skills; creativity; and analytical skills. All these skills should be combined with a strong desire to learn and keep current with technological changes.

In addition to possessing these traits, maintenance systems analysts must also be skilled detectives. The ability to rapidly diagnose and locate the source of a problem in an operational information system is a much prized skill. Maintenance systems analysts also need to be especially skilled in analysis, as well as in its opposite technique, synthesis. **Analysis** is the process of examining the whole in order to understand its component parts; in contrast, **synthesis** is the process of examining and organizing the parts so as to understand the whole. A maintenance systems analyst who is working on only a part of an information system must understand how that part fits into the whole system, and he or she must determine how to perform the required maintenance on that part without compromising or destroying the whole system.

Management in many organizations assigns the applications programmers and systems analysts to one of two groups: one group performs all the new development and the other group performs all the maintenance. The advantage of this approach is that individuals in the maintenance group can develop and enhance the skills that are most important for maintenance projects.

A few organizations do not subdivide their applications staff; programmers and systems analysts are assigned to projects as they arise. One advantage of this approach is the additional flexibility in making project assignments. A second advantage is that the team who developed an information system frequently assumes responsibility for maintaining the system as well. The organization, therefore, need not commit additional time and money for the maintenance team to learn the system. If the development team knows they will also be responsible for maintaining the system, they might take even greater care in designing the system to enhance maintainability; they might tend, however, to be less careful with the documentation because they already know the system.

Unfortunately, maintenance work often carries a stigma. Many systems analysts consider new development to be more interesting, more challenging, more visible, and, as a result, more rewarding. Few people in the information systems department and even fewer people outside that department recognize that maintenance is usually more difficult than new development. The greater difficulty results from the fact that creating new programs is typically easier than understanding and changing someone else's programs.

Some organizations that have separate maintenance and new development groups periodically rotate people from one group to the other in order to achieve some of the advantages of the single-group method and to counteract the stigma against maintenance. When people have a chance to develop all types of skills, project assignment flexibility is enhanced. When necessary, management can rapidly shift staffing in the two groups to meet changing needs. Systems analysts working on maintenance projects gain an understanding of maintenance analysis, enabling them to better design maintainable information systems when they serve as development systems analysts. Similarly, systems analysts working on new development gain a greater appreciation of the design process and the necessity for design compromises; this understanding helps them to become better maintenance systems analysts.

One disadvantage of this rotation technique is it increases applications group overhead costs, because time is lost when people are shifted from one job to another. When systems analysts are constantly shifted back and forth between maintenance and new development, they might never become highly skilled at any one job. The lack of highly skilled maintenance systems analysts can be especially detrimental to an organization. Another disadvantage is many systems analysts strongly prefer either maintenance or new development analysis; with the rotation method, those systems analysts must spend a portion of their time doing a job they dislike.

Newly hired and recently promoted information systems department employees are usually assigned to maintenance projects only. Why is this phenomenon common in so many organizations? Is it better to assign new people to maintenance or to new development projects?

The most significant reason for assigning new people to a maintenance project is the learning it can provide. Studying existing systems and their documentation is an easy way to learn the organization's standards for programs and documentation. In addition, the mini-SDLC utilized for many adaptive maintenance projects is excellent training for the full-scale systems development life cycle.

There are a number of arguments, however, against the practice of assigning new people only to maintenance projects. First, maintenance is usually more difficult than new development; starting a new person out on an easier, new development project might make more sense. Second, maintenance teams are often smaller than new development teams.

Fewer experienced systems analysts and programmers are available, therefore, to provide guidance to the new person. Similarly, fewer people are available to help verify that the work done by the new person is accurate. The new person's share of the responsibility for the project is also greater; therefore, his or her failure would have greater significance for a smaller project.

On the other hand, a maintenance team being smaller than a new development team is a point in favor of assigning new people to maintenance; that is, a new person assigned to a large project might get lost in the larger group and the larger effort. In a smaller project team, the new person is more visible; other team members are more likely to notice if the new person needs assistance.

For most organizations, the argument that maintenance provides excellent training outweighs all other considerations. The common practice of assigning newly hired and newly promoted employees only to maintenance projects is, therefore, likely to continue. ∎

■ Configuration management

We first discussed configuration management in Chapter 11, where we defined it as the process of managing and controlling requested changes to the system requirements document after the requirements were approved and frozen. Configuration management is equally applicable during systems operation for managing and controlling changes to an operational information system.

One major component of systems operation configuration management is a procedure for handling systems requests for maintenance changes. A typical procedure includes these steps: a systems request is completed, an initial action on the request is taken, and a final disposition of the request is determined.

1. *Complete a systems request.* A systems request for maintenance is usually submitted by an end user; requests for perfective maintenance, however, are more often prepared by information systems department members, and requests for critical corrective maintenance might come directly from operations personnel. For system maintenance records to be complete, a systems request must be filled out for all maintenance that is proposed or undertaken, regardless of who initiates the request.

2. *Take initial action on the request.* In most organizations, one person in either the information systems department or the end user department is designated as the **systems operation manager**. This person is responsible for configuration management of one or more operational information systems. When someone submits a systems request for maintenance on an operational information system, the systems operation manager determines an appropriate initial action. If the request indicates a severe problem, a maintenance team is immediately assigned to the task of corrective maintenance; otherwise, the systems operation manager either rejects, defers, or accepts the request. If the request is deferred or rejected, the systems operation manager returns a copy of the request to the requester and to the systems review committee, along with the reasons for the deferral or rejection. If the request is accepted, the systems operation manager submits it to the systems review committee for final disposition.

3. *Determine the disposition of the request.* The systems review committee evaluates the request, determines its feasibility, and then either rejects the request or assigns it a priority and schedules the maintenance project.

In some organizations, the systems review committee separates maintenance requests from new development requests for purposes of evaluation and prioritizing. In other organizations, the systems review committee considers all requests for system services together, regardless of type. An organization, therefore, might have two separate queues for future information systems projects, or it might have a single queue for all future projects. Which approach is better?

Organizations that recognize that maintenance and new development are equally important often choose to treat them equally with respect to evaluation, selection, prioritizing, and scheduling. The most important project is given top priority, whether it is maintenance or new development. This single-queue approach is considered logical, because maintenance and new development require similar information systems department resources. Perhaps most importantly, single-queue organizations believe that prioritizing all types of projects together will accurately reflect the organization's needs.

The double-queue approach also offers several advantages. In those organizations in which the programmers and systems analysts are organized into separate maintenance and new development groups, considering the work to be done by the two groups separately is more logical. Another advantage of double queues is that maintenance might be more likely to receive a fair share of information systems department resources. Many people believe that the double-queue approach also increases the occurrence of worthwhile perfective maintenance projects.

Choosing either a single- or a double-queue approach will not alone guarantee an ideal distribution of maintenance and new development efforts. In organizations with divided information systems applications groups, the number of programmers and systems analysts assigned to each of the two groups also affects the relative balance of maintenance versus new development. In organizations using a single queue, if the systems review committee tends to assign higher priorities to requests of one type over the other, the relative balance of the two types of projects is affected.

Most organizations are satisfied with whatever approach they use, as long as it enables them to complete the highest priority developmental efforts and the most critical corrective maintenance projects. Attaining an ideal balance among all types of maintenance and all new development, however, is a worthy objective. ■

Configuration management is also concerned with managing all versions of an information system. When an operational information system is implemented on multiple computers, maintenance updates must be applied to each installed version of the information system. In some cases, the installed versions are different from one another because of different hardware configurations. Configuration management includes keeping track of all the different versions of the information system, ensuring that all maintenance updates are applied to all versions and that all versions of the information system work correctly.

Another component of configuration management is the management of information system documentation. An operational information system has extensive documentation. Some of this documentation is stored in the information systems department; this documentation includes the initial systems request, all the development history records, all the end-of-phase reports, the data dictionary, and the operations manuals. Other documentation, such as end user manuals, is distributed to other departments in the organization. Maintenance projects almost always generate updates to the information systems department's documentation and often generate end user documentation updates: you almost always must change end user documentation to reflect adaptive maintenance changes; sometimes you will need to change end user documentation for corrective maintenance; only perfective maintenance rarely requires updates to end user documentation. Keeping track of all the existing documentation and ensuring that appropriate updates to that documentation are made and properly distributed is an important, although difficult, aspect of configuration management.

■ Maintenance releases

The difficulties involved in coordinating maintenance changes to multiple versions of an operational information system and in distributing updates to that system's documentation has led many organizations, especially software vendors, to use a release methodology. When a **maintenance release methodology** is used, all the noncritical maintenance changes made during some period of time are collected and held and then implemented all at once. Each newly implemented version of the information system, along with its appropriate documentation updates, is called a release. The span of time between two successive scheduled releases varies, often with the level of maintenance activity; typical release spans are two, three, or six months, or one year. Additional unscheduled releases may occur for critical maintenance changes. A fix for a critical system error might be immediately implemented in an unscheduled release, or the correction might be saved for the next scheduled release; the decision often depends on the nature of the error and its probability of recurring.

When a release methodology is employed, a numbering scheme is used to distinguish between different releases. In a typical numbering scheme, the initial version of the information system is called version 1.0. The system release that includes the first set of maintenance changes is called version 1.1 of the system. Changes in just the tenths digit of the version number usually indicate that the new version contains only relatively minor changes from the prior version. Whole number changes in the version number, such as a change from version 1.0 to 2.0 or from version 3.4 to 4.0, usually indicate significant upgrades to the system, such as an added capability to interact with a new operating environment.

The release methodology offers several significant advantages. One advantage occurs when two or more maintenance teams are working on the same information system. Without a release methodology, maintenance teams will often hurry their work to be the first to finish, so their changes can be applied to the existing version of the information system; the other teams then have the added burden of verifying that their maintenance changes also work with the newly changed system. If a release methodology is used, all the changes to the system are tested in combination before a new version of the system is released; because there is no advantage to being the first to finish, maintenance teams are not tempted to employ potentially detrimental shortcuts.

The release methodology also results in cost savings for the organization. Expenses are reduced because only one full set of system tests is performed for all the maintenance changes in a particular release. Fewer versions of the information system are actually implemented, and so the time saved in implementation also translates to reduced costs. Each time a new version of an information system is implemented, service to the system's end users might be interrupted; having fewer implementations, therefore, is also better for the end users.

Another significant advantage of the release methodology relates to the information system documentation. Every time a new version of an information system is implemented, all the various forms of documentation, both printed and online, must be updated. If the release methodology is not used for a particularly volatile system, the end users often feel they spend all their time filing documentation changes; even worse, some end users might let the documentation upgrades pile up and eventually ignore or lose them. With the release methodology, all the necessary changes or additions to the documentation for one release are coordinated and made all at one time. The end users, the operations personnel, and the systems operation manager have to integrate updates into their documentation only once for each release.

The release methodology has several potential disadvantages. If new versions of the information system are not released frequently enough, the end users have to wait a long time before they can use new features that have been developed and are awaiting the next release; on the other hand, if new versions are released too often, many of the advantages of the release methodology are compromised.

In some instances, the implementation delays of the release methodology can actually add to systems operation costs. If one of the changes in a particular release significantly improves either the information system's operational efficiency or end user efficiency, the cost savings that could be realized by that change are delayed until the release date. In general, the release methodology is appropriate for all but small information systems and those systems that are changed infrequently.

System performance

The end users of an operational information system are certainly concerned with its level of performance; they want a system that operates efficiently and provides output in a timely manner. Operations personnel are also concerned with the performance level of individual information systems, because they must ensure that all the end users of all the operational systems continue to receive adequate service, even during peak demand periods. Various statistics have been developed to measure system performance. In the following sections, we will first look at some typical performance statistics, and then we will consider capacity planning, a process that uses these performance statistics.

■ Performance and workload measurement

You are already familiar with many of the typical workload measurements. Earlier in this book, we considered the number of report lines printed each day, week, or month; the number of master file records accessed each day; the frequency of master file queries; and the sizes of a system's temporary and permanent files. In addition, systems analysts measure performance by using response time, turnaround time, throughput time, and throughput.

Response time is the time that elapses between a request for computer system activity and the receipt of the response. In a distributed online environment, the response time is the time between the moment the end user presses the ENTER key for a query and the moment the first character of the screen display or printed output appears in response to the query. For a batch report program operating on a centralized computer, the response time is the length of time between the end user's submittal of a request for execution of the program and the delivery of the report to the end user's office.

Response time includes the time necessary to transmit or to deliver the request to the computer system *plus* the time that computer operations and the computer use to respond to the request *plus* the time it takes to transmit or to deliver the result back to the end user. These three components of response time are shown in Figure 14-5 on the next page.

The response time for an online system can be so rapid that the end user is disconcerted or feels rushed. More often, however, the end users are frustrated by response times that are too lengthy. Of all the performance measurements, response time is the one the end users notice the most and the one that is the subject of the most end user concerns and complaints.

Turnaround time is a measure of the efficiency of computer center operations. **Turnaround time** is the amount of time that elapses between the arrival of a request for computer resources at the computer center and the availability of the output for delivery or transmission. Turnaround time is, therefore, one of the components of response time, as shown in Figure 14-5 on the next page. For an online system, the turnaround time includes all the time that elapses between the receipt of a transmitted request and the beginning of transmission of the response; thus, online turnaround time includes time spent waiting for execution plus actual execution time. For a batch report, the turnaround time is the time between the receipt and logging of the end user's request for program execution by the operations group and the release of the completed report by the operations group. Batch turnaround time includes all the following factors: the time necessary for input and output control operations; time spent waiting for execution; actual execution time; and time spent waiting for and using peripheral devices, such as printers and plotters.

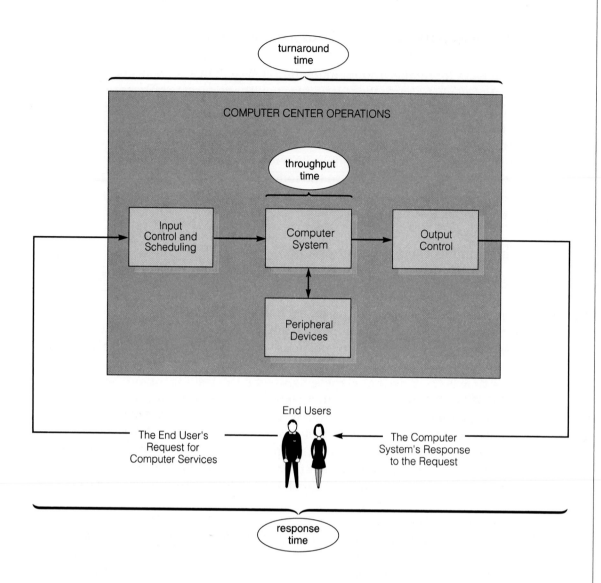

Figure 14-5 *Response time is the total time to complete the path that begins with an end user's request for computer services and ends with the delivery of the response back to the end user. The portion of the path that falls within the box labeled COMPUTER CENTER OPERATIONS represents turnaround time. Throughput time is the time spent in the computer system.*

Throughput time is a measure of the efficiency of the computer. **Throughput time** is the total time from input of a request to the CPU to output of the response from the CPU. Throughput time is, therefore, one of the components of turnaround time. Throughput time is related to throughput, which is another useful measurement of computer system efficiency. **Throughput** is the total amount of useful processing carried out by a computer system in a given time period.

Both the throughput and the throughput times for a computer system can be poor, both can be good, or one can be good while the other is poor. For example, a computer might service a large number of end users in one hour, thus achieving good throughput, whereas the individual computer end users might have to endure considerable delays, producing poor throughput times. Attempts to increase throughput often cause throughput times to worsen. Improving throughput times, however, also tends to improve turnaround times and response times.

The information systems department usually measures response time, turnaround time, and throughput time for each information system. This department also determines average response times, average turnaround times, and average throughput times for the entire computer operation. Management uses these averages, along with throughput and other statistics, such as the proportion of online versus batch executions and the utilization rates for various storage devices, to evaluate the performance of the overall computer operation.

The information systems department periodically evaluates performance and workload measurements for individual operational information systems to identify negative performance trends. Current performance information is also used for cost-benefit analyses of proposed maintenance or of systems that are nearing the end of their economically useful lives. Finally, management uses current performance and workload statistics as input to the capacity planning process.

■ Capacity planning

The role of the operations group within the information systems department is to provide adequate levels of service to all the end users, programmers, and systems analysts, both today and in the future. **Capacity planning** is the process of monitoring current computer equipment activity and performance levels, anticipating future activity levels, and planning for future equipment acquisition to provide necessary levels of service at a minimum cost.

The first step in capacity planning is, therefore, to develop a model of current operations by measuring equipment workloads and performance with statistics such as those we discussed in the previous section. The capacity planners then develop a model of future demand; most often, that model represents a best guess of equipment workloads for one to three years in the future. Once they have developed a future model, the capacity planners analyze the model using a what-if analysis.

With a **what-if analysis**, you vary one or more of the variable elements in a model to measure the effects of the variation. A capacity planner might use a what-if analysis to answer questions, such as *What is the effect on response time if we increase the disk storage capacity by 20%?* or *By how much would throughput improve during peak demand periods if we add one high-speed printer?* Analyses such as these can help the capacity planners decide what changes to make to the current computer equipment configuration to provide adequate levels of service in the future.

As a systems analyst, your role is to supply input to the capacity planning process. To develop the model of current operations, planners need to know details about current activity levels and activity patterns for each operational information system. Useful information includes facts, such as: the number of transactions generated; the daily, weekly, and monthly transaction patterns; the number of master file queries; the number of lines in each report; and how often and when the report is generated. To develop the future model, the capacity planners ask systems analysts to provide estimates of how all these numbers are expected to change in the future. Future information systems must also be included in the future model, so the capacity planners also ask you to provide activity estimates for information systems you are currently developing.

CASE tools for systems operation management

You can use automated tools that provide valuable assistance during all the development phases of an information system. These same tools are equally useful during systems operation. In addition, a number of automated tools have been developed specifically for use during systems operation.

A **CASE maintenance toolkit** includes tools for system evaluation and for maintenance project support. A typical CASE maintenance toolkit includes: a **performance monitor**, which tells you where time is being spent in program execution; a **program analyzer**, which scans source code, provides data element cross-reference information, and helps evaluate the impacts of a program change; an **interactive debugging analyzer**, which helps you locate the source of an error; a restructuring tool, or a reengineering tool; automated documentation tools; and a full-screen editor for making changes to source code.

CASE tools that support capacity planning are also available. These tools include network monitors, workload forecasting software, and capacity planning analysis packages.

System obsolescence

We have focused all our attention in this textbook on developing an information system and keeping it operational. Inevitably, however, an information system will ultimately become obsolete. We must now, therefore, shift our discussion to the final stages in the life of an information system.

An obsolete information system might be a system that is no longer used because its functions are no longer required by the end users. An information system might also become obsolete when the hardware or systems software on which it depends becomes obsolete. Frequently, however, an obsolete system is one that has reached the end of its economically useful life and is to be replaced by another information system. How do you know when an information system is nearing or is at the end of its economically useful life? The following six typical signs will alert you:

1. The system's maintenance history indicates that the amount of adaptive and corrective maintenance necessary to keep the system useful and operational is significantly increasing.
2. Operational costs or execution times are beginning to increase rapidly, and simple perfective maintenance will not reverse or slow the trend.
3. A software package is available that will provide the same or additional services as well or better than the current system.
4. New technological developments provide a means to perform the same or additional services in a different and more efficient manner.
5. Necessary maintenance changes or additions can be integrated into the system only with great difficulty and expense.
6. The end users define a major set of additional requirements that cannot be easily accommodated in the existing information system.

Systems operation continues for an information system that is to be replaced until you implement the replacement system. During the last months of operation for an information system, its end users are unlikely to submit new requests for adaptive maintenance because most of their attention is focused on the development of the replacement system. If new requests for adaptive maintenance on the existing system were submitted, they would probably be rejected for economic reasons. Similarly, new perfective maintenance is rarely undertaken because the existing information system will not continue long enough to realize sufficient benefits to justify the costs of its enhancement. Maintenance activity on an information system in its final stage of systems operation usually consists only of corrective maintenance that is absolutely necessary to keep the system operational. Figure 14-6 shows the typical levels of maintenance activity for an operational information system in its last months of systems operation.

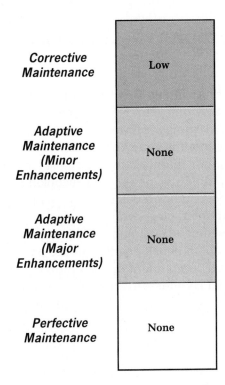

Figure 14-6 *Maintenance activities decrease significantly during the last months of systems operations for an information system while its replacement system is being developed.*

End users often recognize that an information system should be replaced, but sometimes they need convincing by a systems analyst. When the end users decide to replace an information system, they submit a systems request for the development of a new information system. Thus, we have come full circle, as the systems development life cycle begins once again for a new information system.

CHAPTER CASE STUDY 14

James Tool Company — Systems Operation

In mid-June 1998, the payroll package that James Tool Company purchased from Lennox Software Solutions had been operational for nearly one year. Now interfaced with the payroll system, the union system developed by programmer/analyst Howard Coswell has been in systems operation for ten months. The union relations department is generally satisfied with the operation of the union system; they had requested only two minor maintenance changes since the union system was implemented. The only somewhat serious complaint Coswell had received related to difficulties in correctly loading and aligning the special check stock used for printing the checks to the unions. Dean Rosen, the union relations department clerk who performs all the union system microcomputer processing, has evidently become accustomed to the paper loading process, because Rosen has not complained to Coswell about check-printing in the past two months.

No employees in either the payroll department or the union relations department have had to work overtime since last August; Arnold Henderson, the vice president of finance at James Tool Company who initiated the payroll and union system projects, is very pleased with this result. One day in January, Henderson even came to the information systems department to congratulate Coswell on his work; Henderson also took time to thank Don Mard and Kimberly Wallace, who were the primary systems analysts for the implementation of the payroll package.

On June 19, Lennox Software Solutions announced the next release of their payroll package. This new version of the payroll system will include one significant new feature: the package will now be able to handle multiple unions. When he read the announcement, Delbert Donovan, the director of union relations, immediately submitted a systems request for determining if the new version of the payroll system would be able to handle all the company's union processing. Mard and Coswell were in the middle of another large project, so Kimberly Wallace was assigned to handle the request as soon as she completed her current project.

A few weeks later, Wallace began the preliminary investigation phase for Donovan's request by first reviewing the union system processing in the union relations department. She found that the system was running smoothly, and everyone was pleased with the system's contributions to the overall improvement of the accuracy and productivity of union processing. The union relations department, however, was now typing the four monthly checks to the unions because Donovan had decided that typing the checks was less trouble than having the computer print them.

Wallace and Donovan next met with a representative from Lennox Software Solutions and verified that the new payroll package release would definitely handle the James Tool Company union requirements. The new release would also have several other enhancements that would benefit James Tool Company's payroll processing.

Wallace completed her preliminary investigation, prepared her report to management, and presented her findings and recommendation to management. Her recommendation was for James Tool Company to upgrade to the new release of the package, convert union processing over to the package, and discontinue the current union system. Management concurred with Wallace's recommendation and approved the systems analysis phase for the project. The continuation of the systems development life cycle for the new package release, thus, ensured the eventual replacement of the union system.

Summary

Systems operation covers the entire period from the implementation of an information system until the system is no longer used. A systems analyst's primary involvement with an operational information system is maintenance.

Maintenance includes all the changes that are made to an operational information system to correct errors, to satisfy new end user requirements, and to make the system operate more efficiently; these objectives are met by corrective maintenance, adaptive maintenance, and perfective maintenance, respectively. Adaptive and perfective maintenance changes are often called enhancements.

The typical maintenance process is much like a small version of the systems development life cycle. A systems request for maintenance work is submitted and evaluated; if the request is accepted, it is prioritized and scheduled. The maintenance project then follows a logical progression of investigation, analysis, design, development, testing, and implementation.

Corrective maintenance projects occur when an end user or a member of the computer operations staff reports an error. Standard maintenance procedures are usually followed for relatively minor errors. Work often begins immediately, however, for more significant errors. For the most severe errors, programmers devise an immediate fix in a process known as fire fighting.

Adaptive and perfective maintenance projects always follow the organization's standard maintenance procedures. Adaptive maintenance projects occur in response to end user requests for improvements to the information system; these improvements are necessary to meet changes in the business or operating environments. Perfective maintenance projects are usually initiated by information systems department personnel to improve performance or to enhance maintainability. Automated program restructuring and reengineering are forms of perfective maintenance.

A maintenance team consists of one or more systems analysts and one or more programmers. Maintenance systems analysts must have all the same talents and abilities as new development systems analysts; in addition, they must be skilled detectives and must be proficient in synthesis, as well as analysis, to make changes to an information system without destroying or compromising it. In many information systems departments, the applications staff has separate new development and maintenance groups; if so, systems analysts and programmers might be periodically rotated from one group to the other.

Configuration management is necessary during systems operation to manage maintenance requests, to manage different versions of the information system, and to manage and control the distribution of changes to the system's documentation. Maintenance changes can be implemented as they are completed, or a release methodology can be used, in which all noncritical maintenance changes made during a specified period of time are collected and then implemented all at once. A release methodology is usually a cost-effective technique that is also advantageous for end users, because they do not have to deal with an information system that is frequently or constantly changing.

System performance measurements include response time, turnaround time, throughput time, and throughput. Capacity planners use these and other performance and workload measurements to model the current computer environment and to forecast and plan for future needs in an effort to provide the necessary levels of service to the organization.

CASE tools are available to assist you in all aspects of systems operation. Maintenance toolkits provide a wide selection of system evaluation and maintenance support tools. Other tools are available for monitoring network performance, modeling computer environments, and performing capacity planning analyses.

All information systems eventually become obsolete. Signs of the end of a system's operational usefulness include rapidly increasing maintenance or operating costs, the availability of relevant new software or hardware developments, or new requirements that cannot be easily integrated into the existing system. Frequently, an information system that is no longer operationally useful is replaced by a new information system; thus, the entire cycle from preliminary investigation through systems operations begins again for a new information system.

Review Questions

1. What percentage of an information systems department staff's time is typically spent on maintenance activities?
2. What are the three standard classifications of maintenance?
3. How is enhancement different from maintenance?
4. During which stages of systems operation is corrective maintenance most common?
5. What is fire fighting? How does fire fighting differ from other types of corrective maintenance?
6. How does adaptive maintenance differ from perfective maintenance?
7. List six typical perfective maintenance projects.
8. Why is perfective maintenance rarely undertaken late in the life of an information system?
9. Which of the three kinds of maintenance is most likely to generate changes to end user documentation? Which is least likely?
10. Why are newly hired and recently promoted systems analysts and programmers often assigned to maintenance projects?
11. What is a release methodology? What are the advantages and disadvantages of using a release methodology?
12. What is response time? What is turnaround time? What is throughput time? What is throughput? How are they related?
13. What is the purpose of capacity planning?
14. What is a what-if analysis? How are what-if analyses used in capacity planning?
15. What kinds of tools are typically included in a CASE maintenance toolkit?
16. List five signs that can indicate an information system is nearing the end of its economically useful life.

Discussion Questions

1. Updates to a particular operational inventory control system are controlled with a release methodology. The current version of the system is version 2.3. For each of the maintenance changes listed below, decide whether you would number a release including only that change as version 2.4 or version 3.0.

   a. An added optional report
   b. An added graphical screen display
   c. An added input validation check
   d. An added interface to the budget control system
   e. An additional valid product classification code
   f. An additional level in the inventory classification scheme
   g. An added capability for producing graphical output on a laser printer
   h. A changed order of the printed fields in an existing report
   i. A more efficient sort procedure
   j. An increased limit on the number of different warehouses
   k. Renaming a data element
   l. Rewriting a program to streamline its execution

2. A manager of new development in the information systems department was heard to say, "Maintenance systems analysts and programmers don't need any of the new software tools because they are just patching programs." What arguments would you use to try to change that manager's mind?

3. The director of applications in the information systems department of one particular organization has an interesting staffing practice. Programmers and systems analysts are assigned to maintenance projects only if they fall into any of these classifications: trainees; people who have completed no formal education or training courses within the last ten years; and people who received below-average ratings in their most recent evaluation. What misconceptions do you suspect that director holds?

4. Visit the information systems department at your school or at a local company and investigate which performance and workload measurements are used in its production environment. Present to your class a report of the measurements used and the department's assessment of its effectiveness based on these measurements. If the department does not use any performance or workload measurements, present its reasons for not doing so.

MINICASE STUDIES

Hoober Industries

The production support system is a rather complex online information system that runs twenty-four hours a day in all the production shop areas at Hoober Industries; the current production support system was developed in-house and implemented less than two months ago. Late one recent morning, the system developed a problem: when a screen display of certain part master file records was requested, the displayed values were gibberish.

When she was alerted to the problem, Marsha Stryker, the manager of applications maintenance in the information systems department at Hoober Industries, immediately assigned Eric Wu to the correction. Wu, a maintenance systems analyst, was told by Stryker to fix the problem and to get the production control system operating correctly again as soon as possible. Wu had previously worked on two small maintenance projects for the production control system, so he was somewhat familiar with the system.

Wu worked the rest of the day on the problem; by 6:30 that evening, he had developed and implemented a fix. After verifying that the production support system was again producing correct part master displays, Wu went home. Early the following morning, Wu and two other members of the applications maintenance group were called to a meeting in Stryker's office, where she briefed them on a new adaptive maintenance project for another high-priority system and told them to begin work on that new project immediately.

Several nights later, the production control system crashed shortly after midnight. Every time the system was reactivated by an operator in computer operations, the system would immediately crash again. Finally, around 2:30 that morning, all production lines were shut down and all third-shift production workers were sent home. The production support system was finally corrected and full production was restored at noon; by that time, Hoober Industries had incurred thousands of dollars in lost production costs. The cause of the production support system crash was found to be a side effect of the fix that Wu had made to the system.

Questions

1. Is the second production support system failure entirely unexpected?
2. Who is most to blame for the second system failure?

Gallagher Imports

An online customer sales information system was recently developed and implemented at Gallagher Imports. The microcomputers in each of Gallagher's twelve retail stores are networked with two microcomputers and one minicomputer located in the sales support department in the head office. Salespeople in the retail stores use the customer sales information system to record sales transactions, to open, close, or query customer accounts, and to print sales receipts, daily sales reports by salesperson, and daily sales reports by merchandise code. The staff of the sales support department uses the system to query customer accounts and to print various daily, weekly, and monthly reports.

When the customer sales system was implemented, all the salespeople and the entire sales support department staff received intensive training on the new system; the training sessions were conducted by the system's developers. One member of the development team also prepared and distributed a user manual; the system's end users, however, have rarely needed to refer to the manual.

Two weeks ago, Gallagher Imports opened two additional stores, which required hiring six new salespeople. These salespeople were given the user manual and told to read it and to experiment with the customer sales system until they understood how to use it. The salespeople in both of the new stores are having problems using the system. When a representative from the head office visited one of the stores to see why there were problems, she discovered that the new salespeople could not understand the user manual.

The following is a sample of the user manual instructions:

1. Obtaining the authorization of the store manager on Form RBK-23 is required before it can activate a customer charge account.

2. Care should be exercised to ensure that the BKSP key is not pressed when the key on the numeric keypad with a left-facing arrow is the appropriate choice to accomplish nondestructive backspacing.

3. To prevent report generation interruption, the existence of sufficient paper stock should be verified before any option that engenders printing is selected. If not, the option must be reselected.

4. The key labeled F2 should be pressed in the event that a display of valid merchandise codes is required. That same key terminates the display.

Questions

1. Should the sales support department ask the developers of the customer sales system to rewrite the user manual as a maintenance project, or should they ask the system developers to conduct a training session for the new salespeople? Can you offer any better suggestions?

2. Rewrite the user manual instructions presented above so they are clear and understandable.

STUDENT CASE STUDY 14

Western Dental Clinic — Systems Operation

Introduction

Jim Archer successfully implemented the new dental system at Western Dental Clinic, and the staff at the clinic has been using the system for nearly three months. Western Dental is satisfied with the improvements to office productivity and with the new information they receive — both a result of the system developed by Archer.

The office people at the clinic have been calling Archer daily with verbal requests for corrections and for changes, however, and Archer has begun to find it difficult to concentrate his time on a new, major project for a local distributor of health and exercise equipment. In addition, Emily Hendricks, who is the office manager at Western Dental, has just reported to Archer that the system periodically slows down too much during the day; the slowdown makes it difficult for the office staff to keep up with its workload.

Student Assignments

1. Archer wants to be responsive to Western Dental Clinic's requests for correction and change, but in a more organized and productive way. Archer asks you to help him. Prepare a complete, written procedure that Archer can use with Western Dental Clinic for controlling and processing all systems requests for maintenance changes. Include appropriate forms with your procedure.

2. What could be the causes for the periodic slowdowns at Western Dental Clinic? What would you do to determine if a problem does exist? If a problem does exist, which performance and workload measures would you monitor to pinpoint the problem?

3. Investigate one CASE product that would be helpful in detecting, measuring, and analyzing the causes for the performance or workload problem at Western Dental Clinic. Prepare a report that describes the product and its features.